The Penguin Encyclopedia of
Card Games

David Parlett

PENGUIN BOOKS

PENGUIN BOOKS

Published by the Penguin Group
Penguin Books Ltd, 80 Strand, London WC2R 0RL, England
Penguin Putnam Inc., 375 Hudson Street, New York, New York 10014, USA
Penguin Books Australia Ltd, 250 Camberwell Road, Camberwell, Victoria 3124, Australia
Penguin Books Canada Ltd, 10 Alcorn Avenue, Toronto, Ontario, Canada M4V 3B2
Penguin Books India (P) Ltd, 11 Community Centre, Panchsheel Park, New Delhi – 110 017, India
Penguin Books (NZ) Ltd, Cnr Rosedale and Airborne Roads, Albany, Auckland, New Zealand
Penguin Books (South Africa) (Pty) Ltd, 24 Sturdee Avenue, Rosebank 2196, South Africa

Penguin Books Ltd, Registered Offices: 80 Strand, London WC2R 0RL, England

www.penguin.com

The Penguin Book of Card Games first published by Allen Lane 1979
This new edition, entitled *The Penguin Encyclopedia of Card Games*, first published 2000
5

Set in 9.5/12.5 pt Adobe Minion and MT Grotesque
Typeset by Rowland Phototypesetting Ltd, Bury St Edmunds, Suffolk
Printed in England by Clays Ltd, St Ives plc

To Dan Glimne . . . *Ace of Swedes*

Contents

Preface

This book aims to provide a working description of as many card games as possible that are or have been played in the western world with the traditional four-suited pack. It is based on my *Penguin Book of Card Games*, which first appeared in 1979 and is widely regarded as a standard authority, but which, for several reasons listed below, needs to be revised. For instance:

1. Some standard games played at tournament level, such as Bridge and Skat, have undergone revisions to the official rules published by the appropriate authorities.

2. Popular or 'folk' games that are not subject to official rules (but which account for well over 95 per cent of all card games played) are in a constant state of flux, and it is obviously desirable to keep abreast of developments.

3. Many previously unrecorded games have come to light in the past 20 years – some relatively new, some previously thought to be extinct, and some actually extinct but whose rules have now been recovered.

Two modern developments have boosted the discovery, or recovery, of many more games than might have been thought possible a few years ago.

One is a growing awareness that a society's indoor games are as distinctive of its culture as its arts, cuisine, or social customs, and are worth recording for the light they throw on that community's personality. The exploration of card games has become a particular pursuit of the International Playing-Card Society, founded in the late 1960s originally as a forum for playing-card collectors. Many field researchers are members of the Society, and report their findings in its bi-monthly Journal, now known as *The Playing-Card*.

Another has been a growth in the popularity of card-play itself, and that, paradoxically, through the very medium which might have been expected to have led to its decline – namely, computers. A quick trawl though the murky waters of the Internet will soon throw up opportunities to indulge in live play with physically remote opponents, news of clubs and tournaments devoted to an increasing variety of games, newsgroups seeking information as to the availability of cards themselves or rules of obscure games, and websites devoted to a miscellany of cartophilic enthusiasms.

The most important of these is the 'Pagat' website, <http://www.pagat.com>, conducted by John McLeod, a prominent member of the IPCS and himself a well-travelled field researcher. Its intrinsic authority is constantly enhanced by the contributions of interested and knowledgeable players from all over the world, making of it a living, growing, interactive encyclopedia of the cybersphere. This links directly to the home page of the Society via <www.netlink.co.uk/users/pagat/ipcs>. Other interesting and useful sites include <http://www.inmet.com/~justin/game-hist.html>, which is devoted to medieval and renaissance games, and that of Somerville of Edinburgh, <www.playing-cards.demon.co.uk>, for the purchase of national, regional and other specialist playing-cards. The various sets of national suit symbols used throughout this book were taken from a font designed by Gyula Szigri which can be downloaded from <http://www.pagat.com/com/cardsttf.html>. The designer makes no charge for their use beyond the normal courtesy of acknowledgement.

Many thanks are due, and are duly tendered, to John McLeod and Andrew Pennycook, with whom I have shared much information and discussion over the years, and both of whom have read various drafts of the text and rescued me from a number of errors. (Which, however, in the nature of things, I cannot guarantee not to have replaced with others.) Further embarrassments have been saved me by Roger Wells, my eagle-eyed copy editor, with whom I have shared mutually rewarding discussions on matters of grammar and punctuation. My brother Graham has, as usual, been invaluable as a foreign language consultant.

Additional thanks are due to all who have variously sent me games, answered queries, allowed me to quote from their reports, or checked portions of the text from an expert's point of view, in particular: Bob Abbott, Mike Arnautov, David Bernazzani, Thierry Depaulis, Dan Glimne, Lynn King, Veikko Lähdesmäki, Noel Leaver, David Levy (US), Matthew Macfadyen, Babak Mozaffari, Robert Reid, Pamela Shandel, Elon Shlosberg, Anthony Smith, Gyula Szigri, Butch Thomas, Nick Wedd and Jude Wudarczyk.

Introduction

Cards by nature

No man who has wrestled with a self-adjusting card table can ever be quite the man he once was.

James Thurber

Playing-cards are flat, two-sided gaming pieces with identifying marks on one side and a uniform pattern on the other, and are employed in such a way that only their holders can see their identifying marks. Dominoes and Mah-Jong tiles are similar, and all are ultimately related through a common ancestor traceable back to the China of more than a thousand years ago.

Because of their bipartisan nature – secret from one viewpoint and identifiable from another – cards are used for two types of activity: gambling games of chance, in which (basically) you bet on the identity of a card or cards seen only from the back; and games of varying degrees of skill in which you manipulate them in such a way as to win cards from your opponents, or form them into matched sets, or pursue whatever other objective human ingenuity may devise. The skill factor of any given card game is largely the degree to which it enables you to plan your play by reference to information revealed or inferred about the lie of cards in other players' hands. Bridge is a great game (by no means the only one) for the high degree of information that can be acquired before you play a single card, and Eleusis one that bases its whole structure on the acquisition of information.

Everyone knows, even if they do not play, that there are 52 cards in a pack; that they consist of four suits called spades, clubs, hearts and diamonds (♠♣♥♦); that each suit contains numerals 1 to 10, topped by three courtly figures called Jack, Queen, and King; that the '1' is called Ace, and often counts highest of all. Most packs contain one or two additional cards called Jokers. They belong to no suit, are used in relatively few games, and then in various different ways.

Not everybody knows, however, that this particular pack, though universal in extent, is indigenous to only a few countries, including France, Britain and North America, and is native only to France. Its universality is due to two factors. One is inherent, in that it is the simplest in design, therefore the cheapest to produce, and the easiest for newcomers to become acquainted with. The other is cultural, in that it is the pack from which have sprung such internationally favoured games as Whist, Bridge, Poker, Rummy, and Canasta.

Because the pack of international currency coincides with the national pack of France and Britain, and their former colonies, the inhabitants of these countries are generally unaware of any alternatives. In fact, however, other European countries (and their former colonies) still employ packs with different suits, different courts, and different numbers of cards in each suit, and, not unnaturally, prefer them for indigenous games that have never been played with anything else.

Earlier card-game collections published in English describe national or 'foreign' games as if played with standard 'international' playing-cards. In this book they will be described as played with their own cards, but (where practical) accompanied by a translation into their French-suited equivalents in case you cannot find a supplier.

Six basic types of European playing-card systems are shown in the accompanying table. You don't have to learn them in order to use this book, as all will be explained as and when necessary. But you may find the following notes of interest.

The word *spade* probably represents the Old Spanish *spado*, 'sword', while *club* is a direct translation of *basto*, implying that Spanish suits were used in England before the French ones were invented (around 1490). The bells of German and Swiss cards are hawk-bells. The situation is complicated by the fact that some German games are played with French-suited cards but of a German design and with German names (♣ = *Kreuz*, ♠ = *Pik*, ♥ = *Herz*, ♦ = *Karo*, with courts of *König, Dame, Bube*).

The oldest court cards were all male. *Caballo* and *cavallo* mean 'horse', but, as they refer to their riders, are better termed *cavaliers*. *Ober/Over* and *Unter/Under* are taken to mean, respectively, a superior and inferior officer, but originally referred to the position of the suitmark. It has often been pointed out that Latin suits and courts are military, Germanic ones rustic, and Anglo-French ones courtly in nature.

Italian:	swords	batons	cups	coins
Spanish:	swords	clubs	cups	coins
Swiss:	acorns	escutcheons	flowers	bells
German:	acorns	leaves	hearts	bells
French:	trèfle	pique	coeur	carreau
English:	clubs	spades	hearts	diamonds

Above Major European suit systems showing probable lines of evolution from earliest and most complex to latest and simplest.
Below Each system has its own courts (face cards) and range of numerals. Packs often appear in a shortened version (omitted numerals in brackets).

nation	length	courts	numerals
Italian	52, 40	King Cavalier Soldier	(10 9 8) 7 6 5 4 3 2 1
Spanish	48, 40	King Cavalier Valet	(9 8 7) 6 5 4 3 2 1
Swiss	48, 36	King Over Under	Banner 9 8 7 6 (5 4 3) 2
German	36, 32	King Ober Unter	10 9 8 7 (6) 2
French	52, 32	King Queen Valet	10 9 8 7 (6 5 4 3 2) A
International	52	King Queen Jack	10 9 8 7 6 5 4 3 2 A

The numerals are not complete in all traditions. Most French games are played with 32 cards (formerly 36), Spanish and Italian with 40, sometimes 48, rarely 52. Most Spanish and Italian games omit the Tens, and the Ten is replaced by a Banner in Swiss games. Aces are merely Ones in Spanish and Italian games. The Swiss equivalent of an Ace, although so called, is actually a Deuce, as it bears two suit-signs.

Plan of attack

I have made a heap of all I have found.

Nennius, *Historia Brittonum*

Most of the games are accompanied by a 'working description', which means enough of a description to enable you to play the game in its most basic form.

This is not the same as the so-called 'official rules' of play. For one thing, such rules include detailed instructions on how cards should be shuffled and cut, what to do if someone deals out of turn or exposes a card while dealing, etc., and there isn't enough room to be fussy about such niceties. For another, most games are played informally and are not equipped with official rules. Official rules are drawn up for games played at tournament level, and should be regarded as the official rules of the appropriate governing body, not the official rules of the game itself. The vast majority of card games are not book games but folk games. As such, they are played informally, without reference to books, by schools of players who are quite able and willing to make up rules to fit whatever disputes may arise (referring, if necessary, to the local oldest inhabitant as a final arbiter), and to inject new ideas into the game that may, with time, eventually cause it to evolve into something else. The proper function of a card-game observer and collector lies in describing how games *are* played rather than in prescribing how they *should* be played. Far too many card-game books have been perpetrated by writers who, being primarily Bridge-players, imagine that the only true way of playing every other card game is to follow what was written about it in a book whose original text may be a hundred years out of date. (And that's no exaggeration. Nearly all descriptions of Brag published in the twentieth century describe only the nineteenth-century game.)

Since many games are played in different ways by different schools, or even by the same school at different times, I have restricted my descriptions to the most basic form, and have marked additional or alternative items as variations.

In some cases I have given a sample deal and made suggestions as to skilful play, but this is not the primary function of the book, which is designed to be extensive rather than intensive in its coverage. I have preferred to devote space to introductory notes on the historical and ethnic background of the game in question, since, unlike skilful play, this is not something you can pick up for yourself as you go along.

The collection is divided into two dozen chapters, each covering a group of similar or related games. This has necessitated classifying card games according to their various methods of play, which may be introduced and explained as follows.

Trick-taking games

The vast majority of European card games are based on the principle of trick-play. Each in turn plays a card to the table, and whoever plays the best card wins the others. These cards constitute a trick, which the winner places, face down, in a winnings-pile before playing the first card to the next trick. The 'best' card is usually the highest-ranking card of the same suit as the card led – that is, of the first card played to it. Anyone who fails to 'follow suit to the card led' cannot win it, no matter how high a card they play. Winning a trick is therefore doubly advantageous, since you not only gain material but also have free choice of suit to lead next. If you lead a suit which nobody else can follow because they have none of it left, you will win that trick no matter how low a card you play.

The trick-playing principle can be varied in several ways. The most significant is by the introduction of a so-called trump or 'triumph' suit, superior in power to that of the other three, the non-trump or 'plain' suits. If, now, somebody leads a plain suit of which you have none, you can play a trump instead, and this will beat the highest card of the suit led, no matter how low your trump card is.

Trick-games vary in many different ways, and in this book are arranged as follows.

Plain-trick games Trick-taking games in which the object is to win as many tricks as possible, or at least as many tricks as you bid, or (rarely) exactly the number of tricks you bid.

1. Whist, Bridge, and related partnership games with all cards dealt out. Most are games of great skill.

2. Solo Whist and other games resembling Whist-Bridge but played without fixed partnerships, so everyone finishes with a score of their own.

3. Nap, Euchre and others in which not all cards are dealt out, so that only three or five tricks are played. Many of these are gambling games.

4. Hearts, and relatives, in which the object is to avoid taking tricks – or, at least, to avoid taking tricks containing penalty cards.

5. Piquet, and other classic games in which the aim is both to win tricks and to score for card-combinations.

Point-trick games Trick-taking games in which the object is to win point-scoring cards contained in tricks.

6. Pitch, Don, All Fours, and other members of the 'High-low-Jack-game' family.

7. A miscellany of point-trick games including Manille, Tressette and Trappola.

8. Skat, Schafkopf and other central European games of the 'Ace 11, Ten 10' family.

9. Marriage games. These are 'Ace 11' games that give an extra score for matching the King and Queen of the same suit, the best-known being Sixty-Six.

10. Bezique, Pinochle, and other 'Ace 11' games in which scores are made not only for marriages but also for the out-of-wedlock combination of a Queen and Jack of different suits.

11. Belote, Jass and other marriage games in which the highest trumps are the Jack and the Nine.

12. An eccentric family of northern European games derived from a medieval monstrosity called Karnöffel.

13. Tarot games, in which trumps are represented by a fifth suit of 21 pictorial cards. Tarots were originally invented as gaming materials, not fortune-telling equipment, and hundreds of games are still played with them in France, Germany, Italy, Austria and other European states. There is room here only for a small but representative selection.

Non-trick games

Games based on principles other than taking tricks are arranged as follows.

Card-taking games Games in which the aim is to collect or capture cards by methods other than trick-taking.

14. Cassino, Scopa and other so-called Fishing games, in which cards lying face up on the table are captured by matching them with cards played from the hand.

15. A variety of relatively simple capturing games such as Gops, Snap, and Beggar-my-Neighbour, of which some (but by no means all) are usually regarded as children's games.

Adding-up games

16. Games in which a running total is kept of the face-values of cards played to the table, and the aim is to make or avoid making certain totals. The most sophisticated example, Cribbage, also includes card-combinations.

Shedding games These are games in which the object is to get rid of all your cards as soon as possible.

17. Newmarket, Crazy Eights and others, in which the aim is to be the first to shed all your cards.

18. Durak, Rolling Stone and others, in which it is to avoid being the last player left with cards in hand.

Collecting games Games in which the aim is to collect sets of matched cards ('melds').

19. Rummy games, and others, in which the aim is to be the first to go out by discarding all your cards in matched sets.

20. Rummy games of the Canasta family, in which it is to keep collecting and scoring for matched sets before deciding to go out.

Ordering games

21. Patience games, in which the object is to set the shuffled pack in order. Most of these are solitaires (one-player games) but, as there are enough of them to fill an encyclopedia of their own, this section restricts itself to competitive varieties for two or more players.

Vying games

22. Poker, Brag and other gambling games of skill, in which players vie with one another as to who holds the best card-combination, or is likely to finish with the best when their hands are complete.

Banking games

23. A selection of gambling games, such as Pontoon (Blackjack) and Baccara(t), limited to those that can conveniently be played at home.

Original card games

24. Finally, I have appended a selection of some of my own games. Some of these were first published in *Original Card Games* (1977, no longer available). I have invented others since, and include the best of these. One of my originals, Ninety-Nine, has become so widely known, being described also in books by other writers and turned into computer software, that I have included it in the main body of this collection.

Excluded from these contents are games played with non-standard cards, whether proprietary cards (such as Rook cards and Uno™) or with traditional cards other than the four-suited pack, such as the Japanese Hanafuda, the Indian Ganjifa, the European Cuckoo, the Jewish Kvitlakh, and many others.

Included are what might be called children's games, but not in a separate chapter of their own. Many are ancient games of historical interest that throw up enlightening relationships with standard card games.

Also included are several games of mainly historical interest. One reason is that any cultural heritage is worth preserving and needs to be re-assessed and transmitted every generation or so. Another is that many games mentioned only by name in history or literature have recently become playable through the recovery of lost descriptions, or even, in some happy instances, by the discovery of communities that still play them. By far the most important reason, however, is that many of them are simply excellent games, and well worth reviving.

Playing the game

> Well, you were supposed to be teaching me the game, and I saw you were cheating all the time, so I thought it was allowed by the rules.
>
> Leslie Charteris, *Enter the Saint*

Card-play occurs against a backdrop of long-established traditional procedures amounting almost to ritual. They are worth observing, partly as a mark of civility (there is no fun in playing with louts unless you are one yourself), and largely because they are designed to prevent anyone from gaining, or appearing to gain, an unfair advantage by doing anything out of the ordinary.

Love or money?

It is a mistake to characterize all card-play as a form of gambling by definition. All games (even Chess) *can* be played for money and, to that extent, are potential occasions for gambling, but whether or not they *are* so played depends partly on the inherent nature of the game in question and partly on the inherent nature of its players. Some seem incapable of taking any card game seriously unless it is played for money, while others will never, on principle, play for money at all. Extremists of either sort (and I speak from the non-monetary end of the spectrum) have no option but to acknowledge the views of the other, and avoid meeting at the same table.

As to the games, they fall into three groups. At one extreme lie games of skill, such as Bridge, which so engage the intellect as to obviate the need for additional monetary interest. At the other lie entirely chance-determined betting games involving no card-playing skill at all. Some of these are potentially dangerous betting games, but others are played for fun and not necessarily for cash: they include children's games, which can be played for sweets and treats, and drinking games, which are traditional methods of deciding who pays for the next round. Between the two lie games of skill like Poker, in which the actual instruments of play are not cards but money, and the skill involved has nothing to do with card sense but everything to do with money management and *ad hominem* psychology.

Scoring

Gambling games are normally played for hard score – that is, coins, or chips or counters representing coins and eventually redeemable for cash. Intellectual games are played for soft score, meaning points recorded in writing, on which monetary transactions may be based when the game is over. If you are playing for money, the advantage of hard score is that you always know where you stand, and the disadvantage of soft score is that the mind contains an endless supply of points which the pocket may later be unable to match. For those who are not interested in money, the disadvantage of some intellectual games is that they have not developed refined scoring systems but retain the zero-sum format of their ancestral hard-score gambling games, which can make for many complications in any attempt to keep track of all the pluses and minuses on the balance sheet. Unless you have a numerate and trustworthy scorekeeper to hand, you may find it more convenient to play such games for hard score, even if only matchsticks and paperclips.

Some games are played with scoring devices of traditional design, such as Cribbage boards and Piquet/Bezique markers. If you have any of these, they can often be found useful for other games.

Players, partners and positions

Many card games are played by four in two partnerships of two each, partners sitting opposite each other and playing alternately instead of consecutively. If partnerships are to be made at random, it is usual for each player to draw a card from a pack spread face down on the table, and for those drawing the two highest cards to become partners, the one with the highest having choice of seats and dealing first. Tied players draw again. When there are not partnerships, the same system is used to determine seats and first deal. The importance of seating may be regarded as a hangover from more superstitious times, in which hard-bitten gamblers still tend to live.

Rotation

The order in which cards are dealt around the table, the participants take turns to play, and the deal passes from person to person is normally to the left (clockwise, viewed from above) in English-speaking and north European countries, but to the right (anti-clockwise) in southern Europe and many other cultures. The player sitting to the dealer's left in clockwise games, or to the right in anti-clockwise, is called *eldest (hand)* or *forehand*. In nearly all games it is eldest who leads to the first trick or otherwise makes the first move, or who has priority of some sort over everybody else, and the dealer who comes last or has least priority.

The shuffle

The purpose of shuffling is to ensure that cards are randomized before being dealt. Perfect randomness is impossible to achieve in a short time, but that is not the point: the object is merely to prevent anyone from locating the position of any given card and to ensure that, in games based on putting cards in order, such as Rummy, the game is not spoilt by having them come out in order to start with. As a matter of interest (because contrary to expectation), excessive shuffling in trick-taking games is more likely to produce freakish suit distributions than relatively light shuffling or none at all.

Shuffling cannot be taught in words; it can only be copied from watching good practitioners. However you do it, the most important thing is to ensure that none of the cards can be located, especially the bottom one, for which purpose it helps to hold them as close as possible to the surface of the table. In most games (except Bridge, of course, which likes to be different out of sheer cussedness) it is axiomatic that any one or more players may shuffle if they wish, but the dealer is entitled to shuffle last.

The cut

Between shuffling and dealing, the dealer has the pack cut by the player on his other side from eldest. The pack is placed, face down, on the table, the cutter lifts off the top half and places it face down beside the residue, and the dealer completes the cut by placing the former bottom half on top of the other. The purpose of this is to prevent anyone from identifying the bottom card of the pack, which may have been seen during the shuffle. 'Half' doesn't necessarily mean exactly half. Games with codified rules usually specify the minimum number of cards that should be left in each portion of the pack. A sensible minimum is about one-fifth of the total. If any card is exposed in the deal, or if cards are dealt by the wrong player or in the wrong order, anyone may demand a new deal, including a new shuffle and cut.

The deal

Some games specify that cards be dealt singly, one to each player in rotation, others that they be dealt in batches of two or three at a time to each player in rotation. It is worth noting that this is not done in order to 'stack the pack', thereby yielding more unbalanced and 'interesting' hands, but mainly to save time.

Behaviour

When playing with people you do not know, it is advisable to assume that bad manners will get you ostracized. As to what constitutes bad manners, here are some helpful guidelines (adapted from *Esquire* magazine):

1. Remember that shuffling is a dramatic art form, and is at its most impressive when performed in mid-air.

2. Pick up your cards as dealt. You will be ready to bid ahead of the others.

3. Talk about other subjects during the game; it makes for good fellowship.

4. Don't try to remember the rules; they are too confusing.

5. Never hurry. Try several cards on a trick until you are sure which one you prefer.

6. Occasionally ask what is trumps. It will show that you are interested in the game.

7. Trump your partner's ace and make doubly sure of the trick.

8. Always ask your partner why he didn't return your lead; this will remind him to lead it next time.

9. Always explain your play, particularly when you lose. It shows your card knowledge.

10. Eat chocolate caramels or candied fruit while playing; it stops the cards from slithering about.

Irregularities in play

The commonest irregularities are playing out of turn and playing an illegal card, especially revoking – that is, failing to follow suit in a trick-taking game that requires you to do so. Highly codified games, such as Bridge, are equipped with laws specifying corrections and penalties for all conceivable irregularities, as well as some tortuously inconceivable. To detail them all in a book such as this would double its size and is therefore out of the question. Generally, the attempted play of an illegal card in a game involving partners gives useful information to one's partner and ought, strictly, to be penalized by forfeiture of the game by the offending side. An alternative is to play a legal card and to leave the illegal one face up on the table, to be played at the earliest legal opportunity. But in a game where a misplayed card conveys useful information only to the opponents and is corrected before anyone else has played a card, there is no need to impose a penalty.

Game

It is important to establish at the outset what constitutes a game, at what point play will cease and the group will break up. Many games specify what this end-point should be, but if a game is not so defined then you should agree in advance to play up to a target score, or for a fixed length of time or number of deals. If not playing to a target score, it is desirable for all players to have dealt the same number of times in order to equalize the advantages of position.

Cheating

This interesting subject can be mentioned but briefly. To be effective, cheating must be carried out by a dedicated expert, who will normally either have doctored the pack in some way or be working with the aid of a secret partner – not necessarily one participating in the game. When playing with strangers for money, assume everyone guilty until proved innocent, but make no accusations in case you are wrong. If in doubt, just make an excuse and leave. Note that it is your responsibility to hold your cards in such a way that no one else can see them, and that different national traditions, or local schools, may have different views on what is and is not allowable (as Simon Templar observed in the quotation above).

Kibitzers

Taking their name from the German for 'peewits', possibly because of their twittering, kibitzers are onlookers who tend to offer unwanted advice (dictionary definition). Kibitzers by law should sit down, keep quiet, not fidget, and refrain from distracting or encouraging the players.

What shall we play?

Nothing, apart from rumour, travels as fast as a good game of cards.

Rudolf van Leyden, *Ganjifa*

Regular card-players are always on the look-out for games they haven't played before, especially younger players, who have more flexible minds and move in more varied social circles. The advantage of a new game is that everyone starts off on the same footing. So long as you are all having to learn new strategies as you go along, there will be less of a foregone conclusion about the eventual winner.

In choosing something new to try, the two most important selection factors are (1) how many of you are playing and (2) what type of game most suits your mood and personality. As to number, most games are designed for specific numbers of players and don't work well when adapted for others. As to personality, it is obviously self-defeating to play a fixed partnership game if you are all rugged individualists, or a brainless gambling game if you have an average IQ of 150, or a highly complicated bidding game like Bridge if none of you is acquainted with simple trick-taking games like Whist. The following recommendations are therefore made primarily by reference to number, and secondarily by distinction between trick-taking and non-trick games.

Two players

The simplest of the classic trick-takers is probably Ecarté. Piquet is more demanding, and spoilt by some old-fashioned complications; nevertheless, the fact that it has been a favourite with serious card-players for many centuries should give some indication of how deep it goes. At least one of the games Bezique, Pinochle and Klaberjass (Clob), which are substantially similar, should be in every player's repertoire. Sixty-Six (Schnapsen) is similar, but quicker and easier, and packs an extraordinary amount of depth and variety into a game played with so few cards. For something out of the ordinary, try Bohemian Schneider, Sedma or Durak.

The greatest non-trick two-hander is unquestionably Cribbage, though Gin Rummy maintains a huge following. Canasta, though best known as a four-handed partnership game, works surprisingly well for two. Cassino is popular in America, but if you haven't played a game of this type before it may be better to start with a simpler relative such as Scopa. Spite and Malice (Cat and Mouse) is a popular competitive Patience game. For something out of the ordinary, Gops is short and sweet, Zetema long and savoury, and Truc (or Put) a good game of bluff.

Of my own games, Abstrac and Dracula attract the most fan mail. You may prefer Galapagos as an alternative to Piquet; but my favourite is Garbo.

Three players

Don't believe anyone who claims there is no such thing as a good three-handed card game. There are at least as many as good two-handers. That misapprehension is peculiar to English-speaking countries, where most national games are played with the 52-card pack, which divides itself naturally and best into four hands of thirteen. Many other nations use a 32-card pack, which equally naturally divides itself into three 10-card hands and a talon of two. Games based on this pattern include Preference, Skat and Ulti, though it must be admitted that they are all highly complex and not easily learnt from books – a proviso that applies equally to such other excellent games as Ombre and Vira. Simpler three-handed trick games include Ninety-Nine and Terziglio. Tyzicha and Skitgubbe are of intermediate complexity. Many Tarot games are designed for three.

Non-trick games are less well served. Here, however – and this applies as well to trick-takers – three is often the minimum number suitable for a wide variety of games listed below under the heading 'indefinite numbers'.

Four players (partnership)

When it comes to four sitting crosswise in fixed partnerships, you are spoilt for choice. The classic western trick-takers are Whist (simple), Bridge (complex), Euchre, Pinochle, Cinch and Five Hundred. To these might be added Spades and Bid Whist, which have recently achieved enormous popularity in America, the Canadian game of Kaiser, and Don, an increasingly popular British pub game. To extend this repertoire, try national games such as Manille, Doppelkopf, Roque, Sedma, Gaigel, Belote, Durak or Klaverjas. For a real challenge, you might experiment with Karnöffel, Watten, Aluette, or a partnership Tarot game. Quinto and Calypso are two 'invented' games well worth exploring, together with my own game of Tantony.

The classic non-trick partnership game is Canasta, but there is much to be said for Scopone, and Partnership Cribbage has its devotees. If you have ever wondered whether Poker can be played as a partnership game, Mus is a must. Concerto, of my invention, is also based on Poker hands, but is not a gambling game.

Many two-handed games will be found to have partnership equivalents, and vice versa, for obvious mathematical reasons.

Four players (solo)

Four can play in several different arrangements. They may play a three-handed game such as Skat, with each in turn sitting out the hand to which they deal. (This is, in fact, the most usual way of playing three-handers.) Or they may play one of the games listed below under the heading 'indefinite numbers'.

Of games designed specifically for four, some are cut-throat (completely non-partnership), while others are either solo games (the highest bidder plays alone against the other three), or alliance games (an *ad hoc* partnership may be formed between any two players), or a mixture of the two.

Classic trick games include Hearts and Solo Whist. Classic but defunct are Reversis and Quadrille, their respective ancestors. If you like Hearts, you may want to try some of its more recent elaborations such as Barbu and Tëtka. If you like Solo Whist, try Auction or Nomination Whist. Four of my own games with unusual features are Collusion, Mismatch, Seconds and Bugami.

Many Rummy games are suitable for four, the most popular being some form of Contract Rummy, which is played under a vast and confusing array of aliases. Players interested in the history of Poker should try its specifically four-handed ancestor, Bouillotte. A game of Chinese origin that has recently become widespread in the West, and which works best for four, is usually known as Arsehole (or its equivalent, such as Trouduc in French), but in America, whether from prudery or irony, is often bowdlerized to President.

Five players

Very few games are specifically designed for five, but many listed below as 'indefinite' often play best that way. Five is said to be the best number for the Irish game of Spoil Five, though Twenty-Five, its modern equivalent, is largely played by four. My contribution to the genre is called Squint.

Six players
The old French games of Sixte and Sizette are interesting curiosities, and so simple as to be worth making more complicated. My contribution is called Sex (Latin for six, of course).

Indefinite numbers
Games for no specific number of players used to be called 'round' games. Nearly all are suitable for four to six players, some also for three, and some for up to ten. Among the trick-taking games may be mentioned Oh Hell!, Knockout Whist, Nap, Loo, Catch-the-Ten, and the relatives listed alongside them.

To these may be added nearly all the adding-up games (Fifty-One, Hundred, Jubilee, etc.), stops games (Newmarket, Michigan, etc.), Rummy games (notably Manipulation Rummy), vying games (Poker, Brag etc.) and banking games (Pontoon or Blackjack). Crazy Eights and its relatives need no introduction, nor does Spit, but perhaps a word might be put in for Cucumber.

You must remember this ...

Play to the left unless otherwise stated
In English-speaking countries the rotation of play is normally to the left, or clockwise around the table (as viewed from above). In many other countries it is the reverse, with play passing to the right. If you are going to play a game authentically, and especially with the appropriate cards, you might as well play it the right way round (or the left way round, as the case may be). Note, therefore, that if no indication is given, play goes to the left; but if it normally goes to the right in the game's country of origin, there will be a note to that effect.

Eldest hand
This denotes the player to the left of the dealer in left-handed games, or to the right in right-handed games. Each player beyond eldest gets

progressively younger, so youngest is normally the dealer or, if the dealer does not take part, the player on the other side of the dealer from eldest. In games of German origin, Eldest is called Forehand and, if three play, the others are respectively Middlehand and Rearhand. Eldest or Forehand is usually the player who makes the first bid or the first play and who has priority in case of equal bids or results. Other technical terms are explained in an appendix.

Abbreviations

T = Ten. I normally denote the 10 of a suit by the single character T, partly because it is more convenient to represent a card by a single character, especially in a list, and partly because there are many games in which the Ten has special significance.

4p = four players, **4pp** = four in partnerships; **52c** = 52 cards.

† = **trump** e.g. †A reads 'Ace of trumps'. And ☆ = **Joker**

He or she

I employ gender-inclusive language wherever practicable and endorse the use of 'they' as a common-gender singular, but have too much respect for my readers' intelligence to submit to the sort of insti-tutionalized illiteracy that passes for political correctness. Besides, there isn't room.

Don't forget . . .
- Play to the left (clockwise) unless otherwise stated.
- Eldest or Forehand means the player to the left of the dealer in left-handed games, to the right in right-handed games.
- T = Ten, p = players, pp = in fixed partnerships, c = cards, † = trump, ☆ = Joker.

1 Bridge-Whist family

Fifty-two cards are divided equally among four players sitting crosswise in partnerships, the last card is turned for trump, and each side strives to win a majority of the 13 tricks played.

Nothing could be simpler. The game is Whist – lesson one in the education of a card-player – and everything else in this opening section is based upon it.

Contract Bridge comes first in this collection because it is the most prestigious and most widely played card game in the world. Yet, in both complexity and historicity, it follows on from Whist, being its direct descendant and enjoying the high status that Whist had long occupied before.

▍Contract Bridge
4 players (2 × 2), 52 cards

Satirical comments from films and shows of the early 1930s well reflect the impact made by the then newly-developed game of Contract Bridge on the American psyche:

Robert Greig (as butler) – Announce the schedule for the guests tomorrow, your grace.

C. Aubrey Smith (as lord) – Bridge, at three. And dinner, at eight. After dinner – Bridge. Rather an amusing day, Flamand, eh?

Greig – Quite exciting, your grace.

Smith – And what are the guests doing now, Flamand?

Greig – Playing Bridge, your grace.

Smith (delighted) – Aaah!

> (*Cut to shot of apparent corpses propped up at numerous card tables.*)
>
> (*Love Me Tonight*, 1932)

Basically, Bridge is an extension of partnership Whist, with the following additional features:

An auction Instead of randomizing trumps by turning a card, players bid for the right to choose trumps in exchange for contracting to win a certain minimum of tricks. This feature is prefigured in various forms of Bid Whist.

A no-trump bid, absent from ancestral Whist. (The name of the game may derive from *biritch*, pronounced *b'reech*, said to be an obsolete Russian word for this bid.)

The dummy One member of the side responsible for choosing trumps becomes the *declarer* and plays from both hands. For this purpose declarer's partner lays his hand of cards face up on the table for all to see. This feature, the dummy, is prefigured in various forms of Dummy Whist.

The scoring line Scores are recorded above and below a horizontal line dividing the score column in half. Only points scored below the line contribute directly towards winning the game, and these are made only if the contract is fulfilled and only for the number of tricks bid. Above the line go any scores for winning additional tricks, or to the defenders for defeating the contract.

(The terminology is illogical. The declarers obviously *defend* their contract, and their opponents, equally obviously, *attack* it. Bridge is full of such perversities. It is, for example, the only bidding game in which the opening bid is made by the dealer instead of by eldest hand.)

What gives Bridge its bite is the method by which the contract is arrived at – the auction itself. For, although two partners are bidding on what they can see in their own hands, they are also conveying information about their hands to each other in the way they bid, and listening in on their opponents' conversation at the same time. Developments in the structure of Bridge lie less in the play than in the use of bidding systems to convey information.

Bridge has undergone few formal changes since the 1930s, by comparison with the 50 years of development that preceded it. In Biritch or Russian Whist (published 1886), the dealer specified a trump suit or called '*biritch*' (No Trump), dealer's partner put down a dummy, and declarer's aim was simply to win seven or more tricks. In Bridge-Whist (1896), dealer either nominated trumps or 'bridged' this privilege over to his partner. In Auction Bridge (1904), all four players could bid by raising the number of tricks to be won, and all declarer's tricks and overtricks scored below the line. In Plafond (Paris, *c.*1915), only contracted tricks scored below the line. Contract Bridge, a variety of Plafond, first appeared in 1920, but did not displace Auction until several years after its perfection by millionaire Harold S. Vanderbilt on his now famous winter cruise of 1925–6. The first comprehensive bidding system was developed by Ely Culbertson, who was also responsible for launching the publicity campaign which placed Bridge at the summit of social status, from where it has yet to be toppled. Culbertson's system, further refined by Charles H. Goren, remains the basis of the standard American system. The standard British system, Acol, commemorates the Bridge club where it was developed, in Acol Road, London, NW6.

Bridge is played in three distinct forms:
• Rubber Bridge. The home game for four learners and sociable players. A game is 100 points below the line, and a rubber is the best of three games.
• Duplicate Bridge. The club and tournament game for serious and advanced players. Hands are prepared in advance, and every pair plays just one hand against every other pair, in such a way that none benefits from being dealt 'better hands' than any other.
• Chicago Bridge. A home game, ideal for a small number of tables (two to six) where players wish to rotate. It consists of exactly four deals with the scoring of Duplicate.

Beginners should start with Rubber Bridge and progress to Chicago. Complete beginners, with no experience of card games at all, should start with partnership Whist before embarking upon Bridge.

Rubber Bridge

Cards Fifty-two. It is customary to use two packs alternately, one being shuffled while the other is dealt.

Preliminaries Scores are kept on a sheet divided into two columns, one for each partnership, and it is customary for each player to keep a record, as a check on accuracy, in columns headed (ungrammatically) WE and THEY. The sheet – readily obtainable pre-printed from stationers – is divided into vertical halves by a horizontal line. Points that count towards winning a game go below the line, and premiums (bonuses) above.

Partnerships Each player draws a card from a shuffled pack spread face down on the table. Those drawing the two lowest cards become partners against those drawing the highest. If equal, spades beats hearts beats diamonds beat clubs. The higher partners have choice of seats, and the highest deals first. The turn to deal, bid and play passes always to the left. If partnerships are fixed by social agreement, players need draw only to confer choice of seats and first deal.

Game Game is 100 points below the line, which may take several deals to reach. The first to win two games wins the rubber. A side that has won one game is declared *vulnerable* and is subject to certain increased scores or penalties.

Deal Deal thirteen cards each, one at a time, face down.

Rank Cards rank AKQJT98765432 in each suit. Suits rank from high to low: spades, hearts (major suits), diamonds, clubs (minor).

Object In the auction, each side's object is to discover as much as possible about the lie of cards and to arrive at a contract that best suits their combined hands. In the play, the declarer aims to win at least as many tricks as specified in the contract. In any contract the only points which count towards game – below the line – are those made for tricks contracted and won. Any extra or overtricks made by the declarers are scored separately as bonuses, above the line, as are scores made by the defenders for defeating a contract.

The Auction Each in turn, starting with Dealer, may pass, call, double or redouble. If all pass immediately, there is no play, the cards are gathered in, and the deal passes to the left. A pass – pronounced 'No bid' by British players – (but not American) – does not prevent one from bidding again if the opportunity arises. A call is announced as a number of tricks in excess of six which the caller proposes to make, together with the proposed trump.

> Example: The lowest possible bid, 'one club', is an offer to win seven tricks with clubs as trumps; the highest, 'seven no trump', an offer to win all 13 without a trump suit.

Each bid must *overcall* (exceed) the previous one – that is, it must cite either a greater number of tricks, or the same number but in a higher suit. For this purpose suits rank from low to high: clubs, diamonds, hearts, spades, no trump.

> Example: 'One club' may be overcalled by one of another suit, and one of any suit by 'one no trump'. A bid at 'no trump' can only be overcalled by a higher number.

Instead of bidding or passing, a player may announce 'double' if the previous bid was made by an opponent, or 'redouble' if the previous announcement was an opponent's 'double'. The effect of doubling and redoubling is to double and quadruple the declarers' score if the contract succeeds, or the defenders' if not. But if a double/redouble is followed by another bid, it is automatically cancelled. When three players have passed in succession, the last-named bid becomes the contract, whether or not doubled or redoubled. This ends the auction.

Play Whichever one of the contracting partnership first named the prevailing trump becomes the declarer, and plays both hands. The opening lead is made by the player at declarer's left. Declarer's partner then lays his cards face up on the table as a dummy, each suit in an overlapping column of cards. The leftmost column, as seen by declarer, should be the trump suit, or clubs if there is no trump, and the columns should alternate in colour. The second card to the trick is played by declarer from dummy, the third by the leader's partner, and the fourth by declarer from his own hand. Normal rules of trick-taking apply: follow suit to the card led if possible; if not, trump or renounce ad lib. The trick is taken by the highest card of the suit led or by the highest trump if any are played, and the winner of each trick leads to the next. Declarer's partner may not advise or participate in any way except to draw attention to any breach of rules he may be about to commit (such as revoking or leading out of turn). The tricks won by one partnership are kept in one place, face down but overlapping, so that the number taken is clear to all. If declarer wins a trick with a card from the dummy, he leads to the next from dummy; if from his own hand, he leads from his own.

Score See table and example for details. For making the contract, the declarers score below the line the appropriate amount for the number bid and the trump concerned, doubled or redoubled if appropriate. Any overtricks are scored above the line, together with any bonus that may apply for (a) honours, (b) bidding and making a slam, (c) making a doubled contract.

If declarer is beaten ('goes down' or 'is set'), the defenders score above the line for the appropriate number of undertricks. The actual amount depends on whether or not the contract was doubled and whether or not declarer's side was vulnerable.

Regardless of the outcome, any single player who was dealt the top five trumps (AKQJT), or all four Aces if the contract was no trump, scores 150 for honours. A player who held any four of the top five scores 100 for honours. Scoring for honours may, by agreement, be ignored. When a partnership's below-line score totals 100 or more, they win the game and become vulnerable. Another line is drawn across the sheet beneath the bottom-most figure, and the next game begins at zero. When one side wins its second game, it also wins the rubber and adds a bonus of 500 above the line, or 700 if the other side failed to win one game. All above- and below-line scores made by both sides are then totalled, and the difference is the margin of victory.

WE		THEY	
g	50		
g	200		
f	500	150	c
e	100	60	c
a	30	100	b
a	60	100	c
f	120	80	d
g	80		
h	60		
h	500		
	1700	490	
	−490		
	1210		

Example of scoring. (a) We bid 2♠, made 3♠, scoring 60 below for the bid of two and 30 above for the overtrick. (b) We bid 3♥, were doubled, and made only two. They score 100 above for the undertrick, doubled. (c) They bid 3NT and made five, scoring 40 for the first and 30 for the other two below the line, plus two overtricks for 60 above. One of them held four Aces, gaining 150 for honours. They win the first game to our part-score of 60. A horizontal line is drawn to mark the game, and they are now vulnerable. (d) They bid and make 4♣, scoring 80 below the line. (e) They bid 2♠ and make one, giving us 100 above the line for the undertrick, they being vulnerable. (f) We bid and make a small slam, 6♦, for 120 below the line, giving us a game and making ourselves vulnerable. We also count a bonus of 500 above for the slam. (g) We bid 1NT, are doubled, and make three. This gives us 2 × 40 below the line, plus 200 above for the (doubled) overtrick made when vulnerable, plus 50 'for the insult' (making any doubled game). (h) We bid and make 2♥ for 60 below, giving us the second game and 500 for the rubber. Our margin of victory is 1210.

Table of scores at Contract Bridge
tv = trick value (20 or 30), D = doubled, R = redoubled, V = vulnerable

Contract made: *Declarers score below the line for each trick bid and won:*

in a minor suit (♦♣)	20	D 40	R 80
in a major suit (♠♥)	30	D 60	R 120
at no trump, for the first trick	40	D 80	R 160
at no trump, for each subsequent trick	30	D 60	R 120
Declarers may also score above the line:			
for each overtrick (if not vulnerable)	tv	D 100	R 200
for each overtrick (if vulnerable)	tv	D 200	R 400

for making a doubled or redoubled contract			-	D 50	R 100
making a small slam			500	V 750	
making a grand slam			1000	V 1500	

Contract defeated: *defenders score above the line:*

for the first undertrick		50	D 100	R 200	if not vulnerable
	or	100	D 200	R 400	if vulnerable
for the second and third ...		50	D 200	R 400	if not vulnerable
	or	100	D 300	R 600	if vulnerable
plus, for each subsequent undertrick ...		50	D 100	R 200	if not vulnerable

Honours: *scored above the line by either side holding in one hand:*

any four of AKQJT of trumps	100
all five of AKQJT of trumps	150
All four Aces at no trump	150

Rubber scores:

if opponents won one game	500
if opponents won no game	700
for winning the only game completed	300
for being the only side with a part-score in an unfinished game	100

Bidding systems

Chico Marx – He bids one.
Margaret Dumont – One what?
Chico – Never mind. You'll find out. Now I bid two.
Dumont – But two what?
Chico – Er – two the same as what he bid.

(*Animal Crackers*, 1930)

Bidding is the subject of various systems and conventions. A system is a whole process of bidding in accordance with agreed principles so that a partnership which employs it will reach the best contract for their particular combination of hands. A convention is an artificial bid that does not necessarily mean what it says but conveys some other information about the hand. A given convention may be used in more than one system, and a given system may employ alternative conventions for the same purpose. A fundamental principle of Bridge is that each side should know exactly what systems and conventions are being used by the other, so that the information so imparted may be understood by all. Abuse of this principle would render cheating too easy.

Acol, the most popular British system, is based on principles and practices summarized in the table on pages 9–11. The following notes also apply.

The auction Hands are assessed differently according to which type of bid is in question. An *opening bid* is the first bid of the auction (ignoring passes). It is the most important to the side that makes it, as it seizes the initiative and enables them to pursue communications at a lower level than their opponents. The first bid made by the opener's partner is by definition a *responsive* bid, and he may expect the opener to reply in his turn with a *re-bid*. The first bid made by the opponents – if any – interrupts the communication established between the opener and his partner, and is by definition a *defensive* bid.

Doubles A *penalty* double is one you make because you genuinely believe you can defeat the proposed contract. Any double of a No Trump bid is for penalties, as is a double made when the opponents have bid three different suits naturally.

A *take-out* or *informative* double is one that asks your partner to take you out of it by making another bid. Its purpose is to convey useful information rather than to seek to exact a penalty. Suppose you have an openable hand such as ♠AJxx ♥Kxxx ♦xx ♣AQx and your right-hand opponent opens 1♦. A good way of indicating your hand is to use a take-out double. This tells your partner you have a biddable hand which is short in the suit opened but lacks a positive long suit (unlike, say, ♠x ♥AQJxx ♦AQxx ♣QJx, with which you would call 1♥). This double is forcing for one round, requiring your partner to show his best suit in the event of a pass by your left-hand opponent.

Whether a double is meant for penalties or for a take-out may vary with circumstances. Usually, it is a conventional or take-out double when

- doubler's partner has not yet spoken, or
- has spoken, but only to pass;
- doubler has doubled at the first opportunity to do so; and
- the doubled bid was in suit and not above 3-level (unless pre-emptive).

Acol bidding: summary and guidelines

1. Assess your hand by counting strength points as follows:

High-card points (hcp):
> Count for each Ace held 4, King 3, Queen 2, Jack 1 hcp.

Distribution: Add 1 for holding four Aces.
> Deduct 1 for a singleton King, Queen or Jack, or a doubleton Queen or Jack.
> Deduct 1 for a 4-3-3-3 pattern, unless intending to bid No Trump.

In an opening bid only:
> Add 1 for each card above four in any suit or suits, unless intending to bid NT.

If a trump fit is found in the course of the auction:
> Add for a plain-suit doubleton 1, singleton 3, void 5.

Quick tricks: AK = 2 quick tricks, AQ = $1\frac{1}{2}$ qt, A = 1 qt, KQ = 1 qt, Kx = $\frac{1}{2}$qt

2. In general, but not without exception, you should have:

to open 1 of a suit:	13 points and $2\frac{1}{2}$ quick tricks
to support 1 of a suit:	6+ pts and 4-card support
to bid or support NT:	a balanced hand (suit pattern 4-3-3-3, 4-4-3-2, or 5-3-3-2)
for game (NT or major):	25–26 pts in combined hands
for game (minor suit):	28–29 pts in combined hands
for a small slam:	33–36 pts in combined hands
for a grand slam:	37 pts in combined hands

3. Opening bids and responses
• *Opening one of a suit.* You show 13–20 pts and promise to re-bid (unless partner has passed). Of two biddable suits, bid the longer first, or, if equally long, the higher-ranking. But:
> Of two non-touching 4-card suits (♠♦, ♠♣, ♥♣), bid the lower first.
> Of three 4-card suits, bid the suit below the singleton (but 1♥ if singleton ♣).

Partner's response to opening one of a suit.
> With 6–9 points, bid:
> 2 of opener's major suit if you hold at least four.
> 1 of a major over an opening minor if you hold at least four.
> 1 No Trump if your hand is balanced (you need 8–10 to bid 1NT over 1♣).
> Your own biddable suit at lowest level (you need 8 to bid at '2' level).

> With 10–12 points, bid:
> 3 of opener's major suit if you hold at least four.
> 2 of a major over an opening minor if you hold at least four.
> 2 No Trump if your hand is balanced.
> Otherwise: your own biddable suit at lowest level.

> With 13–15 points, bid:
> 4 of opener's major suit if you hold at least four.
> 3 of a major over an opening minor if you hold at least four.
> 3 No Trump if your hand is balanced.
> 3 of a suit of which you hold at least six.

> With 16+ points, bid:
> your own best suit one level higher than necessary (for example, 1♥–2♠, or 1♥–3♦). The jump-bid is mandatory, and forces to game.

- *Opening 2♣ (Two-club convention).* You show 23–24 pts, either balanced or with a strong suit and 5 quick tricks. Partner must respond. Negative response is 2♦.

    Partner's response:
    Having no support, bid 2♦ (conventional).
    With a good suit and 8+ pts or 1¹/₂ quick tricks, bid it.
    With 8+ points but no biddable suit, bid 2NT.

- *Opening 2♠ ♥ or ♦ (Strong two.)* You show anything up to 22 points, at least 8 playing tricks, and one or two strong suits.

    Partner's response:
    You must not pass. Having less than 1¹/₂ quick tricks, bid 2NT (conventional).
    With 1¹/₂ quick tricks and three-card trump support, raise opener's suit to 3.
    To show 1¹/₂ quick tricks and balanced hand, bid 3NT.
    With a 5-card suit of your own and at least 1¹/₂ quick tricks, bid your suit at the
        lowest level.

- *Opening three of a suit (Pre-emptive bid).* This shows weakness in all but the suit bid, which will be a long, strong suit (7+) in a hand counting not more than 10 pts in all. The purpose of this is to hinder the opponents from opening. It is well made from third position, following two passes, but pointless from fourth position.

    Partner's response:
    With 16 pts and at least 2 cards of opener's suit, raise to '4'.
    With 2+ sure tricks and cover in three unbid suits, consider 3NT.
    Otherwise, No Bid unless you can be sure of taking 2 tricks.

- *Opening 1 NT (weak).* You show 12–14 pts (*never* more or less) and a balanced hand. With 15–20 on a balanced hand, bid the best suit first and No Trump next time round. A balanced hand is 4-3-3-3 or 4-4-3-2, or 5-3-3-2 if the 5 is a minor suit.

    Partner's response:
    With 0–10 points
        If balanced, 2NT. If not, 2 of major suit or 3+ of very long suit.
    With 11–12 points
        If balanced, 2NT. If not, 2 of major suit or 3+ of very long suit.
    With 13 points
        If balanced, 3NT. If 5+ suit and 14+ pts, bid '3' of it, forcing to game.
    With 11+ pts and 4 or more ♠ or ♥
        Bid 2♣ to ask for major suit (Stayman convention; see below).
    If you have values for a possible slam
        Bid 4♣, asking for Aces (Gerber convention; see below).

- *Opening 1NT (strong).* Some players prefer a strong NT opening, requiring 15–17 or 16–18 points by prior agreement. Some play strong when vulnerable, weak when not. For the equivalent response to a strong NT, deduct 3 or 4 points from those for a weak NT (above).

- *Opening 2NT.* You show 20–22 pts and a balanced hand.
    Partner's response:
    With 0–3 points, no bid.
    With 4–10 points, raise to 3NT if you hold a balanced hand, or bid 3 of a suit of
        which you hold at least five.
    With 11–12 points, raise to 4NT; with 13–14, raise to 6NT.

4. Opener's re-bids

After opening 1 in a suit and receiving a response:

> With 13–15 pts
>> If partner made a limit bid in your suit or No Trump, No Bid.
>> If partner changed suit, bid '2' of opening suit if five held, or '2' of partner's, or new suit at lowest level.
>
> With 16–18 pts Re-bid your opening suit one level higher.
>
> With 19+ pts Re-bid your suit with jump bid or go straight to game.
>
> With a balanced hand
>> If partner bid at '1' level, bid 1NT on 15–16, 2NT on 17–18, 3NT on 19+.
>> If partner bid at '2' level, bid 2NT on 15–16, 3NT on 18+.

After opening other than 1 in a suit and receiving a response:

> If partner passed, re-bid only to show extra values.
>
> If you opened NT and partner made a limit response, use your discretion.
>
> If you opened 2♣ and partner denied with 2♦ (Stayman), you can bid 2 of a major suit or NT.
>
> If you opened 2 of another suit and partner denied with 2NT, you can pass.

5. Slam bidding

Having in the course of bidding identified a probable trump suit and possible values for a slam, either partner may inquire as to the other's holding of Aces by bidding a conventional 4♣ (Gerber convention) or 4NT (Blackwood). Given an encouraging response, a repeat at the 5 level asks for Kings. Gerber has the advantage of keeping the bidding level low and the bidding space wide, but may be confusing if clubs have been mentioned seriously.

Gerber:

4♣ asks for Aces. Response: 4♦ = none, 4♥ = one, 4♠ = two, 4NT = three, 5♣ = four
5♣ asks for Kings. Response: 5♦ = none, 5♥ = one, 5♠ = two, 5NT = three, 6♣ = four

Blackwood:

4NT asks for Aces. Response: 5♣ = none or four, 5♦ = one, 5♥ = two, 5♠ = three
5NT asks for Kings. Response: 6♣ = none, 6♦ = one, 6♥ = two, 6♠ = three, 6NT= four

6. Defensive bids

A defensive bid is one made by either opponent of the opener. The general requirement is a biddable suit, with length rather than strength. Relative vulnerability is important: you need to be more cautious when playing vulnerable against non-vulnerable. In general, but not without exception, you should have:

> to overcall with 1 of a suit:
>> 5+ in suit and 10–12 pts. Count 1 extra point per card over five.
>
> to overcall with 2 of a suit:
>> 5+ in suit and 13–15 pts. Count 1 extra point per card over five.
>
> to overcall with 1NT:
>> A balanced hand and 16+ points (or 14+ after a bid and two passes).
>
> to overcall a pre-emptive 3:
>> 6+ in suit and 16+ pts. With a strong hand but no long suit, consider 3NT, asking partner for best suit.

7. Defensive double

With 13+ points and fewer than three cards of the suit opened, double. This shows a hand with its own opening values and, in the event of an intervening pass, requires partner to name his best suit at the lowest level.

Bridge: partnership variants

Chicago

As a home game, Chicago has two advantages. One is that a rubber is always four deals, so if two or more tables are operating it is possible for players to swap tables and partners without too much hanging around. The other is that its scoring system, essentially that of Duplicate (Tournament) Bridge, encourages players to bid up to the full value of their hands, so there is no question of 'Why bother to bid up to five clubs if we only need 20 for game?'.

The scoresheet needs only five rows divided into two columns, one for each side. There is no distinction between above- and below-line scoring: if a partnership makes its contract, it scores in its own column; if not, the defenders score in theirs. Part-scores are not carried forward from deal to deal (though they were originally, and many Americans still play this way).

In deal 1, neither side is vulnerable. In deals 2 and 3, non-dealer's side is vulnerable. (A modern development. Originally, dealer's side was vulnerable.) In deal 4, both sides are vulnerable. If a deal is passed out, the cards are gathered and (after the shuffle and cut) re-dealt by the same dealer instead of being passed round to the next as in Rubber Bridge.

The score for a successful contract is the sum of two parts:

1. The natural score for the number of tricks actually made, including overtricks, and with any doubling taken into account;

2. If the contract value was less than game (100), add 50 for a part-score. If it was 100 or more, add for game 300 if not vulnerable, 500 if vulnerable.

The defenders' score for defeating a contract is the same as in Rubber Bridge. There is no score for honours, nor extras for the rubber.

Chicago may be played with so-called 'Russian' scoring, which reduces even further the luck of the deal. This imposes upon a partnership holding 21 or more high-card points between them the obligation to bid and make a contract worth a minimum specified amount. To verify the obligation, play as at Duplicate, with each card played to a trick left face down in front of its player, vertically orientated in a won trick, horizontally in a lost.

hcp	20	21	22	23	24	25	26	27	28
target (not vul):	0	50	70	110	200	300	350	400	430
. . . if vulnerable	0	50	70	110	290	440	520	600	630

hcp	29	30	31	32	33	34	35	36	37+
target (not vul):	460	490	600	700	900	1000	1100	1200	1300
. . . if vulnerable	660	690	900	1050	1350	1500	1650	1800	1950

The difference between the target and the actual score is then converted to International Match Points according to the standard IMP table.

Reverse Bridge

This variant, played by a few heretics, makes 'bad hands' biddable and reduces the incidence of hands being passed out. Here, each natural bid can be overcalled by the same bid 'reversed'. In a reversed contract, all cards rank upside down – Two highest, followed by Three, Four, and so on down to Ace lowest. Otherwise, the play and scoring are precisely the same. As Richard Sharp says (in *The Best Games People Play*, London, 1976): 'Fascinating sequences can be constructed in which many of the reversed bids would have a conventional meaning – e.g. a response of "4NT reversed" to an opening 1♠, asking for Twos!'

Nullo Bridge

Bridge-players acquainted with other trick-taking games such as Solo Whist often bemoan the absence of a misère bid in Bridge. Such a bid was experimented with around 1912 in Nullo Auction Bridge, and can be adapted to Contract if desired. Basically, nullos is a bid ranking between spades and No Trump, and represents an offering to *lose* the stated number of tricks, playing at no trump. Thus a bid of '2 nullos' offers to win no more than five tricks in all, while '7 nullos' is a complete misère. The problem with it, as Milton Work pointed out (in *Auction Developments*, 1913), is that it takes only one card to win a trick, but two to lose it. This makes it essentially a solo game.

Brint

Bridge with a scoring system modelled on that of Vint (q.v.). The value of a trick is not related to whether the contract was major, minor, or no trump, but only to its numerical level – the higher you bid, the more each trick is worth. Brint, as devised by J. B. Chambers in 1929, seems needlessly elaborate. I offer the following simplification.

Below the line If successful, declarers score below the line for all tricks made, including overtricks. The value of each trick is ten times the contract value, i.e. 10 at level one, 20 at level two, and so on up to 70 for a slam. Game is 150 below the line, requiring a contract of 4 for game from a zero score (or 3 bid and 5+ made).

Above the line Defenders score above the line 50 per undertrick.

Doubling Doubling and redoubling affect scores above and below the line. Vulnerability doubles all scores except those made below the line in an undoubled contract.

The rubber bonus is 500 or 700, as at Contract. Honours don't count, and slam bonuses are unnecessary because of the relatively immense differential between contracts of one and seven. (At Contract, 7NT scores eleven times the value of 1 trick bid and made in a minor suit, compared with forty-nine times its value at Brint.)

Non-partnership Bridge

Pirate

A variety of Bridge developed by R. F. Foster (*Foster's Pirate Bridge*, 1917), Pirate replaces fixed partnerships by floating alliances made from deal to deal, so that everyone plays for themselves in the long run. It looks ideal for those who dislike fixed partnerships, but in practice suffered from the fact that the players with the best-matched hands invariably found each other and made their contract.

Dealer bids first. If all pass, the hands are thrown in. When a bid is made, each in turn thereafter must either accept it, thereby offering himself as dummy in partnership with the bidder, or pass. If no one accepts, the bid is annulled, and the turn to bid passes to the left of the player who made it. There is no need to overcall an unaccepted bid. For example, if South opens 2♦, and no other accepts, West may call anything from 1♣ up. If no one accepts any bid, the hands are thrown in.

Once a bid is accepted, each player in turn from the left of the accepter may bid higher or pass, or (in the case of a prospective opponent) double, in which case one of the prospective declarers may redouble. If all pass, the accepted bid becomes the contract. A new bid need not differ in suit from an accepted bid, and may itself be accepted by its previous bidder or accepter, thereby denying the originally proposed alliance. An accepted bidder may himself try to break an alliance by naming a new contract when his turn comes round; but that alliance stands if no higher bid is accepted.

A double reopens the bidding, giving the would-be allies a chance to bid themselves out of the alliance by naming another bid in the hope that someone will accept it. Or they can stay with the accepted bid, and redouble if sufficiently confident.

A contract established, declarer leads to the first trick, his partner lays his hand down as a dummy, and play proceeds as normal. Play in strict rotation even if declarer and dummy are adjacent. Scores are noted above or below the line in the column of each of the players involved.

Three-handed Bridge

Three-handed Bridge is much like the real thing once a contract has been established, but suffers from the lack of partnership bidding. The simplest version is that designated Cut-throat. Towie (Replogle and Fosdick, 1931) is said to still have its devotees, at least in America. Booby (Hubert Phillips, 1953), while not without merit, is complicated by the addition of nullo bids, though it soon becomes obvious why they were introduced.

Cut-throat Bridge

Deal four hands, leaving one face down as the eventual dummy. Whoever bids highest becomes the declarer and turns the dummy face up between the two defenders after his left-hand opponent has led. It may be agreed to turn one or more of the dummy cards face up after each bid is made – for example, face one card after each bid or double at the 1-level, two after a bid or double of 2, and so on.

Towie

Deal four hands and turn six of the dummy cards face up. The highest bidder becomes the declarer, turning up and playing the whole of the dummy hand as at contract. If all players pass, or if the proposed contract is insufficient for game, the same dealer re-deals a 'goulash' hand as follows. Each player sorts his hand into suits so that cards of one suit are together, though not necessarily in ranking order. Dealer sorts all dummy cards in the same way, permitting the others to see how they are arranged. Then dealer lays his own hand face down on the table, upon which are placed, face down and in this order, those of his left opponent, dummy, and fourth player. After a cut, dealer re-deals in batches of 5-5-3. Finally, he shuffles the dummy cards and turns six face up. The same procedure follows until a sufficient contract is reached. Odd tricks contracted and won score as at Contract, except that NT tricks count 35 each throughout. (This more sensible value obtained in the earliest form of Contract.) Overtricks score 50 each, possibly doubled and redoubled to 100 and 200 respectively, and (re)doubled overtricks are doubled again if declarer was vulnerable. Bonus of 50 for making a doubled contract, or 100 redoubled, in either case doubled again if vulnerable. Honours and slams as at Contract. Undertrick penalties are 50 each, or 100 doubled or 200 redoubled, but greater if declarer was vulnerable: 100 for the first and 200 for each subsequent undertrick, these penalties being twice or four times as great if doubled or redoubled. Bonus of 500 for game, 1000 for the rubber.

Booby

Deal seventeen cards each and one face down to an eventual dummy. Each player examines his hand and makes four discards face down to the dummy, leaving all four hands with 13 cards each. Players bid in the usual way, with the addition of a nullo bid ranking between hearts and spades, and valued at 30 per trick. 1 nullo is an offer to win not more than six tricks at no trump, while 7 nullos is a complete misère. Whoever bids highest becomes the declarer and turns the dummy face up between the two defenders after his left-hand opponent has led.
Suggestion Try dealing sixteen each and five face up to the dummy, to which each player then contributes three. Ignore nullos.

Two-handed Bridge

Two-handed Bridge is merely two-handed Whist with Bridge scoring. The traditional forms appear below.

Double Dummy

Deal four hands, two face down. Players bid on what they can see in their own hands. After the auction, the dummy opposite each player is turned face up and each plays alternately from his own hand and from his dummy's. Alternatively (and more realistically), dummies are not open to both players. Instead, after the bidding, each places his own dummy in such a position that the other cannot see exactly how the opposing cards are split. An easily made card-holder for this purpose consists of a shoe box, with lid, placed upside down on the table. The dummy cards are slipped down between the lid and the side of the box. If only one box is available, the players sit at opposite sides of it.

Single Dummy

Deal four thirteen-card hands including two dummies. After the deal, one dummy is turned face up. Bid as at Contract. The established declarer announces whether he will play with the exposed dummy or take his chance with the concealed one. Then the concealed dummy is turned up and play proceeds as at Double Dummy.

Draw and Discard

Shuffle the cards thoroughly and place them face down to form a stock. Starting with non-dealer, each in turn draws the top card of stock, looks at it, and either (a) keeps it, ending his turn, or (b) discards it, face down, and draws the next, which he must then keep. As soon as a player has 13 cards he stops drawing. When both have 13, they bid and play in Contract Bridge fashion. The rejected cards play no further part.

Honeymoon Bridge (Draw Bridge)

Deal thirteen each and place the rest face down as a stock. Non-dealer leads, and tricks are played at no trump. It is theoretically obligatory to follow suit if possible but, as the rule is unenforceable, it may be dispensed with. The winner of a trick discards it face down, as it serves no further purpose, and draws the top card of the stock to add to his hand before leading. His opponent then draws the next before replying. As soon as the last card has been drawn, players bid and play their last 13 cards as at Contract, scoring accordingly. Variant: before leading to each trick, the leader exposes the top card of stock so that each player may gauge whether or not he wishes to win the trick. The loser of a trick draws an unknown card, of course. This improves the strategy of the game.

Memory Bridge

Deal thirteen each and place the rest face down as a stock. The first 13 are played as tricks at no trump. Non-dealer leads and it is obligatory to follow suit. There is no drawing from stock. The player who takes more scores in Contract fashion, as for a bid of 1NT, and adds a premium of 100 above the line. The remaining cards are then dealt, bid on, played and scored as usual.

▌Whist
4 players (2 × 2), 52 cards

> Any good Whist player will be a good Contract player when he has mastered the elements of bidding; but millions of people who pass as good Contract players because they bid their hands well and play them well (after the bidding has located most of the key cards) would be quite beyond their depth at Whist, where the trump depends on chance and the location of the cards has to be inferred from the play.
>
> Elmer Davis, *Harpers Magazine*, 1932

For over 150 years this quintessentially English game was regarded by the whole of the western world as the summit of social and intellectual recreation, a status now claimed by Contract Bridge. Its early history is less illustrious. Whist goes back to a Tudor game called Trump, or Ruff, a relative of Triomphe, the ancestor of Ecarté. Shakespeare's contemporaries regarded it as a rude ale-house pastime, and under the Stuarts it was dubbed Whisk and Swabbers, a rather down-putting piece of word-play on Ruff and Honours. Its reputation as a kids' game was underlined by Charles Cotton's reluctance to describe it in *The Compleat Gamester* (1674), on the grounds that 'Every Child almost of Eight years old hath a competent knowledg in that recreation'. But in 1728 a circle of businessmen, headed by Lord Folkestone, who hob-nobbed at the Crown Coffee-house in Bedford Row, began to apply logic and precision to its deceptively simple structure, and to develop ways of playing the game systematically. One of their acquaintance was an elderly gentleman called Edmond Hoyle, who started teaching it to well-to-do people in their own homes, and eventually published his tutoring notes as a *Short Treatise on Whist* in 1742. So successful was this publication that it made both Hoyle a household name and Whist the game of the élite until its eclipse by Bridge in the 1890s. Since then it has reverted to its original status, remaining a popular family game and still widely pursued in communal Whist drives. By serious players it suffers a quite undeserved neglect. Nobody should learn Bridge without prior experience of it, and many Bridge players would improve their game immensely by going on a crash diet of Whist only.

☞ The name 'Whist' is attached to a number of other games that have little or nothing in common with it beyond being plain-trick games. These will be found in their place, following this description of the classical partnership game.

Preliminaries Four players sitting crosswise in partnerships receive 13 cards each, dealt in ones from a 52-card pack ranking AKQJT98765432. Turn the last card face up to establish trumps.

Object To win seven or more tricks.

Play Eldest leads. Players must follow suit if possible, otherwise may play any card. The trick is taken by the highest card of the suit led, or by the highest trump if any are played, and the winner of each trick leads to the next.

Score Whichever side took more tricks scores 1 point per odd trick. Whichever side held three or four honours (AKQJ), whether in one hand or between the two, scores 2 or 4 points respectively – unless, however, they already stand at 4 towards game, in which case the honours are not counted.

Revoke The penalty for a revoke is 3 points, which the opponents may either add to their own score or subtract from that of the revoking side. In counting towards game, the score for a revoke takes priority over the score for tricks.

Game score The first side to reach or exceed 5 points wins the game, thereby (if applicable) preventing the other side from scoring for honours. The winning side counts a single game point if the other made 3 or 4 points, a double if the other made only 1 or 2, a treble if the other made no score. The side that first wins two games adds 2 game points for the rubber. The margin of victory is the difference between the two sides' total of game points. Thus the highest possible game score is 8 to 0, the winning side having won two trebles plus 2 for the rubber.

Conventions Leading to the first trick gives you the advantage of setting the pace and being best placed to describe your hand by the card you play. For this purpose, some highly elaborate signals or 'conventional leads' were worked out when the game was most in vogue, many of which remain valid for Bridge. They may be condensed and simplified as follows.

Lead from your longest plain suit, or, from two of equal length, from that with the highest cards. If the top cards of the opening suit form one of the following patterns, lead to the first and second tricks as indicated below:

from	lead
AKQJ	K then J
AKQ-	K then Q
AK-J	K then A
A-QJ	A then Q
-KQJ	J

From any other Ace holding, lead the King if you have it, otherwise Ace then fourth best (as it was before the Ace was led). Holding neither Ace nor King, lead fourth best of the suit – for example, the Seven from ♠Q9873.

You may lead trumps if you hold five or more, the appropriate signals being:

from	lead
AKQJ	J then Q
AKQ-	Q then K
AK . . .	if 7+ held, K then A, otherwise fourth highest

The rule of eleven Leading the fourth highest (counting from the top down) enables a partner to get a good idea of the lie of the cards by applying the 'rule of eleven'. Assuming your partner to have led fourth highest, you subtract its face value from eleven to discover how many higher cards are lacking from his hand. By further subtracting the number you hold yourself, you discover how many lie with the other side, and may thereby be able to place key high cards. For example: your partner leads the Seven of a suit of which you hold King-Jack. Seven from eleven means there are four cards against him that lie above the Seven, of which you hold two. He cannot have the Ace, or he would have led it, so it must lie with an opponent. So his original holding must have been any four cards out of QT987 (regardless of anything lower), and the opponents hold between them the Ace and any one of QT98.

Whist variants

The game described above is the classic form of English Short Whist. Also to be noted are:

Long Whist

Until about 1800 the game was played up to 10 (sometimes 9) points, and was subsequently known as Long Whist to distinguish it from the faster 5-point game, which many experts considered too chancy.

American Whist

Honours are not counted, and game is 7 points. Very logical.

Suit-value Whist

Odd tricks score 1 point each with spades as trump, 2 with clubs, 3 with diamonds, 4 with hearts. No honours. Game is 10 points.

Drive Whist

At Whist Drives, and in the home game if preferred, it is usual not to turn a card for trump but to have fixed trumps for each cycle of four deals, respectively hearts, diamonds, spades, clubs. Sometimes also every fifth hand is played at No Trump. Suitably pre-printed scoresheets are obtainable for this purpose. In tournament play it is usual for each person or partnership to play a predetermined number of deals, each scoring the total number of odd tricks they have taken over the number of deals played.

Cayenne

Dating from about 1860, this is worth perpetuating as a stage in the evolution of Suit-value Whist to Bid Whist to Bridge.

At each deal a suit is established as the cayenne suit by cutting either the playing pack or, preferably, a second pack and noting the suit of the top card of the bottom half. This establishes an order of suit preference as follows:

if the cayenne suit is	♥	♦	♣	♠	×4 if trumps
then second colour is	♦	♥	♠	♣	×3 if trumps
third colour is	♣	♣	♥	♥	×2 if trumps
fourth colour is	♠	♠	♦	♦	×1 if trumps

Deal thirteen each in batches of 4-4-5. Dealer either announces trumps or passes this responsibility to his partner, who may not refuse. Whoever decides announces one of the following six contracts: cayenne, second colour, third colour, fourth colour, grand, nullo. Naming cayenne or a colour contracts to win a majority of tricks (7+) with that suit as trump. Grand is a bid to win a majority of tricks at no trump, nullo to lose a majority at no trump. At nullo, an Ace counts as the lowest card of its suit unless its holder specifies otherwise upon playing it. Eldest leads to the first trick.

The side taking most tricks in a suit contract counts a basic 1 point per odd trick taken, and whichever side held the majority of honours (AKQJT of trumps) scores a basic 2 if they held three, 4 if they held four, or 6 if they held five, whether in one hand or between them. In either case the basic score for tricks and honours is then multiplied by the value of the trump suit, as shown in the table above. For example, if the cayenne suit was clubs and the trump suit spades (second colour), the basic score is multiplied by 3.

In a no-trump contract the multiplier is 8 and there are no honours.

(At nullo the winning side scores 8 times the number of odd tricks taken by their opponents.)

Game is 10 points and rubber is the best of seven games, earning a bonus of 8.

Norwegian Whist

There are no trumps (a typical Scandinavian feature), and each deal is played either grand, in which case each side's object is to take a majority of tricks, or nullo, in which case it is to lose the majority. Eldest hand has first option to proclaim grand or nullo, and, if he declines, the privilege passes to the left until someone makes a decision. If all pass, the game is played nullo. If the bid is grand, the player at bidder's left makes the opening lead; if nullo, the player at his right (or at dealer's right if all pass) leads first. At grand, bidder's side scores 4 per odd trick, or, if they fail, opponents score 8 per odd trick. At nullo, either side scores 2 for each odd trick taken by the opponents. Game is 50 points.

Minnesota Whist

Currently popular in northern Minnesota, this game is an obvious development of Norwegian Whist.

Each hand is played either high, in which case each side's aim is to win at least seven tricks, or low, in which case it is to win not more than six. In either case the play is always at no trump. Each player bids high by selecting a black bid-card from their hand, or low by selecting a red, and laying it face down on the table. When all are ready, each in turn, starting with eldest, turns up their bid-card. Since the hand is only played low if all four bid red, as soon as a black card appears the hand is fixed as high and no more cards are turned. The partnership of the player who first showed black is said to have 'granded'. I suggest calling this player the grandee.

The player at grandee's right leads to the first trick. Players must follow suit if possible, otherwise may play any card. The trick is taken by the highest card of the suit led, and the winner of each trick leads to the next.

The winning side scores 1 point for each trick taken in excess of six if playing high, or short of seven if playing low. Game is 13 points.

Chinese Whist

A non-partnership variant, also playable by three or two players. Deal six cards each, face down, which each player lines up (without looking at them) on the table before him. On top of these deal six more cards, face up in one-to-one correspondence. Finally, deal the last single cards, which each player takes into hand. Dealer nominates trumps and the first lead is made by the player at his left. Normal rules of trick-taking apply. A player may play any of his face-up cards or the one in his hand, but not a face-down card. When a faced card is played, the card it covers is immediately exposed and becomes available for play.

Hokm (Troop Chall)

This Iranian game, communicated to me by an e-mail correspondent in Iran (see also Roque), is inexplicably identical with one first reported by Andrew Pennycook as a West Indian game called Troop Chall (phonetic rendering), described to him by a Guyanese player living in London.

Four players in partnerships play to the right. From a 52-card pack deal a batch of five cards to each player. On the basis of these five, eldest nominates trumps and becomes the declarer. Then deal two batches of four to each player. Eldest leads. Players must follow suit if possible, otherwise may play any card. The trick is taken by the highest card of the suit led, or by the highest trump if any are played, and the winner of each trick leads to the next. Play ceases when one side wins by taking its seventh trick, thereby scoring 1 game point, or 2 if the opponents took none. The declaring side continues to declare until it loses, when the other side takes over. Play up to 7 game points.

Comment This game would be strategically more interesting if the winners scored 1 point for each trick taken by the losers!

Dutch Whist

Whist with trumps differently determined in each of four deals: (1) turn the last card, (2) no trump, (3) announced by eldest upon leading to the first trick, (4) cut before dealing. Repeat until bored to death.

Russian Whist

denotes either Vint (below), or Biritch, the earliest form of Bridge.

Bid Whist

Once recorded as a minor forerunner of Bridge, Bid Whist has since developed into a fast and exciting game pursued avidly by black communities in America. Manuals (by R. Wesley Agee, Butch Thomas, and others) and websites confirm that it is now 'played by millions of people across the country at family or social gatherings. A number of big companies sponsor Bid Whist tournaments each year ... [It] has immense popularity on college campuses ... [and] is widely played by military service personnel and their families stationed around the world' (Agee).

Preliminaries Four play crosswise in fixed partnerships using 54 cards – a standard pack, plus two Jokers marked (or equivalently differentiated) 'Big' and 'Little'.

Terminology Book = trick, to cut = to ruff, off-suit = a non-trump suit.

Rank of cards In high bids ('uptown'), cards rank AKQJT98765432; in low bids ('downtown') they rank A23456789TJQK. In trump bids, the top trumps are Big Joker, Little Joker, Ace, and so downwards to Two (uptown) or King (downtown). In no trump bids, Jokers are powerless and are normally discarded before play begins.

Deal Twelve each in ones and six face down as a kitty.

Object A contract is established by auction. If successful, the declarers score 1 per odd book, or 2 at no trump. Game is 5 or 7 points, by prior agreement.

Auction Each in turn, starting at Dealer's left, may pass or bid once only. Each bid must be higher than the last. If the first three pass, Dealer must bid. The lowest bid is 'Three', i.e. to win nine books with a trump suit not yet specified. A bare number is understood to represent a 'high' or 'uptown' bid. This is beaten by 'Three low', which is the same but with reverse or 'downtown' ranking (Big Jo, Little Jo, Ace, Two etc.). This is beaten by 'Three no trump' – whether high or low not yet specified. Thus the bids from lowest to highest begin Three high, Three low, Three no trump, Four high, Four low, and so on.

Taking the kitty If playing in trumps, the highest bidder announces the trump suit, 'sports' the kitty by turning it face up for all to see, and adds it to his hand. If playing at no trump, he announces 'high' or 'low', and takes the kitty into hand without showing it. He then makes any six discards, face down, and these count as the first of his side's won books. At no trump, anyone holding a Joker should then add it to the kitty and draw a replacement at random from it (face down, of course).

Play Declarer leads to the first of 12 books. Players must follow suit if possible, otherwise may play any card. The book is taken by the highest card of the suit led, or by the highest trump if any are played, and the winner of each book leads to the next. If anyone holds a Joker at no trump, it can never win a book, and may only be discarded when its holder cannot follow suit. If a Joker is led, the next card played establishes the suit to follow.

Score The following scores are all doubled in the case of a no trump bid. If successful, Declarer's side scores 1 point per book contracted. If not, they lose 1 point per book contracted; and if the opponents win seven or more, they score 1 point per book won above six. The game ends when one side wins by reaching the target score, or loses by reaching minus the target score.

Winning all 13 books is a 'Boston', and scores quadruple.

Variants With two Jokers, the lowest bid is sometimes 'Four'. Some play with only one Joker and a five-card kitty. Some play without Jokers and either a four-card kitty or none at all. In the latter case, 13 books are played and the lowest bid is 'One'.

Original Bid Whist

Deal thirteen each from a 52-card pack. Each bids a number of odd tricks from one to seven, without mentioning trumps. Bidding continues until three pass in succession, when the last bidder announces trumps and his left opponent leads. A successful contract scores 1 point per odd trick taken, otherwise the opponents score 1 point per odd trick they took and the declarers deduct the amount of their bid.

Contract Whist

(4pp, 52c) Devised by Hubert Phillips in the 1930s, this unjustly neglected game combines the trick-play of Whist with the bidding of Bridge. In effect, it is Bridge without a dummy: all players are active and their hands remain concealed.

The preliminaries, deal and auction proceed as at Contract Bridge.

Bidding systems and conventions employed in Bridge are applicable, except in so far as there is no scoring distinction between major and minor suits, and no bonus for slams. Scores are made above and below the line as at Bridge, and only tricks contracted and won count towards game. The opening lead is made by the left-hand opponent of the declarer who first named the suit of the final contract. Play proceeds as at Bridge, except that declarer's partner plays from his own hand concealed instead of laying it face up as a dummy.

For a successful contract, declarers score (below the line) 3 points per contracted odd trick in a trump suit, 4 at no trump, doubled or redoubled as the case may be. All overtricks score (above the line) 2 each, or 5 or 10 if doubled or redoubled. There is also a flat bonus of 5 for fulfilling a doubled contract, or 10 if redoubled.

For a defeated contract, defenders score (above the line) 10 points for each undertrick, or 20 if doubled, 40 if redoubled.

Game is 10 below the line, a rubber is the best of three games, and the rubber bonus is 50.

Spades

4 players (2 × 2), 52 cards

This game is remarkably popular in America, where it is the subject of numerous clubs, tournaments and websites. Named from the fact that spades are always trumps, it strikes me as having been derived from the pattern of Hearts by changing a suit of penalty cards into a suit of trumps. It is usually played by four in partnerships, but is easily adaptable for other numbers. As befits a genuine folk game of recent origin, it is full of variations and not subject to universally accepted official rules.

Preliminaries Four play crosswise in fixed partnerships, using a 52-card pack ranking AKQJT98765432 in each suit. Deal thirteen each in ones.

Trumps Spades, always.

Bidding There is no competitive auction. Instead, each partnership contracts to win a certain minimum number of tricks. First, the members of the non-dealer partnership discuss how many tricks they think they can win between them. They may say how many certain, probable or possible tricks they think they can win individually, but may not give direct information about specific suit holdings. When their contract number is agreed, it is noted down, and the dealer's side embark on the same process.

A player who thinks he can lose every trick individually may declare 'Nil'. In this case his partner announces how many he proposes to win. This establishes his side's contract, which is lost if the nil bidder wins any tricks. Only one player per side may bid nil, unless otherwise agreed in advance (see Variants).

'Blind nil' is a nil bid made before a player looks at his cards. It is permitted only to a player whose side is losing by 100 or more points. In this case the nil bidder then looks at his cards, and passes two face down to his partner, who adds them to his hand and passes two cards face down in return.

Play To the first trick everyone must play their lowest club. Anyone void in clubs must play any heart or diamond, but not a spade. Whoever plays the highest club wins the trick and leads to the next. Play as at Whist or Bridge, but with the restriction that trumps (spades) may not be led until the suit is broken – that is, until a player has used a spade to trump a trick when unable to follow suit. This does not, of course, apply to a player who has only spades in hand to lead.

Score A side that takes at least as many tricks as its bid scores 10 times its bid, plus 1 per overtrick. There is a penalty, however, for consistent underbidding. When, over a series of deals, a side's overtricks total 10 or more (as witnessed by the final digit of their cumulative score), their score is reduced by 100, and any overtricks above 10 are carried forward to the next cycle of ten. This is called sandbagging. (*Variant*: Each overtrick counts minus 1 point and there is no sandbagging.)

☞ Example: A side has a score of 488, and on the next deal bid five and win nine tricks. This brings them to 538 plus 4 for overtricks, making 542. For the excess of 12 overtricks they deduct 100, bringing them to 442 and leaving them with an excess of 2 towards the next cycle.

For a failed contract, a side loses 10 points per trick bid.

For a successful nil bid, the nil bidder's side scores 50 points, in addition to the score won (or lost) by his partner for tricks made. If it fails, the nil bidder's side loses 50 points, but any tricks taken by the nil bidder may be counted towards the fulfilment of his partner's contract. Blind nil scores on the same principle, but doubled to 100.

Game is 500 points.

Variants Some players include two differentiated Jokers. Big Joker counts as the highest and Little Joker as the second highest spade, followed by Ace (etc.) down to Two. The last two cards go to the dealer (*variant*: to the holder of ♣2), who discards any two face down before (*variant*: after) bidding.

In a variant popular with African Americans the ♣2 and ♥2 are stripped and replaced by differentiated Jokers. Trumps run: Big Joker, Little Joker, ♠2, then ♠AKQJT9876543, but Ace remains highest in the other three suits. Any card may be led to any trick. A lost bid scores minus 10 times the bid value (e.g. a lost bid of 8 scores −80), with no extras for undertricks. There is no nil bid, and instead of a blind nil a partnership can call a 'Blind Seven', undertaking to win at least seven tricks before either partner has looked at his cards. This doubles the score to plus or minus 140, overtricks counting 1 each as usual.

Many special calls are recognized in different circles, in different combinations, and with different procedures and scoring. Here's a small selection to choose from, or to suggest new ideas.

Misdeal may be called by a player with an officially recognized 'bad' hand', such as one lacking spades or face cards, or containing seven or more of a plain suit. The cards are thrown in and a new hand dealt by the same dealer.

10-for-200: A bid to win exactly 10 tricks for a score of 200, or minus 200 if lost.

Moon, or Boston: A bid to win all 13 tricks, also worth plus or minus 200 (or 500 if 10-for-200 is also recognized).

No trump: Anyone bidding a number of tricks 'no trump' thereby undertakes not to win any tricks by ruffing, but only by playing highest in the suit led (which may be spades). Such a bidder must hold at least one trump, and must get his partner's permission by asking 'Can you cover a no trump?' and getting the reply, 'Yes.' The bid wins or loses double.

Double Nil: Both partners may bid nil for a joint win or loss of 500 points (or an automatic win or loss of the game). If either wins a trick, their opponents get a bonus of 100 points.

Bemo: Little Bemo is a bid to win the first six tricks in addition to the normal bid, for a separate bonus of 60 won or lost. Big Bemo is the same for the first nine tricks and a score of 90 won or lost.

Solo Spades

Four can play without partnerships, each bidding individually. If you can follow suit, you must, if possible, beat the highest card so far played to the trick; if unable to follow suit, you must trump, and overtrump, if possible.

▌Kaiser
4 players (2 × 2), 32 cards

Of many interesting games peculiar to Canada, this one is especially popular in the Ukrainian communities of Saskatchewan and neighbouring provinces and has been so since about the mid twentieth century. The following is derived from material posted on the Internet. (The game is not to be confused with Kaiserspiel or Kaiserjass, the modern form of Karnöffel.)

Preliminaries Four players sitting crosswise in partnerships use a 32-card pack basically ranking AKQJT987 in each suit. However, the ♠7 is replaced by ♠3 and the ♥7 by ♥5, both remaining lowest in their respective suits.

Deal Deal eight cards each in ones.

Object For the bidding side to win at least as many points as it bid, counting 1 per trick, plus 5 for winning the ♥5 in a trick, and minus 3 for catching ♠3 in a trick (yielding a maximum possible 12 points).

Bidding Each in turn, starting with eldest, has one opportunity to speak, and may use it to pass or bid. The minimum bid is 5, the maximum 12, and each must be higher than the last. No prospective trump is named when bidding, but a bidder intending to play at no trump should say so (e.g. 'Five no'). There are two exceptions to the need to bid higher. One is that a no trump bid beats one of the same number with trump implied. The other is that the dealer can beat the previous caller by naming the same bid, not necessarily higher.

If all pass, the hands are scrapped and the deal passes round.

Play The highest bidder names trumps, if any, and leads to the first trick. Players must follow suit if possible, otherwise may play any card. The trick is taken by the highest card of the suit led, or by the highest trump if any are played, and the winner of each trick leads to the next.

Score Each side counts 1 per trick, plus 5 for ♥5 and minus 3 for ♠3. The bidding side, if it won at least as many points as it bid, scores the number of points it actually took, doubled if played at no trump. If not, it loses the amount of its bid, also doubled at no trump.

The non-bidders score the amount they actually took, unless their cumulative score is 45 or more, in which case it remains pegged. (But if they finish with a negative count, for example by taking only one trick containing the ♠3, then it is deducted regardless of their total.)

Game is 52 points.

Variations Many are listed on the Pagat website.

Forty-One

4 players (2 × 2), 52 cards

This Middle-Eastern game was observed by Dan Glimne being played by Syrian immigrants in Sweden. It was said to be much played in Syria, less so in Lebanon, but not in Iraq, Jordan or Saudi Arabia. An interesting feature is that partners must play in such a way as to assist each other as individuals.

Preliminaries Four players, sitting crosswise in partnerships and playing to the right, receive 13 cards each, dealt 1-2-2-2-2-2-2 from a 52-card French pack ranking AKQJT98765432.

Object For either member of a partnership to reach 41 points over as few deals as possible, by accurately bidding how many tricks they will win, with hearts as permanent trumps.

Auction Each in turn from the dealer's right examines his cards and states the minimum number of tricks he expects to win. If the four bids total less than 11, the cards are thrown in and the deal passes on. However, bids of seven or more count double, so any such bid automatically ensures that play will proceed.

Play Eldest leads first. Players must follow suit if possible, otherwise may play any card. The trick is taken by the highest card of the suit led, or by the highest heart if any are played, and the winner of each trick leads to the next.

Score Each player's score is recorded cumulatively. Bids of 1 to 6 score, if successful, 1 point per trick bid (even if more were made), or lose 1 per trick bid if unsuccessful. Bids of 7 or more correspondingly win or lose 2 points per trick bid.

The player who first reaches or exceeds 41 points wins for his side.

Vint

4 players (2 × 2), 52 cards

This Russian game is held to be a significant ancestor of Bridge, as it involves above- and below-line scoring and the same trump hierarchy as Biritch. A highly elaborate version of Bid Whist, its name means 'screw', in allusion to the competitive way in which bids are forced up in the auction. The only English-language descriptions I am aware of go back to that by Hoffmann and Rennenkampf in *The Laws and Principles of Vint*, 1900. Whereas the 1900 game is reasonably simple and sedate, the following, based on a Swedish description of the game described as current in Estonia, is extremely complex and elaborate. It embodies, however, an excellent scoring principle – namely, that the value of each trick varies not with the suit but with the level of the contract. In effect, the higher you bid, the more each trick is worth. This could with profit be applied to Bridge (see Brint).

Preliminaries A session consists of three rubbers. Each involves a different combination of two partners sitting crosswise in partnerships to yield an individual final result. A rubber consists of two won games followed by four extra deals. Scores are made above and below a line, as at Bridge, but the scoresheet is necessarily divided into four columns instead of two, and each member of a partnership scores the same in their respective columns for any given deal.

Deal Choose the first dealer by any agreed means. All play goes to the left. Deal twelve cards each face up and four to the table face down.

First auction There are two auctions. The first determines the declaring side, and the second increases their contract. Dealer bids first, and each successive bid must exceed the previous one. Bidding is for a number of tricks to be taken in excess of six, as at Bridge, but starting at the four level, i.e. for ten tricks. The bids from lowest to highest are 4 nullos (undertaking to lose at least ten tricks at no trump), 4♠, 4♣, 4♦, 4♥, 4 grand (= no trump), then 5 nullos, and so on upwards to a maximum 7 grand. There is no doubling. The first auction ends when everyone has passed twice in succession, i.e. after eight consecutive passes. If no one bids and all pass twice, the hand is played as a pass-misère (see below).

Declarers exchange The highest bidder becomes declarer. He turns the table cards face up for all to see, adds them to his hand, and passes any four cards face down to his partner. His partner adds them to his hand, then passes any one card face down to each other player, so that all now have thirteen.

Second auction Declarer now begins the second auction, which takes place only with his partner. His first bid must exceed his last, quoting either more tricks in the same suit or the same number in a higher. This auction ends when both have passed twice in succession, i.e. after four consecutive passes.

Exchange and doubling Before play, eldest hand (declarer's left-hand opponent in a positive contract, right-hand in a nullo) passes one card face down to his partner, who passes him one in return. This does not apply, however, in a slam contract of six or seven. After this exchange, eldest may 'knock' to signify that he doubles the contract, and declarer's partner may then knock to redouble. If eldest declines to knock, his partner may do so; similarly, declarer may redouble if his partner did not. If a contract of four is not doubled, the defenders usually concede it as won without bothering to play.

Play Eldest makes the opening lead. Players must follow suit if possible, otherwise may play any card. The trick is taken by the highest card of the suit led, or by the highest trump if any are played, and the winner of each trick leads to the next.

Pass-misère If all pass, dealer deals the table cards around so all have thirteen. Each player exchanges one card face down with his partner. Dealer's left-hand opponent leads to the first of 13 tricks at no trump, and the aim is to lose the most tricks.

Score Above the line go scores for the contract, overtricks, and honours. The contract score varies only with the number contracted, regardless of whether played in suit, nullo, or grand, thus:

contract	declarers if won	defenders if lost
four	1000 (overtricks ignored)	400 per undertrick
five	2000 + 200 per overtrick	500 per undertrick
six	3000 + 200 per overtrick	600 per undertrick + premium of 400
seven	4500	700 per undertrick + premium of 1000

Honours in a suit contract are all four Aces and the top five trumps – nine in all, as the trump Ace counts twice. They are scorable by either side regardless of win or loss. Whichever side held a majority of honours (after the exchange, if any) scores the number of honours held multiplied by 10 times the contract value.

Example: A side that held the trump Ace and two others, plus King, Queen, Ten of trumps in a contract of five, scores 7 honours times 5 contract times 10 = 350.

Further scores accrue to either side for holding in one hand three Aces for 200, four Aces for 400, trump AKQ 200, plus 200 for each lower card in sequence, non-trump AKQ 100, plus 100 for each lower card in sequence.

At grand, a side that held three or four Aces adds (respectively) 40 or 50 times the contract value. Three or four in one hand count 400 or 800, and suit-sequences headed AKQ count 200 per card involved.

At nullos, there are no honours, but a side that succeeds in discarding an Ace to a trick scores 100 times the number of the trick at which it fell.

At pass-misère, the side winning fewer tricks scores 100 for each trick difference between the two sides, i.e. six tricks 100, five 300, and so on. Scores for discarding Aces also apply as at nullos.

Scores below the line are what count towards game. Both sides score below the line the numerical value of the contract multiplied by the number of tricks it actually won – except in a pass-misère, when neither side scores below the line. This applies regardless of whether the contract was made, and irrespective of doubling.

Example: If the contract was 6 (doubled or not) and the tricks divided 8–5, the respective scores are 48 and 30.

Game and rubber Game is 60 below the line. The first side to win two games scores a bonus of 400, and exactly four more deals are played.

For its third game a side scores 600, for its fourth 800, and so on (improbably) in increments of 200.

Quinto

This delightful and imaginative Whist variant was invented by 'Professor Hoffmann' (Angelo Lewis) around 1900.

Preliminaries Four sit crosswise in partnerships and play to the left. From a 53-card pack ranking AKQJT98765432 in each suit, and including a Joker, deal twelve each in ones and leave the last five face down on the table as a *cachette* (Hoffmann's terminology).

Object Game is 250 points over as many deals as necessary. Points accrue for winning tricks (5 each) and especially for any 'quints' they may contain. The best quint is the Joker, or 'Quint royal', worth 25 points. Additional quints are the Five of each suit, and two cards of the same suit totalling five (A+4, 2+3) and falling to the same trick. A quint in hearts scores 20, diamonds 15, clubs 10, spades 5.

Doubling Before play, each has one opportunity to pass, double or redouble an opponent's double. A double increases the value of won tricks from 5 to 10 points in the current deal, a redouble further increases them to 20 each. An incidental but not insignificant effect is to reduce the relative value of quints to tricks.

Play Eldest leads to the first trick, and the winner of each trick leads to the next. Suit must be followed if possible, otherwise any card may be played. There is no single trump suit. Instead, the suits rank in order from low to high: spades, clubs, diamonds, hearts. A player unable to follow suit to the card led may discard from a lower suit (if any), or may trump by playing from a higher suit (if any). The trick is therefore taken by the highest card of the highest suit played. The Joker may not be led to a trick, and cannot win a trick, but otherwise may be played at any time, whether or not its holder can follow suit. (It follows that a player still holding the Joker at the eleventh trick must play it if the only alternative is to win the trick, otherwise he would have to lead it to the twelfth.)

Score During play, the side winning a trick containing a quint scores immediately for the quint (Joker, Five, A-4, 3-2), according to its suit.

If this brings them to the 250-point target, they win, and play ceases immediately. Otherwise, the side winning the last trick wins also the cachette, which counts as a thirteenth trick, and scores for any quint(s) it may contain. If neither side has reached or exceeded 250, the thirteen tricks are then counted at 5, 10, or 20 each, depending on any doubling. If both sides are still under 250, or both are over but tied, there is another deal.

Whist for three players

Manni (Sprøyte)

Manni is the Icelandic for chap or bloke. The following version is called Hornafjarðar-Manni, of which its Internet contributor says: 'It is one of several versions of card games called Manni . . . The story says that a local minister of our church is the author. This version is the most popular in Hornafjörður as in other parts of the country for the past decades.' (But the fact that an identical game is played in Norway under the name Sprøyte, meaning 'squirt', may absolve the Icelandic minister of any such responsibility.)

Preliminaries Three players use a 52-card pack ranking AKQJ T98765432. Deal a batch of four cards face down to the table (forming the *manni*), then a batch of three to each player, and repeat until there are 16 in the *manni* and 12 in each hand. The player at dealer's right cuts the *manni*, shows the bottom card of the top half to determine what game is to be played, then places the top half face down beneath the bottom half of the *manni*.

Games If the cut card is low (2 to 5), the game is *nolo*. The aim is to win as few tricks as possible, playing at No Trump and with Ace counting low.

If it is intermediate (6–10), the game is *trumps*. The aim is to win tricks, with the suit of the cut card as trump and Ace counting high.

If it is high (Jack to Ace), the game is *no trump*. The aim is to win tricks, playing at No Trump and with Ace counting high.

Exchange Before play, eldest may exchange up to seven cards with the *manni*, second-hand can exchange up to five, and dealer up to as many as remain. (If dealer takes his full entitlement, he will get the card that decided the game.) Source does not state whether the exchange involves discarding first and then drawing replacements, or drawing the stated number and then discarding the surplus. The former seems more likely.

Play Eldest leads. Players must follow suit if possible, otherwise may play any card. The trick is taken by the highest card of the suit led, or by the highest trump if any are played, and the winner of each trick leads to the next.

Score In positive games, each player scores 1 point per trick taken in excess of four, or minus 1 for each trick less than four. In nolo, these scores are reversed. Game is 10 points.

Bismarck

The three-player equivalent of Dutch or Norwegian Whist. A game is 12 deals, each player dealing four times in succession. Dealer receives 20 cards, from which he rejects any four face down; the others receive 16 cards each. Deal (1) is played at no trump. (2) Cut or turn the last card for trump. (3) Dealer announces trumps. In the first three deals, dealer scores 1 point for each trick taken above eight, and each opponent 1 point per trick taken above four. (4) No trump misère: dealer scores 1 point for each trick below four, the others 1 point for each below six.

Sergeant Major (8-5-3, 9-5-2)

Varieties of this modern extension of Bismarck are played in the armed services, and relatives of it in India and the Middle East. Deal sixteen each in ones and four face down as a kitty. Dealer names a trump suit, discards four, and takes the kitty in their place. Eldest leads, and tricks are played as at Whist. The dealer's target is 8 tricks, that of eldest 5, the other's 3; and each wins or loses 1 point (or stake) per trick taken above or below his quota. A player who took more than his quota is 'up', one who took less is 'down'. In subsequent deals, after the cards have been dealt but before the kitty is taken, if just one player was up in the previous deal he gives to each opponent who was down one unwanted card from his hand for each trick by which the other fell short. For each card received, the recipient must return to the donor the highest card he holds of the same suit (the same card, if he has no other). If two players were up, they each do this to the third, starting with the one who has the higher target to reach in the current deal.

(This practice seems borrowed from oriental Climbing games: see page 457.) After any such exchanges, dealer discards four and takes the kitty, as before. The game ends when somebody wins 12 or more tricks in one deal. Variations are inevitable. In a Canadian equivalent, the targets are 9-5-2.

Chinese Whist

Like four-hand Chinese Whist, but deal eight each face down, eight face up, one in hand, and leave the 52nd card face down out of play.

Dummy Whist

> I was delighted to see him, and suggested we should have a game of whist with a dummy, and by way of merriment said: '*You* can be the dummy.' Cummings (I thought rather ill-naturedly) . . . said he couldn't stop; he only called to leave me the *Bicycle News*, as he had done with it.
>
> G. and W. Grossmith, *The Diary of a Nobody*, 1892

Deal three hands and a dummy hand, the latter face up on the opposite side of the table from the person playing it. Each takes the dummy for the duration of a rubber, which is 5 points up, and a game is three rubbers. Lowest cut at the start of the game takes dummy in the first rubber, highest in the third.

| Whist for two players

Double Dummy

Players sit adjacently (not opposite each other), the one cutting the lower card having choice of relative position. Deal four hands including two dummies, one opposite each player, the first card of the pack going to dealer's dummy. Turn the dummies face up. Non-dealer leads and play proceeds to the left, each playing alternately from his own hand and from dummy.

German Whist

Deal six cards each and stack the rest face down. Turn the top card for trump. Non-dealer leads first, suit must be followed if possible, and the winner of a trick draws the top card of the stock and adds it to his hand. The loser draws the next card, and the previous trick-winner, before leading to the next, faces the top card of stock. Play continues normally when the stock is empty, and whoever wins a majority of the last 13 tricks scores the difference between the two totals.

Humbug

Players face each other. Deal four hands, including two dummies. Each announces whether he will play as dealt or exchange his hand for the dummy on his right, which he must then play. Ignoring dummies, play 13 tricks of two cards each. Score as at Whist.

Calypso   4 players, 208 cards (4 × 52)

An ingenious hybrid of Whist and Rummy, invented by R. W. Willis of Trinidad, polished by Kenneth Konstam, and promoted – unsuccessfully – by British playing-card companies in the 1950s as a cross between Bridge and Canasta. Disconcertingly odd at first play, it rewards perseverance.

Cards Use four 52-card packs, preferably of identical back design and colour, and certainly all the same size, weight, and finish. Shuffle them together very thoroughly before play. Cards rank AKQJT98765432.

Partners and trumps The players cutting the two highest cards are partners against the two lowest, and sit opposite each other. Whoever cut highest deals first and has the choice of seats, thereby determining his own and everyone else's personal trumps.

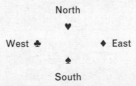

North
♥

West ♣   ♦ East

♠

South

Deal Thirteen cards each face down in ones, and stack the rest face down to one side. These will gradually be used up in subsequent deals. A game consists of four deals, one by each player, the turn to deal passing to the left.

Object A calypso is a 13-card suit sequence. Your aim is to build calypsos in your own personal trump suit, to assist your partner in building calypsos in his, and to hinder your opponents from building calypsos in theirs. The cards used for building them come from those you win in tricks, not directly from hand. The catch is that calypsos must be completed one at a time. That is, you may not start a second calypso until you have completed your first. If any cards won in a trick duplicate those already in a calypso under construction, they cannot (with one slight exception) be retained for future calypsos. It is therefore practically impossible for anyone to complete all four possible calypsos, and even three will be something of a feat.

Play Eldest leads to the first trick, and the winner of each trick leads to the next. Follow suit if possible, otherwise play any card.

If the leader leads his personal trump, then the trick is taken by the card led, regardless of rank, or by the highest personal trump if any are played (by anyone who cannot follow suit).

If the leader leads from any other suit, then the trick is taken by the highest card of the suit led, or by the highest personal trump if any are played.

If the trick is being taken by two identical cards, or by personal trumps of different suits but equal rank, then the first such card wins.

☞ If somebody else leads your personal trump suit, you cannot trump it, but can only hope to win the trick by being the first to play the highest card of it.

The winner of a trick takes from it any cards needed towards the building of his current calypso, and passes to his partner any needed for his. The remainder are stacked face down on a pile of won cards belonging to his partnership, only one such pile being needed for each. These cards will be either of the opponents' suits, or of one's own but unusable because they duplicate cards already contained in the calypso under construction.

A completed calypso is immediately bunched together and stacked face up on the table in front of its builder. Its owner may then start building a new one, and for this purpose may use any valid cards in the trick just taken.

Ending and scoring When thirteen tricks have been played, the next in turn to deal does so, and this continues until four deals have been played. Each side then scores as follows:

500	for each partner's first calypso
750	for each partner's second calypso
1000	for each subsequent calypso
20	per card in an unfinished calypso
50	for each card in the winnings pile

Comment Resist the temptation to lead personal trumps at every opportunity for the novelty of winning easy tricks. Opponents can easily thwart this by playing cards that duplicate those in your current calypso, thus preventing them from being used in future calypsos.

Don't forget . . .

- Play to the left (clockwise) unless otherwise stated.
- Eldest or Forehand means the player to the left of the dealer in left-handed games, to the right in right-handed games.
- T = Ten, p = players, pp = in fixed partnerships, c = cards, † = trump, ☆ = Joker.

2 **Solo family**

The following games are for prima donnas and exhibitionists. They're plain-trick games like Whist and Bridge, but differ in that everyone plays for themselves instead of in fixed partnerships. Typically, in each deal the highest bidder names trumps and aims to win a target number of tricks by playing alone against the combined efforts of the other two (in three-hand games) or three (in four-handers). The basic bid is usually called a solo, and we may refer to its player as the soloist. When four play, a soloist with a dodgy hand may call for assistance in return for a cut of the rewards, so the game is played sometimes one against three and sometimes two against two. A temporary partnership of this type is perhaps better termed 'alliance', from an old game of that name.

Many nations have their own version of a game based on this principle, and many are simply called Solo. The English variety, actually borrowed from Belgium in the late nineteenth century, is known as Solo Whist, though 'English Solo' would be a better title.

The section concludes with two modern games which exploit the historically novel device of bidding to win an exact number of tricks rather than just a minimum.

| Solo Whist   4 players, 52 cards

English Solo became popular in Britain as a relaxation from the rigours of partnership Whist in the 1890s, just as Bridge was appearing on the scene. Were it not for this unfortunate coincidence, Solo might have become more refined and occupied the social position now claimed by Contract. In the event, it became a popular commuters' game in the days of real railways, being more suitable than 'railway Bridge' in that it allowed a single game to go on as commuters got in and out at different stations, cutting in and out of play at convenient points. It now remains an essentially informal game of home and pub, where it is played for the direct interest of small stakes rather than for the more arcane pleasures of ingenious coups and complex scores.

Preliminaries Four players, 52 cards ranking AKQJT98765432. There is no game structure: each deal is settled immediately in coins or counters, though scores can be kept in writing.

Deal Deal thirteen each in four batches of three and one of four. Turn the last card face up to establish a suit of preference for trump. (But see *Variants*, below.)

Bidding Eldest hand speaks first and the turn to bid passes to the left. Each in turn may pass, make a higher bid than the last one, or accept a proposal (see below). A player who passes may not bid again (with one exception noted below), and when a bid has been followed by three consecutive passes the last bidder becomes the soloist and play begins. From lowest to highest, the possible bids are:

1. Proposal and acceptance (Prop and Cop). An offer to win at least eight tricks with the preferred suit as trump, provided that another player is willing to accept the proposal and assist in this enterprise. Bid by saying 'I propose', or just 'Prop'. Provided that no other bid has intervened a subsequent player may accept the proposal by saying 'I accept', or, traditionally, 'Cop'. If no one then bids higher, the arrangement becomes a contract. But any of the following non-partnership bids automatically annuls an attempted Prop and Cop.

2. Solo. To win at least five tricks with the preferred suit as trump.

3. Misère. To lose every trick, playing at no trump.

4. Abundance ('a bundle'). To win at least nine tricks with any trump suit of the bidder's choice, which need not yet be named.

5. Royal abundance. The same, but with the preferred suit as trump.

6. Misère ouverte (or spread misère). To lose every trick, playing at no trump and with one's hand of cards spread face up on the table after the first trick has been played.

7. Slam. To win all 13 tricks at no trump, but with the advantage of leading to the first trick.

If eldest proposes and everyone else passes, eldest may (but need not) raise the bid to a solo. If eldest starts by passing, and another proposes without being overcalled, eldest may (but need not) accept the proposal.

If all four pass, the book-rule is that the hands are thrown in without play and the deal passes to the left. (But see *Variants*.)

Play The contract established, dealer takes the turn-up into hand and the first lead is made by eldest hand, or, in the case of a slam, by the soloist. In a spread misère, the soloist's hand must be faced and spread at the end of the first trick and before the second is led.

Players must follow suit if possible, otherwise may play any card. The trick is taken by the highest card of the suit led, or by the highest trump if any are played, and the winner of each trick leads to the next.

Settlement The soloist (or, in Prop and Cop, each partner) receives from or pays to each opponent in accordance with an agreed schedule, such as:

Prop and cop	10, plus 2 per over/under-trick
Solo	10 plus 2 per over/under-trick
Misère	20
Abundance	30, plus 3 per over/under-trick
Spread misère	40
Slam	60

Some schools omit payments for over- or under-tricks. If preferred, the appropriate amounts can simply be entered on a scoresheet as a plus score in the column or columns of those who make them.

Variations

There are many procedural variations. Some schools shuffle cards at start of play but not again until after the play of a royal abundance: between deals they merely gather up the tricks in order around the table and cut before dealing. Some schools deal first 4-3-3-3, then 3-4-3-3, then 3-3-4-3, and finally 3-3-3-4, thereafter repeating the sequence. Some, instead of turning the last card for preference, follow a pre-determined cycle of suits for each cycle of four deals, typically ♥, ♣, ♦, ♠. Thus each player is associated with a particular dealing pattern and suit of preference. Many aspects of this long-popular game have been subject to local variations. The following are typical.

If all pass One of following may be played in the event that everyone passes.

General misère. No trumps. Whoever takes the last trick loses, at the same rate as a solo.

Competitive misère. No trumps. Whoever takes the most tricks loses, at the same rate as a solo.

Royal misère. The turned suit trumps. Solo value is lost by the first player to win five tricks, or four if no one takes five.

Kimberley (Flying Colours). Re-open the auction and allow a bid of solo in a suit other than the one turned.

First trick trump In some schools, the first trick of a non-royal abundance is played with the turned suit as trump, the announced suit not taking effect until the second. In others, the trump is not announced until the first card has been led to the first trick.

Trump slam Some players allow a slam bid in trumps as an alternative to, or overcall of, the no trump slam. This makes sense only if you ignore the rule allowing the slam bidder to lead, since, if the slam is safe with a trump suit, it is equally safe without.

Notes on play

You are best placed to make a positive (non-misère) bid when sitting eldest hand, as you have the opening lead. With a possible game you should at least propose, because you can always raise it to a solo if the others admit weakness by passing. As dealer, you are well placed for any sort of bid, as you will have heard the others and been able to gauge the possible opposition. Three passes might encourage you to bid solo on somewhat weaker cards than would be advisable for second or third hand. As second hand, you are worst placed for a positive bid, as you will be playing second to the first trick and have no idea what to expect from third hand and dealer. For misère, dealer is best positioned, and eldest worst, as such hands need to be led up to.

But position can also be affected by the shape of the hand. For example, assuming spades turned:

1. ♠AKQT2 ♥J8 ♣JT9 ♦J43
2. ♠AQ2 ♥AQ2 ♣AQ2 ♦A964

Hand 1 offers a solo if you are eldest, as you can lead trumps and probably drop the Jack for five tricks straight off. But it doesn't favour you as dealer: no one leads trumps against a solo, and by the time you have a void suit you could either ruff low and be overtaken by the Jack, or ruff high and so strengthen the Jack in its holder's hand.

Hand 2, however, favours dealer rather than eldest, being risky to lead from. You would have to squeeze a fifth trick from a Queen, requiring you to be so placed as to play last to a trick led in the appropriate suit.

Generally, a solo bid requires length or strength in trumps rather than high cards in plain suits, and trumps are usually best exploited by ruffing rather than leading them, except in hands like (1) above.

Similar principles apply to an abundance. Always resist the temptation to bid abundance instead of solo on the strength of eight tricks and a stroke of luck! This is not only no substitute for nine tricks but also, quite frequently, receives enough strokes of bad luck to yield fewer than eight. It's best to count probable losers rather than winners in assessing the hand – if they exceed four, don't do it.

Abundances are called on hands of various shapes, such as very long trumps (3), overall strength (4), and two-suited hands (5). For example (with spades trump in each case):

3. ♠QJT87642 ♥A2 ♣7 ♦AK
4. ♠AQJ73 ♥AK ♣AKQ ♦AK6
5. ♠AJT953 ♥AKQJ63 ♣8

A slam hand needs only to be recognized when seen. Unbeatable hands obviously contain consecutive top cards in every suit held, whether four lots of AKQ and an odd Jack, or all thirteen of a suit. Whether or not to gamble on such a hand as, say, AKQ in three suits and AKQ2 in the fourth depends on what you can afford to lose should one player be able to hold back the right suit for the last trick.

Prop and Cop, inexplicably abolished in some schools, is an interesting bid, offering as much fun as opportunity for skilful play. Lying behind it is the idea that if no one is strong enough to bid five tricks alone, any two players with hands strong enough for four each may get together in a bid of eight. The important thing is to avoid having both partners bid on trump strength alone, possibly conceding six tricks in side suits, or both bidding on side-suit support alone, possibly finding themselves out-trumped. Experience advises eldest to propose on overall strength and be accepted on the basis of trump support, but other hands to propose on trump strength and be accepted on side-suit support. Either way, it is better to propose on a hand containing many possibilities (6) than on one containing only four certainties (7):

6. ♠Q985 ♥KQJ53 ♣KQ92 ♦–
7. ♠AK85 ♥A53 ♣AJ2 ♦984

When partners happen to sit opposite each other, the play resembles partnership Whist; but when next to each other, more thought is needed. They are clearly best placed when playing first and fourth to a trick, worst when playing first and second. If, as eldest, you are partnering your left-hand neighbour, you should lead top trumps if possible, otherwise weak plain suits. If partnering dealer, lead your best trumps regardless.

The difference between misère and misère ouverte is that the latter is called on a hand that should lose tricks regardless of the distribution of cards in opposing hands, while the former may conceal a possible weakness against an unfavourable distribution. Not that a closed misère is necessarily beatable: with a favourable or merely average distribution it could still be as safe as houses.

An unbeatable spread misère is one which does not have to be led from and enables the soloist to underplay any card led at any time, such as:

8. ♠432 ♥642 ♣AQT8642 ♦–

Here spades are safe because they are the lowest, and hearts because you can underplay any card led and still retain the lowest. An alternating low sequence is therefore every bit as good as a solid one. Clubs show an extension of the alternating low sequence. The suit is safe, not because the AQ can be thrown to diamond leads, but because it is safe against as many club leads as can possibly be made. Even if the missing KJ9753 were in one hand and led consecutively, you could still underplay them, and by the time you're stuck with AQ, no more clubs remain to lead.

But alternating suit patterns are useless for leading. Eldest, from the sample hand, can start only with the unbeatable spades, and an alteration to one card would make the hand unbiddable as a spread:

9. ♠732 ♥642 ♣AQT8642 ♦–

The only sure way of losing that Seven is to throw it to a diamond lead, which cannot reasonably be expected, even though the hand is not exposed till after the first trick. The club-holders, upon seeing this hand, would promptly lead clubs till those with high spades had discarded them, after which three spade leads could force the Seven to take a trick.

Whatever the bid, the opponents must play together as a team, noting and playing into one another's strengths and weaknesses. It always helps to place the trick with the player on the soloist's right, putting soloist in the worst position (second) for playing to a trick.

Belgian Whist (Wiezen, Kleurwiezen, Whist à la Couleur)

4 players, 52 cards

A popular continental game, lying about half way between Boston and Solo Whist.

Preliminaries Four players, 52 cards ranking AKQJT98765432 in each suit. Each player starts with the same number of chips or counters and places an agreed small stake in the pool before each deal. The turn to deal, bid and play passes to the left. Deal thirteen cards each.

Bidding Each in turn may pass, make a proposal or a higher bid, or accept a proposal that has not been overcalled. Eldest hand has the additional privilege of checking ('*J'attends*'), in which case the opening bid passes to the left. A player who has passed may not bid again, apart from the first to speak (whether Eldest or the next player if he checked) who may accept a proposal if no one overcalled it.

The bids are listed below from lowest to highest. Certain bids may be overcalled by the same bid in a higher-ranking suit, for which purpose the suit order is ♠, ♣, ♦, ♥ (highest).

1. Proposal in spades/clubs/diamonds/hearts. To win at least eight tricks with the aid of a partner, the caller to win at least five and partner at least three. Any subsequent player in turn to bid may offer support, provided that no intervening player has bid higher. A player may overcall a proposal, whether accepted or not, by proposing in a higher suit. A player whose proposal is followed by three passes may pass or raise the bid to a solo.

2. Hole. A proposal made by anyone holding three or four Aces. If three, whoever holds the fourth must reply 'Hole' and name a trump suit. If four, he announces this fact, then whoever holds ♥K must reply 'Hole', and the two play a Proposal in hearts. A player holding four Aces and ♥K may bid Hole, in which case whoever holds ♥Q becomes the partner in a heart contract. A bid of Hole may not be overcalled, and so becomes the contract. (Source does not state whether anyone

holding three or four Aces is obliged to bid Hole, but the fact that it cannot be overcalled seems to imply it.)

3. Solo in spades/clubs/diamonds/hearts. To win at least six tricks, playing alone.

4. Petite misère. To lose all 12 tricks at no trump, after everyone has discarded one card before the first trick is played. Two players may bid this, but must then play co-operatively, as both lose equally if either takes a trick.

5. Seven in spades/clubs/diamonds/hearts. To win at least seven tricks, playing alone.

6. Piccolissimo. To win exactly two tricks, playing at no trump.

7. Eight in spades/clubs/diamonds/hearts. To win at least eight tricks, playing alone.

8. Piccolo. To win exactly one trick, playing at no trump. Two players may bid this, but must then play co-operatively, as both lose if one loses.

9. Abundance. To win at least nine tricks alone, playing at no trump and leading to the first trick. It may be played open (the soloist playing with his hand exposed before the first trick) for a higher score.

10. Grande misère. To lose all 13 tricks, playing at no trump.

11. Slam solo. To win all 13 tricks alone, with a specified suit as trump, and leading to the first trick. It may be played open for a higher score.

If all pass, everyone stakes again to the pool and the same dealer deals again.

Play The opening lead is made by the soloist in an abundance or a slam, if any, otherwise by eldest. Players must follow suit if possible, otherwise may play any card. The trick is taken by the highest card of the suit led, or by the highest trump if any are played, and the winner of each trick leads to the next.

Pay-off If successful, the soloist wins the pool, plus an amount from each opponent that varies according to the contract and the result, as listed below. If partnered, both divide the pool equally and each receives the stated amount from one opponent. If unsuccessful, soloist doubles the pool and pays the appropriate amount to each opponent. If partnered, they double the pool between them – half each – and each pays the stated amount to one opponent. A typical schedule of pay-offs might be:

Proposal	4, plus 1 per overtrick
Hole	4, plus 1 per overtrick
Six solo	8, plus 2 per overtrick
Petite misère	10
Seven solo	12, plus 3 per overtrick
Piccolissimo	14
Eight solo	16, plus 4 per overtrick
Piccolo	18
Abundance	22, or 44 if played open
Grande misère	28
Slam	100, or 200 if played open

Solo variants

Auction Solo

An unsuccessful attempt made in the 1920s to increase the variety of bids and so emulate the pattern of (Auction) Bridge. Prop and Cop is abolished. All suit bids may be made in a suit of one's own choice, which is not stated unless overcalled by a bid of the same number in the turned suit. Solo bids may be made for five, six, seven or eight tricks, followed by misère, then 'abundance' bids of nine, ten, eleven, twelve, followed by misère ouverte, a no trump slam with declarer leading, and a slam in the turned suit (only – no alternative) with eldest leading. The pay-offs are solo 2, misère 4, abundance 6, ouverte 8, slam 12, with 1 per over- or under-trick in positive bids.

Nomination Whist

(a name also applied to Oh Hell!). An excellent alliance game, reported to me (by Rodney Jones) as popular in the navy.

Deal thirteen each from a 52-card pack ranking AKQJT98765432. Each in turn either passes, starts the bidding (minimum seven), or overcalls a previous bid. A bid is to win the stated number of tricks in exchange for naming trumps, playing either solo or with a temporary ally. The highest bidder announces trumps and names a card, e.g.

'Hearts, Ace of spades'. The holder of the named card becomes the bidder's ally, but may reveal this fact only by playing it or obviously supporting the bidder in play. The bidder may play a solo by naming a card already held; but this, too, will only become evident in play.

The bidder wins from each opponent if successful, or pays to each opponent if not, one unit for each trick bid. A slam bid wins or loses 26, but if a slam is made unbid, the bidder is penalized by having to pay 13 each instead. If there was an ally, each of them wins from or pays to one opponent.

Knockout Whist

(3–7p, 52c) A popular and highly variegated British game of pub and playground. The simplest rules are:

Deal seven each and turn the next for trumps. Dealer leads first and the winner of each trick leads to the next. Follow suit if possible, otherwise play any card. The trick is taken by the highest card of the suit led or by the highest trump if any are played. Anyone failing to take a trick is knocked out and takes no further part in the game. Whoever took the most tricks gathers and shuffles the cards, deals six to each player, looks at his or her hand, announces trumps, and leads to the second round.

Play continues in this way, with those taking no tricks being knocked out, and the player taking most tricks dealing, choosing trumps, and leading to the next. In case of a tie for most tricks, the tied player cutting the highest card deals next. The number of cards dealt decreases by one on each deal, so only one is dealt on the seventh round. The game will end before that, of course, if one player wins all the tricks in an earlier round.

Boston (Boston de Fontainebleau)   4 players, 52 cards

This great nineteenth-century card game apparently commemorates the American War of Independence, but probably originated in France around 1770. It is a hybrid of Quadrille and Whist, combining the 52-card pack and logical ranking system of the English game with a range of solo and alliance bids borrowed from the French. Both the French and the Americans embraced it as a sort of politico-cultural counter to the popularity of Whist, for which reason it was correspondingly eschewed by their mutual enemy, and so never acquired in Britain the enormous following it subsequently attracted in Europe (except through its descendant, Solo Whist). Original Boston roughly resembled Auction Solo, but boasted an extraordinarily complicated system of payments for bids and over/under-tricks. It rapidly engendered countless topographical variants, such as Maryland, Boston de Nantes, Boston de Lorient, Russian Boston, and so on, and went in for thematic bids such as *independence*, *souverain*, *concordia*, and suchlike. The most widely recorded version, Boston de Fontainebleau, exhibited a rich variety of bids, but was blessed with a comparatively intelligible rate of exchange. This is the form described below, though it was subject to local variations, and no two books describe it in exactly the same way. Boston was invariably played for hard score, with chips and counters of fixed denominations; but in the following account I have translated them into a precisely equivalent written score.

Preliminaries Four players each receive 13 cards from a 52-card pack ranking AKQJT98765432. Whoever bids highest becomes the soloist and plays alone against the other three, unless one of them offers support as an ally.

The auction Each in turn may bid or pass. A bid nominates a contract from the list below and the suit of the proposed trump. Each bid must be higher than the preceding one in accordance with the schedule below, or equal in height but in a higher suit. For this purpose the lowest suit is spades, followed by clubs, diamonds, hearts.

Although misères are played at no trump, a nominal suit must be stated for each, as it can overcall its equivalent positive bid only if made in an equal or higher suit. For example, while 'six diamonds' may be overcalled by seven or more in any suit, a petite misère will overcall it only if announced as 'petite misère, diamonds' (or hearts). This is because its nominal suit governs the amount won or lost.

A player who passes may not bid again, but he may offer support if the eventual declarer subsequently calls for it (see below).

In the following schedule of bids and scores, a higher-numbered bid overcalls a lower. Of two equal-numbered bids, one positive and one misère, priority goes to whichever is made in the higher-ranking suit or, if still equal, to whichever of them was bid first.

Positive bids	Negative bids

1. **Five**. A bid to win at least five tricks in the named suit.
   If supported, the ally must win at least three.
   Base value 4 (+1 per over/under-trick).

2. **Six**. To win at least six tricks in the named suit.
   If supported, the ally must win at least four.
   Base value 6 (+2 per over/under-trick)   *Petite misère.*

   To lose every trick after making one discard,
   face down, and playing to 12 tricks at no trump.
   Base value 16

3. **Seven**. To win at least seven tricks in the named suit.
   If supported, the ally must win at least four.
   Base value 9 (+3 per over/under-trick).   *Piccolissimo.*

   To win exactly one trick at no trump.
   Base value 24

4. **Eight**. To win at least eight tricks in the named suit.
   If supported, the ally must win at least four.
   Base value 12 (+4 per over/under-trick).   *Grande misère.*

   To lose all thirteen tricks at no trump.
   Base value 32

5. **Nine**. To win at least nine tricks in the named suit.
   Base value 15 (+5 per over/under-trick).   *Four-ace misère.*

   Though holding four Aces, to lose all thirteen tricks at no trump,
   but with permission to revoke once in the first ten tricks.
   Base value 40

6. **Ten**. To win at least ten tricks in the named suit.
   Base value 18 (+6 per over/under-trick).   *Petite misère ouverte.*

   To lose every trick at no trump after making one discard, face down,
   exposing one's hand on the table, and playing to twelve tricks.
   Base value 48

7. **Eleven**. To win at least eleven tricks in the named suit.
   Base value 21 (+7 per over/under-trick).

Grande misère ouverte.

*To lose all thirteen tricks at no trump,
after laying one's hand, face up, on the table.*

Base value 56

8. **Twelve**. To win at least twelve tricks in the named suit.
   Base value 24 (+8 per over/under-trick).

9. **Boston**. To win all thirteen tricks in the named suit.
   Base value 100.

10. **Boston Ouvert**.
    The same, but with one's cards face up on the table.
    Base value 200.

Note: In petite misère, whether or not ouverte, only the bidder discards, and only twelve tricks are played.

Support The declarer in a bid of five, six, seven or eight may either play alone or, before the first trick is led, call for a supporter. If anyone accepts the call, the two play as temporary allies and share in any wins or losses. Though playing in concert, they store their won tricks separately, as the supporter is obliged to win a minimum number as stated in the Table, above.

Play In any ouvert game, the hand is exposed before the opening lead. Eldest always leads first. Players must follow suit if possible, otherwise may play any card. The trick is taken by the highest card of the suit led, or by the highest trump if any are played, and the winner of each trick leads to the next.

Scoring In a solo contract (unsupported), the amount won or lost is found by taking the base value quoted in the schedule above and increasing it as follows:

1. Add (except in misères and Bostons) the stated premium for each overtrick, if any, or undertrick, if lost.

2. Add (except in misères and Bostons) the equivalent of two overtricks if the soloist held three honours, or four overtricks if all four. The honours are Ace, King, Queen, Jack of trumps.

3. Double this total if the trump suit (or, in misères, the nominal trump) was clubs, treble it if diamonds, quadruple it if hearts.

If, in a supported contract, both players either fulfil or fail their individual contracts, each one's win or loss is calculated as described above, but is then halved before being recorded. (For a supporter, an overtrick or undertrick is that in excess of, or short of, the three or four that were personally contracted.) If only one member of the alliance succeeds, he scores zero, while the other loses half the value of his lost contract plus half the value of his ally's won contract.

☞ French schedules include an apparent but unexplained contract of *Boston à deux* ranking between bids of five and six tricks. Its base value is 50 – that is, half the value of a solo Boston contract. It sounds like a bid to win Boston with the aid of a partner, though it is hard to see why a bid of six should overcall it. Perhaps it is merely a premium score applied when, in a supported game, each makes his contract and both take all thirteen tricks between them.

Ombre (Hombre, L'Omber) 3 players, 40 cards

A game of cards that the better sort of people play three together at.
Vanbrugh, *The Provok'd Husband* (1727)

A game for card gourmets and snobs . . .
Grupp, *Kartenspiele* (1975)

Ombre is the Anglicized French name of one of the greatest games in card history, the ancestor of all bidding games, including Bridge. It was originally a sixteenth-century Spanish game called Hombre, meaning 'man', and denoting the solo player. Originally for four, it was as a three-hander that Ombre swept Europe towards the end of the seventeenth century. It was the height of fashion at the court of Charles II, a fact exploited to dramatic effect in Magdalen King-Hall's twice-filmed *The Wicked Lady*. The same game is depicted to equal effect by Alexander Pope in *The Rape of the Lock*. The modern game survives in Spain as Tresillo, in Denmark as L'hombre, in Peru as Rocambor, and no doubt elsewhere. All substantially resemble the following nineteenth-century English game, here taken from a treatise by Lord Aldenham, published privately in 1902.

Preliminaries Three players, 40 cards, AKQJ765432 in each suit. Each player starts with at least 40 chips or counters. A game is any number of deals divisible by three. Deal, bid and play to the right. The dealer antes five chips to the pool, deals nine cards each in threes, and sets the last 13 face down in the middle as a stock.

Rank of cards The rank of cards varies with the colour of each suit and whether it is plain or trump. Cards run, from highest to lowest:

black suits (plain)					K Q J 7 6 5 4 3 2
black trumps	♠A	†2	♣A		K Q J 7 6 5 4 3
red suits (plain)					K Q J A 2 3 4 5 6 7
red trumps	♠A	†7	♣A	A K Q J	2 3 4 5 6

Matadors The top three trumps are called Spadille (♠A), Manille (trump 2 if black or 7 if red), and Basta (♣A). They are collectively called matadors and have special powers. In a red trump suit the fourth highest is its Ace, called Punto, but it is not a matador.

Auction Eldest, the player at the dealer's right, speaks first, and each in turn may pass, make an opening bid, or overcall a previous bid. The highest bidder is designated Hombre, chooses trumps, and aims to win more tricks than either opponent individually. Thus five or more always wins, and four wins if the others split three–two. The bids are, from lowest to highest:

1. Entrada. Before play, Hombre announces trumps, makes any number of discards and draws the same number of replacements from the top of the stock.

2. Vuelta (voltereta). Hombre turns the top card of stock face up to determine trumps, then discards and draws as before.

3. Solo. Hombre announces trumps, but plays without discarding.

Each in turn may pass or bid, and, having passed, may not come in again. Each bid must be higher than the last. However, a player who comes earlier in the bidding has positional priority, and may 'hold' (take over) the bid just made by a later player.

Discard and draw Unless playing solo, Hombre may make any number of discards before drawing the same number from the top of the stock. Solo or not, both opponents may then discard and draw for themselves. As it is advantageous for one of them to have the stronger hand, Hombre's right-hand opponent may either discard immediately or pass this privilege to the other player. Whoever does so first may discard and draw any number (up to eight, under English rules). The other may then, but need not, discard up to as many as are left. Discards are always made face down, but rules vary as to whether any cards left untaken from the stock may be turned face up, and this point should be agreed before play.

Play Eldest leads first. Normally, players must follow suit if possible, otherwise may play any card. The trick is taken by the highest card of the suit led, or by the highest trump if any are played, and the winner of each trick leads to the next.

Reneging A player holding a matador need not play it to a trump lead, but may, if lacking lower trumps, instead 'renege' by playing from another suit. However, if a higher matador is led, a player with a lower matador may not renege but must play either it or another trump.

Five and the vole If Hombre takes the first five tricks straight off, he wins without further play. If instead he leads to the sixth, he thereby obligates himself to win the vole (all nine), thus increasing his potential winnings or penalties.

Conceding If Hombre thinks he cannot win, he may surrender at any time before playing to the fourth trick. He may not do this if playing a solo. In a vuelta, his surrender must be accepted by both opponents. In a simple game, however, either opponent may himself take over the role of Hombre and play the rest of the hand as if he had made the bid himself.

Outcomes The possible outcomes are:

1. Sacada = Hombre wins.

2. Puesta = Hombre loses and no one wins a majority of tricks (they fall 4-4-1 or 3-3-3)

3. Codille = Hombre loses and one opponent wins a majority of tricks.

For a win, Hombre takes the contents of the pot and is paid by each opponent as follows: simple game 5, vuelta 7, solo 15, plus any of the following bonuses:

The vole (nine tricks)	25
Primeras (win first five and stop)	1
Estuches (top trumps)	1 each

Estuches are three or more top consecutive trumps from ♠A downwards. Hombre would gain 4 extra if he had held (say) the top four but not the fifth, or, conversely, the fifth highest but none of the top four.

If Hombre loses puesta (4-4-1 or 3-3-3), he doubles the pool and adds to it five chips for each other player in the game.

If Hombre loses codille (one opponent wins a majority of tricks), he pays the same as for a puesta, but to the player who won instead of to the pot.

Penalties payable to the opponents are further increased as described above for *primeras* (losing the first five tricks), and *estuches* (one per top consecutive trump held or not held).

If Hombre fails to win all nine after leading to the sixth, he pays 30 to each opponent, less 2 if he played vuelta or 10 if he played solo, less also the number of *estuches* applicable.

Optional extras

Favorito A bid in diamonds overcalls the same in a different suit, and wins or loses double.

Gascarille Hombre discards and draws eight cards, and then announces trumps. This has a value of 3 chips. It may be bid only if everyone passes, and may be forced upon a player who holds ♠A.

Contrabola (misère). No one discards, Hombre entrumps a suit of which he holds at least one, and aims to lose every trick. If successful, he wins a simple game; if not, it counts as a puesta.

Comment The usual requirement for a simple bid is five trumps including two matadors, or one matador and King, Queen. Vuelta is bid with a few high cards in all suits rather than with two or three long suits. In neither bid is it wise to exchange more than about four cards. Remember that the effect of the exchange, which is also open to the opponents, is that the twenty-seven cards in play will include all eleven or twelve trumps and probably eight top cards in plain suits. Solo needs a long, strong suit with at least one matador and a void suit, or one headed solely by top cards. After winning five tricks, do not attempt the vole if there is a matador out against you. Since higher matadors cannot be forced out by lower ones, it is a common ploy for an opponent to hold one back in order to defeat the bid in the last four tricks.

Scoring by points

The following point-score system (of my devising) works reasonably well and produces interesting results. Agree on the number of deals to be played, and play as described above but with these modifications. The bids and their basic scoring values are:

Obligation	1
Exchange	2
Turn-up	3
Solo	5

If all pass without bidding, Obligation must be played by whoever holds ♠A, or by eldest hand if no one does. It involves discarding all but one card, drawing eight from stock, and then announcing trumps. Exchange is equivalent to entrada, Turn-up to vuelta.

The value of each game is doubled for each of the following feats:

1. *Cuatro*: winning by four tricks (4-3-2).

2. *Primeras*: winning the first five tricks and then stopping.

3. *The vole*: winning all nine. This is doubled in addition to *primeras*, i.e. quadrupled.

4. *Vole declared*: the game value is doubled again (octupled) if Hombre predicts before playing to the first trick that he will win all nine.

The value of a lost game is exactly what Hombre would have won had he succeeded, and is deducted from his current score. If he loses by codille, the same value is also added to the score of the player who beat him. If he loses by puesta, that value is also recorded in a separate column representing the pot. The pot-points are carried forward cumulatively and are eventually credited to the first player to win a solo or the vole. The pot is then reset to zero. If any remain in the pot at the end of the game, it goes to the winner of the last hand – or, if this also resulted in puesta, is distributed evenly between the opponents.

Quadrille

4 players, 40 cards

It will not be unnecessary to acquaint the Reader, that the following game of
Quadrille has been about two years, and is at present, the favourite game at the
French court . . . [It] is more amusing and entertaining than . . . any other Game
on the Cards . . .

Anon., *The Game of Quadrille* (1726)

This four-handed adaptation of Ombre originated in France and spread
to other countries in various forms, giving rise to related games with
different names. In England it was regarded as a ladies' game as opposed
to the relatively spartan rigours of partnership Whist. Whist eventually
won out, partly by virtue of its formal simplicity and universal stan-
dardization, but probably more on patriotic grounds. Quadrille
remained, by any standard of judgement, one of the great European
games of the eighteenth century, but by the start of the nineteenth was
rapidly declining in favour of Boston, its own relatively simplified
descendant.

Preliminaries Four players use a 40-card pack consisting of
AKQJ765432 in each suit. Each player starts with at least 40 chips or
counters. A game is any number of deals divisible by four. Deal, bid
and play to the right. Before each deal, each player stakes one chip to
the pot. (Or the dealer stakes four, if preferred.) Deal ten each in batches
of 4-3-3, 3-4-3, or 3-3-4.

Rank of cards The rank of cards varies with the colour of each suit and
whether it is plain or trump. Cards run, from highest to lowest:

black suits (plain)			K Q J 7 6 5 4 3 2
black trumps	♠A †2 ♣A		K Q J 7 6 5 4 3
red suits (plain)			K Q J A 2 3 4 5 6 7
red trumps	♠A †7 ♣A		A K Q J 2 3 4 5 6

Matadors The top three trumps are called Spadille (♠A), Manille (the
nominally lowest trump), and Basta (♣A). They are collectively called
matadors and have special powers. In a red trump suit the fourth highest
is its Ace, called Punto, but it is not a matador.

Auction Eldest, the player at the dealer's right, speaks first, and each
in turn may pass, make an opening bid, or overcall a previous bid. A
player who passes may not bid later. The bids are:

  1. Alliance. Announced as 'I beg' or 'Propose', this bids to win at

least six tricks after naming trumps and calling as partner the holder of
a specific King.

2. Solo. To win at least six tricks after naming trumps and playing
alone against the other three.

3. The vole (slam). To win all ten tricks after naming trumps and
playing alone against the other three.

If a proposal is not overcalled, Hombre (the declarer) names trumps
and nominates the King of any non-trump suit lacking from his own
hand. If he holds all three, he calls a Queen instead. The holder of the
called card automatically becomes the other partner, but says nothing.
The partnership may be revealed only when the called card is played to
a trick, or when its holder makes some other play that obviously favours
the caller.

If all four pass, the game is *forced Spadille*. Whoever holds ♠A
must play an alliance by calling a King, or Queen if necessary. In
this case, however, he may (but need not) invite his partner to name
trumps.

> ☛ Sources do not remark on the conflict of this rule with that forbidding
> partner's self-declaration. But it is a nice point – perhaps intentional – that the
> caller should either name trumps, or know his partner immediately, but not
> both.

Play Eldest leads first. Players must follow suit if possible, otherwise
may play any card. The trick is taken by the highest card of the suit led,
or by the highest trump if any are played, and the winner of each trick
leads to the next.

Reneging A player holding a matador need not play it to a trump
lead, but may, if lacking lower trumps, instead renege by playing
from another suit. However, if a higher matador is led, a player with
a lower matador may not renege but must play either it or another
trump.

Premiers and the vole If Hombre in a solo bid wins the first six tricks
straight off, he gains a bonus for premiers, and wins without further
play. If, however, he leads to the seventh trick, this automatically raises
his bid to the vole. If unsuccessful, it reduces but does not entirely cancel
his basic win. In an alliance, the same rule applies to the partnership if
they take the first six between them, and they must (obviously) discuss
whether or not to lead to the seventh.

Settlements if contract won For a successful solo, Hombre wins the stake. If, in addition, any of the following bonuses apply, they are paid to him by each opponent. A *unit* means one quarter of the current stake. The stake may be greater than four chips, as it is carried forward when a game is lost.

Hombre held three matadors	1 unit
Hombre held all three and Punto	2 units
Hombre won premiers	1 unit

(Punto, or Ace, only applies when a red suit is trump.)

Settlements for the vole vary enormously. The following is suggested. Having won the game and premiers, and gone for the vole, Hombre receives an additional 2 units from each opponent if successful, otherwise he pays 2 units to each for the loss.

In an alliance or forced Spadille, the stake is divided between the allies, and each opponent pays each partner any of the relevant bonuses listed above. In this case 'matadors held' means 'held between the allies', not necessarily in one hand.

Settlements if contract lost If Hombre wins only five tricks, the loss is called a *remise*; if four or fewer, it is a *codille*, and the same applies to an alliance.

For a remise, Hombre doubles the stake – which is carried forward to the next deal – and, if applicable, pays the opposing side for any matadors held by the contracting side.

Given codille, the stake is won by and divided between the two or three opponents of the contracting side (unless there are three and the stake is not exactly divisible). Hombre also puts up double the stake to be carried forward to the next deal.

In an ordinary alliance, the loss is borne entirely by the player who called a partner, as the latter had no say in joining the partnership. In forced Spadille, however, it is shared, as both played on equally involuntary terms.

Point-score The following is a suggestion. Points for matadors are ignored. If Hombre has an ally, the appropriate winning score is credited to each, but a losing score is deducted only from the ally's in a forced Spadille:

	Forced	Alliance	Solo
Won	3	5	10
Won with premiers	6	10	20
won with vole won	12	20	40
Won with vole lost	1	2	5
Lost remise	−6	−10	−20
Lost codille	−12	−20	−40

If a game is lost, whether by remise or codille, the following game is won or lost double. If two are lost in succession, the next is trebled in value; if three, the next quadrupled; and so on, until a game is won, when the next counts singly again.

Optional extras Countless non-standard variations were played on this basic theme. The commonest, called *Preference*, establishes a preferred trump suit, typically that entrumped in the first deal, which subsequently overcalls a bid at the same level in a different suit, and wins or loses double.

One comprehensive list of additional bids (in 'Q. Quanti', *Quadrille Elucidated*, 1822), runs:

1. Forced Spadille

2. Alliance

3. Médiateur, or Dimidiator. Soloist plays after calling for a King (or Queen if four held) and taking it into his own hand in exchange for any unwanted card.

4. Casco (Respect). The holder of both black Aces makes an alliance by calling a King and letting his partner name trumps.

5. Solo

6. Grandissimo. A solo with no trump suit, apart from the two black Aces, which Hombre does not necessarily hold.

7. Devole (Nemo). Hombre undertakes to lose every trick, playing at no trump except for the black Aces.

Related games

German Solo

The simplest and most straightforward derivative of Quadrille is still recorded in German anthologies. Four players use 32 cards ranking AKQJT987 in each suit, except that the top three trumps are always ♣Q (Spadille), then ✝7 (Manille), then ♠Q (Baste), followed by Ace, etc. The target is always five of the eight tricks played. The trump suit chosen freely in the first deal remains the suit of preference thereafter, and any of the following bids can then be overcalled by the same in the preferred suit:

1. *Frage* (Beg). The soloist announces trumps and names an Ace. Its holder becomes his partner but may not reveal himself except in the play. Worth 2.

2. *Großfrage* (Big-beg). The same, except that the called partner reveals himself and chooses trumps. The Spadille holder is obliged to 'beg big' if all four players initially pass. Worth 4, or 2 if enforced upon the Spadille holder.

3. *Solo.* The soloist declares trumps and plays alone. The bid is compulsory to anyone holding both black Queens and all four Aces, otherwise is optional. Worth 4.

4. *Allstich* (Slam). The soloist declares trumps, plays alone, and guarantees to win all eight tricks. Worth 16.

If the soloist (or ally) in an alliance or solo wins the first five straight off, he may cease play and claim his winnings; but leading to the sixth automatically raises the bid to a Slam, worth 8. All payments are doubled if the preferred suit is entrumped.

Alliance

A 52-card modification of Quadrille from nineteenth-century Germany – despite its French name, from which I derive the term 'alliance' for floating as opposed to fixed partnerships. Cards rank KQJT98765432A in black suits, KQJAT98765432 in red, but in trumps AKQJT98765432 regardless of colour. The black trump Three, or the red trump Nine, is called the Banner. Deal twelve cards each and four as a stock face down, turning the topmost for preference (preferred trump suit). The aim is to win seven tricks. A 6–6 tie favours whoever captures the Banner or, if it is in the stock, a majority of honours (trump KQJ). The bids are:

1. *Alliance.* Bidder names a trump suit and a specific King lacking from his hand – or a Queen, if he holds four Kings, or if the named King is in the stock. Whoever holds the named card declares that fact and becomes his partner.

2. *Colour.* The same, but with the preferred suit as trump.

3. *Turn-up (levée).* The same, but after turning the next card from stock, accepting its suit as trump, adding the stock to his hand, and making four discards.

4. *Solo.* Bidder undertakes to win seven tricks alone in a suit of his choice.

5. *Preference.* The same, but in the preferred suit.

6. *Resistance.* Called by a second player who also wishes to bid solo or preference in the same suit as a previous caller. All then play alone, and he wins who takes most tricks or, if tied, captures the Banner.

An alliance wins or loses 2, turn-up or solo 4, resistance 8. Winning the first seven tricks adds 2, all twelve 4. Side payments: for winning in tricks the trump King 1, Queen 2, Jack 3, Banner 4 (regardless of who played them).

Ligeud

The Danish equivalent of Solo, of which the only published accounts are, unfortunately, totally unintelligible (even in Danish). More promising is . . .

Skærvindsel

A Danish hybrid of Solo and German Schafkopf. From a 36-card pack consisting of AKQJT9876 in each suit deal nine each in three rounds of three. The trumps are always, from highest to lowest, ♣Q, †7, ♠Q, ♣J, ♠J, ♥J, ♦J, followed by AK(Q if red)T986, giving 14 black trumps or 15 red. Plain suits rank AK(Q if red)T9876. Each in turn bids to win from five to nine tricks with the eventual aid of a partner. A higher bid overcalls a lower, and a bid in clubs overcalls an equal bid in another suit. The partner is the holder of a card called after the bidding, usually a high trump or a non-trump Ace lacking from the bidder's hand.

Preference (Austrian)

Preference is a three-hander clearly descended from Ombre, but with two novel features. One is that not only the soloist but also each defender must undertake to win a predetermined quota of tricks – a development of the Ombre situation, which also requires the defenders to keep their won tricks separately. The other is its introduction of a primitive form of suit hierarchy. Previously, only one suit was a suit of preference – clubs in Boston, diamonds in Quadrille, or a suit turned at random, as in Solo Whist. In Preference, the four suits rank upwards in order ♠, ♣, ♦, ♥, a pattern that spread into many nineteenth-century games, including Bridge. (The modern suit order of Contract arose in Auction Bridge through an upgrading of the spade suit that took place around 1910.) The originality of this hierarchical feature is emphasized by the fact that the game itself is named after it. Preference has long been popular in Austria, and can be traced back to about 1820. Other varieties of it are played throughout eastern Europe, from Lithuania to Greece.

Preliminaries Three players are active, but normally four play together, with each in turn dealing and sitting that deal out. All play goes to the left. Play is normally for cash, though accounts can be kept in writing. At the outset, each contributes to the pot an equal sum divisible by ten. The game ends when the pot is empty, unless the players agree to contribute a further stake and play on.

Cards Thirty-two, either French-suited and ranking AKQJT987, or German-suited (acorns, leaves, hearts, bells) and ranking Deuce, King, Ober, Unter, X, IX, VIII, VII. The order and value of suits for bidding and scoring is:

♣	♠	♦	♥
1	2	3	4
🌰	🍃	♥	🔔

Deal Deal ten each in batches of 3-(2)-4-3, the (2) going, face down, to the table as a talon.

Auction This determines who will play solo against the other two. The soloist will name trumps, may take the talon and discard two cards, and must then win at least six tricks in play. The basic bids are from one to four. 'One' entitles the soloist to name any suit as trump. 'Two' prevents clubs from being named, 'three' prevents also spades, and 'four' prevents diamonds, automatically making hearts trumps. Each in turn, starting with eldest, may pass or bid and, having passed, may not come in again. The first bid is 'one'. Each thereafter must either pass or bid one higher – 'jump-bidding' is not allowed. However:

1. An earlier player may 'hold' the bid of a later player. *Example*: if Anton bids 'one', Bertl must pass or bid 'two'. If he bids 'two', Christl must pass or bid 'three'. Bertl and Christl may not hold the previous bid, as they come later in the auction. Anton, however, may then hold Christl's bid of three, as he is the earlier of two players willing to bid the same amount.

2. Any player may immediately declare 'hand' or 'preference', provided they haven't already made a numerical bid. Both bids offer to play the hand as dealt, without taking the talon, but preference undertakes to do so with hearts trump, and cannot be overcalled. If two wish to play 'hand', priority goes to the one nominating the higher-ranking suit as trump (diamonds beats spades beats clubs).

Example of bidding:	Anton	Bertl	Christl
	One	Two	Three
	pass	Hold	Four
	pass	pass	

Anton is willing to play only if given a free choice of suits. Christl's Three offers a red suit. Bertl, also willing to play a red suit, 'holds' this bid by virtue of positional priority. Christl overcalls by committing herself to hearts, which she would have played were it not that numerical bids must go in order. (Had she been willing to play without taking the talon, she could have ended the auction by bidding 'Preference' immediately.) Bertl, whose suit was diamonds, declines to 'hold' hearts. Christl becomes the soloist.

The exchange In a numerical contract, the soloist takes the talon into hand without exposing it, discards any two cards face down, and announces the trump suit, which may not be lower in value than the bid. In a Game contract, he simply announces trumps.

The defence Each defender, starting at the soloist's left, now announces whether he will play or drop out.

If he plays, he must win at least two tricks or be penalized.

If he drops out, he escapes penalty, but this makes it easier for the soloist to win.

If both drop out, the soloist wins all 10 tricks by default.

If only one defender is willing, he may either play alone, in which case the other defender lays his hand face down and tricks are played between the soloist and one defender, or he may invite his partner to assist. An invitation must be accepted, but the guest will not be penalized if he fails to make two tricks. Instead, the host will be penalized if they fail to take four tricks between them.

Play If there is any defence, the soloist leads to the first trick. Players must follow suit and head the trick if possible, otherwise trump and overtrump if possible, and only otherwise renounce. However: if both defenders elected to play, and the soloist leads to a trick, and the first defender can beat that lead, he must do so with the lowest card legally playable. The trick is taken by the highest card of the suit led, or by the highest trump if any are played, and the winner of each trick leads to the next.

Pay-off Whether or not the contract is made, the soloist takes 10 units from the pot and pays each active defender one unit for each trick the latter took – except in the case of a guest, when only the host is paid, and that for each trick taken between them. If the soloist took fewer than six, he then pays 20 units to the pot. Next, any defender who chose to play but failed to win two tricks pays 10 to the pot. If one player was invited and the defence failed to win four tricks, the host pays 10 to the pot and the guest is exempted.

Bonuses The following bonuses, if applicable, are won or lost as between the soloist and each opponent, independently of the pot.

1. Hearts bonus. In a Hearts contract (without the talon), the soloist wins or loses 10 units per opponent.

2. Four Ace bonus. A soloist who held four aces receives 10 from each opponent if the contract succeeded, but does not pay anything if it failed.

3. No Ace bonus. A soloist who held no aces, and announced this before leading to the first trick, wins or loses an extra 10 units per opponent. (You may not discard an Ace to the talon in order to claim this bonus.)

(There are other ways of handling the pot and the various bonuses.)

Illustrated Preference

(*Illustrierte Préférence*) includes at least the first two of the following additional bids.

Five (or Bettel) A bid to lose every trick after taking the talon. There is no trump, but players must still head the trick if possible. Scores 10.

Six (or Durchmarsch) A bid to win every trick at no trump after taking the talon. Scores 20.

Seven (or Bettel Ouvert, or Plauderer) As Bettel, but the soloist's hand is laid face up on the table after the opening lead, and the defenders may discuss their procedure. (A 'chatty' bid: *plaudern* means to converse.) Scores 30.

Eight (*Offener Durchmarsch*) As *Durchmarsch*, but with the soloist's cards exposed after the opening lead. Scores 40.

In these extra contracts neither defender may drop out, the soloist wins or loses as between each defender, independently of the pot, and Ace bonuses are not recognized. Some also allow the same bids and contracts without taking the talon. In this case they outrank suit games in the bidding, and win or lose double.

Kontra and Rekontra In a no-trumper, each opponent in turn may double ('*Kontra*'), thereby doubling the value of the game as between himself and the soloist, but without bearing on the other defender. If the first declines and the second doubles, the former may not then change his mind. If either doubles, the soloist may redouble ('*Rekontra*').

Usurping (*Nachgehen*) When the soloist in a number contract has taken the talon and discarded, another player may, provided he has made at least one positive bid, usurp the role of the soloist by taking the new talon, making two discards, and declaring at least Five (Bettel). However, the original soloist, or the third player if he also bid, may similarly usurp it again for a yet higher contract, and so on.

Sans atout If Six is the highest bid recognized, some play it as a contract called *Sans Atout* (No Trump) instead of *Durchmarsch*. After the exchange, the player at declarer's right makes the opening lead, and declarer's object is to win any six consecutive tricks.

Preference (Russian)

3 players, 32 cards

> Russia, when at home, in dressing gown and slippers, plays chiefly at
> Preference.
>
> Revd Edwin S. Taylor, *The History of Playing Cards* (1865)

Preference reached Russia in the 1830s and remains that country's national card game, albeit hitherto somewhat furtively. Because the old Soviet regime disapproved of card-playing, it was only with the collapse of communism that Preference-players were able to organize themselves and disseminate information about the game that could filter out into the western world. Unsurprisingly, we find it played in various ways. The version described below is that approved by the Moscow-based Preference Lovers' Society, founded in 1996, but that body makes reference to the Leningrad, Sochi and so-called Classical varieties of Preference.

Preliminaries Players, cards and deal, as for Austrian Preference.

Auction Eldest bids first. The bidding sequence from lowest to highest runs 6♠, 6♣, 6♦, 6♥, 6NT, followed by 7 of each in the same order, then 8, misère, 9, and 10. A bid is an offer to win at least the stated number of tricks with the stated or a higher-ranking trump. Misère – played always at no trump – may not be called by a player who has already made a positive numerical bid. Each bid must be higher than the last, but an earlier player may 'hold' the bid of a later player by saying 'Here'.

> Example: If Eldest bids 6♠, Second hand 6♦, and Third hand 6♥, Eldest (or
> Second hand if Eldest passes) can assert priority for 6♥ by saying, 'Hearts here.'
> But Third hand could not have called 'Diamonds here', because Second hand
> enjoys positional priority.

No player may bid again, having once passed. The last-named bidder becomes the soloist, in either the contract named or a higher one. Following two immediate passes, the third can bid or pass, or (in some circles) take the talon silently and become the declarer by default. But if he wishes to play misère after two immediate passes he must say so before taking the talon. If he also passes, they play a round of *raspasovka* (explained later).

Contract announcement Declarer turns the talon face up for all to see, takes it into hand, and makes any two undisclosed discards face down.

He then announces his contract, which must be not lower than his last bid (if any), but may be for a greater number or a higher trump. He may not call a misère if he previously made a positive bid, or if he became declarer by neither bidding nor passing after two immediate passes. No matter how weak the hand or unfavourable the talon, declarer may not concede, but must name a contract and play it through.

Whisting The player at declarer's left now states whether or not he will *whist.* To whist is to undertake one's side to win a minimum number of tricks. This number relates to the contract as follows: at six level, the whister must win at least four; at seven, at least two; at eight, nine and ten at least one. (A misère is not whisted.) The third player then has the same choice. If both pass, declarer wins without play and his opponents do not score for any tricks. If declarer's first opponent passes in a six or seven game, the second opponent may alternatively say, 'Get out for half,' meaning that without play or penalty he would score for taking half the target number of tricks and declarer would score for the rest. In this case, however, the first opponent may change his mind and 'retrieve' the whist, whereupon the second is deemed to have passed.

If only one defender whists, he alone is penalized should the defence fail to reach the target. If both whist, both are liable. To avoid any penalty, they need to win the required number between them – unless only one is needed, in which case it is the second to 'whist' who is penalized if it is not made. If neither player whists, declarer wins by default, and there is no play.

Examples: If, in a doubly-whisted six game:
1. . . . the opponents took only three, then whichever of them took fewer tricks is penalized for the undertrick;
2. . . . they took only one, then each is penalized for an undertrick;
3. . . . they took respectively two tricks and none, the player who took none is penalized for both undertricks, unless there was a prior agreement to share rewards and penalties. (Such an agreement is called 'Gentleman's whist'.)

Light and dark If only one player whisted, he may offer to play 'in the light'. If so, both defenders lay their hands face up on the table before the first lead is made, and the whister plays from both hands – as at Bridge, except that both hands are open, and the defenders may discuss tactics. (Playing with cards concealed is, of course, called playing in the dark.)

Play Eldest leads to the first trick. In a misère contract, both defenders lay their hands face up on the table before the opening lead if one of them is eldest, but immediately after the opening lead if made by declarer. In all contracts players must follow suit if possible, otherwise must trump if possible, and only otherwise may renounce. The trick is taken by the highest card of the suit led, or by the highest trump if any are played, and the winner of each trick leads to the next. Each player keeps his own won tricks apart from the others'.

Raspasovka The aim is to avoid winning tricks at no trump.

If three play, eldest turns the top card of the talon and leads a card of that suit to the first trick. Suit must be followed if possible. Whoever wins the trick adds the turned card to it, turns the second card of the talon, and leads a card of its suit to the second trick.

If four play, the dealer (who normally sits out) treats the talon as a two-card hand. He leads the top card to the first trick, and then, regardless of who wins it, leads the second card to the next. Thus the first two tricks contain four cards, and the dealer may win none, one or both of them. The third trick is led by eldest hand.

Thereafter, the winner of each trick leads any card to the next. After ten tricks, each player records in his dump a penalty of 1 point for each trick he has won. If more than one *raspasovka* is played in succession, the second is scored at the rate of 2 per trick, the third at 3, and so on. (Rules vary. Some stick at 3 in all subsequent rounds. Some follow a geometric progression, such as 1-2-4-8 etc.)

Score Each player's score is kept in three different sections (see the illustration on p. 75), called the dump, the pool, and the bank. (These are more descriptive terms than translations of the Russian, which are: *gorka* 'heap', *pool'ka* 'pool', and *veest* 'whist'.)

- The *dump* chiefly records penalty points exacted for contracts that the player lost.
- The *pool* records points for contracts that the player won.
- The *bank* records points won off each opponent for their various failures and shortfalls. It is therefore divided into two separate accounts – or three, if four play – each associated with a specific opponent.

At end of play, each player scores the total of his bank accounts minus the amount in his dump. Pool points do not enter the equation directly, as they are eventually converted into bank credits. They are recorded separately only in order to measure the length of the game, which continues until every player has made an agreed number of pool points – typically 50.

Scores are based on the following contract values: a contract of six is valued at 2, seven = 4, eight = 6, nine = 8, misère and ten = 10. All scores are recorded cumulatively. (That is, you don't write how many points you just scored, but the new total they make.)

Declarer's score For making a contract, whether by play or by concession, declarer scores the contract value in his pool, with no credit for overtricks. If either opponent failed to take his individual quota of tricks, declarer scores the contract value per undertrick in the bank account identified with that particular opponent.

For failing a contract, declarer drops in his dump the contract value for each undertrick. For failing a misère, he drops in his dump 10 points for each trick he took. Furthermore, whatever he drops in his dump, each opponent scores positively in the bank account maintained against him.

> Example: Declarer bids 8, wins 5. Three down at six each means 18 in his dump, and plus 18 for each opponent in the appropriate bank account.

Opponents' score If any player whisted and fulfilled his quota of tricks, he scores the contract value of each trick won in the bank account relating to the declarer. If not, declarer scores against him in his own bank account, as described above. If only one player whisted, the other has no quota and therefore cannot be penalized.

Endgame and final score When a player has reached the agreed total (say 50) in his pool, he donates any further pool points he may win to either opponent who has not yet reached 50 – conventionally, given a choice, to the one with the higher current total, though which of them gets it makes not the slightest difference to the final outcome. This is not a free gift. (It is sometimes referred to as 'American Aid'.) Instead, the donor adds to his bank account in respect of the recipient 10 points for each pool point donated.

Play ceases when every player has the target number of pool points.

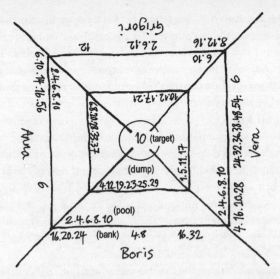

A scoresheet from the viewpoint of Boris, one of four players. (Bracketed words do not actually appear on the sheet.)

In the centre is the target score, 10. The game ends when everyone has reached this target in their pool scoring area. Each row of numbers is a cumulative series, the one at the right being that player's current total. Thus Boris has reached 10 by making five scores of 2 each, some of which may have been 'donated' by opponents who have exceeded 10, in return for points recorded by them in their 'bank' account with Boris. Pool scores record only the progress of the game. They do not figure in the settlement, which is calculated from bank scores and dump scores.

Bank scores are reckoned first. These are scores made 'on the side' by each player against each opponent. Here, Boris has 24 against Anna, 8 against Grigori, and 32 against Vera, total 64; and against him Anna has 6, Grigori 12, and Vera 28, total 46. This leaves Boris 18 up (64 − 46). Similar computations leave Anna 28 down, Grigori 30 down, and Vera 40 up.

Dump scores (penalty points) are counted next. Boris has 29 against him, Anna 37, Grigori 21, Vera 17. These total 104, an average of 26 each. Each player counts 10 times the difference between their personal total and the average. This puts Boris and Anna respectively 30 and 110 down, and Grigori and Vera respectively 50 and 90 up.

The final scores are therefore:

	Boris	Anna	Grigori	Vera
Bank	+18	−28	−30	+40
Dump	−30	−110	+50	+90
Total	−12	−138	+20	+130

Individual accounts are then settled between every combination of two players. For example, if Anna has 16 against Boris, and Boris 9 against Anna, then Anna counts 7 in respect of Boris, and Boris minus 7 in respect of Anna. In this way every player counts plus or minus in respect of every other, and each player's three (or four) plus or minus scores will together yield an overall plus or minus total as the first component of their final score.

For the second component, each player multiplies by 10 the number of penalties recorded in his dump, and then reckons as final penalties the difference between his own tenfold score and that of the average of all three or four players.

Example: Anna, Boris and Grigori recorded respectively 18, 23 and 32 penalties, giving a tenfold average of 243 (i.e. 730 ÷ 3). Anna then reckons 63 minus-points (243 − 180), Boris 13 minus-points (243 − 230), and Grigori 77 plus-points (243 − 320 = a negative penalty = a plus score).

Each player's two scoring components are put together to yield a final plus or minus score. All the players' scores will sum to zero, or to a minute amount caused by the non-integral division of dump scores. It may be agreed that any such fraction or odd point be awarded to the player cutting the highest card.

Asszorti
3 players, 36 cards

A Hungarian game like Preference, but simpler. The following is based on material collected by Anthony Smith, with revisions by Gyula Szigri. **Preliminaries** Three players use a 36-card pack ranking AKQJT9876. Deal eleven each in batches of 3-(3)-2-2-2-2. The (3) denotes three face down to the table as a talon. Play to the left (unlike most Hungarian games).

Bidding Each in turn, starting with eldest, may pass or bid. A bid is an offer to win at least six tricks after exchanging three, two, one or no cards with the talon. Bidding must go in order Three, Two, One, Hand (= none), except that a player sitting earlier in each round of the bidding sequence may 'hold' (take over) the preceding bid of a player sitting later. Jump-bidding is not allowed, though if the first two players pass the third can bid anything.

Exchanging The highest bidder becomes the soloist, and either repeats his last bid or names a higher one. He then draws from the top of the talon as many cards as he bid (if any), discards the same number, and announces a trump suit or no trump.

Arrivázs In a trump contract the soloist may then also bid *Arrivázs*, thereby undertaking to win the last three tricks. There is no reward for doing this unannounced, except at no trump.

Doubling Game (six tricks) and *Arrivázs* are scored separately. Either or both can be doubled and redoubled to a maximum of five levels, announced as *kontra* (2), *rekontra* (4), *szubkontra* (8), *hirskontra* (16), and *mordkontra* (32). If declarer says *rekontra*, then *szubkontra* may be announced only by the partner of the opponent who initiated the *kontra*. If there is a double, the talon is immediately exposed; and if *Arrivázs* was bid, the other announcement can be doubled immediately after the talon is exposed.

Play The soloist's right-hand neighbour leads. Players must follow suit if possible, trump if unable to follow suit, and renounce only if unable to do either. The trick is taken by the highest card of the suit led, or by the highest trump if any are played, and the winner of each trick leads to the next.

Score The basic scores for three, two, one, and hand are 2, 4, 6, 8, respectively, and doubled if played at no trump. Overtricks score half that value each. Undertricks score minus the full value for the first and second, and half value each for any others. All these will be affected by any declared doubles. If declarer wins a bid and the tricks fall 6-5-0, the amount won is reduced by the basic (undoubled) score.

Upon winning six or more tricks, the soloist may save time by ceding the remainder to whichever opponent took more than the other.

Arrivázs (winning the last three tricks) scores 8 if bid and made, or 16 if the game was played at no trump, or (even if played with trumps) if none of the last three tricks was won with a trump. This score is also affected by any doubling and redoubling.

Vira

Sweden's national card game is not only the most elaborate member of the Solo family, but also one of the most complex card games ever devised. With a contract and scoring schedule resembling a railway timetable, this remarkable game could well go under the name of 'Gothic Whist'. It is certainly far too fascinating to omit on grounds of space, especially as it has not (I think) previously been described in any English-language compendium.

Although *vira* means 'to wind' – which, by analogy with the Russo-Baltic game of Vint (meaning 'screw'), reasonably describes what appears to go on in the auction – the game is in fact said to be named after the Vira steelworks, a few miles north of Stockholm, where it was put together in February 1810 by a group of snowbound lawyers who had been trying out all the card games they knew between them. To the basic format of Ombre they added, from Boston, the full pack of 52 cards and some of the more ingenious contracts, including misères of various sizes.

Preliminaries Three are active, but four usually play, with each in turn dealing and sitting out. The game is played for hard score in several denominations, of which the two most essential are chips (*betar*) and points (*pinnar*). Chips are used for payments into and out of the pot, and points for side payments as between individual players. One chip is equivalent to eight points. Everyone starts with an equal number of each sort, and starts by placing an agreed number of chips in the pot. A game ends when the pot is empty, unless it is then agreed to refill and continue. Scores may be kept in writing, with a column for each player and one to record the fluctuating contents of the pot.

Cards and deal Use two separate 52-card packs ranking AKQJT 98765432 in each suit. Before dealing, cut the second pack to establish a suit of preference for trump. The other suit of the same colour becomes the suit of second preference (hereinafter designated 'colour'), and the two remaining suits are designated 'off-colour' (*ofärg*). This is done before each deal, not once for the whole game. All play goes to the left. Deal thirteen cards each in batches of 3-3-3-4 and spread the remaining 13 face down as a talon.

Auction This determines who will play solo against the other two.

Eldest speaks first and may not pass. A player who passes thereafter may not bid again. Each bid must exceed the last, as listed in the schedule. Of equal suit bids, one in preference overcalls the same in colour, which overcalls the same in an off-colour. However, an elder player can 'hold' the bid of a younger. (See Ombre or Preference for explanation.) The various bids are listed in the schedule (see the Table on p. 83) and described more fully below.

Conceding The soloist may surrender before play. This normally counts as a single loss, but a surrendered solo counts double. (See Outcome, below.)

Play Eldest leads to the first trick. Players must follow suit if possible, otherwise may play any card. The trick is taken by the highest card of the suit led, or by the highest trump if any are played, and the winner of each trick leads to the next.

Pay-off The soloist wins or loses a certain number of chips from or to the pot, and a certain number of points from or to each opponent. In trump contracts, the number of points varies with the suit.

A contract that fails by one trick, including one trick taken in a misère, counts as lost singly. One lost by two or more tricks counts as a double loss (*kodille*).

Some contracts are played after a 'second try', as defined below. In this case, immediately after his first try and before making a second, the soloist pays the opponents the appropriate number of points as if the first try had resulted in a lost contract, but he does not pay chips to the pot. A contract played after a second try results in (a) points won to or from the opponents in the normal way, and (b) chips drawn from or paid to the pot as shown under 'second try' in the Table on p. 83. The nett result is that winning after a second try, though unprofitable, loses less than losing after a first. (For details of all these payments, see the Table.)

The contracts There are eight types of contract, described below in a logical order. The first four are positive (draw, solo, turn-up, vira), the next three are negative (cuckoo, misère, solo misère), and the eighth (*gask*) can be either. The order in which they overcall one another, and the appropriate pay-offs, are summarized in the Table.

1. *Draw* (for 6, 7, 8 or 9 tricks). To win at least the said number of

tricks (except that 'Six' is actually announced as 'Beg') after discarding from hand, drawing replacements from the talon, and letting your opponents do likewise. You needn't name a trump when bidding, but can overcall a numerically equal bid by specifying 'in colour', or an equal bid in colour by specifying 'in preference'.

- *Procedure.* Announce trumps, make at least one discard from your hand, and draw the same number of replacements from the top of the talon. If dissatisfied, you may pay points to your opponents and do the same again. This constitutes a 'second try', and reduces the value of the contract, whether won or lost. Your left-hand opponent may now discard and draw in the same way, and so may his partner, if any cards remain. If any remain after that, they must be left face down and not revealed. Players may not examine their discards once play begins.

2. *Turn-up* (for 6, 7, 8 or 9 tricks). A game in which you accept as trump a card turned from talon, and then play to win at least as many tricks as you bid. There are three types of turn-up: *Single*, in which you turn just the top card of the talon and accept it as trump; *vingel*, in which you turn the top two and entrump either of them; and *tringel*, in which you turn the top three and entrump any one. Single and vingel may be bid for six, seven or eight tricks; tringel only for nine. Bid by announcing 'single', 'vingel', or 'tringel', as the case may be. You needn't say how many tricks when bidding, except to overcall.

- *Procedures.* In a bid of Single, turn the top card of talon for trump, make from one to eleven discards, and draw replacements from the talon, starting with the turned card. If dissatisfied, pay the opponents points as if the first turned card made trumps, and turn the next for a new trump. You must accept this, and it counts as a second try. Then discard and draw again up to as many as remain, after which, if any still remain, your opponents may also discard and draw as described above.

  In a Vingel, turn the top two cards of the talon, nominate as trump the suit of either one, and discard and draw as described above. As before, you may pay for a second try. If any cards remain, your opponents may then discard and draw as described above.

  In a Tringel, necessarily contracting to win at least nine tricks, turn the top three cards of the talon and nominate as trump the suit of any one. As before, you may pay for a second try. If any cards remain, your opponents may then discard and draw as described above.

> ☛ In all the above turn-ups, note that the last card of the talon (the *dödsknapp*, or 'death-rattle') may never be used to determine trump. You may therefore not discard in your first try so many as to leave for a second try fewer than two in a single turn-up, three in a Vingel, or four in a Tringel.

3. *Solo* (for any number of tricks from 6 to 13). A bid to win at least a given number of tricks without discarding and drawing, but with your choice of trumps. You needn't say how many when bidding, except to overcall; but a bid of thirteen is announced as 'Solo Vira'.

• *Procedure.* State your trump suit and target number of tricks. Your opponents may discard and draw, as described above.

4. *Vira.* A one-off, all-or-nothing bid to win all 13 tricks after taking the talon, discarding any 13 from 26 cards, and announcing trumps. Opponents may not exchange.

5. *Cuckoo (Gök).* A one-off, all-or-nothing bid to lose every trick at no trump, playing ouverte, after taking up the talon and discarding any 13 from 26 cards. A further peculiarity is that your opponents are virtually obliged to overcall it (even, in some circles, if they have already passed once) unless they hold a safe low combination, such as a 2, a 3-4, a 4-5-6, etc. Anyone who fails to overcall pays an additional chip into the pot if the contract succeeds.

6. *Misère.* A bid to lose every trick at no trump, after discarding a certain number of cards and drawing replacements. Such a bid may be for one, two, three, four, five or six discards. You needn't say how many when bidding, except to overcall.

• *Procedure.* Discard exactly as many cards as you bid, and replace them from the talon. If dissatisfied, you may pay and do the same again, which counts as a 'second try'. Your opponents may also exchange, as described above. If you bid four or more, you make one additional discard and play to only twelve tricks.

7. *Solo misère.* A bid to lose every trick after exchanging one card or none. There are four such bids, namely:

    7.1 Petite misère: Make one discard before play, and play to only 12 tricks. (Opponents do not discard.)

    7.2 Grande misère: Make no discard, and play to all 13 tricks.

    7.3 Petite or grande misère ouverte. As petite or grande above, but with your hand exposed before the opening lead.

    7.4 Petite or grande misère ouverte royale. As above, and the opponents may openly discuss their play, but may not say or show what cards they hold.

- *Procedure.* Only the opponents may discard and draw from the talon. If the contract is designated *royale*, they may discuss their discarding strategy, but not otherwise.

8. *Gask.* An offer to play either a trump game or a no-trump misère after exchanging a certain number of cards but forbidding your opponents to exchange any. Gask may be bid for any number of discards from 0 to 6. You needn't say how many when bidding, except to overcall.

- *Procedure.* Given the contract, keep exactly the number of cards stated in the bid, discard the rest, take the entire talon, and discard down to 13 again. Depending on the number of cards you kept (listed below, left column), you may now have the choice of a trump contract or a misère. In a trump contract, you name trumps and play to win at least the stated number of tricks. In a misère, you play to lose every trick at no trump.

    bid 0 = win 7 *or* discard any two and lose all 11 tricks played

    bid 1 = win 8 *or* discard any one and lose all 12 tricks played

    bid 2 = win 9 *or* discard none and lose all 13 tricks played

    bid 3 = win 10 *or* discard any one and lose all 12 tricks *ouverte*

    bid 4 = win 11 *or* discard none and lose all 13 tricks *ouverte*

    bid 5, 6 = win 12 (no alternative)

☞ Note:

    1. In the auction, a Gask of 5 overcalls a Gask of 6.

    2. In a shortened misère, the opponents have 13 cards each but play only 11 or 12 tricks.

    3. *Ouverte* means with your hand of cards exposed before the opening lead.

Table of bids and contracts, wins and losses at Vira

Bid and explanation of bid	first try			second try			side payment		
	w	l	d	w	l	d	off	col	prf
1 Beg (= Six)	1	1	2	0	3	5	0	0	1
Name trump, change cards, win 6									
2 Single turn for 6	1	1	2	0	3	5	0	0	1
Turn 1 for trump, win 6									
3 Seven	1	1	2	0	3	5	0	0	1
Name trump, change cards, win 7									
4 Vingel 6	1	2	4	−1	6	10	0	1	1
Turn 2 for trump, win 6									
5 Gask with 0	1	1	2	x	x	x	0	0	0
Keep 0, win 7 or 11-card misère									
6 Cuckoo (*Gök*)	1	2	4	x	x	x	0	x	x
Take 13, discard 13, win 0/13									
7 Single turn for 7	1	1	2	0	3	5	0	1	1
Turn 1 for trump, win 7									
8 Misère for 1	1	1	2	0	3	5	0	x	x
Discard 1, draw 1, play 13, win 0									
9 Gask with 1	1	1	2	x	x	x	0	0	1
Keep 1, win 8 or 12-card misère									
10 Eight	1	1	2	0	3	5	0	1	1
Name trump, change cards, win 8									
11 Vingel 7	1	2	4	−1	6	10	1	1	3
Turn 2 for trump, win 7									
12 Single turn for 8	2	1	2	0	3	5	1	1	3
Turn 1 for trump, win 8									
13 Misère for 2	1	1	2	0	3	5	0	x	x
Discard 2, draw 2, play 13, win 0									
14 Gask with 2	1	1	2	x	x	x	0	1	1
Keep 2, win 9 or play 13, win 0									
15 Nine	1	1	2	0	3	5	1	1	3
Name trump, change cards, win 9									
16 Vingel 8	2	2	4	(a)	6	10	1	3	5
Turn 2 for trump, win 8									
17 Misère for 3	1	1	2	0	3	5	0	x	x
Discard 3, draw 3, play 13, win 0									
18 Gask with 3	1	1	2	x	x	x	0	1	2
Keep 3, win 10, or 12-card mis. ouv.									
19 Solo 6	1	1	2	x	x	x	0	0	1
Name trump, win 6 from hand									
20 Misère for 4	1	1	2	0	3	5	1	x	x
Discard 4, draw 4, play 12, win 0									
21 Gask with 4	1	1	2	x	x	x	1	1	3
Keep 4, win 11, or 13-card mis. ouv.									
22 Tringel for 9	3	3	6	(b)	9	15	3	5	11
Turn 3 for trump, win 9									
23 Solo 7	1	1	2	x	x	x	0	1	1
Name trump, win 7 from hand									
24 Misère for 5	1	1	2	0	3	5	1	x	x
Discard 5, draw 5, play 12, win 0									
25 Gask with 6 (c)	1	1	2	x	x	x	1	2	4
Keep 6, win 12									

Bid and explanation of bid	first try			second try			side payment		
	w	l	d	w	l	d	off	col	prf
26 Solo 8 Name trump, win 8 from hand	1	1	2	x	x	x	1	1	3
27 Misère for 6 Discard 6, draw 6, play 12, win 0	1	1	2	0	3	5	1	x	x
28 Gask with 5 (c) Keep 5, win 12	1	1	2	x	x	x	1	3	5
29 Solo 9 Name trump, win 9 from hand	1	1	2	x	x	x	1	3	5
30 Solo petite misère Discard 1, play 12, win 0	1	1	2	x	x	x	2	x	x
31 Vira (13) Take & discard 13, name trump, win 13	1	1	2	x	x	x	2	4	8
32 Solo 10 Name trump, win 10 from hand	1	1	2	x	x	x	3	5	11
33 Solo grande misère Discard 0, play 13, win 0	1	1	2	x	x	x	3	x	x
34 Solo 11 Name trump, win 11 from hand	1	1	2	x	x	x	5	11	21
35 Solo petite misère ouverte Discard 1, play 12, win 0	1	1	2	x	x	x	7	x	x
36 Solo 12 Name trump, win 12 from hand	1	1	2	x	x	x	11	21	43
37 Solo grande misère ouverte Discard 0, play 13, win 0	1	1	2	x	x	x	13	x	x
38 Vira solo (13) Name trump, win 13 from hand	1	1	2	x	x	x	21	43	85
39 Solo petite misère ouverte royale Discard 1, play 12, win 0	1	1	2	x	x	x	27	x	x
40 Solo grande misère ouverte royale Discard 0, play 13, win 0	1	1	2	x	x	x	53	x	x

Notes referring to table of Vira bids

The first six payment columns specify chips received from or paid to the common pool (1 chip = 8 points).

The next three specify points received from or paid to each opponent (8 points = 1 chip).

First try = As played after accepting the cards initially drawn from talon (and, in a turn-up, accepting one of their suits as trump).

Second try = After not accepting the first try, and drawing again.

w = won, l = lost, d = doubly lost, x = not applicable.

prf = suit of preference, col = colour (suit of same colour as preference), off = off-colour (other two suits).

mis. ouv. = misère ouverte.

(a) = 0 for winning 8 tricks, but 1 per overtrick.

(b) = 1 for winning 9 tricks, and 2 per overtrick.

(c) Gask with 5 overcalls Gask with 6.

Variations

Aces low In some circles, if the soloist plays a gask or misère holding all four Aces, they count low (below Two) instead of highest in their suits.

Alternative schedules Some circles vary relative scale of contracts, so that (for example) solo vira is the highest bid.

Additional bids Some recognize additional turn-ups of four cards for 10 tricks, five for 11, and six for 12, called respectively Quadruple, Pingel, and Carousel.

Notes on play

Vira is unique in boasting a schedule of conventional passes rather than of conventional bids. If one player bids and the next passes, the pass is construed as an invitation to the third player to play in partnership against the proposed contract, and if that player also passes then he may be understood to accept the invitation. It is therefore customary to use a 'first pass', and sometimes also a second (by the other player) to convey information about the passer's hand in accordance with an agreed code. For example, if the opener 'Begs' for six tricks, a first pass promises stops in all four suits. Conversely, if that player does not hold four stops, he is expected to indicate that fact by overcalling, even if there is no contract he feels confident about undertaking. Unfortunately, schedules vary from circle to circle, rendering it impractical to continue this description of what is probably the world's most eccentric card game.

Oh Hell! Blackout, Bust, Elevator, Jungle Bridge, Oh Shit!, etc.

3–6 players, 52 cards

Oh Hell! introduces a group of games in which you bid to win an exact number of tricks instead of merely a minimum. Several early relatives of Solo Whist included occasional bids to win exactly one or two tricks, but Oh Hell! – first described by B. C. Westall around 1930 – was the earliest to base the whole game upon this principle. As it appears to be more popular in the USA, the following description is based on the rules of the Oh Hell! Club of America. (Source: Carter Hoerr, via the Pagat website.)

Preliminaries From three to seven players use a 52-card pack ranking AKQJT98765432. A game consists of a fixed number of deals related to the actual number of players. The turn to deal passes to the left.

Deal Cards are dealt singly and face down. In the first deal each player receives ten cards, or eight if six play, or seven if seven. In each subsequent deal the number of cards dealt is reduced by one. Following the one-card deal, the number dealt increases again, one at a time, so that the final deal is of as many cards as the first. Stack the undealt cards face down and turn the topmost card for trumps.

Bid Each in turn, starting at the dealer's left, announces exactly how many tricks he undertakes to win. Dealer, who bids last, may not bid a number that would enable everyone to fulfil their bid.

Play Eldest leads. Players must follow suit if possible, otherwise may play any card. The trick is taken by the highest card of the suit led, or by the highest trump if any are played, and the winner of each trick leads to the next.

Score For making your bid, score 10 points per trick bid and won, or 10 for a bid of nought. For failing, deduct 10 points for each over- or undertrick. In the event of a tie, play another one-card deal.

British Oh Hell!

In the original game, the number of cards dealt is one in the first deal, two in the second, and so on up to the maximum possible for the number of players. If all cards are dealt out, play at no trump. Everyone, including the dealer, is free to bid any number. A successful bid of n tricks scores $n + 10$. A failed bid scores zero.

Variations Many variations may be encountered. The most substantial is that in which players make simultaneous bids by holding their clenched fist face down on the table and, at a given signal, promptly extending as many fingers as tricks bid.

Romanian Whist

(3–6p, 24–48c) This highly refined derivative of Oh Hell! is so popular in Romania as to be called 'Whist', without further qualification. The main differences are as follows:

From three to six players use a pack stripped to eight times as many cards as players – e.g. 24 if three play (AKQJT9), and so on. The first few deals consist of one card each, there being as many one-card deals as there are players. Thereafter, the number of cards dealt increases by one until it reaches a maximum of eight, then it decreases by one and finishes again with as many one-card deals as there are players. For example, if four play there are 21 deals: 1-1-1-1-2-3-4-5-6-7-8-7-6-5-4-3-2-1-1-1-1. (The one-card deals are repeated in order to even out the dealer's probable disadvantage of having to bid a 'wrong' number.)

A successful bidder scores 5 plus the amount bid. An unsuccessful bidder loses the amount bid, plus 1 per overtrick, if any.

Israeli Whist

(4pp, 52c) Another refinement of Oh Hell! currently popular in Israel, with Bridge-style bidding. (Source: Amir Mazuver *et al.*, Pagat website.)

Deal thirteen cards each. There are two phases of bidding, first to determine the trump suit and then to determine the final number.

Each in turn, starting with the dealer, either bids or passes. A bid consists of a number of tricks and a proposed trump. Each bid must be higher than the last. A higher number overcalls a lower, and a given number is overcalled by the same number in a higher suit. As at Bridge, the order is clubs (low), diamonds, hearts, spades, no trump. The lowest permissible bid is 'Five clubs' and the highest 'Thirteen no trumps'. Three successive passes do not prevent the last bidder from bidding yet higher, and this phase ends only when all four pass in succession. The last bidder is the declarer.

If all four pass immediately, play a 'goulash' round (see below). Otherwise each in turn, starting at the declarer's left but excluding the declarer himself, must announce exactly how many tricks he proposes to win, and the last bidder (at dealer's right) must avoid the number that would make exactly thirteen. If the bids total fewer than thirteen, the game is described as 'under'; if more, it is 'over'.

The declarer leads to the first of thirteen tricks played in the usual way.

Your score depends on whether or not you bid zero and on whether the game was 'under' or 'over'.

If you bid one or more, and succeed, you score 10 plus the square of the number you bid. For example, you score 19 for bidding and winning three tricks. For failing, you lose 10 points per over- or undertrick.

If you bid zero and succeed, you score 20 if the game was 'over' or 50 if it was 'under'. For a failed bid of zero, you score minus 50 for the first trick you won, but reduce this by 10 points for each subsequent trick won. This yields a penalty score of 40 for taking two tricks, 30 for three, and so on.

Play up to any agreed target. (Scoring variations may be encountered.)

Goulash If all pass immediately, each player passes any three cards face down to his lefthand neighbour and then picks up the three from his right. This inaugurates another attempt at bidding. Up to three such attempts may be made before the cards are entirely thrown in and dealt again.

Ninety-Nine
2–5 players (best for 3), 24–60 cards

Ninety-Nine was invented by me in 1968 and first published in the February 1974 issue of *Games & Puzzles* magazine. It has since appeared in many card-game books, in many languages, and is now available as computer software. Though equally playable by two, four, or five, Ninety-Nine was specifically designed for three players, and this version is described first.

Deal Three players each receive twelve cards from a 36-card pack ranking AKQJT9876 in each suit.

Object To win, of the nine tricks played, exactly the number you bid by discarding three cards representing that number. For this purpose, the suits of the bid-cards represent numbers of tricks bid as follows:

♣ = 3 tricks ♥ = 2 tricks ♠ = 1 trick ♦ = 0 tricks

> Examples: Bid nine tricks by laying aside ♣♣♣ (3+3+3=9), none by laying aside ♦♦♦ (0+0+0=0). Three may be bid ♣♦♦ (3+0+0), ♥♠♦ (2+1+0) or ♠♠♠ (1+1+1). And so on.

Premium bids Normally, bid-cards are left face down and remain unseen until exposed at end of play to claim a win. For a premium, however, a player may offer to 'declare' by turning their bid-cards face up at start of play, thus declaring their target and revealing more information about the lie of cards. For a higher premium, a player may offer to 'reveal' by not only turning their bid-cards up at start of play but also then playing with their hand of cards exposed on the table before the opening lead. Only one player may declare or reveal. If more than one wish to declare, priority goes to the player nearest the dealer's left, dealer having least priority. An offer to reveal overcalls an offer to declare, regardless of position – but, if two or more wish to reveal, the same priority applies.

Play The first deal is played at no trump. Each subsequent deal is played with a trump suit determined by the number of players who fulfilled their previous contract. The trump suit is clubs if all three succeeded, hearts if two, spades if one, or diamonds if none. Eldest leads first. Players must follow suit if possible, otherwise may play any card. The trick is taken by the highest card of the suit led, or by the highest trump if any are played, and the winner of each trick leads to the next.

Score Whoever claims to have fulfilled their contract must face their bid-cards to prove it. Each player scores 1 point per trick won, regardless of their bid. Anyone who succeeded also gets a bonus score: 10 if all three succeeded, 20 if only two succeeded, 30 if only one succeeded. If anyone declared or revealed, there is a bonus of 30 or 60 respectively. This goes to the declarer if successful, otherwise to each opponent, whether or not they succeeded. *Note*: The highest possible score is 99, obtained if one player bids and wins nine tricks revealed and is the only player to succeed, making 9+30+60.

Game A game is 100 points. The winner, and any opponent who reaches 100 or more in play, adds a bonus of 100. A rubber is won by the first to win three games, each in turn dealing first to a new game. The winner adds 100 for each game played fewer than eight – e.g. 500 for winning three straight off ((8 – 3) × 100).

Two-handed Ninety-Nine (with dummy)

Deal three hands of twelve cards each, face down. Separate the top three cards of the dummy hand as its 'bid'. These remain face down and unseen till end of play. Each player bids in the usual way. Either or both players may declare, but neither may reveal. After the bids and any declarations have been made, the dummy hand only is turned face up and sorted into suits. The first deal is played at no trump; thereafter, the trump suit is determined as in the three-hand game.

Non-dealer leads to the first trick, waits for the second to play, then plays any legal card from dummy. If a live player wins the trick, he leads first from hand and third from dummy. If the dummy wins a trick, the person who played from it then leads first from dummy and third from hand.

At end of play, the dummy's bid-cards are turned up and both live players score as in the three-hand game. However, because the dummy rarely makes its bid exactly, consider it to have failed if it won more tricks than bid, succeeded if it won fewer, and declared if it made its bid exactly. If one live player declares and fails, the other two score the bonus of 30. If both declare and fail, neither gains it but the dummy scores 60 extra.

Two-handed Ninety-Nine (without dummy)

Deal twelve cards each from a 24-card pack ranking AKQJT9. Bid as usual, but without declaring or revealing. Play the first deal at no trump. At any subsequent point, the player with the higher score is 'vulnerable', and if scores are equal both are vulnerable. If both succeed, each adds 10. If only one succeeds, add 20. If a vulnerable player fails, the other, if not vulnerable, adds a further 10, regardless of his own success or failure.

Four-handed Ninety-Nine

Deal thirteen cards each from a 52-card pack. Use three bid-cards to bid up to 10 tricks. A bid of three diamonds represents either 0 or 10 tricks, and either number of tricks automatically fulfils the contract. The contract score is 30 if one player succeeds, 20 each if two, 10 each if three, zero if all four either succeed or fail in their contract. If all four succeed, the next deal is played at no trump, otherwise the trump suit is determined as in the three-hand game. The premium score is 30 or 60 as before.

Five-handed Ninety-Nine

Five players receive twelve each from the Australian 'Five Hundred' pack including Elevens and Twelves (but ignoring Thirteens) and lay aside three cards to bid up to nine. The contract bonus is 10 if all five succeed, 20 if four, 30 if three, 40 if two, 50 if only one. No one may reveal, but any number of players may declare for a premium of 50 points if successful or minus 50 if not. If four or five players succeed, the next deal is played at no trump.

Comments These notes on play relate to the three-handed game, but similar principles apply to other numbers.

Your main strategic task is first to assess how many of your trumps and high cards are probable winners and how many probable losers, and then to select three cards whose absence from the hand leaves exactly the right number of tricks to be made from the remaining nine. Ideally, the three you bid with will be middling cards (Jack, Ten, Nine) whose winning or losing potential is highly unpredictable. Ninety-Nine thus differs markedly from other trick games in which only high cards are really significant. Here, Sixes are as important as Aces, and Sevens as Kings. If you can't bid with middling ranks it is desirable to use Aces or trumps, whose absence from play may confuse the opposition. Sometimes more than one reasonable bid is possible, in which case choose the one that involves confusing discards. For instance, with diamonds as trump:

♦AKQ ♣AT86 ♥76 ♠T86

you can reasonably bid zero by discarding three diamonds (♣A is no problem – you can throw it to a trump lead or the third round of hearts), or bid three by discarding the spades, leaving your diamonds as winners. The better of these is zero, as the holders of lower trumps will almost certainly take too many tricks. Position is also important. Given the lead, a bid of three is easily won by leading diamonds and escaping with ♥7. Without it, hearts could be drawn before you have a chance to trump in. The later you win tricks, the harder it is to lose the lead.

With hearts as trump, and holding

♥J86 ♠AQ9 ♦AQ976 ♣A

... the most sensible bid with or without the lead is two, discarding ♠Q ♠9 ♦A. This loses two middling ranks and offers one certain and one probable trick with a black Ace. Should the ♠A fail, you can probably expect to make the Jack by ruffing a club lead. A psychic bid, designed to confuse the others, would be to discard ♣A and two diamonds for a bid of three, hoping to make two spades and the trump Jack, or else to bid two by throwing the Jack with two diamonds. Either way, your problem is then two middling spades. They could be lost to club leads, but early spade leads – which may be expected from the holder(s) of Six and Seven – would spell defeat.

The most remarkable feature of Ninety-Nine is that the suits have distinctive strength characteristics in play. Because the average bid is three, diamonds and spades are more frequently discarded in bids than hearts and clubs, so that, in play, clubs and hearts tend to be held long and spades and diamonds short. Therefore, clubs are a more 'reliable' suit than diamonds. For example, a plain-suit holding of ♣AK76 will normally win two tricks with the lead, whereas ♦AK76 may be trumped on the first lead and almost certainly will be on the second. Conversely, if leading to the first trick and wishing to avoid tricks, the Seven from ♣AQ987 will almost certainly be overtaken, whereas the Seven from ♦AQ987 could well be followed by the Six and a discard.

Much the same applies to trumps. As we have seen, with diamonds as trump the top three may well be out of play for a bid of zero, but with hearts or clubs as trump you will nearly always find all nine in play. Experienced players find that, as trumps, clubs are reliable to the point of predictability in play, diamonds so unreliable as to shipwreck skill on the rock of chance, hearts somewhat treacherous because not quite as reliable as you might expect, and spades usually the most interesting and skill-demanding. No-trump games tend to favour the opening leader.

Declarations are made on hands containing not more than one uncertain card, and usually for not more than four tricks. Revelations require exceptional hands containing consecutive high trumps, or Sixes and low cards in all suits. They are best played on bids of one or two tricks when you have the opening lead, or of zero when you don't. The opponents of a declared or revealed bid must play co-operatively in order to beat it, as they will score more by failing themselves and defeating the contract than vice versa.

Finally: A long plain suit based on a Six plays safer as a run of definite losers. For example, ♥AK876 counts better as no tricks than as one or two with the top cards, which could well be trumped. From a sequence always play the least informative card – the Eight rather than the Six in the above heart holding.

The Golden Rule of three-hand Ninety-Nine remains: if in doubt, bid three.

Don't forget . . .

- Play to the left (clockwise) unless otherwise stated.
- Eldest or Forehand means the player to the left of the dealer in left-handed games, to the right in right-handed games.
- T = Ten, p = players, pp = in fixed partnerships, c = cards, t = trump, ☆ = Joker.

3 Quick trick games

The following are mostly (but not entirely) gambling and drinking games in which not all the cards are dealt out, which makes it harder to deduce what anyone else has got. Typically, each receives three cards and aims to win at least one trick, or five cards and aims to win at least three, or bids to win a minimum number. The bidding element has given rise to more advanced games of skill such as Euchre, Nap, and Five Hundred. This family may be traced back to the fifteenth-century game of Triomphe, known in England as Trump, or French Ruff, to distinguish it from English Ruff, the ancestor of Whist and Bridge. It is large and rather diffuse, some of its members having apparently interbred with other types such as All Fours (Pitch). Many are associated with particular countries or regions: Euchre with Cornwall and Devon, Five Hundred with Australia, Twenty-Five with Ireland, Ecarté with France, Bourré with Cajun country.

Euchre
4 players (2 × 2), 25 cards

> To win two tricks signifies nothing, to win three or four wins but one, but to win five is the winning of five.
>
> Cotton (on French Ruff), *The Compleat Gamester* (1674)

Besides being the 'national' game of the West Country, especially Cornwall, Euchre is widely played in Canada, some north-eastern States in the USA, and New Zealand, while Five Hundred, its close relative, is the national game of Australia. It was especially popular in America in the nineteenth century, having been brought thither by those German immigrants still referred to as the 'Pennsylvania Dutch'. Its ultimate origin appears to lie in an Alsatian game called Juckerspiel, referring to its two top trumps. (Jucker means Jack. So does Bower, which rhymes with 'flower', and comes from the German *Bauer* = 'farmer' or 'peasant'.) Despite its spelling, which one can only guess to have been inexplicably influenced by 'eucharist', Euchre and Jucker are pronounced almost identically – the J like an initial Y, and the whole probably rhyming better with 'cooker' than with 'snooker'. The word Jucker may also have influenced the choice of the term Joker, an extra card introduced in the 1860s to act as the topmost trump or Jack, originally in a variety of designs, but only from about 1880 in the now well-established guise of a court jester. Our modern Joker therefore has nothing to do with the card called the Fool in Tarot packs, as so often claimed. Rather, it is a fifth Jack, and was specifically invented for the game of Euchre. Another of this great game's legacies is the verb 'to euchre', meaning to force someone into a situation or action they would rather avoid.

Euchre is and has been played in many different versions for various numbers of players. We start with the four-hand partnership game as played (with minor variations) on a tournament basis in the West Country.

Preliminaries Four players sitting crosswise in partnerships receive five cards each (3+2 or 2+3) from a 25-card pack consisting of AKQJT9 in each suit, plus one Joker. Lacking a Joker, substitute a black Two. Lay the other four face down and turn the top card for trump preference. If it is the Joker, dealer must announce trumps before looking at his cards. Game is any agreed number of points (such as 10, 11, 21) over as many deals as necessary.

Rank of cards Trumps cards rank downwards as follows:

> Benny, or Best Bower (Joker)
>
> Right Bower (Jack of trumps)
>
> Left Bower (other Jack of same colour as trumps)
>
> A-K-Q-T-9

In other suits, cards rank AKQ(J)T9.

Bidding Unless the Joker is turned (see below), there is a round or two of bidding to decide which side will undertake to win at least three tricks with the turned suit trump, or, if all decline, with another suit. A bidder who thinks he can win three or more from his own hand may offer to play 'alone'.

Each in turn, starting with eldest, either passes or accepts the turned suit as trump by saying 'Up' (short for 'I order it up') and adding 'alone', if applicable. Any acceptance ends the bidding. In some circles the dealer's partner may only order it up if playing alone.

If all pass, the turn-up is turned down and each in turn may now either name another trump suit or pass. (Choosing the other suit of the same colour is to 'make it next'; choosing either of the other two is to 'cross it'.) If anyone names a suit, the bidding ends. As before, a bidder may offer to play alone. If all pass, the hand is annulled and the deal passes on.

Whichever side chose trumps are the 'makers'. If they are playing in the turned suit, the dealer may, before play, take the turn-up into hand and make one discard face down in its place (unless his partner is playing alone).

If the Joker is turned, the dealer's side automatically become the makers, and dealer must name a suit before looking at his hand.

Play Before play, either of the defenders may offer to defend alone, whether or not one of the makers is doing so. In a lone bid, the loner's partner lays his cards face down before the opening lead, which is made by the player at loner's immediate left, or his partner if the latter is playing alone. Otherwise, the opening lead is made by eldest hand. Players must follow suit if possible, otherwise may play any card. The trick is taken by the highest card of the suit led, or by the highest trump if any are played, and the winner of each trick leads to the next.

Score The makers score 1 point for winning three or four tricks, 2 for the 'march' (all five), or 4 for the march if played alone. If they fail to win three they are 'euchred', and the opponents score 2, regardless of any lone hands.

Variations In North America the Joker is usually omitted. In New Zealand, and occasionally in America, Euchre is still played with its original 32-card pack (AKQJT987, Joker optional).

Euchre for two or three

As for four, but each bids individually and the player who makes trump plays alone against the other two acting in concert. If the turned suit is trump, dealer takes the turn-up in exchange for a discard. Eldest leads to the first trick. The maker scores 1 for point, 2 for the march, or, if euchred, deducts 2 from his score. Game is 5, 7 or 10, by prior agreement.

Euchre for two

As for three, but one player short. Or play Ecarté instead.

Bid Euchre

Original name for the game of Five Hundred (q.v.).

Call-Ace Euchre

Four players use 24 cards, five 28 (AKQJT98), six 32 (AKQJT987), plus Joker as Best Bower. Bid as in the basic game. Before play, the maker names any suit, and the holder of the highest card of it becomes his silent partner, revealing this fact only by the way he plays. The maker may elect to play alone, and may even unwittingly prove to be his own partner. Each member of a side scores the points due to his side as a whole. *Note*: If the absolute highest card of a called suit is undealt, it is the highest card in play that counts.

Jackpot Euchre

Four use 25, five 29, six 33 cards, including a Joker as Best Bower. Each plays for himself, chips one to the pool and receives five cards. Turn the top of the undealt cards for trump. The maker is not obliged to win three tricks. Instead, each player draws a chip from the pool for each trick he wins, or pays one chip if he wins none. The pool is swept by the first player to win a march.

Auction Euchre

Best for five. Use 28 cards, deal five each and leave a blind or widow of three face down (or use 32, make a blind of five and leave two cards out of play). Each in turn has one opportunity to bid at least three tricks using a named trump, or to overcall a previous bid. A bid of 5 is overcalled by a bid of 8, which is an undertaking to play a lone hand after exchanging cards, and that by a bid of 15, which is to play alone with the hand as dealt. The maker, before play, first takes the widow and discards any three cards from his hand (unless he bid 15); he then calls for an ally (unless playing alone) by naming any specific card not in his own hand. The holder of that card becomes his silent partner, revealing that fact only by his play.

Six-hand Euchre

The Cornish version has two teams of three, each player flanked by an opponent. The cards are either 33 (AKQJT987 + Joker) or 50 (2 x AKQJT9 + 2 Jokers). In the double-pack game, the second of two identical cards played to a trick beats the first, though if the Jokers are of different colours then the one matching the trump colour prevails.

One member of either or both sides may play alone, in which case the other two lay their cards down. The loner may make one discard face down and ask one of his partners for a replacement, which that partner must furnish at his own discretion and without consultation.

Almonte Euchre

The Canadian six-hander uses a 31-card pack consisting of AKQJT98 in each suit, plus three Jokers represented by low-numeral spades. Trumps rank downwards ♠4 ♠3 ♠2 Right, Left, A-K-Q-T-9-8. Each receives five cards, leaving one turned for preference. If it is a Joker, dealer names a suit before looking at his cards. (In some circles, this obliges him to become the maker in the nominated suit should all five others pass.) The score for a march or a euchre is 3 instead of 2, or 6 if played alone. Game is 15 points.

▌ **Pepper** (Hasenpfeffer)   4 players (2 × 2), 24 cards

Hasenpfeffer ('Jugged Hare') was an early step in the direction of improving the skill factor of Euchre by reducing the number of undealt cards – in this case by dealing them all out. The modern version, currently popular in Iowa and Ohio, is now called 'Pepper'.

Preliminaries Four players sitting crosswise in partnerships receive six cards each, dealt singly from a 24-card pack ranking AKQJT9. As at Euchre, the top trumps are the Right and Left Bowers. In a no-trump bid cards rank AKQJT9 in all suits.

Auction Each in turn, starting with eldest, either passes or bids a number of tricks he would commit his partnership to winning, given the choice of trumps. The bids are one, two, three, four, five, Little Pepper (six), and Big Pepper, which is also six but for a doubled score. Each bid must be higher than the last. The player whose bid precedes three consecutive passes becomes the maker. The maker announces the trump suit, or declares no trump, and leads to the first trick.

Play Players must follow suit if possible, otherwise may play any card. The trick is taken by the highest card of the suit led, or by the highest trump if any are played, and the winner of each trick leads to the next.

Score If successful, the makers score 1 point per trick won; if not, they score minus 6. Big Pepper scores plus or minus 12. The other side always scores 1 point per trick won. Game is 30 points.

Double Hasenpfeffer

Original Hasenpfeffer was often played without Bowers, cards ranking normally in all four suits. This obtains in Double Hasenpfeffer, which is for four or six players in two partnerships, and employs the 48-card Pinochle pack (AKQJT9, doubled) without a Joker. Deal all the cards around. Each player has one chance to bid or overbid, the minimum being for three tricks, with no trump as yet mentioned. Dealer must bid at least three if the others pass. The high bidder may play alone, in which case he discards any two cards face down and receives from his partner any two cards the latter wishes to give him. If the making side takes at least as many as it bid, it scores 1 point per trick taken; if not, it loses the amount of the bid, except that the dealer, if forced to bid, loses only half that amount. A lone player wins or loses double for his side.

Five Hundred   2–6 players, 33–63 cards

This hybrid of Euchre and Bid Whist was copyrighted by the United States Playing-Card Company in 1904. Though still played in parts of the USA, it has since become the national game of Australia and New Zealand. Southern Cross, the Australian playing-card manufacturer, still produces a special '500' pack containing the 63 cards necessary for the six-handed game, though I have never heard of anyone playing it. This pack includes Elevens, Twelves, two red Thirteens, and a Joker depicting a kookaburra, or laughing jackass, commonly known as 'the Bird'. The Australian game is most widely played by four in partnerships, usually without the Bird. It is also an excellent game for three or five players. The following rules are based on those included in the Southern Cross pack, but there are many local variations, especially regarding the way the Joker is used, the relative ranking of misères, and the non-bidders' scoring.

Preliminaries From two to six may play. The standard game is four, sitting crosswise in partnerships. Six play as two teams of three or three of two, each player being flanked by an opponent. Game is 500 points over as many deals as necessary.

Cards The number of cards used is ten times the number of players, plus two, plus Joker (optional). The special Five Hundred 63-card pack consists in full of A-K-Q-J-(13)-12-11-10-9-8-7-6-5-4-3-2, plus Joker. The Thirteens exist only in red suits. The full pack is used only in the six-player game. For other numbers of players, the cards used are:

> five   52 or 53 (AKQJT98765432 in all suits)
>
> four   42 or 43 (AKQJT98765 in all suits, plus two red Fours)
>
> three   32 or 33 (AKQJT987 in all suits)
>
> two   24 only (AKQJT9 in all suits, no Joker)

Rank of cards In non-trump suits, cards rank in their natural order (Ace high, Two low). In trumps, the order is:

> Best Bower   = Joker (if used)
>
> Right Bower = Jack of trumps
>
> Left Bower   = other Jack of same colour as trumps
>
> A-K-Q-10 . . . etc. (or A-K-Q-13 . . . if six play)

Deal Deal ten each, in batches of 3-4-3. After the first round of three, deal three cards face down to the table as a 'kitty', or two if the Joker is omitted, or four if only two play.

Bidding Each in turn, starting with eldest, either passes or overcalls any previous bid. A bid is an offer to win the stated number of tricks in the stated trump suit playing alone (if two or three play), or with one's partner (if four or six), or with the aid of a temporary ally (if five). A bid may be announced as '6 spades' (for example) or by its value in the following scoring table ('40', etc.):

trump	6 tricks	7 tricks	8 tricks	9 tricks	10 tricks	no tricks, no trump
♠ spades	40	140	240	340	440	misère 250
♣ clubs	60	160	260	360	460	
♦ diamonds	80	180	280	380	480	
♥ hearts	100	200	300	400	500	
no trumps	120	220	320	420	520	open misère 520

Misère, despite its value, is overcalled by any bid of eight or more; open misère overcalls everything.

The highest bidder after three consecutive passes becomes the declarer. If all pass without bidding, tricks are played at no trump and the aim is to win as many as possible.

The kitty Declarer takes the kitty into hand and makes the same number of discards face down before play. If all passed, the kitty remains untouched.

Calling (five players). If five play, declarer either announces that he will 'go alone', or else calls for a partner (except in misère) by naming a non-trump card. Whoever holds it immediately identifies himself as declarer's partner.

Play Declarer leads first, or, if everyone passed, eldest hand. (At open misère, the hand is spread face up before the opening lead.) Players must follow suit if possible, otherwise may play any card. The trick is taken by the highest card of the suit led, or by the highest trump if any are played, and the winner of each trick leads to the next. In a no-trump bid, including misère, the Joker is in fact a trump – the only one – and may be played when its holder cannot follow suit, thereby winning the trick. If led, its holder calls for a suit to be played to it, which may not be one in which he has already renounced.

Score The soloist or each member of the declaring side either wins or loses the value of his contract (see the Table on p. 101). Regardless of success or failure, each member of the opposing side scores 10 per trick won by their side – or, in a misère, 10 for each trick taken by the declarer, for which reason misères must be played right through. If no one declared, each player scores 10 points for each trick that he won.

Game The game ends when either side has scored 500 or more as the result of winning a contract, or has done so badly as to reach minus 500 or more. (The others are then said to have won 'by the back door', or by some even more graphic phrase.) If a player or side reaches 500 only by virtue of scoring 10 per trick rather than by fulfilling a contract, play continues until a qualifying contract is won.

Footnote Under the original rules there was only one round of bidding, so each player had to bid his maximum immediately. The rules published with the Australian pack now declare this to be optional, and it is probably widely ignored. The published rules also state that if the soloist or declarers win all ten tricks in a contract worth 240 or less, they score a flat 250. As this benefit seems designed to compensate for the original one round of bidding, it should be ignored if further rounds are permitted.

Five Hundred (three players). This hand easily bids 6♥, as it contains the top three trumps (the Joker and both red Jacks), a good forcing suit (clubs) and a void (diamonds). The bid can be raised to seven in the expectation that, even if the outstanding hearts are not evenly divided (3–2), some benefit may be derived from the kitty. If an opponent takes the game in spades, this hand bids fair to beat it, as it then holds the Left Bower (♣J) in addition to Best.

American Five Hundred

(4pp, 45c) American varieties are widely played in Ohio and Minnesota, all varying in detail. The following game is as played at St Paul, Minnesota (West Seventh Street rules).

Preliminaries Four play in fixed partnerships with a 45-card pack (4 × AKQJT987654, plus Joker). Agree in advance whether or not to admit nullo (misère) bids. The first to draw a Jack deals first. Deal ten each and a five-card hand called the 'middle' as follows: 3-(3)-2-(2)-3-2, the figures in brackets being those of the middle.

Ace – no face A player dealt exactly one Ace but no courts or Joker may call for the deal to be annulled by claiming 'Ace – no face'. If partner agrees, the deal is annulled without reference to the opponents. If not, play ensues, but the claimant's partnership may not then bid nullo.

Bidding Only one of the first two players may bid six (announced as 'Inkle' – e.g. 'Inkle spades'). If both pass, the minimum bid is seven, otherwise the deal is abandoned.

The first two players who make a bid may, if bidding no trump, announce it in either of two ways in order to convey information to their partner. The standard announcement is 'Seven [or whatever] no trump'. The special announcement 'Seven, No' means that the bidder holds either the Joker or 'split Bowers' (two Jacks of opposite colour). 'Inkle no' is an acceptable bid from the first or second player.

Nullo bids If admitted, a simple nullo counts 250 and a grand nullo, or granola, 510. In a simple nullo the bidder's partner lays his hand face down and the bidder plays alone against two opponents. Granola may be bid only by the partner of a player who bid nullo. If established, this player takes the middle into hand and makes any five discards face down. The original nullo bidder then takes these into hand and does likewise. Both must play, and both lose if either takes a trick.

Play and score As for Australian Five Hundred.

Ecarté

This elegant two-player derivative of Triomphe became all the rage in early nineteenth-century Paris casinos, partly because it encouraged kibitzers to place bets on the outcome. Though now defunct, it is still quite fun to play.

Preliminaries Use 32 cards, ranking KQJAT987 in each suit. (Note the position of the Ace.) Game is five points.

Deal The deal alternates. Deal five cards each in batches of three and two. Stack the rest face down, turn the top card for trump, and lay it to one side. If it is a King, dealer scores a point; and if this makes him five, he wins without play.

Discarding Non-dealer may either lead to the first trick, which obligates him to win at least three, or else propose that both players replace some of their cards. If he proposes, dealer may either refuse, which obligates him to win at least three, or else accept the proposal. If dealer accepts, each in turn, starting with non-dealer, lays aside at least one card and draws the same number of replacements from the top of the stock.

Again, non-dealer may lead or propose, and dealer may accept or refuse. This continues until non-dealer decides to lead, or dealer refuses a proposal, or the stock is exhausted. Neither may call for more cards than remain, and the card turned for trump may never be taken. When either refuses to exchange, or no cards remain, non-dealer must lead to the first trick.

Marking the King Before play, if either player holds the King of trumps he may show it and score 1 point, provided that he has not already played some other card to the first trick.

Play At each trick the second player must follow suit and win the trick if possible. If unable to follow he must trump if possible, and only otherwise may renounce. The trick is captured by the higher card of the suit led, or by a trump to a non-trump lead, and the winner of each trick leads to the next.

Score Normally, the winner scores 1 point for taking three or four tricks, or 2 for the vole (all five). But if either player insisted on playing with the hands as originally dealt, so that no cards were exchanged, and that player fails to win three tricks, the other scores 2 points regardless of how many he took. Further deals ensue until one player reaches 5. He wins a double stake if the other gained only 1 or 2 points, a treble if the other gained none.

Jeux de règle Certain hands are acknowledged to be at least twice as likely to win as not, and should therefore be played without proposing. These are called *jeux de règle*, 'obligatory hands', because in a casino game the house player's job was on the line if he failed to play them as dealt. The full gamut of *jeux de règle* may be abbreviated as follows:

trumps	non-trumps include
3+	any
2	King and a void
	Queen and one of her suit
	any three of a suit
1	KQJ of a suit
	Q-x-x of a suit
	Q-x in each of two suits
0	any four court cards better than four Jacks

Bester Bube ('Best Boy')

(3–6p, 32c) Defunct but interesting; possibly transitional between Ecarté and Euchre, and recorded only by Anton (1889). Dealer puts five chips in the pot, deals five cards each in batches of three and two from a 32-card pack, and turns the next for trump. The highest trump is the Jack ('Bester Bube'), second highest the other Jack of the same colour, followed by AKQT987. Each in turn may discard any number of cards and draw replacements from the stock (excluding the turn-up). Two rounds of discarding and drawing are permitted, so long as enough cards remain in stock. Before play, dealer takes the turn-up in exchange for any discard. Tricks are played without (apparently) any obligation to follow suit. Eldest must lead the Best Boy if held, otherwise any trump. Lacking trumps, he leads any card face down and announces 'Trumps'(!). Whoever holds the Best Boy must play it to the first trick – unless it is the dealer, who may retain it – and no one else need follow suit. The same rules apply at trick two, this time in respect of the second-best Boy. Thereafter any card may be led and played, still without obligation to follow suit. Each player wins one chip per trick taken, but a player taking none pays into the pot the amount it contained at the start of the deal.

Triomphe (French Ruff)

(2p/4pp/6pp, 36c) The ancestor of Ecarté appears in Cotton's *Compleat Gamester* under the title French Ruff. Partners sit next to one another and may overlook one another's hands, but may not verbally consult. Cards rank KQJAT9876 in each suit, though in France the Ace sometimes ranked highest. Deal five cards each in batches of three and two, and turn the next for trump. Anyone dealt the trump Ace may exchange it for the turn-up, together with any further trumps that may lie consecutively below it. Players must follow suit and head the trick if possible, otherwise trump (and overtrump) if possible, and only otherwise may renounce.

Homme d'Auvergne

(2–6p, 32c) An old French game probably ancestral to Euchre. Cards rank KQJAT987, but omit the Sevens if only two or three play. Deal five each and turn the next for trump. There is a round of bidding to see who will undertake to win three tricks in the turned suit, or the first two straight off. If all pass, the turn-up is turned down, there is another round in which players may name any suit, and the first to do so becomes the soloist. Eldest leads. Players must follow suit and head the trick if possible; must trump and overtrump if unable to follow; and renounce only if unable to do either. The trick is taken by the highest card of the suit led, or by the highest trump if any are played, and the winner of each trick leads to the next. The soloist wins 1 game point if successful, or loses it if not. One game point is also scored by anyone holding the trump King, and by anyone who wins a King by trumping. Game is 7 points.

Twenty-Five (45, Spoil Five)   3–10 players (5 best), 52 cards

> They young lads
> So conceity-like and fly with all yon play
> Of euchre and such foolish Yankee fads . . .
> Aru! Twenty-five's not good enough for them!
> > 'Dermot O'Byrne' (Arnold Bax), *An Old Man's Chatter*

Ireland's national card game appeared in nineteenth-century books under the name Spoil Five, your aim being to prevent anybody from winning three of the five tricks played if you were unable to do so yourself. Originally scored in single points up to a target of five, it later came to be scored in fives instead of ones, thereby acquiring the name Twenty-Five. Later still, players adopted a Joker into the game and raised the target to 45 points. All these titles emphasize the peculiar obsession it seems to exhibit for the number five: five is the best number of players; five tricks are played; the top trump is the Five (originally known as Five Fingers), and even the Irish for 'trick', *cúig*, is the word for five. Gaelic through and through, it is first attested under the name Maw as the court game of James VI of Scotland (later James I of England), and was subsequently carried to the New World, where it remains popular in Canada, especially in Nova Scotia ('New Scotland').

Newcomers may find it initially daunting because of the peculiar rank of cards and rules of play, which obviously derive from the ancient Spanish game of Hombre and which take a little getting used to. But it is well worth the effort, as much for its intrinsic interest as for its cultural and historic significance – not to mention the fact that it is one of the very few games for which five is the best number of players.

The following description benefits from additional information collected by Anthony Smith.

Preliminaries From three to ten *can* play, from four to six usually do. Four may play in two partnerships of two, six in two partnerships of three or three of two. For non-partnership play, five is ideal. Each starts with 20 chips or counters, but scores can easily be kept in writing.

Cards Fifty-two. There is always a trump suit, and three or four cards are always the highest trumps, namely (from the top down):

†5	'Five Fingers'
†J	Jack of trumps
♥A	Ace of hearts
†A	Ace of trumps (if not hearts)

The others rank from high to low according to colour:

in ♥♦	KQJT98765432A	'high in red'
in ♠♣	KQJA23456789T	'low in black'

☞ There are usually 14 trumps, but 13 in hearts. In plain suits, the King is always highest.

Deal Everyone chips one to the pool. Deal five cards each in batches of two and three, or four and one, in either order. Stack the rest face down and turn the top card for trump.

Object Primarily, to sweep the pool by winning at least three tricks, and preferably all five. Failing this, to 'spoil five' by preventing anyone else from winning three, thereby increasing the size of the pool for the next deal. If played for soft score, each trick counts 5 points and the target is 25.

Robbing the pack If dealt the trump Ace, you may declare that fact and then 'rob the pack' by taking the turn-up and discarding an unwanted card face down. You are not obliged to declare it if you don't intend to rob, but, if you do, you must rob before playing to the first trick. If the turn-up is an Ace, dealer may rob the pack by exchanging it for any unwanted card.

Play Eldest leads to the first trick.

• To a plain-suit lead, you may either follow suit or trump, as preferred, but may renounce only if unable to follow suit.

• To a trump lead, you must play a trump if possible, unless the only one you hold is a top trump (†5, †J, ♥A) and it is higher than the one led. In this case, you may 'renege' by discarding from another suit. Expressed another way: you can't force a top trump out by leading a lower one, only by leading a higher.

The trick is taken by the highest card of the suit led, or by the highest trump if any are played, and the winner of each trick leads to the next.

Jinking If you win the first three tricks straight off, you may sweep the pool without further play. If instead you 'jink' by leading to the fourth trick, you thereby undertake to win all five, and will lose your stake if you fail to get them all.

Score Anyone winning three or more tricks wins the pool, and for winning all five gains an extra chip from each opponent. If nobody wins three, or a jinker fails to win five, the tricks are said to be 'spoilt'. The pool is then carried forward to the next deal, increased by one chip per player.

Game The game ends when somebody runs out of chips (hard score) or reaches 25 points (soft score).

Forty-Five

Add a Joker, which ranks between †J and ♥A as the third-highest trump. If, in turning the top card for trump, you turn the Joker, you take it into hand, place any unwanted card at the bottom of the pack, and turn the next instead. The aim is simply to score points, not to 'spoil five', and there is no jinking. Each won trick counts 5 points, and an additional 5 goes to the player who was dealt the best card. Normally, the best card is the highest trump, and if the †5 appears in play its holder scores 5 immediately. If no one was dealt any trumps (rare), the best card is the highest-ranking card that actually won a trick, or the first played of cards tying for this honour. Tricks are scored as soon as taken, and the game ends as soon as one player or partnership wins by reaching the 45-point target score.

Variants In some parts of Ireland, the best card counts 6, and the target may be set at 31 (though the game is still called Forty-Five). In Canada, a side scores 5 for winning three or four tricks, or 10 for all five. Another variant has 15 for three, 20 for four, and game for all five. The Joker, if used, ranks as the fourth highest trump, below ♥A.

Auction Forty-Fives

4 or 6 players, 52 cards

The auction equivalent is attributed to Canada and Nova Scotia. I have not heard of its being played in Ireland.

Preliminaries Four or six play in two partnerships, with partners sitting alternately round the table. Game is 120 points. Deal five cards each (2+3).

Bidding Each in turn may bid or pass, and having passed may not come in again. Bids go from 5 to 30 in multiples of five, representing five per trick plus five for holding the highest trump in play. A side standing at 100 points to game may not bid lower than 20. The first time any given number is bid, the next in turn may say, 'I hold,' thereby taking over the bid at the same number. The next in turn, however, must then either raise again or pass. No suit is mentioned till all have passed after the highest bidder, who then announces trumps.

Drawing Before play, each in turn, starting with eldest, may make any number of discards, face down, receiving from dealer the same number of replacements from the rest of the pack.

Play The ranking of cards, method of trick-play and privileges of reneging are as for Twenty-Five or Forty-Five.

Score Count 5 per trick and 5 for whoever proves to have held the highest trump in play. The non-bidding side scores whatever it makes. If the bidding side fulfilled its bid it scores all it made; if not, it deducts the bid from its current total. A bid of 30, if made, scores 60.

Variant In some circles the dealer, having discarded, may 'rob the pack' by examining all the undealt cards and freely selecting replacements.

Bête (Labet, Beast)

Seventeenth-century ancestor of five-card games. From two to five each pay a stake to the pool and receive five cards from a 32-card pack ranking KQJAT987, after which the next is turned for trump. Each in turn may either pass or play, the aim being to win at least three tricks, or the first two straight off. Anyone holding the trump King wins a chip from each player. A player winning three or more tricks sweeps the pool, and for winning all five additionally receives an equivalent amount by each active opponent. If no one wins three, a player winning the first two tricks sweeps the pool. Any active player failing to sweep the pool pays to a side pot an amount equivalent to the pool just played for. These side pots are kept separate, and the largest of them becomes the new pool when the current pool has been won.

Sixte

(6p, 52 or 36c) An eighteenth-century French game worth mentioning for its simplicity and the fact that it is uniquely designed for six. Cards rank AKQJT9876(5432). Play to the right. Deal six cards each in ones. If using 36 cards, dealer exposes his last card for trump; if 52, stack the rest face down and turn the topmost card for trump. Eldest leads to the first trick. Players must follow suit if possible, otherwise may play any card. The trick is taken by the highest card of the suit led, or by the highest trump if any are played, and the winner of each trick leads to the next. One point is scored by the first player to win three tricks or, if everybody wins one trick, by whoever won the first; otherwise no one scores. Game is 6 points, but winning all six in one deal wins the game outright.

Sizette

(6pp, 36c) Partnership version of Sixte. There are two partnerships of three each, each player being flanked by two opponents. Deal six each from a 36-card pack, turning the last for trump. Play as in Sixte. The first side to win three tricks scores 1 point, or 2 if it wins all six. (More interesting scoring schedules are easily devised.) Also recorded is a variant in which all the players of a side sit consecutively – that is, A A A B B B instead of A B A B A B. Equally playable would be a three-partnership version, with players sitting ABCABC.

| **Nap** (Napoleon) | 3–7 players, 28–52 cards |

> We played penny nap after supper. We played for about an hour and a half, by the end of which time George had won fourpence . . . and Harris and I had lost exactly twopence each.
>
> We thought we would give up gambling then. As Harris said, it breeds an unhealthy excitement when carried too far.
>
> Jerome K. Jerome, *Three Men in a Boat*, 1889

This simplified relative of Euchre is played throughout northern Europe under various names and guises. Despite its title and military allusions, it is not recorded under this name before the last third of the nineteenth century, and may commemorate Napoleon III, who probably played either this or one of its close relatives. It is best played by four or five players, using a stripped pack.

Preliminaries Three or more players use a 52-card pack ranking

AKQJT98765432, from which a certain number of lower numerals may be stripped to increase the skill factor. Three may play with 24 cards (AKQJT9), four with 28 (AKQJT98), five with 28 or 32 (AKQJT987), and so on. A Joker may be added, counting as the highest trump – or, in 'mis', the only trump. Each player starts with the same number of chips. It is usual to shuffle the cards at start of play and after a succesful bid of five, but, between other deals, only to cut them. Deal five cards each (2+3 or 3+2).

Bidding Each in turn bids to win a number of tricks if given the lead and choice of trumps. From low to high, the bids are: two, three, mis (lose every trick), four, Nap (five), Wellington (five for doubled stakes), and (if agreed) Blücher (five for redoubled stakes). Wellington may only follow a bid of Nap, and Blücher a bid of Wellington.

Play The highest bidder leads to the first trick, and the suit of that card is automatically trump – except in a mis, if players have previously agreed that mis is played at no trump. Players must follow suit if possible, otherwise may play any card. The trick is taken by the highest card of the suit led, or by the highest trump if any are played, and the winner of each trick leads to the next.

Score If successful, the bidder wins from each opponent 2–4 units for bids of two to four respectively, 3 for mis, 10 for Nap, 20 for Wellington, 40 for Blücher. If not, he pays the same amount to each opponent, though it may be agreed to halve it in the case of Nap.

Peep Nap

Version 1: The soloist, before leading, may peep at the top card of the stock and exchange it for an unwanted card if desired.

Version 2: An extra card is dealt face down. Each player, immediately before making a bid, is entitled to peep at it privately for a unit stake. When everyone has bid, the soloist may exchange it for an unwanted card as above.

Version 3: As above, but each in turn may peep and exchange before making a bid, so that the odd card – the 'floater' – keeps changing. In versions 2 and 3, payments go to a pool which is taken by the next player to bid and win five.

Pool Nap

A losing soloist pays to a pool as if it were an extra player, and the pool is taken by the next player to bid and win five.

Purchase Nap

This radical variant is virtually multi-player Ecarté. After the deal, but before any bids are made, the dealer addresses himself to each player in turn (finishing with himself) and sells him, for a fixed price, as many more cards as he wishes to buy. The purchaser must reject that number from his hand before replacing them and may not subsequently refer to his discards. The price paid goes to a pool, which is taken by the first to win a bid of five.

Seven-card Nap

Deal seven cards each. *Version 1*: Everyone discards two before bidding and playing five-card Nap. *Version 2*: The bids and their values are: three 3, four 4, Nap 10, mis 10, six 18, seven 24. A soloist losing Nap, mis, six, or seven pays half stakes.

Widow Nap (Sir Garnet)

This increases the frequency of Nap bids. Deal an extra hand, face down. Anyone bidding five may take these, add them to his hand, and discard any five before leading off.

Brandle

4 players, 28 cards

I have Anglicized the name of this delightful German Nap equivalent from *Brandeln*, meaning 'smoulder'. Rules vary: the following are typical.

Preliminaries Four players receive seven each (2-3-2) from a 28-card pack, ranking AKQJT97 in every suit but trumps, which rank J7AKQT9.

Bidding The bids and their values are:

Brandle (3 tricks)	1
Four	2
Five	3
Six	4

Bettel (misère, no trump)	5
Mord (trump slam, all 7)	6
Herrenmord (7 no trump)	7

Each in turn, starting with eldest, may pass or bid, and having passed may not come in again. If all pass, there is no play and the deal moves round. Each bid must exceed the previous one, but an earlier (elder) player may 'hold' the bid of a later, thus forcing the latter to pass or raise. The highest bid is Mord ('Death'). Herrenmord is not an overcall, merely a Mord played at no trump.

Play The soloist announces trumps upon leading to the first trick, but is not obliged to lead one. Players must follow suit and head the trick if possible; must trump and overtrump if unable to follow; and may renounce only if unable to do either. The trick is taken by the highest card of the suit led, or by the highest trump if any are played, and the winner of each trick leads to the next.

Score If successful, the soloist receives the value of his bid from each opponent, or scores the appropriate amount. There is no bonus for overtricks. If unsuccessful, he pays it to each opponent, or deducts it from his score.

Redbeard (Rödskägg, Five Up)   3–7 players, 52 cards

The Swedish equivalent of Nap is called Rödskägg (Redbeard, Barbarossa), or Fem Opp, 'Five Up', from the five-point penalty imposed for various faults. Like so many Scandinavian games, it is played without trumps but with a sting in its tail.

Preliminaries From three to seven players start with 12 chips each, or a score of 12, and the winner is the first to reach zero by shedding all chips or points. Cards rank AKQJT98765432. Play to the right.

Deal Deal six cards each in threes, then knock and say, '*Knack för kort och felgiv* (Knock for cards and misdeal).' Anyone picking up their cards before the dealer knocks must go 'five up' (add five chips or points to his account). Dealer himself goes five up if he misdeals, and it counts as a misdeal if he fails to knock or correctly pronounce the requisite incantation.

Bidding Each in turn, starting with eldest, either passes or bids from one to six tricks at no trump, each bid being higher than the last. A bid of six can be overcalled by 'Redbeard', which is an all-or-nothing bid and cannot be overcalled.

Play The highest bidder becomes the soloist and leads to the first trick. Players must follow suit if possible, otherwise may play any card. The trick is taken by the highest card of the suit led, and the winner of each trick leads to the next. There are no trumps.

Drop-outs After the fourth trick, the soloist must (on pain of going five up) ask whether those who have not yet taken a trick wish to go on. Those concerned may then either drop out, suffering no penalty, or continue play, in which case they will go five up if they fail to take at least one of the last two tricks.

Score If the soloist fulfils his bid, he sheds as many points as his bid, otherwise he goes five up. The others shed 1 per trick, but for taking no tricks go five up – unless, however, they dropped out when invited to do so.

A player successfully bidding Redbeard sheds all his points and wins outright. For failing, he goes five up and drops out of the current game.

Game A player wins by reaching zero exactly and announcing, '*Knack för min utgäng* (Knock for going out).' If he fails to announce it, and someone else goes out with the correct announcement, he goes five up for his failure.

A player who wins more tricks than necessary goes down to zero and then comes up again. For example, needing 2 to win, and making 3, he ends with 1. But many schools now disregard this rule.

Bourré   3–7 players, 52 cards

A gambling game in which poor players can be suckered into losing big when they have little chance of winning.

Carl Sifakis, *Encyclopedia of Gambling* (1990)

Pronounced Boo-ray, and sometimes so written, Bourré (French for 'stuffed') has enjoyed a remarkable revival as an 'authentic Cajun game' promoted by the National Cajun Bourré Association of Louisiana, with the usual inauthentic account of its origins and affiliations. On the plus side, their booklet does include some authentic Cajun recipes.

Preliminaries From three to seven players use a 52-card pack ranking AKQJT98765432. Everyone contributes equally to a pool and receives five cards, dealt one at a time, the dealer's last card being shown for trump. (*Variant*: The next undealt card is turned for trump.) Each in turn announces whether or not he will play, thereby undertaking to win at least one trick. (*Variant*: Players secretly put a chip in their fist if they want to stay in or form an empty fist if not; when all are ready, they open their fists simultaneously.) After these announcements, each active player in turn may make any number of discards face down and receive replacements from the top of the stock.

Play First active player left of dealer leads. Players must follow suit and head the trick if possible; must trump and overtrump if unable to follow; and may renounce only if unable to do either. The trick is taken by the highest card of the suit led, or by the highest trump if any are played, and the winner of each trick leads to the next. Anyone holding A, K or Q of trumps must lead his highest trump as soon as possible.

Pay-off A player who wins three or more tricks sweeps the pool. A player who wins none is 'bourréed', and contributes to the next pool the same amount as the pool held when he lost. If two players win two each, it is a 'split pot' tie, and the pool is carried forward to the next deal.

Julep

3–7 players, 40 cards

The Spanish equivalent of Bourré. Julep basically means a sweet drink used as camouflage for a nasty medicine, and is therefore literally a 'sweetener'.

Preliminaries From three to seven, ideally five or six, receive five cards each in ones from a 40-card Spanish pack ranking A3KQJ76542. Turn the next for trump. Play to the right.

Bidding Each in turn may throw his hand in or bid to play, thereby undertaking to win at least two tricks. Dealer may take the turn-up in exchange for a discard, thereby undertaking to play.

Drawing Each in turn may make any number of discards, then receive the same number from the undealt stock (excluding the turn-up). If not enough cards remain, shuffle the cards of those who have passed to form a new stock.

Defending the pack If only one player bids, any one player who passed can offer to 'defend the pack' by drawing six cards from stock and discarding one.

Play The first active player to the right of the dealer leads to the first trick. Players must follow suit and head the trick if possible; must trump and overtrump if unable to follow; and may renounce only if unable to do either.

Pay-off An active player who failed to win two tricks pays an agreed stake, the julep, as explained below. If only one player succeeds, he wins the pot plus a julep from each active player. If two players win two each, they split the pot and the juleps. If all fail, they all pay a julep to the pot, which is then carried forward.

If the pack was defended and lost, the lone player wins the pot but the defender does not pay a julep. If both succeed, the lone player wins half the pot, and the other half is carried forward. If the defender wins, he gets the pot plus a julep from the lone player.

Five-card Loo (Lanterloo) 3–10 players, 52 cards

The English equivalent of Bourré, now defunct, is not be confused with Three-card Loo. The name Pam, denoting the top trump, represents a medieval comic-erotic character called Pamphilus, described by Eric Partridge as 'an old bawd'. (From it derives also 'pamphlet', originally a printed sheet containing a story about him. These educational interpolations come free of charge.) Lanterloo is from the French *lenturlu*, a meaningless refrain used in lullabies ('lullay, lulloo'), and denotes a flush containing Pamphile. An earlier form of the game, lacking Pam, was played under the name Mouche.

Preliminaries From three to ten receive five cards each (3+2 or 2+3) from a 52-card pack ranking AKQJT98765432. Dealer antes five chips to the pot before dealing, and turns the next for trump after dealing.

Pam and flush The highest card in play is ♣J, or Pam, which beats everything, including the Ace of trumps. A flush is five cards of the same suit, or four of a suit plus Pam. The best flush is four of a suit plus Pam, followed by a flush in trumps, then by the plain-suit flush containing the highest top card or cards. Whoever holds the best flush (if any), whether before or after exchanging cards, 'looes the board' immediately – that is, he is deemed to win all five tricks without play, and is appropriately paid by anyone who does not himself hold either Pam or a flush.

Bidding Each in turn may pass or play, thereby undertaking to win at least one trick. (*Variant*: No one may pass if clubs are trump.) Each active player may discard as many as he likes in return for the same number dealt from the top of the pack.

Play Eldest leads. If the trump Ace is led (now or subsequently) its leader may say, 'Pam be civil,' whereupon the holder of ♣J may not play it if he has any other trump. Players must follow suit and head the trick if possible; must trump and overtrump if unable to follow; and may renounce only if unable to do either. The trick is taken by the highest card of the suit led, or by the highest trump if any are played. The winner of each trick leads to the next, and must lead a trump if possible.

Pay-off Each trick earns one-fifth of the pool.

Rams

(Rammes, Ramsch, Rounce, Bierspiel) (3–5p, 32c) The Belgian and Alsatian equivalent of Five-card Loo. Cards rank AKQJT987.

Preliminaries Ante five to the pool, deal five each (3+2) plus a spare hand of five, and turn the next for trump. Each in turn may pass or undertake to win at least one trick; but when the pool contains only five units nobody may pass. One player only may exchange his hand for the spare, sight unseen, but must then play. Rams is a bid to win all five tricks, and obliges everyone else to play. If everybody passes, dealer receives five chips from the player on his right and there is no play. If only one player before him offers to play, dealer himself may not pass. Dealer may take the trump turn-up in exchange for any unwanted card.

Play The first active player left of dealer leads. Players must follow suit and head the trick if possible; must trump and overtrump if unable to follow; and may renounce only if unable to do either. The trick is taken by the highest card of the suit led, or by the highest trump if any are played, and the winner of each trick leads to the next.

Score Each won trick earns one-fifth of the pool. A player who takes none adds five for the next deal. A successful rams bid wins the pool plus five from each opponent. If lost, the bidder doubles the pool and pays five to each (nothing extra for the player who took the trick that ended the play). Variant games include Rounce, using 52 cards, and Bierspiel, in which ♦7 is always the second-highest trump.

Mauscheln, Mousel

(3–5p, 32 or 52c) Mauscheln is the German and Mousel the Danish equivalent of Loo. *Mauscheln* means diddle (swindle).

From three to five players, ideally four, use a 32-card pack ranking AKQJT987. Play to the left. The dealer stakes an amount divisible by four, then deals four cards each, in twos, and turns the next for trump. Each in turn may pass or declare 'Diddle', thereby undertaking to win two tricks. As soon as someone offers to diddle, each in turn may pass, in which case they drop out, or 'Join in', which is an undertaking to win at least one. If no one offers to diddle, the deal passes round. If someone diddles but no one joins in, the diddler wins the pot without play. Otherwise, each active player may now make any number of discards and receive the same number from the top of the stock. If it runs out, make a new stock from the cards of those who passed, or from discards if necessary. The diddler leads any card to the first trick. Players must follow suit and head the trick if possible; must trump and overtrump if unable to follow; and may renounce only if unable to do either. Each won trick earns one-quarter of the pot. An active player who took none, or the diddler if he took only one, pays the value of the pot. If the diddler took none, he pays double.

Variants 1. If the turn-up is an Ace or other high card, the dealer may diddle before looking at his cards. In this case, when his turn comes to exchange, he may look at his cards, discard, and include the turn-up in his replacements.

2. The ♦7, called *Belli*, is the second-highest trump, and its holder pays a premium if he loses it to the trump Ace.

3. A player dealt a flush (four of the same suit) must pay a premium, throw his hand in, and be dealt a new one.

Norrlandsknack (Norseman's Knock)   3–5p, 52 cards

A distinctively Swedish member of the family, literally 'North Country Knock'. Norrland is the northern third of the country, including Lapland. Much the same game is played in Finland under the name Ramina, according to my informant, Veikko Lähdesmäki.

Preliminaries From three to five players use a 52-card pack, ranking AKQJT98765432. Each player stakes one chip to the pot at start of play, but not at each deal. Each also starts with a 10-point score and deducts one for each trick won. The winner is the first to reach zero.

Deal Deal a batch of three to each player, turn the next for trump, then two more each.

Bidding In the first deal, each in turn either knocks, thereby undertaking to win at least one trick, or says, 'I lurk.' Lurking means to play in hope of winning a trick, as there is no penalty for failing to do so at this stage. On subsequent deals, a player can only pass, not lurk. If all pass, the same dealer redeals. After three pass-outs, the deal passes on.

Draw In the first deal only, as soon as someone knocks there follows a draw. Each in turn, starting with eldest, may make any number of discards and then draw the same number of replacements from stock. Dealer must take the trump turn-up before discarding, and correspondingly draws one card fewer to restore his hand to five.

Drop Subsequent deals are played differently. When someone knocks, the other players – including any who have passed – must decide whether they will join in or drop out. (It is also usual to bid, join in or drop out when three cards have been dealt to each and a trump-card is turned. The last two cards are then not dealt till the auction is over.)

Play Eldest leads the trump Ace if he has it, otherwise any card. Players must follow suit if possible, otherwise may play any card. The trick is taken by the highest card of the suit led, or by the highest trump if any are played, and the winner of each trick leads to the next. When at least one player is down to one point – which must be declared by the scorekeeper or the player concerned – the rules change. Trumps must always be led, if possible, and a player failing to do so when possible is 'loafed'.

Score Deduct 1 point for each trick won. If a knocker wins no trick, he is said to be given a loaf, or just 'loafed'. This entails adding five to his score, or raising it to 10 if that would make it more. A player who joins in, but who wins no trick, is also loafed. But this does not apply to the first deal, when everyone may join in for nothing – here, only a knocker can be loafed. Each time a player is loafed, he adds one chip to the pot. The pot is won by (or divided between) the first player(s) to reach zero points.

Femkort (Five-Cards)

2–10 players, 52 cards

A Swedish game, possibly related to Loo, but with an unusual object.

Preliminaries From two to ten players chip an equal amount to the pot and receive five cards each (2+3 or 3+2) from a 52-card pack ranking AKQJT98765432.

Object To win the last trick.

Play Each in turn plays to a trick by laying his card face up in front of himself and leaving it there for the rest of the game so everyone can see who has played what. Eldest leads first. Players must follow suit and win the trick if possible, but if unable to follow may play any card. The trick is taken by the highest card of the suit led, and the winner of each trick leads to the next. There are no trumps.

Pay-off The pot goes to the winner of the last trick, or to the first to win an agreed number of deals.

Variant A common rule is that anyone in course of play may call for 'better cards', i.e. for an annulment and a new deal. If anyone else refuses, play continues with the cards still held.

Three-card Loo

3–10 players, 52 cards

A disreputable old gambling game, harder to describe than to play, and not to be confused with Five-card Loo. It is perhaps best seen as a party game with chips or counters, since 'Unlimited Loo' with real money can prove expensive. The rules of trick-taking are so restrictive as to render the play virtually mechanical. The only skill lies in calculating the odds in favour of staying in.

Preliminaries Everyone starts with an equal number of chips or counters. The dealer stakes three to the pool. A three-chip pool is a 'single'. When it contains more, left over from the previous deal, it is a 'double'. Deal to each player, and to an imaginary extra player called 'Miss', three cards singly from a 52-card pack ranking AKQJT98765432, and turn the next for trump.

Object To win at least one trick. A player who takes none is 'looed', and increases the pool.

Announcements Each in turn announces whether they will play or throw their hand in. Anyone offering to play may exchange their hand for Miss, sight unseen, but may not then drop out or change it back. Only the first player to claim this privilege may exercise it.

If all pass, dealer wins the pool.

If one exchanges and the others all pass, the exchanger wins the pool.

If just one player before the dealer plays, and does so without exchanging, the dealer may not pass but has a choice of play. He may either play for himself, with or without exchanging, or elect to 'defend Miss'. In this case he still plays, but neither wins nor loses anything. Only the other player wins from or loses to the pool, according to the result.

Play Eldest leads, and must lead the trump Ace if held, or the King if the Ace is the turn-up. If not, he must still lead a trump if he has more than one, and it must be his highest if he is playing against only one opponent. Players must follow suit and head the trick if possible; must trump and overtrump if unable to follow; and may renounce only if unable to do either. The trick is taken by the highest card of the suit led, or by the highest trump if any are played. The winner of each trick leads to the next, and must lead a trump if possible.

Pay-off Each trick taken earns its winner one-third of the pool. A player who is looed pays three to the pool, which is then carried forward as a 'double'.

Optional rules If the pool is a single, nobody may pass. In Unlimited Loo, one who is looed (a loo-ee? a loony?) pays the amount the pool contained at the start of that deal. This is where it starts to mount up.

Irish Loo

In effect, Five-card Loo played with three cards. Play as above, except that each active player may discard and receive replacements for any number of cards up to three before the opening lead. If clubs are trump, no one may drop. Dealer is obliged to defend the pool against a single opponent.

Tomato

3–10 players, 40 cards

The equivalent of Loo widely popular in Spain gets its name from a double metaphor. First, *tomate* also means a hole in a sock, from its appearance when filled with a ruddy foot; second, a score of zero is likened to a hole in a sock. Believe this if you will.

Preliminaries Three to ten players use a Spanish 40-card pack, ranking A3KQJ76542, and play to the right.

Deal Dealer antes three to the pot, deals three cards each in ones, and, before looking at his cards, announces 'Pass' or 'Play'. If he plays, he turns and reveals the next card for trump, says, 'It's mine,' and takes it to add to his hand after making a discard (sight unseen). This commits him to winning two tricks, and only then does he look at his hand. If he passes, each in turn has the same option; if all pass, the hands are scrapped and the pot is carried forward. With one player engaged to win two tricks, each in turn who has not already passed looks at his cards and says either 'Pass', in which case he throws his hand in, or 'Play', thereby undertaking to win at least one trick.

Play The first active player to the right of the dealer leads. Players must follow suit and head the trick if possible; must trump and overtrump if unable to follow; and may renounce only if unable to do either.

Pay-off Each trick wins one-third of the pot. A player who takes no trick is tomatoed, and doubles it. If the bidder wins one trick, he is tomatoed, and doubles the pot that remains after first taking one-third for the trick he has won. If the pot does not contain a multiple of three, the odd one or two go to the winner of the first trick.

Defending the pack If all pass except the player who turned trump and undertook two tricks, the lone player wins the pot – unless, however, another player offers to 'defend the pack' (compare 'Defend Miss' in

Three-card Loo). Only one may defend, which he does by drawing a new hand from the top of the stock and leading to the first trick. Whatever the outcome, the defender neither pays nor gets paid, but, if he wins at least one trick, the pot remains untaken and is carried forward to the next deal.

Note To prevent the pot from growing excessively large, tomatoes may be paid into separate side-pots, each of which is fed into the main pot when it contains a multiple of three.

Zwicken (Zwikken, Dreiblatt) 3 players, 20 cards

The Germanic relative of Loo and Tomato, Zwicken is a gambling game of ill repute that was once banned throughout the Habsburg Empire. *Zwicken* means 'pinch' or 'nip', and describes a player who has to replenish the pot for failing to win any of the three tricks played. The basic format is extremely simple, not to mention costly, but gave rise to numerous variations and special features, as thoroughly surveyed by Manfred Zollinger in *The Playing-Card* (XXVI, 5). The game is probably now defunct, as suggested by the lack of any reference to it in late twentieth-century literature, and by the fact that the name has been taken over for an entirely different game related to Cassino. The following description is of Zwikken, the Dutch version.

Preliminaries Three players each chip one to the pot and receive three cards (dealt 1+2 or 2+1) from a 20-card pack ranking AKQJT, the next being turned for trump. Anyone holding the trump Ten may eventually exchange it for the turn-up, but not yet.

Object Each in turn has one opportunity to play for the whole pot, or a portion of it – typically a third or a half – or to pass. Whoever offers to play for the highest amount becomes the shooter. His aim is either to have the best *zwik* (three of a kind), or to win two tricks, or to win one trick containing more card-points than the other two combined (Ace 4, King 3, Queen 2, Jack 1).

If all pass, the dealer may (but need not) require everyone to add a chip to the pool, and he then turns the next card for trump. If all pass a second time, dealer has the same option. If he declines it, or no one bids after three turns, the deal is annulled and the pool carried forward.

Play First, anyone holding the trump Ten may exchange it for the turn-up. Next, anyone holding a *zwik* shows it and wins the pool. Of two *zwiks*, the higher-ranking wins. If no one has a *zwik*, eldest leads to the first trick. Players must follow suit if possible; otherwise must trump and overtrump if possible; otherwise may play anything. The trick is taken by the highest card of the suit led, or by the highest trump if any are played, and the winner of each trick leads to the next.

Winning The shooter wins with two or three tricks, or one trick if it contains more card-points than the other two combined. Equality of card-points will not suffice. If successful, he wins the amount he played for; if not, he adds it to the pot.

Comment A wicked feature of the game is that exchanging the Ten may give a player a *zwik*. Equally crafty is the dealer's ability to pass the first round with a good hand in the hope of shooting later after increasing the pool. Sources vary as to the number of times the dealer may turn another trump, and whether turning the same suit as before counts as a separate turn. It should be added that the card-points are virtually academic, as a single trick will rarely contain enough to beat the other two.

Toepen

This description of a popular Dutch drinking, singing and whistling game is based on one by Nick Wedd, with additional material from Dan Glimne, both from first-hand informants. Details probably vary not only from school to school, but also within the same school as conviviality expands.

Preliminaries From three to eight players receive four cards each, in batches of two, from a 32-card pack ranking from high to low T987AKQJ.

Object In each deal the aim is to win the last trick. The overall aim is to avoid accumulating 10 penalty points, which obliges you to buy the next round of drinks.

Exchange If you have nothing higher than an Ace, or an otherwise poor hand, you may lay it face down and draw a new one from the stock, so long as at least four cards remain. (You may not exchange just one, two or three cards.) If challenged, you turn the old hand face up. If it contains any card higher than an Ace, you incur one penalty; if not, the challenger incurs one.

Warnings A player who holds four Tens must stand up, to warn others of this fact, and one with four Jacks *may* stand up, by way of bluff. Similarly, three Tens obliges, and three Jacks *entitles*, their holder to whistle. A player who can't whistle may sing loudly instead. Failure to give the requisite warning, or giving a false warning without entitlement, incurs one penalty.

Play Eldest leads. Players must follow suit if possible, otherwise may play any card. The trick is taken by the highest card of the suit led, and the winner of each trick leads to the next – or, if he then folds, the next active player to his left leads. There are no trumps. Everyone scores one penalty except the winner of the last trick, who becomes the next dealer.

Raising the penalty The penalty value of each deal may be increased as follows. Any active player may, at any point in the play – in or out of turn – knock sharply on the table to notch the value up by one point. Thus the first knock increases the penalty to 2, the next to 3, and so on. When a player knocks, any still active player (other than the knocker) may immediately drop out by laying their cards face down, thereby incurring only the penalties previously obtaining. If they fail to do so before the next card is played, they must continue play at the new level. If someone knocks during the course of the last trick and you have no cards left, you can escape the new level by saying 'Fold', before the next card is played.

A player may knock more than once in the same deal, but (a) not twice in succession without the intervention of another knocker, and (b) not if this would raise their own score above 10 in the event of loss. A player with 9 penalties, therefore, may not knock at all.

Pay-off The round ends when one player reaches 10 penalties and staggers to the bar. If more than one do so, duty devolves upon the one with most penalties.

Conventions A player who has temporarily disappeared on an errand of mercy or nature is dealt a hand *in absentia*, but is deemed to fold at the first knock. A player who is currently buying a round of drinks is exempt from all penalties while so engaged.

Cucumber

Called Gurka in Swedish and Ogórek in Polish, both meaning 'cucumber', this delightful Baltic gambling game may be played as lightly or as seriously as you wish, either for money or for a simple point-score.

Preliminaries From three to seven players contribute equal stakes to a pot and receive six cards, each dealt singly from a 52-card pack, ranking upwards 23456789TJQKA. The aim is to avoid winning the last trick.

Play Eldest leads any card. Each in turn must play a card which is either

• equal to or higher than the previous card played, regardless of suit; or

• the lowest card they hold.

Whoever plays the highest card – or the last played of equally highest cards – leads to the next trick.

Score Whoever wins the last trick records penalty points equal to its face value, counting Ace 14, King 13, Queen 12, Jack 11, numerals as marked. Anyone else who played a card of the same rank to the last trick also records that number.

A player reaching 30 minus points is a 'cucumber' and drops out of play. He may buy himself back into the game for a new stake, but must restart with the same number of minus points as the player with the next highest total. No one may buy in more than once.

When only three players are left, buying in is barred, and play continues until one of them is sliced (or cucumbered). The pot then goes to the player with the lowest total.

Truc

This is the Catalan version of a unique and highly entertaining group of Spanish and Provençal games in which tricks are won by bluffing rather than by calculation.

Preliminaries Four players sit crosswise in partnerships and play to the right.

Cards Use a 40-card pack, ranking 32AKQJ7654. This should be the Spanish or Catalan pack with suits of cups, coins, swords, clubs, and courts of King, Knight and Valet.

Object In each deal the aim is to win two tricks, or the first trick if both sides win one. A deal is worth from 1 to 3 points, and game is 12 points.

Deal Deal three cards each in ones. (See later for notes on a one-card deal.) In each deal, the dealer and the player at his left, who play the last two cards to the first trick, are the captains of their respective partnerships.

Play Eldest leads first. Any player in turn may play any desired card without restriction. The trick is taken by the highest-ranking card played, provided that it is not tied, and its winner leads to the next. If two or more of the highest rank fall to the same trick, the trick is tied and goes untaken. In this case the same leader leads to the next.

Raising At start of play the deal is worth 1 point. Any player on his turn to play, whether before or after playing his card, can raise it to 2 by calling 'Truc'. The captain of the other side may then either concede the game for 1 point or keep playing for 2. Playing the next card, whether or not intentionally, automatically counts as an acceptance. If one side *trucs*, either member of the other may subsequently, on his turn to play, whether before or after playing his card, raise it to 3 by calling 'Retruc', leaving the first side's captain to concede for 2 or play on for 3.

Score The game value (1, 2 or 3) goes to the side that wins two tricks, or was the first to win a trick if the other side won one or none. Three ties win for the non-dealing side.

One-card deal Provided neither side has yet reached 11 points, the non-dealing side may propose the play of a one-card deal. This is indicated by the player at dealer's left knocking on the pack instead of cutting it after the shuffle. The dealer may then either deal three as usual, or agree the proposal by dealing only one card. The 1-point value, which may not be increased, goes to the side that wins the trick, or to the non-dealing side if it is tied.

Score of eleven The play changes when either partnership stands at 11, needing only 1 point for game. That partnership may concede the hand for 1 point before any card is played, in which case the deal passes on. If it plays, the hand is automatically worth 3 points, and no one may call *truc*. If both have 11, the hand is played for 3, and neither side may concede or call *truc*.

Talking and signalling The members of a partnership are allowed – in fact encouraged – to discuss tactics, tell each other in general terms what to play, and so on, either truthfully to give each other information, or falsely, to bluff the opponents. They may not verbally identify any particular card they hold, yet they may do even this by means of facial signals in accordance with a universally agreed code, the aim being to get such a signal across when neither opponent is looking. For example, to signify the holding of:

Three	wink
Two	pout
Ace	show tip of tongue

French Truc

This is played in the Roussillon (capital Perpignan), also in Poitou under the name Tru, and in Pays Basque as Truka. It originally used a 36-card pack, ranking 76AKQJT98, but, as this is no longer available, players employ the 32-card Belote pack and substitute Eight for Six, giving the curious ranking 78AKQJT9. It is usually played by four in partnerships, as assumed below, but works equally well for two. Game is 12 points over as many deals as necessary, and two games win the rubber. Deal three cards each in ones. Eldest may propose a redeal, and, provided all players agree, the hands are put aside face down and replaced from stock. Play as described above, except for the stake-raising procedure. Any player when about to play a card may raise the game value by any amount, provided that the previous raise was made by the other side. A raise is proposed by saying (for example), 'Three if I play?' thus offering to raise the value to 4, or to 7 if it was already 4. A sudden-death win can be bid by announcing, 'Our [or my] remainder?' which raises the current value to the full dozen. As before, the other side may play on for the new value, or concede for the old.

Truquiflor

Varieties of Truc are played throughout South America. All are partnership games, involving three tricks at no trump and allowing partners to signal with body-language conventions. The most elaborate variety, Truc y Flor or Truquiflor, also includes a preliminary period of vying as to who holds the best *flor* (three-card flush, literally 'flower') and *envido* (highest card-point value). Space precludes description, as the betting procedures are extremely elaborate, and in any case the game does not translate well from Spanish-suited to French-suited cards. But it would be reprehensible not to explain that Truquiflor is known as the 'jolly singing game' because it is traditional to announces one's *flor* by means of a rhyming quatrain which is supposed to be unique to the occasion and made up on the spot. These verses often savour of the limerick, but here is a relatively polite example:

Para pintar a mi chines	To paint the pretty hand I've got
no hay pinceles ni pintor,	you'll neither artist find, nor brush:
ni flores en las jardines	nor blooms to grace your garden plot
comparadas a mi flor.	so lovely as my flow'ry flush.

Put

> If you want to be robbed, my son, play Put in a tavern.
> 'Captain Crawley' (G. F. Pardon), *The Card Player's Manual* (1876)

The English equivalent of Truc was a disreputable old tavern game first described in Cotton's *Compleat Gamester* of 1674. It seems to have died out in Victorian Britain, but remains surprisingly fun to play. 'Put' is short for 'I put it to you that my cards are better than yours and that we therefore play for the whole stake instead of just this point. But I could be bluffing'.

Put for two

Use a 52-card pack ranking 32AKQJT987654. Each in turn deals three cards each in ones. Non-dealer leads first. There is no rule of following: any card may be played to any trick, which is taken by the higher-ranking of the two. If both are equal, the trick is tied and discarded. The winner of each trick, or the leader of a tied trick, leads to the next. A player who wins two tricks, or one trick to two ties, scores a point. If all three are tied, or both win a trick and the third is tied (known as 'trick and tie'), neither player scores. Game is five points.

Either player, when about to play a card, may instead call 'Put'. The other may then resign, in which case the putter scores the point without further play. If the non-putter insists on playing it out, then whoever wins the point jumps to five and wins the game outright. No one scores if the point is put and the result is a tie.

Put for three

Old sources say Put was sometimes played by three, but give no details. Presumably it is trick-and-tie if two or three players win one trick each, and if one player 'puts', then the other two must jointly decide whether to concede or go for broke.

Put for four

'Four-handed Put differs only in this – that on both sides one of the players gives his best card to his partner, who lays out one in lieu of it, and the game is afterwards played as in two-handed Put' (*Hoyle's Games Improved*, by G. H. _____, Esq., 1847).

Aluette
4 players (2 × 2), 48 Aluette cards

Also called Jeu de Vache, 'The Cow Game', l'Aluette is a picturesque extension of Truc mentioned by Rabelais in the sixteenth century and still extensively played down the left-hand side of France, from Vannes to the mouth of the Garonne. What Aluette means is unknown, but *Jeu de Vache* refers to the picture of a cow traditionally depicted on the Two of cups. In fact the game employs a highly idiosyncratic 48-card pack with Spanish suitmarks of swords (♤), batons (◊), cups (☒) and coins (❂), and ranks of Ace, King (Roi), Cavalier (Chevalier, all four depicted as female), Valet, and numerals 9-8-7-6-5-4-3-2, the most important of which bear pictures from which their various nicknames are derived. The following is based on several sources, none of which is complete, and no two of which agree in every detail.

Preliminaries Four players sit crosswise in partnerships and play to the left. A game is five deals.

Object The unusual aim is for both members of a partnership to play in such a way as to ensure that one of them wins more tricks than any other single player.

Deal Deal nine cards each in batches of three and stack the rest, face down.

Le chant (*optional*). If it is agreed to play 'with singing', the following rule is followed. After the deal and before the play, each in turn announces whether he is willing for the remaining cards to be dealt. If all agree, six each are dealt, in threes, to eldest and to dealer's partner. Each of them then examines his hand and makes six discards face down before eldest leads.

Rank of cards The eight highest individual cards, together with their French-suit equivalents, their names, and the actions recognized as signalling their possession, are:

Luettes:	♣3	♦3	Monsieur	look up
	♠3	♥3	Madame	hand on heart
	♣2	♦2	le borgne (one-eyed man)	close one eye
	♠2	♥2	la vache	pout
Doubles:	♠9	♠9	grand neuf	raise a thumb
	♣9	♦9	petit neuf	raise little finger
	◊2	♣2	deux de chêne (two of oak)	raise index finger
	♠2	♥2	deux d'écrit (two of script)	mime writing

These are followed in order by A-R(K)-C(Q)-V(J)-9-8-7-6-5-4-3 without distinction of suit. That is, all Aces are equal in value and beat Kings, which are equal in value and beat Cavaliers, and so on. Of these, the first four are called *les moyennes* and the remainder *les inférieures*. Only two each of the Nines and Threes are inferiors, the others being *luettes* or *doubles*.

Play Eldest leads first. Each in turn thereafter may play any card they please, without necessarily following suit. The trick is taken by the highest card, as explained above, and the winner of each trick leads to the next. If there is a tie for highest, no one wins the trick: it is said to have 'gone off' (*être pourrie*) and is thrown away, the next lead being made by whoever led to the tied trick. A trick containing a *luette* or *double* cannot, of course, be tied.

Score One game point goes to the side of the player who won most tricks individually, or, if tied, who took that number first.

Mordienne (gadzooks) This is an optional but commonly played extra. If a player thinks he can not only win a majority of tricks, but do so by winning them in unbroken succession up to and including the last trick (the ninth), having previously taken none, he may signal his intention to his partner by biting his lip, preferably when neither opponent is looking. If his partner nods agreement, the bidder announces *Mordienne* (an obsolete exclamation equivalent to *Gadzooks!*), thereby committing himself to this feat, which is beaten if any of the last successive tricks are tied. Mordienne carries a score of 2 points, which goes to the bidder if successful or to the opponents if not. If this optional bid is admitted, the target score is set at 10 instead of 5 points. In some circles it is not bid but merely scored if it occurs, and I am told that this is now the commonest practice. In some, it may be declared by the bidder without reference to his partner. In some, it scores 1 point for each of any number of last tricks won in succession, with a bonus of 1 for winning all nine, making 10 in all.

Don't forget . . .
- Play to the left (clockwise) unless otherwise stated.
- Eldest or Forehand means the player to the left of the dealer in left-handed games, to the right in right-handed games.
- T = Ten, p = players, pp = in fixed partnerships, c = cards, † = trump, ☆ = Joker.

4 **Hearts family**

These are games in which your aim is to avoid taking tricks, or, at least, tricks containing penalty cards.

This is not as easy as it sounds. When everyone else is trying to force you to take one, you soon discover that it's not enough just to have a vaguely 'bad hand' for a positive bid: what you need is a positively good hand for a negative bid. Here Twos and Threes are as valuable as Aces and Kings are in Bridge, and middling ranks like Sevens and Eights not just feeble, as in Bridge, but a positive danger.

It takes a particular kind of card-sense to play well a game like Hearts. Where the object is to avoid penalty cards, the required knack is to play your high cards when they are unlikely to win penalties, and to choose just the right point at which to lose the lead and not be forced into taking any more.

▌Hearts (Black Lady, etc.)   3–6 players (4 best), 52 cards

> You don't call playing Bridge or Hearts on Saturday night a very Bohemian sort of life, do you? Damn it all, I do that myself!
>
> Carter Dickson, *She Died a Lady* (1943)

This classic trick-avoidance game has become a popular family and informal game throughout Europe and America, in the USA first recorded as appearing in the 1880s. In its purest form, the aim is just to avoid winning tricks containing hearts. Each player counts a penalty point for each heart taken in tricks, and the winner is the player with the lowest score when one player reaches a critical maximum of penalties. Probably no one, however, plays the purest form. Described here is the current American variety derived from an early twentieth-century development called Black Lady Hearts. There are many local variations, but the following four-player game contains probably the best balance of common features and may reasonably be regarded as standard.

Preliminaries Four players receive 13 cards dealt singly from a 52-card pack ranking AKQJT98765432. The game ends when at least one player reaches a total of 100 penalties.

Object After an exchange of cards, 13 tricks are played at no trump and the aim is to avoid winning tricks containing hearts or ♠Q. Alternatively, you may aim to capture all 14 penalty cards (a slam, or 'hitting the moon'), but need not announce this beforehand.

Exchange Each player first passes three cards face down to his left-hand neighbour and receives the same number from his right. On the second deal, cards are passed to the right and received from the left. On the third they are passed between players sitting opposite each other. On the fourth, there is no exchange, the hands being played as dealt. The same sequence is repeated thereafter. Players may not pick up the cards passed to them until they have passed their own three on. There is no restriction on which cards may be passed.

Play Whoever holds ♣2 leads it to the first trick. Players must follow suit if possible, otherwise may play any card. The trick is taken by the highest card of the suit led, and the winner of each trick leads to the next. There are no trumps. Two special rules apply.

- You may not play a penalty card to the first trick, unless you have no choice.
- You may not lead a heart until the suit has been 'broken' by somebody having discarded one to a previous trick. *Exception:* You may do so if you have nothing else, or your only alternative is ♠Q.

Unless otherwise agreed, it is acceptable to throw all non-penalty cards won in tricks on to a common wastepile, and for players to leave the penalty cards they have won face up on the table before them, so that everyone can see which are yet to come.

Score At end of play each player gets 1 penalty point for each heart taken in tricks, and 13 for ♠Q. For taking all 14 penalty cards, however, you may either deduct 26 from your total, or add 26 to everyone else's. The winner is the player with fewest penalty points when one or more players reach 100. A tie-breaker may be played if necessary.

Sample game Here is an amusing deal that demonstrates some of the problems and pitfalls the game can give rise to.

As dealt . . .

North	♥T93	♠T9732	♦74	♣K76
East	♥K764	♠AJ	♦T85	♣QJ52
South	♥AQ852	♠K6	♦QJ96	♣T8
West	♥J	♠Q854	♦AK32	♣A943

After the exchange . . .

North	♥J93	♠T9732	♦K4	♣K96
East	♥KT764	♠J	♦75	♣QJ752
South	♥AQ852	♠A6	♦QJT986	–
West	♥–	♠KQ854	♦A32	♣AT843

Passing to the left, North gave East ♥T ♦7 ♣7, getting rid of some indeterminate cards and keeping his safe run of spades – safe indeed, as you will see from the exciting finish. East discarded his eminently unsafe ♠A (trusting to luck not to be given the King or Queen), plus ♦T8. South, similarly embarrassed in spades, unloaded its Ace, together with two useless but dangerous clubs. West, facing the awful four-spades-to-the-Queen prospect, decided to hope for an extra covering spade from North, and got rid of ♥J ♦K ♣9, leaving an ideal position in the minor suits. East, holding ♣2, kicks off with it.

	E	S	W	N	(the underlined card wins the trick)
1	♣2	♠A	<u>♣A</u>	♣K	North would have kept the King had South not shown out of clubs
2	♦7	♦Q	<u>♦A</u>	♦K	North seems unnecessarily cautious about diamonds
3	♦5	<u>♦J</u>	♦3	♦4	
4	♠J	♠6	<u>♠K</u>	♠T	West, by playing ♠K second, makes it pretty clear he holds ♠Q safe
5	♥T	<u>♦T</u>	♦2	♥J	East holds up ♥K in case it encourages anyone into a slam bid
6	<u>♥K</u>	♥8	♣T	♥9	Now East can play it and lose the rest
7	♥7	<u>♥A</u>	♣8	♥3	
8	<u>♥6</u>	♥5	♣4	♣9	
9	♣5	<u>♥Q</u>	♣3	♣6	North beats West in spades . . .

At trick 6, with ♥8 led, North 'sacrifices' with ♥9, planning to win the trick and lose the rest, thus preventing anyone from making a slam. East, however, with the same object in view, 'over-sacrifices' with the King.

At trick 4, West could (and perhaps should) have unloaded ♠Q before it was too late. He reckoned, however, that his five-card holding would save him from being forced to take a trick with the Queen, and embarked on the not infrequent dodge of letting everyone know he held the Queen and winding up the suspense by withholding her for the last trick. Unfortunately for him, however, North also held five spades and got rid of the King early on. Coming in at trick 9, North plays from ♠9732 against West's ♠Q854, and West finds himself, at the last trick, hoist by his own petard.

Result: North 2, East 5, South 6, and West 13 penalty points. Truly a wonderful game!

Partnership Hearts

Played by four with either fixed or (my invention) floating partnerships. Each partnership, or each member of a partnership, scores the amount taken by the partnership as a whole.

1. *Fixed partnerships.* The players facing each other across the table are partners for the whole game, and the passing cycle is left, right, across, none.

2. *Rotating partnerships.* In the first deal, NE oppose SW, and each player exchanges three cards with his neighbouring opponent. In the second, NS oppose EW, and each exchanges cards with his partner. In the third, NW oppose SE and each exchanges with his neighbouring opponent. In the fourth, there is no exchange and the first two players to win a trick become partners. A slam requires all penalty cards to fall to one player, not just to one partnership.

3. *Ad hoc partnerships.* The passing cycle is left, right, across, none. The first two players to win a trick – whether or not either trick contains a penalty card – become partners for the rest of the hand, and the other two play in partnership against them. If only one player wins tricks, he will, of course, score a lone slam.

Hearts for 3 or 5–7 players

Divide the cards as evenly as possible. Any extras go face down and are added to the last trick. (*Variant:* Deal all the cards round until they run out. Those with one extra card play two cards to the first trick.) When three play, each passes four cards to the left, then four to the right, then two to each opponent, then none at all.

Hearts for two (Draw Hearts)

Deal thirteen each and stack the rest face down. The winner of a trick draws the top card of the stock and leads to the next trick when his opponent has done likewise. When the stock is exhausted, the remaining 13 cards are played out. Captured cards are counted in the usual way. A Cribbage board may help.

Auction Hearts

Each in turn bids for the right to nominate the penalty suit, not necessarily hearts. Whoever bids highest pays that amount into a pool and leads to the first trick. The player or players who take fewest of that suit take or divide the pool.

Black Maria

First described (and devised?) by Hubert Phillips. Besides ♠Q counting 13, ♠K counts 10 and ♠A counts 7 penalty points. Pass always to the right.

Cancellation Hearts

Shuffle two packs (104 cards) and deal them evenly round as far as they will go. Any undealt cards are laid aside face down and are captured with the last trick. There is no exchange, and eldest leads. If two identical cards are played to a trick, neither wins. Instead, the trick is taken by the highest unduplicated card of the suit led. A trick containing only duplicates is held back and awarded to the winner of the next (or, if it is the last, the previous) unduplicated trick.

Dealer's Choice

Instead of always passing three cards in a predetermined direction, the dealer announces before dealing what method shall be followed in that deal. It may be any of the standard patterns or any other he can think of, such as

• Each player passes one card to each opponent, or two to each, or two to the left and one to the right.

- Three players each pass two cards to the fourth, who passes two back to each of them. The fourth can be the dealer, or the player with the currently smallest or greatest total of penalties.

Domino Hearts

One of the most interesting variants. Deal six cards each and stack the rest face down. Eldest leads. Anyone unable to follow suit must draw cards from the top of the stock until able to do so; but once the stock is exhausted the rules change, and those unable to follow may discard anything. A player who runs out of cards stops play, and, if about to lead, passes the lead to the next in turn to the left. The last player left with cards in hand adds them to those won in tricks. Captured cards are then scored in the usual way.

Greek Hearts

Each numeral heart counts 1 penalty, courts 10 each, ♥A 15, and ♠Q 50.

Heartsette

Everyone receives the same number of cards, but a certain number – ideally three – are laid aside face down and go to the winner of the first trick, who may look at them privately before leading to the second.

Joker Hearts

R. F. Foster described this as 'a most exasperating game'. It replaces ♥2 with a Joker, which ranks between Ten and Jack. If discarded to a non-heart lead, it wins the trick. On a heart lead it falls to any higher heart. If, however, a non-heart is led, and another player throws a heart higher than the Ten, you may discard Joker even if able to follow suit, in which case the highest heart wins the trick and the Joker. It counts 5 against.

Omnibus Hearts

Basic Hearts, except that ♦J (or ♦T) reduces the penalty score of the player who captures it by 10 points. Taking all 15 counters scores 36 for a grand slam; taking all but ♦J scores 26 for a small slam.

Pink Lady

Basic Hearts, except that both ♠Q and ♥Q count 13 against.

Spot Hearts

The penalty value of each heart is that of its denomination, counting 2 to 10 at face value, J-Q-K 10 each, Ace 11, total 95, or 108 if ♠Q is also a penalty.

Widow Hearts

Any form of Hearts in which a few undealt cards are left face down and go to the winner of the last trick – or, in Heartsette, the first.

Related to Hearts...

Polignac

(3–6p, 32c) A French game, probably commemorating Prince Auguste de Polignac, head of the last Bourbon ministry in the 1820s, and not the Mme de Polignac who lost a fortune at cards under Louis XVI. Cards rank KQJAT987 in each suit, but omit the two black Sevens if the number of players is other than four. Deal them around evenly in batches of two or three. The aim is to avoid capturing Jacks, and especially ♠J, known as Polignac. Eldest leads. Players must follow suit if possible, otherwise may play any card. The trick is taken by the highest card of the suit led, and the winner of each trick leads to the next. There are no trumps. Score 2 penalties for taking Polignac, and 1 for each other Jack. The first to reach 10 penalties is guillotined. Or, at least, loses.

Variant 1 A bid of *capot* made before the first lead is an undertaking to win every trick. If successful, all but the bidder score 5 penalties; if not, it is 5 to the bidder.

Variant 2 If you prefer to rank cards AKQJT987, it is Queens that count 1 against, with 2 for the ♠Q.

Slobberhannes

(3-6p, 32c), or 'Slippery Jack' (Hannes = Johannes = John = Jack), is the German equivalent of Polignac. Which came first is a moot point.

Cards rank KQJAT987 in each suit, but omit the two black Sevens if the number of players is other than four. Deal them around evenly in ones. The aim is to avoid winning the first trick, the last trick, and the ♣Q. Eldest leads. Players must follow suit if possible, otherwise may play any card. The trick is taken by the highest card of the suit led, and the winner of each trick leads to the next. There are no trumps. Score 1 penalty for first, last and Queen, or 4 for taking all three. *Variant*: Deduct 4 penalties for taking all three.

Knaves

(3 players, easily adaptable for more). First described by Hubert Phillips, Knaves combines plus-points for tricks won with minus-points for Jacks taken. Deal seventeen each from a 52-card pack and turn the odd card – which plays no further part – for trumps. Eldest leads. Players must follow suit if possible, otherwise may play any card. The trick is taken by the highest card of the suit led, or by the highest trump if any are played, and the winner of each trick leads to the next. Each player scores 1 point per trick taken, less 1 for ♠J, 2 for ♣J, 3 for ♦J, 4 for ♥J. (The suit-order is that of pre-1910 Bridge. More memorable, because easily visualized, would be ♠1, ♥2, ♣3, ♦4.) The first to reach 20 points wins.

Barbu
4 players, 52 cards

Barbu is the most highly developed member of a series of compendium games based on Hearts which first appeared in the early twentieth century, apparently in eastern Europe. A compendium game is one consisting of a fixed number of deals with a different game played at each, the sequence of games being predetermined and invariable. In the series of this type based on Hearts, the first games are negative, each resulting in payment to a pool from the loser or losers, and the last deal positive, the pool being swept by the winner. Early examples are the Hungarian game of Lórum, and a game called King played in Russia, Turkey, Portugal, Brazil, and no doubt elsewhere. (The Russians call it 'King' in preference to their native word *korol*, which denotes a different game). At a higher level of development, the games are not played in a fixed order; instead, each player in turn deals the requisite number of times, and at each deal specifies which game is to be played, subject to the restriction that each available game must be played once. The French game of Barbu takes this further still by introducing a complicated system of doubling. *Le Barbu* means 'the bearded one', and refers to the ♥K, which is the only heart to sport a beard (not, as is sometimes said, the only King to sport a beard – all French playing-card Kings are bearded). A simple version of Barbu, with fixed contracts and no doubling, appears in Gerver's 1966 classic *Le Guide Marabout*. Its more elaborate extension, described below, was developed by Bridge players in the 1970s and was a favourite of the Italian 'Blue Club' Bridge team.

Preliminaries Four players use a 52-card pack, ranking AKQJT 98765432. A game is 28 deals and requires a scoresheet, as illustrated on p. 145. Each in turn deals seven times in succession, dealing thirteen each in ones.

Declaring the contract In each of his seven deals the dealer is automatically the declarer. He examines his cards and declares one of seven possible contracts which has not yet been played in his cycle of deals. Of the seven possible contracts, five give negative scores to the value of −130 points in all, and two give positive scores to the value of +130 in all.

Play All but Domino are trick-taking games, and the opening lead is made by the declarer (or, *variant*, by declarer's right-hand neighbour). The five negative games are played at no trump. Players must follow suit if possible, otherwise may play any card. The trick is taken by the highest card of the suit led, and the winner of each trick leads to the next.

1. No tricks. Each trick taken scores −2 points.
2. No hearts. Each heart taken scores −2, the Ace of hearts −6. Hearts may not be led unless no other suit is held. Captured hearts are left face up so all can see which ones have gone.
3. No Queens. Each Queen taken scores −6. Captured Queens are left face up, and play ends when all four are out.
4. No King. Taking ♥K (*le Barbu*) scores −20. Hearts may not be led unless no other suit is held. Play ends when the King is taken.
5. No last. Taking the last trick scores −20, the penultimate trick −10.
6. Trump. Each trick won scores +5 points. Declarer announces a trump suit and leads any card. To a trump lead, players must follow

suit if possible and head the trick if possible. To a non-trump lead, players must follow suit if possible. If unable to follow, they must beat any trump that may have been played to the trick if they can, but, if none has been played, or if they cannot beat it, may play any card. The trick is taken by the highest card of the suit led, or by the highest trump if any are played, and the winner of each trick leads to the next.

7. Domino. Declarer announces, 'Domino from . . .' and a rank, e.g. 'Domino from Eights', and plays a card of that rank to start the layout. It is permissible to call a rank not held, in which case the layout is started by the next player to the left who is able to do so. This forms the basis of a layout to which each player contributes in turn (if possible), and which will eventually consist of four 13-card suit sequences with one row per suit and one column per rank (see below). The foundation card of each row must be put in place first, and each subsequent card placed to the right or left of the suit row to which it belongs. For example, if the first card played is ♥8, the next in turn must play either ♥7 or ♥9 to one side of it, or another Eight above or below it to start another row. You must play a card if you legally can, otherwise you must pass. First out of cards scores +40, second +20, third +5.

Barbu: the Domino layout. It doesn't matter in what vertical order the suits are arranged.

Doubling Between the announcement of the contract and the play of the hand, each in turn has one opportunity to double one or more specific players, subject to the following rules:

- You must double the declarer at least twice in each seven-deal cycle.
- In a negative contract (but not in Trump or Domino) you may double any other player or players if you think you will achieve a better result than they will.
- You may redouble any player who doubles you. The announcement 'Maximum' means that you double everyone who doesn't double you and redouble everyone who does.
- Declarer may not double independently, but may redouble an opponent's double.

A double amounts to a side-bet between two players as to which of them will do better than the other. A double must be noted on the scoresheet, and a doubling of the declarer is encircled to help ensure that everyone fulfils their quota of two such doubles per cycle of seven.

Score At the end of a hand everyone notes their score in the plus or the minus column as the case may be. The results of any doubling are then calculated for each of the six possible pairs of players. If only one member of a pair doubled the other, the difference between their two results for the deal is calculated, then added to the score of whichever of them did better in the deal, and correspondingly deducted from that of the other. If one doubled and the other redoubled, the same applies, except that the difference is doubled before being credited to one and debited from the other. This procedure ensures that all scores continue to sum to zero.

Example of scoring:

	Annie			Benny			Connie			Denny				*check*	
Q	C	−6	−6	−12	X	6	6	12	24	A	−6	−6	−12	−12		−12	−24	24	24
H	D	0	8	−4		−6	−2		16		−20	−16	−48	X	−4	−8	2	16	−18	30	54

In deal 1, declarer Annie declared No Queens (Q in the leftmost column). Benny, with a good hand for this bid, announced 'Maximum' to double everyone else. The 'X' for 'double all' is underlined to show that it includes the declarer. Connie doubled Annie, the A being underlined to show that she has fulfilled one of her two requisite declarer doubles. Denny passed, having a hand too weak to risk redoubling Benny or doubling anyone else. Annie, finally, felt confident enough as declarer to redouble Connie, but not Benny, whose universal double implied unusual strength. This is indicated by 'C' in Annie's column.

In play, Denny took two Queens, for −12 points, and Annie and Connie one each, for −6 apiece. Now for the doubles. Annie was doubled by Benny, and did worse, causing her to score minus and him plus the difference between their two scores for Queens (6). Annie and Connie were mutually doubled and redoubled, but as they scored the same amount (−6) the difference was zero, so there is nothing to record. Benny doubled everyone, was not redoubled, and beat everyone, gaining 6 each from Annie and Connie, and 12 from Denny. As for the Connie–Denny pair, neither doubled the other. Each player's pluses and minuses are reckoned, and the total entered in their rightmost column.

In the first half of the check column is written the contract value of 24 (four Queens at 6 each). The second half is for the running total.

In deal 2, Annie chose No Hearts (H). Only Denny doubled ('Maximum'), but Annie then redoubled. Annie took no hearts, Benny took hearts worth −6, Connie −20, Denny −4, total −30, as entered in the check column. Denny did better than Benny and Connie, gaining a difference of 2 and 16 respectively. He did worse than Annie, however, who redoubled him, giving her twice the difference between their two totals ($2 \times 4 = 8$).

Variations

Scoring Different scoring schedules may be encountered, especially in the score for Domino. Whichever you follow or however you adapt, the important thing is to ensure that the five negative and two positive games retain a total yield of zero. This is useful for checking, and makes it easier to convert the result into hard score (cash).

Doubling Some circles allow players to double only declarer, not one another. Conversely, a declarer's redouble automatically applies to everyone who doubled, not just some of them.

Ravage city (additional contract) A negative contract played at no trump in the same way as the others. Whoever takes most cards in any one suit scores −36. In the event of a tie, with different players taking the same number of cards in (usually) different suits, it is divided evenly among them (−18, −12, −9). If Ravage City is admitted, there will eight deals per player, making 32 in all, and the scoring schedule of other contracts will need adjusting to preserve the zero-sum feature.

Lórum

(4p, 32c) A Hungarian forerunner of Barbu, first mentioned in 1916 and described in 1928. The name may originally have denoted a simple game of the going-out type (like Crazy Eights), perhaps equivalent to the last deal of the compendium game described below. (*Lórum* means, if anything, a dock-leaf, but it may simply perpetuate the final syllables of an older German game called *Schnipp-Schnapp-Schnurr-Burr-Basilorum*.) Four players use 32 cards ranking AKQJT987, properly Hungarian cards with suits of acorns, leaves, hearts, bells (日, ♠, ♥, ⊖), and courts of King, Ober, Unter. Deal eight each, play to the right. Details vary, but all accounts contain the following core sequence of four deals:

1. *No hearts.* For each heart taken in tricks, pay 1 chip to the pot – or, if one or two players took no heart, pay it to each of those who took none. Hearts may not be led to the first trick.

2. *Obers (Queens).* For taking 日O (♣Q) pay 1 chip to the pot, ♠O (♠Q) 2, ⊖O (♦Q) 3, ♥O (♥Q) 4, total 10.

3. *No tricks.* As (1), but subsitute 'tricks' for 'hearts'. A player who wins all eight receives a total of 8 from the others.

4. *Kirakó (Domino).* Eldest plays a card face up to the table as the starter of a sequence. The next higher card of the same suit will go to the right of it, the next lower one to the left of it, and so on until the eight-card sequence is complete. Each in turn must either add the next higher or lower card to this suit sequence, or play a card of the same rank as the starter immediately above or below it. Thereafter, each player may add a card to either end of any one of the suit sequences, or start a new one with a card of the correct rank. Aces and Sevens are consecutive, so when one of them has been placed, the other can go on the vacant side of it. If you can play a card, you must. The first to run out of cards sweeps the pool and, in addition, wins from everyone else as many chips as they have cards left in hand.

One or more of the following variations may be inserted between the third deal (no tricks) and *kirakó*, which is always played last.

1. *King.* For taking ♥K, pay 4 chips.

2. *Hairy Ape*. Like King, but: Players fan their cards face down and hold them up back to front so that each can only identify those held by opponents. Each in turn plays a card at random face up to a trick. If two or more are of the same suit, the highest of them takes the trick, otherwise each card 'takes' only itself. Whoever wins ♥K, the eponymous Hairy Ape, pays 10 chips to the pot (or 4, in some circles). If both King and Hairy Ape bids are played (rare), then ⊖U is the Hairy Ape.

3. *Acorn Unter (Club Jack)*. The player sitting opposite the one who captures ⊖U (♣J) pays 4 chips.

4. *Seventh Trick*. Whoever wins it pays 4 chips. The eighth is not played.

5. *Mindenrosz (All Bad)*. All the above applied simultaneously, except that there is no reward for taking all the tricks or all the hearts.

6. *Vonat ([Railway-]Train)*. An adding-up game. Each in turn plays a card to the table and announces the running total of all cards so far played, counting each Ace 11, King 4, Ober/Queen 3, Unter/Jack 2, Ten 10, others zero. The first to reach or exceed 25 adds 1 chip to the pot, likewise 2 for 50, 3 for 75, 4 for 100.

7. *Kvart (Quart)*. A going-out game. Cards rank cyclically, Aces and Sevens being consecutive. (*Variant:* Aces are stops.) The leader plays any card, and the next three consecutively higher cards of the same suit are played by whoever holds them. The last player turns this quasi-trick face down and starts a new one with any card. Follow the same procedure, ending each trick when no more can be played to it. Whoever first runs out of cards calls, 'Stop!' and receives 1 chip for each card left in each opponent's hand.

King

(3p, 36c) A Russian game, collected by Anthony Smith from a St Petersburger, whose family traces it back to the 1920s. Cards rank AKQJT9876. Deal twelve each. Six negative games are followed by six positive. Eldest leads. Players must follow suit if possible, otherwise may play any card. The trick is taken by the highest card of the suit led, and the winner of each trick leads to the next. There are no trumps.

1. No tricks. Score −6 per trick.
2. No hearts. Score −8 per heart. You may not lead hearts if you have an alternative.

3. No men. Each King and Jack taken scores −9. (*Variant*: Jacks only, −18 each.)
4. *No Queens*. Each Queen taken scores −18.
5. *No last*. The last two tricks score −36 each.
6. No ♥*King*. Taking it scores −72. You may never lead hearts unless forced, and must play ♥K as soon as you cannot follow suit or when ♥A has been played ahead of you to a heart lead.

Deals 7 to 12 follow exactly the same sequence but with plus-points instead of minus, e.g. +6 per trick won, +8 per heart won, and so on. In positive Hearts and King you may still not lead a heart unless you have no choice, but in the last deal you may play ♥K at any legal opportunity.

Yeralash (Medley) is an optional seventh and fourteenth game. In the seventh, all penalties operate simultaneously, and in the fourteenth all bonuses likewise. This may be the origin of the next game.

Pesë Kate

('Five Levels') (4p, 52c) Albanian equivalent of Lórum, described by Franco Pratesi in *The Playing-Card* (XXVI, 3). Play either cut-throat or crosswise in partnerships. Deal thirteen each. Cards rank AKQJT98765432. Four deals:

1. Each trick taken counts +2 points.
2. Each heart taken counts −2 points.
3. Each Queen taken counts −4 points.
4. The ♠K taken counts −16 points.

Traditionally, this four-deal sequence is played five times (whence the name), so the winner is the player or side with the highest score after 20 deals.

Tëtka (Tyotka)
4 players, 52 cards

Compendium games of the Hearts family often include a deal that incorporates in one go all the penalty features of the preceding deals. Tëtka is Russian for 'Auntie', and refers to the undesired Queen. Source: Mike Arnautov.

Preliminaries Four players use 52 cards, ranking AKQJT98765432. Play to the left. A game is any agreed multiple of four deals.

Deal Deal thirteen each in ones and reveal the last card before adding it to dealer's hand. This is the bum card, its suit is the bum suit for that deal, and its rank is the bum rank.

Object To avoid incurring any of the following nine penalties:

1. Taking a Queen in a trick (1 penalty each = 4).
2. An extra penalty for taking the Queen of the bum suit ('Tëtka').
3. Taking the bum card in a trick.
4. Winning the 'bumth' trick (i.e. the first if the bum card an Ace, the second if a Two, and so on).
5. Winning the last trick. (If the bum card is a King, this is also the bumth trick, and so counts 2 penalties.)
6. Winning the greatest number of tricks. (Tie-break by the greatest number of cards of the bum suit, or, if still tied, the highest-ranking card of that suit.)

Play Eldest leads. Players must follow suit if possible, otherwise may play any card. The trick is taken by the highest card of the suit led, and the winner of each trick leads to the next. There are no trumps.

Score One penalty point per penalty incurred. Note that several penalties may fall to the same trick. To take the most extreme and unlikely example, if a Queen is the bum card, and a player leads a Queen at trick 12, and everyone discards a Queen because unable to follow suit, the total number of penalties in that trick will be seven: 2 for Auntie, 1 for each other Queen, 1 for taking the bum card, and 1 for the bumth trick.

Reversis

4 players, 48 cards

Modern Hoyles contain Reversis, but no one ever seems to play it.
'Cavendish' (Henry Jones), *Card Essays*, 1879

Reversis (no relation to the board game Reversi) is the probable ancestor of the Hearts family and was one of the great games of continental Europe from the seventeenth to the nineteenth centuries. It is supposedly so called because the aim of avoiding tricks in general and penalty cards in particular is the reverse of conventional trick games, though the name also denotes an exceptional slam bid – like 'hitting the moon' in Hearts

– which itself reverses the practice of the rest of the game. Reversis was long thought to be of Spanish origin because played to the right, with a 48-card pack lacking Tens, and from such technical terms as Quinola (name of a seventeenth-century Spanish admiral) and *espagnolette*. But these are later additions, and the original game, first cited as Reversin in France in 1601, was played with the full 52-card pack. More probably it originated in Italy, where they still play a negative variety of Tressette under the name Rovescino. Details differ from source to source. The following is based on an article by John McLeod in *The Playing-Card*.

Preliminaries Four play, to the right, with a 48-card pack ranking AKQJ98765432 (no Tens) and the equivalent of at least 100 chips each. A full set of Reversis chips comprised 36 units called *fiches* (Anglicized to 'fish'), 24 counters worth 6 fish each, and 6 contracts worth 8 counters each, total 468 fish.

The pool Before play begins, a pool is formed by the contribution of 5 chips from each player. At each deal the dealer (only) adds 5 chips to the pool, bringing it to 25 at the start of the first deal.

Deal Deal eleven cards to each player in batches of 4-3-4, plus a twelfth to the dealer, and finish by dealing one card face down in front of each non-dealer. Dealer discards any unwanted card face down. Each other player may either make a discard and then take the card in front of him as a replacement, or look at his undealt card without taking it, but not both. This leaves everyone with eleven cards, and four on the table constituting a talon.

Object Tricks are played and the main object is to take as few card-points as possible: this is called winning the party. For this purpose each Ace counts 4, King 3, Queen 2, and Jack 1 point. Secondary objects are:

- to discard the ♥J when another suit is led of which you have none, and,
- whenever possible, to discard an Ace when unable to follow suit to the card led.

Alternatively, given a suitable hand, it is either to win every trick (the *reversis*) or to lose every trick (the *espagnolette*).

Play Eldest leads. Players must follow suit if possible, otherwise may play any card. The trick is taken by the highest card of the suit led, and the winner of each trick leads to the next. There are no trumps.

Pay-off The party is normally won by the player who took fewest card-points and is lost by the player who took most. A tie, in either case, favours the player who took fewest tricks. If still tied, preference goes first to the dealer, then passes to each succeeding player to his left.

The value of the party – that is, the amount paid by the loser to the winner – is 4 plus the card-point value of any counters in the talon. For example, if it contains a King and a Queen, the payment is 4+3+2 = 9 chips. (By some accounts, ♦A counts 5 in the talon, and ♥J counts 3.) If the loser is sitting opposite the winner, he pays double.

Side payments These occur whenever an Ace or Quinola is *placed* (thrown to a trick when unable to follow suit), or *forced* (played to the lead of its suit), or *led* to a trick.

- Anyone who places an Ace or Quinola is paid by the winner of the trick.
- Anyone forced to play the Ace of the suit led pays the leader of the trick.
- If anyone plays Quinola to a heart lead, the leader of the trick is paid by all three opponents.
- If anyone leads an Ace or Quinola at any time, the eventual winner of the hand may claim the appropriate payment in addition to his other winnings (provided he remembers to do so before the next deal).

The appropriate payments are:

event		♥J	♦A	♥♠♣A
placed:	trick-winner pays holder	5	2	1
forced:	holder pays leader	10	2	1
	others pay leader	5	0	0
led:	holder pays winner	10	2	1
	others pay winner	5	0	0

These amounts are doubled as between players sitting opposite each other, and doubled as between everyone if occurring in either of the last two tricks. Thus a player who leads a heart to the last trick, and is lucky enough to draw the Jack from the player sitting opposite, will receive 40 from the Quinola player and 10 from each neighbour.

Quinola and the pool Whoever plays Quinola to a trick not only wins or loses the side-payments detailed above but also either wins or enlarges the pool.

If Quinola is forced, or is led to a trick, its player pays a *remise*. This is an amount equivalent to the latest (most recently formed) pool. The first remise that occurs is used to double the only pool there is. The second and subsequent remises go to form new pools, which are kept separate from one another. The dealer always adds his 5 to the latest pool, which is therefore also the largest.

The latest pool is won by the Quinola holder when he succeeds in placing it on the lead of another suit. If at this time no pools remain, a new one is formed by the contribution of 5 from each player, and 10 from the dealer, as at the start of the session.

Optional rule Once a remise has been paid, everyone is obliged to discard and draw before the first trick is played, and it is illegal to discard Quinola. This rule (if agreed) applies until all pools have been won and a new one started, when it is held in abeyance until a remise is paid.

The reversis To make the reversis, a player must win all eleven tricks. A player who wins the first nine is held to have undertaken the reversis and may not renounce it. No further payments may be made for aces or Quinola, and all payments between the players or to or from the pool which may have been made during the first nine tricks are returned. The only payments that apply relate to what happens in the last two tricks, as follows.

- If successful, the reversis player receives 16 from each neighbour and 32 from the player opposite. If he played Quinola during the first nine tricks, he also wins the Quinola pool.
- If unsuccessful, he pays 64 to the player who broke the reversis by first taking a trick against him, and if he played Quinola during the first nine tricks, he also pays a remise.
- If the reversis is broken, and the breaking trick is taken by Quinola, the reversis player pays his 64 as above, but receives the appropriate side-payment for forcing Quinola, though nothing is paid either to or from the Quinola pool.

Espagnolette This later addition to the game is a sort of misère contract, but may be undertaken only by a player who holds all four Aces, or Quinola and at least three Aces. Throughout the first nine tricks this player need not follow suit but may renounce at will. Having done so, he has automatically contracted to lose every trick, and is obliged to follow suit in the tenth, if possible. (If in fact he followed suit throughout, he is held not to have undertaken the bid of espagnolette.)

The espagnolette player wins if he loses every trick – even if a better-placed player also took no tricks – and provided no one else makes the reversis. Besides winning the party, he also gains the appropriate amounts for the Aces he placed and, if he held and therefore placed Quinola, the amount for that and the pool as well.

If he loses by taking a trick, he must return, doubled, all the side payments he received for the placement of Aces and, if he placed Quinola, for that too, together with double the pool he won. He also loses the party, in place of the player who took most card-points, and pays the player who took fewest in the usual way.

If he loses because another player makes the reversis – an occupational hazard of undertaking the espagnolette – he pays the reversis winner 64 chips and the others pay nothing. If, however, he breaks the reversis himself by taking either of the last two tricks, he is absolved from all penalty, as the reversis attempt cancels all side payments to or from the pool, and there is no payment as between winner and loser.

Schieberamsch
3 players, 32 cards

Skat-players will know Ramsch – meaning 'junk' – as the game played when a hand is passed by all three players, even though the 'official rules' forbid it. In fact it is a highly intriguing and skilful game in its own right. Schieberamsch (from *schieben*, 'to shove') is the most popular modern form.

Preliminaries Three play with a 32-card French or German pack having the following card-point values:

French	Ace	Ten	King	Queen	Jack	9-8-7
German	Ace	Ten	King	Ober	Unter	9-8-7
counting	11	10	4	3	2	0

The Jacks or Unters do not belong to the suits marked on their faces but form a separate four-card trump suit of their own, ranking from high to low as follows:

♣J – ♠J – ♥J – ♦J   *or*   ☐U – ♁U – ♡U – ☐U

In non-trump suits, the order is A-T-K-Q(or Ober)-9-8-7.

Deal Deal ten each in batches of 3-(2)-4-3, the (2) going face down to the table to form the *skat*.

Object Normally, to avoid taking most card-points in tricks. Before play begins, however, each in turn has one chance to bid 'grand hand', which is an undertaking to win at least 61 card-points in tricks and without picking up the skat. (See Grand hand, below.)

The skat Forehand may take the skat, add it to his hand, and discard any two cards face down in its place. Each in turn thereafter may do the same, taking as the skat the previous player's discards. (Hence the title: the skat is shoved round from player to player.) It is permissible to discard either or both of the cards picked up, but many players forbid the discard of any Jack. A player with sufficient confidence in his hand may simply pass the skat on to the next player without looking at it. This has the effect of doubling the eventual score, so that, for example, if all three play 'from the hand' the score will be octupled.

Play Forehand leads. Players must follow suit if possible, otherwise may play any card. The trick is taken by the highest card of the suit led, or by the highest Jack if any are played, and the winner of each trick leads to the next. At end of play, any card-points contained in the skat are added to those of the player who took most (or, *variant*, to whoever won the last trick).

Score Whoever won most card-points records that number as a penalty score, increased by as many doubles as apply, and rounded down to the nearest 10. For example, if two players doubled by not taking the skat, and the loser took 82 card-points, he scores $4 \times 82 = 328 \div 10 = 32$ (ignoring remainder). If two tie for most, they both count the same penalty. The amount is doubled (before rounding down) if one opponent took no trick at all. If, however, both took no trick, then the player who took all ten wins. His penalty score is then reduced by 120, doubled for each opponent who did not look at the skat.

Grand hand If one player bids 'grand hand', the skat remains untaken but is turned up and added to the soloist's won tricks at end of play.

An opponent may double the contract ('*Kontra*'), and the soloist may then redouble ('*Rekontra*'). The score at grand hand is calculated in the manner of Skat, from which it is borrowed, and which see for further explanation. (Briefly: base value 24, multiplied by the following factors: number of consecutive top trumps originally held or not held, 1 for game, 1 for hand, 1 if schneider made, 1 if schwarz made, 1 if schneider bid, 1 if schwarz bid.) Doubles and redoubles are applied before rounding down. If the soloist took 61 or more card-points, the resultant score is deducted from his penalty total, otherwise it is added.

> ☞ Note that Jacks constitute a separate suit and do not belong to the suits marked on their faces. If a Jack is led, you must play a Jack if possible. If a non-trump is led, you cannot follow suit by playing its Jack, but may trump with any Jack if unable to follow.

Ramsch

In the original game the skat was not touched but merely taken in with the last trick, and whoever took fewest card-points won an agreed stake from each opponent. A player who took no tricks at all (a 'virgin'), or who took all ten, won double. There was no grand hand bid.

Augenramsch (Point-Ramsch)

As Ramsch, but whoever takes most card-points counts that number as a penalty.

Mittelramsch (Middle-Ramsch)

As Augenramsch, but whoever takes the middling number of card-points loses, and records that number as a penalty.

Vierzigeramsch (Forty-Ramsch)

As Schieberamsch, but the aim is to take the middling number of card-points, which in practice means as close to 40 as possible. This is recorded as a positive score. If two players tie, the third scores either what he makes, or the amount scored by each opponent, whichever is the greater. If all take 40, it is scored by the winner of the last trick.

Bassadewitz (Bassarovitz)   3–6p (4 best), 32 cards

A forerunner of Ramsch, probably defunct, but not without interest.

Preliminaries Cards rank and count as follows:

A	K	Q	J	T	9	8	7
11	4	3	2	10	0	0	0

Dealer contributes 12 chips to a pool (or each of four players contributes three) and deals the cards round evenly. If two remain, leave them face down and add them to the last trick.

Object To take as few card-points as possible of the 120 available.

Play Eldest leads. Players must follow suit if possible, otherwise may play any card. The trick is taken by the highest card of the suit led, and the winner of each trick leads to the next. There are no trumps.

Pay-off Whoever takes fewest card-points collects 5 chips, second-fewest 4, third 3 chips. Ties are settled in favour of the eldest player, but a player taking no tricks beats one who merely takes no card-points.

A player winning every trick receives 4 chips from each opponent. A player winning 100+ card-points, but not every trick, pays 4 chips to each opponent. In either case the pool is carried forward and the same player deals again, as also if everyone takes the same number of card-points.

Variant: In an earlier incarnation, Ace counts 5 penalties instead of 11, and each player adds 1 per trick to his card-point total (a maximum of 88 when four play).

Coteccio ('Reverse')   2–7 players, 40 cards

Of several similar Italian games so named, the most interesting is that played in Trieste, as it is one of the few games extant that retain the card-point values associated with the ancient game of Trappola. The following derives from McLeod's description in *The Playing-Card* (XXV, 5).

Preliminaries From two to seven players pay an agreed stake to a pool and start with a notional four lives. Play to the right. Deal five each from the 40-card Italian pack ranking 1, Re, Caval, Fante, 7, 6, 5, 4, 3, 2. The top four cards (equivalent to AKQJ) count respectively 6, 5, 4 and 3 points each. Another 6 for winning the last trick makes 78 card-points in all. The aim is either to avoid taking the greatest number of card-points, or to win all five tricks.

Play Eldest leads. Players must follow suit if possible, otherwise may play any card. The trick is taken by the highest card of the suit led, and the winner of each trick leads to the next. There are no trumps. A player who wins the first four tricks straight off may either annul the hand, in which case the same dealer deals again, or undertake to win the fifth trick by leading to it.

Score Normally, the player who takes most card-points loses a life. If two or more tie for most, they all lose a life. If you win four and successfully go for the fifth, you gain an extra life and the opponents lose one each. If you fail, you lose a life and the actual winner of the last trick gains one.

Theoretically, players drop out upon losing their fourth life, and the winner is the last left in. However, the game can be long drawn out. By agreement, a player upon losing his last life may, provided at least two other players remain alive, 'call the doctor' by paying (say) a half stake to the pool and receiving in return as many lives as remain to the player who currently has fewest.

If all live players tie for most and so 'die' simultaneously, the whole game is annulled and re-started with four lives each and a new pool added to the old one.

The turn to lead first always passes to the next live player to the right of the previous first leader, and the deal is always made by the next live player to the leader's left.

Don't forget . . .

- Play to the left (clockwise) unless otherwise stated.
- Eldest or Forehand means the player to the left of the dealer in left-handed games, to the right in right-handed games.
- T = Ten, p = players, pp = in fixed partnerships, c = cards, † = trump, ☆ = Joker.

5 Piquet and others

Piquet is the best known of a group of games following a similar pattern. First, you score for any card combinations that you have been dealt, or can acquire by making discards and drawing replacements from a stock. Next, you make further scores by playing your cards out to tricks. Most are now defunct, but Piquet itself retains a following among card connoisseurs.

▌Piquet (Picquet, Picket, Cent)   2 players, 32 cards

... the French consider the invention of Piquet as a national point of honour, and that the native author who should call it into question would render himself liable to a suspicion of incivism.

William Chatto, *Facts and Speculations on Playing-Cards* (1848)

God send you better lucke at pickott than I have with Harry Bennett at cribbadge.

Charles II *in a letter to Ormonde*
(*Clarendon State Papers*, Vol. 3, 1656)

Piquet has long been regarded as the best card game for two. In 1534 Rabelais placed it high on the list of games played by Gargantua, and in 1892 (according to *Le Guide Marabout*) the delegates to a card congress held at Vienna voted it the most 'classic' of all card games. Perhaps because it was also regarded as essentially aristocratic and upper-class, and because it takes a good many words to explain, it has been little played since the First World War. Despite French ancestry, Piquet has been played in England long enough – probably since the marriage of Charles I to Henrietta Maria of France in 1625 – to have become thoroughly naturalized. For most of its English history its vocabulary has been either replaced by English equivalents or at least pronounced as English. Use of French terminology like *carte blanche* for 'blank', and the pseudo-French pronunciation 'P.K.' for what was previously pronounced 'Picket', date from the nineteenth century.

The game's popularity among the literate is suggested by its prominence in the earliest books of instruction in card-playing, an activity previously regarded as something you just picked up, like the common cold. It held pride of place for three centuries in various editions of *The Compleat Gamester,* formed the subject of a treatise by the real Edmond Hoyle in 1744, and still remains a staple component of all self-respecting card-game compendia. In the eighteenth and nine-teenth centuries the home of intensive Piquet play for real money, along with Whist, was at Bath. In the late nineteenth century the game of Piquet au Cent, or Hundred-up Piquet, was replaced by a new structure under the name Rubicon Piquet. In the old game, play continued until one player reached 100 points, whereas the Rubicon game (or *partie,* equivalent to a rubber at Bridge) consists of exactly six deals, the loser being penalized if then short of the 100 points necessary to 'cross the Rubicon'.

Like Cribbage, Piquet is a game of almost continuous point-scoring: traditionally, you recite your score as you go along and write down the result only at the end of each round. As this tradition is now lost, and special Piquet markers are a thing of the past, a Cribbage board may be found helpful.

Preliminaries Two players, 32 cards (AKQJT987). A game is six deals. The aim is to gain a majority of points for scoring combinations and winning tricks, and, in the loser's case, to reach at least 100 points overall.

Deal The deal alternates. The dealer is called Younger and non-dealer Elder. Deal twelve each in twos or threes and spread the last eight, face down. These form the talon.

Blank A player whose hand contains no court cards scores 10 for 'blank' (*carte blanche*) and must prove it by playing his cards rapidly face up on the table. Elder does so immediately, but Younger waits until Elder has exchanged before proving it.

The exchange Elder discards up to five cards face down and replaces them from the top of the talon. He must discard at least one. If he discards fewer than five, he may privately peep at the cards he would have taken had he exchanged all five. Younger may exchange up to as many as remain (at least three), but need not exchange any. If he draws fewer, Younger may expose those untaken for both to see, or leave them face down for neither to see. Players may examine their own discards at any time during the play.

Declaring combinations The players now state what combinations they hold in the following order. In each class, Elder always declares first. If Younger has a higher combination of the same class, or any combination of a class in which Elder has none, he says 'Not good' and scores it himself. If he cannot match it, he says 'Good', and Elder scores. If he says 'Equal', neither scores.

1. *Point.* Whoever has the longest suit scores 1 point for each card in it. If equal, the point goes to whichever of the matched suits has the highest value, counting Ace 11, courts 10, numerals at face value. If still equal, neither scores for point.

2. *Sequences.* A sequence is three or more cards in suit and sequence. Whoever has the longest sequence scores for it and any other sequences he may declare. If both tie for longest sequence, it goes to the one with the higher-ranking cards. If both still tie, neither scores for sequences. Sequences of three and four score 3 and 4 respectively, five to eight score 15 to 18 respectively.

3. *Sets.* A set is three or four cards of the same rank but not lower than Tens. Three is a *trio* and scores 3, four a *quatorze* and scores 14. Any quatorze beats any trio, and as between equal sets a higher-ranking beats a lower. A tie is impossible.

Announcing the score Elder now summarizes the scores he has made so far, leads a card to the first trick, and adds 1 point 'for leading'. Younger, before playing a card, then fully identifies and scores for any combinations he holds which enabled him to describe Elder's as 'Not good', and announces his total score for combinations.

Repique If either player reaches 30 for combinations before the other has scored any, he gets a bonus of 60 for *repique*. For this purpose, points accrue strictly in order blank, point, sequences, sets.

Examples:
1. Elder scores 7 for point, sequences of 15 and 4 and 3, and 3 for a trio, giving him 32 + 60 = 92. But if Younger had already called a blank, Elder fails the repique, because the blank counts first.
2. Neither scores for point or sequence because Younger replied 'equal' to both, but Younger then calls two quatorzes and a trio for 31, earning 60 more for

repique. But if Elder had scored for blank, point or sequence, Younger's sets would not earn the repique.

Pique If Younger scores nothing for combinations, and Elder reaches 30 as the result of scoring 1 point for each card he leads to a trick in unbroken succession, then Elder gains a bonus of 30 for *pique*. Younger can't score for pique, being prevented by Elder's '1 for leading'.

Play Elder leads first. Second to a trick must follow suit if possible, otherwise may play any card. The trick is taken by the higher card of the suit led, and the winner of each trick leads to the next. There are no trumps.

Score A trick scores 1 point if won by the player who led to it, otherwise 2. Winning from seven to eleven tricks earns a bonus of 10 'for cards', and winning all twelve a bonus of 40 for *capot*.

Game If the loser reaches 100 ('crosses the rubicon'), the winner scores 100 plus the difference between their final totals. If not (the loser is 'rubiconed'), the winner scores 100 plus the *total* of their final scores. If tied, play two more deals to break it.

Sample deal Younger deals twelve cards each as follows:

Elder									*Younger*							
♠	-	-	Q	-	T	9	-	-	-	K	-	-	-	-	8	7
♥	A	-	Q	J	-	-	8	-	K	-	-	T	-	-	-	
♣	-	-	Q	-	-	-	-	-	A	K	-	J	T	-	8	7
♦	A	K	-	-	-	9	8	-	-	-	-	-	T	-	-	-

Elder will keep three Queens, hoping to draw the fourth, and retain one of the four-card suits for point. Since he wants a specific card (♦Q), he must exchange five, so out go two spades and all diamonds below the Ace.

Younger has a good club point, but it is gappy and probably pitted against a better diamond point in Elder's hand. His only hope lies in drawing the fourth King (the fourth Ten would not be good against the cards, as Elder may have four Queens to beat it), or either of the missing clubs. A club would give him a quint, which would be good, as it is clear from his own holding that Elder cannot possibly hold better than a quart in any suit. Faced with three possibilities, Younger throws ♦T and two low spades. In other circumstances it would be wiser to keep the Ten as a guard on the possible draw of the King, and to throw one or two low clubs in order not to unguard the King of spades.

Elder draws the top five cards and is pleased to get the fourth Queen and two of his point suit. Younger successfully draws ♣9 and is fortunate in also finding ♠A to cover his previously bared King. The hands are now:

Elder										Younger								
♠	–	–	Q	J	–	–	–	–		A	K	–	–	–	–	–	–	–
♥	A	–	Q	J	–	9	8	7		–	K	–	–	T	–	–	–	
♣	–	–	Q	–	–	–	–	–		A	K	–	J	T	9	8	7	
♦	A	–	Q	–	–	–	–	7		–	–	–	J	–	–	–	–	

Elder – Point of six.
Younger – Not good. (*Having seven.*)
Elder – Fourteen Queens. (*The low three-card sequence is not worth mentioning.*)
Younger – Good.
Elder – And one for leading, fifteen. (*Leads* ♥A)
Younger – Point of seven for 7, quint to the Jack 15, makes 22. (*Plays* ♥T)

Elder next leads ♦A ('sixteen'), ♦Q ('seventeen'), ♦7 ('eighteen'), to which Younger plays, respectively, ♦J, ♣7, ♣8. Whatever Elder leads next, Younger is bound to win (saying 'twenty-four'), as well as all seven remaining tricks, bringing him to 31, plus '10 for more', total 41 to Elder's 18.

The outcome is untypical, as Younger rarely wins more than once in three or four deals. Elder's weakness lay in his lack of Kings and in the fact that Younger's Kings were covered. Elder had no alternative play: anything other than his ♥A and three diamonds would have put Younger in sooner for at least ten tricks.

Notes on play Piquet is an asymmetrical game, and the assessment of a given hand depends on whether you are playing it as Elder or as Younger. For example:

♠	–	–	Q	J	T	–	–	–
♥	A	–	Q	–	T	9	–	–
♣	–	–	Q	–	T	9	8	–
♦	–	–	–	J	–	–	–	–

As Elder, keep the hearts for point, the spades for sequence, and discard clubs and diamonds. Three Queens are not worth keeping, with a possible four Kings against. If you keep the clubs, hoping for a quint, you'll lack a fifth discard. As the cards lie, Younger can't get a quint against you.

♠	–	K	Q	–	–	–	–	–
♥	A	K	Q	–	–	–	–	–
♣	–	–	Q	J	–	–	–	–
♦	A	–	–	–	T	9	8	7

As Elder, don't waste high cards for the sake of keeping a low point in diamonds, but dump the Jack and four diamonds and go for the fourteen Queens. As Younger, however, consider discarding ♥AK and ♣J. You may conceivably get the fourteen Queens or a diamond quint, are in no danger of capot, and may even, with a lucky club break, divide the tricks.

♠	A	–	Q	J	–	9	–	7
♥	A	–	Q	–	–	–	–	–
♣	–	–	Q	–	–	9	–	7
♦	–	–	–	J	–	9	–	–

A scrappy hand, full of loopholes. As Elder, you must choose between the spade point and the potential fourteen Queens. If you keep both, you must either throw ♥A, assuring Younger of at least 20 for tricks, or discard four, thus reducing your chances of improving the point or the quatorze. You may as well forget the Queens and discard all the clubs and diamonds.

As Younger, though, you certainly can't expect to pick up a Queen *and* the necessary King in a three-card draw, and would be justified in abandoning the point by discarding three low spades in order to remain safe in at least three suits. The draw of any high diamond could enable you to at least divide the tricks.

Variations

1. *Carte rouge* Some traditions include a bonus of 40 for *carte rouge*, defined as a hand of which every single card forms part of at least one scoring combination.

2. *Point and sequence of nought.* A void suit may be counted as a

point and sequence of nought worth 50½. It therefore beats any five-card point and sequence lower than AKQJT (worth 51). It scores 5 for point (if good) and 10 for sequence (likewise).

3. *10 for last.* Players approaching Piquet from other games may find the trick-scoring more fiddly than the final result is worth. A simpler and strategically more interesting variation is to score a flat 1 per trick and to award a 10-point bonus not to the player who wins a majority of tricks but to the player who wins the last trick.

Saunt (Piquet au Cent)

The original form of Piquet is played up to 100 points over as many deals as necessary, and the winner scores a double game if the loser fails to reach 50. A partie is won by the first to win three games, a double counting as two. Minor differences of procedure are not essential, and many are optional. The main one is that Elder is free to play without exchanging.

Elder does not lead until all announcements and scores have been made. In trick-play, score 1 point for leading a card higher than a Nine, and 1 point for winning the opponent's lead with a card higher than Nine. Score 1 more for winning the last trick, unless also scoring for capot, 10 for more, and a further 30 for capot.

The first to reach 100 points scores the difference between the two totals. If the loser fails to reach 50 points he is rubiconed, or lurched, and the winner scores twice the difference.

Auction Piquet

One of the less successful attempts to apply Bridge principles to other games, Auction Piquet originated in Oxford and was developed by prisoners of war in 1914–18.

Bidding After the deal, each in turn, Elder first, may bid 'seven' or more or pass. If both pass there is a new deal. A bid of seven offers to win at least seven tricks in the play-off – or, if so stated, to *lose* at least seven tricks (i.e. win five at most). Since plus and minus bids are equal in value, a bid can be overcalled only by raising the number of tricks to be won or lost. A given bid may be doubled by the opponent and redoubled by the maker, but any doubling is cancelled if the next player then bids higher.

Exchange The exchange takes place as usual, except that Elder is free to exchange none.

Declarations In a minus bid the bidder scores everything 'good' in his opponent's hand, so the exchange should be made with this in mind. Point, sequence and set are declared and scored as usual, except that they may be declared in any order (with a view to scoring repique). In minus deals, obviously, 'sinking' (deliberate under-declaring) is not permitted.

Pique and repique In a plus deal pique or repique is made upon reaching a count of 29 (not 30); in a minus deal it is made at 21.

Score for tricks Score 2 points for winning a trick led by yourself, 1 point for a trick led by your opponent (the reverse of normal Piquet). In addition, the bidder scores 10 per overtrick, or 20 if doubled or 40 if redoubled. Failing the contract entitles the opponent to score the same amount for undertricks. For example: bid seven, take ten, score 30 extra; bid seven, take six, opponent scores 10. Bid minus seven, take seven, lose 20 (because you undertook to lose at most five). Doubling and redoubling affect only the score for overtricks or undertricks.

Game The rubicon is 150 points. If tied, play a seventh deal; but if still tied, the partie ends.

Contract Piquet (Counterpique)

A version developed by myself and Andrew Pennycook.

Preliminaries Scores are kept on a Bridge-pad divided by a horizontal line. Scores made for combinations go above the line, those for tricks below. Although 12 tricks are played, the last trick counts double, making the number of tricks nominally thirteen.

Deal Lowest cut deals first. Each subsequent deal is made by whichever player scored for tricks below the line in the previous hand. Deal as in the parent game. A player who has a blank may declare and score for it (above the line) immediately.

Bidding There follows a round of bidding for the privilege of becoming Elder. Dealer starts by announcing a bid, and non-dealer replies 'Yes' if he can bid the same or higher, or 'Pass' if he can't match it. Dealer continues raising the bid, jumping to any higher level as desired, until one of them passes, leaving the other as Elder hand. (If both pass immediately, the game is misère: see below.)

The lowest bid is 5-7 (announced 'Five-Seven'). This is a bid to win at least seven tricks after discarding and drawing five cards. It can be raised by increasing the number of tricks to be won – for example, 5-8, 5-9, 5-10, etc., up to 5-13. Or it can be raised by reducing the number of cards to be drawn. Thus any bid of '5', even 5-13, can be bettered by 4-7, any bid of 4 by 3-7, and so on. The highest possible bid is '0-13'.

If non-dealer becomes Elder, he may state a higher-valued game than the one he accepted. Dealer, however, upon becoming Elder, must play the game he last bid, and may not raise it.

Play Elder then makes exactly the number of discards stated in the bid, and draws replacements from the talon. He may not see the faces of any cards he leaves to Younger. Younger discards and draws as in the parent game, and combinations are declared and scored in the usual way, except that Elder does not score '1 for leading'. This makes it possible for either player to score 30 for pique.

Score Tricks are scored below the line, and by one player only.

For winning at least as many tricks as bid, Elder scores the number of tricks actually taken, multiplied by the number of cards left to Younger in the draw. For example, a bid of 5-7 scores 21 if seven tricks were taken, 24 if eight, 27 if nine, and so on. There is no special bonus for *capot*.

If Elder falls short of the number bid, Younger scores for 'counter-pique'. This amount is what Elder would have won for making the bid exactly, multiplied by the number by which Elder fell short. For example, if Elder bid 5-7 and took only six, Younger would score 21. If Elder bid 4-9 and took only seven, Younger would score 72. And so on.

Game The first to reach 100 below the line wins a game, and a new line is drawn. The first to win two games wins the partie (rubber). Both players then total their above- and below-line scores, and the winner adds a bonus of 300, or 500 if the loser did not win a game, plus (in either case) 100 for any game in which the loser failed to make any score.

Misère If both pass immediately, there is no draw and no declaring of combinations. Elder leads to the first trick, and whoever wins the smaller number of tricks scores below the line 5 points for each trick won by the other, giving a range of 35 to 65.

Piquet for three and more

Piquet Chouette

(for 3). Not so much three-hand Piquet as two-hand Piquet played by three players in rotation. Highest cut has choice of deal and plays against the other two in combination (the latter are said to play *à la chouette*). Lowest cut sits out and participates in his partner's hand by advising him on play and making the same score. If the soloist wins the partie, the others swap their active and passive roles. If he loses, he becomes the passive opponent and the active opponent who beat him becomes the new soloist. The soloist always has choice of deal and, if the game is played for stakes, plays double.

Piquet Normand

(for 3). Three take part in play, all against all. Deal ten each and lay the last two aside. Dealer (but nobody else) may discard two and take the undealt cards in their place. Eldest announces first: only the player with the best point, sequence or set may score it and, in the case of sequence or set, may score any lower ones he may also hold. Bonuses: 90 for repique upon reaching 20 in combinations before either opponent has scored, 60 for pique upon reaching 20 in combinations and tricks before either opponent scores, 10 for taking more tricks than either opponent, plus 30 for taking all ten. If two players take ten between them, each scores 20 for capot. Game is 100 points.

Partnership Piquet

(for 4). Deal eight each. Eldest announces his best combinations in all classes, and leads. His left-hand opponent follows, announcing any better combinations that he may have. This establishes which side may score in each category. As the rest of the first trick is played, the partner of the player scoring for sequence or set may announce any score for any sequence or set held by himself. Repique of 90 is scored for making 20 in combinations before the opposing partnership has anything to count, or pique of 60 for reaching 20 in combinations and play before the opponents score.

Duplicate Piquet

(for 4). A and B are partners against Y and Z. With the aid of a fifth person to deal identical hands and talons at both tables, A plays Elder against Y's Younger at one, while B plays Younger against Z's Elder at the other.

Round Piquet

(for 3 or more). Three or more may play a series of two-hand games, each playing a hand first as Elder against the player on his right, then as Younger against the player on his left. When all have played an equal number of times, each pays to any with a higher score the difference between their two scores. This works best with an even number of players, all active at the same time but in different combinations.

Imperial (Piquet Imperial, Trump Piquet, Vingt-quatre)

2 players, 32 cards

This sixteenth-century hybrid of Triomphe and Piquet remains popular in the Midi and offers many points of interest to card-game explorers. Descriptions vary: the following is typical.

Preliminaries Two players use a 32-card pack nowadays, ranking AKQJT987 in each suit (but originally KQJAT987, as may still be encountered in some books). Scores can be written, but counters are better. Each starts with five reds and six whites on his left, and passes one white from left to right for each point won in play. Six points make an imperial, indicated by moving a red to the right and returning six whites to the left. Game is 36 points, being won by the first to pass all eleven counters from left to right.

Deal Deal twelve each in twos, threes, or fours. Turn the twenty-fifth card for trump, and place the rest face down across it. If the turn-up is an honour (K Q J A or 7), dealer scores a white. If it is a King or an Ace, and dealer holds the Seven, he may exchange it for the turn-up.

Point Whoever now has the better point scores one white. Point is the total face value of all cards held in any one suit, counting Ace 11, courts 10 each, numerals as marked. If equal, Elder scores. (It is usual, but not legally binding, to declare and score for point before announcing imperials.)

Imperials Each in turn, starting with Elder, scores for any of the following imperials he may have been dealt. Imperials must be declared in this order, and shown on request:

1. K Q J T of trumps (*impériale d'atout*)   2 reds
2. K Q J T of non-trump suit   1 red
3. All four of A, K, Q, J or 7 (*impériale d'honneur*)   1 red
4. No court cards (*impériale blanche*)   2 reds

Play Elder leads to the first trick. Second to a trick must follow suit and head the trick if possible; must trump if unable to follow a non-trump lead; and may renounce only if unable to do either. The trick is taken by the higher card of the suit led, or by the higher trump if any are played, and the winner of each trick leads to the next.

Score Score one white for leading an honour to a trick, and one for leading to a trick and thereby capturing an honour. At end of play, whoever won a majority of tricks scores one white per trick in excess of six, or two reds for *capot* if he won all twelve. Neither scores if the tricks are divided.

Throughout play, whenever one player scores a red – whether for an imperial or by getting his sixth white across – his opponent's odd points are promptly annulled, and he must shift all his whites back to the left. The sole exception is the *impériale blanche*, which does not annul the odd points. With this exception, however, the rule is also applied at the start of the second and subsequent deals when reds are scored for imperials in hand. Hence it is important, especially near the end of a game, that scores be made strictly in order: turned trump, imperials in hand, *impériale blanche*, the point, leading and capturing honours, number of tricks taken.

Optional extras Some players recognize two additional imperials, each earning one red but not forcing the opponent to cancel his whites. An *impériale de retourne* occurs when a player has all but one card of an imperial, and the card missing is the trump turn-up. This counts immediately before the score for point. An *impériale de rencontre*, or *impériale tombée*, occurs when a player wins the four top trumps in tricks without having been originally dealt all four. This counts immediately before the score for honours.

Gleek

An old English game described in various, slightly differing ways between 1533 and 1674. It could be described as the three-player equivalent of Piquet. I will call the unit stakes 'p' for pence.

Preliminaries Three players use 44 cards ranking AKQJT987654. Deal twelve each in fours, set the remaining eight face down as a stock, and turn the top card for trump. If it is a Four ('Tiddy'), the dealer receives 4p from each opponent.

Bidding Each in turn bids to take in the stock (excluding the turn-up) in exchange for seven discards. Eldest starts at 12p, and each in turn raises by 1p. The highest bidder pays half his bid to each opponent (any odd penny going to the elder of them), makes seven discards, and takes the stock, other than the trump turn-up. (Sources vary as to whether you discard before drawing or draw before discarding.)

Vying the ruff The ruff, or flush, or point (as at Piquet) is the total face value of cards held in one's longest suit, counting Ace 11, courts 10 each, numerals as marked. Each in turn pays 2p or more to the pot so long as he thinks he has the highest-counting ruff. This pot is won by the player showing the best ruff when all bets are equalized, or, without showing, by the player remaining when neither of the others has matched his last bet. If all pass without vying, the pot is carried foward to the next deal. An oddity of the game is that a player holding four Aces may vie the ruff, without warning, and will inevitably win it.

Gleeks and mournivals A gleek is three Aces, Kings, Queens or Jacks, a mournival four of the same. These are declared, not vied. Whoever has the best mournival wins, from each opponent, for Aces 8p, Kings 6p, Queens 4p, Jacks 2p. Failing mournivals, whoever has the best gleek wins half the appropriate amount. It is not clear whether the player who wins this is also entitled to payment for any lower gleeks and mournivals he may hold, so this should be decided beforehand.

Play Eldest leads. Players must follow suit if possible, otherwise may play any card. The trick is taken by the highest card of the suit led, or by the highest trump if any are played, and the winner of each trick leads to the next.

Score Each player counts 3 points per trick won, plus additional points for top trumps won in tricks as follows: Ace ('Tib') 15, King 3, Queen

3, Jack ('Tom') 9. If one of these counters is the turn-up, it counts in favour of the dealer. Since the combined total is 66, anyone who scores less than 22 pays the difference into a trick-pot, and anyone who scores more than 22 takes out the difference, yielding a zero-sum result.

Comment In *The Compleat Gamester* of 1674, Charles Cotton counts also 5 for the trump Five ('Towser') and 6 for the trump Six ('Tumbler'). These presumably represent only side payments made upon being turned for trump, otherwise they make nonsense of the 22-point target for tricks. They are absent from earlier accounts of the game.

Romestecq (Rum und Stich, Rumstick)

An eighteenth-century Dutch game, played also in France and Germany, by two, or more usually by four or six in partnerships, with partners sitting adjacently in order to communicate their holdings. Deal five each from a 36-card pack ranking AKQJT9876 and play five tricks at no trump. Game is 21 points if four play, 36 if six. Anyone dealt a quartet (four Aces, Kings etc.; German *Wirlik*, French *virlique*) wins the game immediately. Other features score thus:

Quartet (*Wirlik, virlique*)	wins outright
Two pairs (*Doppelnieger, double ningre*)	3
Triplet (*Tritsch, triche*)	2 (or 3 if Aces)
Two suit pairs (*Dorf, village*)	2 (e.g. ♣K ♣Q ♥9 ♥8)
AA or KK (*Doppelrome, double rome*)	4, or 2 if 'duped'
Lower pair (*Rome, rome*)	1
Win last trick (*Stich, stecq*)	1

A combination held and scored in the hand is announced by saying 'part of a triplet' (or whatever) upon first playing a card of it to a trick. You can also score for capturing combinations taken in tricks from the other side, when they are said to be *grugé* ('duped').

Rumstick (only once so mentioned in English) enjoyed brief popularity as a fad game, but was soon condemned as being more complicated than it was worth, which may explain why contemporary descriptions are barely intelligible.

Guimbarde (Jew's Harp) or **La Mariée (The Bride)**

(France, eighteenth century.) A two-part gambling game played by three to five with 32 cards; from six to eight with all 52, ranking KQJAT987(65432).

Staking Everyone places 1p (point, penny, pound, whatever) in each of five staking compartments marked *guimbarde* (♥Q), *roi* (♥K), *fou* (♦J), *mariage* (♥KQ), *point* (3+ cards of the same suit). Deal five each and turn the next for trump. Anyone dealt a scoring card or combination wins the contents of the appropriate compartment. Thus a player lucky enough to be dealt ♥KQxx ♦J, or ♥KQ ♦Jxx, would sweep the lot. Any content remaining untaken is carried forward to the next deal.

Play Everyone adds 1p to the *point*, and eldest leads to the first trick. Players must follow suit if possible, otherwise may play any card. The top trumps are always *guimbarde* (♥Q), *roi* (♥K), *fou* (♦J) followed by KQJAT . . . etc. of the trump suit, omitting any that are top trumps by definition.The trick is taken by the highest card of the suit led, or by the highest trump if any are played, and the winner of each trick leads to the next. The contents of *point* are won by the first player (if any) to win two tricks. During play, the following side-payments may be made:

- For playing a King followed immediately by the Queen of the same suit (*mariage*), 1p from all but the Queen-player.
- For winning with one of the three top trumps a trick containing a marriage, 1p from the King- and Queen-players.
- For playing ♥K and winning ♥Q (*grand mariage*), 2p from everyone.

Guinguette

(France, eighteenth century.) A three-part gambling game, played by from three to eight with a 52-card pack ranking KQJT98765432A. A guingette is a public dancing-place, whether a hall or a garden, and all the features of this game have names related to dancing and dance steps.

Staking Everyone stakes 1p to each of three compartments labelled *guingette* (♦Q), *cabaret* (sequence of three), and *cotillon* (two tricks). Deal four each in twos and stack the rest face down, forming the talon or *cotillon*. Whoever has ♦Q shows it and wins the stake for *guingette*. If no one does, each draws another card from the stock and tries again. If still unclaimed, the stake goes forward to the next deal.

Vying Next, players vie as to who has the best *cabaret*. A cabaret is three cards in sequence, not necessarily of the same suit. KQJ and QJT don't count, so the highest possible is JT9. Each in turn either raises the stake, equalizes the last stake, or drops out. When all bets are equal, whoever has the highest *cabaret* wins these bets plus the contents of that compartment. If two or more tie for highest, that of the eldest player prevails. If nobody has one, the stakes are carried forward.

Exchanging Each in turn has one opportunity to make a discard and draw a replacement from the top of the stock, adding for this privilege 2p to the *cotillon*. Eldest then chooses and announces a trump suit. Each in turn announces whether he will pass or play. Each active player may make one discard and draw a replacement from the stock upon payment of 2p to the *cotillon*, and may keep doing so until satisfied. Before the next in turn does so, the previous player's discards are shuffled in with the stock.

Play When all are ready, Eldest leads to the first trick. Players must follow suit and head the trick if possible; must trump and overtrump if unable to follow; and may renounce only if unable to do either. The trick is taken by the highest card of the suit led, or by the highest trump if any are played, and the winner of each trick leads to the next. The contents of the *cotillon* are won by the player who wins most tricks. For winning only one trick, add 2p to the *cotillon*. For winning none, start another pot containing as much as was in the *cotillon* when tricks began, and carry it forward. Taking every trick wins not only the current pot and an additional 1p from each opponent, but also the contents of all these previous pots.

Don't forget . . .
- Play to the left (clockwise) unless otherwise stated.
- Eldest or Forehand means the player to the left of the dealer in left-handed games, to the right in right-handed games.
- T = Ten, p = players, pp = in fixed partnerships, c = cards, † = trump, ☆ = Joker.

6 High-low-Jack family

A number of games current throughout the English-speaking world derive from the Restoration game of All Fours, whose title refers to its four principal scoring points: High, Low, Jack, and the Game.

- *High* is scored by the player dealt the highest trump in play,
- *Low* by the player dealt the lowest trump in play, or (in later versions) winning it in a trick,
- *Jack* by the player capturing the Knave of trumps in a trick, and
- *Game* by the player capturing the greatest value of counting-cards in tricks (or, in later versions, winning the trump Ten).

As not all cards are dealt out, it is possible for Jack to be the only trump in play, in which case it scores three points, one each for High, Low, and Jack.

All Fours may be of Dutch origin, as it was from Holland that the retinue of Charles II arrived when the monarchy was restored. It was subsequently regarded as a low-class game, played mainly in alehouses and 'below stairs' (in servants' quarters), as well as 'below decks' in the British navy. Its great mark of distinction is having bequeathed us the proper name 'Jack' for the card previously known as 'Knave'. In *Great Expectations*, Dickens has Pip betray his social status in Estella's snooty complaint, 'He calls the knaves *Jacks*, this boy!'

All Fours underwent its greatest expansion in the United States, becoming the foremost card game by the beginning of the nineteenth century. Subsequently challenged by Poker and Euchre, it responded not by disappearing but by developing novel elaborations to compete with them for interest.

The modern British descendant of All Fours is an equally lively folk-game called Don. Its relations with mid-nineteenth-century American games are unclear.

All Fours (Seven Up)   2–4 players, 52 cards

> All Fours is a game very much play'd in Kent ... and I have known Kentish
> Gentlemen and others of very considerable note, who have play'd great sums of
> money at It
>
> > Charles Cotton, *The Compleat Gamester* (1674)

> We have played together,
> Many a time and oft, at Put and Crib,
> And at All-Fours have cheated with the best.
>
> > 'Captain Crawley' (G. F. Pardon), *The Card-Player's Manual* (1876)

The ancestral game of All Fours became popular with plantation slaves in America, adopting the name Seven Up from its characteristic target score.

Preliminaries From two to four play, four either cut-throat or in fixed partnerships.

Deal From a 52-card pack deal six cards each in threes, and turn the next as a prospective trump. If it's a Jack, dealer scores 1 point.

Object To win as many as possible of the four points for high (playing the highest trump), low (winning the trick containing the lowest trump in play), Jack (winning a trick with or containing †J), and game (winning the greatest value of cards in tricks).

Cards The rank of cards in descending order, and the value they count towards the point for 'game' when taken in tricks, is:

A	K	Q	J	10	98765432
4	3	2	1	10	0 each

The total value of cards in the pack is therefore 80, but not all of them are likely to be in play.

Choosing trumps Eldest may accept the turn-up as trumps by saying '(I) stand', in which case play begins, or refuse it by saying 'Beg'. If he begs, dealer may accept by saying '(I) give you one', in which case eldest scores 1 point and play begins, or 'Refuse the gift', in which case the turn-up is turned down and the cards are 'run'.

Running the cards If the first turn-up is turned down, three more cards are dealt to each player and the next is turned up. If it is the same suit as before, the cards are run again, and so on until a different suit appears. When a new suit appears, it is automatically entrumped and, if it is a

Jack, the dealer scores 1 point. If none appears before the cards run out, the hands are thrown in and the same dealer deals again.

Discard If the cards were run, everyone reduces their hand to six by discarding the extras face down before play begins. (*Variant*: This is usually ignored if the first run produced a new trump, so there are nine tricks instead of six.)

Play Eldest leads first. Players may freely follow suit or trump, but may renounce only if unable to follow suit. The trick is taken by the highest card of the suit led, or by the highest trump if any are played, and the winner of each trick leads to the next.

Score Up to 6 points may be scored in all: 1 for 'gift', 1 for turning a Jack, if applicable, and thereafter 1 each for high, low, Jack, and game. If two or more players or sides tie for 'game', by taking the same number of card-points, that point is not scored.

Game Play up to 7 points. If tied, the winner is the first to reach 7 as the result of counting high, low, Jack, game, in that order of priority.

Revoke If a player renounces when able to follow suit, he may not score for Jack or game, and each opponent scores 1 point, or 2 if the Jack is in play.

Variants The following are 'book' games, which means they are probably no longer current.

All Fives

(2p, 52c) As All Fours, but with additional scoring features. Upon winning a trick with or containing the trump Ace, a player immediately scores 4 points, the King 3, Queen 2, Jack 1, Ten 10, Five 5. Add 1 point each for high, low, Jack, and the game. In assessing the point for game, the trump Five counts 5, and *all* Aces, Kings, Queens, Jacks and Tens count respectively 4, 3, 2, 1, and 10 each. Game is 61 up, and is best scored on a cribbage board.

California Jack

(2p, 52c) Deal six each in threes and stack the rest, face up. The suit of the top card is trump for the whole of the deal. Non-dealer leads. Second to a trick must follow suit if he can, otherwise may play anything. The winner of a trick draws the top card of stock; the loser draws the next. When the stock is finished the last six tricks are played out as usual. At the end of play either player scores 1 point for high, low, Jack and the game. Game is 10 up.

Shasta Sam

(2p, 52c) As California Jack, but with the stock set face down instead of up. This removes the desirable feature of playing to win or cede the top card of stock, which, in California Jack, is the best part of the game.

Troeven ('Trump')

(4pp, 32c) This simple partnership game, played in southern Limburg, reinforces my suspicion of a Dutch origin for All Fours. Virtually identical is Couillon, or Couyon, played in Normandy on a tournament basis.

Deal a batch of four cards each from a 32-card pack ranking and counting as follows: Ace 4, King 3, Queen 2, Jack 1, T-9-8-7 zero, total 40 card-points. Eldest announces trumps on the basis of the first four cards, then the rest are dealt out in fours. Eldest leads to the first of eight tricks. Players may freely follow suit or play a trump, but may renounce only if unable to follow suit. The trick is taken by the highest card of the suit led, or by the highest trump if any are played, and the winner of each trick leads to the next. If the trump-makers take more card-points, they score 1 game point. If not, they lose 1 game point and their opponents score 1 plus. If tied, the game point is held in abeyance and goes to the winners of the next deal. Play up to 7 game points. (There are versions for two or three players.) [Troeven from: Harry Tiggelovend, *The Playing Card* (XXIV, 6); Couillon from Daynes, *Le Livre de la Belote* (Paris 1996).]

| **Pitch** (Auction Pitch, Setback) | 2–7 players (4 best), 52 cards |

Pitch is a variety of All Fours characterized by the fact that, instead of turning a card for trump, that suit is fixed by whoever bids to win a minimum number of the points available. Furthermore, the trump suit is not announced verbally, but is indicated by 'pitching' – that is, leading a card of that suit to the first trick.

Preliminaries From two to seven play with a 52-card pack ranking AKQJT98765432.

Deal Deal six each in batches of three and stack the rest, face down, out of play.

Object Up to four points are played for in each deal, one each for high, low, Jack and game (see All Fours).

Bidding Each in turn bids to win from 1 to 4 of the points available, without naming a trump (yet). Each bid must be higher than the last. No one may bid more than once.

Dealer's right An optional but common rule permits the dealer to take the previous bid over at the same level. For example, if the bidding goes 'one', 'two', 'three', the dealer may also bid 'three'. But if the first three pass, dealer is obliged to bid at least one.

Play The highest bidder declares trumps by 'pitching' one of them as the lead to the first trick. Players may freely follow suit or trump, but may renounce only if unable to follow suit. The trick is taken by the highest card of the suit led, or by the highest trump if any are played, and the winner of each trick leads to the next.

Score The points for high, low, Jack, and the game go to whoever earns each of them, except that there is no point for game if two players tie for counters. If the pitcher fails to make what he bid, he is set back by the amount of his bid, which can result in a minus score.

Game The game is won by the first player or side to reach an agreed target (e.g. 7, 11, or 21 points, depending on the number of optional scoring features included). If two players reach the target in the same deal, the pitcher wins; or, if neither is the pitcher, the winner is the one who reached it first, counting strictly in order the points for high, low, Jack, and the game. Anyone with zero or a minus score pays a double stake.

Sample deal

North:	♠9 ♥2 ♣AQT4
East:	♠AQ73 ♦6 ♣J
South:	♠85 ♥3 ♣K8 ♦2
West	♠6 ♥Q74 ♦T7

North bids two, hoping to win for 'high' and 'game'. East bids three for the same reasons plus the hope of either winning 'low' with his Three or, more desperately, catching the Jack if it is in play. South and West pass. East pitches the Ace, making spades trump.

	N	E	S	W
1.	♠9	♠A	♠5	♠6
2.	♣4	♠Q	♠8	♥4
3.	♣A	♣J	♣K	♦T
4.	♥2	♦6	♥3	♥7
5.	♣Q	♠3	♦2	♦7
6.	♣T	♠7	♣8	♥Q

At trick 3, West carefully threw his high counter away from the pitcher. At trick 4, East could have trumped, but would eventually have had to lead the ♦6, possibly with disadvantage. He therefore abandons it to a trick which so far contains nothing of value to his opponents.

East wins with points for high, low, and the game, having taken cards counting 20 as against North's 18. Had he trumped at the fourth trick, he would have lost 'game' by North's subsequent discard of ♣T to a losing lead of ♦6.

Variants Pitch is very much a 'pick'n'mix' game. Here are some of the possible ingredients.

Smudge (1)

A player who is not in the hole may bid 4 by announcing 'smudge'. If he then makes 4 he immediately wins the whole game. Dealer cannot take over a bid of smudge.

Smudge (2)

A 'slam' bid to win all six tricks. This counts for a fifth point, and necessarily includes the other 4 – which means you can sensibly bid it only if holding the trump Jack, otherwise you can't be sure of making that particular point.

Racehorse Pitch

A variety played with a 32-card pack (AKQJT987). Game is usually 11 up.

Sell-out

In this version eldest hand either pitches, which automatically counts as a bid of four, or offers the pitch for sale to the highest bidder. If he offers it, the others bid from 1 to 3. Eldest may then pitch for the amount of the highest bid, in which case the player who made it marks that score to his credit. Alternatively, eldest may mark that score himself, in which case the player who bid it becomes the pitcher and leads to the first trick. But an important restriction applies. No player, if invited to bid, may bid as many points as would give eldest the game if he sold it. Conversely, eldest must sell out if the high bidder would otherwise mark enough points to win immediately.

Joker Pitch

If a Joker is added, it ranks as a trump below the Two. It does not, however, count as 'low' but scores an additional (fifth) game point to whoever wins it in a trick. This point is counted after Jack but before 'game'. If the Joker is pitched, it counts as a spade. Joker Pitch has given rise to a range of games involving one or two Jokers, notably the following.

▌ Smear (Ten-point Pitch, Trey Pitch)　　4 or 6 players, 53–54 cards

Lynn King of Lakeview, Texas, tells me, 'I have encountered this variation in locales ranging from eastern New Mexico to southern Nebraska, sometimes by the name Trey Pitch.' John McLeod's Pagat website lists other varieties from Minnesota, Wisconsin and Ontario. Details vary, but the most full-blown version runs as follows.

Preliminaries Four players sitting crosswise in partnerships receive nine cards each from a 54-card pack including two Jokers, or six in two partnerships and sitting alternately receive eight each.

Cards Cards rank AKQJT98765432 except in trumps, where the order is:

　　　A-K-Q-Jack-Jick-T-9-8-7-6-5-4-3-2-Joker-Joker

or, if the Jokers are distinguishable from each other:

　　　A-K-Q-Jack-Jick-High Joker-Low Joker-T-9-8-7-6-5-4-3-2

Jick, the fifth-highest trump, is the other Jack of the same colour as trumps. (Also called the Off-Jack or, as in Euchre, the Left Bower.)

Bidding Each player may bid once only, and each bid must be higher than the last. A bid is an undertaking for the bidder's side to win from 1 to all 10 of the points available in exchange for appointing trumps. Points are:

1 for high	having been dealt the highest trump
1 for low	having been dealt the lowest trump
1 for Jack	capturing the trump Jack
1 for Jick	capturing the Jick
1 for Joker-1	playing the first Joker (or high, if distinguished)
1 for Joker-2	playing the second (or low) Joker
1 for game	capturing the trump Ten
3 for trey	capturing the trump Three

The point for low can't be won for holding either of the Jokers when they rank below the Two.

Some circles don't recognize the Trey point, so the maximum bid is 7, not 10.

Play Trumps declared, everyone discards their non-trumps and is dealt as many replacements as necessary to bring their hand up to six cards (not the eight or nine as dealt). Anyone who was dealt more than six trumps must play the excess number to the first trick: they may not include more than one point-scoring trump, which must be placed on top. The highest bidder pitches to the first trick. All play is in trumps only, and players drop out when they have none left. When necessary, the lead passes to the left of a player who should be on lead but has no trump left. (*Variant:* Such a player may lead a non-trump before folding.)

Game is 21 or 31. If both sides go over in the same deal, points are counted strictly in the order quoted above. If only the non-bidding side reaches or exceeds the target, play continues until a bidding side does go over, and they are the winners even if the other side has more.

Cinch (Pedro, Pidro)
4 players (2 × 2), 52 cards

Other extensions of Pitch attach significance to the trump Five, which is called Pedro and counts 5 points when won in a trick. In Double Pedro, the other Five of the same colour as trumps ranks as a trump between the Five and the Four, and also counts 5, making 14 points in all. The two are distinguished as, respectively, the Right and the Left Pedro. From this derived a fad game called Cinch, in which the point for 'game' was simplified by crediting it to whoever won the trump Ten in a trick. 'Cinch' means to play a trump high enough to prevent an opponent winning with a Pedro. The game originated in Denver, Colorado, around 1885, but is still current in various forms. John McLeod says: 'Pedro (Cinch) is currently popular in the Southern USA (Louisiana, I think) and Central America (e.g. Nicaragua). I recently discovered to my great surprise that an identical game Pidro is enthusiastically played in Österbotten, a Swedish-speaking region in the east of Finland. 83 and 63 are played in Maine, USA.' Here's the US/Finnish version:

Preliminaries Deal nine cards each in threes.

Cards Cards rank normally (AKQJT98765432), except that between the trump Five (Right Pedro) and trump Four there ranks a card called Left Pedro, which is the other Five of the same colour as trumps. This gives 14 trumps, 12 cards in the other suit of its colour, and 13 in each of the others.

Object For the side that announces trumps to win at least as many points for counters as they bid. The counters are:

high	1	game	1 (trump Ten)
low	1	Right Pedro	5
Jack	1	Left Pedro	5

Bidding Each in turn, starting with eldest, may bid once only. A bid is any number from 7 to 14, no suit being mentioned, and each bid must be higher than the last.

Draw and discard The highest bidder announces trumps; all but the dealer discard all their off-suit cards (non-trumps); and dealer then deals enough cards to restore each player's hand to six. Dealer then discards his own non-trumps, sorts through the undealt cards, and adds all the trumps they contain to his own hand. If his hand is less than six, he adds as many off-suit cards as necessary.

Play The bidder leads to the first trick. Players are free to follow suit or trump, as they please, but may renounce only if unable to follow suit. Anyone holding more than six trumps must play the excess to the first trick, leaving five in hand. These are played face up in a stack, of which only the top card counts towards contesting the trick. The others may not include a counter.

The trick is taken by the highest card of the suit led, or by the highest trump if any are played, and the winner of each trick leads to the next.

Score The non-bidders score what they make. So do the bidders if they take at least as many as they bid; otherwise, the amount they bid is deducted from their total.

Game Play up to 62 points. If both sides have 55 or more, the next bidders win the game if they make their bid, regardless of the non-bidders' score; but they lose it if they fail and the non-bidders reach 62. If both sides reach 62 when one of them previously had less than 55, another hand is played, and the side reaching the higher total wins. If tied, the bidders win.

Variations Some set the minimum bid at 6, and require the dealer to bid 7 if the first three players pass. Some score 28 for making all 14 points. Some retain the older rule whereby all hands are reduced to six even if this means discarding trumps, but forbid the discard of counters. Some require the bidder to pitch a trump. Some have abandoned the traditional method of trick-play, and require suit to be followed if possible (probably through ignorance, as it is hard to think of any good reason for doing so deliberately).

Variants

Sixty-Three

As Cinch, but with a maximum of 63 game points to be bid and played for. The additional scores are 25 for winning the trump King, 15 for the Three, and 9 for the Nine. Game is 152 points.

Eighty-Three
Reported by Linda Moran (via the Pagat website) to have been played by her mother's family in Maine for several generations. Four playing in partnerships receive twelve each from a 53-card pack including a Joker, the other five going face down to a kitty. Trumps rank and count as follows:

A	K	Q	J	T	9	8	7	6	5	5	4	3	2	☆	
1	25	20	1	1	9	0	0	0	5	5	0	15	1	0	= 83

Eldest bids first and each bid must be higher than the last. The maximum 83 can be overcalled by '83 double', which simply scores double (166) whether won or lost. Bidding continues until three pass in succession. The highest bidder takes the kitty and declares trump. Everyone discards down to a hand of six. Trumps may not be discarded. A player with more than six trumps may pass the excess to his partner. A side with more than 12 trumps must discard the extras, but these may not include counters. The bidder leads. Players may freely follow suit or trump, but may renounce only if unable to follow suit. The trick is taken by the highest card of the suit led, or by the highest trump if any are played, and the winner of each trick leads to the next. The non-bidders score what they make. So do the bidders if they take at least as many as they bid; otherwise, the amount they bid is deducted from their total. Game is 200 points.

Auction Cinch (Razzle Dazzle)
(5–6p, 52c). Each receives six cards and bids independently (up to 14) but reckoning on the aid of an *ad hoc* partner. The highest bidder then chooses a partner by naming a specific card – often the highest trump – whose holder becomes bidder's partner for that round only. The partner may not reveal himself except by playing the called card, and scores the same as the bidder. Play as at Cinch.

Sancho Pedro
Deal six each, or more if agreed, so long as all have the same number. Bids range from 1 to 18 and the highest bidder pitches. Score points immediately upon capturing any of the following trumps (†). Note that the point for Game is redefined as for capturing the trump Ten.

1 for High	1 for Game (†10)
1 for Low	9 for Sancho (†9)
1 for the Jack	5 for Pedro (†5)

Game is 50 up.

Dom Pedro

As above, but with the addition of 3 for winning †3 ('Dom'). Highest bid is 21.

Snoozer

As either of the above, but with the addition of a Snoozer (Joker). This ranks as a trump below the Two for trick-taking purposes. It counts 15 to whoever wins it in a trick but does not count as 'low' for the winning of that point, which still applies to the otherwise lowest trump in play. Highest bid is 33 without Dom or 36 with. Game is 100 up.

Blind Cinch

(4p, 52c) Deal nine each plus a packet of four each, which remains face down until a high bidder has been established. Highest bidder (maximum 14) adds the four extra cards to his hand before announcing trumps, then he discards seven, reducing his hand to six. Each opponent then does likewise. Play as at Cinch.

Widow Cinch

(6p, 52c) Deal eight each and a face-down widow of four. This is taken by the highest bidder (maximum 14) before naming trumps, who discards six to reduce his holding to six. Others discard two each. Play as at Cinch.

Don
4 players (2 × 2), 52 cards

Evidently derived from the 'Dom' of Pedro, Don is widely played on a league basis in England and Wales. An interesting but regrettable twentieth-century development has been the abandonment of the traditional freedom to follow suit or trump as preferred, in favour of the method of trick-play more appropriate to Whist and Bridge. Whether this has been done out of ignorance, or deliberately because of the higher card-point values, requires further research.

First described is the Lancashire version as played by the Bolton Don League, based on information from Simon Roberts and others (via the Pagat Card-Game Website). It is almost identical to the Blackburn version described by Arthur Taylor in *Pub Games*.

Preliminaries Four play in partnerships. The aim is to win counting cards in tricks. Scores for cards won are pegged on a cribbage board both during the play and at the end of each hand. Game is 91 points (up, down and then up the board again).

Cards Cards rank AKQJT98765432 in plain suits, but in trumps 59AKQJT876432.

Counters The following cards are scored as and when captured in tricks during the course of play:

trump Five	10	trump Queen	2
trump Nine	9	trump Jack	1
trump Ace	4	each non-trump Five	5
trump King	3		

Deal Deal nine cards each in ones and stack the rest face down. The player at dealer's right may not touch his cards until his partner has pitched – just to prevent any possibility of indicating which suit to pitch.

Play Eldest hand pitches a card to the first trick, and its suit establishes trumps. Players must follow suit if possible, otherwise may play any card. The trick is taken by the highest card of the suit led, or by the highest trump if any are played, and the winner of each trick leads to the next. (This differs from the rules of play traditional in this family.)

Score At end of play each side counts the total value of card-points contained in its won tricks, following the traditional schedule of each Ace 4, King 3, Queen 2, Jack 1 and Ten 10. (The theoretical pack total is 80, but some of the counters may not be in play.) The side taking a majority by this schedule pegs an additional 8 points, but neither side does so if equal. Thus the total peggable for the whole deal is 44 for card-points captured during play plus a possible 8 after play.

Play out of turn A player who plays out of turn leaves the offending card face up on the table and must play it as soon as he legally can. In League play, the offending side also deducts 19 points from their score.

Revoke Failing to follow suit when able to do so results in abandonment of the game and a re-deal by the same dealer. In League play, the offending side also deducts 52 points.

Welsh Don

Almost the same game is widely played in South Wales. Play as above, except that trumps rank in their natural order (AKQJT98765432), though the Nine and Five still count respectively 9 and 10 when taken in tricks. Game is 121 up – twice round the board. (Information from Ian Morgan, of the Abercarn Crib and Don League.)

Phat

An even more complex extension of Don, played on a League basis around Norwich, according to Arthur Taylor (1974). All cards are dealt out, thirteen to each player. Peg for the following cards, as and when taken in tricks:

trump Ace	4	trump Nine	18
trump King	3	any other Nine	9
trump Queen	2	trump Five	10
trump Jack	1	any other Five	5

The side capturing a majority of the 80 counters pegs an additional 8 towards game, which is 121 up – twice round a normal Cribbage board or once round a specially made Phat board.

Don't forget . . .
- Play to the left (clockwise) unless otherwise stated.
- Eldest or Forehand means the player to the left of the dealer in left-handed games, to the right in right-handed games.
- T = Ten, p = players, pp = in fixed partnerships, c = cards, t = trump, ☆ = Joker.

7 Point-trick games

These are a miscellaneous collection of card-point games – that is, games where winning and losing depend not on the number of tricks taken but on the point-value of cards taken in tricks. Otherwise, all they have in common is that the card-point values are generally lower than the 'Ace 11, Ten 10' schedule of the great Skat–Bezique–Jass family – typically 5-4-3-2-1, as in Manille.

Manille

3–7 players (4 best), 32 cards

This classic French game originated in Spain, where it is known as Malilla (Catalan Manilla), but spread throughout France in the early twentieth century and for a while looked as if it might become the major national card game. However, its popularity was soon eclipsed by that of Belote, which now occupies that position together with French Tarot, and Manille is now (according to *Le Guide Marabout*) vigorous only in the south-west of the country. It forms a good introduction to point-trick games for players accustomed only to plain-trick games. There are several varieties for several different numbers of players. The most straightforward is Manille muette (Manille without talking), as follows:

Preliminaries Four players sitting crosswise in partnerships play with a 32-card pack consisting of AKQJT987 in each suit. A game is won by the side that first wins two deals, or (if preferred) by the first side to reach an agreed target score, such as 100 or 200 points. All play goes to the right.

Deal Deal eight cards each in fours. Dealer turns his last card face up for trumps and leaves it on the table until the first card has been led.

Card values and object Cards rank TAKQJ987 in each suit and count as follows:

each Ten (*manille*)	5
each Ace (*manillon*)	4
each King	3

| each Queen | 2 |
| each Jack | 1 |

These total 60, and each trick counts 1 point, making 68 in all. The aim is to win a majority of points – 35 or more.

Play Eldest leads to the first trick and the winner of each trick leads to the next. The rules of trick-play vary, depending on who is currently winning the trick to which you are playing.

• If your partner is winning, you are required to follow suit only if you can, otherwise you may play any card.
• If an opponent is winning, you must not only follow suit but also head the trick if possible and, if unable to follow a plain suit lead, you must play a winning trump if possible. If unable either to follow suit or to play a winning trump, you may play as you please.

The trick is taken by the highest card of the suit led or by the highest trump if any are played.

Score The side with the higher score wins.

Manille Parlée (Manille with Talking)

(4pp, 32c). This more popular variety permits spoken communication between partners, but only in accordance with strict rules. When about to lead to a trick, you may give your partner a single piece of information about your hand, or request such information about your partner's, or you may instead invite your partner either to do the same or to give you some instruction as to what card or suit to lead. Such information may relate to the number of cards held of a specific suit or rank, or whether a particular card is held. Question and answer must be succinct, explicit, intelligible to the opponents, and not replaced or accompanied by any non-verbal conventions. Questions must be answered truthfully, and instructions followed if possible.

Auction Manille, I

(3–7p, 32c) Deal all the cards out evenly. If two or four are left over, leave them, face down, as a widow.

Each in turn, starting with eldest, may pass or declare, and the first to declare becomes the declarer. The declarer's object is to take at least 21 points in tricks and cards, or at least 15 if more than four are playing.

Before play, declarer may draw any number of cards from the widow and discard a like number before announcing trumps.

The amount won by the declarer from each opponent if successful, or paid to each if not, varies with the number of cards exchanged – for example, 4-3-2-1, 8-4-2-1, 10-6-3-1, as agreed.

Auction Manille, II

(3–7p, 32c) Remove as many Sevens as necessary to enable everyone to receive the same number of cards. Each in turn, starting with eldest, may pass or bid. A bid states the number of points the bidder undertakes to make in exchange for choosing trumps. Each bid must be higher than the last, and a player who has passed may not come in again. The highest bidder announces a trump suit, or declares no trump, and eldest leads to the first trick – unless the bid was to win every trick, in which case the bidder leads. The bidder scores the amount bid if successful, or loses it if not. Everyone deals the same number of times, and the winner is the player with the highest score after any agreed number of deals.

Auction Manille, III

(3–7p, 32c) A number of cards are dealt to each player in a particular manner, and the rest are laid, some face up and some face down, on the table, as follows:

players	deal each	remainder
3	9 (3-3-3)	3 down, 2 up
4	7 (3-2-3)	2 down, 2 up
5	6 (2-2-2)	1 down, 1 up
6	5 (3-2)	1 down, 1 up
7	4 (2-2)	2 down, 2 up

Play as in Version II, above, but the highest bidder may exchange cards with the widow before naming trumps. In some circles the score is doubled if the bidder undertakes to win every trick, or plays without exchanging. If both apply, it is quadrupled.

Butifarra

(4pp, 32c). A popular Catalan game. My Spanish–English dictionary defines *butifarra* as 'Catalonian sausage; ill-fitting trousers; ham sandwich'. Take your pick.

Four players sitting crosswise in partnerships (and ill-fitting trousers) are dealt twelve cards each in fours from a 48-card pack ranking 9AKQJ8765432 in each suit. Each Nine (*manilla*) counts 5 points, A-K-Q-J count 4-3-2-1 respectively. An additional 1 point per trick makes 72 points in all, and the declaring side must take at least 37 to win. Play to the right.

The dealer may announce trumps, declare *butifarra* (no trumps), or delegate this choice to his partner, who must then exercise it. Either opponent may double, and either declarer may then redouble. Eldest leads, and tricks are played as at Manille. The winning side scores whatever it makes, doubled if played at no trump, and in any case doubled or quadrupled if doubled or redoubled.

Spanish Solo

3 players, 36 cards

A variety of Manille with bidding, once popular throughout Spain and Latin America.

Preliminaries Three players use a 36-card pack, typically consisting of AKQJ76543 in each suit. The game is played for hard score (coins or counters). The Spanish suits of ◊ clubs, ⚔ swords, ⊠ cups, ❂ coins, are equivalent to the French ones of ♣ ♠ ♥ ♦, respectively.

Deal The turn to deal and play passes to the right. It is customary to shuffle at the start of a game, but not between deals. Each player antes one chip to the pool. Deal twelve cards each in fours.

Rank and value The top cards in each suit rank and count as follows:

Seven	5
Ace	4
King	3
Queen	2
Jack	1

The Seven is called *mallilla*. The card-point total is 60, but each trick also counts 1 point, bringing the total available to 72.

Bidding Each in turn, starting with eldest, must pass or make a higher bid than any gone before. A player who passes adds a chip to a pool, and is then out of the auction. The bids are:

- *Juego* (solo). To take at least 37 points in cards and tricks, or 36 if bid by eldest. Scores 2, or 4 in diamonds.
- *Bola* (slam). To win every trick, after first naming a wanted card and receiving it from its holder in return for any unwanted card. Scores 8, or 12 in diamonds.
- *Solo*, or *Bola sin pedir* (no-call slam). To win every trick without first calling a wanted card. Scores 16, or 20 in diamonds.

The highest bidder becomes the soloist and announces trumps. No suit is named while bidding unless the proposed trump is diamonds, as this always beats the same bid in a different suit.

If all pass, the dealer names trumps, all play for themselves, and whoever takes most points wins.

Play Eldest leads to the first trick. Players must follow suit if possible, otherwise may play any card. The trick is taken by the highest card of the suit led, or by the highest trump if any are played, and the winner of each trick leads to the next.

Pay-off The soloist receives the appropriate amount from each opponent if successful, otherwise he pays that amount to each opponent.

Comment Sources do not state what happens to the pool. Probably it goes to the soloist if successful, who doubles it if not. Nor do they state the pay-off for the case when all pass and all play alone. It would be reasonable for whoever takes fewest points to pay 2 to whoever takes most.

Nor do they adequately detail two optional misère bids. In *bola pobre*, the soloist aims to lose every trick after first calling a wanted card in exchange for an unwanted one. *Bola pobre sin pedir* is the same, but without calling a card. It is unstated where these fit into the bidding hierarchy, whether they are played with or without trumps, and how they are valued.

Fifteens (Fünfzehnern)

4 players (or 3), 32 cards

This old German game belongs here by virtue of its 5-4-3-2-1 card-point system.

Preliminaries Four players each receive eight cards dealt singly from a 32-card pack ranking AKQJT987. Three may play by omitting a suit and playing with 24 cards. Aces count 5 each, Kings 4, Queens 3, Jacks 2, Tens 1, making a total of 15 per suit and 60 in all.

Play Eldest leads. Players must follow suit if possible, otherwise may play any card. The trick is taken by the highest card of the suit led, and the winner of each trick leads to the next. There are no trumps. Each player counts the total value of the cards he has won in tricks, and either pays 1 chip to the pot for each point by which he fell short of 15, or wins 1 for each point by which he exceeded that number. An optional rule is that if two players win all the tricks between them, they divide the pot equally.

In case this sounds too simple to be true, here's the inevitable complication.

Inevitable complication Upon winning the lead, you must not only continue leading the suit in which you just won the trick (if possible), but you must also, if possible, start by leading any winners you may hold in that suit. Only if void of that suit may you lead from another. The second player to win the lead must also, if possible, lead his winners of the suit by which he came in. When he has none of these, he must, if possible, return to the suit of the first player who won tricks. The same applies again, in that no player may break into a new suit until he has led from the suit by which he gained entry, or the previously played suit or suits.

Forced play A King and Queen of the same suit in one hand is a 'force' (*Zwang*). A player holding a force in a suit of which the Ace has yet to be played may announce 'force' upon leading the Queen. This forces the Ace-holder to play it and win the trick, leaving the King high. Unless the leader declares 'force', the Ace-holder is free to underplay in hope of winning the King later.

Forty for Kings (Quarante de Roi, Vierzig vom König)

4 players (or 3), 32 cards

An eighteenth-century game of some interest.

Preliminaries Four players sitting crosswise in partnerships receive eight cards each in batches of 3-2-3 from a 32-card pack ranking KQJAT987. Dealer exposes his last card to establish trumps. Play to the right.

Cliques Each in turn announces and scores for any cliques he may hold. A clique is three or four court cards of the same kind. The scores for four or three of each court, and its individual score when captured in a trick, are:

	four	three	each
Kings	40	10	5
Queens	20	8	4
Jacks	13	6	3

Play Eldest leads. Players must follow suit if possible, otherwise may play any card. (*Variant*: Some sources say they need not follow suit but may play any card they like.) The trick is taken by the highest card of the suit led, or by the highest trump if any are played, and the winner of each trick leads to the next.

Score Each partnership scores for all the courts they have captured and adds these to their score for cliques. Game is 150 points.

Comment Anton (1889) mentions scores of 50, 60, 70 and 80 for 'valid cliques of five or more'. Presumably these are sequences of five to eight cards in the same suit.

Tressette

4 players (2 × 2), 40 cards

Tressette is one of Italy's major national card games, together with Scopone and Briscola. Although it appears very old, in that it lacks trumps, and ranks Threes and Twos above Aces, it is known only from the early eighteenth century. Its name, meaning 'three Sevens', may refer to a scoring combination no longer recognized, or to the fact that it is played up to 21. The game appears in many formats and for any number of players up to eight. Mediatore is a non-partnership version for four, Rovescino a trick-avoidance variety, Madrasso a uniquely Venetian hybrid of Tressette and Briscola. Described below are the standard partnership game for four and a classic three-hander popular in Lombardy under the name Terziglio, sometimes called Calabresella. Sources: Giampaolo Dossena, *Giochi di Carte Italiani* (Milan, 1984); Rino Fulgi Zaini, *Giochi di Carte* (Milan, 1934-77), Anon., *Giochi di Carte* (Milan, 1969).

Preliminaries Four players sit crosswise in partnerships and play to the right.

Cards A standard 40-card pack, lacking numerals 8–10, with suitmarks of swords, batons, cups, coins (♤ ♯ ♨ ✿ equivalent to ♠ ♣ ♥ ♦), and courts of Re (King), Cavall (Knight), Fante (Footsoldier).

Object A stake is agreed, and the winners are the first side to reach a score of 21, 31 or 51 (as agreed) over as many deals as necessary. Points accrue for declaring combinations, winning card-points in tricks, and winning the last trick.

Rank and value of cards Cards rank and count in descending order as follows:

3	2	A	K	Q	J	7	6	5	4
1/3	1/3	1	1/3	1/3	1/3	0	0	0	0

Any fractions occurring in the final total are ignored (they are said to 'drop on the floor').

Deal Deal ten cards each in two batches of five. A player whose counters total less than 1 point may annul the hand, and the same dealer deals again.

Declarations Before the opening lead, a player dealt a particular card combination may announce '*Buon gioco*', then declare and score it when the trick is over (regardless of who won it). The valid combinations are:

Four Threes, Twos or Aces:	4 points
Three Threes, Twos or Aces:	3 points
3-2-A of a suit (*napoletana*):	3 points
All 10 cards of a suit (*napoletana decima*):	wins the game outright.

The suit of a napoletana must be stated, as must the suit missing from three of a kind. It may be agreed not to include combinations, in which case the game is normally played up to 21.

Play Eldest leads. Players must follow suit if possible, otherwise may play any card. The trick is taken by the highest card of the suit led, and the winner of each trick leads to the next. There are no trumps.

Signals Each player, upon leading to a trick, may signal to his partner by making an announcement or performing an equivalent action as follows.

- *Busso* (bunch one's fist on the table): 'Win the trick if you can, and return this suit.'
- *Volo* (slide the card slowly on to the table): 'This is the last or only card I have of this suit.'
- *Striscio* (skim the card rapidly on to the table): 'This is my best suit.'

The third convention is not always admitted.

Score The side winning the last trick scores an extra point. The total value of points available in one deal is $11^{2}/_{3}$, rounded down to 11 by counting 1 for each group of three fractional cards and ignoring the final fraction. Normally, the game ends as soon as one side claims to have reached 21, any remaining cards being left unplayed. If the claim is correct, that side wins the stake (even if the others scored more without claiming); if it is false, they lose it. Alternatively, any of the following special events ends the game:

- *Cappotto.* One side takes all ten tricks. This wins a double stake.
- *Cappottone.* A single player takes all ten tricks. This wins sixfold.
- *Stramazzo.* One side takes all the counters, but not all the tricks. This wins treble. Its also prevents the losing side from scoring a point for winning the last trick, as also does:
- *Strammazzone.* A single player takes all the counters, but the opponents win at least one trick. This wins eightfold.
- *Collatondrione.* A player declares all 10 of a suit. This wins sixteenfold.

Comment The challenge of Tressette lies in accommodating oneself to the absence of trumps. This increases the incidence of 'squeezing', whereby players unable to follow suit may be uncertain which other suits to discard and which to keep guarded. It also tends to reduce the amount of information obtainable by conventional play, which is why partners are instead allowed to convey information through conventional announcements. Scoring for declarations also imparts useful information, and is therefore significant to the play in a way that scoring for honours in Whist and Bridge is not.

Variants

Tressette con la Chiamata del Tre

(4p) A version with floating instead of fixed partnerships. After each deal, eldest hand before leading to the first trick calls a suit in which he lacks the Three. Whoever holds that card becomes his partner for the deal, sharing in any wins or losses, but may reveal himself only by playing the called card.

Rovescino

(3–8p) This is the negative member of the Tressette family, the main aim being to avoid taking card-points in tricks. Its name originally applied to an early seventeenth-century game, the ancestor of Reversis and, ultimately, Hearts. In fact it has many names (Traversone, Perdivinci, Vinciperdi, Ciapanò and others) and is played throughout Italy in a multiplicity of local variations.

Deal all the cards out until everyone has the same number and as many as possible. Any leftovers are dealt face down to the table as a monte. Play as at Tressette. The monte, if any, goes to the last trickwinner, together with any card-points it may contain. Points are counted and rounded down as at Tressette, including one for last, but are recorded as negative or penalty points. The first to reach 21 loses, or the winner is the player with the lowest score when that happens.

Four or more may play it as an elimination game, with each successive loser dropping out of play until only three remain.

Tressette in Due

(2p) Deal ten each and play as above, but leave 20 face down as a stock. So long as any cards remain in stock the winner of each trick draws the top card, waits for the other to do likewise, then leads to the next trick.

Terziglio (Calabresella)   3 players, 40 cards

See, those priests enter a café . . . They call for cards, and sit down to their
national game. The glassy eyes become bright, and the dull countenances full
of life. They are playing Calabrasella [*sic*], which we mentioned last month, and
which we now proceed to explain.

'Cavendish' (Henry Jones), *The Westminster Papers* (Nov. 1870)

Cavendish's misspelling of Calabresella, now more often known as
Terziglio, and his rationalization of the scoring system by multiplying
everything by three, resulted in an inaccurate English-language description that remained current through much of the twentieth century.

Preliminaries Terziglio is Tressette for three players, using the same
cards and card-point system as in the parent game (see above), but
disregarding card combinations.

Deal Deal twelve cards each and spread the last four face down, forming
a *monte*.

Object The overall aim is to be the first to reach 21 points. In each
deal, one person plays against two with the aim of capturing in tricks
cards totalling at least 6 of the 11 points available for counters and the
last trick

Bidding Each bids in turn, starting with eldest. Each successive bid
must be higher than the last, and a player who has once passed may
not come in again. The bids from low to high are:

- *Chiamo* (Call). The soloist plays after calling for a card lacking from
  his hand, and receiving it from its holder in exchange for any card
  he doesn't want. If the called card is in the monte, he may not call
  another. Having called, he turns the monte face up for all to see,
  adds it to his hand, and makes any four discards face down in its
  place. Whoever wins the last trick will win the monte, and benefit
  from any card-points it may contain.

- *Solo*. The soloist doesn't call a card, just takes the monte and discards
  as above.

- *Solissimo*. The soloist plays without calling a card or taking the monte,
  which remains face down and out of play.

- *Solissimo aggravate*. The soloist not only does not take the monte,
  he even allows the opponents to use it. If he says, 'Half each' (*Dividete*),

each of them takes two cards without showing them, and makes any two discards, face down, also without showing them. If he says, 'You choose' (*Scegliete*), they turn the four face up and may agree to split them 2–2, 3–1 or 4–0. Each then discards, face down, as many as he took.

Pass-out (optional rule). If all pass without bidding, the monte is left intact and the hands are gathered up and redealt by the same dealer without being shuffled. This time, the minimum bid is a solo.

Play Eldest normally leads to the first trick, but it may be previously agreed that the soloist always leads in a bid of solissimo. Players must follow suit if possible, otherwise may play any card. The trick is taken by the highest card of the suit led, and the winner of each trick leads to the next. There are no trumps. The two opponents may not signal or communicate with one another unless so agreed beforehand.

Score Whoever wins the last trick not only scores 1 point for last but also wins the monte as if it were an extra trick. The soloist counts the points he has won in tricks, as in Tressette, ignoring fractions. If he has taken at least 6 points, he scores the appropriate amount, or is paid it by each opponent; if not, each opponent scores the appropriate amount, or is paid it by the soloist. The appropriate amounts are: call 1, *solo* 2, *solissimo* 4, *aggravato dividete* 8, *aggravato scegliete* 16. The appropriate score is doubled for winning every trick, or trebled for taking all 11 points without winning every trick.

Game Normally 21 points, but 31 or 51 may be agreed.

Comment The main aim in exchanging through the monte is to secure guards for your Aces and only secondarily to replace low cards with high ones. If not leading to the first trick, you need at least all four suits headed by 3, or 2-A, or A-x-x, or three suits headed 3-2. Given the lead, a single suit will do, if it is long enough and headed by top cards. Play centres largely on the trapping or saving of Aces and winning the last trick. The partners must study each other's play carefully to discover their strong suits.

Stovkahra (Trappola) — 4 players (2 × 2), 32 cards

> The whole male population of Šumice seems to know the game; they play fast, enthusiastically and loudly, banging the cards down on the table. Many of the players are farmers; in the winter months when they have little to do, and are sometimes cut off from the outside world for long periods by snow, they play cards every day.
>
> John McLeod, *The Playing-Card* (XXVI, 2)

Playing-card enthusiasts have long been fascinated by a pack of cards called Trappola, bearing Italian suitmarks and courtly figures, but distinguished by its peculiar omission of numerals Three to Six. Early researchers were mystified by the regular appearance of examples from different parts of Europe at different periods of time, suggesting various lines of continuity that no one could disentangle convincingly. Some considered it to be the oldest European pack, perhaps ancestral to the Tarot. We know from Cardano, 'the gambling scholar', that Trappola was played in Venice as early as 1524, and was probably invented there. By the end of that century it was no longer played in Italy, but was beginning to fan outwards. It continued in Bohemia and Moravia under the names Trapulka, shortened to Bulka, and Šestadvacet (meaning 'Twenty-six', from a significant score), certainly until the nineteenth century and perhaps into the twentieth. In the eighteenth and nineteenth centuries it flourished in Austria and southern Germany under the alias Hundertspiel, from its target score of 100 points, while the closely related game of Špády persisted in Silesia and Czechoslovakia into the twentieth century. Trappola cards were last manufactured at Prague in 1944. A Greek dimension is also suggested by the fact that the everyday Greek word for any pack of cards is *trapoula*.

Field researches conducted in 1997 by Tomáš Svoboda of Prague have now established that Trappola survives under the name Stovkahra (the Hundred-Game), or Brčko (a splinter or matchstick), which is still played in the Romanian village of Šumice (population 500). Šumice is one of nine villages which are all that remain of a Czech community settled in the Banát region in the early nineteenth century. Trappola cards being no longer available, the game has been adapted for play with the readily obtainable 32-card German-suited pack. It is distinguished by bonuses for winning tricks with the lowest card of a suit, the Seven. Originally the key card was a Two, which explains the original omission of numerals Three to Six instead of the more usual Two to Five.

This description is based on a revision of an article by John McLeod in *The Playing-Card* (Sept.–Oct. 1997), itself based on Svoboda's findings.

Preliminaries Four players sit crosswise in partnerships and play to the left. The aim is to be the first side to reach 100 points. Points are scored for declaring card combinations, for taking card-points in tricks, for winning any trick with a Seven, especially the first, and for winning the last trick, especially with a Seven.

Cards The game is normally played with a 32-card German-suited pack, with ♣ acorns, ♠ leaves, ♥ hearts and ♦ bells equivalent to ♣ ♠ ♥ ♦ respectively. Cards rank in descending order as follows, and the top four have point-values as shown:

Ace	King	Over (*svršek*)	Under (*spodek*)	10	9	8	7
6	5	4	3	0	0	0	0

Deal Shuffle the cards only at start of play. In subsequent deals they are merely cut by the player at dealer's right. The bottom card of the pack is displayed after the cut to establish trumps. Deal eight cards each in batches of 3-2-3, all face down except the first batch of three to eldest hand. These go face up, purportedly to compensate the dealer's side for not having the first lead.

Declarations A player holding three or four of a kind, other than Eights or Nines, can declare them before the opening lead. They score as follows:

	four	three
Aces	40	30
Tens, Sevens	20	10
Kings, Overs, Unders	12	6

Combinations need not be declared, but score only if they are. Declarations must specify how many cards are held and of which rank, but not necessarily which card is missing from a set of three.

If a player believes that a combination just scored by his side brings their total to 100+ points, he can end the game by announcing '*dost*' (enough). The same applies upon winning any of the bonuses scored in the play. A false claim loses the game.

Play When all declarations have been made, eldest leads to the first trick. Players must follow suit and win the trick if possible; must trump if unable to follow a plain-suit lead; and may renounce only if unable to do either. The trick is taken by the highest card of the suit led, or by the highest trump if any are played, and the winner of each trick leads to the next. The following bonuses accrue as they occur:

winning the first trick with a Seven	52
winning an intermediate trick with a Seven	10
winning the last trick with a Seven	26
winning the last trick other than with a Seven	6

Score To the score for declared combinations and for winning particular tricks, each side adds the total value of counting-cards they have taken in tricks. (These total 72.)

The first team to reach 100 points or more wins a game, for which they get one matchstick (*brčko*) if the losers had 50 or more points, or two matchsticks if they failed to reach 50. A game ended by a call of '*dost*' scores the same, but if the claim proves false the other side get two matchsticks regardless of their own score.

The winners may, if they prefer, deduct one or two matchsticks from the opposing team's winnings instead of adding to their own. This has the effect of lengthening the session, which is won overall by the first side to collect 10 or more matchsticks.

Comment A partnership wins with a correct claim of *dost* even if the other side had already reached 100 without claiming it or, on examination, find they have a larger score. This makes it important to claim 100 as soon as you make it, otherwise you risk letting the other side win with a correct claim first.

The only way of winning the first trick with a Seven, for the huge bonus of 52, is to trump a plain-suit lead with the Seven. If the player to dealer's right has the Seven of trumps and is void in another suit, it is accepted practice for him to signal to the leader to play this suit by mouthing its name when the opponents are not looking. (But no penalty is specified for doing so when they *are* looking.)

It may be agreed that when a side reaches 10 matchsticks, play continues up to 20. If then the same side also reaches 20 first, they win a double series; if not, the result is a draw.

▌Roque

There is a group of card-point games in which Kings and Tens count 10 each, and Fives 5 each, making 25 per suit and 100 in total. This schedule is common to many Chinese games, not all of them trick-takers, and some of them highly convoluted. But it is also found elsewhere, and the relatively straightforward Iranian game of Roque (communicated by 'Babak' on the Internet) makes a good starting point, though the high-scoring card is not the King but the Ace. Roque is remarkably similar to an American game played with proprietary 'Rook' cards, and it would be interesting to know who got what from whom.

Preliminaries Four players sit crosswise in partnerships and play to the right.

Cards Deal twelve cards each, in batches of four, from a 52-card pack ranking AKQJT98765432. The last four go, face down, to the table.

Object For the declaring side to win at least the number of points it contracted in exchange for nominating trumps. Points are scored for winning tricks (5 each), Aces and Tens (10 each), and Fives (5 each) – a total of 165.

Auction Each in turn, starting with eldest, bids to win a minimum number of points, which must exceed that of any previous bid. The lowest bid is 85. No trump suit is mentioned in the auction.

Play Declarer takes the four table cards, discards any four, face down, which will count as a won trick to the declaring side, and leads to the first trick. The suit of the card led is automatically trump. Players must follow suit if possible, otherwise may play any card. The trick is taken by the highest card of the suit led, or by the highest trump if any are played, and the winner of each trick leads to the next.

Score The non-declarers always score what they make. So do the declarers if successful, with a special score of 250 for winning all 13 tricks. If not, they lose the amount of their bid, doubled if they take less than their opponents. The scores are recorded like this:

125 /	135	30	= bid 125, made 135 to opponents' 30.
125 /	−125	50	= bid 125, made only 115 to opponents' 50.
125 /	−250	90	= bid 125, made only 75 to opponents' 90.

Game Play up to 505 points, or any other agreed total.

Roque for three

Omit ♣2, deal fifteen each and six face down to the table. The lowest bid is 95, the highest 185. As in the four-hand game, the counting cards total 100, but there are 15 tricks at 5 points each, and the declarer's six discards count 10, making 185 in all. The slam score is 350. Game is 650.

Da Bai Fen ('Competing for a Hundred') 4 players (2 × 2), 54 cards

A rich and skill-demanding Chinese game, first described by John McLeod in *The Playing-Card* (Vol. VIII, No. 3). (A similar game for six to twelve players in *ad hoc* partnerships, appropriately called Zhao Pengyou, 'Looking for Friends', appears on the Pagat website. Unfortunately, it would take about ten pages to explain here.)

Format Four players sit crosswise in partnerships and play to the right. The full game can go on for hours, but may be shortened by prior agreement.

Cards Use a 54-card pack including Jokers distinguishable as black and red. In each deal there are eighteen trumps: the two jokers, plus all the cards of a suit appointed trump during the deal (the trump suit), plus all four cards of a particular rank (the trump rank), which at the beginning of the game is the Two. Trumps run from highest to lowest as follows:

1. Red Joker
2. Black Joker
3. The card of the trump rank and suit (e.g. ♠2 initially if spades are trump)
4–6. The other three cards of the trump rank (e.g. ♥2, ♣2, ♦2, all equal-ranking)
7–18. A-K-Q-J-T-9-8-7-6-5-4-3-2 (omitting the card of the trump rank)

Cards in plain suits rank AKQJT98765432, omitting the trump rank.

Object To win counting-cards in tricks, and to win the last trick. The counters are: each King 10, each Ten 10, each Five 5, making 25 in each suit and 100 in all.

Declarers and opponents In the first hand the declaring partnership is that of the player who first draws a Two in the deal. In subsequent hands the declarership remains with the previous declarers until they lose a contract, when it passes to their opponents.

Deal Cards are not dealt in western fashion but are drawn from a stock in Chinese fashion. For the first hand one player is randomly designated the Starter. The Starter shuffles the cards, has them cut by either opponent, and sets the pack face down on the table. He then draws the top card of stock to start his hand, and each in turn to the right does likewise until everyone has 12 cards and six remain untaken. A trump suit may be declared during the draw as follows.

Trumps The trump rank is always that which corresponds to the score of the declarers. At the beginning of the game, each side starts with a score of 2 points, thus making Twos the initial trump rank. During the draw, a player who draws a card of the trump rank may set it face up on the table and declare its suit trump. He need not do this immediately – or even at all – but may hold on to it until he sees how his hand is shaping up and declare it later. He may not, however, consult with his partner. Note that the trump suit is always that of the first player to declare it, and any player who previously drew a card of the trump rank without declaring it has no comeback.

Last six cards In the first hand the Leader is the player who declared trumps; in subsequent hands, the Starter is also the Leader. Assuming a trump suit has been declared, the Leader takes the last six cards into hand without showing them, and discards any six face down out of play. (*Variant*: In some circles the six undealt cards are exposed before being taken into hand.) The Leader's discards are not shown until the end of play, and must be kept separate from all other cards that are played out.

In the rare event that no one declared trumps during the draw, the Starter turns the last six cards face up, one at a time. The first card of the trump rank to appear establishes the trump suit, and the rest are not exposed. If none of the trump rank appear, the trump suit is that of the highest of the six exposed cards (other than Jokers), or the first exposed of equally high cards.

Trumpless hands Any player who has not a single one of the 18 trumps may, before the opening lead, expose his hand and claim a draw, but may not consult his partner about this. This happens so rarely, and the consequences are so elaborate, that the best thing to do is shuffle the cards and go through the whole procedure again.

Play The Leader leads to the first trick, and the winner of each trick leads to the next. A player may lead any single card (I use the term 'singleton' for this) or several cards of the same suit, but he may lead several only if all of them are the highest cards remaining of that suit in anybody's hand. In other words, they must be unbeatable unless trumped. Failure to meet this requirement constitutes a revoke, for which the penalty is that play ceases and the offended side scores as if it had won every trick. Note that a led singleton need not be the highest remaining of its suit.

Each of the others in turn must play as many cards as were led, and must follow suit as far as possible. Having run out of that suit, they may play as they please.

A singleton trick is taken by the highest card of the suit led, or by the highest trump if any are played. A multiple trick is taken by the highest card of the suit led, unless one or more followers had none of that suit and played as many trumps as cards led, in which case it is taken by the highest trump played. Of equally high trumps, the first played always prevails.

As play proceeds, the opponents extract from their won tricks all Kings, Tens and Fives, and place them face up on the table in front of one of them. All other cards won by both sides go face down to a single wastepile.

Score At end of play the declarer's six discards are turned up, and any counters they may contain count double (20, 20, 10) to the opponents if they won the last trick. The outcome is based on how many card-points were won by the opponents. This determines who scores how many game points (column 2 in the Table below), who will be the declarers for the next hand (column 3), and who is to be the Starter/Leader in the next hand, as follows:

opponents' card-points	score	declarers in next hand	next hand started by
0	declarers 2	as before	previous leader's partner
5–35	declarers 1	as before	previous leader's partner
40–75	no score	as before	previous leader's partner
80–95	opponents 1	opponents	previous leader's right opponent
100+	opponents 2	opponents	previous leader's right opponent

> Example: Both sides start at 2 game points. In the first hand South declared trumps upon drawing a Two, and East–West took 15 card-points. The Declarers score 1, bringing North–South to a total of 3 game points and leaving them as declarers in the next hand with North as the Starter/Leader. Because they now have 3 game points, the trump rank in the next hand will be Threes.

Game Each side's score is represented by the rank of the card that will be trumps when they become declarers. For example, when they have 10 game points they are on Tens, 11 puts them on Jacks, 12 on Queens, 13 on Kings, and 14 on Aces. A side wins the whole game when they reach Aces and win a hand with Aces as the trump rank.

Shorter game To shorten the game, it may be agreed to play up to a lower rank, for example from Twos to Sevens, or (McLeod's recommendation) to start at Sevens and play up to the Aces.

Comment A multiple lead is normally made in the expectation that each opponent has at least one card of the suit led and so cannot win by ruffing, or does not have enough trumps to match the number of cards led. For this reason it is neither usual nor useful to lead multiple trumps, though it is not illegal.

Zheng Fen ('Competing for Points') 3–6 players, 54 cards

A cross between a point-trick game such as Da Bai Fen and a climbing game such as Zheng Shàngyóu, this Chinese oddity was first described, in *Die Pöppel-Revue*, by Axel Schmale, who learnt it in China during a railway journey. The following is based on John McLeod's English rewrite.

Preliminaries Three to six players play to the right.

Cards 54, including two distinguishable Jokers. They rank: High Joker, Low Joker, then 2AKQJT9876543 in each suit.

Object To win counters in tricks, counting 10 for each King and Ten, and 5 for each Five, making 100 in all.

First deal The pack is cut by the player to the right of the shuffler and set face down on the table. Each in turn, starting with the cutter, draws a card from the top of the pack and takes it into hand. This continues until all 54 have been taken. It doesn't matter if some players have one more than others.

Play Whoever holds ♥3 leads to the first round. The leader may play any of the combinations listed in the table below. Each in turn thereafter must either pass or else play a combination which is (a) of the same type as the one led and (b) higher in rank than any so far played to that round. Alternatively, they may play one of the three special combinations, which in its turn can be beaten only by a higher special combination.

Play may continue for several rounds. A player who has once passed is still permitted to play if the turn comes round to him again. The round ends, however, when one person plays and everyone else passes. Whoever played last (and highest) may not play again, but wins all the cards played to that round. The winner of a round leads to the next, and is free to play any of the legal combinations.

combination	definition or example	won by
singleton	one card	highest card
pair	two of the same rank	highest pair
triplet	three of the same rank	highest triplet
quartet	four of the same rank	highest quartet
pair sequence	at least three pairs in sequence, e.g. 2-2-A-A-K-K	highest cards, or, if equal, longest sequence
triple sequence	at least three triplets in sequence, e.g. Q-Q-Q-J-J-J-T-T-T	highest cards, or, if equal, longest sequence
quadruple sequence	e.g. 9-9-9-9-8-8-8-8-7-7-7-7	highest cards, or, if equal, longest sequence
suit sequence	at least five in suit and sequence, e.g. ♥7-6-5-4-3	highest cards, or, if equal, longest sequence

full house	triplet and two cards: the two must be:	highest triplet (the other two cards have no effect)
	(a) of the same rank (e.g. 7-7), or	
	(b) of the same suit and consecutive in rank (e.g. ♣7-♣6), or	
	(c) any two counters (e.g. K-5), or	
	(d) a Three and any other card	
special (1)	King-Ten-Five not all the same suit	beats any of the above, but is beaten by special (2) and special (3)
special (2)	King-Ten-Five of the same suit	beats any of the above, but is beaten by special (3)
special (3)	four Twos	beats everything

Jokers are wild, and one or both may represent any natural card(s) in any combination except

(a) a singleton, where the High Joker beats everything, and the Low Joker beats any natural card; and

(b) any of the three special combinations.

☞ There is no ranking of suits, and in no circumstance may you play a combination equal in rank to that of the previous player. For example, you cannot follow 8-8-8 with 8-☆-☆, or vice versa; nor 9-9-9-A-A with 9-☆-☆-3-6, or vice versa.

A player who runs out of cards drops out of play. If that player was due to lead, having won the round, the lead passes to the next active player on the right. When the penultimate active player runs out, the only player with cards remaining is allowed, if able, to win the round by playing a higher combination. It is highly advantageous to be the first out of cards and severely disadvantageous to be the last.

Score Before the scoring, whoever was the last left in must surrender all the cards they won in tricks, plus any cards still remaining in their hand, to the player who went out first. Everyone scores the total value of all the counters they have won (which will be zero in the case of the last left in). The scores for each deal will total 100.

Second and subsequent deals Whoever came last in the previous hand shuffles the cards and sets them down when they have been cut. Whoever came first then draws first to the next 'deal' and also leads to the first round of it.

Game Play up to any agreed target, such as 500 or 1000 points.

8 Ace-Ten games

Many of Europe's most popular card games feature cards counting Ace 11, Ten 10, King 4, Queen 3, Jack 2. Lower numerals usually have no value, and tricks as such are pointless in themselves. With 30 points in each suit and 120 in the whole pack, games are typically won by taking at least 61 card-points in tricks. There is usually a penalty for taking less than 31 (called *schneider,* from *schneiden*, 'to cut', because the losers are thereby cut down to size), and a heavier one for losing every trick (*schwarz*, 'black', because their reputation is thereby blackened).

The 'Ace-11, Ten-10' pattern is first recorded in 1718 for the French game of Brusquembille, but may now be described as the Skat Schedule from its most illustrious manifestation in Germany's national card game. Many of its relatives also enjoy the status of national or regional games and are played with the short pack associated with the area in which they are practised. The schedule has even spread southwards into Spanish and Italian games, where, because Ten does not appear in those countries' native cards, the 10-point value is ascribed instead to the Seven or the Three.

A notable feature of these games is that all are played with packs stripped down to 40, 36, 32, 24 or even 20 cards. This speeds up the game by dropping the uninteresting non-counters, and has two interesting repercussions. One is the preponderance of games suitable for three players, which has never been a suitable number for the Anglo-American 52-card pack. The other is the variability of trick values, in that some are worthless, while others may carry enough card-points to win the game. Once you have got used to the possibility of winning a ten-trick game by taking only two tricks – provided they contain sufficiently high counters – it is hard to work up much enthusiasm for plain-trick games like Whist or Solo.

As some of the following games are extremely complicated, it is worth mentioning that good introductory examples are Bohemian Schneider for two players, Six-Bid or American Solo for three, and Einwerfen or Sueca for four.

Skat

3 active players, 32 cards

Skat was developed between 1810 and 1820 by members of the Tarock Club of Altenburg, some twenty miles south of Leipzig. It was based on Wendish Schafkopf, with additional features borrowed from Tarock, Ombre and German Solo. By the end of the century it had become Germany's national card game, having been embraced and disseminated by the military and the studentry, thereby acquiring countless local rules and variations. A 'pure' form of the game promulgated by the newly formed German Skat Congress at Altenburg in 1886 was considerably modified in 1928–32. Altenburg remains the Mecca of all Skat players, though the modern Deutscher Skatverband has its headquarters at Bielefeld. Thousands of local Skat clubs exist and annual national tournaments are held. Worldwide tournaments are organized by the International Skat-Players Association, to which are affiliated local associations in Australia, Belgium, the Bahamas, Canada, Germany, France, Namibia, Austria, Switzerland, Spain, South Africa and the USA.

The rules below are those prescribed for both national and international tournaments by the Deutscher Skatverband and the International Skat-Players Association. Having followed different rules for many years, these two bodies agreed on a compromise between the two which became effective on 1 January 1999. Although both organizations like to be strict about their rules, they are not always followed in domestic play, and a select list of common variations follows the main description.

Preliminaries Three players are active, but four usually play, with each in turn dealing but not playing. A game is any number of deals exactly divisible by the number of players. (In tournament play a session is 48 deals, or 36 at a three-player table.) Choose first dealer by any agreed means. Play to the left.

Cards Thirty-two, either French-suited (♣♠♥♦AKQJT987) or German (♣♠♥♠AKOU10987).

Rank and value The rank of cards for trick-taking purposes, and their point-value when captured in tricks, is as follows.

in trumps	♣J	♠J	♥J	♦J	A	T	K	Q	9	8	7
card-points	2	2	2	2	11	10	4	3	0	0	0
non-trumps					A	T	K	Q	9	8	7

The total number of card-points in play is 120.

Note that, in trump bids, the four Jacks belong to the trump suit, regardless of their individual suitmarks, and rank as the four highest in the order shown. Consequently, while an Ace is the highest card of a non-trump suit, it is only the fifth highest in trumps.

Deal Deal ten each in batches of 3-(2)-4-3. The (2) denotes 2 cards dealt face down to the table immediately after the first three batches of three. These constitute the skat.

Object There is an auction to establish a soloist. The soloist normally aims to capture at least 61 card-points in tricks, but may instead bid to capture at least 90 (*schneider*), or to win every trick (*schwarz*), or to lose every trick (*null*).

There are three types of contract:

1. *Suit.* A suit is declared trump. The entire trump suit then contains eleven cards, headed by the four Jacks, and followed by ATKQ987.

2. *Grand.* Only Jacks are trumps. They form a fifth suit of four cards ranking from high to low ♣♠♥♦. The other four suits rank ATKQ987 each.

3. *Null.* The aim is to lose every trick. There is no trump, and cards rank AKQJT987 in every suit.

Any of these contracts may be undertaken in either of two ways:

1. *With the skat.* Before announcing his contract, the soloist adds the skat to his hand and makes any two discards face down.

2. *From the hand.* The skat remains untouched until after the last trick.

Either way, the skat belongs to the soloist, and any card-points it contains count for him at the end of play as if he had won them in tricks (except at null, where they are irrelevant).

Game values Players bid by announcing not the *name* of the contract they wish to play, but the minimum score they expect to make for it if successful. The score is not the same as the number of card-points: it is the *value* of the contract they wish to undertake; and this must be calculated in advance from a number of relevant factors as follows.

1. Trump games are valued by taking the base value of the suit selected as trump (if any) and multiplying this by a number of additional factors called multipliers. The base values are:

diamonds 9, hearts 10, spades 11, clubs 12, grand 24

The multipliers are reckoned in the following order, all being added together as you go along.

- Tops (*Spitze*). This denotes the number of consecutive top trumps, counting from the ♣J downwards, which you do or do not hold in your hand. Thus:

    If you hold ♣J, then you are 'with' as many tops as you hold. For example: holding ♣J but not ♠J, you are 'with 1' top. Holding ♣J ♠J but not ♥J, you are 'with 2'. Holding ♣J♠J♥J but not ♦J, you are 'with 3'. And so on, up to a maximum 'with 11' in a suit game, or 'with 4' at grand.

    If you do not hold ♣J, then you are playing 'without' as many top trumps as lie above the highest trump you *do* hold. For example: if your highest trump is ♠J, then you are 'without 1'. If it is ♥J, you are 'without 2'. If it is ♦J, you are 'without 3'. And so on, up to a maximum of 'without 11' in a suit game (which is unusual but not impossible), or 'without 4' at grand (which is not unusual).

    In counting tops, all that matters is the *number* of consecutive top trumps involved: whether you are *with* or *without* them does not affect the score – though it may affect the playability of your hand.

- Next, to this number add '1 for game' – that is, for undertaking to take at least 61 card-points. If you think you can take at least 90, you can mentally add another 1 for *schneider*. If you think you can win every trick, you can add yet another 1 for *schwarz*.

- If intending to play from the hand, without taking the skat, then add another '1 for hand'.

- If – and only if – playing from the hand, you may further increase your game value by declaring in advance that you will win *schneider* (90+ card-points) or *schwarz* (all 10 tricks), for 1 or 2 extra multipliers in addition to the 1 or 2 for actually winning it.

- If – and only if – playing from the hand and declaring *schwarz*, you may further increase your game value by playing *ouvert*, that is with your hand of cards exposed on the table before the first trick.

The valuations described above for suit and grand bids are summarized in the following Table:

if taking the skat	if playing from the hand
1 per top trump	1 per top trump
+1 for game (61+)	+1 for game
+1 for *schneider* (90+)	+1 for hand
+1 for *schwarz* (10 tricks)	+1 for *schneider*
	+1 for *schneider* declared
	+1 for *schwarz*
	+1 for *schwarz* declared
	+1 for *ouvert*

The lowest possible game value is therefore 18 (diamonds, with or without 1, game 2, times 9 for diamonds = 18). The highest valued suit game would be 216 (clubs, with 11, game 12, hand 13, *schneider* 14, declared 15, *schwarz* 16, declared 17, *ouvert* 18, times 12 for clubs = 216). The highest grand would be 264 (grand *ouvert* with 4, game 5, hand 6, *schneider* 7, declared 8, *schwarz* 9, declared 10, *ouvert* 11 = 264).

   2. Null games have invariable values as follows:

Null (with skat)	23
Null hand	35
Null *ouvert*	46
Null *ouvert*, hand	59

Auction The player at dealer's left is designated Forehand, the next round is Middlehand, and the next Rearhand (who will be the dealer if only three play). The auction is started by Middlehand bidding against Forehand until one of them passes, whereupon Rearhand may continue bidding against the survivor until one of them also passes, leaving the other as the soloist.

   Middlehand bids by naming successive game values from the lowest upwards, i.e. 18, 20, 22, 23, 24, 27, 30, 33, 35, 36, etc. It is not necessary to name every single one: you are allowed to jump-bid, even to bid your highest possible game immediately; but it is illegal to quote any number that does not correspond to an actual game value.

   To each of these, Forehand says 'Yes' if he is prepared to play a game of equal or higher value. When one of them passes (either Middlehand because he will not make a higher bid, or Forehand because he can't accept the last bid named), Rearhand may similarly continue against the survivor by naming the next higher bid. When one of them passes, the survivor becomes the soloist, and must play a game at least equal in value to the last bid made. If neither Middlehand nor Rearhand will open at 18, Forehand may play any game; but if he also passes, the deal is annulled and the deal passes round (unless it is agreed to play Ramsch: see below).

Game announcement If wishing to take the skat, the soloist adds it to his hand without revealing either card, makes any two discards face down, and then announces his contract by naming a suit, or declaring grand, or null, or null *ouvert*. The contract he names need not be the one he had in mind when bidding (if any), so long as what he does announce is going to be worth at least the amount he bid.

If playing from hand, he leaves the skat untouched and immediately announces his game, adding 'hand' and any other declaration that may be applicable, such as *schneider* or *schwarz* or *ouvert*. If playing *ouvert*, he lays his hand of cards face up on the table before the opening lead.

Conceding The soloist may concede the game at any time before playing to the first trick. The commonest reason for conceding is that, having bid 'without' a number of Jacks, he takes the skat and finds it contains one that reduces his game value, so that he has bid a greater amount than he can actually score. (Ways of overcoming this are outlined in the notes on play, below.)

Play Forehand leads to the first trick. Players must follow suit if possible, otherwise may play any card. The trick is taken by the highest card of the suit led, or by the highest trump if any are played, and the winner of each trick leads to the next.

> ☞ At grand, leading a Jack requires Jacks to be played if possible, and the highest Jack wins the trick. In a suit contract, leading any trump calls for the play of any other trump, which may or may not be a Jack.

Cards won by the partners are kept together in a single pile. All ten tricks must be played – except at null, if the soloist wins a trick – and the skat then faced to ensure that the game is correctly valued.

Score if won The soloist wins if both the following apply:
(a) he took at least 61 card-points, or at least 90 if he declared *schneider*, or every trick if he declared *schwarz*, or no trick at all if he bid null; and
(b) the game as valued in retrospect is worth at least the amount bid.

If successful, the bidder adds to his score the total value of the game he has actually won, which may be higher than his original bid, but may not be lower.

☞ (a) A hand game played 'without' two or more tops may be reduced in value if the skat is found to contain a top, and may therefore be lost by default.

☞ (b) The skat counts as part of the hand for game valuation purposes, so it is possible to be 'with' or 'without' eleven even though only ten cards are actually played.

Score if lost A lost game loses double the amount it would have won if successful, but, before being doubled, this amount may have to be increased.

First, if the soloist is *schneidered*, by failing to take at least 31 card-points, his lost game value is increased by an extra multiplier before being doubled.

Second, if the game value is less than the bid, the amount to be lost is the next higher multiple of the relevant base value above that of the bid.

Example: You bid 36, intending to play 'hearts, without two, game three, hand four, times hearts 10 = 40'. You make your bid, but then find one black Jack in the skat. This devalues your game to 'with (or without) one, game two, hand three, game 30'. This being less than your bid, you must lose the next higher multiple above your bid, i.e. 40, which is then doubled to 80. Had you been *schneidered*, you would have reckoned 'with(out) one, game two, hand three, *schneidered* four, lose 40 doubled'. You don't have to add another multiplier here, as the fact of being *schneidered* does it for you.

Tournament score Tournament scoring is adjusted so as to attach greater weight to winning and losing contracts than to their relative values. First, each player adds 50 for each game he has bid and won, and deducts 50 for each he has bid and lost. Next, each player adds 30 for each game bid and won by each opponent at a four-player table, or 40 each at a three-player table.

Variations The following practices (strictly non-tournament) may be followed by prior agreement:

(a) Either partner may double the announced game (by announcing *kontra*), and the soloist may redouble (*rekontra*), before the first trick has been led to. In this case the score or penalty, as detailed above, is doubled or quadrupled before being applied.

(b) If all three pass, play Ramsch instead of annulling the hand. Ramsch is played like grand, with only Jacks trump, and the aim is to avoid taking the greatest number of card-points in tricks, each playing on his own account. The commonest of several versions is Schieberramsch (Push Ramsch). In this, Forehand takes the skat and passes two cards face down to Middlehand, who passes any two face down to Rearhand, who discards any two to the skat. (Some hold it illegal to pass or discard Jacks.) The winner of the last trick adds the skat to his won cards, and whoever takes the most card-points deducts that number from his score. (Ramsch is a game in its own right: see Hearts family.)

(c) Grand counts 20 instead of 24.

(d) If the soloist holds the lowest trump (Seven in a suit game or ♦J at grand) he may before play declare his intention of winning the last trick 'with a spit' (*mit Spitze*), indicating this fact by turning the spit back to front so that it faces outwards in his hand. This adds an extra multiplier to the game value, which is lost if the soloist fails to win the last trick with it. A player may take this possibility into account when bidding, to increase the level to which he can raise. ('Spit' as in spit-roast, not as in spittoon.)

(e) Even unorthodox German players no longer seem to admit the old bid of tournée (see American Skat for description), but my own Skat group has adopted it into the German game by giving it a base value of 13, regardless of the suit turned.

Notes on play Start by putting your Jacks and potential trump suit together in high-low order. Without Jacks, you probably have no game on unless you have one of the following three types of hand:

1. ♣AKQ987 ♥AKQ ♦A

With six or more trumps and safe side suits you can risk bidding 'without four', or even five, in the long suit. With a fair break of the remaining cards, you could take up to about 80 card-points for a score of 72 (without four, game five, hand six, times clubs 12). One or more Jacks could be in the skat, but if it contains only one black Jack, your game will be devalued to 36, so be cautious if pushed into bidding beyond this level.

2. ♣AT7 ♠AT7 ♥AK7 ♦A

If you are prepared to chance a balanced distribution of Jacks and suits in the adverse hands, this is a 'grand' hand without four for 144.

3. ♣AT97 ♠T87 ♥97 ♦8

Given the lead (♦8), this is a virtually unbeatable null *ouvert* hand for 59. Even without the lead, it would require a freak distribution and clever play to fail.

Holding one or more Jacks, consider whether your hand looks best for a suit bid, grand, or null, and be prepared to pass if it doesn't. Most hands are either a suit bid or nothing; relatively few are right for grand or null. Roughly speaking –

• If about half your cards are Nines, Kings and Queens, pass.

• If about half consist of Jacks and a good suit, consider game in that suit. With six or more trumps and a void suit, consider playing it from the hand. With both black Jacks and a long suit headed Ace-Ten, consider grand.

• If about half are Jacks and Aces, especially Ace-Tens, consider grand.

• If about half are Sevens, Eights and Nines, and you have no more than one Ace, King or Queen, consider null. If you can lose every trick with the hand as dealt, you can bid up to 35, or 59 if you can play it *ouvert*. If you need to take the skat to get rid of a dangerous card, you can bid up to 23, or 46 if the remaining cards offer an *ouvert* possibility.

Suit bids For a safe suit bid you normally need at least five trumps including Ace or Ten, at least two side suits which are void or headed by an Ace, and not more than five losers. If dealt such a hand, you can reckon on playing it from the hand – for example:

4. ♣J ♥J ♣AK9 ♥AT8 ♦Q9

This enables you to bid up to 36 (with 1, game 2, hand 3, times clubs 12). The opposition will probably take up to 20 in clubs and 28 in diamonds, giving you a safety margin of 12 card-points to compensate for one partner's dropping an Ace or Ten on his partner's winning trump.

For a 'hand' game, worth an extra multiplier, you generally need six trumps plus a non-trump Ace or void. Consider it especially if you have a void, as taking the skat all too often produces just two middling cards of that very suit, which you might as well throw out again. A hand game also entitles you to declare *schneider* in advance though, to do this, you should be confident of winning nine of the ten tricks.

The time to think of a skat game is when you need the draw and discard in order to produce the sort of hand on which you would have bid 'hand' if originally dealt it. For example:

5. ♣J ♥J ♣AK9 ♠K ♥AT8 ♦Q

In a hand game, the opposition could make 49 straight off in spades and diamonds, and finish you off with the trump Ten. Here, you need the skat to enable you to ditch the two dangerous singletons, or one of them if the skat offers support to the other.

Two points to watch in bidding suit games are Jacks and non-trump Tens.

The danger besetting a Ten is that of being caught by the Ace, giving the opposition, in a single trick, one-third of the points needed to win. A Ten in hand is obviously safest when covered by the Ace, and most dangerous when held singleton. With a singleton Ten, therefore, you should consider playing from hand only if you can be sure of winning most of the other tricks. It is not unknown for the soloist, playing third to the first trick, to win it with a singleton Ten; but of course it would be unwise to count on it. A singly-guarded Ten is an obvious risk. On a low lead from your right, you may play the Ten and have it captured by the Ace on your left; or you throw the guard, and then lose the Ten to the Ace on a subsequent trick. A twice-guarded Ten is safer, but still risks being trumped on the third round of the suit. If dealt one T-x combination and taking the skat, it is usually acceptable to keep it; if dealt two, it usually best to lay both Tens aside to ensure 20 towards your card-points.

The danger of Jacks is that of bidding 'without' too many of them. Suppose you have only the diamond Jack and take the game at 36, reckoning yourself without 3, game 4, times spades = 44. You turn the skat and find it contains, say, the heart Jack. Now your game is devalued: you are 'without 2, game 3, times spades = 33'. Having bid 36, you are 'bust', and threatened with loss. The best thing to do is to play on, hoping to win *schneider*. This will give you the extra multiplier you need to justify your bid. If you turned a black Jack, you would be 'with (or without) 1, game 2, times spades = 22' – worse still. In this case you must look for other ways of justifying your bid. Can you entrump clubs and win *schneider*? If so, you will score 'with 1, game 2, *schneider* 3, times clubs = 36'. If not, can you make a brave attempt at a grand (48), or a clever discard for null ouvert (46)? Generally, it is unwise to bid too high when playing without Jacks, unless you can assume from the auction that the higher trumps are in one player's hand rather than lurking in the skat. Being double-crossed by Jacks in the skat tends to disconcert inexperienced players. Experts take this danger into account intuitively and are rarely caught out by it.

Grand bids To bid grand hand, you need at least five of the nine power factors represented by Jacks, Aces, and the opening lead. You therefore bid Grand hand on:

6. ♣J ♦J ♣TKQ ♠AT ♥A98 and the lead
7. ♣J ♠J ♣ATK9 ♠7 ♥98 ♦A and the lead
8. ♠J ♥J ♦J ♣A ♠TKQ9 ♥AK, the lead unnecessary

If just short of these values, you may consider playing grand with the skat. For example:

9. ♣J ♥J ♣AK9 ♥AT8 ♦Q9

This is the hand identified earlier as a bid of clubs, hand. Given the lead, you have five of the nine power factors, but five probable losers – one Jack, and two each in clubs and diamonds. If the auction forces you beyond 36 for your clubs bid, you may make the mental switch to grand and raise to 48.

Null bids For any null bid, a void suit is an unbeatable advantage. Any other suit should include the Seven, and no higher card than Seven should be separated by more than one gap from the one below it. Thus a holding of J-9-7 is unbeatable, and even A-J-9-7 would lose only if one opponent held the other four of that suit and had the lead. A singleton Eight is not bad, especially if you have the lead and get rid of it immediately. With only one dangerous card, you can play hand for 35, but not *ouvert*. For example:

10. ♣KJ97 ♠Q87 ♥8 ♦97

The Queen is the danger card, and you could be forced to take a spade trick if you played *ouvert*. An alternative approach would be to take the skat, dump the Queen, and then play *ouvert* for 46. But if the skat yielded, for example, two high hearts, you could be lost. A simple null for 23, in which you take the skat and do not play *ouvert*, is very chancy, and you should call it only as a substitute for drawing a bad skat on a lower bid. Some circles permit null bids only from the hand.

Play Skat is full of opportunities for clever and subtle play. Here are a few pointers.

As the soloist in a suit game, lead trumps at every opportunity. With five or six trumps, it's customary to lead high then low, then high again, attempting to win the third trick in order to prevent an opponent with probably no trump left from throwing a high counter to a trump trick won by his partner.

From a side suit headed T-K, it is often best – sometimes even vital – to play the Ten at the earliest opportunity. This forces the Ace out, leaving your King in command at a time when the other opponent is still able to follow and hence unable to 'stuff' (*schmieren*) a 10-point trick by dropping another Ace or Ten on it. If you play the King and the Ace-holder ducks, you could lose 31 or more card-points on the next round of the suit, giving the opponents what is known as 'half the rent'.

Always keep track of the number of card-points currently won by both sides, and the number of trumps left in play. This takes practice, but soon becomes second nature, and is well worth while. For example, when a suit is led which you cannot follow, don't automatically trump. Always be ready to slough useless Kings and Queens to dud tricks in order to void your side suits without giving too many away, but remember you can do this with safety only so long as you know the score.

At grand, don't hesitate to lead a long suit to force Jacks out if your own are either vulnerable or needed for a later entry. For example:

11. ♥J ♦J ♠ATK87♥AT7

Given the lead, this is a grand hand without two. Leading a Jack could be fatal. Instead, play spades from the top down. If the Ace is trumped, re-enter with a top heart or red Jack, and play the spade Ten. If this also is trumped, you are left with the only Jack in play and at least five more tricks to win. You will try to throw the heart loser cheaply, rather than rely on clearing the suit with your Ace-Ten.

The partners' main object is to exploit every opportunity of 'stuffing' tricks being won by the other by throwing high counters on them, especially vulnerable Tens. A typical suit-game opening sees the soloist leading a red Jack and the second dropping a black Jack in case his partner can stuff it with the Ace or Ten, which might otherwise be lost. Alternatively, the second to play, having no black Jack, will himself drop the Ace or Ten, hoping his partner can play a high Jack. If not, they are both in the soloist's hand – or skat (same thing in practice) – and the high trump would probably be lost anyway, so there was no harm in trying.

A vital rule of play for the partners is to seek, wherever possible, to keep the soloist in the middle, i.e. playing second to a trick. If, for example, soloist is lying third to a trick to which you have the lead, and you have no probable winner, lead low from a suit which your partner can either head or trump, in order to get him into the lead. Associated with this endeavour is a mnemonic applying to the opening lead, namely 'Long route, short suit; short route, long suit'. In other words, lead from a short suit if the soloist is playing third to the first trick, long if he is playing second.

North American Skat

The form of Skat still played (though dwindlingly) by members of the North American Skat League, based in Milwaukee, and the subject of an excellent treatise by Joe Wergin, reflects the nineteenth-century form of the game introduced by New World immigrants. The old game offered three types of suit-bid, namely skat, tournée, and hand. German Skat has retained the first and dropped the second, but America has retained the tournée and dropped the skat-exchange bid (except at grand). The hand bid, here called solo, remains unchanged. The games and base values of American Skat are:

Tournée Diamonds 5, hearts 6, spades 7, clubs 8, grand 12. The soloist takes one card of the skat and may accept its suit as trump, in which case he shows it, adds the other, and discards two to the skat. If it doesn't suit him (*'Paßt mir nicht'*) – either because he hasn't enough of that suit or because its value is lower than his bid – he adds it to his hand without showing it, and must then turn up and accept the suit of the second card as trump, even if it is the same. Either way, if he turns a Jack he may either entrump the suit it shows, or play at grand. (A tournée bid normally requires at least two Jacks, one of them black, and three biddable suits.)

Solo Diamonds 9, hearts 10, spades 11, clubs 12, grand 20, grand ouvert 24. The soloist announces trump and plays without touching the skat. There is no extra multiplier for this, the base values being higher instead. Extra multipliers may be added for making or declaring schneider and schwarz. Suit solos are not playable ouvert.

Guckser The soloist takes the skat without showing it, makes any two discards, and must play at grand. This bid, called *guckser* or *gucki*, has the base value 16.

Null Null may only be played solo, without skat-exchange. It counts 20, or 40 ouvert.

Ramsch If Middlehand and Rearhand make no bid, Forehand may call Ramsch. The skat is untouched, Jacks are trumps, and the player taking the fewest card-points scores 10, or 20 if he took no trick. A player careless enough to win every trick loses 30 instead of the others' winning 20.

As in German Skat, the game value is found by multiplying the base value by: 1 per 'top', plus 1 for game (61+), or 2 for schneider (91+), or 3 for schwarz (win every trick), plus another 1 or 2 for schneider or schwarz declared.

Auction, rules of play, and scoring are basically as for German Skat. But note:

• Bidding starts at 10 (diamonds, tournée, with or without one), and continues: 12, 14, 15, 16, 18, 20, 21, 22, 24, 25, 27, 28, 30 . . .

• The soloist needs at least 91 card-points to win schneider (not 90 as in German Skat), and at least 30 to escape it.

• Lost *gucksers* are lost doubled, as also is a lost tournée if played 'second turn', the soloist having rejected the suit of the first-turned card (even if the second was the same).

Texas Skat

This is still played at tournament level under the aegis of The Texas State Skat League (Austin, Texas), founded in 1924. It resembles German rather than North American Skat in that the basic game is skat-exchange rather than tournée.

The base values are: diamonds 9, hearts 10, spades 11, clubs 12, grand 16. This is multiplied by the number of 'tops' played with or without, plus 1 for game, and an additional 1 each for hand, schneider, schneider declared, schwarz, and schwarz declared. You may declare schneider or schwarz whether you take the skat or play from the hand. If declaring schwarz, you may also play ouvert. This doubles the score instead of adding an extra multiplier.

The soloist needs at least 91 card-points to win schneider (as in North American Skat), and at least 31 to escape it (as in German Skat).

Null is 20, ouvert 30, hand 40, ouvert hand 60.

Ramsch (played if all pass) is 10 for taking fewest card-points, 20 for winning no trick, minus 30 for winning every trick.

Schafkopf (Schaffkopf, Sheepshead)   4 players, 32 cards

Schafkopf is widely played in southern Germany and is claimed as the national card game of Bavaria. First recorded in 1811, but with so many variations as to suggest a substantial history, it evidently borrowed from Quadrille and Tarock, contributed to Skat, and is the immediate ancestor of the more complex Doppelkopf, now popular in the north. It exists in many variations for three and four players. The following partnership game is that specified by the First Bavarian Schafkopf Congress (Munich, 1989), as described by Wolfgang Peschel in *Bayerisch Schaffkopfen* (Weilheim, 1992). Schafkopf means Sheepshead, popularly explained as reflecting a hypothetical original played up to nine points, supposedly marked as nine lines on a board gradually building up to the stylized representation of a sheep's head. The spelling Schaffkopf is preferred by those who assert that its original players typically used a barrel (*Schaff*) as an *ad hoc* card table, with its lid as the playing surface – a practice well attested for several other games of this period. Another possibility is that it derives from an earlier German game called Scharwentzel (see also the Danish game of Skærvindsel).

Preliminaries Four players each play alone in the long run but form *ad hoc* partnerships from deal to deal. A game is any multiple of four deals, each being settled in hard score (coins or counters). Play goes to the left.

Cards and deal Schafkopf normally employs a 32-card German pack consisting of Daus, König, Ober, Unter, 10-9-8-7 and suits of acorns, leaves, hearts, bells, but here we will assume AKQJT987 in spades, hearts, clubs, diamonds. Deal eight each in two rounds of four.

Rank and value Cards have point-values as follows: Ace 11, Ten 10, King 4, Queen 3, Jack 2, others zero. The rank of cards for trick-taking purposes is peculiar. Queens and Jacks are normally the eight highest trumps, known collectively as *Wenz* or *Wenzel*, ranking downwards as follows:

♣Q ♠Q ♥Q ♦Q ♣J ♠J ♥J ♦J

In suits, the order is A-T-K-9-8-7. If there is a trump suit, it contains 14 cards, headed by the eight Wenzels and followed by the other six of the specified suit – which, in a partnership bid, is always hearts.

☞ Note that Wenzels normally belong not to the suits marked on their faces but to the trump suit, whatever that may be.

Object One player undertakes to capture in tricks cards totalling at least 61 of the 120 card-points available, and will get a bonus for taking 90 or more (*schneider*), or winning all eight tricks (*schwarz*). In the simplest bid he attempts this with the aid of a temporary partner. In higher bids, he plays solo against the other three, and is then entitled to vary the trump suit.

Contracts From lowest to highest, the contracts that may be bid are as follows.

1. *Call-Ace*. Queens, Jacks and hearts are trumps, and the bidder finds a partner by naming the Ace of a suit other than hearts. Of that suit he must himself hold at least one card, other than the Queen, Jack, or Ace. Whoever holds it becomes his partner, but must not announce this fact until it is revealed by the play.

This is the only partnership contract. It cannot be bid by a player holding all three non-trump Aces, or no card of the called suit. However, some schools allow a player to call the Ace of a void suit provided that he announces 'Void' when doing so. The next higher bids are all solos.

2. *Wenz*. Only the four Jacks are trumps, ranking in their normal order (♣♠♥♦), and forming a fifth suit of their own. Queens rank between the Kings and Nines of their nominal suits.

3. *Suit Solo*. The soloist nominates a trump suit, which, headed by all eight Wenzels, forms a series of 14 trumps. He himself, however, may not hold any trumps apart from Wenzels (otherwise it is too easy).

4. *Wenz-Tout*. Same as Wenz (only Jacks trump), but the soloist must win all eight tricks.

5. *Solo-Tout*. As solo, with Queens, Jacks, and a specified trump suit, but the soloist must win all eight tricks. (The bid is usually announced and known as *Du*, literally 'thou', but punning on the French words *tout*, meaning 'all', or *atout*, meaning 'trump'.)

6. *Sie.* Same as Solo-Tout, but announced in the rare event of the soloist's having been dealt all eight Wenzels. (*Sie* is another piece of word-play, being the 'polite' equivalent of *Du.*)

Bidding procedure Each in turn, starting with eldest, says 'Pass' or 'Play'. If all pass, the deal is annulled and passes on. If only one player says 'Play', he either calls an Ace or declares a higher contract. If a second bidder says 'Me too', he is automatically making a solo bid on the assumption that the first to speak was seeking a partner. The competing bidders must then state what contract they wish to play, and whoever bids highest becomes the soloist. If two or more wish to play the same solo contract, priority goes to the eldest of them – that is, the player entitled to speak first in each round of bidding. (In competing suit-solo bids, all suits are equal. Priority is still determined by position, not by suit.)

Doubling An opponent who thinks the contract can be beaten may double (by announcing 'Kontra') at any time before the second card is played to the first trick. This increases the game value, but obliges his side to take at least 61 in order to beat the contract. (The soloist would then need only 60 to win.) The soloist – or his partner, if any – may in turn redouble; in which case they must again make 61. Some circles impose no limit on doubles, redoubles, etc., but whichever side doubled last must always make 61 or more to win.

Play Eldest leads. Players must follow suit if possible, otherwise may play any card. The trick is taken by the highest card of the suit led, or by the highest trump if any are played, and the winner of each trick leads to the next.

In a partnership game, whoever holds the called Ace:
• must play it when its suit is led, or
• must lead it the first time he chooses to lead from its suit, unless he holds at least four of that suit, and
• (in some circles) may not discard it when unable to follow suit.

Settlement A typical tariff of '10 and 50 *Pfennig*' yields the following basic results, which will be increased by as many doubles as may have been applied.

1. *Call-Ace.* Each member of the losing side pays a different member of the winning side a basic 10pf, or 20pf if schneidered, or 30pf if schwarzed.

2. *Suit-Solo* or *Wenz*. The soloist wins or loses 50pf from or to each opponent, or 60pf for schneider, 70pf for schwarz.

3. *Tout*. Win or lose double, i.e. 100pf per opponent.

4. *Sie*. Win or lose quadruple, i.e. 200pf per opponent.

Runners (*Laufende*) Runners – the equivalent of honours in Whist and Bridge – are the top three trumps held in one hand, or by one partnership (of two in a Call-Ace or three in a Solo), together with any further trumps held in downward succession. They are paid at the rate of 10pf each, increased by any relevant doubling.

> Examples. In a Call-Ace or Suit Solo, a player or side holding ♣Q-♠Q-♥Q but not ♦Q may claim 30pf; holding ♦Q but not ♣J 40pf, and so on to a maximum of 80pf in a Suit Solo or 140pf in a Call-Ace. A soloist winning Tout with three runners would gain 100 for the contract plus 60 for the runners.

Variations The following is a list of bids and contracts expanded by the addition of local and regional variants. They are listed from lowest to highest, and include the standard bids in order to show the order of priority. Unless otherwise stated, the settlements are the same as for a Suit-Solo (base value 50pf).

1. *Hochzeit* (*Wedding*). A player who has been dealt only one trump – whether a Wenzel or a heart – may, before the bidding begins, lay it face up on the table and 'Call a wedding'. Any other player may then take that trump in return for any card passed face down from his own hand, thereby forming a partnership with the caller which cannot be overcalled by any higher bid. Its base value is 20pf. If no one takes it, bidding continues.

2. *Call-Ace*. Standard bid.

3. *Bettel* (*Misère*). A bid to lose every trick. There are no trumps or Wenzels, and cards rank AKQJT987 in each suit. Wins or loses 30pf.

4. *Farb-Dame* or *Farb-Geier*. There are 11 trumps: the four Queens, followed by ATKJ987 of a nominated trump suit. Jacks rank between Kings and Nines of their nominal suits.

5. *Farb-Wenz*. There are 11 trumps: the four Jacks, followed by ATKQ987 of a nominated trump suit. Queens rank between Kings and Nines of their nominal suits.

6. *Wenz*. Only the four Jacks are trumps. Queens rank between Kings and Nines of their nominal suits.

7. *Geier*. Only the four Queens are trumps. Jacks rank between Kings and Nines of their nominal suits.

8. *Farbsolo*. Same as solo in the standard game.

9. *Farb-Dame(Geier)-Tout, Farb-Wenz-Tout, Dame(Geier)-Tout, Wenz-Tout, Farb-Solo-Tout, Sie*. As above, but bidding to win all eight tricks. These pay double (100pf).

If all pass without bidding, it may be agreed that the fourth player can demand either a sweetener (*Stock*) or a round of Ramsch. A sweetener is an agreed amount that everyone pays into a pot. The hand is annulled, the next player deals, and the pot goes to the next player to win a bid. Or:

Ramsch Each plays for himself and the aim is to take as few card-points as possible. Wenzels and hearts are trumps, as in a Call-Ace. Whoever takes most points pays 20pf to each opponent. If equal, the loser is the tied player who took the most tricks; or, if still equal, the most trumps; or, if still equal, the highest trump (*sic*. Presumably the ♣Q).

Comment With trumps accounting for half the cards in play, you need at least four to call an Ace, as there is no guarantee that the Ace-holder will have any. In practice, the number of trumps held is less significant than their power (three Queens is better than five low hearts), the relative positions of the partners (whether crosswise or adjacent), and how they are distributed among the four hands. In a called game, it is usual to lead trumps if you are the soloist or a called partner, otherwise the called suit, in order to clarify who the partners are. The soloist should make early trump leads in order to clarify the trump distribution and to draw adverse trumps to clear the way for side-suit Aces. With only six cards in a plain suit it is likely to go round only once, if that. Partners will seek in play to throw high-scoring cards on tricks being, or likely to be, won by their own side. It is theoretically possible to capture 44 card-points in a single trick, and to make or defeat the contract by winning three or even two of the eight tricks played.

Sjavs

(3–4p, 20c) The Danish equivalent of Schafs[kopf]. A four-player version is popular in the Faeroes. Klørsjavs – *klør* = 'clubs' – is played with a 20-card pack ranking and counting as follows:

permanent trumps	♣Q	♠Q	♣J	♠J	♥J	♦J	♣A	♣K	–	♣T
card-points	3	3	2	2	2	2	11	4	(3)	10
in non-trump suits							A	K	(Q)	T

If three play, deal six cards each in batches of 3-(2)-3. The (2) are dealt face down as a skat. Each in turn may pass or make a higher bid than any that has gone before. A player holding four or more trumps is obliged to bid (*sic*; but presumably only if no one has already done so). The basic bid, 'Play', is to take at least 61 card-points in tricks after discarding any two cards and taking the skat in their place. This can be overcalled by 'Strike' (*Jeg stryger*) – indicated by thumping the skat with one's fist – which is to win without exchanging cards. In either case, the two cards out of play eventually count to the soloist as if he had won them in tricks. 'Strike' can be overcalled by 'Slam' (*Tout*), an undertaking to win all six tricks without exchanging. Eldest leads to a simple game, the soloist to a Strike or Slam. Players must follow suit if possible, otherwise may play any card. The trick is taken by the highest card of the suit led, or by the highest trump if any are played, and the winner of each trick leads to the next. Each player starts with 65 game points. If the soloist wins, the opponents each deduct 5 from their game-points, or 10 if they failed to reach 31, or 15 if they lost every trick. If unsuccessful, the soloist deducts 5 for losing a simple game, 10 for a strike or 15 for a slam. (My interpretation of ambiguous Danish rules.) The first to reach zero loses the game. In some circles, a player down to his last game-points cannot be brought to zero except by becoming the soloist and losing his bid.

Variant Omit the red Queens, and deal five each with three to the skat. The soloist must take at least 59, and wins double if the opponents fail to reach 29.

Four players Omit the red Queens and deal 2-(2)-2. Alternatively, retain the red Queens and deal five each with no skat.

Farvesjavs

(*farve* = 'suit') is the same, except that the suit of which A-K-T are trumps below the permanent Jacks and Queens is not necessarily clubs but is specified by the soloist.

American Sheepshead

(Shep). Like Skat, Schafkopf crossed the Atlantic in the nineteenth century and developed independently. The following games, reported by Joseph Wergin in *Wergin on Skat and Sheepshead* (McFarland, Wis., 1975), are typical.

Trumps are always ♣Q ♠Q ♥Q ♦Q ♣J ♠J ♥J ♦J ♦ATK987, and cards rank ATK987 in the three plain suits.

Three players Deal ten each and two face down as a blind. Eldest has first choice of taking the blind, making any two discards, and playing against the other two with the aim of taking at least 61 card-points in tricks (including also any that may be contained in the blind). If he passes, second hand has the same choice, then dealer. If all pass, a 'Leaster' is played, in which each plays for himself with the aim of taking fewest card-points in tricks, the blind going to the winner of the last trick.

Eldest leads to the first trick and the winner of each trick leads to the next. Follow suit if possible – noting that all fourteen trumps belong to the same 'suit' – otherwise play any card. The trick is taken by the highest card of the suit led, or by the highest trump if any are played. The bidder wins 2 units from each opponent for taking 61+, 4 for 91+ (schneider), or 6 for winning every trick (schwarz). If unsuccessful, he pays each according to the same schedule. In a Leaster, the player taking fewest card-points wins 2 from each opponent, or 4 if he takes no trick. An improved schedule, proposed by Wergin, is 3-4-5 for a positive game and 2-3 for a Leaster.

A solo bid may be included, ranking higher than an ordinary game. In this case the soloist aims to take 61 or more card-points without using the blind, except at the end of play to score for any counters it may contain. The appropriate pay-offs are 4-5-6.

Four players, partnership Each receives eight cards and there is no blind. Ties are avoided by counting an additional point for winning the ♦A in a trick. This is known as 'catching the fox'.

Four players, solo Remove the black Sevens, deal seven each and two to the blind. Whoever takes the blind (eldest having first choice, and so round the table) aims to take 61+ either alone or with the aid of a partner. If he holds ♦J he *must* play alone, but does not announce that fact. If he does not hold ♦J he *may* play alone, but must say so immediately, otherwise whoever does hold it automatically becomes his partner, without announcing that fact.

Doppelkopf
4 players, 48 cards (2 × 24)

Doppelkopf is basically Schafkopf with a doubled pack and a vast array of eccentric variations. It has become enormously popular throughout northern Germany, where it is normally played with French-suited cards rather than the German-suited ones preferred in the south. The following is based on rules promoted by the Deutscher Doppelkopf-Verband (which has its own website), with additional material from Claus D. Grupp, Ralf Wirth, Matthias Noelting and Noel Leaver.

Preliminaries Four play, each on their own account. It is normally played for hard score (coins or counters), or is scored in writing in the form of such accounts.

Cards A double 24-card pack with Nines low. (*Variant*: 40 cards, with the Nines removed.) Cards have the following point-values:

A	T	K	Q	J	9
11	10	4	3	2	0

There being two of every card, the total value of all in the pack is 240.

Rank of cards The basic game involves a trump suit of 26 cards, ranking downwards as follows:

♥T ♥T ♣Q ♣Q ♠Q ♠Q ♥Q ♥Q ♦Q ♦Q ♣J ♣J ♠J ♠J ♥J ♥J ♦J ♦J ♦A-A-T-T-K-K-9-9

Plain suit cards rank A-A-T-T-K-K-9-9, except in hearts (A-A-K-K-9-9), whose Tens belong to the trump suit.

The heart Tens are called *die Tollen*, 'Loonies'. The club Queens are *die Alten*, 'the grannies'. The diamond Aces are *Füchse*, 'foxes'. Aces and Tens are *Volle*, 'big-'uns'.

Deal Deal twelve each in batches of three, or (with Nines omitted) ten each in batches of 3-4-3. Any player may demand a redeal upon receiving (a) five or more kings, (b) eight or more big-'uns, or (c) exactly one trump.

Object In the basic game, the players who were dealt the two grannies are partners, but do not reveal themselves except by their play. A player holding both of them may seek a partner or play a solo, one against three. The partners' or soloist's object is to take at least 121 card-points in tricks; that of their opponents to take at least 120. Higher calls are possible, but the grannie-holding side always aims to take at least 121 card-points unless otherwise specified.

Bidding Each in turn, starting with eldest, makes one of two announcements, namely:

- 'OK' (*Gesund* – literally 'healthy'). This indicates a willingness to play the basic game, with the position of the grannies determining who the partners are. Anyone who says 'OK' when holding two grannies will automatically be playing a 'Silent Solo', a situation that will become apparent only as play proceeds.

- 'Special' (*Vorbehalt*, literally 'Reservation'). This indicates a desire to play one of the specialist games. If two or more players bid Special, they must announce which game they wish to play, and the highest bid determines the game. The most usual specialist games are as follows. The first two are partnership quests.

1. Wedding (*Hochzeit*). This is called by a player who holds both grannies but is not confident of playing solo. It offers to accept as partner the first of the other three players to win a trick, provided that it is one of the first three tricks – otherwise the bidder must continue playing Solo. (*Variant*: The caller may specify as partner the first to win a trump trick, or a non-trump trick, or any trick. In every case, however, it must still be one of the first three tricks.)

2. Poverty (*Armut*). This may be bid only by a player who holds three or fewer trumps and would like to find a partner. He takes from his hand three cards, which must include any trumps he holds, and offers them, face down, to each other player in turn. The first player to accept them (without first seeing them) adds them to his hand and passes, face down, to the bidder three cards, which may (but need not) include any or all of those he accepted. These two players thereby become partners. If no one accepts the offer, the hands are annulled and redealt.

The other bids are solos, of which there are several types. Traditionally, the following solos are all equal, and if more than one player bids solo then priority goes to the eldest of them (first one round from dealer's left). A more recent tendency is to rank them from lowest to highest as follows:

1. Ace solo. The soloist must take at least 121 card-points at no trump. All four suits then rank A-T-K-Q-J-9. This is also called a *Fleischloser* ('meat-free') solo, or *Knochenmann* ('skeleton').

2. Heart solo. As above, but with hearts as the trump suit following downwards from the Loonies, Queens, and Jacks. (With hearts, there will be only 24 trumps instead of 26.)

3. Spade solo. As above, but with spades trump instead of hearts.

4. Club solo. As above, but with clubs trump.

5. Diamond solo. As above, but with diamonds trump.

6. International solo. As above, but with only the eight Queens and eight Jacks as trumps. The other four suits then rank A-T-K-9. (This bid is not recognized by the Deutscher Doppelkopf-Verband.)

7. Jack solo (*Bubensolo*). As above, but with only the eight Jacks as trumps. The other four suits then rank A-T-K-Q-9.

8. Queen solo (*Damen*). As above, but with only the eight Queens as trumps. The other four suits then rank A-T-K-J-9.

Play Eldest leads first, and the winner of each trick leads to the next. Players must follow suit if possible, otherwise may play any card. The trick is taken by the highest card of the suit led, or by the highest trump if any are played. Of two identical winning cards, the first played beats the second. (*Variant*: If both Loonies are played to the same trick, the second one wins.)

During play, the value of the game can be increased by various announcements, and by achieving certain feats, as described below.

Announcements Either member of the grannie side, or the soloist holding both grannies, may double the game value by announcing 'Double' (*'Re'*), provided that he has at least 11 cards in hand when making that announcement. (In the case of a Wedding, however, this privilege may be delayed until a trick is taken which establishes who the marriage partner is.) Conversely, any member of the non-bidding side may double the game value by announcing 'Counter-double' (*Kontra*), subject also to the 11-card requirement. In this case the *Kontra* side must take at least 121 card-points to beat the grannie side or soloist.

Once a side has doubled, any of its members may subsequently further increase the game value by making one of the following announcements, in the order given, provided that he still holds the minimum stated number of cards.

1. *No 90* (at least 10 cards in hand). The caller's side will prevent the other side from taking as many as 90 card-points in tricks (by taking at least 151).

2. *No 60* (at least 9 in hand). The caller's side will prevent the other from reaching 60 (by taking at least 181).

3. *No 30* (at least 8 in hand). The caller's side will prevent the other from reaching 30 (by taking at least 211).

4. *Schwarz* (at least 7 in hand). The caller's side will prevent the other from winning a single trick (by winning them all).

Following any such announcement, any member of the other side may double it, holding not more than one card less than was required for the announcement they are replying to.

Special feats Each of the following feats adds to the score of the side achieving it, regardless of whether it wins or loses the contract.

1. *Catching a fox*. Winning a trick containing a ♦A played by a member of the opposing side. (Not valid in a solo.) The Ace is left face up to mark the fact.

2. *Charlie Miller* (*Karlchen Müller*). Winning the last trick with a ♣J, or winning the last trick if it contains a ♣J played by the opposing side (not a partner, and not valid in a solo). This is not doubled if both fall in the same trick. *Variant*: The specified card may be ♦Q, called Lizzie Miller (*Lieschen Müller*).

3. *Doppelkopf*. Winning a trick containing four big-'uns. (*Variant*: Winning a trick containing two pairs of identical cards.)

Score or settlement Scores are normally kept in writing, with a column for each player, but in zero-sum format – that is, showing negative amounts for payments made and positive ones for payments received.

Partnership game If the partners take at least 121 card-points, they each win 1 unit from a different member of the opposing side, so the scores are [+1 +1 −1 −1]. If their opponents take at least 120, they each win 2 from a different partner – one for the game, and one for playing 'against the grannies'. This makes the scores [+2 +2 −2 −2].

Solo game As above, except that the soloist wins 1 unit from each opponent [+3 −1 −1 −1], or pays 1 unit to each [−3 +1 +1 +1]. The opponents do not count extra for playing against the grannies.

The winning side gets an extra 2 units if one side doubled, or 4 if both did.

The winning side also gets 1 extra unit if the other side went 'off 90', 2 if they went off 60, 3 if off 30, or 4 if they were *schwarz* (lost every trick).

A side that announced No 90 (etc.) gets yet another extra unit for each such announcement they made, provided that they took enough card-points themselves to fulfil the announcement. If not, they lose the game, and the other side scores everything that would otherwise have been scored by those who failed their announcement.

> Example. The Queen-partners double and announce 'No 90', and the other side
> counter-double. If the Queen-partners take at least 151 card-points, they score 7
> (1 for the game, 2 for the double, 2 for the counter-double, 1 for No 90, and 1 for
> announcing it). If they fail to reach 151, the opponents each score 8, since they
> add 1 for playing against the grannies.

Further variations

Poverty Some disallow this bid. Others allow it to be played in conjunction with a Wedding. For example, if a Wedding is called, a player with three or fewer trumps may wed the caller by pleading Poverty with him, and proceeding accordingly.

King solo A soloist undertakes to take at least 121 points using only the eight Kings as a trump suit, in the usual suit order (♣♠♥♦). The other four suits then rank A-T-Q-J-9.

Piglets (*Schweinchen*). A player with both ♦Aces (or, *variant*, both ♥Aces) may declare 'Piglets' before play begins. In this case the two Aces count as the two highest trumps, beating both loonies. That done, another player holding both ♦Nines (or ♦Tens if the Nines are stripped out) may declare them to be 'Hyperpiglets' (*Hyperschweinchen*), in which case they become top trumps and beat the ordinary piglets.

Doubling Some play that doubling literally doubles the game value, rather than adding 2 units. Some play that all Solo contracts are automatically doubled.

Catching a Loony Gain a point for playing a ♥T and capturing the other ♥T off the opposing side.

Notes on play (Based on those by Noel Leaver on the Pagat website.)

The rule that the first of equal cards wins makes it very important to lead the Ace of a side suit before an opponent can lead theirs, as the second round is almost certain to be trumped – there are only eight cards in a plain suit, or six in hearts. This is obviously less urgent if you hold both Aces of a suit. Therefore, if leading to the first trick, your priorities are usually to lead:

- a single black Ace (shortest suit first if you have ♣A and ♠A);
- a single ♥Ace;
- one of two identical Aces.

After this, you normally try to give the lead to your partner. If you are on the Queens' side you will normally lead a trump to your partner's ♣Queen. If you are on the other side you may lead a plain suit, which gives a good indication of which side the leader is on (but is not always done as a matter of course). However, if your partner has counter-doubled, you should lead a trump, as they should have at least one ♥Ten and may want you to lead trumps.

If you are trumping in, and fear being overtrumped, play at least a Jack so that the fourth player cannot win with a Fox or trump Ten. Similarly, if trumps are led, and you are the last of your side to play to the trick, with one or both opponents after you, play a Jack or higher if no high card has been played so far.

It is important to double if things seem to be going well, not only to increase the score for the game but also to entitle you to announce 'No 90' if things keep going well.

You can signal a particularly strong hand, especially one rich in high trumps, by doubling earlier than necessary – for example, on your first play rather than your second, this indicates a possession of additional strength.

If on the opening lead the fourth player doubles before second hand plays, he probably expects to trump the lead and wants his partner to put a valuable card on it.

It is nearly always right to announce a marriage, as you will rarely have a hand strong enough for Solo. It is always desirable to become the partner of a player with a marriage, as you get a partner with at least two high trumps. Therefore, if on lead against a marriage, you might lead a ♥Ten to win the trick; otherwise you could lead an Ace in your shortest suit. (However, the variant whereby the second ♥T beats the first is specifically designed to prevent this.)

A Poverty game is easier to win than it sounds, because the Poverty player can discard valuable cards on partner's tricks, and also the accepting player gets the chance to create voids.

In considering a solo, having the opening lead is usually a great advantage. Trump solos require a much stronger hand than you may think, and such hands will also play well in a normal game. For an Ace solo, a five-card suit headed A-A-T will normally capture over 60 points. For a Queen or Jack solo four trumps will often suffice, but you also need a reasonable number of Aces.

Before announcing No 90 (or 60 or 30), remember you will be changing the target, and gambling 1 extra point against the possible loss of the whole game. You must be confident of achieving this to announce it.

Beware leading the second round of hearts. With only six cards in the suit, you may be giving a ruff and discard to the opponents.

Avinas
4 players (2 × 2), 32 cards

The Lithuanian game of Avinas ('Rams' in English) is especially popular around the town of Jurbarkas on the river Niemen, between Kaunas and the western border. Albinas Borisevicius of Vilnius taught it to John McLeod at a 1991 meeting of the International Playing-Card Society, and the following description is based on the Pagat website composite subsequently prepared by McLeod and Anthony Smith.

Preliminaries Four players sit crosswise in partnerships and play to the left. Two slightly different types of game are played and both are scored negatively – that is, by marking penalties against the losers or by cancelling penalties previously marked against the winners. One game is scored by means of circles, called 'rams' (*avinas*), which can be cancelled. The other is scored in 'pips', which are written down as a running total. Pips cannot be cancelled, and a match ends when one side has accumulated 12 pips.

Cards The 32 cards, consisting of ATKQJ987 in each suit, rank and count as follows:

in trumps	♣Q	†7	♠Q	♥Q	♦Q	♣J	♠J	♥J	♦J	A	T	K	9	8
card-points	3	0	3	3	3	2	2	2	2	11	10	4	0	0	0
plain suits										A	T	K	9	8	7

Deal The dealer deals eight cards each in batches of four. He exposes each opponent's fourth and eighth cards. He also examines the fourth and eighth of his own and his partner's cards, but only exposes any of these that are Sevens. The game takes different forms according to whether or not any Sevens have been exposed. Either way, the aim of the declaring side is normally to take at least 61 of the 120 card-points available.

If any of the exposed cards is a Seven, the suit of the last Seven exposed becomes the trump suit for that deal. Its holder automatically becomes the declarer, and leads to the first trick. This is a Sevens game, and is scored in rams.

If no Seven is exposed (which happens about three deals in ten), the player at dealer's left either passes or chooses a suit as trump and, without saying what suit it is, states how many trumps he holds (including Queens and Jacks). The other players in turn then either pass or quote a greater number of cards held in a suit of their choice. If all pass, the deal is annulled and passes on to the next in turn. Otherwise the player stating the greatest number of trumps becomes the declarer and leads to the first trick. This is a No Sevens game and is scored in pips.

> ☛ Players need not choose the suit of which they hold most cards, but if it later transpires that declarer held fewer trumps than he claimed, his side loses the whole game.

Doubling (sevens game only) Before leading to the first trick, declarer or his partner may knock on the table to signify that they undertake to win every trick, thereby doubling the value of the game. If so, either opponent may knock again, thereby betting they don't, and doubling the value again.

Play (sevens game) Declarer leads. Players must follow suit if possible, otherwise may play any card. The trick is taken by the highest card of the suit led, or by the highest trump if any are played, and the winner of each trick leads to the next. Normally all eight tricks are played and the declarers win if they take at least 61 card-points in tricks. In a doubled game, however, the declarers lose as soon as they lose a trick, and the rest are not played.

Play (no sevens) Declarer leads to the first trick, and must lead a trump. If it is a Queen or Jack, the player at his left must ask what the trump suit is, and be truthfully told.

The winner of the first trick must lead a trump to the second. If he has none, he may lead any card, and may (but need not) lead it face down. If he does, he may indicate to his partner by a facial expression whether or not it is a high counter. The others then follow as if a trump had been led, the led card is exposed, and the highest trump played wins the trick.

In all other tricks any card may be led, and players must follow suit if possible. Play ceases when either member of the declaring side claims his side to have reached at least 61.

Score (sevens game) If the declarers win, the opponents record against themselves as many rams as there were Sevens exposed in the deal (1 to 4); if not, declarers record twice that number against themselves (2-4-6-8). These scores are doubled if they bid all eight tricks, and doubled again if the opponents redoubled.

In subsequent deals, a ram is primarily scored by crossing out a ram of the opposing side. If they have none, then it is recorded by drawing a circle against the losing side. At any given time, therefore, not more than one side will have uncancelled rams against them.

N/S | E/W

N/S	E/W
1	⊗
3	⊗
	⊗
◯	⊗
◯	1
◯	2
◯	4
◯	7
◯	8
◯	10
◯	12
◯	
◯	

Score (no sevens) If the declarers win, the opponents count 1 pip against themselves if they took from 31 to 59 card-points, 2 pips if they took 30 or fewer, or 3 pips if they took none at all (even if they took one or more worthless tricks). If the declarers lose, they count respectively 2 (for 31–60), 4 or 6 pips against themselves.

Ending The match ends when either side has at least 12 pips marked against them. Normally, the winning side is the one that has no uncancelled rams marked against it. If neither side has any rams, the one with the fewer pips wins. However, if one side has no pips at all, then the rams are ignored and the side with 12 or more loses disgracefully, being designated 'Cats' until the next match. In this event it is traditional to play no more that day, and to break open new cards for the next game.

In the illustration, East–West have won because they have no rams against, but North–South would have won if they had had no pips instead of three.

Comment McLeod points out the anomalous fact that it can be good tactics for both sides to wish to lose a No Sevens game. Suppose one side has no rams and 11 pips while the other side has at least one ram and at least one pip. The players on 11 pips will wish to lose in order to reach 12 and so end the match while their opponents still have rams. Conversely, their opponents can avoid this only by themselves losing. Since the declarers at No Sevens can choose when to end the game, they can deliberately lose by claiming to have reached 61 when they have not. Thus there will be no underbidding for the right to be declarer.

Owcy Glowa ('Sheep's Head') 3 players, 24 cards

This unusual variety of Schafkopf is played by American Poles. It was described to me by Jude Wudarczyk, who subsequently published it in *The Playing-Card* (XXII, 23).

Preliminaries Three active players play to the right. If four play, the dealer sits out. Each has six coins to use as markers, placing four of them heads down in a row on his left, and two heads down away from them towards the middle.

Cards and deal Deal eight cards each, in ones, from a 24-card pack ranking and counting A11, K5, Q4, J2, Ten 10, Nine 9, making an overall total of 160.

Object For the soloist (as defined below) to take at least 54 card-points, and the partners to prevent this. Optionally, players may also bid to win a number of card-points falling within a given range.

Bidding Each player, upon playing a card to the first trick, may (but need not) bid to win a number of card-points falling within a certain range. Turning heads up the leftmost coin in one's row of four represents a bid to take from 0–40 points, second from the left bids 41–80, third 81–120, fourth 121–160. Note that each in turn after eldest hand can see what has been already bid and played before deciding on their own bid.

Play Eldest leads first. Players must follow suit if possible, otherwise may play any card, apart from restrictions on the black Queens. These are called *babki*, 'grannies'. You may not declare your granny holding except by your play, nor play a granny until it is the only card you hold of its suit. The trick is taken by the highest card of the suit led, and the winner of each trick leads to the next. There are no trumps.

Soloist and partners Upon playing a granny, turn one of your two further coins heads up. If you have both grannies, you are the soloist. If you have one, the other player with a granny is your partner and the third player the soloist. If you have none, you won't know until later whether you are the soloist or a partner.

Score For taking a number of card-points falling within the range of your bid, score 1 game-point. If you take more or fewer, each opponent scores 1 game-point. In addition: if, as soloist, you take at least 54 card-points, you score 1 game-point; if not, the other two score 1 each.

Game The winner is the player with most game-points when at least one player has reached nine. If tied, more deals are played until the tie is broken. Game-points are recorded as vertical strokes, with three in the two top rows, two in the next, and one in the last. The final arrangement is traditionally said to represent a sheep's head.

Six-Bid (Slough, Sluff, American Solo)   3 players, 36 cards

First recorded in 1924 and particularly associated with Salt Lake City, Six-Bid is an extension of a game called Frog (see below).

Preliminaries Three play with 36 cards ranking and counting as follows:

A	T	K	Q	J	9	8	7	6
11	10	4	3	2	0	0	0	0

Deal Eleven each in batches of 4-3-(3)-4. The 3 in brackets are dealt face down to the table to form a blind.

Object Whoever bids the highest valued game plays it against the combined efforts of the other two.

Bidding The player at dealer's left bids or passes. If he bids, the next in turn may pass or overbid. If he overbids, the first may pass or bid even higher. The next in turn then bids against the survivor in the same way. A player who passes may not bid again. If all pass, the cards are thrown in and the deal rotates. From lowest to highest the bids are:

1. *Solo.* Bidder undertakes to win at least 60 of the 120 card-points after announcing as trumps any suit except hearts. The blind is left

down, but any card-points it contains count for the soloist at the end of play.

2. *Heart solo*. The same, but with hearts as trumps.

3. *Misère*. Bidder undertakes to lose every trick at no trump. The blind is not touched.

4. *Guarantee solo*. Bidder undertakes to capture at least 74 card-points if he plays in hearts, or 80 if he entrumps any other suit.

5. *Spread misère*. Same as misère, but the bidder plays with his hand exposed and his left-hand opponent leads first.

6. *Call solo*. Bidder names trumps and undertakes to capture all 120 card-points (not necessarily taking all the tricks). Any contained in the blind belong to him at end of play. Before play, he may call for any card not in his hand, and whoever has it must give it to him in exchange for any card the bidder does not want. If the called card is in the blind, he may not exchange or make another call.

Play Eldest leads to the first trick except in a spread misère (see above). Players must follow suit if possible, otherwise must trump if possible, otherwise may play freely. The trick is taken by the highest card of the suit led, or by the highest trump if any are played, and the winner of each trick leads to the next.

Score Settle in hard score (coins or counters) or record transactions in writing. Bidder receives the following amount from each opponent if successful, or pays it to each if not.

Solo: 2 per card-point taken over or under 60 (no score if 60–60).

Heart solo: 3 per card-point taken over or under 60 (no score if 60–60).

Misère 30, Guarantee solo 40, Spread misère 60, Call solo 100, Call solo in hearts 150.

Frog (Rana)

Ancestor of Six-Bid played in Mexico under the name Rana. Although this is the Spanish for Frog, 'frog' itself has nothing to do with amphibians but is an Americanization of the German *Frage*, meaning 'request', the lowest possible bid in games of this type. There are only three bids:

1. *Frog*. To take at least 60 card-points, accepting hearts as trump but first taking the three cards of the blind, adding them to his hand, and then discarding three face down, any card-points they contain

counting for him at the end of play. He wins, or pays, 1 chip per point taken over or under 60.

2. *Solo* or *Chico*. The same, but bidder nominates any other suit as trump and plays without exchanging three cards, though anything in the blind counts for him afterwards. Payments are double those of Frog.

3. *Heart solo* or *Grand*. The same, in hearts. Payments are treble those of Frog.

Play as at Six-Bid.

▌ Bavarian Tarock (Haferltarock)   3 players, 36 cards

One of several German varieties of a game related to Six-Bid and obviously derived from true Tarock by omitting the 22 tarocks. This version, still played, dates from the 1930s.

Preliminaries Three players play to the left. They start by each contributing 100 units to a pot, and the game ends either when the pot is empty or by mutual agreement.

Cards Thirty-six, either German- or French-suited. Cards rank and count as follows:

A	T	K	Q	J	9	8	7	6
11	10	4	3	2	0	0	0	0

Deal Eleven each in batches of 4-3-(3)-4. The 3 in brackets are dealt face down to the table to form a stock.

Bidding Each in turn, starting with eldest, may pass or say 'Play'. 'Play' is an offer to take at least 61 of the 120 card-points in tricks after naming trumps and playing alone against the other two. If not overcalled, he further announces Pick-up or Hand. Pick-up means he will take the stock and discard three unwanted cards before announcing trumps. Hand means he will play the hand as dealt. In either case, any card-points contained in the stock will count at the end of play as if he had won them in tricks.

If he says Play, the next in turn (or, if he passes, the third player) may try to take the game off him by bidding Hand. The first bidder may then pass, or assert priority by bidding Hand himself. If he also bids Hand, the other bidder may contest it by raising the number of card-points he undertakes to catch in successive multiples of five. Thus 'And five' guarantees at least 66, 'And ten' at least 71; and so on. This continues until one of them passes. If the third player has yet to speak, he may bid the next higher multiple of five; and so on.

Play Eldest leads to the first trick. Players must follow suit and head the trick if possible; must trump and overtrump if unable to follow; and may renounce only if unable to do any of these. The trick is taken by the highest card of the suit led, or by the highest trump if any are played, and the winner of each trick leads to the next.

Score The soloist, if successful, wins a basic 5 chips, plus 5 per whole or part of every 5 points he took in excess of his contract. If not, he loses 5 chips per whole or part of every 5 card-points by which he fell short of it.

> Example: In a basic contract, the value is 5 for taking 61–65, 10 for 66–70 etc. or minus 5 for 56–60, etc. In a 66-contract, it is 5 for taking 66–70, minus 5 for 61–5; and so on.

For winning a Pick-up, the soloist takes the appropriate amount from the pot; for winning a Hand game, he receives the appropriate amount from each opponent, plus 10 units for each additional 5 points by which he raised his contract above 61.

For losing a Pick-up, he pays out of pocket to one opponent, the other taking that amount from the pot; for losing a Hand game, he pays it to each opponent instead.

The game ends when the pot is empty. If the last soloist wins, and the amount due from the pot is more than it contains, he can take only what is there. But if he loses, and the amount due from him is more than the pot contains, he need not pay one player more than the other can take from the pot.

Variant If an opening bid is uncontested, and the bidder announces a hand game, he may raise the amount of his contract by any multiple of five.

Einwerfen (Zählspiel)   4 players (2 × 2), 32 cards

This old German game has a distinctly ancestral air about it and forms a good introduction to the Ace-11 family for those unacquainted with that principle.

Four playing in partnerships receive eight each from a 32-card pack ranking and counting

A	K	Q	J	T	9	8	7
11	4	3	2	10	0	0	0

If the dealer forgets to turn the last card for trumps, a suit may be nominated by eldest hand. Eldest leads. Players must follow suit if possible, otherwise may play any card. The trick is taken by the highest card of the suit led, or by the highest trump if any are played, and the winner of each trick leads to the next. A side wins a single game for taking 61+ card-points, a double for 90+, a treble for winning every trick. A 60–60 tie doubles the value of the following deal. The trump of the first deal remains 'favourite' throughout play, doubling the value of any subsequent deal played in it.

Sueca

(meaning 'Swedish') is a Portuguese game remarkably similar to the above. Four play in partnerships, or three with a dummy (*manca*), usually with a 40-card Spanish pack with suits of swords, batons, cups and coins. Cards rank and count as follows:

A	7	K	J	Q	6	5	4	3	2
11	10	4	3	2	0	0	0	0	0

| ☛ Note the reverse ranking of Jack and Queen.

Deal ten each and turn the last for trumps. Eldest leads. Players must follow suit if possible, otherwise may play any card. The trick is taken by the highest card of the suit led, or by the highest trump if any are played, and the winner of each trick leads to the next. A side wins one game point for taking 61+ card-points, two for 90+ (*capote*), three for winning every trick. A 60–60 tie doubles the value of the following deal, quadrupling it in the unlikely event of two tied rounds. Game is 4 points.

Yukon

This fun game looks as if it had been invented by someone who had forgotten how to play Skat. The earliest book description dates only from 1945 (Ostrow), but Andrew Pennycook reports that his father learnt it in Canada before the First World War.

Two to four players use a 52-card pack. Three must discard one of the deuces; four may play in partnership. Each receives five cards and the rest are stacked. After each trick, each in turn draws the top card of the stock, starting with the previous trick-winner. The aim is to capture card-points in tricks, for which purpose cards rank and count:

Grand Yukon (♠J)	15
Other Yukons (Jacks)	10
Each Ten	10
Each Ace	5
Each King	3
Each Queen	2

These total 125, and the winner is the first to reach 250. Yukons (Jacks) form a separate, four-card trump suit. Eldest leads to the first trick and the winner of each trick leads to the next. Players must follow suit if possible, otherwise must play a Yukon if possible. The trick is taken by the highest card of the suit led, or by a Yukon if any are played. If more than one Yukon falls to the same trick, the first beats the second, except that the Grand Yukon always wins.

Catch-the-Ten (Scotch Whist)

Also called Catch-the-Lang-Tens (lang = long), and older than previously thought: Sir Walter Scott refers to the 'lang ten' in *Old Mortality*, set in the mid-eighteenth century. (Reported by Robert Reid.)

Preliminaries Cards rank AKQJT9876 except in trumps. If five or seven play, omit a Six; if eight, omit all Sixes, or (better) add the Fives. Four, six, or eight may play in any agreed partnership arrangement. Deal all the cards out in ones and turn the last for trumps. If two or three play, deal (respectively) three or two 6-card hands face down to each. Each hand is picked up and played separately, the others remaining face down until the previous hand has been played out.

Object To win tricks, especially those containing any of the top five trumps, which rank and count as follows:

Jack 11, Ace 4, King 3, Queen 2, Ten 10

These total 30. No other cards count.

Play Eldest leads to the first trick and the winner of each trick leads to the next. Follow suit if possible, otherwise play any card. The trick is taken by the highest card of the suit led or by the highest trump if any are played. Each player scores the point-value of any top trumps won in tricks, plus 1 point per card taken in excess of the number originally held (if any). Game is 41 points. If previously agreed, play ends when anyone reaches 41 by winning a counter; otherwise, play the last hand out.

French Whist

is similar, but play with 52 cards and count 10 for capturing ♦10 instead of the trump Ten. Game is 40 points.

Reunion

3 players, 32 cards

This eighteenth-century Rhenish game feels like a cross between Euchre and Skat. Harjan (below) is still played in Norway.

Preliminaries Three players, 32 cards, play to the left. A game is three deals, one by each player. Points are recorded in writing and settlements made in hard score.

Cards Cards rank from high to low in the following order, and bear the stated point-values:

RB	LB	A	T	K	Q	(J)	9	8	7
12	12	11	10	4	3	(2)	0	0	0

The highest trump is the Jack of trumps, or Right Bower; the second highest is the other Jack of the same colour as trumps, or Left Bower. These count 12 each. Non-trump Jacks rank between Nine and Queen, and count 2 each. With an additional 10 for the last trick, the total number of points in play is 150.

Deal Deal ten each in batches of 3-4-3 and 2 face down to the table, turning the second of them for trumps. The dealer then makes two face-down discards, which may not include an Ace or a Bower. Any card-points they contain will count for him at end of play as if he had won them in tricks. The two undealt cards belong to him, and he may take the face-down card immediately, but must leave the turn-up in place until the second trick has been quitted.

Play Eldest leads first. Players must follow suit if possible, otherwise must trump if possible. The trick is taken by the highest card of the suit led, or by the highest trump if any are played, and the winner of each trick leads to the next. If both Bowers fall to the same trick, the holder of the Left Bower immediately pays a single stake to whoever played the Right.

Settlement The player with most card-points after three deals is paid a single stake by any opponent who took between 100 and 149 card-points. An opponent with 150 or more pays nothing, but the other then pays double. Anyone with under 100 pays double, under 50 triple. If two tie for most, the loser pays each of them according to how many he took.

Harjan

(2p, 52c) A Norwegian two-hander resembling Sixty-Six, but without the marriages. Deal six each in threes, turn the next for trump, and half cover it with the remaining 39 cards, face down. Cards basically rank ATKQ(J)98765432, but the highest trump is the Jack, followed by the other Jack of the same colour. These count 12 points each, the other Jacks 2 each, and the top cards Ace 11, Ten 10, King 4, Queen 3. The leader to each trick must lead three or more cards of the same suit if possible (otherwise two of one suit and an unmatched third), and the follower can win only by beating every card, either with a higher one of the same suit or with a trump. Before making the next lead, draw from stock to restore each hand to six. With 10 for the last trick, the maximum possible is 150 points. Play up to a target of 121 over as many deals as it takes. Score 1 game-point for winning, or 2 if the loser fails to reach 30 (*jan*), or 3 if the loser fails to win a trick (*harjan*).

Hundredogen

(2p, 36c) As Harjan, except: deal three cards each from a 36-card pack ranking ATKQJ9876; only one card is led to a trick; and the target is 101 points. It is sometimes played with the Jack as highest trump, followed by the other Jack of the same colour (see Harjan).

Madrasso (Mandrasso, Magrasso)   4 players (2 × 2), 40 cards

This cross between Tressette and Briscola has in the last fifty years replaced Scaraboción as the most popular and widespread card game of Venice and its surrounds. It is normally played with the Venetian or Trevigiane patterned 40-card Italian pack with suits of swords, batons, cups, coins (♠ ♣ ♥ ♦, respectively equivalent to ♠ ♣ ♥ ♦), and courts of *Re* (King), *Cavallo* (Horse), *Fante* (Jack). French-suited cards, however, will suffice to render this relatively simple but strategically deep game accessible to players unable to obtain (or cope with) Italian cards. The following description is adapted from John McLeod's translation and revision of one prepared by Paolo Valentini for the 1997 convention of the International Playing-Card Society.

Preliminaries Four players sit crosswise in partnerships and play to the right. A game consists of at least 10 deals (*battute*) and is won by the first side to correctly claim to have reached a target score of 777 points.

Cards The 40 cards rank and count as follows (R-C-F equivalent to K-Q-J):

A	3	R	C	F	7	6	5	4	2
11	10	4	3	2	0	0	0	0	0

Aces and Threes are called *carichi*, court cards are *punti*, and non-counting cards *scartine* or *lisci*.

Deal Deal ten cards each in the following way: three each, two each, one (the twenty-first) face up in front of the dealer to determine trumps (*trionfi*), then three each but only two to the dealer, and finally two each.

The dealer's faced card stays on the table until it is played to a trick.

Whoever holds the trump Seven may (but need not) exchange it for the turn-up immediately before playing a card to the first trick.

Play Eldest leads first. Players must follow suit if possible, otherwise may play any card. The trick is taken by the highest card of the suit led, or by the highest trump if any are played, and the winner of each trick leads to the next.

Revoke If a player revokes, play ceases and the opposing side scores 130 points.

Scoring and winning At the end of a deal each side totals the value of counters they have taken in tricks, and the winners of the last trick add 10. As the two totals always make 130 it suffices for one side to write down what they have scored. Normally no running total is kept – one side simply writes their own score for each deal in a single column.

If after 10 deals one side has scored at least 777 points, it wins. The score of the non-scorekeeping side is calculated by subtracting the scoring side's total from 1300. If neither side has that many, more deals ensue until one side reaches the target.

Only a player who has just won a trick may claim to have reached 777. Play immediately ceases and the points so far taken by the claimant's side are counted. If the claim is upheld, the declaring side wins, otherwise they lose. If at the end of a deal both sides are found to have more than 777 and neither has declared, the side with the higher total wins.

If a side wins all 10 tricks in one deal (*cappotto*), it wins the entire game outright, even if the other side has reached 777 points but failed to claim a win.

Briscola (Brisca)   2–5 players, 40 cards

A popular Italian game, first recorded in 1828, and played also in Spain under the name Brisca. Madrasso is an elaboration of it.

Preliminaries From two to four play the basic game, four playing crosswise in fixed partnerships. For five, see Briscola Chiamata. All play goes to the right.

Cards Properly played with a 40-card Italian or Spanish pack, but a stripped Bridge pack will do. Cards rank and count as follows:

Italian	Asso	Tre	Re	Cavallo	Fante	7	6	5	4	2
Spanish	As	Trey	Rey	Caballo	Sota	7	6	5	4	2
equivalent	Ace	Three	King	Queen	Jack	7	6	5	4	2
card-points	11	10	4	3	2	0	0	0	0	0

If three play, remove one of the Deuces.

Deal Deal three cards each face down, turn the next for trumps, and slide it face up and partly projecting from beneath the face-down stock. Eldest leads to the first trick. There is no requirement to follow suit (ever). A trick is taken by the highest card of the suit led or by the highest trump if any are played. The winner of each trick draws the top card of stock (so long as any remain), and waits for the other(s) to do so in turn before leading to the next.

Game The game is won by the player or partnership taking most of the 120 card-points, the hands being played right through. A two- or three-way split (40-40-40 or 60-60-0) is a stand-off. A rubber is the best of five games (first to three).

Signals When four play, partners may signal certain trump holdings to each other by means of conventional signs codified as follows, seeking to do so when neither opponent is looking.

Ace	Go tight-lipped.
Trey	Twist mouth sideways.
King	Raise eyes heavenwards.
Queen	Show tip of tongue.
Jack	Raise one shoulder.

They may also secretly show each other their final hand of three cards when the stock is empty.

Briscola Chiamata

(4–5p, 5 best). Deal eight each in fours, or, if four play, 10 each in batches of 4-2-4. There follows an auction to decide who will play against the others, either alone or with a secret ally. A bid is made by naming a card by rank only (e.g. Ace, Trey, King, etc.). Whoever names the lowest card becomes the soloist and announces trumps. Whoever holds the called rank of the declared trump becomes his partner, but may reveal himself only by the play. A bidder may call a card in his own hand, thereby playing without a partner, but does not announce this fact.

Eldest leads. Players must follow suit if possible, otherwise may play any card. A trick is taken by the highest card of the suit led, or by the highest trump if any are played. The winner of each trick leads to the next.

If the declarer takes 61+ card-points without an ally, he scores 4 game-points, otherwise it is 2 to him and 1 to his ally. Either way, each opponent loses 1 point. These scores are doubled for winning every trick, and reversed if the declarer loses. Game is 11 points.

Variant A Deuce bid may be overcalled by raising in fives the minimum number of card-points required to win, e.g. '66', '71', etc.

Briscolone

(2p) As two-handed Briscola, but with five cards each and no trumps. Theoretically, suit must be followed throughout; but, as the rule cannot be policed, players may agree to ignore it.

Brusquembille

(2p) A probable ancestor of this family, Brusquembille is first recorded in 1718 and takes its name from that of a famous French actor of the day. Play as Briscola, but with a 32-card pack, ranking and counting A11, T10, K4, Q3, J2, Nine-Eight-Seven zero. Aces and Tens are *brusquembilles*, and a side-payment is made for winning a trick with, or containing, each of them.

Bisca

(2–4p, 40c) A relative of Briscola played by Asian Indians in Guyana; description elicited by Andrew Pennycook from informants at an ethnic party in London, *circa* 1975. Two or three play for themselves, four crosswise in partnerships. Forty cards, ranking and counting as follows:

A	7	K	J	Q	6	5	4	3	2
11	10	4	3	2	0	0	0	0	0

If three play, remove a low card. Deal three each, stack the rest face down, establish trumps by cut and show. Play tricks, drawing from stock (winner first) after each one. To the lead of a non-trump you may follow suit or trump as preferred, but may renounce only if unable to follow. To a trump lead you may play anything (*sic*). When the stock is exhausted, play the remaining cards out. The winner is the player or side with the greatest value in card-points. There is, however, a 'sudden death' win, made by capturing a Seven with the Ace of the same suit.

Bisca is also played in Brazil, but with a 52-card pack headed Ace 11, Ten 10, King 4, Jack 3, Queen 2, and with a hand of nine cards each. To the lead of a trump, you must follow suit and head the trick if possible, but to any non-trump lead you are free to play any card without restriction.

Brisca

(2–4p, 40c) Three-card Bisca as played in Spain. One source says that players must follow suit to the card led, another says they do not. The latter seems more likely.

Bohemian Schneider   2 players, 32 cards

A nice little two-hander from central Europe.

Deal six cards each, in two rounds of three, from a 32-card pack ranking and counting as follows:

A	K	Q	J	T	9	8	7
11	4	3	2	10	0	0	0

The aim is to win card-points in tricks, which are played in an unusual way. Non-dealer leads to the first trick and the winner of each trick leads to the next, after having drawn the top card of stock (so long as any remain) and waited for the other to draw the next. The second to a trick may play any card regardless of suit, but can win the trick only by playing the next higher card of the suit led. For example, ♥T, if led, can be captured only by ♥J. Count a single game or stake for taking 61+ card-points, double for 91+, treble for all 120 (not necessarily winning every trick).

Variations

1. By agreement, an Ace is captured by the Seven of its suit.

2. By agreement, a card is captured by any card of the next higher rank, regardless of suit.

3. In a simpler version, possibly ancestral, the counting-cards all count 1 each. You score 1 for taking 11+, 2 for 16+, 3 for all 20.

Elfern

(2p, 32c) A primitive German game akin to Bohemian Schneider. Elfern means 'making elevens'. Its alternative title, Figurenspiel, means 'the honours game'. Though not an 'Ace-11' game, it may be ancestral to the family.

Deal six each from a 32-card pack ranking AKQJT987 and stack the rest face down. The aim is to capture, in tricks, at least 11 of the 20 honours – Aces, Kings, Queens, Jacks and Tens. Eldest leads. Suit need not be followed. The higher card of the suit led wins the trick. There are no trumps. The trick-winner draws the next card from stock, waits for the other to draw, and leads to the next. When none remain, suit must be followed if possible in the play of the last six tricks. Count a single win for taking 11–14 honours, double for 15–19, treble for all twenty. *Variant.* Before play, turn the top card of stock for trumps and half cover it with the pack, to be taken by the loser of the sixth trick. A trick can then be taken by the higher trump if any are played. In the last six tricks, a player unable to follow suit must trump if possible.

| Bura
2–6 players, 36 cards

A game played in Russian prisons, as described in *The Playing-Card* (XXVII, 2) by John McLeod, from information supplied by Dr Alexey Lobashev.

Preliminaries Best played by two, with a 36-card pack, ranking and counting Ace 11, Ten 10, King 4, Queen 3, Jack 2, numerals Nine to Six nothing.

Deal When everyone has added an agreed stake to the pot, deal three cards each and stack the rest face down. Turn the next card for trump and half bury it under the stack.

Object To be the first to claim (correctly) to have captured cards totalling 31 or more.

Play Eldest leads first. The leader may play one card, or two or three of the same suit. The followers must each play the same number of cards, but may freely choose which, there being no need to follow suit. A single trick is taken by the highest card of the suit led, or by the highest trump if any are played. If two or three cards were led, each one is played to as a separate trick. You can win a multiple trick only by winning both or all three tricks individually.

> Example: Diamonds are trump. Alex leads ♠K-J. Boris plays ♦9 ♣J, which beats one card (by trumping) but not the other. Grigori plays ♦A♠Q, which respectively beat ♦9♠K and ♠J♣J, giving him a multiple trick worth 22.

Draw Won tricks are stored face down and may not be referred to. After each trick, each in turn, starting with the trick-winner, draws cards from stock until all have three again. If not enough remain to go round, take as many as possible for all to have the same number and play the hand out without drawing any more.

Pay-off Play ceases when someone claims to have made 31 or more, which must be done by memory and without checking. The claimant's cards are then examined. If the claim was successful, he wins the pot. If not, he doubles it. Each subsequent deal is made by the previous claimant, even if he claimed wrongly. If no one claims, the pot is added to and carried forward, and the same dealer deals again.

Special hands Certain hands entitle their holder to lead to the next round of tricks, even if they didn't win the previous trick. These are, from lowest to highest:

1. *Modolka*. Three cards of the same suit.
2. Three Aces.
3. *Bura*. Any three trumps.

A player who holds such a hand must declare it before the previous trick-winner leads if he wishes to lead instead. If two or more players have the same special hand, priority goes to whichever of them would be playing earlier to the trick if it were led by the previous trick-winner.

Sedma

2–4 players, 32 cards

Sedma, the Czech for 'Seven', is an appropriate title for this Bohemian game with rules as simple as they are unique. It appears here because I suspect it was probably originally played with the old 11-10-4-3-2 schedule.

Preliminaries Two or three may play, each for himself. The game is best for four, sitting crosswise in partnerships and playing to the right.

Cards Thirty-two, consisting of ATKQJ987 in each suit. Deal eight each, one at a time. The aim is to win Aces and Tens in tricks, each counting 10 points. A further 10 for winning the last trick makes 90 in all, so preventing ties.

Play Eldest leads first, and the winner of each trick leads to the next. Subsequent players need not follow suit but may play as they please. A trick is taken, when the leader deems it complete, by the last played card of the same rank as the one led. Sevens are wild, and therefore duplicate the rank led. *Examples*:

played	winning card	score
9-J-A-J	Nine, neither matched nor trumped	10
9-A-A-9	second Nine	20
9-T-7-J	Seven (counts as a Nine)	10
A-7-Q-A	second Ace	20
7-7-7-7	fourth Seven	0

When four cards have been played, the leader to the trick may, regardless of who won it, leave it in place and lead to another round with a card of the same rank as the previous lead, or a Seven. The others then play another card, as before. In fact, the leader may lead yet a third and fourth time, if he wishes, so that the trick may contain 4, 8, 12 or 16 cards.

When the leader is unable or unwilling to lead again, the trick is taken by the last-played natural or wild duplicate of the card originally led. Each in turn, then, starting with the trick-winner, draws from stock until he has four cards, or until none remain, and the winner of the trick leads to the next.

When the stock runs out, the remaining cards are played with however many remain in hand.

Score Each player scores the points made by his own partnership. The scores are carried forward, and the winner is the player with the highest total after 12 deals, or any other agreed number.

Hola

(2p or 4pp, 52c) The Polish equivalent of Sedma uses a full pack and is typically played, to the left, by four in partnerships. If three play, reduce the pack to 51 by removing any card other than an Ace, Ten, Seven or Two. Play as Sedma but with these differences:

• Twos are wild in addition to Sevens;
• At the end of a round the leader is allowed to lead to another round with any card, not necessarily of the same rank as the previous lead.

Each side scores 10 for each Ace and Ten taken in tricks, and one side adds 10 for winning the last trick. In the rare event of winning every trick, a side scores 170 instead of 90. This feat is called *hola*, from a Slavic word meaning 'nakedness'.

If the non-dealing side take 50 or fewer points, the same player deals again for the next hand. If they take 60 or more, the deal passes to the left-hand opponent of the previous dealer.

Play up to any agreed total, e.g. 500 points.

(Source: David Przednowek, via the Pagat website.)

Zsírozás

(2p or 4pp, 32c) The Hungarian equivalent of Sedma is normally played with the national 32-card pack, the so-called 'Tell pattern' (after William Tell) with German suit symbols. If you haven't any, use an international pack with AKQJT987 in each suit. Four play crosswise in partnerships, and to the right.

Play as Sedma, but with these differences.

The trick leader must pass if his side is winning the trick. He may lead again only if it is being won by the other side, and even then he must lead a duplicate of the original lead, or a Seven to represent it.

The side taking a majority of Aces and Tens (known as *zsír*, 'grease'), or who took the last trick in the case of equality, scores 1 game-point. For taking all the grease but not all the cards, they score 2, and the losers are said to be *kopasz* (bald). Winning every trick scores 3, and the losers are said to be *csupasz* (naked). Play up to 5 or 10 game-points.

Zsírozás means larding, greasing, or basting. In the partnership game, a player may give his partner one of four instructions, namely 'Win it [if you can]', 'Don't win it', 'Lard it' (by playing an Ace or Ten if possible), or 'Don't lard it'.

Ristiklappi ('Crossclap')

(2p or 4pp, 52c) A Finnish relative of Sedma, sent me by Veikko Lähdesmäki. The rules were written in very unreliable English (albeit miles better than my Finnish), and I have had to adjust them to make the game playable. In particular, Ländemäki says the trick is taken by the first-played duplicate; but I find this incredible, and have made it the last, as in Sedma.

Four players sitting crosswise in partnerships receive five cards each in batches of three and two from a 52-card pack, ranking and counting as follows:

A	T	K	Q	J	9-8-7-6-5-4-3-2
11	10	4	3	2	0

The rest go face down as a stock. The total of card-points available is 120. The aim is to be the first side to reach 121 from the capture of counting-cards over as many deals as necessary. Eldest leads to the first trick. Subsequent players may play any card. The trick is taken by the last-played card of the same rank as the one led, or by the one led if nobody duplicates it, and the winner of each trick leads to the next. So long as any cards remain in stock, each in turn, starting with the trick-winner, draws the top card of stock before playing to the next trick. Having drawn from the stock, the trick-winner has the privilege of 'spicing' the trick by adding to it the card just drawn, and taking back into hand the card he won the trick with. Furthermore, any player upon playing to a trick need not play from hand but may speculatively turn the top card of stock and play that instead.

Don't forget . . .

- Play to the left (clockwise) unless otherwise stated.
- Eldest or Forehand means the player to the left of the dealer in left-handed games, to the right in right-handed games.
- T = Ten, p = players, pp = in fixed partnerships, c = cards, † = trump, ☆ = Joker.

9 King-Queen games

These games also belong to the 'Ace 11, Ten 10' family, but extend it by awarding points to anyone declaring the 'marriage' of a King and Queen of the same suit in the same hand – typically 20 for a plain-suit marriage, 40 for a 'royal' or trump marriage. A further bonus of 10 for winning the last trick raises the card-point total from 120 to 130, and the winning target from 61 to 66, thereby giving rise to the great game of that name (also called Schnapsen). Counting marriages towards the target score makes Sixty-Six and its descendants even more exciting, in that marriages are normally unpredictable: they may not occur at all, or they may bring a sudden win to a player who was previously trailing.

Sixty-Six (Marriage)   2 players, 20 or 24 cards

The oldest Marriage game remains one of the best two-handers ever devised. Despite claims for its invention at Paderborn, Westphalia, in 1652, it is not attested earlier than 1715, appearing first under the title Mariagespiel, later Sechsundsechzig from its target score. Though still played in Germany, it is in Austria that it ranks (with Tarock) as a truly national game. Here it is called Schnapsen, or Schnapser – possibly with bibulous connotations – but, as you need a really clear head to play it well, it may instead relate to *schnappen*, meaning 'grab'. Schnapsen differs from Sixty-Six only in that it is played with the Nines stripped out of the 24-card Schnapsen pack. This makes for an even tighter and snappier game, one full of speed and variety yet demanding a high degree of skill.

Cards 24, ranking and counting Ace 11, Ten 10, King 4, Queen 3, Jack 2, Nine 0.

Deal Deal six each in two batches of three, turn the next for trump, and half cover it with the rest of the stock face down.

Object To be the first to correctly announce that you have reached 66 or more points for cards, marriages (if any), and 10 for winning the last trick (if applicable). Counting must be done mentally, not orally or in writing.

Play Elder leads first, and the winner of each trick leads to the next. Suit need not be followed. The trick is taken by the higher card of the suit led, or by the higher trump if any are played. The trick winner then draws the top card of the stock and waits for the other to do likewise before leading to the next trick.

Trump Nine When in possession of the trump Nine, whether dealt or drawn, you may exchange it for the turn-up immediately before leading or following to a trick, provided that (a) you have won at least one trick, and (b) the turn-up is still covered by at least two cards.

Marriages When holding a King and Queen of the same suit, you may score 20 for the marriage, or 40 in trumps, by showing both cards when leading either of them to a trick (but not when following). If as elder you are dealt a marriage, and declare it, but never win a trick in that deal, the marriage score is annulled.

Last six When the last card of stock (the turn-up) has been taken, the last six tricks are played to different rules. Now you must follow suit if possible, otherwise must trump if possible; and in either case must beat the card led if possible. Marriages are no longer declarable. The winner of the last trick scores 10.

Closure If, before the stock is exhausted, you think you can reach 66 on the cards remaining in hand, you may close the stock by turning the turn-up card face down. You may do this either before or after drawing, so the number of tricks remaining will be either five or six. These are then played as above, but without 10 for last (which applies only if all twelve tricks are played).

Score Play ceases when the last trick has been taken, or when either player claims to have reached 66. If both have 65, or it transpires that one player reached 66 without declaring, it is a draw, and the next deal carries an extra game-point. A player correctly claiming 66 scores:

   1 game-point, or

   2 if the loser failed to reach 33 (*schneider*), or

   3 if the loser took no trick (*schwarz*).

If a player claims 66 incorrectly, or fails to reach 66 after closing, the opponent scores 2 game-points, or 3 if he took no trick.

Notes Keep track of the other player's points as well as your own throughout play. In the first half, try to reserve plain-suit Aces for capturing Tens, but be prepared to lead them if you have no trumps and wish to draw them from your opponent's hand. The trump Ace is always best reserved for capturing an Ace or Ten rather than for drawing a low trump. Trumps in general are best not led before the last six tricks. Keep careful track of the Kings and Queens played, so as to know whether or not it is worth aiming for a marriage. The main point of the game is to know when to close it. Expert players conclude more games by closing than by playing them through to the bitter end.

Schnapsen

(2p, 20c) Same as Sixty-Six, but drop the Nines, and deal five each (3+2 or 2+3), from the resultant 20-card pack. Play as above, except that it is the trump Jack that may be exchanged for the turn-up.

Auction Sixty-Six

(4pp, 24c) American partnership version. Game is 666 points over as many deals as necessary, compiled from the actual point-scores made for counting-cards, marriages and last tricks. Deal six each, leaving no stock. Each in turn bids for the right to name trumps, but without actually naming a suit until a contract is established. The lowest bid is 60, succeeding bids are made in multiples of 6 (66, 72 etc.) or 10 (70, 80), jump-bids are allowed, and the highest bid is 130. A player who passes may not bid again unless his partner bid.

When three players pass in succession, the last (highest) bidder declares trumps and leads first (not necessarily a trump). Players must follow suit if possible, otherwise may play any card. The trick is taken by the highest card of the suit led, or by the highest trump if any are played, and the winner of each trick leads to the next.

If the bidding side takes at least what it bid, it scores what it makes. If not, the other side scores what it makes, plus the amount of the bid. The 'grand bid ' (130), whether won or lost, counts 260 to the scoring side.

Tausendeins

(2p, 32c) This Austrian variant is played also in Switzerland under the name Mariage, in Denmark as Deliriumseksogtres, and in the Ukraine as a three-hander called Tyzicha (q.v.). Deal six each from a 32-card pack ranking ATKQJ987, and stack the rest face down. Play as at Schnapsen, but at no trump until a marriage is declared. This is done by leading a King or Queen to a trick and showing its partner. The first marriage establishes a trump suit, and each subsequent marriage changes it to that of the marriage suit. The score for a marriage is 40 in diamonds, 60 in hearts, 80 in spades, 100 in clubs. Marriages may not be made in the last six tricks, and there is no score for winning the last. The winner is the first to reach 1001 over as many deals as it takes, and play ceases the moment either player claims to have done so.

Mariage

(2p, 24c) As Schnapsen, but deal five each from a 24-card pack. The first marriage declared scores 20, regardless of suit, the second 40, the third 60, and the fourth 80. There is a bonus of 100 for winning the last five tricks. Actual scores are divided by ten, remainders are ignored, and the winner is the first to reach 100.

> ☛ Mariage also denotes several similar but slightly varying games. One, the ancestor of Sixty-Six, is virtually identical, but is played with 32 cards, and recognizes, in addition to the marriage, a combination called *amour*. It consists of the Ace and Ten of a suit, and scores 30 points, or 60 in trumps.

Chouine

(2p, 32c) A variety of Sixty-Six or Mariage played in championships at Lavardin, in Loir-et-Cher – '*le plus français des villages de France*' (Daynes, *Le Livre de la Belote*, Paris 1996). Deal five each from a 32-card pack. Game is 101 points. A marriage scores 20, or 40 in trumps. A *tierce* (K-Q-J of a suit) scores 30, or 60 in trumps; a *quarteron* (A-K-Q-J) scores 40, or 80 in trumps; a *cinquante* (five 10-point cards) scores 50; and a *chouine* (A-K-Q-J-T in any suit) wins the deal outright. A game is the best of five deals, a rubber the best of three games.

Briscan (Brisque)

(2p, 32c) An extraordinary elaboration of Mariage from late eighteenth-century France, Briscan is an ancestor of Bezique, lacking only that game's distinctive Queen-Jack combination. But there are plenty of others to be getting on with.

Deal five each from a 32-card pack ranking ATKQJ987. Dealer scores 30 if the turn-up is an Ace, or 10 if any other card higher than Nine. Play as at Sixty-Six/Schnapsen/Bezique. Game is 600 points, scoring as follows:

Sequences Ten ranks between Jack and Nine for sequential purposes. The scores for sequences are all doubled in trumps.

top card of sequence	A	K	Q	J	T	9
sequence of five	300	150	100	50		
sequence of four	100	80	60	40	30	
sequence of three	60	50	40	30	20	10

You cannot score a particular sequence twice. For example, if you declare JT9 for 30, you can't then add the Queen for 40 or the Eight for 30; nor, having scored 40 for QJT9, may you play the Queen or Nine and then rescore JQT.

Quartets Aces 150, Tens 100, Kings 80, Queens 60, Jacks 40.

Marriages 40 in trumps, 20 otherwise. Declarable from the hand or as won in a trick by taking a Queen with the King of the same suit (*mariage de rencontre*).

Carte rouge (a hand composed entirely of courts) 20.

Carte blanche (a hand composed entirely of numerals) 10.

☞ Each of these two is repeated every time the hand is re-formed by the draw of another matching card.

You may exchange the †7 for the turn-up at any time before the stock is exhausted, but score nothing for it. For taking the last card of stock, score 10. For a hand composed entirely of trumps when the last card has been taken, 30. For winning the last five tricks, 30. For winning nine or more in all, 10. Taking all sixteen wins the game outright.

Finally, score for each Ace taken in tricks 11, each Ten 10, King 4, Queen 3, Jack 2.

▌ Bondtolva ('Farmer's Dozen')   2–4 players, 24 cards

The Swedish equivalent of Sixty-Six, Bondtolva (pronounced *boontolva*) has peculiarities of its own. The simplest version is for two.

Preliminaries Two players, each dealing in turn. Deal six each in threes from a 24-card pack ranking ATKQJ9, and stack the rest face down.

Object To be the first to reach 12 points over as many deals as necessary. Points accrue for declaring marriages, for winning the most 'matadors' (Aces and Tens), and for winning the last trick.

Play Elder leads first. Suit need not be followed. A trick is taken by the higher card of the suit led, or, when trumps have been made, by the higher trump. The trick-winner draws the top card of stock, waits for the other to draw, and leads to the next.

Marriages Upon leading to a trick you may declare a marriage by showing a King and Queen of the same suit and leading one of them. The first marriage, called 'trump', scores 2 points and establishes trumps for the rest of the deal. Subsequent marriages score 1 each, but don't change the trump.

End-game When the stock is empty, no more marriages may be declared. Second to a trick must then follow suit if possible, head the trick if possible, and trump if unable to follow.

Score The last trick winner scores 1 point, as does the player who took a majority of Aces and Tens. If equal, that point goes to the player who took most card-points, reckoning each Ace 4, King 3, Queen 2, and Jack 1. If still equal, neither scores it.

Variant You must attain exactly 12 points to win. If the amount you win would take you over 12, you must instead deduct it from your current total.

Comment The first marriage is called a 'trump' for obvious reasons, and each subsequent marriage a 'score' (*tjog*). The latter reflects its original score of 20 points, as in Sixty-Six, Bezique and related games.

Bondtolva for 3–4 players
The cards are all dealt out, and the rules of trick-play are those applying to the two-hander when the stock is empty, except that marriages are declarable throughout.

The four-hander is played in partnerships. Before trumps are established, the leader to a trick may do one of the following:

(a) If holding a marriage, show and lead from it. This scores 2 and fixes the trump suit.

(b) If not, ask if partner holds a marriage. If so, partner shows it for 2 and this establishes trumps. Any card may then be led.

(c) Holding one card of a marriage, ask if partner can pair it, by saying (for example) 'Hearts?' If partner says 'Yes', the trump is established for 2 points and the qualifying King or Queen must be led. If 'No', any card may be led of that suit, but no other.

Note that only one marriage query may be made on the same turn. Given a negative to (b) or (c), the asker must win a trick and be on lead before asking again. Subsequent marriages score only 1 each and do not change the trump.

Upon leading, once trumps have been established, you may:

(a) declare a marriage yourself by showing and leading from it; or

(b) ask if your partner has one. If so, you must lead the stated suit in order to score the point; or

(c) lead a King or Queen and ask if your partner can wed it. If so, the marriage partner must be shown, but need only be played to the trick in order to comply with the rules of following – i.e. head the trick if possible, and trump if unable to follow suit.

Marjapussi

The Finnish equivalent of Bondtolva. (See Kurki-Suonio, *Korttipelit ja Pasianssit*, Otava Publications Inc., 1992, Pekka Ranta, *Marjapussissa Porvooseen*, WSOY, Porvoo, 1993, and <www.pagat.com>).

Tute   2 players, 40 cards

Tute (pronounce both syllables) has replaced Tresillo in the playing affections of Spain and Latin America. The name is from Italian *tutti*, 'everyone', but the game itself is obviously a Hispanicized version of Sixty-Six. It is played in many forms by two, three or four. The following two-hander, of which no two native accounts appear to be identical, is called Tute Habañero.

Preliminaries Two players, each dealing in turn. Deal eight each in ones from a 40-card pack, ranking and counting as under, and stack the rest, face down. Turn the next for trump and half cover it with the stock.

A	3	K	Q	J	7	6	5	4	2
11	10	4	3	2	0	0	0	0	0

Object To be the first to correctly claim to have reached 101 points for cards and combinations. These must be totalled and remembered as play proceeds.

Play Eldest leads first, and the winner of each trick leads to the next. Second to a trick must follow suit if a trump is led, but otherwise may play any card. If unable to follow to trumps, you must lay your cards face up on the table and keep them there until you draw a trump, when you may take them up again. The trick is taken by the higher card of the suit led, or by the higher trump if any are played. The winner of a trick draws the top card of stock and waits for the other to do likewise.

Turn-up exchange If the turn-up is a Jack or higher, you may take it in exchange for the Seven, but not before you have won a trick. Similarly, if it is a Seven – whether initially dealt or subsequently substituted for a Jack – you may take it in exchange for the Two. Exchanging is optional.

Combinations Before leading, the previous trick-winner may show and score for a marriage or a tute. A marriage is a King and Queen of the same suit and scores 20, or 40 in trumps. A tute is all four Kings or all four Queens, and wins the game outright. A combination may be declared only upon winning a trick, and only one may be declared per trick.

Last eight When the stock is exhausted and the turn-up taken in hand, you may, before the last eight are played, declare *capote*, thereby undertaking to win all eight. If successful, you win the game outright; if not, you lose. The last eight tricks are played to different rules. Combinations may no longer be declared. Second to play must follow suit if possible and win the trick if possible, and, if unable to follow suit, must play a trump if possible. Count 10 for winning the last trick.

Winning Play ceases with a tute or capote, or when one player claims to have reached or exceeded 101 points, or when either player is found to have reached 101 without claiming it. A correct claim of 101 wins the game, a false claim loses. If neither has claimed 101 by the end of play, but it transpires that both have made it without declaring, the winner of the last trick wins. If no one wins in the first deal, the winner of the last trick deals to the next.

Variant Some accounts give the target score as 121.

Gaigel

3–4 players, 48 cards (2 × 24)

A multi-player extension of Sixty-Six, much played in Württemberg, sometimes by three but mainly by four in partnerships. There is no universally accepted standard version and the game is subject to many local variations and extras. The following is based on Claus D. Grupp, *Schafkopf, Doppelkopf* (Wiesbaden, 1976).

Preliminaries Four players sitting crosswise in partnerships play to the right. The winning side is the first to correctly claim to have reached 101 points, which usually happens before all cards have been played out. Points are scored for capturing counters in tricks and for declaring marriages. Players must remember their points as they accrue, and may not announce or write them down.

Cards Deal five cards each (3+2 or 2+3) from a 48-card pack containing two in each suit of the following ranks:

A	T	K	Q	J	7
11	10	4	3	2	0

(Eights and Nines were dropped to speed the game up, and Sevens retained because they play a significant part.) Turn the top card for trumps and half cover it with the stock.

Play Eldest leads. So long as cards remain in stock players may lead and follow with any desired card regardless of suit. A trick is taken by the highest card of the suit led, by the highest trump if any are played, or by the first played of two identical winning cards. Each trick winner draws the top card of stock, waits for the others in turn to do likewise, then leads to the next. When the stock is empty, players must follow suit and head the trick if possible; must trump and overtrump if unable to follow; and may renounce only if unable to do either.

Marriages Upon playing to a trick you may declare a marriage by showing a King and Queen of the same suit and playing one of them. Count 20 for a plain marriage or 40 in trumps, but only if your side has already won a trick, or wins the trick to which you are playing.

> Example: The leader's side has not yet won a trick. Trump Ace is led. As this is bound to win, leader's partner may declare a marriage upon playing to it. The same principle may be extended to any other certain trick.

No player may declare more than one marriage in the same deal. A note may be kept of declared marriages to avoid argument.

Taking the turn-up You may at any time take the trump turn-up in exchange for †7 (called the *dix*), provided that (a) your side has won at least one trick, and (b) the turn-up is covered by at least three cards. Alternatively, you may place your †7 under the turn-up. If, then, your partner has the other †7, he may either take the turn-up and give you his †7, or invite you to take the turn-up if he thinks it would be better in your hand. If he hasn't, neither opponent may take the turn-up, and, if either of them plays the other Seven to a trick, you may promptly take the turn-up to restore your hand to the correct number. You must do this before the last draw of cards, and if the last draw includes a *dix* it may not be exchanged.

Score Play ceases when anyone claims either that their own side has reached or exceeded 101 in counters and marriages, or that the opposing side has done so and failed to claim before leading to the next trick. If correct, his side wins a single game, or a double if the other has not yet won a trick. (Even if they were about to win the trick in which the winning side reached 101 by declaring a marriage.) If incorrect, the other side wins a double game, or gaigel. (Incorrectly claiming a win is called 'overgaigling', and incorrectly failing to do so 'undergaigling'.)

Variations The version described above is that played in Remstal, which also includes the following local elaborations.

1. By agreement, the first trick in each deal (only) is played as follows. Eldest leads a non-trump Ace, the opponents refrain from trumping, and his partner throws him a high-counting card. Having no such Ace, he may lead any other non-trump, face down (this is called 'diving'). The others also play face down; the played cards are faced; and the trick is taken by the highest card of the suit led, trumps being powerless. It is

also permissible to 'dive' an Ace, by playing it face down and announcing 'second Ace'. In this case, however, it can be lost if someone else plays the other Ace of the same suit, which then counts as if it were the first Ace played. (But it is permissible to dive an Ace if you hold its twin yourself, so that there is no danger of losing it.)

2. A player showing five Sevens, whether dealt or drawn, wins for his side without further play. The same result may be applied for holding five cards of the same suit.

3. An extension of the above is that a player holding four Sevens or four of a suit, and waiting for the fifth, must announce 'I'm on Sevens' or 'I'm on a flush'. In this case, so long as cards remain in stock, he is not permitted to win a trick. Whatever he plays counts as a plain-suit Seven, even if it happens to be the Ace of trumps!

4. Some circles play with 'winking' – that is, conventional signals, such as nods, winks, and grimaces, to indicate to a partner the holding of certain cards or suits. Winks must be common and intelligible to both sides, the aim being to make them without being spotted by an opponent.

Homme de Brou

(3–4p, 32c) An interesting marriage game recorded in an *Académie Universelle des Jeux* published at Lyon in 1802. Four play in fixed partnerships or three with a dummy. Use a 32-card pack ranking ATKQJ987 or AKQJT987 (whether Ten ranks high or low is not specified). Deal eight each and turn the last for trump. Rules of trick-play, also unspecified, are probably those of Whist. King-Queen of the same suit is a marriage, and K-Q-J of a suit is a tierce. Before play, any marriage or tierce held in one hand may be declared and scored by its holder. During play, a trick containing a marriage or tierce (*de rencontre*) is scored by the side that wins it. The basic score of 20 for a marriage and 30 for a tierce is doubled if made in trumps, and doubled if made *de rencontre*. At end of play each side adds the card-points they took in tricks, counting each Ace 11, Ten 10, King 4, Queen 3, and Jack 2. Game is 300 points.

Tyzicha

An enjoyable but skill-demanding three-hander, Tyzicha is short for *tyzicha odin*, which is Russian for one thousand and one, its target score. It was first described in English in *Games and Puzzles* magazine by Don Laycock, an Australian games expert with a Ukrainian mother-in-law. The following account is based on his (or, rather, her) rules, but with slight modifications from Czech and German sources.

Preliminaries Three players use a 24-card pack, ranking and counting thus:

A	T	K	Q	J	9
11	10	4	3	2	0

Deal Deal a batch of three cards each, then a widow of three cards face down to the table, and the remainder one at a time till each player has seven.

Object To be the first to reach 1001 points. Points accrue for winning counters in tricks (120 in all) and for declaring marriages.

Bidding Players bid to become the soloist. The first bid is made by the player at dealer's right (not by eldest), who must bid at least 110 or pass. Higher bids are made in multiples of 10. When two have passed, the third is the soloist. If the first two players pass, eldest is forced to bid at least 100.

Card exchange The soloist turns the widow up for all to see, except in a forced game, when he takes it up without showing it. If the widow is unhelpful, he may concede defeat by announcing 'Forty each', in which case each opponent scores 40 and the soloist deducts the amount he bid from his current score. Otherwise he either repeats his bid or raises it to any higher multiple of ten – unless he bid a forced 100, which may not be raised. He then passes one card from his hand, face down, to each opponent, so everyone has eight cards.

Play The soloist leads first, and may establish trumps by declaring a marriage (see below). If not, play begins at no trump. Players must follow suit if possible, otherwise must trump if possible, otherwise may play any card. The trick is taken by the highest card of the suit led, or by the highest trump if any are played, and the winner of each trick leads to the next.

Making trumps If you are on lead and hold a marriage, you may declare it by showing both cards and leading one of them. The suit of this marriage is thereby entrumped and remains so until changed by another marriage (if ever). Your score for the marriage depends on its suit as follows:

♠40, ♣60, ♦80, ♥100

Score Each opponent scores whatever they have made for counters and marriages, unless this brings them to more than 1000, in which case their score remains pegged at 1000. The soloist either adds or subtracts the amount of his bid, depending on whether or not he has taken at least as many points as he bid. The game can be won only by a successful soloist, and that when his score exceeds 1000.

Variations Scores are often rounded off to the nearest five, though the soloist may not round up if he took less than he bid. An opponent's score is then pegged at 995 or 1000 as the case may be, but the soloist wins by exceeding 1000, if only by one point.

Notes on play Players unused to variable trumps may find it difficult to bid convincingly at first. As soloist, and given an even distribution, you can normally expect more than your fair share (40) of the 120 available card-points. Your advantage of the widow and the lead should yield something like 50 to 60, and more if you can quickly establish a good trump suit, while a marriage in hand will add to this anything from 40 to 100, thus explaining the minimum forced bid of 100. Multiple marriages are not advantageous, as the card led from one generally loses the trick, and it may then be impossible to get back in again to declare the next – especially if another suit is entrumped, or one of the marriage partners is lost under the obligation to follow suit. Given four marriage partners of different suits, the chances of mating one of them from the widow are better than even; with three, they are less than even, but worth taking if you are either sufficiently in the lead to be able to afford the risk, or sufficiently behind not to be able to afford not to. Having overcome the hurdle of accurate bidding, the actual play should be relatively straightforward for a skilled soloist, as there are not enough tricks to enable the partners to communicate and co-operate very effectively. The soloist often thereby ends up with considerably more than he bid – which is a good reason for allowing him to score only what he bid, thus exerting even greater pressure to bid up to the full potential of the hand. The game can get very exciting when someone is close to the thousand, as careless bidding at this critical point may induce irrecoverable reversals of fortune.

| Mariáš

This extension of Mariage is the Czech national card game. Of several versions, each with its own range of variations, the following three-hander is essentially that described by V. Omasta and S. Ravik in *Hráči Karty, Karetní Hri* (Prague, 1969).

Preliminaries Three active players, but four may play with each in turn dealing and sitting that hand out. The player at dealer's left is Forehand, and bids and plays first; the next player in rotation is Middlehand, the third Rearhand. The 32-card pack is normally German-suited, but if necessary you can substitute French. Cards rank and count as follows:

German	𝇋 ♤ ♡ 🙂	Daus	Zehn	König	Ober	Unter	9	8	7
point value		10	10	0	0	0	0	0	0
French	♣ ♠ ♥ ♦	A	T	K	Q	J	9	8	7

Object In each deal there is a soloist who aims to take a clear majority of the points available. The total available is at least 90, including 10 for winning the last trick, but may rise to as high as 190 with marriage declarations, which count 20 each, or 40 in trumps.

Deal Deal ten each in batches of 3-2-(2)-3-2. The (2) denotes an extra two dealt to Forehand, giving him 12 in all. Each player's second batch of five must be kept separate from the first.

Bidding Forehand is expected to choose trumps and play a basic game. He starts by examining his first seven cards, leaving his other five face down. If willing to entrump the suit of any of these seven, he lays it, face up, on the table. If not, he picks one of his other five at random, turns it face up, and must accept its suit as trump. He then takes all his cards except the turn-up, and discards any two, face down, as a widow. They may not include an Ace or Ten, and if they include a trump, he must say so.

Forehand then asks the others – Middlehand first – if they will let him play a basic game. One of them can prevent it by offering to play either *betl* (lose every trick playing at no trump), or *durch* (win every trick after nominating any desired suit as trump).

If neither does so, Forehand is the soloist in a basic game, which he is at liberty to embellish by making any of the following announcements:

1. *Seven Last.* An undertaking to win the last trick with †7.

2. *Hundred.* An undertaking to take at least 100 points without making more than one marriage. (But subsequent marriages are scorable once this has been achieved.) There is a bonus for doing this anyway, but it is doubled for announcing it beforehand.

3. *Hundred and Seven.* Both the above bids may be combined.

4. *Double Seven.* An undertaking to win both the last trick with †7 and the penultimate trick with any other Seven. (If either of these fails, the other is also considered to have failed.)

5. *Betl.* A bid to lose every trick at no trump. Cards rank AKQJT987, and there are no scores for Aces, Tens or last. Betl may be played open, with all players' hands face up on the table, for double the score.

6. *Durch.* A bid to win every trick, playing with the turned suit as trump. (Unlike the others, Forehand may not entrump a suit other than the one turned.)

Other announcements and doubles Either opponent, if holding †7, may announce 'Seven last', thereby undertaking to win the last trick with it. (There is a penalty for playing †7 to the last trick and losing it, whether announced or not.) Similarly, either opponent may call 'One hundred', thereby obligating his partnership to take 100 points with the aid of not more than one marriage.

It is possible to double the basic game, and either or both of the announcements. Each may be doubled at different levels: *double* (×2), *redouble* (×4), *tutti* (×8), *retutti* (×16). As to the basic game, either opponent may double the soloist, the soloist may then redouble, and so on, alternating between the soloist on one hand and the opposing partnership on the other. As to the announcement of Seven last or One Hundred, it can be doubled by either opponent if the soloist bids it, or vice versa, and further levels of doubling continue alternately.

It is necessary to specify what is being doubled. For example, a round of bidding might go:

Forehand	Clubs, hundred
Middlehand	Double
Dealer	Seven last
Forehand	Redouble the game, double the Seven
Middlehand	Pass
Dealer	Tutti the game
Forehand	Pass

Automatic concession If Forehand bids a basic game, and no extras are added or doubles made, it is considered not worth playing. Forehand is deemed to have won, and scores accordingly.

Play The soloist leads first. Players must follow suit if possible and head the trick if possible. If unable to follow, they must trump and overtrump if possible. The trick is taken by the highest card of the suit led or by the highest trump if any are played, and the winner of each trick leads to the next.

A player holding a marriage announces 'Twenty' or 'Forty' upon playing either of the relevant cards to a trick. The cards of a marriage are not gathered into the trick but left face up on the table in front of the player scoring them, for ease of checking afterwards.

In an open betl or durch, all hands are laid face up on the table at the end of the first trick, and the partners may discuss with one another how best to play.

Score The basic scores for betl and durch are 5 and 10 respectively, or 10 and 20 if played open, and they are affected by whatever level of doubling may have been applied. The appropriate amount is added to the soloist's score if won, deducted if lost.

The scores for a trump game are as follows. All are doubled if hearts were trump, and are subject to whatever additional doubling may have been applied:

Basic game	1
plus	
for each additional 10 points	$1/2$
plus	
Seven last (silent)	1
or Seven last (announced)	2
or Double Seven (announced)	8
plus	

| Hundred (silent) | 2 |
| or Hundred (announced) | 4 |

The relevant score for winning the last trick with †7 goes to both partners if one of them makes it. Playing it to the last trick and failing to win it incurs 1 penalty point, or 2 if it was announced. If this happens to the partners, both are penalized even if one of them wins the trick to which the other played the Seven. If Seven last was announced, its holder may not play it to any earlier trick unless forced to do so.

Ulti (Talonmariáš)   (3 players, 32 cards)

Hungary's national card game is an elaboration of Mariáš, formerly called Talonmariáš, but now more usually Ulti from its bid of winning the last trick with the lowest trump. Though virtually unknown outside its home borders, Ulti is well worth exploring, as it offers some unusual and intriguing features. The following account is based on an article by John McLeod and additional material from Gyula Zsigri. It reflects recent changes in the play, but, as usual, the game is subject to local variations.

Preliminaries As for Mariá (see above). Deal and play to the right.

Deal Lowest card deals first. The player at dealer's left either cuts or knocks. If he cuts, deal seven cards to Forehand and the rest round in batches of five. If he knocks, deal a batch of 12 to Forehand and batches of 10 each to the others.

Object In each deal the highest bidder becomes the soloist and plays alone against the other two. The soloist's aim in a basic game is to take, in tricks, more points than the other two take between them. The points available are basically 90, counting 10 for each Ace and Ten taken in tricks, plus 10 for winning the last trick; but this may be increased (to a maximum of 190) by the declaration of marriages, which count 40 in trumps and 20 in each non-trump suit.

Contracts The biddable contracts are listed below. Any of those involving a trump suit may be increased in value by adding 'ulti' to the basic bid. Ulti is an undertaking to win the last trick with †7, and adds 4 points to the game value (or 8 with hearts trump).

    1. *Game*. An undertaking to win a majority of points for Aces, Tens,

and marriages. It is bid by announcing 'Play' if the intended trump is not hearts, otherwise 'Play in hearts'. A game in hearts overcalls one in a relatively minor suit (one of the other three). The contract is worth 1 game point, or 2 in hearts.

2. *Hundred.* The bidder undertakes to win at least 100 points in play, including the score for not more than one marriage. It is bid by announcing '40-hundred' or 'hearts 40-hundred' if the marriage to be scored for is in trumps, or '20-hundred' or 'hearts 20-hundred' if not. In either case, a heart bid overcalls the same bid made without suit specification. A 40-hundred is worth 4 points and a 20-hundred worth 8, both doubled in hearts.

☞ 20-hundred is a higher bid than 40-hundred, as you can afford to lose only one Ace or Ten, whereas in a 40-hundred you can afford to lose three.
☞ It is legal to bid 20-hundred or 40-hundred without holding a marriage, but hoping to find a required marriage-partner in the talon.

3. *Betli.* An undertaking to lose every trick, playing at no trump, and with each Ten ranking between its Jack and Nine. There are three such bids: simple betli for 5, hearts betli for 10, and open betli for 20. The first two are identical, except for the scores ('hearts' is purely nominal). In open betli, all three play with their cards spread face up on the table after the first trick has been won, and the partners may not confer.

4. *Plain durchmars.* An undertaking to win every trick at no trump, with Tens ranking between Jacks and Nines. As with betli, there are three such bids: simple for 6, hearts for 12, and open for 24. (*Variant:* Only two such bids are recognized: simple durchmars for 12 and open durchmars for 24.) In open durchmars, all three play with their cards spread face up on the table after the first trick has been won, and the partners may not confer.

5. *Trump durchmars.* The soloist undertakes to win every trick with a trump suit specified by himself, and with Tens ranking between their Aces and Kings. This may be bid alone, or with an ulti, a hundred, or both. Trump durchmars scores 6 game points, or 12 in hearts. Open trump durchmars scores 12, or 24 in hearts. (*Variant:* Open durchmars scores 24 whether in hearts or a minor suit.)

Bidding The auction is conducted in a manner unique to Ulti. Forehand may not pass, but must make two discards face down and make an opening bid by naming any contract.

Thereafter, each in turn may (a) pass, or (b) take the two discards, make a higher bid, and discard any two, face down, or (c) bid without taking the discards (but this is unusual). Passing does not prevent anyone from bidding again later, but the auction ends when all three pass in succession, and the last bidder becomes the soloist in the last-named contract. This makes it possible for the last bidder to make one final exchange and a higher bid than his previous one.

➤ The soloist should note that if the final two discards include any scoring cards, they will count to the opponents at end of play as if they had won them in tricks.

A higher bid is one carrying a higher potential score, but there are so many of equal value that they can only be listed in order of priority (see the Table below). Note that any 'heart' bid overcalls the same bid in a relatively 'minor' suit (one of the other three):

Conceding, doubling In a basic 'Play' in a minor suit and without extras, the soloist may concede without play before the first trick is led. This prevents the opponents from doubling or scoring bonuses that might have accrued in the play. Otherwise, either opponent upon playing to the first trick may announce 'double' to the soloist's basic bid, or to his additional ulti announcement, or both. The soloist may then announce 'redouble', thus quadrupling the appropriate score, and either opponent may then announce 'surdouble', thus octupling it. A double or surdouble made by one partner is binding upon the other, except in respect of a betli or durchmars bid. In these cases (only), one or both partners may double, and any such double is binding only upon its maker's final settlement with the soloist.

Ulti: table of bids in order of priority

bid	trump	score
1 play	minor	1
2 play in hearts	hearts	2
3 40–100	minor	4
4 ulti	minor	1 + 4
5 betli	NT	5
6 durchmars	NT/min.	6

bid		trump	score
7	40–100 ulti	minor	4 + 4
8	hearts 40–100	hearts	8
9	20–100	minor	8
10	hearts ulti	hearts	2 + 8
11	40–100 durchmars	minor	4 + 6
12	ulti durchmars	minor	4 + 6
13	hearts betli	NT	10
14	20–100 ulti	minor	8 + 4
15	hearts durchmars	NT/min.	12
16	open durchmars	minor	12
17	40–100 ulti durchmars	minor	4 + 4 + 6
18	20–100 durchmars	minor	8 + 6
19	hearts 40–100 ulti	hearts	8 + 8
20	40–100 open durchmars	minor	4 + 12
21	ulti open durchmars	minor	4 + 12
22	hearts 20–100	hearts	16
23	20–100 ulti durchmars	minor	8 + 4 + 6
24	40–100 ulti open durchmars	minor	4 + 4 +12
25	hearts 40–100 durchmars	hearts	8 + 12
26	hearts ulti durchmars	hearts	8 + 12
27	20–100 open durchmars	minor	8 + 12
28	open betli	NT	20
29	20–100 ulti open durchmars	minor	8 + 4 + 12
30	hearts 20–100 ulti	hearts	16 + 8
31	open durchmars	NT/hearts	24
32	hearts 40–100 ulti durchmars	hearts	8 + 8 + 12
33	hearts 20–100 durchmars	hearts	16 + 12
34	hearts 40–100 open durchmars	hearts	8 + 24
35	hearts ulti open durchmars	hearts	8 + 24
36	hearts 20-100 ulti durchmars	hearts	16 + 8 + 12
37	hearts 40–100 ulti open durchmars	hearts	8 + 8 + 24
38	hearts 20–100 open durchmars	hearts	16 + 24
39	hearts 20–100 ulti open durchmars	hearts	16 + 8 + 24

Play The soloist leads first. Players must follow suit and head the trick if possible; must trump and overtrump if unable to follow; and may renounce only if unable to do either. The trick is taken by the highest card of the suit led, or by the highest trump if any are played, and the winner of each trick leads to the next.

In a basic game, any player holding one or more marriages announces them upon playing to the first trick, by saying (for example) 'Twenty', 'Two twenties', 'Forty and a Twenty', or whatever it may be. Any marriages announced by either partner count to the credit of the partnership, not of the individual.

In a 20-hundred or 40-hundred contract, only one marriage may be counted, and that is the Twenty or Forty implicit in the soloist's bid. If the soloist did not in fact have a marriage, he of course loses the contract.

In an ulti contract, the soloist may not lead or play †7 before the last trick unless he has no other legal play.

Score To win, the soloist must:

- in the basic game, win at least one trick and earn more points from cards and marriages than the other side. (Neither the soloist nor the partners can win by scoring only for marriages.)
- in a hundred bid, take at least 100;
- in a betli, lose every trick; or
- in a durchmars, win every trick.

The value of his bid and announcements, with whatever degree of doubling may apply, is received from each opponent if successful, or paid to each opponent if not. These values are listed in the scoring table (see overleaf).

Bonuses A bonus applies for making ulti, hundred, or durchmars, even if not bid in advance. Thus:

1. *Silent ulti.* If the soloist or a partner plays †7 to the last trick, and it wins, he scores 2 points (4 in hearts) for himself or his side. If the soloist does so, and it loses, he pays twice that amount to each opponent. If a partner does so, and it loses, each opponent pays the soloist, even if the trick was won by the other partner.

2. *Silent hundred.* For taking 100 or more unannounced, the score for the basic game is doubled. A silent hundred may include more than one marriage.

item	bid			unbid	
	min.	♥	*NT*	*min.*	♥
game	1	2	–	–	–
conceded	2	4	–	–	– *a*
100	–	–	–	1	2
40–100	4	8	–	–	– *b*
20–100	8	16	–	–	– *b*
ulti (won)	4	8	–	2	4 *c*
ulti (lost)	4+4	8+8	–	4	8 *c*
betli	–	–	5	–	–
betli hearts	–	–	10	–	–
betli open	–	–	20	–	–
durchmars	6	12	6	3	6 *d*
hearts durchmars	–	(12)	12	–	(6)
open durchmars	12	24	24	–	–
open hearts d.	–	(24)	(24)	–	–

a. Amount paid if the soloist concedes without play.

b. Only one marriage can be counted towards the 100.

c. When ulti is bid, doubled (etc.), and lost, the doubling applies only to the first 4 points (8 in hearts), not to the extra 4 (8) for losing the ulti bid.

d. Unbid durchmars replaces the score for a basic game, if any. If the basic game was doubled (etc.), any bonus for unbid durchmars is also doubled (etc.).

3. *Silent durchmars.* Winning every trick without having bid durchmars earns a bonus of 3 (6 in hearts).

☛ The silent hundred and silent durchmars are affected by any doubling or redoubling that may have been announced, but not the silent ulti.

Ending the game By tradition, a player can bring the game to a close by announcing 'Ace of hearts deals and deals not' ('*Piros ász oszt, nem oszt*'). At the end of the hand following this announcement it is noted who held ♥A when the auction ended. When that player deals next, three more hands are played, and the session ends when the said player would have been about to deal again.

Comment It may take a while to grasp the details and relative values of the various contracts. Once these are overcome, the play of the game, though requiring much skill, offers a greater degree of clarity than many other three-handers similar in format, such as Skat and Tyzicha. Its greatest and most original feature is the fact that the talon changes from bid to bid. This enables players to see and even use one another's discards, and to convey genuine or misleading information through them. With helpful discards, it may be possible to build up a stronger hand, which in turn tends to make the bidding more competitive.

Pip-Pip! 4–10 players, 104 cards (2 × 52)

This jolly little game is of unknown provenance. First described in the 1920s, it looks as if it was invented by an English player with an imperfect knowledge of European marriage games, possibly picked up during the First World War.

Preliminaries From four to ten players use two 52-card packs shuffled together. Deal seven each, turn the next for trumps, and stack the rest face down on top of it. The aim is to score points for (a) declaring marriages and thereby changing the trump suit, and (b) capturing card-points in tricks. For this purpose cards rank and count as follows:

2	A	K	Q	J	T9876543
11	10	5	4	3	0 each

(But the game works just as well with the more authentic European schedule of Ace 11, Ten 10, King 4, Queen 3, Jack 2.)

Play Eldest leads first. Subsequent players must follow suit if possible, but otherwise may play any card. The trick is taken by the highest card of the suit led, or by the highest trump if any are played. Of identical winning cards, the second played beats the first. The winner of each trick draws the top card of stock (so long as any remain), then waits for the others to do likewise in rotation from his left before leading to the next.

Pipping Immediately before the first card is led to a trick, any player holding a King and Queen of the same suit other than trump may change the trump suit to that of the marriage by laying it face up on the table in front of him and calling 'Pip-pip!', thereby scoring 50 points. The two cards remain on the table but continue to belong to his hand until played to tricks. Neither of them may be remarried to the other partner of the same suit, but there is nothing to stop the same suit from being pipped again when the other King and Queen are both shown together. If two players pip before the same trick, both score 50, and the suit is changed to that of the second one called (or, if called simultaneously, that of the player nearest the dealer's left, dealer counting as furthest from his own left).

Ending and scoring When the last card is drawn from stock, play continues until everyone has played out all their cards. It doesn't matter if some players have no card left to play to the last trick. Each player scores for all the marriages he has made, and adds to this total that of all the counters in the tricks he has won.

Zetema

Zetema is not a traditional marriage game but an invented one, first marketed by J. Hunt around 1870. It seems to have been soon forgotten, but (fortunately) not before making its way into *Cassell's Book of Indoor Amusements, Card Games and Fireside Fun* (1881), whence it was enthusiastically rescued and revised by Sid Sackson in *A Gamut of Games* (1969). It is in fact an excellent and unusual game, obviously inspired by Bezique and Poker – then relative novelties – but less earnest and more fun than either. The following account incorporates Sackson's improvements to the scoring system. It also drops the word 'trick', originally used to denote a set of five discards, as it conveyed the false impression of a conventional trick-play game. These sets of discards are better called 'zetemas' in order to give employment to the otherwise redundant and unexplained title.

Preliminaries From two to six may play, three being an ideal number, and four or six playing best in partnerships. Make a 65-card pack by shuffling in a whole suit – it doesn't matter which – from a second pack of identical back design and colour. Deal six each (or five if six play), and stack the rest, face down.

Object To score points for declaring melds in the hand and for winning zetemas. A zetema is a set of five discards of the same rank.

Play Each in turn, starting with eldest, draws a card from stock, adds it to his hand, may declare a meld if he has one, and (usually) ends by making one discard, face up, to the table. Discards are made in sets of the same rank. That is, thirteen wastepiles are formed, one for each rank. A completed wastepile is called a zetema and is discarded, face down, to a common wastepile. The player adding the fifth card to the wastepile scores for the zetema before discarding it. A zetema of Kings or Queens scores 50, Jacks 20, Aces or Fives 15, other ranks 5 each.

Combinations Upon drawing a card, a player may show and score for one of the following combinations:

1. *Sequence* (scores 20). Six cards in sequence, not all the same suit. For this purpose, cards run A23456789TJQK.

2. *Flush* (scores 30). Six cards of the same suit, not all in sequence.

3. *Flush sequence* (scores 50). Six cards in suit and sequence.

4. *Assembly*. Five cards of the same rank. An assembly of Kings or Queens scores 130, Jacks 120, Aces or Fives 110, other ranks 100.

Having declared one of the above, the player ends his turn by discarding one of the declared cards to its appropriate wastepile.

5. *Marriage*. A marriage is a King and Queen of the same suit. They may both come from the hand, or one of them may come from the hand and be matched to a partner lying in the appropriate discard pile on the table. Kings and Queens may be collected quietly and scored simultaneously – the more at one time, the better. One marriage scores 10, two declared simultaneously score 30, three 60, four 100, all five 150. If fewer than five are declared, each marriage in the doubled suit counts an additional ten. Having declared one or more marriages, the player discards them face up to the common wastepile (they do not contribute to zetemas), and restores his hand to six by drawing from the stock. He does not make any other discard.

☞ If you draw the marriage-partner of a King or Queen forming part of a six-card combination already in hand, you may not declare that combination and the marriage in one turn.

End-game If some players run out of cards before others, they simply stop playing. The whole game ceases the moment anyone reaches the target score of 200 or 300, even in mid-play. Otherwise, it ends, very neatly, when the last zetema has been taken and turned face down to the wastepile, leaving an otherwise empty table.

Zetema. South discards the fifth Three, scoring 5 for the zetema. The draw of a King would give a sequence to score on South's next turn.

Comment Assemblies originally scored 100, 90, 80, 60; but they are so difficult to acquire that even with the revisions quoted above they are rarely worth aiming for. The exceptionally high scores for King and Queen zetemas are somewhat academic, as neither of them can ever be completed if so much as a single marriage is declared.

10 Queen-Jack games

A further variation on the marriage theme occurs in the European game of Bezique and its American counterpart, Pinochle. These tend to simplify the card-point counters almost out of existence, replacing them with scores for combinations such as sequences and quartets, whether as originally dealt, or collected by drawing from a stock, or counted by the winner of a trick to which the appropriate cards were played. Their most significant and amusing feature, however, is their characteristic parodying of the marriage theme by the introduction of an extra-marital but high-scoring relationship between a specified Queen and a Jack of the wrong suit – from the other side of the tracks, so to speak. French researchers trace this feature back to an old Limousin game called Besi or Besit, though the still popular Provençal game of Marjolet has primitive features that might make it vie for ancestry.

Bezique
2 players, 2 × 32 cards

> He . . . with a shamed and crimson cheek
> Moaned 'This is harder than Bezique'
>
> Lewis Carroll, *The Three Voices* (1869)

Bézique is basically the name of the two-card combination consisting of ♠Q and ♦J. There are many theories as to its meaning. Some derive it from *bazzica,* the Italian for companion, others from a supposedly Spanish word for a little kiss. Its ancestor *besi* or *besit* means eye-glasses or spectacles. This is also the meaning of *binocle*, from which derives *pinochle*. In the regional pattern of cards first used for this game these two figures were the only ones depicted in profile, thus exhibiting only one eye apiece, and so two eyes in combination. There could be a hint of voyeurism in the whole idea.

In another dialect *besi* means an immature figure, reminding us that ♦J appears as trickster or a wild card in other old games like Reversis, Boston and Guimbarde. This role may be of German origin, as the German equivalent of diamonds is bells, and bells are traditionally

Bezique and **Binocle.** In the traditional French pack, the Queen of spades and
Jack of diamonds are each depicted with only one eye visible, and so are
'binocular' between them. 'They only have eyes for each other' (so to speak).

associated with fools. ('Pull the other one . . .') His partner, ♠Q, has
less of a history, though exhibiting some significance in cartomancy and
her role as Black Maria. Both together formed a winning combination in
Hoc, the court game of Louis XIV, 'the Sun King', at Versailles.

Two-pack Bezique, an improvement on its 32-card ancestor, became
a craze in the Paris clubs of the 1840s. It subsequently spread through
the cultural centres of Europe, was first described in English in 1861,
and soon sprouted larger and more elaborate forms. Like many elaborate
games, it has fallen victim to the ever-increasing need for speed and
simplicity, in this case having been ousted by the vaguely comparable
Gin Rummy. Playing-card manufacturers still occasionally produce
boxed sets containing the appropriate number of 32-card packs and
specially designed Bezique markers for keeping score, and those with
the time and inclination to pursue the game will find themselves well
rewarded by its depth and variety.

Preliminaries Two players each receive eight cards dealt 3-2-3 from
two 32-card packs shuffled together, ranking ATKQJ987. Turn the next
for trump and stack the remainder, face down, half covering the turn-up.

Object To be the first to reach 1000 points over as many deals as
necessary, dealing alternately. Points are scored for capturing brisques
(Aces and Tens) in tricks, and for acquiring and declaring any of the
combinations listed opposite.

Play Elder leads first. Second to a trick may play any card. A trick is
won by the higher card of the suit led, or by the higher trump if any
are played, or by the first played of two identical cards.

trump sequence (A T K Q J)	250
trump marriage (KQ)	40
non-trump marriage	20
double bezique (♠Q♠Q♦J♦J)	500
single bezique (♠Q♦J)	40
any four Aces	100
any four Kings	80
any four Queens	60
any four Jacks	40
trump Seven	7

Brisques For each Ace or Ten won in a trick, score 10 points immediately. (*Variant*: Some players wait until the end of the hand before counting them, but this is not recommended.)

Declarations Winning a trick entitles you to declare a scoring combination. This is done by taking the relevant cards from your hand and laying them face up on the table, where they remain, and continue to form part of your hand, until played to tricks. You then draw the top card of stock, wait for your opponent to draw the next, and lead to the next trick. If the draw gives you a combination, you must wait until you win a trick before you can declare it.

You may declare more than one combination upon winning a trick, but may score only one of them per trick won. Any others must be left in place until another trick is won, and then are scorable only if no card has been played from them.

A card that has been declared once in a combination may later be combined with one or more others, from hand or table, to form a combination of a different type (sequence, marriage, bezique, quartet), but it may not be used twice in the same combination. Thus, the Queen in a spade marriage may not be remarried to the other King, but may later be counted in a bezique or a quartet of Queens. Similarly, with 'eighty Kings' and 'sixty Queens' declared, each possible marriage may be scored in a subsequent trick so long as it remains intact. It is perfectly legal to make a meld entirely from cards already on the table, so long as none of them has already been scored in a combination of the same type.

If you score a trump sequence, you may not subsequently score the marriage it contains; but you may count the marriage first, and then score the sequence upon winning a subsequent trick.

You may declare double bezique by laying out all four cards at once, or by adding a second bezique to a single bezique already scored and still on the table; but if you score for two singles, you may not count the double as well.

Trump seven You may show a †7 and score 10 for it at any time, usually upon playing it to a trick. You may also exchange it for the trump turn-up, but only upon winning a trick, and instead of declaring any combination. (Sources differ as to the detail of this procedure. This is my recommendation.)

End-game The winner of the last trick before the stock is emptied may make one declaration before drawing the penultimate card. When both last cards have been drawn, no more declarations may be made, and each player takes all his cards back into hand. In playing the last eight tricks, the second must follow suit if possible, win the trick if possible, and trump if unable to follow suit. Combinations are no longer declarable. The winner of the eighth trick scores 10 for last.

Score Play continues, with the deal alternating, until one player reaches or exceeds 1000 points, whereupon it immediately ceases. If the loser has failed to reach the 'rubicon' of 500 points, the winner scores a double game or stake.

Variations

1. Instead of turning a card, start at no trump and entrump the suit of the first marriage declared.

2. If spades or diamonds are trump, bezique may be redefined as ♣Q♥J.

Comment The main point of the game is to judge which cards to collect for possible melds and which to throw to tricks, especially when the hand consists entirely of meldable cards. It is important to remember which cards are not available because declared by the opponent or previously played to tricks. Win tricks with Tens wherever possible, as they have no melding value but score 10 each. Lead Aces and Tens to tempt out trumps if weak in trumps yourself. Win tricks only if they

North

In hand   On table

South

Stock and
turn-up

Bezique North has scored 60 for Queens and an earlier bezique for 40, from which the Jack and one Queen have since been played. South has scored 100 for Aces and has a marriage to declare upon winning a trick.

contain brisques, or if you have something to declare, or think your opponent has.

Fildinski (Polish Bezique)

Play as above, but with the following differences. Cards held in the hand may not be melded. Instead, those won by each player are left face up on the table in front of him. Either or both cards of a won trick may be used to form and score for a meld in conjunction with one or more cards already won. More than one meld may be scored at a time, provided that each incorporates a card won in the trick just played, and that no card is used simultaneously in different melds.

Multi-pack variants

Bezique may be played with four, six or eight 32-card packs shuffled together. Four is called Rubicon (or Japanese) Bezique, six Chinese Bezique. The following general rules apply to all. See also the Table below for other scores and details.

Cards See the Table. No card is turned for trump, and no score or significance attaches to the trump Seven.

Four-, six- and eight-pack Bezique features

	Four	Six	Eight
Number of cards dealt	9	12	15
Carte blanche	50	250	–
Sequences			
Trump sequence (ATKQJ)	250	250	250
Non-trump sequence	150	150	150
Marriages			
Royal marriage (trump KQ)	40	40	40
Common marriage	20	20	20
Beziques			
Double	500	500	500
Treble	1500	1500	1500
Quadruple	4500	4500	4500
Quintuple	–	–	9000
Quartets, quintests			
Any four Aces	100	100	100
Any four Tens (*if agreed*)	90	90	90
Any four Kings	80	80	80
Any four Queens	60	60	60
Any four Jacks	40	40	40
Four trump Aces	–	1000	1000
Four trump Tens	–	900	900
Four trump Kings	–	800	800
Four trump Queens	–	600	600
Four trump Jacks	–	400	400
Five trump Aces	–	–	2000
Five trump Tens	–	–	1800
Five trump Kings	–	–	1600
Five trump Queens	–	–	1200
Five trump Jacks	–	–	800
Extras			
Winning the last trick	50	250	250
Add for game	500	1000	1000
The rubicon is:	1000	3000	5000
If loser fails to reach it, add	500	*loser's total*	

Carte blanche Except in eight-pack Bezique, a player dealt no court may show the hand and score for carte blanche (see the Table). Thereafter, so long as each successive card drawn fails to be a court, he may show the drawn card and score *carte blanche* again.

Trump suit Play starts at no trump. The first marriage or sequence declared establishes a trump suit, which remains unchanged throughout.

Bezique If agreed, bezique may be redefined as the Queen of trumps and the appropriate Jack of opposite colour – spades with diamonds, clubs with hearts. In this case, the trump may be established as that of the Queen if a bezique is declared before a marriage. Also, the same suit may not be entrumped twice in successive deals. The score for a multiple bezique obtains only if all cards involved are on display at the same time.

Additional melds

1. Sequences may be declared in plain suits as well as trumps.

2. In six- and eight-pack Bezique, trump quartets are declarable as shown in the Table.

3. It may be agreed to double the score for a quartet if all four suits are represented.

4. Four Tens may be admitted for a score of 90, or 900 in trumps.

Re-forming melds A meld that has been broken up by the play of one or more cards to a trick may be re-formed and scored again by the addition of matching replacements.

Brisques do not count in multi-pack variants, except to break ties in the four-pack game.

Game score Final scores are rounded down to the nearest 100 and the winner scores the difference, plus a bonus if the loser fails to 'cross the Rubicon' – that is, fails to reach the target score specified in the Table for that purpose.

Single Bezique (Cinq Cents, Binage)

(2p, 32c) The ancestor of two-pack Bezique, played with 32 cards and up to 500 points. Captured cards count Ace 11, Ten 10 etc.; ♠Q♦J is called binage; a trump sequence scores 250, plain sequence 120; royal and common marriages count, but not quartets.

Marjolet

2 players, 32 cards

A simpler relative of Bezique, popular in the west of France (Vendée, Marais poitevin, Aunis, Saintonge). The Queen-Jack liaison appears in an unusual and possibly ancestral form. Marjolet, the name attached to the trump Jack, relates to *mariole*, denoting someone sly and crafty, a trickster. It may also be significant that *mari* means 'husband'.

Preliminaries Deal six cards each in twos or threes from a 32-card pack, ranking ATKQJ987 in each suit. Turn the next for trump and half cover it with the face-down stock. If it is a Seven, dealer scores 10 for it.

Object To reach 500 (or 1000 or 1500) points over as many deals as necessary, each dealing alternately. Scores accrue for collecting and declaring melds, as detailed below, and for winning brisques (Aces and Tens) in tricks, these counting 10 each.

Play Elder leads any card to the first trick. Suit need not be followed. The trick is taken by the higher card of the suit led, or by a trump to a plain-suit lead. The winner of a trick draws the top card of stock, waits for his opponent to do likewise, and leads to the next. Before drawing, the trick-winner may show and score for any of the following melds:

- Four Aces 100, Tens 80, Kings 60, Queens 40. (No Jacks.)
- Trump marriage 40, common marriage 20
- *Mariage de Marjolet* = trump Jack and trump Queen 40, or any other Queen 20

More than one combination may be scored at a time. Combinations remain on the table but continue to form part of the hand. Marjolet may be retained and married on different occasions to different Queens, and any given Queen may be married both to Marjolet and to her matching King.

Trump Seven A player drawing or dealt the trump Seven may exchange it for the turn-up and score 10. He may do so only upon winning a trick and before making a draw. The loser of the tenth trick scores 10 upon drawing the last, faced card.

End-game The stock exhausted, players take their melds into hand for the last six tricks. The second to a trick must follow suit and head the trick if possible, otherwise play a trump. The winner of the final trick scores 10, or 50 if he took all six.

Score Each player then sorts through his won cards and scores 10 for each brisque he has taken. The winner is the player with the higher score at the end of the deal in which either player reached the target. (Presumably. Source not explicit.)

Pinochle

Pinochle, pronounced *pea-knuckle* and formerly spelt Penuchle or Pinocle, ranked second only to Bridge in the affections of American cardplayers in the first half of the twentieth century, but has subsequently declined in popularity. American Pinochle developed in nineteenth-century immigrant communities from Binokel, which still remains a popular family game in Württemberg and parts of Switzerland. There are versions for various numbers of players. Two-hand Pinochle is much like two-hand Bezique. Auction Pinochle is an excellent game for three, but is equally playable by four. Adaptations for more than four seem long past their sell-by date.

Pinochle: general features

Cards Forty-eight cards (double-24) ranking and counting as follows.

	A	T	K	Q	J	9
traditional	11	10	4	3	2	0
modern	10	10	10	0	0	0
simplified to	1	1	1	0	0	0

Agree beforehand which card-point system to follow. The traditional is now largely restricted to two-handed play.

Melds The following melds apply. When the simplified point-count system is used, all scores quoted below are divided by 10 (flush scores 15, etc.).

standard melds in all versions of the game		
meld	*definition*	*score*
flush	A T K Q J of trumps	150
royal marriage	trump K Q	40

plain marriage	non-trump KQ	20
Aces around	four Aces, one of each suit	100
Kings around	four Kings, one of each suit	80
Queens around	four Queens, one of each suit	60
Jacks around	four Jacks, one of each suit	40
pinochle	♠Q♦J	40
dix *or* deece	trump Nine	10
additional melds used by agreement		
double flush	2 × ATKQJ of trumps	1500
double pinochle	♠Q♠Q♦J♦J	300
K & Q flush	ATKKQQJ	230
K or Q flush	ATKKQJ or ATKQQJ	190
grand pinochle	♠K♠Q♦J	60

Note:

• Two distinct but identical melds both score.

• The royal marriage contained within a flush does not score separately.

Auction Pinochle for three

Deal fifteen each in batches of 3-(3)-3-3-3-3. The (3) denotes three dealt face down to the table as a widow.

Object The highest bidder becomes the soloist and aims to make at least as many points as he bid from (a) melds declared from hand after taking the widow, (b) card-points taken in tricks, and (c) 10 for winning the last trick. The total available for card-points and last is 250.

Bidding Each in turn, starting with eldest, either passes or makes a higher bid than any that has gone before. The minimum bid is 300 (unless agreed otherwise), and subsequent bids must rise in tens. A player having passed may not come in again. If all pass, the hand is annulled and the next in turn deals.

Widow The bidder turns the widow face up and announces trumps. From the 18 cards now in his possession he shows and scores for as many melds as possible. If these fulfil his bid, there is no play and he scores the value of his game. If not, and he doubts he can fulfil it in play, he may concede immediately for a smaller penalty.

Play The bidder takes all 18 cards into hand and discards, face down, any three which have not been used in melds. Any counters among them will count in his favour at the end of play. He then leads to the first trick.

If a trump is led, subsequent players must not only follow suit but must also beat any other trump already played, if possible. If a plain suit is led, they must follow suit if possible, otherwise trump if possible, but need not overtrump. A trick is taken by the highest card of the suit led, or by the highest trump if any are played, or by the first played of two identical winning cards. The winner of each trick leads to the next.

Score If successful, the bidder scores or receives from each opponent an agreed stake related to the size of the bid. If not, he loses or pays it double, unless he conceded without play. A game valuation scheme might be 1 chip or game-point for a bid of 300, plus 1 or 2 points for each additional 50.

Auction Pinochle for four

Preliminaries Four play crosswise in fixed partnerships. Deal twelve cards each in threes.

Object Each side's aim is to score 1000 or more points over as many deals as necessary. Points are scored for standard melds in individual hands, counters taken in tricks, and winning the last trick, as scheduled above.

Bidding A bid is the minimum point-score a player claims his partnership will make if allowed to name trumps. Eldest may not pass but must make an opening bid of at least 100 (*variant*: 200). Each in turn may thereafter pass or bid any higher multiple of ten. A player having once passed may not bid again. A bid followed by three passes establishes the bidding side, and the player who made it announces trumps, without consulting his partner.

Play Eldest leads to the first trick, and the winner of each trick leads to the next. (*Variant*: Declarer leads first.) As each plays to the first trick, he scores for any combination that he holds and shows. If a trump is led, subsequent players must not only follow suit but must also beat any other trump already played, if possible. If a plain suit is led, they must follow suit if possible, otherwise trump if possible, but need not overtrump. A trick is taken by the highest card of the suit led, or by the highest trump if any are played.

Score The bidding side counts its score first. If they took at least the amount bid, they score whatever they make; if not, they deduct from their score the amount they bid. If the bidding side thereby reaches or exceeds 1000, they win, and the opponents add nothing to their score. Otherwise, the opponents score everything they make – unless they fail to win a single trick, in which case their meld scores are cancelled and they score nothing.

Comment Most hands are worth opening for the minimum 100. By convention, an average-looking hand would be opened at 100 plus the value of melds it contains – for example, 120 shows a plain marriage held, 140 a trump marriage. Another convention is to bid an odd number of tens (e.g. 250, 270) to show a flush held, an even number (e.g. 180, 200) to deny this. As in all point-trick games, players will seek every opportunity to stuff their partners' tricks by throwing high counters to them.

Two-hand Pinochle

(2p, 48c). Deal twelve each in threes and fours, turn the next for trump and half cover it with the face-down stock. Play as at two-hand Bezique, but scoring for melds as at Pinochle. Double pinochle counts only 80, but can be declared in one trick rather than requiring one each. (*Variant.* Many players now give it 300.) Similarly, grand pinochle (♠K♠Q♦J) may be declared at one trick for 60, or 80 if spades are trump. Game is 1000. The first to reach that total calls 'Out' to end the play, and loses if he is wrong. If both have over 1000, play up to 1250, and increase the target by 250 each time this happens. (One recent description allows a trick-winner to draw first then meld from 13 cards, which seems somewhat over-generous.)

Three-hand Pinochle

(3p, 48c) This forerunner of Auction gives everyone a chance to meld, enabling beginners to gain experience faster. Deal sixteen each in fours and turn the last for trump. The first player left of dealer holding a *dix* (✝9) may exchange it for the turned card, the dix then being taken by dealer. This scores 10, so long as that player subsequently wins at least one trick. Players meld and note their scores. Eldest leads, and tricks are played in the usual way, with 10 for last. Each player counts towards game the value of cards captured in tricks plus the value of his melds, unless he won no trick, in which case his melds are also cancelled. Game is 1000, increasing by 250 each time two players reach the target score in the same deal.

Widow Pinochle

(3p, 48c) Played like Auction Pinochle, the highest bidder making his melds from eighteen cards including the widow. Each opponent, however, also scores for melds he makes and separately for counters taken in tricks. The partners keep their tricks separate in case one of them takes no tricks, in which case his melds are annulled. The bidder scores the amount he bid if successful, otherwise zero. Game is 1000. The bidder's score is counted first, and the others' only if he fails to reach the target. If bidder exceeds the target he wins, even if one opponent reaches a higher score on the same deal. If both opponents reach the target but bidder does not, the target is increased by 250 each time this happens.

Non-partnership Pinochle

(4p, 48c) Play as three-hand Pinochle without a widow. Each receives twelve cards and the game is played up to 1000. A player taking no tricks, which happens more often with four, scores nothing for melds.

Widow Partnership Pinochle

(4p, 48c) As Partnership Pinochle, but deal eleven each in batches of 4-(4)-4-3, the (4) denoting a four-card widow dealt face down to the table. Highest bidder takes the widow, melds from 15 cards, then buries four, which count to his side at end of play.

In the 'one-bid' version, each player may make only one bid in the auction and must therefore either pass or bid his hand to the limit.

Firehouse Pinochle

(4p, 48c) – so-called because the players could answer a call, extinguish the fire, and get back to the game without forgetting where they were in the auction – is an extension of the 'one-bid' game, in which each bid from 200 to 300 conveys previously agreed information to one's partner. For example, 200 shows a barely biddable hand, 210 offers a good trump suit but less than 60 in melds, 220 shows good trumps and

60 to 120 in melds, but lacking four Aces; and so on. If the first three pass, the dealer must take the game at 200.

Check Pinochle

(4p, 48c) This extension of Firehouse, not restricted to 'one bid', introduces a bonus feature comparable to above-line scoring at Bridge. Each partnership has a number of checks (chips or counters) which it pays to the other at agreed rates for certain scoring features in addition to those recorded in the scoring.

A player must hold a marriage in order to bid, but this does not apply to the dealer if the first three pass, as he is then obliged to make a bid and may do so at any level. Numerous bidding conventions obtain. For example, 250 implies four Aces held, 290 a roundhouse, 300 a flush. If the bidding side justifies its bid, it scores what it makes; if not, it loses the amount of its bid, the value of its melds, and the total value of counters won in play.

Certain melds made by either partner are immediately rewarded in checks by the opponents as follows:

roundhouse (four marriages)	5
flush (trump sequence)	4
four Aces	2
double pinochle	2
four Kings, Queens or Jacks	1

But these checks are returned if the partnership then fails to make its bid. If the bidding side wins, it collects a number of checks appropriate to the bid made, as follows: 2 for 200+, 4 for 250+, 7 for 300+, 10 for 350+, and thereafter 5 extra for every 50 jump. If the bidding side fails, it pays the opponents twice the appropriate amount.

Additional checks are paid for yet other feats as follows:

10 for game (1000 up) plus 1 per 100 extra scored over 1000

5 more if the losers finish with a minus score

5 for winning all 12 tricks, or

4 for taking 250 card-points but not all the tricks

Contract Pinochle

(4p, 48c) Deal twelve cards each in threes. The lowest bid is 100 and raises go in multiples of ten. Each bid must also mention a prospective trump suit, as at Bridge (e.g. '100 spades – 120 diamonds – 160 hearts', etc.), but all suits are equal and each new bid must be numerically higher. A bid may be doubled by an opponent and redoubled by a defender. The bidding ends when three players have passed.

The opponents do not meld, but the bidding partner lays his melds on the table and scores for them, and his partner does likewise. Scores may then be made for melds made between the partners. Thus the bidder may lay out one or more cards which, considered in conjunction with those of his partner, form valid melds; after which his partner may then lay out more; and so alternately until neither can make any further improvement. At that point the bidder may nominate one card which he needs for another meld. For example, holding ♠Q he may call for ♦J or ♠K to make a pinochle or marriage respectively. If his partner can oblige, the meld is made and scored and bidder may call for another desired card. This continues until his partner can't contribute. It is then the partner's turn to call for a card and, as before, more melds can be made so long as the bidder can supply a nominated card or either partner can add to the cards already melded. As soon as he cannot, the melding is over.

The cards are then taken into hand and, if the bid has not yet been fulfilled by melds alone, the high bidder leads to the first trick. Won cards are counted in the usual way. If the bidding partnership succeeds, it scores the amount of its bid; if not, that amount goes to the opposing side. The score may be doubled or quadrupled as a result of doubling or redoubling earlier.

Two-pack Pinochle

(4p, 80c) Partnership Auction Pinochle using the ATKQJ of four packs. Deal twenty each in fours or fives. Because of the inflated scores, those of the traditional schedule are divided by 10 (see the Table below). The minimum bid is 50. Raises go singly up to 60, thereafter in fives (. . . 55, 60, 65, 70, etc.). If the first three pass, dealer must bid at least 50. As now played, a player who can follow suit to the card led must head the trick if possible.

	single	*double*	*triple*	*quadruple*
flushes	15	150	225	300
pinochles	4	30	60	90
royal marriages	4	8	12	16
common marriages	2	4	6	8
Aces around	10	100	150	200
Kings around	8	80	120	160
Queens around	6	60	90	120
Jacks around	4	40	60	80

4, 8, 12, 16 of a kind must contain an equal number of each suit

Army and Navy Pinochle

(3–4–6p, 80–120c) Played with the Nines stripped out of either four packs (80 cards) or six (120). Three play with twenty-five cards and a five-card widow; four (partnership) with twenty; six (three teams of two each) with twenty. Trumps may be established by turning, by one-bid, or by free auction. Multiple melds with inflated scores are recognized as follows: four Aces, Kings, Queens or Jacks at 100, 80, 60, 40 as usual; eight Aces, etc., score 10 times those values; twelve score 15 times; sixteen score 20 times (for example, sixteen Jacks count 800). Pinochles count 40 single, 300 double, 600 triple, 3000 quadruple. With 120 cards, 20 Aces count 2500, Kings 2000, Queens 1500, Jacks 1200, quintuple pinochle 4000, sextuple pinochle 5000.

Pinochle for Six or Eight

(6/8p, 96c) These realms of addiction are entered with a quadruple 24-card pack and the following scores:

		single	*double*	*triple*	*quadruple*
flushes		150	1500	3000	*a*
royal marriages		40	300	600	1200
common marriages		20	300	600	1200
pinochles		40	300	600	1200
	b	*four*	*eight*	*twelve*	*sixteen*
Aces		100	1000	2000	3000
Kings		80	800	1600	2400

Queens	60	600	1200	1800
Jacks	40	400	800	1200
dixes	10	20	30	40

a. Not possible with only 16 cards dealt.

b. Four, eight, twelve and sixteen of a kind are valid only if represented by an equal number of each suit.

Six receive sixteen each and play as three teams of partners. If a trump is turned, the first holder of a dix left of the dealer exchanges it for the last card and counts 10 for it; otherwise, trumps are established by one-bid or free auction. The last trick may be set at 20 instead of 10 to give a maximum of 500 for cards (instead of 490). Game is 3000, 4500 or 6000 up.

Eight receive twelve each and play as four teams of partners. Quadruple melds cannot be made.

Binocle

(2/4p, 32c) Swiss variety of one-pack Bezique. The 32 cards rank ATKQJ987 per suit, the top five counting 11-10-4-3-2 respectively. Two start with eight cards each and play as at Bezique, the first marriage determining trumps. The ♠Q♦J combination, called binocle, counts 40; grand binocle is ♠K♠Q♦J for 80. If four play, all the cards are dealt and the holders of ♠Q♦J are automatically partners, or one player is the soloist if dealt both. Players must follow suit and head the trick if possible; otherwise they must trump and overtrump if possible. Only the winner of a trick may meld.

Binokel

(2–4p, 48c) The still-popular German game from which Pinochle derives is played, if by three, as at Auction Pinochle but with some differences. Melds are: family (ATKQJ of a suit) 100, trump family 150, double family 1500, marriage 20, trump marriage 40, diss (†7) 10, binokel (♠Q-♦J) 40, double binokel 300, four Aces l00 or Kings 80 or Queen 60 or Jacks 40, eight of a kind 1000, roundhouse (four marriages, one in each suit) 240. A marriage may not be scored separately if forming part of a family or roundhouse. Bidding starts at 200 or 300 as agreed. Besides taking the widow, highest bidder may call for any card not in his hand. Whoever has it must exchange it for whatever the soloist gives him (face down). The opponents may also individually meld, but they score only if they win a trick. A player who takes all 15 tricks scores a bonus of 1000; this may be bid beforehand. Some localities recognize a bid of *bettel* (misère). Players must follow suit and head the trick if possible; otherwise trump and overtrump if possible. If the soloist makes his bid, he scores everything he makes; if not, he loses twice the value of his bid. Game is 1500 up. Four play as partners with eleven cards each and a four-card widow. Two play as at two-hand Bezique/Pinochle with twelve cards each.

Don't forget . . .
- Play to the left (clockwise) unless otherwise stated.
- Eldest or Forehand means the player to the left of the dealer in left-handed games, to the right in right-handed games.
- T = Ten, p = players, pp = in fixed partnerships, c = cards, † = trump, ☆ = Joker.

11 Jack-Nine games

Clob, Clobiosh or Klaberjass, a two-hander of widespread popularity, is probably the best-known member of a family of games originating in the Netherlands and most highly developed in Switzerland.

Jass games are distinguished by the promotion of the Jack to highest position in trumps, with a point-value of 20 like the marriage itself. It is followed as second-highest trump by the trump Nine, which counts 14 points and bears some such name as Menel, or Nel (from *manille*). As in Euchre, the result is that the ranking order of cards differs as between trumps and plain suits, and you have to take this into account when deciding which suit to entrump. The games are all much alike, so if you can play one you can easily learn another. Belote is the national game of France, Klaverjas of the Netherlands, and Jass of Switzerland. (J sounds like Y, as you can easily remember by singing 'Jass, we have no bananas' in a Cockney accent.)

First mentioned in the Netherlands in 1721, Jas(s) is supposedly short for Jasper, a name being applied by the Dutch to the Knave at about the same time as the English were dubbing him 'Jack' in the game of All Fours (also probably of Dutch origin). In 1796 a writer in Switzerland describes it as a new game introduced by Dutch mercenaries. Since then the Swiss have developed countless varieties of it, typically played with cards bearing the traditional Swiss suit symbols of acorns, flowers, shields and bells, and now known as *Jasskarten* from their most characteristic use. So popular have they become that many so-called Jass games are in fact adaptations of completely unrelated games for use with the same cards, such as Hearts and Crazy Eights.

Klaberjass (Clob, Clobby, Clobiosh, Klob, Kalabriasz, Bela, Cinq Cents, Zensa)   2 players, 32 cards

This popular and widespread two-hander has so many names, mostly variations on the same one, that it is hard to know which is best for universal recognition. Klaberjass is probably closest to the original.

Kalábriász or Kalabaer is an ancestor of Alsós, long popular in Hungary, where Klaberjass itself is known as Klob. Bela, which denotes the combination of the King and Queen of trumps, is a Hungarian male forename (as in Béla Bartók), but is better spelt *bella* as it ultimately derives from the French *belle*. An old game recorded in German as Belle-Bruid means royal marriage. However spelt, Klaberjass has always enjoyed greatest favour as a Jewish game, which undoubtedly accounts for its travels and consequent variations.

Preliminaries Two players, 32 cards. In each deal one player becomes the maker by choosing trumps and thereby contracting to score more than the other. Points are scored for declaring melds and winning card-points in tricks, and the winner is the first to reach 500 over as many deals as necessary.

Cards Deal six each in threes. Stack the rest face down, turn the next card for trump and place it beside the stock. Cards rank ATKQJ987 except in trump, which is headed by the Jack (Jass), followed by the Nine (Menel).

trump suit	J	9	A	T	K	Q			8	7
card-points	20	14	11	10	4	3	2	0	0	0
plain suits			A	T	K	Q	J	9	8	7

The total of trick-points available is 162, consisting of 62 in trumps, 90 in plain suits, and 10 for winning the last trick.

Bidding There is an initial round of bidding to see if either player will accept the turned suit as trump. Elder may Take it, or Pass, or Schmeiss. The last is an offer to become the maker with the turned suit as trump if Dealer agrees, or to annul the deal if he doesn't, thereby preventing Dealer from becoming the maker himself. If Elder passes, Dealer has the same three choices. If a schmeiss is rejected by the opponent, the deal is annulled and Elder deals the next. (*Note* The Schmeiss option, though still recorded in books, is now rarely played.)

If both pass, Elder turns the trump card down and may propose another suit as trump, or pass, or schmeiss, which is now an offer to name a suit or abandon the deal. If he passes, Dealer has the same options. If he also passes, the deal is annulled and Elder deals next.

Completion of deal If trumps are made, Dealer deals another batch of three cards each, then turns the bottom card of the stock face up and places it on top. This card is for information only: it may not be taken, and it plays no part in tricks or melds.

Dix If the originally turned suit was entrumped, either player holding the trump Seven (*dix*) may exchange it for the trump turn-up, provided that he does so before declaring any melds.

Melds A score is available for holding a sequence of three or more cards in the same suit, sequential order being invariably AKQJT987 in every suit. A sequence of three counts 20, of four or more 50. Only the player holding the best sequence may score. For this purpose a longer sequence beats a shorter. If equal, the best is the one with the sequentially highest cards. If still equal, a trump sequence beats a plain. If still equal, neither scores. (*Variant*: If still equal, Elder scores.)

To determine which player has the better sequence, Elder announces, on leading to the first trick, 'Twenty' if he has a sequence of three cards, 'Fifty' if four or more. In responding to the first trick, Dealer announces 'Good' if he cannot match 20 or 50, or 'No good' if he can beat it. In case of equality, he asks first 'How many cards?', then, if necessary, 'How high?', then, if still necessary 'In trumps?' At the end of the first trick, the player who has the best sequence (if any) must show and score for his best sequence, and may show and score for any others also held.

Tricks Elder leads first, and the winner of each trick leads to the next. The second to a trick must follow suit if possible, otherwise must trump if possible. If a trump is led, the second must play higher if possible. The trick is taken by the higher card of the suit led or by the higher trump if any are played.

Bella A player holding both King and Queen of trumps may score 20 for the marriage upon playing the second of them to a trick and announcing 'Bella'.

Last trick Winning the last trick scores 10 points extra.

Score Both players then declare their respective totals for melds and card-points. If the trump-maker made more points, both score what they make; if less, his opponent scores the total made by both players. If equal, the opponent scores what he took and the maker scores nothing. (*Variant*: the maker's points are held in abeyance and go to the winner of the next deal.)

The game ends at the end of the deal in which either player has reached or exceeded 500 points. (*Variant*: It ends as soon as either player correctly claims to have reached 500, the rest of that deal not being played out.) The higher total wins.

Comment Scoring for sequences introduces an element of chance, especially since three more cards are dealt between bidding and playing, and the maker's opponent may do very well out of the draw. In the long run, this factor evens itself out, and it should not be taken too much into account when bidding. In particular, don't bid on the probability of filling a potential sequence. Look, rather, to the hand's trick-taking potential, on the certainty of bella if held, and on the probability that a four-card or high three-card sequence already held will prove to be the best.

To succeed as maker you must usually take about 60 card-points in tricks, of which you need to see at least 40 when bidding. Better than a long trump suit for this purpose is the Jack of your proposed trump, or three including the Nine and Ace. Without Jass and Menel, you can easily lose even with a four-card trump; conversely, you can win on as little as Jass alone and two plain-suit Aces.

Don't swap the dix for the turn-up unless it yields a good sequence, or bella, or a safe trump worth 10 or more.

Alsós (Kaláber)

Alsós denotes a Hungarian variety of Klaberjass for two or three players with extra bids borrowed from Tarock. It is extremely complicated and became defunct in the 1950s with the rise in popularity of Ulti. Alsós means 'the Jacks game', as distinct from its predecessor, Felső's, the 'Queens game', also called Kalábriász.

Smoojas (Smousjass)

(2p, 32c) The probable ancestor of Klaberjass and Belote first appears in a Dutch book of 1821 with this name meaning 'Jewish Jass'. Deal nine each in threes from a 32-card pack, turn the next for trump and half cover it with the rest of the stock, face down. The turn-up may be taken in exchange for the trump Seven when possible. Cards rank and count thus:

trump suit	J	9	A	K	Q		T		8	7
card-points	20	14	11	3	2	1	10	0	0	0
plain suits			A	K	Q	J	T	9	8	7

The †J is called Jas, the †9 Nel. Trick-points total 146 (60 in trumps, 81 in plain suits, 5 for last). Melds rank and score from high to low as follows: quint (five or more cards in suit and sequence) 100, four Jacks 200, four Kings 100, four Queens 100, four-card suit-sequence 50, three-card suit sequence (*tierce*) 20. Note that a quint beats four Jacks but scores less.

Non-dealer leads. Second to a trick may play any card so long as cards remain in stock. Thereafter, in the play of the last nine tricks, the second must win the trick if possible, and trump if unable to follow suit, with this exception: that the holder of Jas, if holding no other trump, is not obliged to play it but may renege for as long as he thinks fit. The trick is taken by the highest card of the suit led, or by the highest trump if any are played. The winner of each trick draws the top card of stock, waits for the other to do likewise, then leads to the next.

Before leading, a player may declare any combination he may hold. The other player must then either declare a higher-ranking combination, or acknowledge the other's 'Good'. Whoever declares the higher meld scores it. Sequences of equal length are determined by the highest card. As between equal sequences, that in trumps beats that in a plain suit. If still equal, that of the first declarer prevails. It is permissible to declare a longer sequence containing cards that have already been declared in a shorter.

A player holding the King and Queen of trumps scores 20 for the marriage upon leading one of them to a trick and showing the other. This applies independently of other melds.

When no more cards remain in stock, melds and sequences cease to be declarable. There is a bonus of 100 for winning all nine of the last-played tricks. At the end of play each player adds to his score for melds that of all counters taken in tricks, and the winner of the last adds 5. Game is 500 points.

Belote

Belote replaced Bezique as France's national card game early in the twentieth century, though not without stiff opposition from Manille. It probably derives from one or more varieties of Jass played in the east of the country, especially in Alsace and Flanders, and was introduced and disseminated throughout the country by French soldiers returning from the most active theatres of the First World War. Belote (spelt Belotte until the late 1920s) is the name of the trump marriage. Some explain it as a contraction of *bel atout*, and there is an obvious but not easily explained connection between it and the Hungarian Bela. More plausibly, however, it could be a diminutive of *belle*, which in older card games denoted the card turned to propose a suit for trumps, or the suit itself, and in this game may originally have denoted the top Jack. There are many varieties of Belote, and many local variations on each variety, but for tournament purposes a standard version is promoted by the Fédération Française de Belote, founded in 1984. The following descriptions derive from Daniel Daynes, *Le Livre de la Belote* (Paris, 1996).

Basic Belote. Two, three or four play to the right. (For partnership game, see below.)

Cards Thirty-two, ranking and counting as follows:

	J	9	A	T	K	Q		8	7
trump suit	J	9	A	T	K	Q		8	7
card-points	20	14	11	10	4	3	2	0	0	0
plain suits			A	T	K	Q	J	9	8	7

Three often play with only 24 cards, omitting Sevens and Eights.

Deal If two or three play, deal six cards each (3+3); if four, five each (3+2). Turn the next card for trump.

Object To score as many points as possible for tricks and melds, and, in the case of the maker, to score more than any other single player.

Trick-points The total of trick-points is 162 (see above), consisting of 62 in trumps, 90 in plain suits, and 10 for last (*dix de der*).

Melds There are four kinds, from high to low:

meld	definition	score
foursome (carré)	all four Jacks	200
	or Nines	150
	or Aces, Tens, Kings *or* Queens	100
hundred (*cent*)	suit sequence of five or more	100
fifty (*cinquante*)	suit sequence of four	50
tierce	suit sequence of three	20

A card may count twice, once in a foursome and once in a sequence. A higher type of meld beats a lower. As between foursomes, the highest is Jacks, followed by Nines, and so on down to Queens, with Sevens and Eights not counting. A sequence is three or more cards of the same suit and in sequential order, which is AKQJT987 in every suit, including trumps. As between hundreds, the highest is that containing the highest top card, regardless of length – e.g. five to the Ace beats six or seven to the Ten. As between any two sequences of equal height, priority goes to a sequence in trumps, or, if none, to the one declared first (thus favouring eldest most and dealer least).

Bidding In the first round of bidding, each in turn, starting with eldest, may pass or agree to make the turned suit trump. As soon as a player makes, the bidding ends. If all pass, the turn-up is turned down and there is a second round of bidding. This time the maker is the first player to name a different suit as trump, thereby undertaking to score more than either of the others. If all pass again, the cards are gathered in and the deal passes to the next in turn. (*Variant*: Dealer is obliged to make trumps if no one else will. This rule is called *vache*, 'cow'.)

La valse (optional bid when two play). In either round of bidding, a player may propose either to become the maker or to annul the deal, as his opponent dictates. This prevents his opponent from becoming the maker. This practice (equivalent to the schmeiss in Klaberjass) is no longer current.

Dix If the trump suit is that of the turn-up and you hold the †7 (*dix*), you may exchange it for the turn-up at any time before playing to the first trick, and may use it in a meld.

Further deal If two or three play, once the maker is established deal another batch of three to bring everyone's hand up to nine cards. Then turn the bottom card of the stock face up and place it beside the original turn-up. This card – variously called *la bergère*, *la fille*, etc. – is for information only.

If four play, the maker takes the turn-up, or the Seven that may have been exchanged for it, and receives two additional cards instead of three. Since everyone now has eight, no card can be turned for information.

Melding Each player, upon playing to the first trick, announces the best meld he holds (by type only, e.g. foursome, hundred, etc.), provided that it is higher than any previous announcement. If it is lower, he says 'Good'. If it is equal, he asks 'How high?', and the previous announcer then specifies the rank of the foursome or the top card of the sequence. Whoever declares the best meld, or has priority in case of equality, scores for it and any other melds he may declare. All declared melds must be shown when that player plays to the second trick (if so demanded).

Play Eldest leads first. To a trump lead, you must follow suit if possible and must head the trick if possible. To a plain-suit lead, you must follow suit if possible, but need not head the trick. If unable to follow suit, you must play a trump if possible, and, if the trick has already been trumped, must overtrump if possible. The trick is taken by the highest card of the suit led, or by the highest trump if any are played, and the winner of each trick leads to the next.

Belote Holding the King and Queen of trumps entitles you to score 20 for belote, provided that you announce '*belote*' upon playing one of them and '*rebelote*' upon playing the other to a subsequent trick.

Score All scores are rounded up to the nearest ten if ending in 5–9, otherwise down. If the maker scores more than any opponent individually, everyone scores what they took in tricks and melds. If he scores lower than any opponent, he scores nothing, and whatever he counted is added to the score of the player who took most. If tied, his points are held in abeyance (*en reserve*, or *en pénitence*) and go to the winner of the next deal.

Capot A player who wins every trick adds 100 for capot. If a player fails to win a trick, 100 for capot is added to the score of his opponent if two play, or divided between any opponents who did take tricks if three or four play. If two take no tricks in a four-player game, 100 goes to each of the others. A capoted player may score for melds and belote, but not if this would enable him to reach the target score.

Game Two play up to 500 points, three to 750 or 1000, four to 1000 or 1500.

Belote Marseillaise (à la Découverte)

(2p, 32c) Deal sixteen cards each in eight packets of two as shown in the illustration. The suit of the last card is the proposed trump. Bid and play as at two-hand Belote. Each player's top eight cards are available for playing to tricks in the usual way. As each top card is played, it reveals the one beneath, which then becomes available in its turn.

Upon winning a trick, a player may claim the value of any meld appearing in his top eight cards. The values are noted, but they are not recorded until the end of play, since only those of the player with the best meld count, the opponent's all being annulled. Belote scores in the usual way. Apart from that, no card may be declared twice in a sequence.

If the play of a card to a losing trick reveals a scoring combination, the trick-winner will obviously attempt to lead in such a way as to force out a card of that combination before it can be scored.

In the illustration, North announces the tierce in clubs and plays ♥J, drawing ♥8. North's Jack uncovers ♥K and South's Eight uncovers ♠9, giving him a fifty in spades, which beats North's tierce. North, hoping to uncover the fourth Queen for 100, must win the next trick to prevent South from forcing a Queen out by leading his ♦8. He therefore plays ♥9. This happens to uncover ♠Q, giving him the fourth Queen and so beating South's fifty.

Partnership Belote

(4pp, 32c) Four playing in fixed partnerships follow the rules of Basic Belote but with these differences:

1. The †7 may not be exchanged for the turn-up, which automatically goes to the maker. (Some schools ignore this rule.)

2. The partner of the player with the highest meld may also count his melds towards their combined total.

3. When unable to follow suit to a plain-suit lead which is being trumped by an opponent, you must also trump and overtrump if possible; but if your partner is winning it, whether with a trump or a higher card of the suit led, you may play as you please.

4. A side winning all tricks between them adds 100 for capot instead of 10 for last. Since all cards are in play, the total of trick-points is always 162, or 252 with capot (rounded down to 160 and 250). Game is 1000 points.

Belote Bridgée

(4pp, 32c) This partnership game appeared in the 1930s, borrowing from Bridge the features of a no-trump contract and of doubling and redoubling. In Bridge-playing circles it also borrowed the suit hierarchy of Bridge, so that, for example, a bid in clubs was overcalled by the same bid in diamonds or a higher suit. With greater originality, it introduced the novel concept of an all-trump bid, thus producing a game known as Toutat-Sansat (from *tout atout, sans atout*). After the Second World War, Belote Bridgée developed into the now classic game of Belote Coinchée, or Coinche.

Coinche (Belote Coinchée, Belote Contrée)

4 players (2 × 2), 32 cards

Coinche means 'fist', and it is so called because if you make a bid, and an opponent doubles it – traditionally by banging a fist on the table – the auction ends, and you're stuck with it. It takes only a few rounds of play to see why this has become France's national card game.

Preliminaries Four play in fixed partnerships and, traditionally, to the right, but many now play to the left. Game is 3000 points, or 300 if counted in tens.

Cards and deal Cards number, rank and count as at basic Belote.

	J	9	A	T	K	Q		8	7
trump suit or all trump									
card-points	20	14	11	10	4	3	2	0	0	0
plain suits or no trump			A	T	K	Q	J	9	8	7

Deal Shuffle before the first deal, but thereafter only cut before each successive deal. Deal eight each in batches of 3-2-3. Do not turn a card for trump.

Contracts Coinche allows contracts to be played with a suit as trump, or at no trump (*sans atout*), or at all trump (*tout atout*).

• In a suit contract, the total of trick-points is 62 in trumps, plus 90 in plain suits, plus 10 for last, total 162.

• At no trump, all Jacks and Nines rank in their plain-suit position, Jacks counting 2 each and Nines zero. The total of trick-points is therefore 120 for cards, plus 10 for last, total 130. There being no trump suit, there can be no belote.

• At all trump, all Jacks and Nines rank in their trump-suit position – that is, above Aces and Tens – and count respectively 20 and 14 each. The total of trick-points is therefore 248 for cards, plus 10 for last, total 258. Since every suit is a quasi-trump, the King and Queen of every suit counts as a belote.

Foursomes score as usual in a suit or all trump contract, but differently at no trump:

suit or all trump		no trump	
Jacks	200	Aces	200
Nines	150	Tens	150
A,T,K,Q	100	K,Q,J	100
8,7	n/a	9,8,7	n/a

Bidding A bid is an offer to win (a) more than half the trick-points available and (b) more points than the opposing side in tricks and melds. It consists of a number and a contract, e.g. '80 hearts', '90 all trump' etc.

☞ A nominal bid of 80 is actually a bid of at least 82, as 80 is less than half of the 162 available. In some circles, the principle is extended, so that 90 requires at least 92, and so on. The number quoted is that of the actual score made after rounding the minimum requisite number of points down to the nearest ten.

Eldest speaks first, and each in turn may pass, bid, double, or redouble. Bidding may start at any level, but the lowest is 80, and each subsequent bid must quote a higher multiple of ten. Jump-bidding is allowed, and a player who has passed is not thereby debarred from bidding again. A contract is established when a bid is followed by three passes, or by an opponent's 'Double', which may then be redoubled by the bidder or his partner.

If all pass on the first round, the deal is annulled and passes to the next in turn.

Melds Each in turn, upon playing to the first trick, announces his highest meld, provided that it is not lower than any already announced. If equal, he asks 'How high?', and the previous announcer details the rank of a foursome or the top card of a sequence, as the case may be. Whichever player has the highest meld notes the total value of all melds declared by himself and his partner. A meld declared at the first trick must be shown (on demand) at the second.

Play Eldest leads first. Rules of trick-play vary, the laxest being those of eastern France.

• To a trump lead you must follow suit if possible and head the trick if possible. (*Variant*: If your partner is winning, you need not overtrump.)

• To a plain-suit lead you must follow suit if possible, but need not head the trick.

• If you can't follow suit, and an opponent is currently winning the trick with a trump, you must trump and overtrump if possible. (*Variant*: If you cannot overtrump, you need not undertrump but may discard at will.)

• If you can't follow suit, and your partner is currently winning the trick, you may play anything. (*Variant*: But may not undertrump if able to overtrump.)

The trick is taken by the highest card of the suit led, or by the highest trump if any are played, and the winner of each trick leads to the next.

Belote A player holding the King and Queen of trumps, and announcing *'belote'* upon playing one of them and *'rebelote'* upon playing the other, scores 20 for his side. Belote is declarable in any suit in an all trump contract, but not at all in no trumps.

Score At end of play each side calculates its total for trick-points (including 10 for last) and melds. To win, the declaring side must have scored more than their opponents and at least as many as they bid. If successful, both sides score (rounded to the nearest 10) the amount they took for tricks and melds, and the declarers add the value of the contract. If not, the declarers score nothing, and the opponents 160 for trick-points plus the value of their melds plus the value of the lost contract. These scores are all affected by any doubling that may have taken place.

Notes on play Belote players have been quick to exploit the possibilities of the bidding system for conveying information about their hands. No code is unversally accepted, but the following opening bids and responses are fairly typical.

Opening bids

80	four sure tricks and: trump Jack or Nine, or four good tierces, or a 34 (= trump Jack and Nine) plus two Aces, or a sequence of five
90	four sure tricks, with a 34 in three suits
100	five sure tricks and a promising game
110	four Aces, Kings, or Queens
120	sequence of four, including belote but lacking the Nine
130	sequence of four including Jack, Nine
150	four Aces, no Jack
160	four Nines
180	sequence of five, or four Aces and a Jack
220	four Jacks

Response to partner's opening 80 (add another 10 if necessary to overcall intervening bid)

+10	Nine and at least one other of partner's suit
+20	Jack of partner's suit, or two side Aces
+30	Jack and Nine, or three side Aces
+50	four Tens, Kings, or Queens
+70	meld worth 100
+100	four Aces

+120 meld worth 150
+130 four Nines
+170 meld worth 200
+200 four Jacks

Response (to 80) in another suit if unable to support opener's suit

+10 three including 34, plus one side Ace
+20 five including 34, or five sure tricks
+40 sequence of four including belote
+50 as above, and the Nine

If your partner opens 90, ignore the above and instead add 10 for each Ace you can offer.

Jo-Jotte
2 players, 32 cards

Not tonight, Josephine . . .

Ely Culbertson devised Jo-Jotte in response (he claimed) to urgent requests from players throughout America to apply his mind to the development of a hitherto unrealized game for two that would be as intellectual and jazzy as Bridge was for four. The result, first published in 1937, melds the scoring of Bridge to the mechanics of Belote, which Culbertson had played in France but thought 'too tame and too mono-tonous to satisfy the quick-witted impatience of American psychology'. He gallantly named it Jo-Jotte after his wife Josephine. The game flopped, and Jo ungallantly divorced him the year after.

Preliminaries Scores are kept in columns ruled in half with a horizontal line as at Bridge. Below the line go scores made for trick-play, above it scores for melds and various bonuses. A game is won by the first to reach 80 points below the line, and a rubber by the first to win two games.

Cards As for Klaberjass, but with simplified card-points:

trump suit	J	9	A	T	K	Q			8	7
card-points	20	15	10	10	5	5	0	0	0	0
plain suits			A	K	Q	J	T	9	8	7

The total of trick-points available is 160 (60 in trumps, 90 in plain suits, 10 for last).

Deal Deal six each in ones and turn the next for trump. Non-dealer may accept the turned suit as trump, or pass, leaving dealer with the same choices. If both pass, the turn-up is turned down and non-dealer may name another suit or call no trump. If he passes, dealer has the same choices. If either names a suit, the other may overcall by bidding no trump. If both still pass, the deal is annulled and the present non-dealer deals to the next. Any contract may be doubled by the opponent, and redoubled by the declarer. Doubling affects only the scores for tricks, not for melds.

A contract established, deal three more cards each, and turn the bottom card of the stock 'for information'. Declarer's opponent may now claim his melds, or bid nullo, which is an undertaking to lose every trick playing at no trump, and disregarding melds. If he bids nullo, declarer may overcall by bidding a slam (win every trick), which cannot be overcalled. If he claims melds, he does so by announcing the scoring value of the highest meld he holds in each of two classes: quartets and sequences.

Melds The player with the best four of a kind scores above the line 100 for the quartet and 100 for any other quartet he may declare. In a trump contract the highest quartet is of Jacks, followed by Nines, Aces, Tens, etc.; at no trump, it is Aces, then Tens, etc.

The player with the longest sequence of three or more cards – or the highest if equal, or the one in trumps if still equal – scores for it and any other sequences he may declare. Sequential order is invariably AKQJT987. A sequence of three scores above the line 20, of four 40, of five or more 50.

Play The opponent leads first. To a non-trump lead the follower must follow suit if possible, otherwise must trump if possible, otherwise may play anything. To a trump lead he must not only follow suit but must also head the trick if possible. The trick is taken by the higher card of the suit led, or by the higher trump if any are played, and the winner of each trick leads to the next.

Jo-Jotte is the King and Queen of trumps. A player holding both cards scores 20 above the line provided that he (a) plays the King to an earlier trick than the Queen, and (b) announces 'Jo' upon playing the King and 'Jotte' upon playing the Queen.

Score At end of play each player calculates his total for melds and tricks. If the declarer's total is greater, he scores his trick-total (only) below the line. If not, his opponent scores below the line the total of their combined trick-scores.

The winner of a doubled or redoubled contract scores below the line the total of both players' trick-scores, doubled or quadrupled respectively.

In the event of a tie for totals, and in any nullo contract, the combined trick-score is held in abeyance and subsequently goes above the line to whichever player has the higher total score (for tricks and melds) on the next untied hand other than nullo.

A successful nullo scores 200 above the line. Failure gives the opponent 200 above the line for the first and 100 for any subsequent trick taken by declarer.

Winning every trick gains 500 above the line if bid, otherwise 100. If bid and lost, the opponent scores above the line the combined trick-scores of both players.

Add 300 for winning the rubber.

Klaverjas (Klaverjassen)   4 players (2 × 2), 32 cards

Klaverjas has been the Dutch national card game since about the end of the nineteenth century. A delightful and relatively simple member of the Jass family, it is distinguished by its predilection for scoring melds as made in tricks rather than as resulting from the luck of the deal. It makes a good introduction to point-trick games for players accustomed only to plain-trick games like Whist and Bridge.

Preliminaries Four players sitting crosswise in partnerships receive eight cards each dealt in batches of four from a 32-card pack ranking and counting thus:

in trumps	†J	†9	A	T	K	Q		8	7
	20	14	11	10	4	3	0	0	0	0

plain suits		11	10	4	3	2	0	0	0
		A	K	Q	J	T	9	8	7

The †J is called *Jas* and the †9 *Nel*. The trick-points total 162 (62 in trumps, 30×3 in plain suits, 10 for winning the last trick).

Object Both sides seek to win a majority of points for counters and melds taken in tricks, but the side that makes trumps is penalized if it fails.

The melds are:

four of the same rank	100
four in suit-sequence	50
three in suit-sequence	20
stuk (marriage of †K-Q)	20

Sequence order is AKQJT987 in every suit including trumps. Four of a kind occurs so rarely as to be hardly worth remembering.

Bidding Each in turn, starting with eldest, passes or becomes the maker by announcing a trump suit. Bidding ends as soon as trumps are made. Following three passes, the dealer is obliged to make trumps.

Play (Rotterdam rules) Eldest leads to the first trick. To a trump lead you must follow suit if possible and head the trick if possible. To a plain-suit lead you must follow suit if possible, but need not head the trick. If you can't follow suit, you must trump and overtrump if possible, even if your partner is winning the trick.

The trick is taken by the highest card of the suit led, or by the highest trump if any are played. The winner of each trick, before leading to the next, scores to his partnership the value of any meld it may contain. If a trump sequence includes K-Q, the marriage counts 20 in addition.

Score If the maker's side has scored more than the other, both sides score what they make. If not, the makers score nothing and the opponents score 162 plus the value of all melds made by both sides. There is a bonus of 100 for winning every trick. Game is 1500 points.

Variations

Amsterdam rules of following (1) If you cannot follow to a plain-suit lead and the trick is being won by an opponent, you must trump and overtrump if you can. However, if they are winning with a trump which you cannot beat, you may only undertrump if you cannot discard from a plain suit. (2) If you cannot follow to a plain-suit lead and the trick is being won by your partner, you may play anything, other than a lower trump if your partner played a higher (unless you have no alternative). (3) If trumps are led, you must follow suit and head the trick if you can, even if your partner is winning it.

Trump selection A preferred trump suit is proposed by revealing the dealer's last card or by cutting a second pack. In one round of bidding each in turn may pass or make the preferred suit trump. If all pass another round follows, in which each in turn may pass or make another suit trump. If all pass again there is a new deal.

Melds Originally, each player upon playing to the first trick could declare and score for any melds his hand contained, apart from quartets of Sevens, Eights and Nines. Although this is outmoded, some still allow the hand declaration of a *stuk*. One effect of abolishing hand declarations is the virtual elimination of the quartet as a scoring feature, even though it has been extended to include four of any rank. Some players compensate by scoring for three of a kind taken in a trick.

Doubling Some schools allow the opponents to double and the makers to redouble. This game is known as Kraken.

Sample game North deals:

East	♠87	♥A	♣97	♦AKJ
South	♠KQ	♥TQJ	♣J8	♦7
West	♠AJ9	♥9	♣KQ	♦T8
North	♠T	♥K87	♣AT	♦9Q

East makes diamonds trump, preventing South from making hearts and West spades. East, as eldest, leads. Winning tricks are underlined. The trick score is marked (+) if won by the makers, otherwise (−), and where there are two values the second is for a meld made on the table, or for the last trick.

	East	South	West	North	*score*
1	♠7	♠Q	♠A	♠T	+24
2	♦J	♦7	♦T	♦9	+44, 20
3	♦K	♣8	♦8	♦Q	+7, 20
4	♣8	♣K	♣9	♥K	−8
5	♥A	♥J	♥9	♥7	+13

6	♣9	♣J	♣Q	♣T	−15, 50
7	♦A	♥Q	♣K	♥8	+18
8	♣7	♥T	♠J	♣A	−23, 10

East–West count 146 and North–South 106 towards game.

East's lead of a low non-trump at trick 1 is conventional, asking partner to lead his highest trump as soon as possible. At 2, West obliges with the Ten. North's Nel gives the bidders 20 for a sequence of three after West plays the Jas. At 3, East leads the King to marry the Queen, virtually a foregone conclusion. At 4, East gets off play with a worthless spade. North might reasonably have been expected to stuff the trick with the Ace or Ten of clubs rather than with a rather thin King. At 6, the makers carelessly yield a sequence of four for 50: East should have led the Seven rather than the Nine, as the Eight had already gone, and West should have played the King instead of the Queen to restrict any possible sequence to only three cards. At 7, West is legally required to trump, otherwise he might have preferred to throw the ♣7 and add a second worthless card to the trick. At 8, North is lucky to have made his ♣A as well as his earlier Ten, as there was a strong chance that either would fall to the last trump or a lead in a 'wrong' suit.

Handjass (Sack-Jass, Poutze, Pomme)   2–5 players, 36 cards

Of the countless varieties of Jass played in Switzerland and western Austria, the following may be recommended as the simplest and most basic non-partnership game. Four may prefer the partnership game of Schieber, or the more elaborate solo game of Pandour. For authenticity, all Swiss Jass games should be played with the traditional 36-card Jass pack distinguished by suits of acorns, shields, flowers and bells, and ranks of Daus (Deuce), King, Over, Under, Banner, 9-8-7-6. If international cards are used, the following suit correspondences apply:

Swiss suits	acorns	flowers	shields	bells
	🌰	❀	🛡	🔔
	♣	♠	♥	♦
international	clubs	spades	hearts	diamonds

Terminology In Switzerland the trump Jack is rarely called Jass. It sometimes has other names, such as 'Puur', but often is merely referred to as the trump Jack, e.g. *Trumpfbauer* or its dialectal equivalent. The Nine is *Nell* or *Näll*. A meld or combination is *Wys* (in a variety of spellings), and the trump marriage either *der Stöck* or *die Stöcke*.

Format Two to five players, each playing alone. If five play, each in turn deals and sits that hand out. All play goes to the right.

Cards The 36-card pack ranks and counts as follows.

Jass cards	†U	†9	D	K	O	(U)	B	(9)	8	7	6
card-points	20	14	11	4	3	2	10	0	0	0	0
International	†J	†9	A	K	Q	(J)	T	(9)	8	7	6

The trick-points total 157 (62 in trumps, 30×3 in plain suits, 5 for winning the last trick).

Jass. Flowers are trumps, and the top trumps are Jack, Nine, Ace. The suitmark is doubled because the Ace was originally a Deuce.

Deal Deal nine each, in batches of three.

If two play, deal two extra hands of nine: one is 'spare' and may be taken as described below; the other is 'dead', and its top card is turned for trump.

If three play, lay the remaining cards face down as a spare hand but turn the top card for trump.

If four play, show the dealer's last card for trump.

Object To score for melds in hand and counters taken in tricks, and particularly to score at least 21.

Exchange Each in turn, starting with eldest, has the right to turn his hand down if it is unsatisfactory and replace it with the spare, sight unseen and without right of re-exchange. Only one player can do this, thereby forcing the others to play as dealt.

Melds The following count:

- Four Jacks 200, Nines 150, anything else 100. As between fours worth 100, a higher rank beats a lower.
- Sequence of three 20, four 50, five 100, six 150, seven 200, eight 250, nine 300. Sequence order is AKQJT9876 in every suit including trumps. A longer sequence beats a shorter, or, if equal, a higher beats a lower.
- Marriage of †K-Q (*Stöck*) 20

Only the player with the best meld in hand may score for melds, but then may score for every meld he declares. Any single card may count once as part of a quartet and once as part of a sequence. The trump King-Queen may count both as a marriage and also as part of a sequence or (individually) in quartets as well.

If two or three play, whoever has the †6 may exchange it for the turn-up before declaring melds.

Each player in turn upon playing to the first trick announces the best meld he has, giving no more information than needed to establish its superiority over someone else's. (For example, eldest may merely say '100' and need not say any more about it unless and until other players whose best melds are also worth 100 rise to the challenge.)

As between apparently equal hands, the 'best' is the one which, reading from the top down if equal:

1. scores most, or
2. contains most cards, or
3. contains the highest-ranking card, or
4. is in the trump suit, if applicable, or
5. was declared first (Forehand having priority).

Tricks Forehand leads first. To the lead of a trump you must follow suit if you can, unless the only trump you have is the top Jack, in which case you may renege. To a plain-suit lead you may either follow suit or play a winning trump, as you please; and if unable to follow suit you may either discard or play a winning trump, as you please; but in neither case may you play a lower trump than any already played to the trick – unless you hold nothing but trumps, in which case you may play any of them. A trick is taken by the highest card of the suit led, or by the highest trump if any are played, and the winner of each trick leads to the next.

Score The two players making the most in melds and tricks each score one game point, or 'stick'. Anyone who fails to make at least 21 scores minus one point, or a 'potato' (because it is marked as a circle), and is said to be 'in the sack'. Any opponent who is not himself in the sack marks a stick for each player who is. In subsequent deals, a game point can be indicated by either marking a stick or cancelling a potato. A player drops out of play upon accumulating five sticks. Whoever remains when everyone else has dropped out is the loser, and pays for the drinks (or potatoes).

Variation Only the player taking most in melds and tricks scores a game point, and a player taking less than 21 loses a point. Players drop out on reaching seven points. A player with a bad hand may throw it in and decline to play, rather than risk losing a point. The 21-point threshold is often increased to 26, making it impossible for a player to stay safe by holding the Puur back till the last trick.

Schieber (Kreuzjass)   4 players (2 × 2), 36 cards

Probably the most popular member of the Swiss family Jass is the partnership game known as Schieber, so called because the player entitled to name trumps may 'shove' (*schieben*) this duty over to his partner. This distinguishes Schieber from its predecessor Kreuzjass, in which the last card was turned for trump, only suit contracts were played, and they all counted single. The terminology, cards, scores and method of trick-play are as at Handjass, with these additions: *Obenabe* (literally 'top down') is a no trump contract with cards ranking in their normal order, *Undenufe* (pronounced *un'enu'e*, literally 'bottom up') is a no trump contract with cards ranking upside down. I will refer to these contracts respectively as 'no trump' and 'reverse'. Players of Bid Whist may prefer 'Uptown' and 'Downtown'.

Preliminaries Four players sit crosswise in partnerships (whence the name 'Kreuz'jass) and play to the right. Deal nine cards each in threes.

Choosing the contract Forehand – the player at dealer's right – starts by either naming the contract or 'shoving'. The possible contracts are:

acorns *or* flowers (*or* black suit)	scores single
shields *or* bells (*or* red suit)	scores double
Obenabe, Undenufe (no trumps)	scores treble

The factors single, double, etc., apply to all scores made for tricks and melds in the contract played.

> ☞ In some circles, Undenufe (reverse no trump), scores quadruple.

Rank and value of cards In a suit contract, cards rank and count as at Handjass. In the no trump contracts there is no top Jack or Nell, and their additional point-values are compensated by counting 8 card-points for each Eight. In the reverse contract, cards rank 'upside down', with Six highest and Ace lowest.

suit contract	†J	†9	A	K	Q	(J)	T	(9)	8	7	6
	20	14	11	4	3	2	10	0	0	0	0
Obenabe			A	K	Q	J	T	9	8	7	6
(*no trumps*)			11	4	3	2	10	0	8	0	0
Undenufe			6	7	8	9	T	J	Q	K	A
(*reverse*)			11	0	8	0	10	2	3	4	0

The total of trick-points is always 157, consisting of 152 card-points and 5 for the last trick.

Play Forehand leads to the first trick, even if his partner named the contract. If he leads without either naming a contract or shoving, then the contract is automatically that of the suit led: he cannot afterwards claim to have intended a no trump or other contract. The rules of trick-play are as at Handjass, except that, in a no trump contract, players must always follow suit if possible.

Declaring melds Upon playing to the first trick, each in turn announces the highest meld they hold. The partnership of the player holding the highest meld scores for all the melds in both their hands, multiplied by the factor applying to the contract.

> ☞ Melds count and outrank one another as at Handjass (above), except that, in a reverse contract, sequences of equal length are decided in favour of that with the higher trick-winners. For example, 6-7-8 is the highest and Q-K-A the lowest of a

three-card sequence. As to quartets, Kings beat Aces, Queens beat Kings, and so on.

Stöck (marriage) In a no trump contract there can, by definition, be no marriage. In a suit contract the marriage does not count as a meld at this point, but if anyone holds it they score 20 upon playing the second card of it to a trick, also multiplied by the relevant contract factor.

Score At end of play, each side totals their trick-points, including 5 for last, and adding 100 if they won every trick. This sum is multiplied by the relevant contract factor before being added to their cumulative total.

Game Play up to 2500 points, or 3000 if Undenufe counts quadruple. If during the course of play a player believes his side has already taken enough card-points to have reached this total, the play ceases, except that anyone who holds the marriage but has not yet scored for it may now do so. If the claim proves correct, the claiming side wins; if not, they lose.

If a side claims to have won in the first trick of a hand, and the other side makes a counterclaim, the matter is settled in the order '*Stöck–Wys–Stich*'. This means that the winners are the first side to reach 2500 (3000) as the result of counting, first, the marriage, if anyone has it; or, failing that, second, the scores just made for melds; or, failing that, the point-value of any cards just won in the first trick (when completed).

☛ The Stöck–Wys–Stich rule is not invariable, and the Schweizer Wirteverband of Zurich claims the original form to have been Stöck–Stich–Wys. 'In some Swiss cafés, you will see a notice saying "Stöck–Wys–Stich" or whatever: this is the local house rule, hung up by the management to avoid disputes among customers.' (Nick Wedd, on the Pagat website.)

Variations There are too many variations in all these games of Swiss Jass to justify listing them here. See, for example, *Puur, Näll, As*, published by A. G. Müller, Neuhausen am Rheinfall.

Note on play As Forehand, don't bid a black or 'vegetable' suit (acorns or flowers) unless you either have a strong hand, or you have reason to believe that your partner may be able to nominate a more profitable contract.

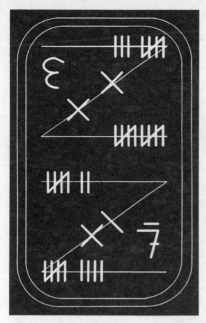

Schieber. Scores are typically chalked on a blackboard marked with a Z-shaped grid for each partnership. From each side's viewpoint, the top bar shows hundreds bundled in fives, the oblique bar fifties bundled in twos, and the bottom twenties bundled in fives. Here the southern partnership has 7 hundreds, 3 fifties, and 9 twenties, making 1030. Odd points above or below 20 are written as a numeral on the right, with a bar above to show a minus, and being erased and replaced after each deal (if it changes). The actual score represented is therefore 1023. The northern partnership stands at 1363. It is possible to buy specially designed scoreboards in Swiss shops.

Pandour

2–4 players, 24 cards

Pandours were eighteenh-century Croatian or Austrian militiamen of just the sort who would have played a game like this. It is the Jass equivalent of Boston or Solo Whist, and one of the oldest members of its family. A similar game (Pandoeren) was formerly popular in the Netherlands.

Preliminaries Three players are active, but four often play, with each taking turns to deal and sit that hand out. Play to the right. The normal Jass pack is stripped to 24 by the removal of Sixes and Sevens. Deal eight each. If two play, leave a spare hand, face down.

Bidding Forehand bids first. The lowest bid is 100, which is an undertaking to make at least 100 points in melds and tricks. Subsequent bids rise in tens up to the maximum 300, with four extra bids inserted. Misère is a bid to lose every trick, pandour is a bid to win every trick, and each of these may be bid at no trump or (higher) with a trump suit. The bidding sequence runs:

100, 110, 120, 130, 140, 150, 160, 170, 180, 190, misère without, misère with, 200, 210, 220, 230, 240, pandour without, 250, 260, 270, 280, 290, 300, pandour with.

Whoever bids highest becomes the soloist. Pandour with a trump cannot be overcalled, and if anyone absent-mindedly bids 310 or higher they are obliged to play a trump pandour themselves.

Play The soloist leads to the first trick, and if playing misère in trumps must start with a trump. During the course of the first trick melds are called and scored as at Handjass or Schieber, but with the addition of four Nines and a sequence of six, both scoring 150. The rules of trick-play are as at Handjass and Schieber, except that in a trump misère you are allowed to undertrump if unable to follow suit.

Score The contract scores are 1 game-point for each 50 bid (100–140 = 2, 150–190 = 3, etc.). Misères count 4 each, pandour without trumps 5, with trumps 6. If successful, the soloist scores the number of game-points appropriate to his bid (not more). If not, this amount is scored by each opponent, including the dealer if four play, but not if this would give him the game: you can only reach the target on active service. Game is 15 points, or any other agreed total. A player upon reaching the target score drops out of play. The last player left in loses.

Variations Any of the following additional bids may be included by agreement.

Push Bids may be made with a 'push' (*stossen*) of one, two or even more cards. A bid of '100, push 2', for example, means that if that contract is played, everyone first passes two cards face down to his right-hand neighbour and then picks up the two passed from the left. Raising the number of cards to be pushed raises the level of bidding. For example, a bid of 100 is overcalled by 100 pushing one card, that by 100 pushing two, and so on.

Piccolo is a bid to win exactly one trick, either without or (higher) with trumps. It counts 4 game-points, and is overcalled by any misère.

Under-pandour is a bid to lose exactly one trick (by winning exactly seven). Without trumps it counts 5 and is overcalled by pandour without; with trumps it counts 6 and is overcalled by pandour with.

Differenzler

(3–4p, 36c) Deal three batches of three cards to four players, or four batches of three to three players, and turn the last for trumps. Melds don't count, only trick-points, which are the usual 157. Each in turn bids to win an exact number of trick-points. Play as at Handjass. At end of play, each scores the difference between what he bid and what he took. The winner is the player with the lowest total after 12 deals. A player who fulfils his bid exactly deducts 10 from his current total.

Mittlere

(3p, 36c) Deal twelve cards each in threes and play as at Handjass but without scoring for melds. The aim of the game is to win at least one trick, to take not more than 99 of the 157 trick-points available, and to avoid taking the middling number of trick-points. Play begins at no trump. As soon as one player cannot follow suit to the card led, the suit of whatever card he plays immediately and automatically becomes trump for the rest of the deal. This means that if a Jack or Nine was played earlier, and lost the trick, whoever won it will have to count it as 20 or 14 respectively instead of 2 or 0 points!

With three players there will be either one winner, who scores plus 2 to the others' minus 1 each, or one loser, who scores minus 2 to the others' plus 1 each. If everyone takes at least one trick but under 100 points, the player in the middle loses. If one takes no tricks or 100+ points, then he loses to the others. If one takes no tricks and another takes 100+, then the one in the middle wins. If one takes 100+ points but succeeds in taking all the tricks, then he wins. My sources do not state what happens if two players tie, but I think the third should then win if he has at least one trick and not more than 99 points, and otherwise lose. A game is 12 deals.

Schmaus

(2p, 36c) The Swiss version of Smousjas, the two-player trick-and-draw member of the family. From the usual 36-card Jass pack deal nine each in threes, turn the next for trump, and half cover it with the remaining cards, forming a face-down stock. So long as at least two cards remain in stock the holder of the †6 may, upon winning a trick, exchange it for the turn-up. Non-dealer leads to the first trick. So long as cards remain in stock there is no need to follow suit. The trick is taken by the higher card of the suit led, or by the higher trump if any are played. The winner of each trick takes the top card of the stock, waits for the other to do likewise, and may declare a meld before leading to the next. The usual melds apply, with the exception of four Nines for 150, but with the addition of sequences of six for 150, seven for 200, eight for 250, and nine for 300. King and Queen of trumps can be declared for 20 independently of a longer sequence, but not at the same trick. No single card may be declared more than once in sequences of the same length, but may be declared in longer sequences. For example, declaring A-K-Q prevents the later declaration of K-Q-J, but not of K-Q-J-T. When the last card of the stock has been taken, the last trick-winner may declare a final meld. Strict rules of trick-play then apply: follow suit and head the trick if possible, otherwise trump if possible. Winning the last trick counts 5 as usual. Game is 1500 points.

Grevjass (Grivjass)   4 players (2 × 2), 32 cards

This variety of Jass is played in the Faeroe Islands, though it is less popular than Sjavs. The following account derives from researches conducted by Dr Anthony Smith.

Preliminaries Four players sitting crosswise in partnerships use a 32-card pack ranking and counting as follows:

†J	†9	A	K	Q	(J)	T	(9)	8	7
20	14	11	3	2	1	10	0	0	0

The trick-points total 146, consisting of 60 in trumps, 27×3 in plain suits, and 5 for winning the eighth trick (if play gets that far). The trump Jack is called *Jass*, the trump Nine *Manella*.

Object To be the first side to correctly claim to have reached 100 points for tricks and melds, which may take one or two deals. Scores are translated into chalk-strokes, equivalent to game-points.

Deal The player drawing the lowest card deals first, but subsequent deals are made by the winner of the last trick in the previous deal. There are two ways of dealing, depending on whether the player at dealer's right cuts the pack or merely thumps it with his fist. If he cuts, he shows the bottom card of the top half to determine trumps before the dealer completes the cut. Dealer then deals eight cards each in batches of 3-2-3. If he thumps, the bottom card is shown for trump and the pack is dealt out in batches of eight. Either way, dealer gets the trump-determining card.

Melds Each in turn, starting with Forehand, may declare any of the following melds:

Sequence of three 20 points, of four 50 points, of more 2 strokes.

Four Jacks 1 stroke, Queens 2, Kings 3, Aces 4 strokes.

Sequence order is AKQJT987 in all four suits including trumps. A sequence of five or more, or four of a kind, being worth at least 100 trick-points, wins the stated number of strokes without further play – unless, however, a member of that partnership bids *vol* (to win all eight tricks: a slam), in which case play proceeds for a score of 4 strokes if successful. Melds are scored only by the partnership of the player declaring the best meld. For this purpose the best is that scoring most, or (if equal) that containing the most cards, or that containing the highest-ranking cards.

Play If no one scores 100 for melds, Forehand leads to the first trick. To the lead of a trump you must follow suit if you can, unless the only trump you have is the Jass, in which case you may renege. To a plain-suit lead you may either follow suit or play a trump, as you please; and if unable to follow suit you may either trump or discard.

Stikk (marriage) A player holding the King and Queen of trumps – a *stikk* – scores 20 upon playing the second of them to a trick. (One account says this applies only if the declarer wins that trick, but this is unprecedented. More likely it is annulled if the declarer, or his partnership, fails to win a single trick.)

Score The side first correctly claiming to have reached 100 in play wins a single stroke, or a double if the other side has less than 51 (when they are said to be in *jan*). Winning all eight tricks scores 4 strokes. If neither side reaches 100, the points for tricks and melds are carried forward and the winner of the last trick deals next. Play up to any agreed number of strokes.

Comment As in all Jass games, the top Jack is a most powerful card. If it fails to capture a high counter, or remains in the hand of an opponent when the other side has reached 100, the Jass is said to have 'gone in his socks'.

Don't forget . . .

- Play to the left (clockwise) unless otherwise stated.
- Eldest or Forehand means the player to the left of the dealer in left-handed games, to the right in right-handed games.
- T = Ten, p = players, pp = in fixed partnerships, c = cards, † = trump, ☆ = Joker.

Quasi-trump games

Karnöffel is the oldest known card game. Its rules were thought to be lost beyond recovery until the late twentieth century, when researchers discovered a game that almost exactly fitted its description being played in one or two remote valleys of Switzerland under the name Kaiserspiel, or Kaiserjass. (Not an ideal title, as Kaiser also applies to other, unrelated games.) Since then, further exploration has opened up a whole family of related games still played throughout northern Europe.

So now we can introduce and explore a fascinating group of trick-taking games distinguished by several peculiar habits. One is that players need not follow suit but are free to play any card they like. Another is that, instead of a trump suit in the usual sense of the word, certain individual cards have special names and act as quasi-trumps, or enjoy particular powers of their own. Some, especially Sevens, always win the trick, but only when led; some win only when played from other positions and are powerless when led; some only beat other specific cards; and some are totally powerless, serving only to pad the hand out so that no one can tell how many power cards the other players hold. Another amusing feature (though not unique to this family) is the practice, in partnership varieties, of signalling the holding of certain high cards to one's partner by means of codified nods, winks and grimaces, ideally made when the other side is not looking. This does not constitute 'organized cheating', as some believe: it is merely a system of conventions, like opening 'Two clubs' at Bridge to denote a hand worth 23 points.

Because Karnöffel itself is first mentioned some 10 years before the invention of real trumps (in Tarot games), it may be that some of these features go right back to games played when cards first reached Europe, around 1360, and that the invention of a trump suit may have been inspired by the concept of individual cards with special powers.

Karnöffel (Kaiserspiel, Kaiserjass)   4 players (2 × 2), 40 cards

The oldest identifiable card game is first mentioned in Bavaria in 1426 under the name Karnöffel, which rhymes more or less with 'kerfuffle' (appropriately), means a hernia (literally), and was then a rude word for a cardinal (scandalously). A low-class game of soldiers and peasants, it is early recorded because regularly banned by legal and ecclesiastical authorities, who vehemently objected to its satirical promotion of an anarchic world order. Certain cards were given names, such as the Pope, the Devil, and the Kaiser, and those one would normally expect to be highest were beaten by Twos and Fours and bolshie-looking Jacks.

The Swiss game now called Kaiserspiel seems closer to its original than any other member of the family, and the following is based on current practice at several localities in Nidwalden, south of Lake Lucerne. It has long been played with Swiss-suited cards in default of the medieval pack, which partly explains why the game was not recognized earlier. Although 36-card Swiss-suited packs are readily obtainable from specialist suppliers, the 48-card version required for Kaiserspiel may be harder to find. In case this inhibits you from sampling its peculiar delights, several other games of the same family follow which are (or were) played with French-suited cards.

Cards Kaiserspiel is properly played with a 40-card pack consisting of King, Ober, Unter, Banner, and numerals 765432 in suits of acorns, shields, flowers and (hawk-)bells. The symbols and abbreviations used here, with their Anglo-American equivalents are:

acorns	♣ clubs	King	K	King
flowers	♠ spades	Ober	O	Queen
shields	♡ hearts	Unter	U	Jack
bells	♦ diamonds	Banner	B	Ten

Preliminaries Four players in fixed partnerships. Deal one card to each player. Whoever gets the lowest, or the first dealt of equal cards, deals to the first hand after shuffling and cutting. The dealer and eldest hand are the captains of their respective partnerships, for purposes explained below.

Rank of cards In common suits, cards rank KOU(B)765432. The Banners may be promoted to Kaisers, in which case they belong to the 'special' suit. The suit chosen to be special varies from deal to deal, and some of its cards are equivalent to trumps.

Cards of the special suit (indicated †), and Banners if promoted to Kaisers, rank in the following order and have the powers quoted.

King-beaters	♣B (*Mugg*) †5 † U (*Joos*) † 6 † 2 ♣B (*Blass*)	these beat any common card or lower trump
Ober-beaters	† 3 ♡B	these beat any commoner but are beaten by the King of the suit led
Unter-beaters	† 4 ♢B (*Wydli*)	these beat any commoner but are beaten by the King or Ober of the suit led
Non-trumps	† K (*Fuil*) † O (*Hiratä*) † 7	beats only the Ober of the special suit beats nothing wins only if led to a trick, and even when led is beaten by †U

☞ Note that only the top six cards are full trumps. The next four are only partial trumps, and the King, Ober and Seven of the special suit are not trumps at all. Example: Assume ♡ trump. The cards played to a trick are ♣O ♡3 ♣K ♡6. Of these:

♣O	Establishes the suit led
♡3	Beats it, because it is an Ober-beater
♣K	Beats ♡3, because the King is of the suit led, and the Three is not a King-beater. Had a different King been played, the Three would have beaten it for not being of the suit led.
♡6	Takes the trick, as it is a King-beating trump. It would have beaten any other King.

Initial deal Before the deal, the player at dealer's left cuts the cards and shows the bottom card of the top half, which will be at the bottom of the pack and so out of play when the cut is completed. This is for information only. If it is a Banner, he must cut again elsewhere until some other card appears. Each player receives seven cards, but not all at once. First, deal one card face up to the right and to partner, then pause. If either card is a Banner, its owner should immediately declare it to be a Kaiser, otherwise it remains a commoner. Then deal a card face up to the left and to self, and pause again for making Kaisers and raising the game value.

Raising the game value At the start of a hand, the value of the game is 4 points. During the deal, this may be increased in either of two ways.

1. Whenever a Kaiser is declared, the captain of the team declaring it must offer to raise the game value by 1 or 3 points. The second captain may either accept the raise and play on, or resign, losing only the game value that obtained before the raise was announced. If a 1-point raise is accepted, the first captain may increase the raise from 1 to 3, with the same consequence. (It is usual to raise by 3 immediately.)

2. At any point during the deal, either captain may announce 'Three up' (*Spieldrei*), thereby offering to raise the stake by 3 points. The other captain may accept and play on, or resign for the previously existing value. Three up may be called any number of times, but not by the same team twice in succession.

Trump With four cards dealt, one to each player, the special suit is now declared to be that of the lowest card so far showing, other than Banners (Kaisers). Of equally low cards, it is that of the one dealt first.

Remainder of deal All additional cards are dealt face down. Deal two to the right and to partner, then pause, then two to the left and to self and pause again. The pauses are to allow for any declaration of Kaisers and for any raising of the game value that may ensue. Banners need not be declared immediately: their holders may delay declarations until the dealing is finished. Next, deal four more cards each, in two rounds of two, and without pausing for raising, until everyone has seven cards in all. Finally, each player reduces his hand to five by throwing out any two unwanted cards, face down.

More Kaisers Each in turn, starting with eldest, may now promote any unannounced Banners they hold into Kaisers, and the team captain may accordingly raise the game value by 1 or 3 points for each. A player holding two or more should promote them one at a time, enabling the opponents to resign after each one if they wish, or to accept the game without knowing that another may be declared against them. This continues until one side resigns or everyone has declared their Kaisers.

Play Eldest leads to the first trick and the winner of each trick leads to the next. Any card may be played: there is no need to follow suit. It is usual to play each card in front of oneself rather than to the centre of the table. It is also usual to play a losing card face down, but if it is a Kaiser this fact must be announced, though its actual suit need not be stated. (It is legal to play any card face down, but it can never win a trick.)

If a common suit is led, or the King or Ober of the special suit, the trick is taken by the highest card of the suit led, unless it contains a trump of sufficient power to beat it.

If a trump is led, the trick is taken by the highest trump played.

If the †7 is led, it wins the trick unless the Joos (†U) appears. The Joos itself can then be beaten only by †5 or ⊕B. (Neither of these, however, beats the Seven if the Joos is not played.) If †7 is not led, it loses.

Signalling Both during the deal and in the course of the game, players may indicate to their partners the holding of particular cards by means of facial and bodily signals, preferably when neither opponent is looking. This is not cheating, so long as the signals accord with a universally recognized code (like bidding conventions at Bridge). The recognized signals are as follows:

Mugg (⊕B)	puff up one cheek
Trump Five	wink
Joos (†U)	stick tongue out
other K-beater	shrug shoulder
low trump	waggle finger as though writing
trump Seven	silently mouth the word 'seven'
⊛King	wrinkle nose
◌King	glance sideways
⍟King	look up
⊖King	look down

Also, there is no restriction on table talk. You may announce what cards you hold (truthfully or untruthfully), or expose any of them, provided that everyone can see them, and either ask or tell your partner what card to play at any given point.

Score The increasing game value and current score are recorded with chalk on a slate. Game is 101 points.

Watten

2–4 players (2 × 2), 32 cards

A member of the Karnöffel family popular in Bavaria. Though hard to describe, Watten is fun to play and easy to learn. (Source: Claus D. Grupp, *Kartenspiele*, Wiesbaden, 1975.)

Preliminaries From two to four may play, four sitting crosswise in partnerships and all play going to the left. The 32-card pack is normally German-suited (A-K-O-U-10-9-8-7) but French-suited will do. Suit equivalents are acorns ♣ (clubs), leaves ♠ (spades), hearts ♥ (hearts), bells ♦ (diamonds)

Deal Deal five each in batches of 3+2 and stack the rest face down.

Object To score one or more game-points, either by winning three tricks or by bluffing the other side into folding. Game is 15 points.

Rank of cards Three cards are permanent top trumps (*Kritischen*, 'criticals'), namely:

Maxi	♥K	or	♥K
Belli	♦7	or	♦7
Spitz	♣7	or	♣7

After examining his cards, eldest nominates a rank for trump promotion. All four cards of that rank (or fewer, if one is a critical) become the next highest trumps, called 'strikers' (*Schlage*).

Dealer then nominates any suit as trump. The striker of trumps, or 'chief striker', becomes the fourth-highest trump (unless it is a critical), and the other strikers rank equally below it in fifth position. Below them follow the remaining cards of the trump suit: A-K-O(Q)-U(J)-10-9-8-7, omitting any that may be a critical or a striker.

Examples:
1. Eldest promotes Unters (Jacks), and dealer promotes leaves (spades), giving as trumps:

♥K ♦7 ♣7 ♥U (♣ = ♠U = ♦U) ♥A-K-O-10-9-8-7

or ♥K ♦7 ♣7 ♠J (♣J = ♥J = ♦J) ♠A-K-Q-10-9-8-7

2. Eldest announces Kings and dealer hearts. Trumps are:

♥K ♦7 ♣7 (♠K = ♣K = ♦) ♥A-O-10-9-8-7

or ♥K ♦7 ♣7 (♠K = ♣K = ♦K) ♥A-Q-J-10-9-8-7

In (2) there is no chief striker, as ♥K is always a critical. Bracketed cards are equal in rank.

Play Eldest leads first and the winner of each trick leads to the next. Suit need not be followed except in one instance: if the chief striker is led, everyone else must play a trump if possible, and beat any others already played if possible. All criticals, strikers and trumps count as trumps. The trick is taken by

- the highest trump played; or,
- if headed by equal strikers, the first played; or
- if containing no trumps, the highest card of the suit led.

Raising and scoring A player or side upon winning three tricks scores the point, and play ceases. At any time during the game, however, once the trumps and strikers have been established, any player may raise the game value by saying 'Double'. The other side may then fold, or accept the double, or raise it further by saying 'Three'. If they fold, play ceases and the challenger scores the pre-raise game value. If they accept, either verbally or by continuing play, then play continues at the new level. (If three play and one challenges, the other two must jointly agree whether to accept or fold.) Further raises of 'Four', 'Five', etc., are made alternately between the two sides. A player or side standing at 13 or more may not raise. If they do, it is discounted, and they lose 2 points.

Signals When four play, partners may signal certain card holdings to each other by conventional body-language. Maxi is indicated by pursing the lips, Belli by winking the right eye, Spitz by winking the left.

Brus (Bräus)   4 or 6 players (2 × 2, 3 × 3), 36 cards

A member of the Karnöffel family peculiar to Gotland, Brus (or Bräus) underwent a brief revival in the 1980s for reasons possibly related to the touristic rediscovery of folklore and customs. This account is based on articles in various Swedish magazines, notably by Nils Lithberg and Göran Åkerman. Brus is also the name of a related Jutish game in Denmark.

Preliminaries Four players sit crosswise in partnerships, or six sit alternately in two partnerships of three. Four players receive nine each, or six players six each, dealt one at a time from a 36-card pack consisting of AKQJT9876 in each suit. Play to the left.

Object the ultimate aim is to win six strokes (game-points) over as many deals as it takes. In each deal a stroke is scored by the side that wins six tricks, or five tricks if one of the partners holds ♣K. Winning six straight off is a lurch (*jan*) and earns two strokes. It is possible for the outcome to be a no-score draw.

Rank of cards The pack consists of 'live' cards, which may be played to tricks, and 'duds', which may not (in Swedish respectively *spelbara* and *odugliga korte*). The top three live cards are called matadors (*makdorar*) and have individual names. Live cards rank from high to low as follows. Those equal in face value beat one another in the suit order shown (clubs highest):

♣	♠	♥	♦		
♣	-	-	-	Jack	*Spit*
-	♠	-	-	Eight	*Dull*
-	-	♥	-	King	*Brus*
♣	♠	♥	♦	Nines	
♣	♠	♥	♦	Aces	
-	♠	♥	♦	Jacks	
♣	♠	♥	♦	Sixes	

The Sevens are winners, as explained below. All others – Tens, Queens, and unlisted Eights and Kings – are duds.

Play Eldest starts by laying, face up on the table, any Sevens he may hold. Each of these counts by itself as a won trick. He then leads a live card to the first trick. Each in turn thereafter must, if possible, play a higher live card than any so far played, otherwise pass. Whoever plays highest wins the trick, turns it face down, and leads to the next. Before leading, he may similarly lay out Sevens, counting each as a won trick. If a player on lead has no live card, the turn passes to the left until somebody has one, which must then be led.

Score Play ceases when one side has won six tricks, including any declared Sevens. That side scores 1 stroke, or 2 for the lurch. If neither has won six tricks when no live cards remain to be led, a side with five tricks scores 1 stroke if one of its members holds ♣K. Game is six strokes.

Comment The effect of dud cards is to distribute playing hands of unequal length, while camouflaging the number of live cards in each player's hand. Duds might as well be discarded before play begins, but this would spoil the fun. Certain cards other than matadors also have individual names, of varying degrees of formality and propriety. The ♣9 is commonly called *plågu*, literally 'torment', because it may force the play of a matador when its holder would have preferred to hold it

back till later. The ♠A is called *grodballen*, 'frog's scrotum', which makes
no apparent sense at all.

Stýrivolt

The national card game of the Faeroe Islands has been played there for
over 200 years and probably originated in Denmark 100 years before
that. It is now severely in decline, but fortunately has been well docu-
mented. The following is based on John McLeod's website description,
which benefits from comments by Jógvan Bærentsen, and on Anthony
Smith's translation of an article by Bærentsen. Dr Smith also had the
benefit of playing the game at Tórshavn in 1996.

Terminology The Faeroese word *stikkar* I render by the related English
word cognate 'sticker', in the archaic sense 'slaughterer'. *Karnifl* obviously derives from *Karnöffel*. The Nines of the chosen suit are each
called *ryssa*, meaning 'mare'; in fact, the ♥9 is called *Hoygarðsryssa*,
'hay-yard mare'. The so-called 'postmen' (*postar, pavstar*) represent a
corruption of, or pun on, the word for 'pope'. Picturesque as these and
other terms are, I employ them sparingly, as the game has quite enough
other complications to be getting on with.

Preliminaries Four players sitting crosswise in partnerships use a 48-
card pack lacking Tens. Play goes to the left. The aim in each deal is to
be the first side to win five of the nine tricks played, and over the whole
session to win the largest number of crosses (game-points). Scores are
usually chalked on a slate, as described later.

Deal The cards are usually shuffled between deals, but not cut. Deal
nine each in threes and stack the last twelve face down.

Rank of cards Before the actual play, which is very simple, it is necessary
to learn which cards beat which other cards in which circumstances.
This is very complicated, so pay attention.

First, note that instead of a single trump suit, there are two so-called
'chosen' suits, which vary from deal to deal. (How they are chosen is
explained later.)

There are nine top cards called stickers (*stikkar*), which beat all lower
cards except 'lambs' (Sevens). The highest stickers are five specific cards,
in descending order ♥2 ♣4 ♠8 ♥9 ♦9, which remain invariant regardless

of the chosen suits. The other four are the two Aces, called *stýrivolts*, and the two Jacks, called *karnifls*, of the two chosen suits.

These are followed by eight cards called beaters, four in each chosen suit. They are called 'beaters' because they beat certain lower cards but not all. In descending order, they are the 6, 2, 3 and 4 of each chosen suit.

This leaves twelve cards in the two chosen suits (six each). Ten of these may be called 'leaders', because they win a trick only when led to it, and even then only if not beaten by a sticker or a high enough beater. (They are not actually called leaders, but the term may be found helpful.)

The nine stickers, eight beaters, and remaining twelve cards of the chosen suits are listed below in descending order of trick-taking power:

category	ranks	names	powers
9 stickers:	♥2	bird	
beat all	♣4	fyrik	
lower	♠8	áttuni	
cards	♥9	mare of hearts	
except	♦9	mare of diamonds	
led Sevens	A A	stýrivolts	
	J J	karnifls	
8 beaters:	6 6	postmen	beat Aces and lower
beat only			(but not stýrivolts)
certain	2 2	tvists	beat Kings and lower
cards			(but not karnifls)
	3 3	trists	beat Queens and lower
			(but not karnifls)
	4 4	unfortunates	beat Jacks and lower
			(but not karnifls)
10 leaders:	7 7	lambs	unbeatable
win only	9 9 8 8	free cards	beaten only by stickers
when led	K K Q Q	kings and queens	K beaten only by tvists and higher
			Q beaten only by trists and higher
	5 5	traders (chapmen)	no value, but trade for turn-up

In the two unchosen suits, cards rank in descending order AKQJ98765432 (omitting the five individual cards that are permanent stickers).

Four of a kind If anyone holds all four cards of the same rank, they all assume the value and powers of the best of them. For example, if you hold four Twos, they all count as 'birds', being as powerful as the unbeatable ♥2.

Chosen suits The chosen suits are chosen as follows. Dealer takes cards from the top of the stock one by one, holding them in such a way that only he can see them. As soon as a third different suit appears, he stops. The first two suits are the chosen ones. He shows what they are by placing the best card of each chosen suit face up on the table, and half covering them with the remaining ten cards of the stock, face down.

For this purpose only, the best card in a chosen suit is the Trader (Five), followed by the Lamb (Seven), followed by the highest sticker, followed by the Six, Eight or Nine (ad lib.), Two, Three, King or Four (ad lib.), Queen (lowest). If the exposed card is a Lamb, and one or more stickers have also been turned, then the highest sticker is exposed as well as the Lamb of that suit, so there may be three or even four exposed cards.

Examples of chosen suits:

♥2 ♠K ♠3 ♥J ♦9= hearts and spades chosen: expose ♥2 ♠3

♣6 ♣4 ♦A ♣A ♦7 ♥5= clubs and diamonds chosen: expose ♣4 ♦7 ♦A

♥9 ♥5 ♥4 ♣7 ♣6 ♥2 ♠9 = hearts and clubs chosen: expose ♥5 ♣7

A player who holds the Trader (Five) of an exposed suit may at any point in the game exchange it for the exposed card of its suit (or either card if one of them is the Lamb). If he doesn't, but plays it to a trick, it behaves exactly as if it were that exposed card.

Taking the stock If your hand contains not a single sticker, you may exchange it for the stock. More than one player may do this, if so entitled, but they must do it in order of play and before individually playing to the first trick. The exchange is made by laying your hand face down and taking the stock up in its place. This gives you ten cards instead of nine, but you may freely discard one before play, or play two to the first trick, or have one left over at the end.

If you then find that the stock also contains no sticker, you may trade it in again for your original hand, provided that you have not, with either hand, exchanged a Trader for an exposed sticker. If neither hand contains a sticker or a Trader, you may keep both hands and play with 19 cards.

Another player may also exchange in the same way at any time during the game (unless the first one kept all 19 cards), provided that (a) the stock was taken for the first time during the first trick, and (b) the whole of the original hand of the exchanging player was devoid of stickers.

Taking the stock without entitlement incurs a penalty when it comes to the scoring.

Play Eldest leads to the first trick any card except a Lamb (Seven). Each in turn may play any card he chooses, with no obligation to follow suit. The trick is taken by the highest card played, or by the first played of two equally high cards, and the winner of each trick leads to the next. A Lamb (Seven) may be led to a trick only by a player who has already won a trick (individually).

The winning card is determined by the Table above, or by the following notes:

• A sticker can be beaten only by a higher sticker.
• A beater can be beaten only by a higher beater or a sticker. If the two highest cards played are equal in rank, the first played beats the second.
• If a leader is led, it wins the trick unless it is beaten by a sticker or a high enough beater. The four Eights and Nines of the chosen suits are equal in rank, and if two or more of these are the highest cards played, the first one played beats the others. The same applies to Kings and Queens.
• If an unchosen suit is led, the trick is taken by the highest card of that suit, unless it is beaten by a sticker or a high enough beater. (It is not beaten by a leader.)

Play continues until one pair has won five tricks, and may then stop. Winning the first five straight off is called 'keeping in', or, more distinctively, '[making] the vol'. A pair that makes the vol may elect to continue play, thereby undertaking to win all nine tricks. This earns a bonus if successful; if not, it incurs both the loss of the deal and an additional penalty.

Score Scores are recorded as strokes, crosses, and double crosses (known as monks' crosses). A cross is equivalent to three strokes, and a double cross to two crosses. The scores are:

the game (five tricks)	1 stroke
the vol (five straight off)	2 strokes
winning all nine	3 strokes
the vol made by one partner	1 cross
all nine won by one partner	1 double cross
illegally taking the stock	1 cross to the opponents

Scores are kept on a chalk-board. Start by drawing a vertical line with three shorter cross-lines. This is called the chalk-up (a):

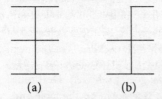

(a)   (b)

Record each stroke you win by erasing a bar from your side of the vertical line (b, assuming yours is the left side). When you have erased all three bars, you may draw a cross on your side of the chalk-board, unless your opponents already have a cross on their side, in which case you erase their cross instead of drawing yours. Then erase the chalk-up (leaving only the crosses, if any) and draw a new one.

If you earn more strokes than you have bars to erase, erase as many as are left on this chalk-up, and erase the balance from the next one.

The general principle is that only one partnership at a time may have crosses on their side of the board. Upon earning a cross, therefore, you draw one only if your side (or neither side) has any crosses, or erase one if only the other side has any.

If you make three strokes before your opponents have made one, you score a double or monk's cross, which looks like this: ‡. As before, you either draw it on your side, or erase it on their side. Earning a single cross entitles you to erase one of their single crosses, a double cross to erase one of their doubles. If you earn a double and they have only singles, you may erase two of them. If you earn a single and they have only a double, you may erase one bar of it to make it a single. This is called, in polite terminology, 'gelding the monk'. It is supposed to be impolite to geld a monk when it is possible to erase a single cross.

The first chalk-up is done by the first dealer, but, as chalking is regarded as messy work, the task is subsequently delegated to whichever side currently has no crosses. The actual scoring, though, is done by the side entitled to it.

Alkort

This obvious descendant of Karnöffel could have been described as the national card game of Iceland until perhaps a century ago, Icelanders having since become fiendish Bridge fanatics. The following is based on Þórarinn Guðmundsson, *Spilabøk AB* (Reykjavik, 1989).

Preliminaries Four payers sitting crosswise in partnerships use a 44-card pack lacking Tens and Fives. All play goes to the left. Deal nine each in batches of three. The last eight go face down on the table and have no further part to play. The aim is to win five of the nine tricks played, ideally the first five straight off.

Rank of cards Cards rank from high to low as follows:

1. Sevens always win the trick when led, but lose otherwise.
2. ♦K ♥2 ♣4 ♠8 ♥9 ♦9, in that order.
3. Aces, Jacks, Sixes, Eights (except ♠8), in that order but regardless of suit.

The remaining cards (black Nines, three Fours, four Threes, three Twos, three Kings, four Queens) are all equal and have absolutely no trick-heading power, except that Twos beat Kings and Queens, and Threes beat Queens.

Exchange A player who holds no card capable of beating an Eight may immediately declare himself 'under-eight' (*friðufær*).This entitles him to discard eight cards from his hand and draw those undealt as replacements.

Play Before play, each player secretly shows his partner his highest card. Eldest leads to the first trick and the winner of each trick leads to the next. Any card may be played: there is no need to follow suit. The trick is taken by the highest card played, or by the first played of cards equal in rank or equally worthless.

Score Play normally ends when one side has won its fifth trick, thereby scoring 1 point. However, if one side wins the first five straight off (a *múk*), play continues for as long as they continue to win tricks, after which they score from 5 to 9 points according to the number they won in unbroken succession. Six or more is called a 'stroke' (of six, seven, etc.).

Treikort

In this three-hand equivalent of Alkort each player receives nine each in threes from a 27-card pack consisting of Aces, ♦K, ♣Q, Jacks, red Nines, Eights, Sevens, Sixes, ♣4, ♠2 and ♥2. Cards rank as follows:

1. Sevens win if led, otherwise lose.
2. ♣Q ♠2 ♦K ♥2 ♣4 ♠8 ♥9 ♦9 in that order.
3. Aces, Jacks, Sixes, Eights (except ♠8), all equally worthless.

Play as at Alkort. A player who wins 13 or more tricks in three deals is designated 'Pope', and remains so until he fails to win 13 within any three consecutive deals. After each deal and before play begins, the current Pope (if any) may demand a Seven from one player and the highest card other than a Seven from the other. They are obliged to give him these in return for any low card of his choice. If the first player has no Seven, the Pope must do without.

Voormsi (Wumps)

2–4 players, 36 cards

Greenland's national card game, much played on the coastal ferry, is also recorded as 'Wumps' by a Swedish respondent. The following description is based on research by Dr Anthony Smith, and is subject to local variations.

Terminology *Voormsi* (pronounced *woormsi*) is a non-Greenlandic word of unknown meaning. *Toqu* means 'death'. This card is also called *Toqutsit*, literally 'he who kills you' (pronounced *dogutsit*).

Preliminaries Four usually play sitting crosswise in partnerships. Three play without partners. When two play, a trick is four cards. Two play as if they were two partnerships, as explained below.

Cards and deal Deal four each in ones from a 36-card pack consisting of AKQJ98765 in each suit except diamonds, whose King is normally replaced by the Three. (Note Fives instead of Tens.) There will be nine tricks if two or four play, twelve if three.

Object The aim is to win tricks and either bring home certain high cards, or at least prevent the others from doing so. Game is 9 points (12 if three play) over as many deals as necessary. Scores are normally kept by erasing or crossing off the appropriate number of arms of cross-strokes from a diagram like this:

N–S
E–W

Rank of cards Below the top three cards, ranks beat one another in the order shown – any Nine beats any Ace, etc.

♣	♠	♥	♦		
♣	-	-	-	Jack	*Toqu* or *Toqutsit*, equal in rank with ...
-	-	♥	-	King	*Voormsi*
-	♠	-	-	Eight	Third highest card (no special name)
♣	♠	♥	♦	Nines	i.e ♣9 beats ♠9 beats ♥9 beats ♦9, and
♣	♠	♥	♦	Aces	... the same suit-order applies
-	♠	♥	♦	Jacks	... to Aces and lower ranks
♣	♠	♥	♦	Sixes	...
♣	♠	♥	♦	Fives	...
♣	-	♥	♦	Eights	...
♣	♠	♥	♦	Queens	...
♣	♠	-	-	Kings	nominally lowest, but have special powers

The following cards have special properties:

♦3   Powerless if led to a trick, but unbeatable if played from any other position.

any 7   Powerless unless led to a trick, when it can be beaten only by ♦3, ♣K, or a higher-suited Seven. A Seven counts as 'led' if played second following ♦3. It loses in all other circumstances.

♣K   Normally the second lowest card of all, but it beats a winning Seven, and in that event can then be beaten by ♠K or ♦3. If led, or played second to the lead of ♦3, it holds the trick only if nothing else but Sevens or ♠K are played.

♠K   Normally the lowest card of all, but it beats ♣K when the latter is beating a Seven. If led, or played second to the lead of ♦3, it holds the trick only if nothing else but Sevens are played.

Play Eldest leads to the first trick and the winner of each trick leads to the next. The lead to any trick may be of a singleton, pair, triplet or quartet of the same rank – any rank, including Sevens and Kings. (Whether ♦3 counts as a King for this purpose is unclear, and must be agreed beforehand.) The followers must play the same number of cards as those led, and they may be any cards at all, not necessarily of the same rank or suit. (*Exception*: If Voormsi is heading the trick, and an opponent holds Toqu, he must play it.) A singleton trick is taken by the highest card played, as detailed above. A multi-card lead is beaten only by a group of cards of which each and every one beats a different card of the group led. Before the next lead, each in turn, beginning with the trick-winner, draws a card from stock until the hands are restored to four cards, or none remain to draw. (When two play, they each draw one after playing each card.)

Two-player rule Whoever plays the higher of the first two cards draws one from stock, waits for the other to do so, then plays third to the trick, which is won by whoever plays the highest of the four.

Score Points are scored for the following feats. Remember that Toqu (♣J) and Voormsi (♥K) are equal in rank, and if both fall to the same trick the second one played beats the first.

1. Score 2 points for playing Toqu and thereby capturing Voormsi played by an opponent. However, you may not capture it from your partner, otherwise you immediately lose all your points and the game ends.

2. Score 1 point for playing ♦3 and thereby capturing Voormsi, no matter who played it, provided that Voormsi would otherwise have won the trick. (Thus the bonus does not apply if Voormsi has been discarded on a Seven, or played to a doubleton trick won by Toqu and ♦3.)

3. Score an additional 1 point for playing ♦3 if, besides capturing Voormsi, you also thereby capture Toqu, provided that it was itself capturing Voormsi by virtue of being played after it. This nullifies the Toqu player's 2-point bonus.

4. Score 1 point for playing Voormsi and winning the trick, but not if you played it last to the trick, or if Toqu has already gone, or if you hold Toqu yourself. In other words, you get the bonus for playing it only when, so far as you knew, it risked being captured by Toqu. If challenged, you must show that you are not holding Toqu yourself. (Logically, therefore, you don't get the point if you capture Toqu with Voormsi in the same trick.)

5. Score 1 point for winning any five tricks, and 1 for each trick in excess of five. However, winning all nine tricks (or 12 if three play) nullifies the hand.

6. Score an additional point for winning the first five tricks in succession, but don't stop playing until the sequence is finished – in case you win them all, or more than needed for game.

A side scoring more points than needed for game deducts the excess from their target score. For example, if you stand at 7 and score 5, you go up to 9 then down to 6.

Examples: To illustrate the trick-winning powers of special cards, here are some examples. In each case, the first card is the one led and the others follow in order.

♥7-♣K-♦3-♠K won by ♦3 (always wins if not led)

♥7-♠K-♦7-♥K won by ♥7 (in winning position because led, and no better card played)

♦3-♥7-♠K-♣A won by ♥7 (in winning position after ♦3, and no better card played)

♦3-♥7-♠K-♣7 won by ♣7 (higher suit than Seven previously played in winning position)

♥7-♣K-♦7-♥K won by ♣K (it beats a Seven led)

♦3-♥7-♠K-♠7 won by ♣K (the ♥7 counting as 'led')

♦3-♥7-♠K-♣K won by ♣K (black Kings cannot capture in advance, only in retrospect)

♥7-♦3-♠K-♣K won by ♦3 (beats anything when not led)

♦3-♠K-♥7-♠7 won by ♠K (♦3 and Sevens are powerless, so ♠K, though lowest, is the only 'real' card)

♣K-♥7-♠K-♣7 won by ♣K (Sevens are powerless; ♣K is the higher of two 'real' cards)

Don't forget . . .

- Play to the left (clockwise) unless otherwise stated.
- Eldest or Forehand means the player to the left of the dealer in left-handed games, to the right in right-handed games.
- T = Ten, p = players, pp = in fixed partnerships, c = cards, † = trump, ☆ = Joker.

13 Tarots and tarocks

People are often surprised to learn that Tarot cards were originally invented for playing games, that such games are still widespread and popular in continental Europe, and that the employment of tarots for divination and fortune-telling is a relatively recent perversion of their proper use, dating only from the eighteenth century.

Tarots were invented in Italy in about 1430-40 by adding to the existing four-suited pack a fifth suit of 21 specially illustrated cards called *trionfi*, and an odd card called the Fool – which, despite appearances, is not the origin of the modern Joker. (For its true origin, see Euchre.) The pack to which it was added was the then current one of 56 cards, bearing the standard Italian suitmarks of swords, staves, cups and coins, and headed by not three but four courts: King, Queen, Knight (best abbreviated to C for Cavalier), and Valet or Equerry (conveniently abbreviated J for Jack). The original full pack therefore consisted of 78 cards.

Austrian Tarocks. The Fool (Sküs), Trump XXI ('Moon'), Queen of hearts, and Cavalier of spades.

From *trionfi*, meaning 'triumphs' in the pageantry sense of the word, comes the English word 'trumps', their original function being to act as cards that would beat any ordinary card played to the same trick. It was not until nearly 1500, when players found they could duplicate this effect more cheaply by simply entrumping the suit of a card turned at random from the pack, thereby giving rise to the game of Triomphe, that a new word was required for the former special cards. Why they were then called *tarocchi*, and what it means, was a mystery even to their contemporaries. From it, however, derive the German *tarock* and the French and English *tarot*.

Tarot games subsequently spread throughout Europe, with the exception of Britain, the Iberian peninsula, and the Balkans. They still thrive in Italy, France, Austria, Hungary, Czechoslovakia, Slovenia and parts of Switzerland and southern Germany. Most follow the same underlying pattern, being trick-taking games for three to five players in which win or loss is determined both by the number of tricks taken and also by the value of the counting-cards they contain. The counters are normally the lowest and the highest trumps, the Fool, and the four court cards of each suit.

The only complete and authoritative survey and classification of Tarot games is that of Sir Michael Dummett, *The Game of Tarot*, and its briefer accompaniment *Twelve Tarot Games* (both London, 1980). Additional descriptions, based on the authority of first-hand experience, appear on John McLeod's card game web-site (www.pagat.com). From all these I have selected for description several different games, of which the first is chosen for its relative simplicity, and the remainder for the variety they display in exploring the possibilities of just a few basic ideas.

Scarto

3 players, 78 cards (Italian tarocchi)

The Piedmontese game of Scarto ('Discard'), though now in decline, makes a good starting-point for the exploration of Tarot games, being less complicated than most, and probably differing little from their common fifteenth-century ancestor.

Preliminaries Scarto is normally played by three with the 78-card Tarocco Piedmontese pack, in which the Angel trump, †20, is actually the highest, beating †21. But any 78-card Italian-suited pack will do, and the 21 can then resume its normal high position. The pack consists of:

- the Fool (Matto)
- twenty-one trumps, headed by the Angel (20), followed by 21, 19, 18, and so numerically down to No. 1, called Bagatto
- fifty-six plain cards, fourteen in each of the four suits, swords, batons, cups and coins (♠♣♦♥). The highest cards are King (*Re*), Queen

(*Dama*), Cavalier (*Cavallo*), Jack (*Fante*). These are followed by the ten numerals. In swords and batons they rank downwards from Ten high to Ace low. In cups and coins they rank in reverse order from Ace high to Ten low.

A game is three deals, each dealing in turn. Points are scored for capturing certain cards ('counters') in tricks. They are the Angel, the Bagatto, the Fool, and all sixteen courts. Each plays for himself, and whoever has the lowest cumulative score after three deals is the loser.

Deal Choose first dealer by any agreed means. The turn to deal and play then passes to the right. Deal all the cards around in fives, Dealer himself taking the remaining three.

Discard Dealer examines his hand and discards three cards face down which will count for him at end of play as if he had won them in tricks. He may not discard the Angel, the Fool, or any King, and may not discard the Bagatto unless he holds no other trump or the Fool. Every player now has twenty-five cards.

Play Eldest leads to the first trick. Subsequent players must follow suit if possible, otherwise must trump if possible, otherwise may play any card. The trick is taken by the highest card of the suit led, or by the highest trump if any are played, and the winner of each trick leads to the next. Tricks need not be kept separated: everyone just makes their own pile of the cards they win.

Playing the fool Whoever holds the Fool may play it at any time, in contravention of any of the above rules. It cannot win the trick, but neither can it be lost. Instead, its player simply shows it as his played card, then adds it to his own pile of winnings, where it stays for the rest of the deal. It is legal, if pointless, to lead it to a trick. In this case, any card may be played second, and the third player must follow suit to that.

Score At end of play, everyone sorts through their won cards and reckons their values in batches of three at a time. The counting cards and their values are:

The Angel (20)	5	Each King	5
The Bagatto (1)	5	Each Queen	4
The Fool	4	Each Cavalier	3
		Each Jack	2

A batch of three counters scores 2 less than the total value of its individual counters. Two counters and a blank score 1 less than the two counters together. One counter and two blanks score just the value of the counter, and three blanks score exactly 1 point. Whoever played the Fool counts 4 for it without including it in a batch. Whoever won the trick to which the Fool was played will have two odd cards left over. He counts these exactly as though they were three, the third being a non-counter.

No matter how the cards are batched in threes, the total of points distributed between the three players will always be 78. Since the average score is 26, each player counts towards game the difference between 26 and the points he took. Thus, if the counters divide 30, 27, 21, the respective scores are +4, +1, and −5.

The player with the lowest score after three deals pays a small stake to each of the others.

> ☞ The scoring is typical of Tarot games. There are two ways of simplifying it. One is to try to make all batches of three contain at least two blanks, as these give the simplest scores, namely, 1 point or the value of the single counter. The other is to assume a notional value of 1 point per blank, in which case any three cards count 2 less than their total face value. For example: Angel, Cavalier, Ten counts $(5 + 3 + 0) − (1) = 7$ by the first method, and $(5 + 3 + 1) − (2) = 7$ by the second.

Notes on play All Tarot games are deep and subtle, and an ounce of play is worth a pound of book. Suffice here to say that the dealer will use the discard to bury a vulnerable counter, or to create a void suit: and, since he has this advantage, the other two may find it mutually profitable to play to some extent as if they were partners against a soloist. Much of the interest centres on saving or capturing the Bagatto, as it counts 5 points and is vulnerable because it is the lowest trump. If the dealer has it, he cannot (by law) save it by putting it in his discards, unless it is the only trump he holds. One of his aims in voiding a suit as soon as possible will be to enable him to win the trick with the Bagatto when that suit is led. Conversely, this is one good reason for his opponents not to lead a King until they have discovered, by playing lower cards, in which suit the dealer may have voided himself. A player holding the Bagatto may, if he holds significantly more than the average of seven trumps, try to save it by drawing his opponents' trumps whenever possible – either by leading them, or by leading suits in which they are void, as they are then obliged to trump.

Ottocento (Tarocco Bolognese, Tarocchino)

4 players (2 × 2), 62 cards

In 1725, however, it came to the notice of the Papal authorities that the citizens of Bologna were playing with a pack of cards containing the figures of the Pope, Emperor, Empress and Popess: duly scandalised, they ordered these to be replaced by others. They were henceforward replaced by four Moors, royal figures of a vaguely Eastern appearance

Michael Dummett, *Twelve Tarot Games* (London, 1980)

This remarkable Tarot game has remained popular in and around Bologna for some five centuries. It lacks bidding, but boasts, besides an unusual range of scorable card combinations, the rare feature of scoring for card combinations contained in individual tricks, and a distinctively shortened pack, causing it once to be known by the diminutive title 'Tarocchino'. The 62-card pack is easily obtainable in Bologna, or from specialist card suppliers. If necessary, you can use a stripped-down Tarot de Marseille or Tarocco Piemontese, making the appropriate substitutions in trumps. But this is recommended only as a last resort, as the individuality of the Bolognese cards is one of its chief attractions. If the game seems complicated, take heart from Professor Dummett's assurance that it has been considerably simplified since the eighteenth century.

Players Four play in fixed partnerships. Play goes to the right.

Object To score points for (a) card combinations declared from individual hands as dealt, (b) card combinations that can be made from cards captured in tricks by each partnership, (c) individual counting-cards captured in tricks by each partnership, and (d) winning the last trick. The target score is 800 points, whence the name of the game.

Cards The Tarocco Bolognese contains 62 cards: 21 trumps; a card called the Matto, which belongs to no suit; and ten each of swords, batons, cups and coins. The trumps, of which only twelve are numbered (and somewhat anomalously) rank downwards as follows:

	Angelo	Angel
	Mondo	World
	Sole	Sun
	Luna	Moon
16	Stella	Star
15	Saetta	Thunderbolt
14	Diavolo	Devil
13	Morte	Death
12	Traditore	Traitor
11	Vecchio	Old Man
10	Ruota or Roda	Wheel
9	Forza	Strength
8	Giustitia	Justice
7	Temperanza or Tempra	Temperance
6	Carro	Chariot
5	Amore	Love
	Mori (×4)	Moors (four, all equal in rank)
	Bègato or Bagattino	the lowest trump

The Angel, World, Bègato and Matto are called *tarocchi*. The Matto is not a trump and has no ranking order. Plain suits rank downwards as follows:

in swords (♠) and batons (♣):

King, Queen, Knight, Jack, 10, 9, 8, 7, 6, Ace

in cups (♡) and coins (♦):

King, Queen, Knight, Jack, Ace, 6, 7, 8, 9, 10

Tarocchi and court cards when captured in tricks count as follows:

Tarocchi	5 each
Kings	5 each
Queens	4 each
Knights	3 each
Jacks	2 each

Deal The dealer shuffles and his left-hand opponent cuts. Deal fifteen cards each in batches of five. The last two cards go to the dealer, who then reduces his hand to 15 by making any two discards – other than 5-point cards – face down. At end of play these will count to his side as if won in tricks.

Declarations During the first trick, players may declare and score for certain card combinations. Declarations are not compulsory, nor need they be made in full – for example, you may declare a sequence of four when actually holding five – but, of course, you score only for what you declare. Each in turn makes any such declarations by placing all the relevant cards face up on the table immediately before playing his card to the first trick, and then returning them to hand. The dealer may not use any discards in combinations.

If either side reaches 800 from points scored for declarations, the game ends with no further play.

The combinations and their scores are:

1. *Cricche.* A cricca is three or four cards of the same kind, namely:

cards	three	four
Tarocchi	18	36
Kings	17	34
Queens	14	28
Knights	13	26
Jacks	12	24

If three or more different *cricche* are scored simultaneously by the same player, their total score is doubled.

2. Sequences. Combinations of three or more cards score a basic 10 points, plus 5 points for each card in excess of three. A single gap in a sequence may (with some restriction) be plugged by the use of the Matto or Bègato as a wild card (*contatore*). Each wild card held can be used in every sequence – that is, its use in one sequence does not preclude its use in another. If either or both is held but not used wild, they may be added to the sequence to increase its length and hence its score.

Trump sequence (*grande*). The minimum trump sequence consists of the Angel and at least two of the next three trumps (World, Sun, Moon). It may be extended by any further sequence running downwards from the 16 until a gap is reached. Matto and Bègato can be used wild, but neither of them may replace the Angel, nor may they be put together to represent consecutive numbered trumps. (But a sequence of, say, World-Sun-Matto-Bègato is valid because Matto stands for Moon, which is unnumbered.)

Suit sequence The minimum suit sequence consists of the King and at least two of the next three cards (Queen, Knight, Jack). It may then be extended by the Ace, if held. It may contain one wild card, which may not replace the King; and at least one of the other courts must be natural.

Moors sequence (*mori*). At least three Moors, of which at least two must be natural.

Ace sequence At least three Aces, of which at least two must be natural.

Three or more different sequences scored simultaneously in one hand are doubled in value.

> ☞ Moors and Aces are not sequences in the strict sense of the word, but they are so regarded here. The fact that they count as sequences and not *cricche* is important when it comes to doubling.

Combination	score
Angel, World, Moon, 16	15
Four-card grande	
Angel, Matto (= World or Sun), Moon, 16, 15, Bègato (=14), 13, 12	35
Eight-card grande. (It is not necessary to replace both the World and the Sun with wild cards)	
Angel, World, Sun, Moon, Matto, Bègato, 14	25
Six-card grande. (Not seven: the 16 and 15 are both missing, making the 14 irrelevant.)	
King, Queen, Bègato (for Knight or Jack), Ace	15
Four-card suit sequence	
King, Queen, Knight, Jack, Ace, Matto	25
Six-card suit sequence	
four Aces, Bègato, Matto	25
Six-card Ace sequence	

Play Eldest leads first. Players must follow suit if possible, otherwise must play a trump if possible, and only otherwise may renounce (unless holding the Matto: see below). The trick is taken by the highest card of the suit led, or by the highest trump if any are played, and the winner of each trick leads to the next.

Matto You can play the Matto to any trick at any time, even if able to follow suit, and it is automatically added to the tricks won by your own side. If the other side wins the trick you play it to, you take it back and give them a worthless one in exchange. This can be any card you have already taken, or you can wait until you win a trick containing a card you are willing to abandon, in which case the Matto can be left face up as a reminder. You will lose the Matto only if your side loses every single trick.

Score There are several parts to the scoring, with points made for both individual cards and card-combinations captured in tricks, and to some extent for tricks themselves, and these all in addition to those scored originally for declaring combinations in the hand. It is important to note which side won the last trick, as they will score 6 for it.

The rest is best calculated by taking all the cards captured by the side that won fewer tricks and spreading them out on the table in an ordered layout, with trumps and plain suits clearly distinguished and in proper sequence. This makes it easy to see what combinations they can score, and to deduce, from the cards missing, what combinations can be counted by the other side.

Score first for all the *cricche* that can be made from the visible cards, remembering to double the total if there are three or more of them. The other side then scores similarly for the *cricche* that can be made from their own cards.

Score next for all the sequences that can be made from the visible cards, remembering to double the total if there are three or more of them. The other side then scores similarly for the sequences that can be made from their own cards.

Finally, count the individual card-points in the following specific way. We will call point-scoring cards 'counters' (these are the tarocchi and court cards), and non-counting cards 'blanks' (the remaining trumps and the plain-suit numerals). Count all cards in pairs consisting either of two blanks or of one blank and a counter. Score 1 point for each pair of blanks, and for each pair consisting of a blank and a counter score the value of the counter. In the rare event of necessarily pairing two counters, score them as 1 less than their sum. Add 6 points if this side won the last trick. Record this total towards game.

The other side's score can be found by the same method, or by simply deducting the first side's score from 93, which will always be the combined total no matter how the cards are paired off and counted. (Check: Twenty pairs consisting of a counter and a blank will total 76. This leaves 22 blanks scoring 1 per pair, total 87; and 6 for last makes 93 in all.)

Game The winning side is the one with the larger score when at least one side has reached 800.

Signals Upon leading to a trick, you may make any one of three conventional signals to your partner:

1. *Volo* (toss the card in the air): 'This is my last card in this suit'.

2. *Busso* (strike the table with the fist): 'Play high and return this suit if you win (and can)'.

3. *Striscio* (scrape the card along the table): 'Please lead trumps'.

Two signals may be made at the same trick. Hence a *volo* made without a *busso* can be taken as a request *not* to return the suit. Partner is not obliged to comply with any signalled request.

No other signals are normally permitted today.

French Tarot

3–4 players (4 best), 78 cards

French Tarot became remarkably popular in the late twentieth century, helped largely by the fact that there is basically only one main French game and that it is promoted by a national body called the Fédération Française de Tarot. The following account is based on Dummett (see introduction), with reference to Patrick Arnett, *Le Tarot* (Paris, 1977) and Claude-Marcel Laurent, *Le Jeu de Tarots* (Paris, 1975). It is customary to use the 78-card Tarot Nouveau, but details of play vary from circle to circle and the following account is typical rather then definitive.

Terminology Three significant cards in the game are called *bouts*, meaning 'ends' or 'extremities'. I have reluctantly decided not to translate these as *butts*, which comes from the same root and has the same meaning, as the word sounds vaguely ridiculous in this context. The six undealt cards, which constitute what in classical games would be called a talon, are in fact collectively called *le chien*. This term, though jocular, really does mean 'dog', and gives rise to all sorts of punning remarks when a player picks it up. Hence there is no reason not to call a dog a dog, and that's what it will be. The term *poignée*, for a bonus-earning number of trumps, literally means 'fist'. I will call it a 'bunch' (as in 'a bunch of fives').

Preliminaries Four players play to the right. The 78-card pack consists of

- 21 trumps (*atouts*) numbered 1–21, with scenes of eighteenth-century everyday bourgeois life;
- the Excuse (*excuse*), unnumbered, and depicting a Fool or Jester;
- 14 cards in each of four suits, spades, clubs, hearts, diamonds, ranking from high to low: King (R for *roi*), Queen (D for *dame*), Cavalier (C for *chevalier*), Jack (V for *valet*), 10 9 8 7 6 5 4 3 2 1.

Three of these are special cards called 'bouts'. They are the lowest and the highest trumps (1 and 21), and the Excuse. Certain cards, called counters, carry point-values as follows:

Each bout	5 (†21, †1, and the Excuse)
Each King	5
Each Queen	4
Each Cavalier	3
Each Jack	2

Object An auction determines who will play alone against the other three. The soloist's aim is to win a minimum number of points which varies with the number of bouts contained in his won tricks, *viz.*

3 bouts	36 points
2 bouts	41 points
1 bout	51 points
0 bouts	56 points

The missing value, 46, is one point more than half the total available (91).

Deal Whoever draws the lowest card deals first. For this purpose trumps count higher than plain suits. The turn to deal and play then passes to the right. After cutting to the left, deal eighteen cards each in batches of three, and six face down to the table. The six down-cards – collectively referred to as the 'dog' (*chien*) – are also dealt in batches of three, but they may not be the first three or the last three from the pack, nor may both threes be dealt consecutively.

Void deal A player who happens to have been dealt †1, but no other trump at all, must declare the deal void, and the next in turn to deal does so. (There are other options, but the event is rare and the relevant rules excessively complicated.)

Auction Each in turn, starting with eldest, has one opportunity to bid or pass, and each bid must be higher than the last. The bids from lowest to highest are:

1. *Petite.* The soloist will turn the dog face up, add it to his hand, and make any six discards, face down, before play. These discards will count for him at end of play as if he had won them in tricks. He may not discard a bout or a King, and may discard trumps only if he hasn't enough plain cards. In this case, he must say how many he has discarded, but need not identify them.

2. *Garde.* Same as *petite*, but for a higher score.

3. *Garde sans le chien* (*without the dog*). The soloist will play without touching the dog, but its six cards will still count for him at end of play as if he had won them in tricks.

4. *Garde contre le chien* (*against the dog*). As above, but the six dog cards will count to the opponents as if they themselves had won them in tricks.

Declarations Each player, just before playing to the first trick, may make one or more of the following applicable declarations:

1. Anyone holding ten or more trumps may declare a bunch (*poignée*). The possible declarations are 'Ten', 'Thirteen', or 'Fifteen' trumps. Such a declaration must be supported by showing the stated number of trumps. The Excuse does not count as a trump unless the hand is one short of a declarable number, in which case it may be used to make it up. A player holding a bunch is not obliged to declare it; nor, if he holds cards in excess of a bunch, need he state whether or how many extra he holds; but it is not legal to declare a smaller relevant number than actually held. (*Example*: You may declare 'Ten' if you hold ten, eleven, or twelve trumps; but if you hold thirteen, or twelve and the Excuse, you must declare, if anything, 'Thirteen'.) A bunch declared by the soloist will score for him alone if he wins, or by each opponent if he fails. One made by any partner will be credited to each of them if they beat the contract, or to the soloist if he wins.

2. The soloist may declare 'Slam', undertaking to win all eighteen tricks.

☞ The following variants may be encountered but are no longer recognized by the FFT. (a) A partner may declare 'No trumps' if he holds neither any trump nor the Excuse; 'No courts', if he holds no court card; or 'Misère', if he has either of the above but prefers not to say which. This earns him a private and personal bonus at end of play. (b) In some circles, a slam bid overcalls a bid 'against the dog'. (c) Some also recognize a 'Little Slam' bid of seventeen tricks.)

Play The soloist either takes the dog and discards, as detailed above under 'Auction', or moves it to his side of the table if playing 'without', or to the opposite player's side if playing 'against'. Eldest leads to the first trick, and the winner of each trick leads to the next. Subsequent players must follow suit if possible, otherwise must play a trump if possible. In playing any trump – whether to a plain-suit or a trump-suit lead – it is obligatory, if possible, to play a higher trump than any so far played to the trick, even if it is already being won by a partner. The trick is taken by the highest card of the suit led, or by the highest trump if any are played. All tricks won by the partners are kept together in a single pile.

The Excuse Whoever holds the Excuse may play it at any time and in contravention of any rule stated above. If it is led, the suit to be followed is that of the second card played. The Excuse normally loses the trick. If, however, it is led to the last trick, and its holder has won all seventeen previous tricks, then it wins.

If the soloist plays the Excuse, he may, when the trick has been taken, retrieve the Excuse from the won trick, and replace it with any card (preferably worthless) that he has himself already won in a trick. If he has not yet won a trick, he lays the Excuse, face up, in front of him and, upon winning a trick, passes one of its cards to the opposing side. In either case, the Excuse is then incorporated into one of his tricks, and cannot be played again.

If a partner plays the Excuse to a trick, and it is taken by the soloist, he has exactly the same privilege of retrieving it in exchange for a card from a trick won by his own side, and of retaining it for this purpose if his side has yet to win a trick.

Obviously, if the partners (or, improbably, the soloist) win not a single trick, they cannot reclaim the Excuse.

Last trick There is a bonus (see below) for winning the last trick if it contains the lowest trump – No. 1, called *le petit*. This is paid by the soloist to each of the partners if either of them wins it, or by each of them to the soloist if the latter wins it, regardless of who actually played *le petit*.

Score At the end of play, the opponents count the value of all the tricks and counters they have won, including the six dog cards if the soloist played 'against'. Cards are counted in pairs, each pair consisting of two blanks or a blank and a counter. A pair of blanks counts 1 point; a blank and a counter take the value of the counter.

The partners' count is then subtracted from 91 to yield the soloist's count. As stated above, he needs 36, 41, 51 or 56 to win, depending on whether he took three, two, one or no bouts. If he wins, he is paid the appropriate amount by each opponent; if not, he pays it to each of them. If scores are kept in writing, it is necessary to record only the amount as won or lost in the soloist's own score column, since a settlement properly made on the basis of the final scores will come to the same thing as if each deal had been settled in coins or counters when it occurred.

For the main contract, the score won or lost is a basic 25, plus 1 for each point by which the soloist exceeded or fell short of his required count. This total is then doubled in a *garde* contract, quadrupled at 'no dog' (*garde sans*), or sextupled at 'against the dog' (*garde contre*).

Example. The soloist bid *garde* and took two bouts for 52 points, or 11 over the target. He scores (25 + 11) × 2 = 72. With two bouts and 40, he would have been one short, and lost (25 + 1) × 2 = 52 points. With three bouts and 40, he would have been four over, and scored (25 + 4) × 2 = 58 game-points.

The score for a misère (if recognized) is 10, for a bunch of Ten 10, of Thirteen 20, Fifteen 30, and Eighteen 40. This is scored independently of winning or losing the main contract; it is not multiplied according to the bid made; and it goes to the soloist if he declared it, or to each opponent if one of them did.

The score for *petit* (the lowest trump in the last trick) is 10. This is scored independently of the main contract and goes to the soloist or to each opponent as described in the appropriate paragraph. Some make it a fixed score; others multiply it by two, four or eight, according to the contract.

The score for a declared slam may be set at 500 for a little slam and 750 for a grand, and is won or lost as a fixed amount.

Notes on play The first two players should bid cautiously, especially the second as he hasn't even the advantage of the lead. The third and fourth may be bolder if the first two pass. The average number of trumps dealt is about five; no bid should be undertaken with fewer. Few players now bid *petit*: if you can fulfil a basic contract you might as well bid garde for the higher score. A bid 'without' would be undertaken with the hand on the left, and a bid 'against' with that on the right (X = Excuse):

```
†21 17 16 14 12 11 5 4 X    †21 19 18 16 14 10 9 8 I X
♠ K C J T 4 2               ♠ Q 2
♣ J 3                       ♣ K 6
♥ 7                         ♥ K Q 3
♦ none                      ♦ K
```

The interest of the play rests as much on the outcome of *petit*, the lowest trump, as on the main contract, since it both counts as a bout and carries weight in the last trick. If you hold it, decide from the outset whether or not to save it for the last trick. As soloist, try to ensure its safety by leading trumps whenever possible so as to draw them all and leave the lowest safe.

French Tarot for three

The same, but with these variations. Deal twenty-four cards to each player in batches of four, and six to the dog. The lowest declarable bunch is Thirteen (score 10), the highest Twenty-one (score 40). A little slam is 22 or 23 tricks. If an odd card remains after counting in pairs, ignore it.

▌Tapp Tarock   3 players, 54 cards (Austrian tarocks)

Tapp, or Tappen, makes a good introduction to the general principles of Tarot play as it developed in central Europe, and can lead to more advanced 54-card, French-suited games such as Point Tarock and Königsrufen. The following is based on Babsch, *Original Tarock* (Vienna, 1975), but details vary from place to place. The French origin of Austro-German Tarock games is revealed in their terminology. *Sküs* comes from *excuse*; *Mond*, though meaning moon, is a corruption of *monde* ('world'); *pagat*, the smallest trump, is related to *bagatelle*; and *trull* is a corruption of *tous les trois*.

Cards The Austrian Tarock pack contains 22 trumps ('tarocks') and 32 plain cards.

- The highest tarock, called Sküs, depicts a Fool or Joker
- The second highest, called Mond, is numbered XXI
- Others follow in descending order: XX, XIX, XVIII . . .
- The lowest, called Pagat, is numbered I.

Sküs, Mond and Pagat form a trio called the trull. In plain suits, cards rank downwards as follows:

In ♠ and ♣   King Queen Cavalier Jack T 9 8 7

In ♥ and ♦   King Queen Cavalier Jack A 2 3 4

Deal Whoever cuts the highest card deals first (trumps beat plain suits). The deal and turn to play then pass regularly to the right. Deal a talon of six cards face down to the table in threes, the second batch lying crosswise atop the first, then sixteen cards to each player in eights. Anyone dealt no tarocks at all may call for a new deal.

Object There is an auction to decide who plays alone against the other two. The soloist's primary aim is to win cards totalling at least 36 of the 70 points available. For this purpose, cards won in tricks count as follows:

Sküs, Mond, Pagat	5 each
King	5 each
Queen	4 each
Cavalier	3 each
Jack	2 each
All others	1 each

This gives a theoretical total of 106. However, won cards are counted in threes, and each batch of three counts 2 less than its face value. As there are 18 batches (54 ÷ 3), the final total is 70 (106 − 36). Thus the target of 36 points represents just one point more than half the total.

☞ Make a mental note if you hold two or three cards of the trull, or all four Kings, as these earn a bonus at end of play.

Types of bid There are basically only two bids: Exchange and Solo.

- In an exchange game, the soloist turns up the six cards of the talon, adds either the top three or the bottom three to his hand, and discards three cards face down in their place. These three discards will count for him at end of play as if he had won them in tricks, while the other three, which are turned face down again, will similarly count for the opponents.

- In a Solo, he leaves the six cards of the talon unturned, and all six will count for the opponents at end of play as if they had won them in tricks.

Bidding procedure Although there are only two basic bids, 'Exchange' can be bid at three different levels, namely Dreier ('threes') for a score of 3, Unterer ('lowers') for 4, and Oberer ('uppers') for 5 points. (These terms originally denoted which of the two batches of three cards, lower or upper, the Soloist had to take. Nowadays the choice is free.)

Each in turn, starting with eldest, may pass or bid. A player who has once passed may not come in again. So long as no one has yet bid Solo, the procedure is as follows.

The first bid (if not Solo) must be Dreier. This can be overcalled only by Unterer (or Solo), and Unterer only by Oberer (or Solo). However, if a player who comes earlier in the bidding order has made a bid and been overcalled, and has not yet passed, he may raise his bid to that of the previous player by saying 'Hold', thereby exerting positional priority.

Anyone may bid Solo in their proper turn, and this normally ends the auction, as it cannot be overcalled. (Theoretically, an earlier player can 'hold' the solo bid of a later one; but it is most unlikely that two players would hold cards strong enough to contest it.)

Announcements Unless the highest bidder is playing Solo, he now turns up the six cards of the talon, takes either the top three or the bottom three, and makes three discards face down in their place. These may not include a King, or a card of the trull. They may include other tarocks only if he has no other legal discard(s), and in this case he must show his opponents which tarocks he has discarded. Before a card is led, any of the following announcements may be made:

- The soloist may announce 'Pagat', thereby undertaking to win the last trick with the lowest trump (I). If he is forced to play it to an earlier trick, he loses this bid. He may not play it earlier voluntarily, if he can legally avoid it, even though he may wish to do so in order to save his basic contract.
- The soloist may announce 'Valat', thereby undertaking to win every trick. (Very rare!)
- Either opponent may announce 'double the game', 'double the Pagat', 'double the Valat' (as the case may be), if he believes the soloist will

not fulfil his contract or achieve whatever feat he announced. In return, the soloist may announce 'redouble' to anything that was doubled. These announcements respectively double and quadruple whatever scoring feature the soloist wins or loses.

Play Eldest leads to the first trick, and the winner of each trick leads to the next. Players must follow suit if possible, otherwise must play a tarock if possible, otherwise may play any card. The trick is taken by the highest card of the suit led, or by the highest tarock if any are played, and the winner of each trick leads to the next. Tricks need not be separated, and all cards won by the two partners are thrown face down to a single pile.

Score Each side counts the card-points it has won as described above. If the soloist has reached his 36-point target he scores the appropriate game value, or is paid it by each opponent. If not, each opponent scores the appropriate game value or receives it from the soloist. The basic game values are: Threes = 3, Lowers = 4, Uppers = 5, Solo = 8. These amounts are doubled or quadrupled if the game was respectively doubled or redoubled.

If the soloist wins every trick, he scores the above amount fourfold, or eightfold if he previously announced 'Valat'. But if he announced Valat and failed to win every trick, he loses the above amount eightfold, regardless of how many card-points he took. This amount is doubled or quadrupled if the announcement was respectively doubled or redoubled.

If the soloist wins the last trick with Pagat, he scores 4 points, or 8 in a solo bid. Conversely, if he leads Pagat to the last trick and loses it – or, having announced it, plays it to any earlier trick – he is deemed to have been attempting to make the bonus, and the appropriate 4 points (8 in a solo) are scored by each opponent. These amounts are doubled, won or lost, if he previously announced his intention of winning the last trick with Pagat, and further doubled or quadrupled if the announcement was respectively doubled or redoubled. Note that the score for Pagat obtains independently of the main contract: it is possible for the soloist to score for game and the partners for Pagat, or vice versa.

Finally, any player whose original hand contained one of the following features may now claim and score for it:

All three cards of the trull:	3 points
Any two cards of the trull:	1 point
All four Kings:	3 points

(In some circles, these scores are doubled in a solo game.) Play continues for any agreed number of deals, which should be a multiple of three.

Variants Many variations of procedure and scoring will be encountered. Some permit additional redoubles, and some credit any player with a score of (say) 2 points for capturing trump XXI with the Sküs. Of greatest interest is that whereby the holder of Pagat may bid to win the last trick with it even though he is not the soloist. In this case:

1. The soloist may double the announcement, and its maker or his partner may redouble.
2. The Pagat announcer may not play it to any earlier trick if he can legally avoid doing so.
3. If the Pagat holder plays it to the last trick and loses it to an opponent – or, having announced it, plays it to any earlier trick – he is deemed to have been trying to win the last trick with it, and the other side scores the appropriate bonus. (Four points, doubled in a solo, doubled if announced, and doubled or redoubled as the case may be.)
4. Prior agreement must be made as to what happens if, in the above case, one of the partners plays Pagat to the last trick, and the other partner wins it. Strictly, the Pagat-player has lost it, and the soloist scores; but it may be agreed to call it a stand-off, and leave the bonus unearned.

Notes on play The game is often won on tarocks, plain cards being used to plump the value of tricks rather than intentionally to win them. In assessing a hand for the bid, think first of the possible split of the tarocks and then of the seven 5-point cards (Kings and trull). The most even split is about seven tarocks in each hand and one in each half of the talon. A minimum bid of threes therefore requires at least eight tarocks, including several high ones and at least one card of the trull, but this can be reduced if you have four Kings. Higher bids require correspondingly higher strength. A very short side suit is a possible strength factor, as one aim of taking the talon is to create a void. Solo should not be bid with fewer than three of the 5-point cards, eleven good tarocks, and at least one void suit or a singleton King.

In play, the soloist normally leads tarocks first in order to draw two for one from the partners, while the partners lead long plain suits to force out the soloist's tarocks. A key point occurs when one of them is out of tarocks and can throw high counters to his partner's tricks. As in any three-hander, it is always desirable to keep the soloist in the middle, i.e. playing second to the trick.

Winning the last trick with the Pagat should not be attempted without at least ten tarocks in hand, and they of above-average strength. In attacking this feat, aim to get rid of all plain-suit cards before the last trick, as a diminished hand consisting entirely of tarocks is then bound to capture the Pagat.

▌ **Paskievics** (Hungarian Tarokk)   4 (or 5) players, 42 cards

An important part of the apparatus of this game is the mayor's hat – one version is a felt hat with feathers and other decorations, but anything ridiculous looking will do . . . The player who is unfortunate (or careless) enough to lose the XXI is called the mayor (*polgármester*), and is obliged as a penalty to wear the hat until someone else suffers the same misfortune.

Macfadyen, Healey, McLeod: *Paskievics* www.pagat.com (1996)

The classical Tarot game of the former Austro-Hungarian Empire first appeared around 1870. Its name commemorates Ivan Fyodorovich Paskevich, the prince of Warsaw whose Russian troops put down the Hungarian revolution and war of independence in 1848–9. It is played with a 54-card pack but stripped down to the 42 quoted below. These cards, sometimes unusually large (up to 127 × 74 mm), are widely available in eastern Europe: I bought mine in Sibiu, Romania. Paskievics is distinguished by a bidding system designed to convey a considerable amount of advance information about the lie of cards, thus rendering it a game of extreme skill. The following is condensed from the Pagat website, with revisions by Gyula Zsigri.

Terminology *Skíz* is from French *excuse*, *tulétroá* from *tous les trois*, *pagát* is related to *bagatelle* in the sense of something trifling.

Preliminaries Four players are active, but five often play, with each in turn acting as a non-playing dealer. All play on their own account in the long run, but the declarer in each deal may call for the aid of a temporary ally, who will share in the profits or losses for that deal. Play rotates anti-clockwise, so eldest is the player at dealer's right. Settlements are usually made in hard score (coins or counters), but may be kept in writing.

Special equipment Besides cards and counters, a silly hat is essential (see above).

Cards The 42-card pack consists of 22 tarokks (trumps) and 20 French-suited plain cards. Tarokks rank downwards as follows:

- Skíz: a figure resembling a jester. It is unnumbered, but equivalent to XXII. Then:
- XXI, XX, XIX, XVIII, XVII, XVI, XV, XIV, XIII, XII, XI, X, IX, VIII, VII, VI, V, IV, III, II, I (Pagát).

The two highest tarokks and the lowest one – Skíz, XXI, Pagát – are 'honours'. In plain suits, cards rank:

In black (♠ ♣)	King, Queen, Knight, Jack, Ten (low)
In red (♥ ♦)	King, Queen, Knight, Jack, Ace (low)

Cards count as follows when taken in tricks:

Honours	5 each= 15 in all
Kings	5 each= 20
Queens	4 each= 16
Knights	3 each= 12
Jacks	2 each= 8
all others	1 each= 23 (Aces, Tens, and 19 tarokks)

Object Of the 94-point total, the soloist's aim is to take in tricks cards amounting to more than half (i.e. at least 48), either alone or with a partner.

Deal After a cut from the left, deal the first six cards face down as a talon, followed by nine to each player in batches of five then four. If five play, the talon is placed in front of the dealer; if four, to his right.

Bidding Before bidding, you need to know that the eventual declarer will call for a partner by naming a particular card. Whoever holds that card will become his partner, but may not reveal himself except by playing the called card in the normal course of events (though it may become apparent from the bidding). Furthermore, the declarer may elect to play alone against the other three by naming a card that he holds himself, in which case the fact that he is his own partner will become apparent only when he plays the called card in the normal course of events.

The bids, and their basic scores, from lowest to highest are:

Three	1 point
Two	2 points
One	3 points
Solo	4 points

A bid indicates how many cards the prospective declarer will draw from the talon with a view to improving his hand. Solo is equivalent to drawing none, and playing with the hand as dealt.

Each in turn, starting with eldest, may pass or bid, and having passed may not come in again. No one may bid unless he holds at least one honour. Each bid must be higher than the last, except that an elder player (one who comes earlier in the bidding sequence) may 'hold' (take over) the previous bid if it was made by younger. A bid once held may not be held again.

Should all four pass at once (a rare occurrence), the deal is annulled and the same dealer deals again. This automatically doubles all scores made in the next round of deals – four if four play, five if five. If another pass-out occurs, so does the doubling, making it possible for some successive deals to be quadrupled, octupled, and so on. In some schools, however, a deal following any number of pass-outs is merely doubled.

If the first three pass, the fourth may bid the minimum Three though holding no honour in his hand. But if he then finds none in the talon either, the hand is annulled and he pays the others 1 chip each.

If one of the first three players bids Three and the others all pass, that bidder may raise his contract to any higher level. Otherwise jump-bids are allowed only in accordance with a code of cue bids called 'invitations'.

Example of bidding: A 'Three', B 'Two', C 'Pass', D 'One', A 'Hold', B 'Pass', (C is out), D 'Solo', A 'Hold'. The declarer is A, as there is nothing higher than a solo, and a held bid cannot be held again (nor, in any case, can anyone 'hold' a bid by A, who is in prime position).

Invitations (cue bids) An invitation indicates that you wish someone else to become the declarer and pick you as their partner by calling a card that you hold. You may make it only if you hold two particular cards, namely:

(a) Skíz or XX (or both; and many players allow cue bids with the Pagát provided that you subsequently announce Pagát ultimó); and

(b) a particular card which you invite the player with another honour to call should they become the declarer. This must be one of the following:

- Tarokk XIX. This you indicate by jump-bidding to one level higher than necessary. For example, as first to speak you would bid Two instead of Three; or, following a bid of Three, you would bid One instead of Two. You then hope that another player with an honour (preferably higher, but it could be Pagát) will bid higher still (or at least hold your bid), take the contract, and call your card. None of which, however, is he obliged to do, so you may well find yourself left in the declaring position.

The bidding sequence A 'Three', B 'Two', A 'One' also signals the XIX, because A could have held B's 'Two'.

- Tarokk XVIII. As above, but bid two levels higher than necessary (if possible).

In either case, a player who bids higher is deemed to accept the invitation, and, if he becomes declarer, is obliged to call the card he was invited to. If two players each hold one honour, they may both accept the invitation, and must fight it out between them.

> ☛ You are allowed to make either of these jump-bids without holding the card it relates to, provided that it is obvious that no invitation was intended because no one could legally accept it. For example, if the first three pass, the fourth may bid anything, since those who passed are prohibited from bidding again. Or again, if the bidding goes A 'Three', B 'Two', C 'Pass', D 'One', A 'Solo', then A can't have been inviting to the XIX by bidding Solo instead of Hold, as no one is in a position to hold his solo bid.

- Tarokk XX. Holding this card and a high honour, you can invite it only in the following circumstances. Being the first to make a bid (as eldest, or following nothing but passes), you bid Three. Of the other players, two pass, and the other, regardless of position, bids Two. If you then pass, the player who bid Two is deemed to have accepted your invitation and must then enlist your aid by calling the XX. But you are not obliged to pass and thereby put him in this position. For one thing, you may also hold XIX, and invite it to be called by jumping to a bid of One. For another, you might have bid Three without intending the XX to be called – or even without actually holding it – in which case you must cancel the apparent invitation by 'holding' the bid of Two.

> ☛ Unlike XIX or XVIII, you cannot cue bid the XX with the Pagát.

Drawing and discarding Declarer draws from the top of the talon as many cards as he bid (if any), adds them to his hand, and discards the same number face down. Each other player in turn from his right draws from the rest of the talon either the top two cards, so long as this will leave at least one for the last player to draw, otherwise one card. If five play, these cards are not drawn by the players themselves but dealt to them by the dealer.

No one may discard any five-point card (an honour or a King), and some schools also prohibit the discard of trump XX.

Declarer places his discards, if any, face down (but tarokks up) on his left. Any card-points they contain will count to him at end of play as if he had won them in tricks. The other three place theirs, face down, on dealer's right. Any card-points they contain – even those of declarer's partner, if any – will count to the opposing side as if they had won them in tricks.

Annulling the hand A player holding an officially recognized 'bad hand' after the draw may (but need not) show it and call for a new deal, provided that no announcements have yet been made. The following holdings justify an annulment:

- all four Kings (because they can't be discarded and are likely to be trumped);
- no tarokks; or XXI or Pagát alone; or XXI and Pagát but no others.

The cards are then gathered, shuffled and cut, and redealt by the same dealer. This automatically doubles all scores made in the next round of deals, exactly as if all four had passed (see above).

Calling a card Declarer now names a card whose holder is to become his partner. If he accepted an invitation, he is obliged to call the invited card. If not, he is obliged to call tarokk XX unless any of the following applies:

1. He holds the XX himself. In this case he may either call it and play alone, or else secure a partner by calling the highest tarokk below XX that he does not hold himself.

2. Anyone other than the declarer discarded a tarokk. In this case, he may call any tarokk not in his own hand, other than an honour. This makes the holder of that card his partner, who must not reveal himself except by the play. If, however, the called tarokk was discarded, the player who discarded it must double the game by saying

Kontra (as described below). This does not necessarily prove that the declarer has no partner, as the discarder might have doubled the game anyway.

Announcements After calling a card, the declarer may make one or more of the following announcements. There are three types of announcement: tarokks, feats, and doubles. He finishes by saying 'Pass', whereupon each subsequent player in turn from his right may also make any valid announcements before saying 'Pass'. Play does not begin until three players in succession have said nothing but 'Pass'. The possible announcements are:

1. Eight or nine Tarokks. This is an individual (non-partnership) declaration. If you hold eight or nine tarokks, you may immediately claim payment of (respectively) 1 or 2 units from each opponent, and from your partner if any. If you hold nine, you may not declare only eight. But, whether you hold eight or nine, you are not obliged to declare them, unless you are also bidding Pagát ultimó – or saying *kontra* to somebody else's bid thereof – in which case the declaration is compulsory.

2. Feats. These are feats that you commit your partnership to performing. Each of them earns a fixed payment even if achieved unannounced, but, if announced, it scores double if successful, or incurs a loss if not. They are:

announcement	meaning	score
double game	take at least 71 card-points	×2, or ×4 if announced
volát	win all nine tricks	×3, or ×6 if announced
tulétroá (or trull)	win all three honours in tricks	1, or 2 if announced
four Kings	win all four kings in tricks	1, or 2 if announced
Pagát ultimó	win the last trick with Pagát	5, or 10 if announced
catch XXI	capture tarokk XXI with Skíz	21, or 42 if announced

☞ The scores for double game and volát *multiply* the basic game score. For example, a successful bid of One is worth a basic 3, and so pays 18 if made with an announced volát. The others are flat bonuses.

3. Kontra. Any feat announcement may be *kontra'd* (doubled) by an opponent if he thinks his side will beat it. This is done by saying 'Kontra' to the particular announcement – for example, 'Kontra all four', 'Kontra

the double game', and so on. It is also possible to 'Kontra the game', whether or not any announcements have been made: it means that you are not the declarer's partner and that you think declarer's side will fail to take the requisite 48 card-points in tricks. Note, in this connection, that if you have discarded the called card into the talon, you must announce 'Kontra' at your first turn to speak in the round of announcements. An announcement that has been kontra'd can subsequently be re-kontra'd by the player who made it, and the doubling process can go up to five levels. The full range of terms is *kontra* (2), *rekontra* (4), *szubkontra* (8), *hirskontra* (16), *mordkontra* (32).

All bonuses and announcements are scored independently of each other and of the game; you can win some and lose others. Although most announcements will be made by declarer's side, it is possible for the opponents to make them too. However, if you want to announce a bonus against the declarer, you must make it clear which side you are on, for example by saying kontra to the game. (This restriction does not apply to declaring eight or nine tarokks, as it is done on a purely individual basis.)

> Example of call and announcements: A (declarer): 'Call XX, pass.' B: 'Trull, four Kings, pass.' C: 'Pass.' D: 'Kontra the trull, pass.' A: 'Pagát ulti, pass.' B: 'Pass.' C: 'Pass.' D: 'Pass.' B's announcement of trull and Kings signals the XX and identifies him as A's partner, and encourages A to bid the Pagát.

Play Eldest leads to the first trick. Players must follow suit if possible, must play a tarokk if unable to follow a plain-suit lead, and may renounce only if unable to do either. The trick is taken by the highest card of the suit led, or by the highest tarokk if any are played, and the winner of each trick leads to the next.

Settlement If two played against two, each member of the losing team pays one of the members of the winning team the net score for the game and any bonuses that may have been earned in the play. If you played alone against three, you receive the net score from each of them, or pay it to each of them if you lose, making the value of such contracts three times as much. When five play, anyone who received an honour from the talon is supposed to pay the dealer for it at the end of the hand: 3 points for the Skíz, 2 for the XXI, and 1 for Pagát.

In calculating the settlement, note the following.

1. If neither double game nor volát was announced, and the game

was not kontra'd, then only the highest of game, double game and volát is scored.

2. If a side wins the volát (every trick), they cannot score for thereby winning the trull or four Kings unless they previously announced their intention of doing so. (Consequently: when the bid is three, and nothing has been announced, and you have already won all the honours and kings, it is better to lose one trick and make double game, trull and four kings for 4 points (2+1+1), than to win every trick and make the volát, which counts only 3!)

3. If a team announces double game, they cannot score for the basic game, but can score additionally for volát if they win every trick. If they lose not only the announcement but the game as well, the opponents will score for the ordinary game as well as the failed announced double game (5 times the game in total). If the opponents managed to make their own double game or even volát, they would score that instead of the ordinary game, in addition to the failed announced double game.

4. If a team announces both double game and volát, each of these bonuses is scored separately, and it is possible to win the double game but lose the volát. The basic game is not scored unless the announcing team loses it, in which case the opponents score for it. (They could even, albeit improbably, make and score a double game or volát in place of the basic game.)

5. If a side announces volát but not double game, only the volát is scored (won or lost). The announcing side cannot score for game or double game, but if the opponents beat it they can score for game, double game, or volát, whichever they make.

6. If the game is kontra'd it is always scored. If either side makes an unannounced double game or volát, that is scored in addition to the kontra'd game (but not both the double game and the volát).

7. If the game is kontra'd (or re-kontra'd), and either side announces double game or volát (or both), the basic game is scored as well as the announcements. An unannounced volát can be scored in addition to a kontra'd game and an announced double game.

Pagát ultimó (announced) If you announced Pagát ultimó then you must try to win the last trick with it, and must hold it back for as long as possible, even if it becomes clear that you can't win the last trick. If you fail – whether by losing it to the opponents or to your partner in the last trick, or by being forced to play it prematurely – you and your partner each pay 10 points.

Pagát ultimó (not announced) If Pagát is played to the last trick, and takes it, not having been announced, the winners of that trick earn 5 points. If it is played to last trick and is captured by a trump, then the opponents of the Pagát-player earn 5 points. (Playing Pagát to the last trick and having it taken by your partner is like scoring an own goal.)

Catching the XXI This bonus can be won only if the Skíz and the XXI were dealt to opposite sides, and you succeed in capturing the XXI with the Skíz (the only card that outranks it). There is no bonus or penalty if you and your partner play the Skíz and the XXI to the same trick. If you lose the XXI to the Skíz played by an opponent, both you and your partner must pay for it, but you are the one who must don the silly hat.

Eight or nine tarokks A player who held originally eight or nine tarokks, but did not announce them, may nevertheless claim the appropriate payment from his partner (not the opponents) at end of play.

Comments The following notes are based on those of Matthew Macfadyen.

At any stage during the play of a hand there will normally be one objective much more important than the others. The normal order of priorities is:

> Capture the XXI
> Make Pagát ultimó
> Make the game
> Capture the Pagát so as to make trull
> Capture four Kings.

The fact that one may bid only when holding an honour means that there is often a lot of information about who holds the honours before any cards have been played. By the time the argument about the XXI has been resolved it should be clear what might happen with the Pagát – either someone is keeping it for the end or it has already been played.

The ideal hand for catching the XXI is the Skíz and a lot of small trumps. The attempt depends mostly on the player with the Skíz playing after the player with the XXI on every trick. This works best if the Skíz holder is on the victim's right. The Skíz holder will try not to take a trick before the XXI appears, so as not to have to lead. The player with the XXI will probably try leading side suits in order to get the player with the Skíz to trump them. A conspicuous sign of a player trying to catch the XXI is that they play high trumps without heading the trick – for example, the XVIII when XIX is led. This should be taken as a signal to partner to abandon all other objectives in pursuit of the XXI. If you are partnering someone who is apparently after the enemy XXI, and you actually hold it yourself, play it as soon as possible, so as to allow normal play to resume.

Don't bid double game in a solo unless you are almost strong enough to announce volát. Even in a three bid the talon may contribute 12 points, so a trick with King, Queen of a suit and two small cards would be enough. Normally if the contract is three or two you can afford to lose one trick and still make double.

As it is extremely difficult to predict making four Kings, you may make that announcement more as a general encouragement to your partner to continue making more realistic announcements, and you can kontra such an announcement fairly freely.

Cego

3–4 players, 54 Cego cards

Cego has been the national card game of Baden and Hohenzollern since the early nineteenth century, and remains extremely popular in these south-western regions of Germany. It uses a distinctive 54-card pack produced in two main designs, with animals depicted on the trumps of one, and domestic scenes on those of the other. (But you can, if necessary, substitute a standard Austrian 54-card Tarock pack, or French Tarots stripped of numerals 1–6 in black and 5–10 in red suits.) Besides the special pack, it differs from most Tarot games in having an extra hand dealt to the centre of the table, variously known as the Cego, the Tapp, or the Blind (*Blinde*). Many bids involve playing with this extra hand, retaining only one or two of one's original cards and discarding the rest. This feature originated in a version of Hombre, and survives in a few other games, such as Vira. Cego is played with many local variations.

The following description is based on John McLeod's website account of games played in Bräunlingen in April 1997, at the Gasthaus zum Löwen, and also with young members of the Bräunlingen Ministranten (the local church).

Players This version is for four, each playing alone. If five play, each in turn deals and sits that deal out. A version for three is appended. Play rotates to the right. The player at dealer's right (eldest) is called Forehand (*Vorhand*), as in all German games.

Cards There are 54 cards: twenty-two trumps called Trocke, and eight cards in each of the four suits clubs (*kreuz*), spades (*schippen, schip*), hearts (*herz*), diamonds (*karo, eckstein, eck*).

The highest Trock is called *der Gstieß* (or *Geiger*). It depicts a musician and is unnumbered, though in effect it is No. 22. The others rank downwards from 21 to 1, and are readily identifiable by large Arabic numbers in the top centre. No. 1, the lowest, is called the Littl'un (*der kleine Mann*).

Plain-suit cards rank downwards as follows:

in black suits ♠, ♣	King, Queen, Rider, Jack, 10, 9, 8, 7
in red suits ♥, ♦	King, Queen, Rider, Jack, 1, 2, 3, 4

Object To win counters in tricks, namely

Gstieß, Trock 21, Trock 1	5 each
Kings	5 each
Queens	4 each
Riders	3 each
Jacks	2 each
all other cards	1 each

These total 80, but the scoring system reduces this to 70, as explained later.

Deal Highest cut deals first. The dealer shuffles and the player at his left cuts. Deal the top ten cards face down to the middle to form the cego, then a single batch of eleven cards to each player.

The contracts An auction establishes who the soloist is in what kind of contract. Whoever bids highest plays alone against the other three players in partnership (the defenders), except only in the game called Räuber (robbers), where all play for themselves.

There are two types of contract: counter games and special games.

- In counter games, the soloist aims to win at least 36 card-points for counters won in tricks and contained in the cego. The various counter games are:

1. Solo. Everyone plays with the cards as dealt. No one may look at the cego till after the play.

2. Cego. The soloist keeps two cards (usually high Trocke), discards the other nine, picks up the ten cego cards, and finally makes one discard to restore his hand to eleven. None of these cards are exposed to the defenders.

3. One Card (Eine). The soloist keeps one card (usually a high Trock), discards the other ten, and replaces them with the cego to restore his hand to eleven.

4. One Blank (Eine Leere). The soloist keeps one card, which must be a plain-suit numeral. He places it face up on the table, discards the other ten, and takes up the cego cards as his new hand, without showing them. He must then lead to the first trick either the exposed 'blank' card, or another card of the same suit.

☞ A soloist holding no blank card may nevertheless play One Blank. In this case he may keep a court card instead, and nominate it as blank. It thereby counts as the lowest in its suit, and cannot win a trick in any circumstance.

5. Two blanks (Zwei Leere). The soloist places two numerals of the same plain suit face up on the table, and discards the other nine, face down. He then takes the cego, and from it must discard the lowest Trock, showing it to his opponents before adding it to the other discards. He must then either lead the two exposed cards to the first two tricks, or replace one or both of them by cards of the same suit from hand and lead those. As in One Blank, neither of the exposed 'empty cards' can ever win a trick. A player who hasn't got two numeral cards of the same suit may designate any two cards of the same suit as 'empty' and expose them. As in One Blank, these become low cards and can never win tricks.

6. Two different (Zwei Verschiedene). The soloist places two numeral cards of different suits face up on the table, discards the other nine face down, picks up the cego, and from it must discard the highest Trock, showing it to the defenders before adding it to his discards. He must then lead the two exposed cards to the first two tricks (not other cards of the same suits). A player who hasn't got two numeral cards of different

suits may substitute a court card for either, or both if necessary. As before, these then become the lowest cards of their suits.

7. The Littl'un (Der kleine Mann). This can be bid only by a player who holds the Littl'un (Trock 1). He places it face up on the table, discards the other ten, replaces them with the cego, and must lead the exposed card to the first trick, which (of course) it will lose.

- The special games have different objectives from that of counter games, and from each other. In all four, the cego is set aside and everyone plays with the hand they were dealt. They are:

1. Ulti. The soloist's only object is to win the last trick with Trock 1 (the Littl'un). He will lose if forced to play it before the last trick, or if it fails to win the last trick.

2. Piccolo. The soloist's object is to win exactly one trick, neither more nor fewer.

3. Bettel. The soloist's object is to lose every single trick.

4. Räuber. There is no soloist. Whoever captures the highest number of card-points loses.

Bidding procedure There are two phases of bidding. The first is to see if anyone wants to play Solo or Ulti. If not, there is a second phase in which anything else may be bid.

Each in turn, starting with Forehand, may pass or bid Solo or Ulti. If someone bids Ulti, the auction ends, as it cannot be overcalled. If there was a bid of Solo but not Ulti, skip down to (b) below.

(a) If everyone passed, Forehand must start phase two by bidding either Cego or Piccolo or Bettel. He may not pass. If he bids Cego, anyone else wishing to play Piccolo or Bettel can say so now, or at any time up to and including their normal turn to bid. A bid of Piccolo or Bettel ends the auction and establishes the contract. In the unlikely event that two wish to play Piccolo or Bettel, priority goes to the elder of them (the earlier in turn to bid).

If no one interrupts with Piccolo or Bettel when Forehand bids Cego, players may now bid any of the normal counter games. In ascending order, these rank: One Card, One Blank, Two Blanks, Two Different, the Littl'un. If two players wish to play the same game, the younger of them has priority, which he asserts by saying 'Hold' (actually *Selbst*, meaning 'Myself'). Jump bids are not allowed, and each player enters the bidding only after the bidding between the previous players has been resolved.

If Forehand bids Cego and everyone else passes, Forehand can choose whether to play Cego or Räuber. This is the only way Räuber gets to be played. (Its purpose is to punish a player who failed to bid Solo despite having a good hand, which will probably lose the Räuber.)

Examples A is Forehand, D is dealer:

A	B	C	D	*Outcome*
Pass	Pass	Pass	Pass	
Cego	Pass	One Card	-	
Hold	-	One Blank	-	
Pass	-	-	Two Blanks	
-	-	Hold	Pass	C plays Two Blanks
Pass	Pass	Pass	Pass	
Cego	One Card	-	-	
Pass	-	Pass	Pass	B plays One Card
Pass	Pass	Pass	Pass	
Cego	One Card	-	Piccolo	D plays Piccolo
Pass	Pass	Pass	Pass	
Cego	Pass	Pass	Pass	A plays Cego or Räuber

(b) If there was a Solo bid in phase one, phase two proceeds more or less as described in section (a), above, but with these differences:
• The Solo bidder has highest priority, then Forehand, and then the other players in anticlockwise rotation.
• The next bid above Solo is Gegensolo (identical with Cego), then One Card, One Blank, etc., as usual.
• No special games (Piccolo, Bettel) can be bid over a Solo.

Examples (A is Forehand; B, C and D are the other players in anticlockwise order; D is dealer.)

A	B	C	D	*Result*
Pass	Pass	Solo	-	
Pass	Pass	-	Pass	C plays Solo
Pass	Solo	-	-	

Pass	-	Gegensolo	-	
-	Pass	-	Pass	C plays Gegensolo (Cego)
Pass	Pass	Solo	-	
Gegensolo	-	Selbst	-	
Pass	Pass	-	One Card	(A rather unlikely sequence)
-	-	Selbst	Pass	C plays One Card

Play The soloist leads to the first trick. Players must follow suit if possible; must play a Trock if unable to follow a plain-suit lead; and may renounce only if unable to do either. The trick is taken by the highest card of the suit led, or by the highest Trock if any are played, and the winner of each trick leads to the next.

If the soloist played a discard game, he may refer to his discards (the *Legage*) up to the completion of the first trick, but not thereafter. In Solo, Ulti, Piccolo, Bettel and Räuber, no one may look at the cards of the cego before play ends.

In Two Blanks and Two Different, the soloist leads to the first two tricks. The two cards kept from the soloist's original hand (which in the case of Two Blanks may be replaced by other cards of the same suit found in the cego) are placed face up on the table to begin the tricks, and each opponent in turn plays to both tricks. If the first two tricks are won by different players, whichever of them won with the higher card leads to the third trick. In Two Different, they could conceivably have won with equally high cards. If so, the leader is the one who played the higher suit, counting clubs highest, then spades, hearts, and diamonds (lowest).

In One or Two Blanks, the exposed blank(s) can never win a trick. If the soloist chooses to lead a different card of the same suit, the originally exposed card automatically loses any trick to which it is played later.

> Example: The soloist keeps ♣8, but, finding ♣K in the cego, prefers to lead the King, which wins. He subsequently manages to draw all the opponents' trumps and clubs. If he now leads ♣8, it is not allowed to win. Instead, the second player may play any card, and this determines the suit to be followed for the rest of the trick.

Score The cards are counted in groups of three, each group scoring 2 less than its total face value. If one or two odd cards remain, they score

1 less than their combined face value. The total is always 70, regardless of how they are grouped.

In a counter game, the soloist counts the card-points he won in tricks plus those contained in the cego (provided that he won at least one trick), and wins if he makes at least 36 of the 70 available. If he loses every trick, the cego counts for the opponents, so they win by 70 to 0 points.

The amount the soloist wins or loses is the difference between 35 and the number of card-points taken, multiplied by a factor which depends on the game which was played. The result is rounded up to the next multiple of 5, and this is the amount (in Pfennig) which the soloist receives from or pays to each opponent.

The factor for a Solo is 2 if the soloist wins, but 1 if he loses. The factors for the other counter games are as follows:

Cego	1	or 2 if played as a Gegensolo
One Card	2	. . . 3 if bid against a solo
One Blank	3	. . . 4 . . .
Two Blanks	4	. . . 5 . . .
Two Different	5	. . . 6 . . .
The Littl'un	6	. . . 7 . . .

A 35-point tie is called Bürgermeister, and the soloist pays 5 Pfennig to each opponent.

Examples: (1) The soloist wins a Solo by 41–29. The difference from 35 is 6; multiplying by 2 (the factor for a won Solo) gives 12; this is rounded up to 15, and the soloist wins 15 Pfennig from each defender.

(2) The soloist loses a Solo by 29–41. The difference is 6 and the multiplication factor is 1 (for a lost Solo); 6 is rounded up to 10, and the soloist pays 10 Pfennig to each opponent.

(3) The soloist wins Two Blanks by 39–31. The difference is 4 and the multiplying factor is 4; the product 16 is rounded up to 20 and the soloist wins 20 Pfennig from each opponent.

The special games have fixed scores as follows:

Ulti	80
Piccolo	30
Bettel	30
Räuber	30

In Ulti, Piccolo or Bettel, each opponent pays the appropriate amount to the soloist if the soloist wins; otherwise the soloist pays each defender.

Hungarian Tarokks. Paper wrapper from pack bought in Romania.

In Räuber, all players count the points in their own tricks. The cego is not counted. The player who has most points loses. If Forehand loses, the payment to the other players is doubled (60 instead of 30). If there is a tie for most, and Forehand is involved in the tie, he loses; otherwise, all the tied players pay 30 to each other player.

Game A player who wishes to end the session says '*Der Gstieß gibt ab*' ('The Gstieß winds it up'). On the following deal players note who holds the Gstieß. Play continues until that player's following turn to deal, which is the last of the session.

Cego for three

Strip the pack to 51 cards by removing the two black Sevens and ♦4. Deal twelve cards to the cego and thirteen to each player. Play as above, but omit bids of Piccolo, Bettel and Räuber.

Räuber is replaced by a different way of penalizing a player who fails to bid Solo with a strong hand. A strong hand is here defined as one containing (a) nine or more trumps, or (b) eight trumps, including two higher than the 17, and two void suits. Anyone who passes such a hand in the first phase of bidding is said to 'skin' a solo (*soloschinden*).

If everyone passes, the eventual highest soloist can, after looking at the cego cards, claim that someone has skinned a Solo. All then expose their cards, and if one of them has indeed skinned, he loses exactly as if he had played in the game of the final bid and lost every trick. If, however, it transpires that no one has skinned, the accuser loses as though having lost every trick.

If you become the soloist and find that your own hand plus the cego contains fewer than five Trocke, you can safely claim that someone has skinned.

Don't forget . . .
- Play to the left (clockwise) unless otherwise stated.
- Eldest or Forehand means the player to the left of the dealer in left-handed games, to the right in right-handed games.
- T = Ten, p = players, pp = in fixed partnerships, c = cards, t = trump, ☆ = Joker.

14 Catch and collect games

This section covers various card-catching and card-collecting games. With the notable exception of Gops, they are mostly either gambling or children's games.

Catching games are extremely old. The fact that they include some classic children's games doesn't necessarily mean they require no skill, only that the skill required is not that normally associated with 'card sense'. For instance, Snap depends on speed of recognition and reaction, Pelmanism on memory, and Gops on something akin to extra-sensory perception.

The collecting games may not go back so far, but are much older than those of the Rummy type.

Card-catching games   2–6 players, 32 or 52 cards

Snap

Deal all the cards round as far as they will go. Everyone either holds their pack face down in one hand or lays it face down on the table in front of them. Each in turn, as fast as possible, plays the top card of their pile face up to the middle of the table. When the card played matches the rank of the previous card (Ace on Ace, Jack on Jack, etc.) whoever first calls 'Snap!' wins the central pile and places it face down beneath their own playing-pile. A player who runs out of cards drops out of play.

If one player snaps mistakenly, or two or more snap simultaneously, the central pile is placed face up to one side as a pool (or on top of an existing pool) and a new pile is started. Whenever a card played to the main pile matches the top card of the pool, the pool is won by the first player to call 'Snap pool!'

Win by capturing all 52 cards.

Variant There is no central pile. Instead, each card in turn is turned face up on to a pile in front of its owner. Whenever a card played matches the rank of any other player's face-up pile, the first to call

'Snap!' wins his own and the other player's pile and adds them to his playing-pile. Whenever a player runs out of face-down cards, he takes his face-up cards, turns them over, and continues playing from them.

Battle
Deal all the cards out face down. It doesn't matter if some have one more than others. Everyone holds their cards face down in a stack, without looking at them, and each in turn plays the top card of their stack face up to the table. Whoever plays the highest card, regardless of suit, wins all the cards played in that round, or trick, and places them at the bottom of their pile. If there is a tie, the cards stay down and are won by whoever wins the next untied round. Win by capturing all the cards.

Beat Your Neighbour out of Doors (Beggar-My-Neighbour)
Deal all the cards out face down. It doesn't matter if some have one more than others. Everyone holds their cards face down in a stack, without looking at them, and each in turn plays the top card of their stack face up to a central pile. When one of them plays a Jack, Queen, King or Ace, the next in turn must play (respectively) one, two, three or four cards immediately to the top of the pile. If they are all numerals, the pile is won by the earlier player and added to the bottom of the winner's stack. If one of them is a pay-me card, however, then the next in turn must pay the appropriate number of cards. Win by capturing all 52 cards.

Slapjack
Deal all the cards round as far as they will go. Everyone stacks their cards face down in a neat pile on the table in front of them. Each in turn, as fast as possible, takes the top card of his pile and plays it face up to a pile in the middle of the table. Whenever a Jack appears, whoever is first to slap it with their hand wins the central pile, shuffles it in with their own pile to make a new one, then leads any card to start a new central pile.

A player who slaps a card other than a Jack forfeits one card to whoever played the card so slapped. A player who runs out of cards has one opportunity to win a pile by correctly slapping a Jack, but drops out if unsuccessful. Play continues until only one player remains, or utter boredom sets in, whichever is the sooner.

Egyptian Ratscrew (Bloodystump)

A cross between Beggar-My-Neighbour and Slapjack. Play as at Beggar-My-Neighbour but with this addition: that whenever two cards of the same rank are played in succession to the pile, the first player to slap the top card wins the pile. (Hence 'Bloodystump'. It is advisable not to wear metal rings or knuckledusters.) The same right may be attached to any other agreed combination, such as a sequence. Players who have run out of cards may get back in by successfully slapping. One set of rules, published on the Internet by 'Oxymoron', adds: 'Beware of slapping triple sixes – which results in everyone losing, and mandates that the deck be completely burned by midnight and that no one else can play Ratscrew until the next day. This isn't superstition, this is pyromania.' (This rule may be regarded as optional.)

Memory (Pelmanism)

Shuffle the cards and deal them face down at random all over the table. The aim is to collect pairs of matching ranks (two Kings, Fives, or whatever). Each in turn picks up two cards and looks at them in secret. If they form a pair, he wins them; if not, he replaces them face down in the same positions. The player with the best memory, or concentration, or both, will usually win. A score or pay-off can be devised based on the number of pairs collected, their ranks, or both. Some play that upon winning a pair you get another go. Some insist that unmatched cards be shown to all before being turned down.

| Gops | 2–3 players, 39 or 52 cards |

Alex Randolph, the great games inventor, says this game derives from one popular with the 5th Indian Army during the Second World War. Some say the name is an acronym for 'Game of Pure Strategy', but 'Game of Psychological Strife' would be more like it, as the skill involved is more like extra-sensory perception than calculation.

Preliminaries Divide the pack into suits. Shuffle the diamonds and set them face down as a stock. Give one other suit to each player. If two play, ignore the fourth suit.

Object To win the greatest value of diamonds, counting Ace 1, numerals at face value, Jack 11, Queen 12, King 13.

Play At each turn the top diamond is turned face up. The players then bid for it by choosing any card from their hand and laying it face down on the table. When all are ready, the bid cards are turned face up. Whoever plays the highest card (Ace low, King high) wins the diamond. The bid cards are put aside, and the next turn played in the same way.

If two play, and both bid the same amount, the bid cards are put aside and the current diamond is held in abeyance, being won by the winner of the next diamond. If the last card or cards are tied, they belong to neither player, unless it is agreed to credit them to the winner.

If three play, and two tie for best, the diamond is won by the third player. A three-way tie is decided as in the two-player game.

Winning The winner is the player who wins the greatest face value of diamonds (maximum 91).

Thirty-One

3–8 players, 52 or 32 cards

This game is played in various ways under various names. Basically:

Deal three cards each and three face up to the table as a spare hand.

The aim is to collect cards of the same suit totalling 31 or as near as possible, counting Ace 11, faces 10 each, numerals as marked. Alternatively, to get three of a kind, which counts 30½.

Each in turn draws one card from the spare and replaces it with a card from hand. As soon as anyone thinks they have the best hand they end the game by knocking. Each opponent then has one more opportunity to exchange. Cards are revealed and whoever has the highest suit-total wins the pool, unless beaten by three of a kind. Tied hands share it.

Examples: ♣2 ♣3 ♣5 (counting 10) is beaten by ♥A ♣7 ♦3 (11 for the Ace), this by ♠J ♠Q ♠K (30), this by ♣9 ♦9 ♠9 (30½), and this by ♦J ♦K ♦A (31).

Commerce

French forerunner recorded as early as the 1718 edition of the *Académie des Jeux*. The aim is to acquire the best Commerce hand, ranking from high to low as follows:

Tricon Three of the same rank, Aces highest, Twos lowest.

Sequence Three cards in suit and sequence, from A-K-Q high to 3-2-A low.

Point The greatest face-value on two or three cards of the same suit. If equal, a three-card beats a two-card flush. If still equal, the tied player nearest in turn after the dealer wins, but dealer himself has absolute priority.

Whisky Poker

(Spelt with an 'e' if Irish or Bourbon, but undiluted if Scotch.) An adaptation of Thirty-One involving Poker hands. Deal five cards to each player and to a spare hand face down on the table. Everyone antes and looks at their hand. Eldest, if dissatisfied with his hand, may lay it face up on the table and take the spare in its place. If he declines, this option passes round the table till somebody exercises it or all refuse. If all refuse, the spare is turned up and play begins.

At each turn a player may do one of the following:

- exchange one card with the spare, or
- exchange his whole hand for the spare, or
- knock.

When somebody knocks, the others have one more turn each, after which there is a showdown and the best hand wins the pot. Or, originally, the worst hand pays for the drinks.

Variant You may exchange any number of cards from one to five. (Exchanging one *or* five was the original rule.)

Bastard (Stop the Bus)

The same as Whisky Poker, but with three cards each instead of five, and Brag hands instead of Poker hands. You may exchange one or three cards, but not two.

Schwimmen (Schnauz, Knack, Hosen 'runter)

(etc.) A version of Thirty-One popular in Germany and western Austria, there played with 32 cards (Seven low). Everybody starts with (typically) three chips. In this version three Aces counts 32, and any other three of a kind 30½. Anyone dealt a 31 or 32 must show it immediately, thereby ending the play and winning. The dealer deals the spare hand face down and, if not satisfied with his own hand, may exchange it for the spare, sight unseen. Whether he does or not, the spare is then faced and eldest plays first.

Each in turn may exchange one card, or pass. If all pass, the spare hand is swept away and three more cards dealt from stock. If none remain, there is a showdown. When somebody knocks, everybody gets one more turn, but this does not apply if someone goes down with a 31 or 32.

The worst hand loses a chip. Ties (rare) are decided in favour of the best suit, for which purpose the order is clubs (high), spades, hearts, diamonds (low). If the winner has a 32 (three Aces), everyone else loses a chip.

A player who has lost three chips is said to be 'swimming'. The swimmer may continue to play, but must drop out upon losing again. (You might as well play with four chips in the first place.) The overall winner is the last player left in.

Variant You may exchange one or three cards, but not two.

Kemps

(4pp, 52c) Unusually, a partnership game of the Commerce type. Any even number may play, but assume four. Before play, each pair of partners agree between themselves on a visual signal by which either can indicate to the other when he has collected four cards of the same rank. They can also agree on meaningless signals that merely act as camouflage. The signals may include nods, winks, grimaces, twitches, and suchlike, but may not be verbal. False signals may not be used to convey relevant information, such as having got three of a kind.

The aim is to correctly call 'Kemps' when you think your partner has made four of a kind, or 'Stop Kemps' when you think an opponent has done so.

Deal four cards each face down, and four face up to the table. Play does not take place in rotation. Anybody at any time can take from one to four cards from the table and replace them with the same number of (different) cards from their hand. If two or more players want the same card, the first one to touch it gets it.

When everyone has stopped exchanging, the dealer sweeps the spare hand away and deals four more cards from stock.

Play ceases the moment anyone calls Kemps or Stop Kemps. On a call of Kemps, the caller's partner reveals his hand, and, if it contains four of a kind, the opponents lose a point. If not, the caller's side loses a point. On a call of Stop Kemps, both members of the opposing partnership (or, if more than four play, of the partnership specifically challenged by the caller) reveal their hands. If either has four of a kind, their side loses a point; if not, the caller's side does.

The first side to get five points loses the game. The first point lost is marked as a letter K, the second as E, and so on, until a side loses by completing the name of the game. Its origin is not explained. [Source: Elena Anaya, via the Pagat website.]

Other collecting games

The following resemble shedding games, in that the object is to get rid of all your cards first. The difference is that, whereas in shedding games you play only by discarding, in collecting games you also collect new cards, and can 'go out' by discarding sets of cards that match one another by rank or suit. In this respect they form a transition to Rummy games.

Go Fish

A game of this name, *Andare e piscere*, was current in Italy at the end of the fifteenth century, but no description survives.

From three to six can play, using a 52-card pack. Deal five to each player and stack the rest, face down. The aim is to run out of cards, largely by collecting matching groups of four, such as four Tens, or Jacks, etc.

The player at dealer's left starts by addressing any player and asking them for a particular card, such as ♥6 or ♣Q. The rank asked for must, however, be one of which the asker has at least one in his own hand. The player so asked must comply with that request if possible. If so, the asker gets another turn and does the same thing, asking the same or another player for a particular card of the same rank as one he already holds. This continues until a player who is asked for cards has none of that rank. He then replies, 'Go and fish.' The asker must then draw a card from stock – so long as any remain – and add it to his own hand, leaving the asked player to take over the turn to ask.

Whenever you get four of a kind you can lay them down like a won trick after showing them to the others. The winner is the first to run out of cards by giving them away when asked and discarding them in fours when collected. If more than one go out at the same time, the winner is the one who collected more groups of four.

Authors

Authors is so called because the Victorians got their children to play it with special cards depicting famous authors and their works. This was considered 'educational' and therefore A Good Thing – unlike ordinary cards, which are only mathematical and therefore A Bad Thing.

From two to four players use a 52-card pack. The cards are shuffled and dealt round one at a time as far as they will go. It doesn't matter if some people get more than others. The aim is to lose your cards by discarding them in 'books' – that is, in sets of four, such as four Aces, four Jacks, or whatever.

The player at dealer's left starts by addressing any other player and asking them for all the cards they have of a particular rank. The rank asked for must, however, be one of which the asker has at least one in his own hand. The player so asked must comply with that request if possible. If so, the asker gets another turn and does the same thing, asking the same or another player for cards of any rank of which he holds at least one. This continues until a player who is asked for cards has none of that rank. He then replies, 'None,' and takes over the turn to ask somebody else.

Whenever a player gets all four of a given rank he shows them to the others and lays them down like a won trick. The winner is the first to run out of cards by the process of giving them away and discarding them in fours.

My Ship Sails

From four to seven players use a 52-card pack. Deal seven each and throw the rest away. The aim is to be the first to collect seven cards of the same suit.

Everybody looks at their cards and places one of them, face down, on the table at their left. This should be one of a suit they are not planning to collect. When all are ready, they each pick up the card lying at their right and add it to their hand. If anyone now has seven of a suit, they say 'My ship sails' and lay their cards face up, thereby winning. If not, keep playing likewise till somebody wins.

If two fill their hands at the same time, the winner is the first to call 'My ship sails' – or, if you prefer, the one with higher-ranking card, or the second highest if tied, and so on.

Donkey (Pig)

From three to thirteen can play, but five or six is about right. Remove from a 52-card pack as many groups of four as there are players. For example, with five players you might use all four Aces, Fives, Tens, Queens and Kings. Shuffle these cards together and deal them round in ones so everyone gets exactly four. The aim is to get four of a kind, or to notice when somebody else has done so.

Each player now takes one card from his hand and passes it face down to the player at his left. Everyone does this together, not one by one in turn.

Repeat this process until one player gets all four of a rank in his hand. He then, as slyly and quietly as possible, lays his hand of cards face down on the table and rests one finger wisely against his nose. Anyone who notices him doing so also puts his cards down and rubs his nose, even if he hasn't got four of a kind. Eventually, everybody will notice what's going on and do the same thing. The last player to do so is the donkey, or pig, or triceratops, or whatever.

Don't forget . . .
- Play to the left (clockwise) unless otherwise stated.
- Eldest or Forehand means the player to the left of the dealer in left-handed games, to the right in right-handed games.
- T = Ten, p = players, pp = in fixed partnerships, c = cards, † = trump, ☆ = Joker.

15 **Fishing games**

Given a number of cards face up on the table and a number of cards in your hand, can you play a card from the hand that matches one or more of those on the table? If so, you play it, take them, and add them to your pile of winnings. If not, you'll have to add another card to those on the table for the next player to 'catch'.

This is the pattern of games widely played in China under the general title 'Fishing'. They resemble trick-taking games to the extent that the aim is to capture cards: it's the method that differs. Whereas trick-taking is the commonest form of card-capture in the West, the reverse is the case in the East. Fishing games are also widely played in the Middle East and round the shores of the Mediterranean, being especially popular in Turkey, Greece and Italy. Only one of them, Cassino, has regularly formed part of the western repertoire, though it is by no means the easiest to learn or the most exciting to play. The fact that it is often presented as an arithmetically 'educational' game for children can't have done much for its image. A better starting-point is the Italian national game of Scopa, for two, or its partnership equivalent, Scopone. Once you get the hang of this family, you'll find more elaborate variations to enjoy.

▌Cassino   2–4 players, 52 cards

There are two kinds, sorts, descriptions, species, manners, classes, natures and qualities of Casino. As you love me, child, avoid that which contains but a single S.

G. A. Sala, *Lady Chesterfield's Letters to her Daughter* (1860)

Cassino is the only member of the Scopa family to have penetrated the English-speaking world, and that in America rather than Britain, possibly brought thither by Italian immigrants in the nineteenth century. There it seems to have been heavily elaborated by the addition of single and multiple 'builds', a feature absent from its first recorded description in Piggott's *Hoyle* of 1797, where it more resembles Scopa in relative simplicity. Though spelt in English with a double 's' from the outset, it has recently become fashionable to favour the spelling Casino, for no particularly useful or sensible reason.

Preliminaries Up to four can play, but the game works best for two. From a 52-card pack deal two to each opponent, two to the table, two to the dealer, then the same again so everyone has four. Turn the four table cards face up in a row. Place the rest of the pack to one side. When everyone has had four turns and run out of cards, deal another four each in batches of two, and so on throughout the game. No more cards are dealt to the table, however, at any time.

Object To capture cards, especially spades, Aces, Big Cassino (♦T) and Little Cassino (♠2). Each player's captured and capturing cards are stored face down in a pile on the table in front of him.

Play Each in turn, starting with eldest, plays a card to the table to do one of the following:

1. Capture one or more table cards by pairing. For example, an Ace captures one or more Aces, a Jack one or more Jacks, and so on.

2. Capture one or more table cards by summing. For example, a Ten captures two or more cards totalling ten, a Nine two or more cards totalling nine, and so on. Court cards have no numerical value and are therefore never involved in summing.

3. Build a combination that the player can capture on a subsequent turn (provided no one else captures it first). For example, with two Sixes in hand and two on the table, play a Six to the table, put all three Sixes together, announce 'Building sixes', and capture them with the fourth Six on the next turn. Or: with 2-3 on the table and 4-9 in hand, build the Four to the 2-3, announce 'Building nine', and capture all these with the Nine on the next turn. Note that a build can be captured only as a whole: none of its component cards can be captured individually. An existing build can be extended, but in a non-partnership game it is not permissible to make a build for which one does not hold an appropriate capturing card. A build may be captured by another player, whether an opponent or a partner. In the partnership game, you may increase builds made by your partner without yourself holding a capturing card, provided that it is evident from his announcement that he can capture on the next turn. (*Example*: He plays a Four to a Three and announces 'Building seven'. You may play a Seven and announce 'Building sevens', even if you do not hold another Seven yourself.)

A possible source of confusion in building cards must be avoided by clearly announcing the total. For example, a player may add a Three from his hand to a Three on the table. If he announces 'Building threes', the two cards may be captured only with a Three (by multiple pairing). But if he announces 'Building six', the build may be captured only by a Six. Furthermore, the build of six could be increased by the addition of another card to make a higher build, but the build of Threes could be increased only by the addition of another Three.

A card played from hand may make as many captures as possible, whether by pairing or summing. Capturing all the cards on the table is called a sweep. This is a scoring feature and is indicated by leaving the capturing card face up in the winnings pile.

A player who neither captures nor builds must simply trail a card by playing it face up to the table and leaving it there as an additional table card – though, if it can capture a card, it must. When one player makes a sweep, the next in turn has no option but to trail.

Ending and scoring When all cards have been played from hand and none remain in stock, the player who made the last capture adds to his won cards all the untaken table cards, but this does not count as a sweep unless it is one by definition.

Players then sort through their won cards and score 1 point for each sweep, Ace and Little Cassino (♠2), and 2 points for Big Cassino (♦T). For taking most spades add 1 point, and for taking most cards 3 points. The 3 for cards is not counted in the event of a tie. The game ends at the end of the deal on which a player or side reaches a previously agreed target score, typically 11 or 21.

Game There are several different ways of scoring for game. (a) Each deal is a complete game and the higher score wins. (b) The first player or side to reach 11 points wins a single game, doubled if done in two deals, or quadrupled if in one deal, the loser's score being subtracted to determine the margin of victory. If both exceed 10, the higher score wins, but if tied there is no pay-off. (c) Game is 21 up. If tied, the winner is the side with the majority of cards, or, if still tied, of spades.

Variants When two play, sweeps may be ignored.

Some players allow a court card to capture only one card or three by pairing, but not two, as the consequent invulnerability of the fourth prevents any sweeps from being made. (Which may not matter if sweeps are not counted anyway.)

It may be agreed that play ends the moment someone makes a capture that brings his score to the target.

Comment Concentrate always on the objectives: to capture most cards, most spades, Aces, the ♦T, and the ♠2. Avoid trailing any of the latter, and work on builds rather than individual cards. Beware of capturing a court if this leaves only numerals on the table, as these may enable the next in turn to make a sweep. Do so only when you have a good chance of making the sweep yourself.

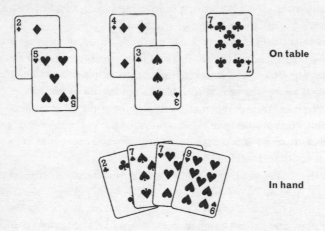

On table

In hand

Cassino. With this hand you can sweep the board with a Seven. Better, though, is to play a Seven to the Seven, announce 'Building Sevens', and sweep the board on your next turn – provided your opponent does not hold a Seven with which to sweep it first. You can't increase the 2-5 or 4-3, as they form a multiple build.

Diamond Cassino

(2–4p, 40c) A cross between Cassino and Scopa. Deal three each and four to the table. Game is 11 up, counting 1 for cards (capturing 21 or more if two play), 1 for diamonds (capturing six or more of them), 1 extra for ♦7, 2 for capturing all four Sevens or Sixes or Aces, and 1 per sweep.

Draw Cassino

Any two-hand version of Cassino played in the following way: after playing a card, each completes his turn by drawing the top card of stock to restore his original number of cards. There are no extra deals. When the stock is exhausted the last cards are played out in the usual way.

Royal Cassino

(2p, 52c) Basic Cassino but counting each Jack 11, Queen 12 and King 13, so that court cards may be built or captured by combining as well as by pairing. As an optional extra, Ace may count 1 or 14 *ad lib*.

Spade Cassino

Cassino variant that replaces 1 for taking a majority of spades with 1 point for each spade captured, with an extra point each for ♠J, ♠2 (Little Cassino) and ♠A (by virtue of the score for Aces).

Royal Spade Cassino

A mixture of Royal Cassino and Spade Cassino.

Zwicker   2–4 players, 52 cards + 6 Jokers

A simpler and jollier version of Cassino, Zwicker is described (by Claus D. Grupp, in *Schafkopf, Doppelkopf*, Wiesbaden, 1976) as a popular family game of Schleswig-Holstein.

Preliminaries From two to four players use a 52-card pack, to which it is usual to add six Jokers of (preferably) the same back design and colour as the main pack. Deal four cards each, and four face up to the table. Stack the rest face down. When everyone has played four cards, deal four more each so long as any remain in stock.

Object To capture Aces, ♦7, ♠7, ♦T, and to make sweeps.

Play Each in turn, starting with eldest, plays a card face up to the table, where it may capture either:

• one table card by pairing; e.g. a Two captures a Two, a Jack a Jack, etc.; or

• two or more table cards by summing. For this purpose each Ace counts 11, Jack 12, Queen 13, King 14; so a Queen might capture 6-7, or 2-3-8, etc.

A played card may make as many captures as possible in one turn. Capturing all the table cards is a sweep and is marked by placing the capturing card face up instead of face down in the pile of won cards. A sweep leaves the next player in turn no option but to trail.

Building A player unable to capture must trail by adding a card to the pool. He may, however, use it to form a 'build' by placing it half over another card. In this case the build counts as if it were a single card of their combined value, and may be captured but only as a whole. For example, a Five played to a Seven makes a build of 12, which can later be captured by a Jack – or, if there is also a Two on the table, by a King in conjunction with the Two, since the Two and the 12-build are equalled by the value of the King. More discards may be added to a build, so long as it does not exceed 14 in total value.

Jokers may be captured by matching. In addition, a Joker counts as any desired value from 2 to 14, and may be played or captured accordingly. Of course, it may only count as one value at a time: it cannot capture two different cards, or builds of different values, in the same turn.

Ending No cards are added to the pool when extra cards are dealt. On the last deal, it does not matter that there may not be enough cards to go round. The last person to play a card from the hand also wins any cards left in the pool, but this does not count as a sweep, unless it happens to be one by definition.

Score At end of play everyone sorts through their won cards and scores as follows:

> 1 for ♦7
> 1 for ♠7
> 2 for each Ace
> 3 for each sweep
> 10 for ♦T

Play up to any agreed target.

Variants Restrictions may be imposed on the power of Jokers. In some circles, for instance, a Joker on the table may never be captured, thus preventing any more sweeps.

Cuarenta

2 or 4 players, 40 cards (from 52)

Cuarenta is played in Ecuador, mostly in mountainous regions, including the cities of Cuenca and the capital Quito. The play is supposed to be full of bravado, loud, exciting, even silly (reports Paul J. Welty on the Pagat website). Glenn Maldonado Vaca of Guayaquil publishes a Cuarenta website in Spanish, which includes rules, information about the World Championship, and a downloadable software program.

Preliminaries Two play alone, four crosswise in partnerships. If four play, one partner keeps the score and the other stores their won cards.

Cards The cards in play are KQJ7654321(=A), usually taken from a 52-card pack, of which the Eights, Nines and Tens are used for marking scores. At start of play they are stacked face up between the two opposing scorekeepers.

Deal Deal a single batch of five cards to each player and stack the rest face down. When five each have been played, five more are dealt.

Announcements Immediately after any deal, and before play begins, a player may declare and score for either of the following:

1. *Four of a kind*: Four cards of the same rank. These are shown, and that player's side wins the game without play.

2. *Ronda*: Three cards of a kind. These are declared, but not shown or identified, and their holder's side scores 4 points.

Play Each in turn plays a card to the table and either captures with it or leaves it to trail. Captures are made by pairing numerals or courts, or by summing numerals, or by footing a sequence. That is, if a table card captured by pairing is accompanied by one or more cards in ascending numerical sequence the whole sequence is thereby captured. For example, playing a Three captures a Three alone, or any sequence beginning Three-Four-(etc.). Given a choice of captures, you may choose any one of them, but not more. You may also trail a card even if you could make a capture with it. A card played to an empty table, as at start of play or following a sweep, is necessarily trailed.

Caída Capturing the card just played by the previous player by matching it is called a *caída* (a fall), and scores 2 points. However, it is not a *caída* when the first player after a new deal matches and captures the last card played at the end of the previous deal.

Limpia Capturing all the cards on the table is a *limpia* ('clean-up'), and scores 2 points. Since the next player can only trail, it often happens that the player or partnership scoring for *limpia* also scores for *caída* on their next turn, making 4 in all.

Score Any table cards remaining untaken at end of play do not count to either side. A player or side that took exactly 20 cards scores 6 points, but if both do, only the non-dealing side scores. For each card taken above 20, add 1 point, but round up to the nearest even number. For example, score 8 for 21 or 22 cards, 10 for 23 or 24, and so on. If both sides take fewer than 20, the side that took more cards, or the non-dealing side if equal, scores just 2 points. Game is 40 (*cuarenta*) points.

Special scoring rules If a player makes a *caída* by capturing a card that was part of a *ronda* (trio), and remembers this event and the rank of the *ronda* cards, he can score 10 points at the end of the hand for correctly announcing this fact and the rank of the *ronda* involved. This cannot be announced before the end of the hand, or after the next deal has begun.

A side standing at 30 or more cannot score for *rondas*, nor for capturing a card of the opponents' *ronda* by means of a *caída*. However, if the opposing team has less than 30, they may still score 10 points if they capture a card of an 'unannounced' *ronda* by a *caída*, and correctly announce it.

A side standing at 38 points cannot score for *limpia*. They can win only by counting cards or with a *caída*. Standing at 36, however, they can win the game by scoring 4 for both feats (*caída y limpia*).

Scorekeeping with eights, nines and tens Each of these cards represents 2 points face up or 10 points face down. Each scorekeeper takes a scorecard from the stock and places it face up before him for every 2 points scored. Upon reaching 10, four cards are returned to the stack and the fifth is turned down to represent 10 (when it becomes known as a *perro*, 'dog'). A score of 38 is indicated by returning all one's score-cards to the stack. There are just enough cards to keep score in all situations.

Scopa

2–4 players, 40 cards

One of Italy's major national card games, Scopa is easy to learn and grows deeper with repeated play. It forms by far the best introduction to games of this family. Its partnership equivalent, Scopone, is described separately.

Players Scopa is basically for two players, but three or four can play as individuals. Play to the right.

Cards Forty, normally an Italian pack with suits of swords, batons, cups, coins (♠ ▯ ♇ ✿), courts of Re (King), Cavall (Knight), Fante (Footsoldier), and numerals 7654321. The equivalents and numerical values are:

				R	C	F	7	6	5	4	3	2	1
♠	♣	♥	♦	K	Q	J	7	6	5	4	3	2	A
face values:				10	9	8	7	6	5	4	3	2	1

Deal Deal three cards to each player, singly, and four face up to the table. When everyone has played out their three cards they are dealt three more, and so on throughout the game so long as any remain.

Object To capture as many cards as possible, especially diamonds and high numerals (not courts). If the table cards include three Kings, it is usual (but not official) to deal again.

Play Each in turn, starting with eldest, plays a card face up to the table, where it may capture either:

• one table card by pairing – for example, a Two captures a Two, a Jack a Jack, etc., or

• two or more table cards by summing – for example, a Queen might capture 4-5, or 2-3-4, etc.

Only one capture may be made in one turn, and if pairing is possible this must be done in preference to summing. For example, if the table cards are 2-4-6-J, a Jack captures the Jack but not the 2-6. Each player stacks his capturing and captured cards face down in a pile on the table before him.

A card that cannot capture must be trailed – that is, left in place as a new table card. If a card intended to trail can actually make a capture, it must do so.

Scopa A sweep (*scopa*) is made when only one card is on the table and a player captures it by pairing, or when all the cards on the table are captured by summing. This is a scoring feature and is marked by placing the capturing card face up instead of face down in the pile of won cards. When a player makes a sweep the next in turn can only trail.

Ending Play continues until no cards remain in hand or stock. Any cards remaining on the table then go to whoever made the last capture, but this does not count as a sweep, even if they are all validly captured.

Score Players sort through their won cards and score, where relevant, as follows:

> 1 for winning the most cards (no score if tied)
>
> 1 for winning the most diamonds (no score if tied)
>
> 1 for the *sette bello* or 'best Seven' (♣7 or ♦7)
>
> 1 for *primiera*, as explained below
>
> 1 per sweep

For *primiera*, each side extracts from its won cards the highest-valued card it has taken in each suit, and totals their face values according to the following schedule:

Seven	21	Four	14
Six	18	Three	13
Ace	16	Two	12
Five	15	K,Q,J	10 each

Whoever took the highest value of cards on this basis scores 1 for *primiera*. A player who has taken cards in only three or fewer suits cannot compete for this point.

> ☞ You rarely need to count these exactly, as it is usually obvious from just looking at the Sevens and Sixes who has the best *primiera*.

Game Play up to 11 points. If there is a tie, the points made on the last deal are counted strictly in order: cards – diamonds – best Seven – *primiera* – sweeps; and the first to score on that basis wins.

Variants Scopa is rich in alternative rules and optional extras.

Some start by dealing nine cards to each player. When both (or all) players have had a turn, they draw a replacement card from stock before playing again, so long as any remain to take.

Points may be scored for other cards or combinations found among a player's won cards, notably notably ♠2, and three-card suit-sequences such as ♦A-2-3, ♠6-7-J, or ♦J-Q-K.

In some circles, points are remembered as they accrue, and the winner is the first to claim correctly that he has reached 11. A false claim loses the game.

Some use a 52-card pack, and count Jack 11, Queen 12, King 13.

In **Scopa d'Assi**, an Ace from the hand sweeps all the cards from the table. This may or may not be permitted if the table cards include an Ace, and may or may not score as a sweep.

In **Scopa de Quindici**, a card from the hand may capture one or more cards on the table which, together with the capturing card, total fifteen. For example, with A 3 7 K on the table, a Five could be played to capture the 3 + 7 (or, less profitably, the King). In some versions, point-count captures may be made only in this way, to the exclusion of other forms of addition.

In **Sbarazzina**, cards may be captured only by fifteening. Courts have a count of zero, so that, for example, if the table cards are 2-7-K they are all captured with a Six (2 + 7 + 0 + 6 = 15). A player unable to capture in this way must trail. An Ace sweeps the board provided that no other Ace is on the table. Score as at Scopa, but with the addition of 1 for capturing ♦K (*re bello*).

Scopa de Undici

resembles Scopa de Quindici, but has 11 as the key total.

Hurricane

Italian game here quoted from a German source. A hurricane is a sweep. Deal six each and four to the table. Play as Scopa and score: 1 for cards, 1 for most hearts, 1 extra for ♥7, 1 for *primiera* (see Scopa). Game is 16 up, and won double if the loser fails to reach 8.

Scopone
4 players (2 × 2), 40 cards

An excellent and unusual partnership game, recommended to players seeking something quite different from the usual run of trick-and-trump games, easy to learn but of considerable depth.

Preliminaries Four players sit crosswise in partnerships and play to the right.

Cards and deal As Scopa, but deal nine cards each and four face up to the table, in batches of 3-(2)-3-(2)-3. If the table cards include three Kings, it is usual (but not official) to deal again.

Play and score As at Scopa, with each pair of partners keeping all its won cards in a single pile.

Variant Deal ten cards each and none to the table, thus forcing the first player to trail.

Comment If at the start of the hand each player were to capture exactly one card, the dealer would score a sweep, eldest would be forced to trail, and there would be a strong tendency for the dealer's side to be continually sweeping while the opponents continually trail. The elder partnership must therefore seek to break up this potential pattern. Suppose the table cards dealt are A-3-4-J. Eldest plays a Five and captures A-4. Dealer's partner is now awkwardly facing 3-J, a combination worth 11 and so unsweepable. If he pairs either card he leaves his next opponent one card and the chance of a sweep, though his own holding may enable him to assess this risk. For example, holding two Jacks and a Three he could capture the Three, arguing that it is two to one against the next player's holding the other Jack. Otherwise, his safest play is to trail, which scores, but costs, nothing.

The first move (5 = 1 + 4) leaves in play three each of Aces, Fours, and Fives, and these ranks are consequently said to be unpaired (*sparigliato*). Generally, it favours the non-dealers' side to maintain as many ranks as possible unpaired. To redress the balance, dealer's side should seek to trail the lower cards of three or more unpaired ranks so that they may capture by summing – an attempt which the opponents will try to frustrate by trailing the highest unpaired rank before the others can get both of the lower ranks into play. In the above example, dealer's side will now seek to trail a Four and an Ace so as to capture both with a Five of their own. But if the non-dealers can themselves trail a Five before a Four and an Ace get into play, then the dealer's side will not be able to catch them, since, by the rules of the game, capture by pairing has priority over capture by summing.

Another common sequence of play is the *mulinello* ('whirlwind'). Suppose the table cards are A-3-4-5 and eldest has two Threes. Trusting that his next opponent does not have the fourth, he plays K = A + 4 + 5, leaving the Three *in situ*. Dealer's partner does not have the Three and must trail a court to prevent a possible sweep. Suppose he trails a Jack. Now third-hand, who does have the fourth Three, pairs the Jack, thus leaving dealer in exactly the same fix as his partner. As the fourth Three is a constant threat, this painful situation can be dragged out for some time.

When forced to trail it is natural to choose a rank of which two or three are held, a fact which can give useful information to one's partner and possibly enable him to reap a whirlwind as described above. For example, suppose the first move is 6 = 2 + 4. Second-hand trails a Four from a pair. If now his partner, dealer, has the other Four, the two of them can set up a whirlwind based upon that rank – rather like a squeeze at Bridge.

The single most important card in the pack is ♦7 – the *sette bello* or Best Seven. It is worth a point in itself, counts towards the majority of diamonds, and counts most for *primiera*. Much of the play is directed towards catching this card, or at least preventing the opponents from catching it too easily. The other three Sevens come next in importance, as the *primiera* point can be won on three Sevens if the fourth card is a Three or better. A side that has already lost a majority of Sevens must chase after the Sixes, then the Aces, and so on down the scale.

Varieties of Scopa/Scopone

Cicera

(2–4p, 52c) Normally played in partnership form in the province of Brescia, with Italian-suited cards of the Bresciane pattern. Reported by Virgilio Ferrari on the Pagat website.

Play to the right. Deal twelve each and four to the table. Each in turn plays a card to the table and either makes a capture or leaves it to trail. Capture is by pairing or summing of numeral cards (1 to 10 at face value) or pairing only of courts. Given a choice of captures, the player may make any but only one. It is permissible to trail a card even if it could capture.

Points are scored during play for any of the following feats. These are indicated by leaving the capturing card face up in the partnership's pile of winnings.

Scùa Capturing all the table cards in one turn.

Picada Capturing, by pairing, the card just trailed by one's left-hand opponent.

Simili When the capturing card is of the same suit as the card or all the cards it captures.

Quadriglia Capturing three or more cards from the table.

More than one of these points can be scored with a single play. For example, if ♦9 captures ♦2-3-4 it scores 1 for *simili* and 1 for *quadriglia*, and, if no cards remain on the table, another 1 for *scùa*. It is obviously necessary to leave some of the captured cards face up to mark these points.

The last player to make a capture also wins any remaining table cards.

At end of play, either side scores as follows:

2 for most cards (unscored if split 26–26)

2 for most swords (♠, equivalent to spades)

3 for *napula*, which is the sequence ♠1-2-3 (♠A-2-3) if the Four is not held. If it is, *napula* scores the value of the highest card in unbroken suit-sequence from the ♠3 upwards.

1 for *mata*, i.e. ♠2 (♠2)

1 for ●10 (♦T)

1 for ♦Fante (♥J)

Play up to 51 points.

Cirulla

(2–4p, 40c) Played in Genoa and the Liguria region, usually in partnerships.

Deal three cards each and four to the table, and stack the rest face down. If the table cards include more than one Ace, bury them and deal again.

If all four table cards initially dealt total 15 exactly, the dealer takes them immediately, scores for a *scopa*, and leaves the next player to trail. If they total exactly 30, he does likewise and scores 2 *scope*. The ♦7 (♥7), if among them, is wild, and represents any valid count the dealer wishes.

So long as cards remain in stock, deal three more each when all are out of cards. If, after any such deal or re-deal, a player's three cards total less than 10, he may 'knock' (*bussare*), reveal them all, and score 3 *scope*, indicated by turning three captured cards face up. A player dealt three of a kind at any time may also knock for 10 points. In either case, the ♣7 (or ♥7) may be used as a wild card for the purpose of knocking for a low total or three of a kind. It must be designated as a particular rank, and then played as such. For example, if it is called an Ace, it can be used to sweep the table.

Each in turn plays a card to the table and either captures with it or leaves it to trail. Captures are made by pairing or by summing in the usual way (Fante/Jack counting 8, Cavall/Queen 9, Re/King 10). Capture can also be effected by fifteening. For example, a Seven takes an Eight, or vice versa, or a King takes a Two and a Three (10 + 2 + 3 = 15).

Given a choice of captures, the player may make any but only one. It is permissible to trail a card even if it could capture.

An Ace captures all the table cards, but only if there is not another Ace among them.

Capturing all the table cards is a *scopa*, and is indicated by leaving the capturing card face up in the player's pile of winnings.

At end of play points are scored for won cards as follows:

1 for each *scopa*

1 for most cards (unless tied)

1 for most *denari* (diamonds) (unless tied)

1 for *sette bello* ♣7 (♦7)

1 for *primiera* (as in Scopa)

5 for *scala grande* – ♣F-C-R (♦J-Q-K)

3 for *scala piccola*, which is the sequence ♣1-2-3 (♦A-2-3) if the Four is not held. If it is, *scala piccola* scores the value of the highest card in unbroken suit-sequence from the ♣3 upwards.

Capturing all the *denari* (diamonds) wins the game outright. Otherwise, play up to 26, 51, or 101, as agreed.

▌ Basra (Ashush)   2 players, 52 cards

An Egyptian and Lebanese game widely played in coffee houses through-out the Middle East, reported by Bonnie Smith and Thierry Depaulis on the Pagat website. Ashush, in the Lebanon, means Jack, but it is also colloquial Arabic for imam.

Preliminaries Deal four each and four to the 'floor', and when these are gone deal four more each so long as any remain. If the floor cards include any Jacks or ♦7, put these at the bottom of the stock (they will eventually go to the dealer) and deal replacements.

Play Capture by pairing or summing or both. A card that makes no capture is merely trailed. Capturing all the cards from the floor is a *basra*, and the capturing card is stored face up to mark it.

Kings and Queens have no numerical value, and can capture or be captured only by pairing.

A Jack sweeps all the cards from the floor, but this does not count as a basra. So does ♦7, and this can count as a basra, but only if the floor cards are all numerals, and their combined values do not exceed 10. Trailing a Jack or ♦7 is legal but pointless.

Any cards remaining on the floor after the final capture are taken by the player who last made a capture, but (presumably) this does not count as a basra.

Score 3 for cards, 1 per Jack, 1 per Ace, 2 for ♣2, 3 for ♦T, and 10 for each basra. Game is 101 points. A rubber is won by the first to win three games. If both players have won two, the fifth is usually played up to 150.

Basra is easily adaptable for three and four players. The Lebanese version differs mainly in that each player receives six cards and ♦7 has no special power.

The following games are self-evidently related.

Pishti

(2p, 52c) Reported by Harbin (*Waddingtons Family Card Games*, London, 1972) as a Turkish contribution to the genre. Dealer cuts, non-dealer takes the bottom card of the top half, and dealer half covers it with the stock face down – unless it is a Jack, which is immediately won by the non-dealer. Deal four each and four to the table face up in a stack. If the top card is a Jack, it is won by the dealer and replaced from stock. Each in turn plays a card. If it matches the top card, or is a Jack, it sweeps the whole stack. If not, it is placed face up on the stack. When the stack is taken, the next player can only trail. If the next player immediately pairs the trailed card, he calls 'Pishti!' (said to mean 'cooked'), and scores 10. When both have run out of cards, deal four more each so long as any remain. Score 3 for most cards, 3 for ♦T, 2 for ♣2, 1 per Ace, 1 per Jack. Play up to 101.

Dry Game

(2–4p, 52c) Transmitted by Harbin (see above) from a Greek informant. Deal six each, then four face up to form a stack of which only the top card is available. When players run out of cards there is a new deal, including four to the stack. Each in turn plays a card face up to the stack. If it matches the top card by rank it captures the whole stack, and the next in turn has no option but to start a new one by playing any card face up. If not, it is left on top. Any Jack captures the whole stack regardless of the top card. A player capturing a stack consisting of only one card immediately scores 10 for a 'dry trick'. Score 3 for most cards, 3 for most clubs, 2 for ♦T, 1 extra for ♣2, and 1 per Jack.

Pástra

(2 or 4p, 52c) Cypriot equivalent of Basra described to me by Kyriakos Papadopoulos. Deal four each and four to the table, and keep dealing fours when players run out of cards. Score 3 for winning most cards, 3 for ♦T, 2 for ♣2, 1 per Ace and 1 per Jack, total 16, plus 10 per sweep (*pástra*). Play up to 101.

Ladies' Game

(2–4p, 52c) Another of Harbin's discoveries. Deal six each and four to the table. Play as Scopa except that courts count 10 each. Score as in the Dry Game (see above).

Tablanette

(2p, 52c) Described only by Hubert Phillips (*Complete Book of Card Games*, London, 1939), and said to be of Russian provenance, but evidently related to the Basra group. Deal six each and four to the table.

Capture by pairing or summing. Ace counts 1 or 11 as preferred, Queen 13, King 14. The play of a Jack sweeps all the table cards in one turn. This is a *tablanette* (possibly from French *table nette*, 'clean table'), and entitles the player to score the combined pip-count of all the cards so captured, the Jack itself being valueless. Apart from the potentially huge scores for tablanette, players score 1 for each Ace, King, Queen, Jack and Ten captured, an extra 1 for ♦T, 1 for ♣J, and 3 for cards. Game is 251 up.

Tenteret
(2–8p, 52c) A Russian game described in 1809. Possibly the ultimate source of Tablanette (above), except that players are dealt three cards each.

Konchinka
(2–4p, 52c) Early nineteenth-century Russian equivalent of Basra.

Zing
(2p or 4pp, 52c) Albanian relative reported by Franco Pratesi in *The Playing-Card* (XXVI, 3). Four each, four to the table in a face-up pile. At each turn either capture the stack by matching the top card or playing a Jack, or play a card face up to the stack. Capturing a one-card stack is called a 'zing' (an apparently meaningless word), and is marked by storing the capturing card face up. Deal four more each whenever hands are depleted. Cards left untaken at the end are ignored. Score 5 for cards, 5 for ♦7, 5 for ♣T, and 10 per zing. Game is said to be 51 points, which suggests that there is more to the scoring system than reported here.

Other fishing games

Callabra
(2–3p, 52c) A fast and simple forerunner of Cassino for two or three players. Deal three each and five to the table. The rest remain out of play and the simple object is to capture a clear majority of the cards in play – six if two play, eight if three. Numerals count face value, plus

J11, Q12, K13. Each in turn (passing to the right) plays a card face up to the table and leaves it there unless able to capture one or more table cards with it. A card played from the hand may capture one or more cards by pairing or by summing, and multiple captures are permitted. The game ends when one player has taken a majority of cards, or one player has run out of cards and no one has won, or no more cards are available for capture.

Papillon (= 'Butterfly')

(2–4p, 3 best, 52c) A defunct but delightful French game, characterized by an elaborate system of side-payments for special coups, and by its almost exclusive suitability for three players. Deal three cards each and seven to the table (or only four if four play). When all have been played deal three more, and so on so long as any remain in stock. Each in turn plays one card and captures by pairing or summing, with certain restrictions. One King, Queen, Jack or Ten will capture as many cards of the same rank as possible, but lower numerals may not pair with more than one of their kind. They alone, however, may capture by summing. The last to capture a card from the table takes all those remaining.

Payment as follows: pay 1 to the pool each time a card is trailed; receive from each opponent 2 for capturing an Ace with an Ace, 4 for capturing two Aces with a Two, 6 for capturing three Aces with a Three, 8 for capturing four with a Four, 1 for capturing any three cards of the same rank with the fourth (a feat known as *hanneton*, 'cockchafer'), 1 for a sweep (*sauterelle*, 'grasshopper') – after which the next in turn must lay out his remaining cards to form a new table – 1 for winning a majority of cards (not counted in the event of a tie, but the winner of the next counts 2), and various others which are not 100 per cent clear but may easily be extended by exercise of the imagination.

It is clear that all variants must be named after arthropods.

Chinese Ten

(2–4p, 52c) A game reported by Jennifer Bullock on the Internet.

From a 52-card pack deal two players twelve cards each, three players eight, or four players six. Deal the next four face up to the table and stack the rest face down.

Each in turn, starting with eldest, plays a card to the table, thereby capturing any card with which it sums to 10. For example, an Ace captures a Nine, or a Nine an Ace, and so on. Cards above Nine are captured by pairing – Ten takes Ten, Jack takes Jack, and so on. A non-capturing card is left on the table. Having either captured or trailed, you then turn the top card of stock, and may make a capture with it if possible. If not, leave it on the table for subsequent capture. Not more than one card may be turned from stock.

Players sift all the red cards from their winnings and count them as follows: Aces 20 each, Nines and higher 10 each, lower numerals at face value.

Black cards don't count when two play. When three or four play, ♠A counts 30 extra points, and when four play ♣A counts 40 in addition.

Each player scores towards game the difference between the value of card-points taken and the mean total, which is 105 if two play, 80 if three, or 70 if four. For example, if two players count 114 and 96, the former scores +9 and the latter −9.

Laugh and Lie Down

(5p, 52c) A simple and eccentric member of the family, the oldest of all recorded, and the only one known from English sources. The title, at least, is first mentioned in 1522, and the game itself described in Francis Willughby's *Volume of Plaies, c.* 1665. The following is based on Justin du Coeur's redaction on the Medieval and Renaissance Games website.

A mournival is four of a kind, and a prial (pair-royal) three of a kind.

The dealer stakes 3 units and everyone else 2 to the pot. Deal eight cards each in ones and the last twelve face up to the table. Any mournivals found among the table cards are promptly won by the dealer. Any player holding a mournival 'wins' its constituent cards and places them face down before himself. Any player holding a prial similarly 'wins' two of them, retaining the third for making a subsequent capture.

Each in turn plays a card to the table in order to make a capture if possible. A capture is made only by pairing, and the card so played may capture either one or three cards of the same rank, but not two.

When a card is captured by pairing, any other player holding the other pair of the same rank may add them to his pile of winnings.

When a player cannot make a capture on his turn to play he must add all his remaining cards to the table ('lie down') and drop out. Willughby attributes the name of this game to the way people laugh at someone who must lie down.

Play continues until only one player has any cards left. He may not make any more captures, but wins 5 units from the pot. All uncaptured cards are finally won by the dealer.

Each player then either wins 1 unit for every pair of cards he has won in excess of eight cards, or pays 1 unit for every pair of cards he has won short of eight cards.

If the dealer overlooks a mournival on the table, the person who notices it first can take it.

If a player captures only one table card when he could have taken three, anyone who notices can take the other pair.

16 Adding-up games

'Adders' appropriately describes those arithmetical games where each in turn plays a card to the table and announces the total value of all cards so far played. Such games are popular in eastern Europe, but have percolated through to the West only towards the end of the twentieth century. The process is the same as that part of Cribbage where the cards are played and counted up to thirty-one, so Cribbage itself can be regarded as an adder with added attractions.

Cribbage (Six-card Cribbage)   2 players, 52 cards

Uncle Mort – Hey up, Lil, I'm sorry your Bob's snuffed it.
Mr Brandon – You'll have to look for a new Crib partner now, won't you?
Auntie Lil – There'll never be another one to equal my Bob. I'll never forget the way he used to add up the cards in his box. 'Fifteen 2, fifteen 4, 2 for me pair of Sevens and 1 for his nob.' Ooh, there was poetry and magic in them words, Mort.
Uncle Mort – Mebbe, Lil. But he'd got a bloody awful hand, hadn't he?

> Peter Tinniswood, *I Didn't Know You Cared*
> (BBC-TV, 1975)

Britain's national card game is, by any reckoning, one of the world's great games, albeit restricted to the English-speaking nations. First recorded in 1630, the invention of Cribbage is traditionally ascribed to Sir John Suckling (1609–42) – poet, playwright, soldier, wit, courtier, eventual rebel and probable suicide – though it obviously derives from a sixteenth-century game called Noddy. Throughout the seventeenth and eighteenth centuries Cribbage enjoyed the patronage of royalty and the aristocracy, which, however, it subsequently lost to the challenge of Whist and Bridge. It currently enjoys the status of being the only game legally playable on licensed premises (pubs and clubs) without special permission from the local authorities, and boasts an estimated minimum of two million tournament players, in addition to an unknown, but hardly smaller, number of domestic players.

A distinctive feature of the game is its associated scoring equipment.

The Cribbage board is a handy device, as old as the game itself, and designed to keep simple but accurate track of the respective scores which are made in dribs and drabs as play proceeds. The basic model contains 60 holes on each side and an extra one at each end. Each player sticks a coloured peg (or a plain old match-stick) in the end-hole nearest himself, and throughout the game advances it one hole per point scored, up the outside line and back down the inside, returning to the end-hole for a winning count of 61. When the game is played up to 121, the peg travels 'twice round the board' before returning to the end-hole, though 121- and even 181-hole boards are also obtainable. Each player uses two pegs, and, upon scoring one or more points, takes out the trailing peg and replaces it ahead of the former leading peg by the appropriate amount. This serves as a double-check on accuracy, otherwise one could easily take a lone peg out, do the calculation, and then forget where it came from. The posher boards contain storage compartments for the pegs, and some sport additional holes in which to record the number of games won.

Described first is Six-card Cribbage, the standard modern game for two players.

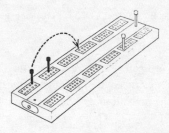

Cribbage board designed for play up to 61, or 121 if played twice round. Scores are recorded up the outside and down the inside row of holes on one side of the board for each player. In this illustration 'black' stands at 8 points and is about to increase his score to 16 by transferring his back peg 8 holes in front of his leader, while 'white' stands at 10 points made on one deal, as can be seen from the fact that his back peg has not yet moved from the '0/61' position. The two-peg system guards against inaccurate scoring.

Preliminaries Two play, using a 52-card pack ranking A23456789 TJQK.
Object To be the first to score 121 over as many deals as necessary.

Scores are recorded by moving pegs round a Cribbage board ('pegging').

Deal The player cutting the lower card deals first (Ace lowest), after which the deal alternates. (That's the traditional rule. Modern players corrupted by Bridge tend to declare, 'Ace high, high card deals.') Deal six cards each in ones, starting with non-dealer.

The discard Each player discards two cards face down to form a 'crib' of four cards. Their aim in discarding is to keep a hand of four cards which form scoring combinations. The four crib cards belong to the dealer. He may not turn them up yet, but any scoring combinations they may contain will eventually be added to his total.

Combinations The combinations and their scores are:

1. *Fifteen* (2). Two or more cards totalling 15, counting Ace 1, numerals at face value, courts 10 each.

2. *Pair* (2). Two cards of the same rank.

3. *Prial (Pair Royal)* (6). Three of the same rank.

4. *Double Pair Royal* (12). Four of the same rank.

5. *Run* (1 per card). Three or more cards in ranking order.

6. *Flush* (4 or 5). Four cards of the same suit in one hand.

Starter Non-dealer lifts the top half of the undealt pack, the dealer removes the top card of the bottom half and sets it face up on top as the starter. If it is a Jack the dealer pegs 2 'for his heels', provided that he remembers to claim it before any card is played.

Play Starting with non-dealer, each in turn plays a card face up to the table in front of himself and announces the total face value of all cards so far played by both.

For making the total exactly 15, peg 2 points. For making exactly 31, peg 2 points. You may not bring the total beyond 31, but must play if you can do so without reaching or exceeding 31. If you can't play without going over 31, you say 'Go'. The other then adds as many more cards as possible without exceeding 31, scoring 2 for making 31 exactly, or 1 for anything less (not both). If any cards remain in hand, the cards played so far are turned face down, and the next in turn to play begins a new series. When one player runs out of cards, the other continues alone.

Points are also pegged for pairs and runs made by cards laid out successively in the play. A card matching the rank of the previous one played scores 2 for the pair; if the next played also matches, it scores 6; and the fourth, if it matches, 12.

If a card just played completes an uninterrupted run of three or more in conjunction with the cards played in immediately preceding succession, the run is scored at the rate of 1 per card.

> Example: Annie plays 5, Benny 7, Annie 6 and pegs 3 for the run. If Benny then plays 4 or 8 he pegs 4. If instead he played 3 he would peg nothing, having broken the sequence; but Annie could then play 4 and reconstitute it for 5 points.

> ☞ Flushes are ignored in the play to 31. Some wrongly believe that runs also don't count in the two-hand game. They may be confused by the fact that a run is broken by the interruption of a paired card. For example, in the consecutive play of 6 7 7 8, the second Seven breaks the run, which therefore doesn't count.

The show Each player, starting with non-dealer, picks up his four hand cards and spreads them face up. Counting these and the starter as a five-card hand, he then scores for any and all combinations it may contain – fifteens, pairs, prials, runs and flushes. A given card may be used in more than one combination, and more than once in the same combination, provided that at least one other associated card is different each time.

A flush in the hand counts 4, or 5 if its suit matches the starter's. A player holding the Jack of the same suit as the starter also pegs 1 'for his nob'. (If the starter is a Jack, neither player reckons for his nob, as it is overridden by the '2 for his heels'.)

3	3	6	6	9	= 14		7	7	7	A	A	= 20		5	5	J	J	J!	= 21
J!	Q	Q	Q	K	= 16		7	8	8	9	9	= 20		5	5	5	10	10	= 22
6	7	8	9	9	= 16		7	7	7	8	8	= 20		4	5	5	5	6	= 23
2	6	7	7	8	= 16		6	6	9	9	9	= 20		5	5	5	J	J!	= 23
A	A	2	2	3	= 16		6	6	7	7	8	= 20		7	7	7	7	A	= 24
2	3	4	4	4	= 17		3	3	4	4	5	= 20		4	4	4	4	7	= 24
5	5	J	Q	K	= 17		3	3	6	6	6	= 20		4	5	5	6	6	= 24
3	3	3	6	6	= 18		3	4	4	4	4	= 20		6	7	7	8	8	= 24
5	5	J!	Q	K	= 18		7	7	7	8	9	= 21		7	7	8	8	9	= 24
3	3	4	5	5	= 20		3	3	3	4	5	= 21		5	5	5	5	10	= 28
4	4	4	7	7	= 20		4	5	6	6	6	= 21		5	5	5	5	J!	= 29

Some hands requiring care at counting. J! denotes 1 for his nob. No possible five-card combination can score 19.

Counting the crib Finally, dealer turns the crib face up and pegs for it as a five-card hand exactly as above, except that a flush only counts if all five are in suit.

Score Play ceases the moment either player 'pegs out' by reaching 121, no matter what stage of the game has been reached. If the loser has failed to reach 91, he is lurched (or 'in the lurch', or, in American parlance, skunked), and loses a double stake.

Muggins (optional rule). If a player fails to notice a feature he could have scored for, his opponent may point it out and peg it himself.

Cribbage variants

Five-card Crib

The original five-card game for two players remains the standard version in English club, tournament and championship play, probably because its practitioners more frequently play the partnership game, in which a five-card deal remains the norm. The differences are as follows:

At start of play, non-dealer pegs '3 for last' as compensation for dealer's having the first crib. Deal five each, discard two. Play up to 31 once only: any cards left in hand remain unplayed. A flush in hand counts 3, or 4 with the starter. A flush in the crib scores 5 if it matches the suit of the starter, but is otherwise worthless. Game is 61 points, and a loser who fails to reach 45 is in the lurch.

Seven-card Crib

Deal seven cards each and discard two. Game is 181. Rarely played.

Eight-card Crib

According to *Hoyle's Games Improved* (1820): 'Eight-card Cribbage is sometimes played, but very seldom.' I can find no contemporary account of it, and suspect it to be a joke name for what is described under that heading as follows:

> Some ingenious folk invented a game of chance they styled playing at cribbage by hackney-coaches; that is, two persons placed themselves at a window in some great thoroughfare or street; one would take all the coaches from the

right, the other from the left; the excise duty figures on the doors of the carriages were reckoned as cards in the show, the coachman as ten for turn-up, and every other person that happened to sit, stand, or hold at the back of any of them, was a called a noddy, and scored one.

Losing Cribbage

Play as at any form of standard Crib, but the first to reach 121 is the loser.

Auction Cribbage

(by Hubert Phillips) Before the starter is turned (see note on starter above), each in turn, Dealer first, states how many points he will pay (deduct from his score) in return for the privilege of the crib. The higher bidder promptly subtracts that amount, and play proceeds as in any of the above games as if he were the normal dealer.

Three-hand Crib

(cut-throat) Deal five cards each and one card face down to the crib, to which each then discards another one, making four in all. Eldest leads and counts his hand first; dealer plays and counts his hand and crib last. Each player scores for himself.

Three-hand Crib

(solo) The dealer's two opponents play as a partnership. Deal five each and six to the dealer. The partners pass one card each to the dealer, who from his hand discards four to the crib. Play as above, except that each partner scores the total made by them both.

Four-hand Crib

(partnership) Deal five each, discard one each to the crib. Eldest leads and shows first. Pegging is done by dealer's and leader's partners. Each partnership scores the amount made by both its members.

Cribbage Patience

Deal sixteen cards face up to form a square of four rows and columns, placing each new card adjacent to any previous one. Turn the 17th up as a starter. Score for each row and column as for a five-card hand including the starter. Win if you make at least 61.

Noddy

2 players, 52 cards

O beastly nody, wythoute brayne . . .
Bale, *Apology* (1550)

'Noddy' means a fool or simpleton – one who tends to nod off at any opportunity. This parent of Cribbage is known from 1589, but could conceivably have been identical with, or an elaboration of, an earlier game called One-and-Thirty.

Deal three cards each, then cut the pack to enable non-dealer to turn the top card of the bottom half and set it face up on top. If it's a Jack, dealer immediately pegs 2 for 'Knave Noddy'.

A game is 31 points over as many deals as it takes.

Each in turn, starting with non-dealer, announces and scores for (but does not reveal) any combination he can make from the four cards comprising the turn-up and the three in his own hand. The possible combinations and their scores are:

pairs	pair	2
	pair royal	6
	double pair royal	12
points	fifteen	2
	twenty-five	2
run	three	1
	four	2
flush	three	3
	four	4

If a Jack was not turned, then Knave Noddy is the Jack of the same suit as the turn-up, and its holder (if any) pegs 1 point for it.

If non-dealer reaches 31 for combinations in hand, dealer does not count his, and the game ends. If dealer reaches 31, the game ends and there is no play-off.

If neither reaches 31, then each in turn, starting with non-dealer, plays a card face up to the table and announces the combined total of all cards so far played. Ace counts 1, numerals at face value, and courts 10 each.

If in the play-off a card makes a pair, run or flush with those immediately preceding it, its player pegs the appropriate amount. For this purpose, runs and flushes of more than four cards count 1 point per constituent card.

> Example: If the cards played are ♥6 ♣4 ♣7 and the next plays ♦5, he pegs 4 for the run. Or, if he plays ♣5, he scores 4 for the run plus 3 for the successive clubs.

Peg 2 for making the total 15, 25, or 31 exactly. Play ceases either when one player reaches a total score of 31 for game, or when the total value of cards played reaches or exceeds 31. If it is exceeded, the player who last kept it under 31 pegs 1 point.

There is only one round of play up to 31, unlike the play of Six-card Cribbage.

Costly Colours
2 players, 52 cards

This fascinating relative of Cribbage and probable co-descendant of Noddy was first described by Cotton in 1674 and was occasionally mentioned as a regional game in the eighteenth century. The following description communicated by Robert Reid derives from an 1874 edition of *Shropshire Folklore*, itself partly based on a booklet entitled *The Royal Game of Costly Colours* published in Shrewsbury in 1805. Arthur Taylor, the pub-game researcher, tells me that he saw it played in a Lancashire pub under the name 'Costly' in the 1980s, but, unfortunately, did not realize its historical significance at the time and has since forgotten the location.

Preliminaries Cards rank A23456789TJQK. Numerals count face value, courts 10 each, Ace 1 or 11 as its player declares. Deal three each in ones and turn the next for trumps. This is called the 'deck card'. If it's a Jack or a Deuce, Dealer pegs 4 'for his heels'.

Mogging The players may now 'mog'. This is done by each passing a card from his hand face down to the other. If either refuses, the other pegs one point for the refusal. If either gives away a Jack or a Deuce, he may first peg 2 points for it (4 if in trumps). If he neglects to do so, the other may score for it when the final declarations are made.

Play Each in turn, starting with non-dealer, plays a card face up to the table in front of himself, announcing the total face value of all cards so far played. In play, scores are pegged for making sequences and points, at the rate of 1 per card.

A *sequence* is three or more cards in ranking order (Ace low).

Example: Annie plays 8, Benny plays 6, Annie plays 7 and pegs 3 for the sequence. If Benny then plays 5 or 9, he pegs 4.

The *points* are 15, 25, 31, the last known as the 'grand point' or 'hitter'. A player making any such total pegs as many points as cards involved. Example: 7 4 4 scores 3 for the fifteen. If the next adds a court or a Ten, he pegs 4 for the twenty-five; and if the next plays a Six, he pegs 5 for the 'hitter' or 'grand point' of thirty-one.

The count may not exceed thirty-one. The first player unable to play without busting says 'Go!', whereupon the other may add as many more cards as he can without busting. The last to play scores 1 for the go, plus 1 per card if he hits thirty-one exactly.

If any cards remain in hand, those so far played are turned down, and the next in turn to play begins another series as before.

Hand scores The players then reveal their cards and score for any of the following features they can make. Non-dealer counts first. Each player's hand is considered to consist of four cards, i.e. his own three plus the deck card. Four types of combination are recognized:

1. *Points*	15	1 per constituent card
	25	1 per constituent card
	31 (Hitter)	1 per constituent card
2. *Jacks and Deuces*	Jack or Deuce of trumps	4 'for his nob'
	Any other Jack or Deuce	2
3. *Pairs and prials*	Pair (two of same rank)	2
	Prial (three alike)	9
	Double prial (four alike)	18
4. *Colours*	Three in colour	2
	Three in suit	3
	Four in colour, two in suit	4
	Four in colour, three in suit	5
	Four in suit	6 for 'Costly Colours'

Sequences don't count.

A given card or cards may be counted as belonging to more than one combination, but may not be counted more than once within each of categories 3 and 4. For example, if you count a prial you cannot count separately for any pair it contains, and if you count four in suit, you cannot also count for three in suit or any in colour.

Examples (spades are trumps):

hand   *deck card*

fifteens 2-4-6-8, twenty-fives 3-6, pair 2, colours 5 = total 21

fifteens 2-4-6; twenty-fives 3-6-9; Jacks 4-6-8, prial 9, colours 2 = total 34

fifteen or twenty-five 4 (Ace counts 1 or 11, but not both), Deuces 4-6, pair 2, colours 4 = total 16.

Game Play up to 121.

Four-hand Four may play in partnerships. Each player mogs with his partner, and the dealer, if refused, may mog alone by taking the card below the deck-card and substituting a card he does not want.

Comment According to the Shropshire source, 'his nob' denotes the Jack or Deuce of a suit other than trump. I query this, and have here followed Cribbage terminology. In Salopian dialect, a score of zero in a single hand is called 'a cock's nist'.

Counting games (Adders)

Fifty-One

(2–5p, 32c) Deal five each from a 32-card pack and turn the next face up to start a discard pile. Cards count as follows:

A	K	Q	J	T	9	8	7
11	4	3	2	−1	0	8	7

Each in turn draws a card from stock (so long as any remain), plays a card face up and announces the total value of all cards so far played, including the starter. Whoever raises the total above 50 loses.

Hundred

(2–6p, 32c) Divide the cards as evenly as possible. If any remain, leave them face up to start the discard pile and announce their total; otherwise, start at zero. Cards count as follows:

A	K	Q	J	T	9	8	7
11	4	3	2	10	9	8	7

Each in turn plays a card to the table, adding its value to the previous total and announcing the new one. A player wins by making the total exactly 100, but loses by causing it to jump over the 100 mark. It may be agreed to continue play with another scoring point at 200.

Jubilee

(2–7p, 57c + 4☆) A Czech game. Make a 61-card pack containing one heart of each rank, two spades of each rank, two each of club numerals from Ace to Nine only (no Tens or courts), and four Jokers. Cards count as follows, plus in black suits, minus in hearts:

A	K	Q	J	T	9	8	7	☆
15	10	10	10	10	9	8	7	0

Deal eight each and stack the rest face down. Eldest starts by playing a black card and announcing its value. Each in turn thereafter plays a further card, announces the total value of all cards so far played, and draws a replacement from stock so long as any remain.

No one may bring the total below zero. Anyone unable to make a legal play must show his hand and pass.

Making the total an exact multiple of 25, whether by addition or subtraction, scores 10 for a 'jubilee', or 20 if it is also a multiple of 100. Anyone causing the total to skip over a jubilee instead of hitting it exactly, whether by addition or subtraction, loses 5 points.

When all cards have been played the final total should be 189.

Ninety-Nine

(3–13p, 52c) Said to be a Gypsy game. Deal three cards each and stack the rest face down. Play goes to the left, but may change. Each in turn plays a card face up to the table, announces the total face value of all cards so far played, and draws a replacement from stock.

Cards count as follows:

black Ace	*ad lib.*	Seven	7
red Ace	2	Eight	8
Two	2	Nine	*makes* 99
Three	0	Ten	*minus* 10
Four	0	Jack	10 *and reverse*
Five	5	Queen	10
Six	6	King	10

A black Ace brings the total to anything its player chooses, from 0 to 99.

A Nine automatically makes the total 99, and can therefore be followed only by a Three, Four, Ten, or black Ace.

A Jack, besides counting 10, reverses the order of play – that is, the next card is played by whoever played the card preceding the Jack, and so on.

The total may not exceed 99. The first player unable to play without busting loses a life. The first to lose three lives is the overall loser.

Obstacle Race (Hindernislauf)

(2–6p, 32c) Recorded only by Jürgen Göring in *Stich um Stich* (Berlin, 1977); possibly his invention. It has some nice points, and lends itself to further elaboration.

Divide the cards evenly. If other than four play, the two remaining cards are laid face up on the table to start the sequence, and the dealer announces their combined point-total. Cards count as follows:

A	K	Q	J	T	9	8	7
11	4	±3	2	10	9	8	7

Queens count plus or minus 3, ad lib, and are the only cards able to reduce the total.

Each in turn plays a card face up to the sequence, announcing the combined total of all cards so far played. The 'obstacles' are 55, 66, 77, 88, 99, and 111. A player scores one point for hitting an obstacle precisely, but loses a point for skipping over one, regardless of direction.

Play continues until the total reaches or exceeds 120, then starts again at zero. The winner is the player with the highest score when all cards have been played.

Twenty-Nine

(2–8p, 52c) Best played by four sitting crosswise in partnerships. If other numbers play, remove as many Tens as necessary to ensure everyone gets the same number of cards. Deal them all out in ones. Eldest leads to the first 'trick', announcing the face value of the card led. Aces and courts count 1 each, other numerals at face value. Each in turn plays a card and announces the new total, provided it does not exceed 29. Anyone who cannot play without busting must pass. Keep going until someone makes it exactly 29. That player wins the trick for his partnership, turns it down, and leads to the next. The winning side is that which takes the majority of cards. If any Tens were removed, the last trick is not played. The earliest description of this game (Ostrow, 1945) says the remaining unplayed cards don't count, but there seems no good reason not to simply add them to one's own pile of winnings.

Twenty-Nine is said to be a children's game. Adults find it boring; but, with a bit of creative imagination, it can easily be elaborated into something more interesting and skill-demanding.

Wit and Reason

(I) (2p, 52c) The game which Cotton (1674) rightly qualifies as '*so call'd*' results, like Noughts & Crosses, in a foregone conclusion. One player takes all the red cards and one all the black. Each in turn plays a card face up to the table and announces the total value of all cards so far played. Ace counts 1, numerals face value, courts 10 each. If you can't play without exceeding 31 you must pass. The other player will then win by making it 31 exactly. (You can easily work out which card wins for the first player.)

(II) (2p, 24c) The mathematical hustlers modern equivalent of this game requires more wit and reason than Cotton's original. Take out all the lower numerals from Ace to Six and arrange these 24 cards face up on the table. Each in turn takes a card from the array and announces the total value of all cards so far taken. The player who makes exactly 31 wins. This version has two levels of strategy. When the punter discovers what appears to be a winning move, the hustler raises the stakes and thwarts it by switching to Strategy Two.

Don't forget . . .
- Play to the left (clockwise) unless otherwise stated.
- Eldest or Forehand means the player to the left of the dealer in left-handed games, to the right in right-handed games.
- T = Ten, p = players, pp = in fixed partnerships, c = cards, † = trump, ☆ = Joker.

17 **First out wins**

There are many and various games where you shed cards from your hand in accordance with certain rules, and seek either to be the first to go out by getting rid of them all, or to avoid being the last player left in when everyone else has gone out. This chapter covers the 'first out wins' variety. Typically, everyone seeks to reduce their hand by playing to a discard pile one or more cards that match or beat the card last played. They include:

Stops group
(Newmarket etc.) Light-hearted staking games where players contribute one at a time to a sequence of cards in numerical order, but, instead of each playing in rotation, the next higher card is added by whoever happens to hold it. The defining feature is that some cards are left undealt and never drawn, and thereby stop the sequence from following its proper course.

Eights group
(Crazy Eights etc.) An ever-popular group in which players try to shed cards by matching the preceding ones, and, if unable, must enlarge their hands by drawing from a stockpile.

Eleusis
An invention of Bob Abbott that has become a classic. It belongs here because players try to shed their cards by matching, as in Crazy Eights, but the rule of matching is known only to the player who devised it, which means the others have to deduce it.

Climbing games
(Zheng Shàngyóu etc.) Variations on a Chinese game that have recently migrated to the West under a distinctive range of somewhat unsavoury titles.

Newmarket

A light-hearted staking game still played among friends and family, and the chief British representative of the Stops family. These started out as serious gambling games of the French aristocracy, being much favoured by Cardinal Mazarin. Later, they became genteel family games, played for penny stakes, as suggested by references in both Sheridan and Dickens to the popularity of Pope Joan with the rural clergy. Their subsequent decline in domestic favour may have been caused by the success of Rummy games, which occupy a similar social position. But they are far from dead, and nowadays keep re-emerging in various forms as pub games, providing the researcher with a promising field of study. The rules of Newmarket vary. The following are those current at my local (South London) Day Centre.

Preliminaries Each player deals in turn and the turn to deal passes to the left. The four Kings are placed in the centre as a staking layout. The remaining cards are dealt round one at a time, the last card of each round going to a dead hand. It doesn't matter if some players get one more card than others. Everybody stakes an agreed amount on each King and to a separate kitty.

Object A game consists of several deals and ends when all the Kings have gone. In each deal the aim is to be the first out of cards.

The buy One player may 'buy' the spare hand in exchange for the hand dealt him. Dealer has the first option, which passes to the left until someone exercises it. Whoever buys pays a fixed stake to the kitty, except the dealer, who exchanges free.

Play Cards run in sequence A23456789TJQ. Whoever holds the lowest diamond starts by playing it face up to the table. The holder of the next higher consecutive diamond plays it, then the next, and so on for as long as the sequence continues. Cards are played face up in front of their holders, not to a spread on the table.

Eventually the sequence will come to an end, usually because the next higher diamond is in the dead hand. A new sequence is then started by whoever played the last card. That player must start with a suit of different colour, and with the lowest card held of it.

Example. Annie leads ♦3-♦4, Connie plays ♦5, Barney adds ♦6-♦7. No one has the Eight. Barney, to play, holds ♠3-9-J ♥A-2-9-Q ♣8-Q ♦2, and must therefore start the new sequence with either ♠3 or ♣8.

If the player on lead has none of the required colour, the turn passes to the left until someone can change colour. If no one can, the round ends and the next deal ensues.

Alternatively, the sequence ends when someone plays a Queen. That player immediately wins everything staked on the King of that suit, and starts a new sequence with the lowest card held of a different colour. The stripped King is then removed, and remains out of play till the end of the game. In subsequent deals, whoever plays the Queen of an absent King has nothing to win, and merely starts a new sequence.

End of round The round ends in either of two ways. Whoever plays the last card from their hand thereby ends the play and wins the kitty.

Alternatively, it ends when a sequence has been finished and no one can change colour to start a new one, though all have at least one card in hand. In this case the kitty is carried forward and increased on the next deal.

Last King When only one King remains, a new rule applies. A player who is dealt the Queen of that King's suit says 'Bury the Jack' (or 'Johnny'). If it is not in the dead hand, then whoever holds that Jack must swap their hand for the dead one, free of charge. If the Queen-holder also holds the Jack, or any longer sequence, they order the burial of the next lower card. For example, the holder of T-J-Q says 'Bury the Nine'. If the Queen is in the dead hand, the Jack-holder says 'Bury the Ten'. If the Jack is in the dead hand . . . (etc.).

End of game The game ends as soon as someone plays the Queen matching the fourth and last King, thereby winning both the stake on the King and the kitty.

Original Newmarket

Ace counts low and the layout is an Ace, King, Queen and Jack, one of each suit, taken from another pack. Deal the same number of cards, as many as possible, to each player and to a dead hand, and add any remainder to the latter. Eldest leads from any suit, but must lead the

Newmarket. West dealt. No one bought the spare hand, though South, holding too many low cards and an imbalance of black and red suits, would have benefited by it. The lowest diamond was led by West and followed by North, who played ♠4 when the ♦4 failed to appear. The play continued: ♣4–Q, ♦5–Q, ♣5, ♥A–3, ♣A–4, 'No red', ♥9–10, ♣Q, ♥6, ♠2 and East is out. Depositing three Kings in one deal is quite rare.

lowest he holds of it. The starter of a new sequence need not change colour, but in some circles must at least change suit. Whoever plays a card matching one in the layout by rank and suit wins everything staked on it, but the layout card is not removed from the table. Whoever plays their last card ends the current deal and wins one chip from each opponent for each card left in hand.

Michigan (Boodle, Stops)

The equivalent American game plays like the original version of Newmarket, except that Ace counts high (23456789TJQKA). Before play the dealer may exchange his hand for the dead hand if he wishes, sight unseen, or may auction this privilege to the highest bidder. The staking layout may be elaborated with additional cards or combinations, such as Jack-Queen of the same suit. In this case whoever plays both cards wins that stake.

Pink Nines

A pub game in line of descent from Comet. Everyone stakes an equal amount. Deal four random cards face down to a dead hand and distribute the rest evenly, any surplus also being dead. Cards rank 23456789TJQKA. Eldest starts by playing his lowest card and as many more as he can in ascending sequence on it, regardless of suit. When he is stuck, the next in turn takes over and continues the sequence. Both ♥9 and ♦9 are wild and may be played as any card. If you can play, you must. When no one can go, the first who was blocked starts a new sequence. Aces are stops, and whoever plays one starts a new sequence. A new sequence must be based on one's lowest card, but, given two or more equally low cards, the choice is free. First out wins the pool.

Comet (Commit)

Ancestor of Pink Nines, named upon the appearance of Halley's comet in 1758. Strip out ♦8 and enough Eights and Sevens to divide the cards equally. A single pool is formed, which goes to the first player to go out. Play cards in ascending suit-sequence. The ♦9, or Comet, must be played either when the game is blocked or when its holder, having played regularly, cannot otherwise continue the sequence. The player on his left may follow it with ♦T or the card in sequence with the one before it, this privilege passing round, if he cannot, until somebody can. Whoever plays the comet wins 2 chips from each opponent, and each King played wins 1. First out wins the pool, plus 2 from each opponent and 1 extra for each King unplayed.

There is also a ridiculously complicated two-hand version played with a doubled pack.

Pope Joan

Delightful Victorian family game played with an elaborate piece of stake-and-layout equipment for which substitutes can easily be made. The 51-card pack lacks ♦8, making it difficult to play ♦9, known as Pope Joan (also, in other contexts, as the Curse of Scotland). The eight

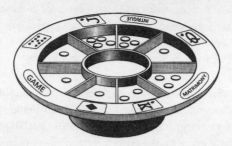

Pope Joan. Stakes are deposited in the labelled compartments. All games of the Stops family involve such layouts, which may be simply made by sticking old playing-cards on sheets of paper – or, more elaborately but attractively, card cut-outs in the compartments of small cake-baking tins.

divisions of the board are labelled Pope (♦9), Matrimony (K-Q), Intrigue (Q-J), Ace, King, Queen, Jack, Game. Ace is high.

Dealer starts by setting 6 counters on Pope, 2 on Matrimony, 2 on Intrigue, and 1 on each other. He deals all the cards around as at Newmarket, including a dead hand. The last card of all is turned for 'trumps', and, if it is Pope, Ace, King, Queen or Jack, he wins the stake from the appropriate division. Eldest leads by playing the lowest card held of any suit he chooses. Whoever holds the next higher card of the same suit plays it, and so on until no one can play. The last to play then starts a new sequence with the lowest card held of any desired suit.

Whoever plays the Ace, King, Queen or Jack of trumps wins the contents of the corresponding compartment. The contents of Matrimony can be taken only when the same player plays both King and Queen of the trump suit, and of Intrigue only by someone who plays both Jack and Queen. (Anyone fortunate enough to hold and play J-Q-K-A of trumps, therefore, collects from six of the eight pools.) First out wins the stake on Game. Everybody else pays him one counter for each card remaining in his own hand, except that a player who is left with ♦9 in hand is exempt from this penalty. Unclaimed stakes are carried forward to the next deal.

Spinado

Simplified Pope Joan played with a 47-card pack made by stripping out ♦8 and four Deuces. Dealer sets 12 counters on a position marked Matrimony (♦K♦Q), 6 on Intrigue (♦Q♦J), and 6 on Game, and everyone else stakes 3 on Game. Deal and play as at Newmarket. Aces are low, and are necessarily stops because there are no Deuces. The ♦A is known as Spinado, or Spin. Its holder may turn any card he plays into a stop by promptly covering it with ♦A and declaring 'And Spin!' This nets him 3 counters from each opponent, and he starts a new sequence. Anyone playing a King immediately receives 1 counter from each opponent, or 2 for ♦K. The contents of Matrimony or Intrigue go only to a player able to play both cards concerned, and the player of all three wins both pools in addition to the ♦K payment. First out wins the stakes on Game, and need not then stake on it in the next deal, unless he happens to be dealer. He also receives from each opponent 1 counter for each card left in hand, doubled from the holder of Spin if he failed to play it.

Yellow Dwarf

(Gelber Zwerg, Nain Jaune) The European ancestor of Pope Joan had staking compartments for ♥K ♠Q ♣J ♦T and a yellow dwarf representing ♦7. Aces are low and cards go in sequence regardless of suit.

Play or Pay

Deal all the cards out as far as they will go. Eldest starts by playing any card face up to the table to start a discard pile. Each in turn thereafter must either play the next higher card of the same suit or else pay a counter to a pool. The sequence ends when it reaches an Ace, or any other card that can't be followed. Whoever played the last card of the sequence starts a new one with any card. First out of cards wins the pool, plus 1 chip for each card left in other players' hands.

Snip-Snap-Snorum (or -Snorem)

A distant relative of the Stops family, referred to by Fanny Burney as early as 1782, and still recorded as a children's game. Deal the cards round as far as they will go. Eldest plays any card. The next in turn who is able to pair it does so and says 'Snip', the next also matches rank and says 'Snap', and the next plays the fourth of its kind, announces 'Snorum!', discards the quartet, and leads afresh. Anyone unable to match the previous card misses a turn, and in some versions pays a counter to its player. If two or more are able to play consecutively, the first of them is 'snipped' and pays 1 counter to a pool if he played the first of its rank; if he played the second he is 'snapped' and pays 2, if the third, he is 'snored' and pays 3. The pool goes to the first out of cards, who also receives one counter from each opponent for each card left in hand.

Earl of Coventry

differs only in its announcements: (1st card) 'There's as good as [Ace] can be', (2nd) 'There's an Ace as good as he', (3rd) 'There's the best of all the three', (4th) 'And there's the Earl of Coventreeeee' . . .

Jig

As above, but each in turn plays the next higher card of the same suit, and the player of the fourth in sequence starts a new series. The sequence is cyclic, passing through K-A-2.

Schnipp-Schnapp-Schnurr-Burr-Basilorum

The German equivalent of Jig, with five cards to a sequence instead of four.

Muggins

A game played by Victorian children, including Mr Pooter (see *Diary of a Nobody*). Deal one card face up to the table if three play, four if four, two if five, four if six, three if seven. These cards are the mugginses. Divide the rest evenly among the players. Players may not examine their cards but must stack them face down on the table in front of themselves. The aim is to be the first out of cards.

Each in turn flips the top card of his stack and places it face up on a muggins that is one rank higher or lower than the one turned – for example, a Six turned will go on a Seven or a Five. Aces and Kings may not be played on each other.

Anyone unable to place the card they turn must place it face up on the table before them to start a discard pile. Thereafter, a turned card must be played to a muggins if possible, otherwise to the next higher- or lower-ranking card on top of the faced pile of the nearest player to one's left, otherwise – if it won't legally fit anywhere – to one's own discard pile, where it need not match.

Anyone who is correctly challenged for breaking a rule – by discarding to his own pile if it will fit that of a player nearer his own left, or to a player's pile if it will fit on a muggins – is himself a Muggins. Everybody else takes the top card from their face-down pile and gives it to the offending Muggins, who must place them at the bottom of his own.

When no cards remain in your playing pile, turn your discard pile face down and continue from there. The winner is the first to have no cards remaining in either their playing or discard pile.

Domino (Card Dominoes, Fan Tan, Parliament, Spoof Sevens) 3–8 players, 52 cards

A two-dimensional relative of Eights, very suitable for children, but not without elements of skill.

Preliminaries Any number of players, but ideally six or seven, use a 52-card pack running A23456789TJQK in each suit. Use small cards or a large table. Everyone starts by paying an agreed sum into the pool. Deal all the cards out in ones. It doesn't matter if some players have one more than others.

Object To be the first to shed all one's cards.

Play Eldest starts by playing any Seven face up to the table. If unable, he pays 1 to the pool and the turn passes. With a Seven in place, the next in turn must play one of the following cards: the Six of the same suit to the left of the Seven, or the Eight of the same suit to its right, or any other Seven below it. Thereafter, each in turn must play either a Seven, or the next higher or lower card of a suit-sequence, in such a way as to build up four rows of thirteen cards, each of the same suit and reading from Ace at the extreme left to King at the extreme right. (See the illustration on page 144.)

Penalties Anyone unable to play at his turn contributes 1 counter to the pool. Anyone who fails to play, although able to do so, pays 3 to each opponent, plus 5 to the holders of the Six and Eight of a suit if he holds the Seven of it and fails to play. Not that this obliges him to play a Seven if prefers to play otherwise: holding up Sevens is all part of the strategy.

Going out. First out sweeps the pool and gets 1 counter from each opponent for each card left in hand.

Variant In Five or Nine (or Five and Nine), the first person able to play may start with a Five or a Nine. Whichever is chosen must be adhered to as the foundation rank for each row for the rest of that hand.

Crazy Eights (Swedish Rummy)

2–7 players, 52 cards

Crazy Eights is not so much a game as a basic pattern of play on which a wide variety of changes can be rung. Anyone can invent new rules for it, and combine them with old rules to produce a version that can be explored for fun and then changed again when new ideas come up. The basic pattern itself forms a game that was called Eights when it first appeared in the 1930s. Crazy Eights is what it became when players started elaborating it.

A feature that has become common to most games of this group in recent years is that of prohibiting anyone from explaining the rules to beginners, who must be left to pick them up by trial and error, and will of necessity lose many deals before being able to play with consistent success.

Cards 52, or 104 (two packs) if six or more play.

Deal Five each, or seven if only two are playing. Stack the rest face down as a stock, then take the top card and set it face down on the table to start the discard pile. If the starter is an Eight, bury it in the stock and turn up the next card.

Object To be the first to shed all one's cards.

Play Each in turn, starting with Eldest, plays a card face up to the discard pile, which is spread slightly so all remain visible. Each card played must match the previous card by either rank or suit. Eights are wild: you can play one whenever you like, and nominate a suit for the next player to follow, which needn't be that of the Eight itself. Anyone unable or unwilling to follow must draw cards from the top of the stock, adding them to his hand until he eventually plays one, or the stock runs out.

Ending Play ends the moment anyone plays their last card, or when no one can match the last card. The player who went out collects from each opponent a payment equivalent to the total face value of cards remaining in the latter's hand, counting each Eight 50, courts 10 each, others face value. If the game blocks, the player with the lowest combined face value of cards remaining in hand scores from each opponent the difference between their two hand values. In the four-hand partnership game both partners must go out to end the game.

Rockaway

The same, but Aces are wild instead of Eights and count 15 each at end of play.

Hollywood Eights

Eights count 20 each and Aces 15. Several games are played and scored simultaneously, as at Hollywood Gin (q.v.). Game is 100 points.

Mau-Mau

(3–5p, 32c) This is apparently the earliest member of the family to require beginners to learn the rule by play rather than by instruction. Deal five each from a 32-card pack, turn the next as a starter, and stack the rest face down. Play as Crazy Eights, except that Jacks are wild instead of Eights. You must call 'Mau' upon playing your last card, or 'Mau-Mau' if it is a Jack, in which case you win double. The penalty for not doing so is to draw a card from stock and keep playing. Cards left in others' hands score against them thus: each Ace 11, Ten 10, King 4, Queen 3, Jack 2 (or 20), others zero (or face value). End when someone reaches 100 penalties.

Neuner

('Nines') (3-5p, 32c) As Mau-Mau, except that a Joker is added, and it and all Nines are wild.

Go Boom

(3–10p, 52c) This game only differs from Rolling Stone (see Durak family) in that players who cannot follow draw from stock instead of from the played-out cards.

Deal seven cards each (or, by some accounts, ten) from a full pack – or, if more than six play, a doubled pack of 104 cards – and stack the rest face down. Eldest leads any card face up. Each in turn thereafter must play a card of the same suit or rank if possible. A player unable to do so must draw cards from stock until able, or, when no cards remain in stock, must simply pass. When everyone has played or passed, the person who played the highest card of the suit led turns the played cards down and leads to the next 'trick'.

Play ceases the moment anyone plays the last card from their hand. That player scores the total values of all cards remaining in other players' hands, with Ace to Ten at face value and courts 10 each.

Switch (Two-Four-Jack, Black Jack)   2–7 players, 52 cards

This game became popular in the 1960s, and gave rise to a successful proprietary version called Uno. Play as Crazy Eights or Rockaway, except that a player unable to follow draws only one card from stock, and with the following special rules.

Aces are wild.

Twos Playing a Two forces the next in turn either to play a Two, or, if unable, to draw two cards from stock and miss a turn. If he draws, the next in turn may play in the usual way; but if he does play a Two, the next after him must either do likewise or draw four cards and miss a turn. Each successive playing of a Two increases by two the number of cards that must be drawn by the next player if he cannot play a Two himself, up to a maximum of eight.

Fours have the same powers, except that the number of cards to be drawn is four, eight, twelve or sixteen, depending on how many are played in succession.

Jacks Playing a Jack reverses ('switches') the direction of play and forces the preceding player to miss a turn, unless he, too, can play a Jack, thus turning the tables.

Twos, Fours and Jacks operate independently of one another. You cannot escape the demands of a Two by playing a Four instead, or of a Jack by playing a Two, and so on.

The game ends when a player wins by playing his last card. A player with two cards in hand must announce 'One left' or 'Last card' upon playing one of them.

The penalty for any infraction of the rules (including playing too slowly) is to draw two cards from stock.

The winner scores the face value of all cards left in other players' hands, with special values of 20 per Ace, 15 per Two, Four or Jack, and 10 per King and Queen.

Bartok (Warthog)

A form of Crazy Eights in which the winner of each round makes up a new rule of play. For example, Oedipus Jack means any Jack can be played on any Queen, regardless of suit, but not on any King, even of the same suit. (From Lisa Dusseault's website.)

Eleusis   4–8 players, 104–208 cards

Eleusis formally resembles a game of the Crazy Eights type, but turns the whole idea on its head by concealing the rule of matching that determines whether a given card can legally be played to the discard pile. The current dealer invents the rule and the players have to deduce what it is before they can successfully play their cards off. This involves a process of inductive thinking similar to that which underlies scientific investigation into the laws of Nature: you observe what happens, hypothesize a cause, test your hypothesis by predicting the outcome of experiments, modify it until it appears to work, then accept it as a theory so long as it continues to produce results. Eleusis was invented by American games inventor Robert Abbott in his student days, and was first described in Martin Gardner's *Mathematical Games* department of *Scientific American* in 1959. A more refined version appeared in *Abbott's New Card Games* (1963), and this further extension separately in 1977, to which the inventor has recently added some scoring refinements incorporated below. Abbott's brilliant innovation probably generated the current craze for requiring newcomers to games of the Crazy Eights family to pick the rules up as they go along.

Preliminaries From four to eight players start by shuffling two 52-card packs together. At least one other pack should be available, but must be kept apart until needed (if ever). Cards rank A23456789TJQK. Unless otherwise stated, an Ace counts as numeral 1, Jack as 11, Queen 12, and King 13.

Deal Nobody deals twice in the same session, but the dealership should not rotate regularly but be allocated at random to someone who has not yet dealt. The dealer receives no cards and plays a different role from the others. Deal fourteen to each other player, then one card face up as a starter, and stack the rest face down.

Players' object To deduce the rule that will enable them to play off their cards to a mainline sequence extending rightwards from the starter. A card can be played to the mainline only if it correctly follows a rule of play secretly specified by the dealer. Deductions are made by formulating and testing hypotheses as to what the rule might be, on the basis of information gained by noting which cards are accepted and which rejected by the dealer.

Dealer's object To devise a rule that is neither too easy nor too hard to deduce. A typical elementary rule is: 'If the last card is red, the next card played must be even; if it is black, the next must be odd.' The dealer writes this rule down on a piece of paper, and may refer to it at any time, but does not say what it is (though he may give clues, such as 'Colours are significant, but not individual suits').

Play Each in turn tries to play a card to the mainline. If the dealer says 'Right', it stays put and the player's turn ends. If not, it is replaced below the last card played in a 'sideline' extending at right angles to the mainline. If a sideline already exists for that card, it goes at the end of the sideline.

If you think you know The Rule, you can attempt to play a 'string' of two, three or four cards, of which you believe the first correctly follows the last mainline card and the others correctly follow that rule among themselves. Again, if the dealer says 'Right' they stay in place, but if 'Wrong' (and he won't say how many or which ones are wrong) they must be added to the latest sideline. In this case they should be overlapped, to show that they were attempted as a string and not one per turn.

When an attempt is declared wrong, and the incorrect card or cards have been added to the sideline, the dealer deals to the defaulting player twice the number of cards made in the attempt – that is, from two to eight cards as the case may be.

Can't play If you think you know The Rule, but have no card in hand that will go, you can declare 'Can't play'. In this case you must expose your cards so everyone can see them, and the dealer will say whether your claim is right or wrong.

If you're wrong, the dealer must play to the mainline any one of your cards that will fit, then deal you five more from the stock.

What happens if you're right depends on how many cards you have left. If five or more, the dealer counts your cards, puts them at the bottom of the stock, and deals you from the top of the stock a number of cards equivalent to four less than the number you held when you made the claim. If four or fewer, they go back into the stock and the game ends.

Adding another pack If four or fewer cards remain in stock after someone has been dealt more, shuffle them into the spare pack and set it face down as a new stock.

The Prophet If you think you know The Rule, you may, instead of simply playing all your cards out, seek to improve your eventual score by declaring yourself a Prophet and taking over the functions of the dealer (who, as the Ultimate Rule-maker, is known in some circles as God). But there are four conditions:

1. There can only be one prophet at a time.
2. You cannot become a prophet more than once per deal.
3. At least two other players must still be in play (discounting yourself and the dealer).
4. You may declare yourself Prophet only when you have just played a card (whether successfully or not), and before the next in turn starts play.

On declaring yourself a prophet, you place a marker (such as a coin) on the card you just added to the layout, whether or not on the mainline, and stop playing your cards – but keep hold of them, in case you get deposed and have to play again. You then proceed to act as if you were the dealer, making the appropriate announcements of 'Right' or 'Wrong' as other players attempt to play. The dealer must either confirm or negate each decision as you make it, and you remain the Prophet so long as they are confirmed. As soon as you make a wrong decision, you are deposed as Prophet, are debited with a 5-point penalty, and must take up your hand of cards and become an ordinary player again. The dealer takes over again and immediately places correctly the attempted card or cards that you wrongly adjudicated. Furthermore, whoever played them is absolved from having to take extra cards even if their attempted play was wrong.

Expulsion There comes a point at which it is assumed that everyone has had long enough to deduce The Rule. Once that point is reached, as soon as you make a play that is rejected as illegal you are expelled from the remainder of the deal, and place your cards face down on the table. The expulsion point is reached when there is no Prophet in operation and at least 40 cards have been played to the mainline, or, if a Prophet is currently operating, at least 30 cards have been added to it since the Prophet took over. To keep track, it helps to place a white piece on every tenth card from the starter until a Prophet takes over, and then a black piece on every tenth card from the Prophet's marker. If a Prophet is overthrown, the black pieces are removed and a white piece is placed on every tenth card from the starter, but nobody can be expelled on that turn.

> ☞ A round can go in and out of expulsion phases. For example, one player may be expelled when there is no Prophet and more than 40 cards have been placed. But if the next player then plays correctly and becomes a Prophet, and the player after that fails to place a card, the latter is not expelled, as fewer than 30 cards have been placed since the Prophet took over.

Ending and scoring Play ceases when somebody plays the last card from their hand, or when everybody except the Prophet (if any) is expelled. Everybody scores 1 point for each card left in the hand of the player with the most cards, and deducts 1 point for each card left in their own hand. The player with no cards in hand (if any) adds 4 points.

A bonus also accrues to the Prophet, if any. This bonus is 1 for each card on the mainline following his marker, and 2 for each card on any sideline following his marker.

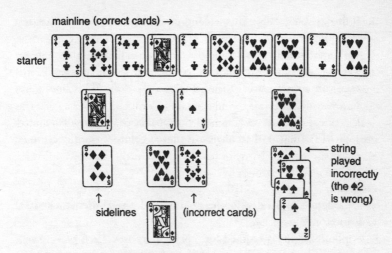

mainline (correct cards) →

starter

string
played
incorrectly
(the ♣2
is wrong)

↑
sidelines

↑
(incorrect cards)

Eleusis. Sample layout (from Abbott, *The New Eleusis*). It shouldn't take more than fifteen seconds to deduce the governing rule of play.

The dealer, finally, gets a score equal to the highest score made by anyone else, but with one possible exception. If there is an undeposed Prophet at end of play, count the total number of cards played (to mainline and sidelines) before the Prophet's marker, and double it. If this total is smaller than the highest score, the dealer scores that smaller total instead.

Game If not enough time remains for everyone to have a turn as dealer, those players who never dealt add 10 points to their score (to compensate for the dealer's inbuilt scoring advantage which they did not enjoy).

Comment Beginners should keep rules simple to start with. It is fatally easy to be too clever too soon. If you play regularly, it is worth keeping a notebook of rules devised and their relative success rate. The rule must be one which, on average, would give a randomly played card at least a one-in-five chance of being acceptable. For example:

1. Each card must be higher than the last until a face card is reached, which must then be followed by a numeral.
2. If the last card correctly placed was odd, play red; if even, play black.

3. If the last two cards match colour, play a high number, otherwise a low number.
4. If the last three cards form an ascending sequence, play a spade; if descending, a heart; if they go up and down, a diamond; if they contain any two of the same rank, a club. (This one is not easy!)

If a rule is not meaningful until two or more cards are down, as in examples (2) and (3), then any cards played before it takes effect must be accepted.

Delphi

(3–7p, 52c) A simpler development of Eleusis devised by Martin Kruskal of Princeton University.

A pool of chips is requied for scoring purposes. Each player starts with one chip and a card or counter marked YES on one side and NO on the other. One player, designated the Oracle, secretly writes down a rule of card-matching, as at Eleusis, and the other players (supplicants?) seek to deduce what it is. The rule may not be related to any factors extrinsic to the cards themselves, such as the current clock time, or the way in which each card is announced, but the Oracle may give a clue as to its nature before the first card is placed.

The pack is stacked face down and the top card is turned and placed face up beside it to start a sequence. Each subsequent card is turned face up and will eventually be placed next in the main sequence if it correctly follows the previous card in accordance with the rule. If not, it is put in a vertical line above the last card validly placed in the main sequence.

At each move the Oracle turns the top card of stock and announces its identity. Each player decides whether or not it will fit the main sequence and places their decision counter on the table with either the YES or the NO face side up according to their decision, but as yet covered by their hand. When all are ready, their decisions are revealed simultaneously.

The Oracle then attaches the card to the main sequence if it fits, or to the vertical column it if does not, and pays one chip to each player who correctly foretold the oracular decision, and wins all the chips of those who did not.

When all the cards have been placed, each player scores (a) the difference between their own total of chips and the totals of all who won fewer, less (b) the difference between their own total of chips and the totals of all who won more. Their total for the deal may therefore be positive or negative, or zero.

The Oracle scores the sum of all the part-scores made in category (b). The scoring system ensures that the Oracle's best interests are served by formulating a rule which about half the players will correctly deduce by the end of the deal.

Ideally, a game consists of as many deals as there are players (or a multiple thereof), so that all can be the Oracle the same number of times.

Arsehole (Asshole, Bum Game, Hûbéres, Pits, President, Scumbag, Trouduc, etc., etc.)   4–7 players, 52 cards

This is the westernized version of a distinctive group of oriental games, aptly dubbed 'climbing games' by John McLeod. No one knows exactly when it reached the West, or in what form, but closely related varieties of it seem to have become popular with children and students in Britain, France and America some time in the last quarter of the twentieth century. A notable feature is the prominence they attach to the relative social status of the winners and losers, which also accounts for their common range of graphic titles. Following the pattern of some old four-hand games in which the place-holders are designated, in descending order, King–Nobleman–Poorman–Beggar, western games exhibit such gradations as Boss–Foreman–Worker–Bum, or President–Vice-President–Citizen–Asshole. In Hûbéres, the six-player Hungarian equivalent, the positions are King, Big Landowner, Small Landowner, Big Peasant, Small Peasant, 'Swampy'. A peculiarly western innovation is the requirement for each of these characters to occupy a particular seat, ranging from a comfortable armchair to a rickety old crate, and for these to remain fixed so that players have to physically change places. In some versions they also wear different hats.

The following rules are typical rather than definitive.

Preliminaries From four to seven play, to the left, using a 52-card pack

ranking 2AKQJT9876543 in each suit. (*Or*: AKQJT98765432.) Two
Jokers may be added. Deal all the cards out one at a time. It doesn't
matter if some players have one more card than others.

Object To play out all one's cards as soon as possible.

Play In the first deal, eldest leads by playing face up to the table any
single card, or two, three or four cards of the same rank. (*Or*: The player
holding ♣3 leads.) Each in turn thereafter may pass or play. (*Or*: Must
play if legally able.) One who plays must put out the same number of
cards as the leader, and all of the same rank, which must be higher than
that or those of the previous player. (*Or*: May be equal in rank.) One
who passes will still be allowed to play on the next round if the turn
reaches them again. (*Or*: Not.) The round finishes when one person
plays and everyone else passes. The last player may not play again but
must turn all the played cards face down and lead to the next round.
If he has run out of cards, the lead passes round to the next player
who has any left. Play ceases when all but one player have run out of
cards.

Jokers If there are Jokers, either or both of the following rules apply:

They rank above Twos; and, if they are distinguishable, one of them
outranks the other (and everything else).

They are wild, but are beaten by the equivalent natural combination.
Thus 6☆☆ counts as, but is beaten by, 666.

Social status The first and second to run out of cards are designated,
respectively, Boss and Foreman (or whatever titles may be agreed). The
last to run out of cards is the Worker, and the one left with cards in
hand is the Bum (or whatever). Intermediate positions may be graded
accordingly.

Score and seating The Boss scores 2 points, and in the next round
occupies the most comfortable chair. The Foreman scores 1 point, and
occupies the next best chair, which should be at the Boss's left. The
others score nothing; the Bum sits at the Boss's right, and the Worker
at the Bum's right – opposite the Boss, if four play.

Next deal and card exchange The Bum is entirely responsible for
gathering cards in and shuffling and dealing, getting the others' drinks,
wiping their noses, and so on.

☛ In some circles, anyone else who so much as touches a card between deals,
even accidentally, is obliged promptly to swap places with the Bum.

The first card is dealt to the Boss, and so on round. Before play, the Bum gives the Boss the highest card in his hand, and the Boss gives the Bum any card he doesn't want. (*Or*: The Worker and Foreman exchange respectively their highest and least-wanted card, the Bum and Boss their two highest and two least-wanted cards.) The Boss then leads to the next round. (*Or*: The Bum leads.)

Game Play up to any agreed target, preferably at least 11, as the system of card exchange makes it hard for the Bum and the Boss ever to change positions in the short term. (*Or*: Ignore point-scores and play for final position after any previously agreed number of rounds.)

Variations A vast range of variations is listed on the Pagat website. Many include rules and features borrowed from related games. The following may be worth mentioning.

Single or multiple sequences may be played, as at Zheng Shàngyóu. A variety called Big Two includes Poker combinations.

A given play may be followed by one containing more cards, provided that it is the same type of combination and higher in rank.

The play of a given card or combination may induce a change in the rotation of play (clockwise becomes anti-clockwise, and vice versa), or in the ranking of subsequent combinations (each new one must be lower instead of higher), or both.

Cards other than Jokers may be declared wild.

Suits may be ranked as at Bridge (♠♥♦♣). Consequently, ♦5 may be followed by ♥5 or ♠5, but not by ♣5, and competing pairs of equal rank are won by the pair containing the spade.

Zheng Shàngyóu 'Struggling Upstream'   4–6 players, 54 cards

This skill-rewarding but very jolly Chinese game, ancestral to Arsehole (above), was first described in English by John McLeod in the February 1980 issue of *The Playing-Card*.

Preliminaries Four (or more) play, to the right, with a 54-card pack including two distinguishable Jokers – e.g. one red and one black. Four may play crosswise in partnerships.

Deal Shuffle the pack thoroughly and stack it face down. Each player in turn draws a card to build up a hand until none remain in stock. It doesn't matter if some have more cards than others. (This is the Chinese method, but westerners may prefer to have them distributed by a single dealer.)

Rank of cards The highest card is the red Joker, followed by the black Joker, then all Deuces, Aces, Kings, and so on down to Threes. Within certain limits, Deuces and Jokers are wild.

Object To get rid of all one's cards. Players drop out as they do so until only one remains with cards in hand, thereby losing.

Play In the first deal eldest leads to the first of a number of rounds of play. The leader to a round may lead any one of the following patterns:

- a single card
- two, three, or four cards of the same rank
- a single sequence of three or more cards, not necessarily of the same suit. Twos don't count, so the lowest sequence is 3-4-5, and the highest will be topped by an Ace.
- a multiple sequence of six or more cards. For example, 33-44-55, JJJ-QQQ-KKK, etc.

Each in turn thereafter may either pass or play, but in the latter event must play (a) the same number of cards, which (b) form exactly the same pattern, and (c) outrank the previous play. For example, a pair can be followed only by a higher pair, a single sequence by a single sequence of the same length but with a higher-ranking top card, and so on. A player who passes although able to play is allowed to come in later if the turn reaches him again. However, as soon as a play is followed by a pass from everyone else, the last player turns down all the cards so far played and leads to the next round. If he hasn't any cards, the lead passes round to the next player who has.

The following rules govern the constitution and relative values of the playable patterns:

1. *Single card.* Any single card is beaten by one of higher rank, suit being irrelevant. A Deuce can be beaten only by a Joker, and the black Joker only by the red.

2. *Pair.* Two of a kind can be beaten only by a pair of higher rank, Jokers being highest. A Deuce or Joker may be paired with a natural card, but a natural pair beats a wild pair of the same rank. Deuce +

Joker counts as a wild pair, and is therefore beaten by two natural Deuces.

3. *Triplet, quartet.* The same, with the additional note that a wild set can be beaten only by a higher rank or a natural set of the same rank, not by a wild set containing fewer wild cards. Note: if a three-card lead contains both jokers, the leader must state whether it is to be counted and followed as a triplet or a three-card sequence. For example, ☆-☆-7 could be interpreted as three Sevens or 9-8-7.

4. *Single sequence.* A sequence is three or more cards in numerical order, anywhere from Three (low) to Ace (high). Deuces may not be used in sequences at all, but either or both Jokers may be used to fill any gaps. A sequence is beaten by a higher one of the same length, or a wild one by a natural one of the same length and height. For example, 3-4-☆ is beaten by 3-4-5, and so on. It is not beaten by a longer sequence, nor is it even legal to play one. However, a mixed suit sequence can be beaten by a flush sequence (all the same suit), even if lower in rank. Once a flush sequence has been played, all subsequent sequences must also be flush – not necessarily in the same flush suit – and higher. For this purpose Jokers count as belonging to the desired suit.

5. *Multiple sequence.* Two or more sequences of the same length and rank – or, to put the same thing another way, three or more pairs, triplets, or quartets of consecutive ranks, regardless of suit. The lowest possible multiple sequence is 33-44-55. A Joker may represent any desired card, and a Deuce may represent an accompanying natural card, but not an entire missing rank. (For example, 33-42-25 is legal, and 33-☆2-55, but not 33-22-55.) A multiple sequence is beaten only by one of higher rank, except that, as between sequences of the same height, an entirely natural one beats one containing any wild cards.

Going out and scoring The first player to run out of cards scores 2, and the second 1 point. The others score nothing, but third out has the slight advantage of leading to the next round, to which – if western practice is followed – the loser (not out) has the onerous task of dealing. After the deal, but before the opening lead, the two losers must each place their highest-ranking card (regardless of suit) face up on the table. The winner of the previous round takes whichever of these he prefers, and second out takes the other, each laying out any single card face up in exchange. Of these two discards, the previous third out adds whichever he prefers to his hand, leaving the loser to take the other.

If four play in partnerships, each partnership's score is that of its two partners added together.

If five or more play, for 'third out' read 'second to last player out'. Those in intermediate positions between the top two and the bottom two neither score nor exchange any cards.

Play up to any agreed total, such as 10 points.

Comments The skill of this game lies in deciding how best to divide your cards into matching ranks as opposed to sequences, and even then in being prepared to switch plans for tactical reasons. For example, the combination J-J-Q-Q-K-K may be regarded as a multiple sequence, or as two separate sequences (J-Q-K)(J-Q-K), or as three pairs (J-J)(Q-Q)(K-K). Always get rid of low cards when you have the lead, as there is no other way of losing a Three, or a sequence based on one, than by leading it – though a nice coup, if you can pull it off, is to win a round with a high combination, leaving yourself with only a Three in hand, which you then lead to go out. It is rather like winning a trick at Bridge with a Two after drawing all the trumps. Don't hold on to a high-ranking, multi-card combination for too long, or you may reach a point at which no one can lead a low version of the right sort of combination to enable you to come in.

Tieng Len
4 players (best), 52 cards

Said to be the national card game of Vietnam (and to mean something like 'Speak up'), Tieng Len is a relatively simple member of the 'climbing' family.

Preliminaries Three or four players use a single 52-card pack; more than four may use a doubled pack.

Cards Suits rank from high to low ♥-♦-♣-♠. In each suit, cards rank 2AKQJT9876543. Thus ♥2 is the highest card and ♠3 the lowest.

Deal The first dealer is chosen at random; thereafter, the loser of each deal deals to the next. Deal thirteen each, in ones. Any excess cards are turned down and not used. (*Variant*: Three players may be dealt seventeen each and one card left out.)

Object To avoid being the last player with cards remaining in hand.

Play In the first deal, whoever holds ♠3 starts by playing it face up to the table, unaccompanied by any other card. In each subsequent round, and in every round of every subsequent deal, the leader to a round may start by playing any of the following:

    1. A single card

    2. A pair (two cards of the same rank)

    3. A triplet (three of a rank)

    4. A quartet (four of a rank)

    5. A sequence (of three or more cards regardless of suit)

    6. Three or more consecutive pairs (e.g. 33-44-55, QQ-KK-AA-22, etc.)

Sequences may not turn the corner. Thus 2-3-4 is illegal because Twos are high and Threes low, hence not consecutive.

The highest of two or more otherwise equal combinations is the one with the highest-suited top card. For example, ♦7-♣6-♥5 beats ♣7-♥6-♦5 because ♦7 beats ♣7. Similarly, the pair ♥7-♠7 beats the pair ♦7-♣7.

Each in turn must then either pass or play. If they play, it must be the same number of cards, forming the same type of combination, and outranking the previous player's contribution. A player who has once passed must keep passing throughout that round of play. Play continues round the table, omitting those who have passed, until someone plays and everyone else passes. Whoever played last turns the played cards face down and leads to the next round.

Beating Twos There are four exceptions to the rule requiring the play of similar combinations, and all involve beating the play of one or more Deuces (but no other rank). Namely:

    1. A single Deuce is beaten by four of a kind.

    2. A single Deuce is beaten by a double sequence of three (e.g. 3-3-4-4-5-5).

    3. A pair of Deuces is beaten by a double sequence of four (e.g. 6-6-7-7-8-8-9-9).

    4. Three Deuces are beaten by a double sequence of five (e.g. T-T-J-J-Q-Q-K-K-A-A).

These combinations apply regardless of whether the Deuce(s) were led or played as the highest of a series. When one or more Deuces are beaten by the play of an appropriate longer combination, anyone who has not already passed may, if possible, play a higher combination of the same length and type, as if it had been led.

Ending As players run out of cards, they drop out of play. If a player who runs out did so by winning a round, the lead passes to the next player in turn with cards remaining. The last player left in loses, and pays a fixed stake to each of the others.

Viet Cong (VC)

Variants of Tieng Len are played in America under this title. A version reported by Kelly Aman (via the Pagat website) has the following features:

1. Anyone dealt four Deuces automatically wins.
2. Whoever holds ♠3 must include it in his opening combination.
3. In a single sequence the highest permissible card is an Ace. Only multiple sequences may include Deuces.
4. The special combinations that beat Deuces are called slams. The slam rules are:
   - A single Deuce is beaten by three consecutive pairs.
   - A pair of Deuces is beaten by five consecutive pairs, or by two consecutive fours of a kind.
   - Three Deuces are beaten by a sequence of seven consecutive pairs, or by three consecutive fours of a kind.
5. Some play the game with trading (in which case, four Deuces do not automatically win). Before the first lead, any two players may trade a mutually agreed number of cards between themselves, provided that they can agree on which cards to trade.

Don't forget . . .

- Play to the left (clockwise) unless otherwise stated.
- Eldest or Forehand means the player to the left of the dealer in left-handed games, to the right in right-handed games.
- T = Ten, p = players, pp = in fixed partnerships, c = cards, † = trump, ☆ = Joker.

18 **Last in loses**

Durak, that most popular of Russian pastimes, is the chief of a more elaborate clan of going-out games than Newmarket and Crazy Eights. While still striving to get rid of your cards, you are primarily aiming to avoid being the last one in, rather than to be the first one out, and the method of play is more like trick-taking, which demands a greater degree of skill. This character is well reflected by the fact that many such games are called 'Fool', in the various different languages of the countries that play them – Russian *durak*, Swedish *tok*, Finnish *hörri*, and so on. Some go further, and attach less salubrious and even positively scatological titles – such as 'Shithead' – to the humiliated loser.

The only member of this family regularly recorded by western Hoyles is the much simpler and possibly ancestral game called in English Rolling Stone, together with its negative version Sift Smoke. Also attachable to the family, however, are 'scapegoat' games – my proposed term for traditional gambling and drinking games like Old Maid and Chase the Ace, where the last one in is disgraced by being stuck with a penalty card.

▌**Rolling Stone** (Enflé, Schwellen)   3–6 players, 32-52 cards

A simple but maddening game, whose French and German titles imply inflating or swelling, from the way one's hand tends to grow in size. With accurate play, it threatens to go on for ever.

Preliminaries From three to six players use a number of cards ranking AKQJT98765432 in each suit. Ideally, the number of cards is eight times the number of players, so strip out lower numerals from the Twos upwards as necessary. Shuffle thoroughly and deal eight each.

Object The aim is to be the first to run out of cards.

Play Play to the left. Eldest leads any card face up. Each in turn thereafter must play a card of the same suit if possible. The first person unable to do so must take up all cards so far played and lead to the next trick. If all follow suit, whoever plays highest wins the trick, throws it away, and leads to the next.

Winning Play ceases the moment anyone plays the last card from their hand. That player scores the total values of all cards remaining in other players' hands, with Ace to Ten at face value and courts 10 each.

Variant As described in *Le Guide Marabout*, a player who cannot follow suit must draw from stock until he can, or until it runs out.

Stortok

(2–5p, 36c) This more ingenious Swedish equivalent employs a 36-card pack ranking AKQJT9876 in each suit. Deal five each and stack the rest face down. Turn the top card of stock to start the discard pile. The suit of this card is the high trump, and the other suit of the same colour automatically becomes the low trump.

Eldest starts by playing a better card than the turn-up and drawing a replacement from stock, and each in turn thereafter must similarly beat the previous card played and then draw a card from stock. A better card is a higher card of the same suit, or any trump to a non-trump, or any card of the high trump to a card of any other suit. Anyone unable or unwilling to beat the previous card must pick it up and take it into hand, but does not then draw from the stock.

If everybody plays to the trick, it is turned down and a new one started by the person who played last. If anyone picks up instead of playing, the trick is turned down and a new one started by the person to that player's left. When the stock runs out, play continues with the cards left in hand. As players run out of cards they drop out of play, and the last one left with cards in hand is a *stortok*, or 'great fool'.

Sift Smoke
3–6 players, 32/52 cards

Also called Lift Smoke (mistakenly) and Linger Longer (appropriately), Sift Smoke can conveniently be classed as the negative version of Rolling Stone.

Preliminaries From a 32- or 52-card pack, ranking AKQJT987(65432) in each suit, deal three players eight each, four players six, five players five, or six players four each. Turn the last card (dealer's) face up for trump, and stack the rest face down.

Object To be the only player with cards in hand when everyone else has run out.

Play Eldest leads to the first trick, and the winner of each trick leads to the next. Follow suit if possible, otherwise play any card. The trick is taken by the highest card of the suit led, or by the highest trump if any are played.

The winner of each trick, and no one else, draws the top card of stock and adds it to hand before leading to the next. As players run out of cards, they drop out of play, and the winner is the last player left in. If all play their last card to the same trick, its winner wins the game.

If the stock runs out before anyone wins, the won tricks are gathered up, shuffled, and laid down as a new stock.

Score The winner scores a point for each card remaining in hand. Credit is sometimes given for tricks won. For example, each may score 1 per trick taken, the winner's trick-score being then multiplied by the number of cards left in hand.

Durak ('Fool')   2–6 players, 36 cards

Dealing is traditionally regarded as menial work, undertaken as a punishment by the loser of the previous hand. Only the dealer handles the cards – they are not usually cut, as in other card games. If any other player touches the cards they become the fool and take over the job of dealing. Sometimes the dealer may offer the cards to be cut after shuffling; if the player to whom they are offered falls into the trap of cutting the cards, that player becomes the dealer and takes over the role of the fool. Hence the expression: *'Shapku s duraka ne snimayut'* ('One should not take the hat away from a fool').

John McLeod and Alexey Lobashev, <www.pagat.com> 1998

Russia's most popular card game is played in many versions, some of which have spread to neighbouring countries in recent years. It is usually played by four in fixed partnerships, but is easier to describe in its two-handed form, as follows.

Preliminaries Deal six cards each, in threes, from a 36-card pack ranking AKQJT9876. Turn the next for trump and half cover it with the remaining cards turned face down as a stock.

Object To be the first out of cards when the stock is exhausted. The loser is *durak* – 'a fool'.

Play In each bout, one player attacks and the other defends. Non-dealer attacks first; thereafter, the winner of each bout attacks in the next. Each bout proceeds as follows:

Attacker leads any card. Defender must then either pick it up and add it to his hand, or beat it by playing a higher card of the same suit or a trump if a plain suit was led. Attacker continues with any card of the same rank as either of the first two, and, again, defender must either beat it or else take all cards so far played up into hand. If at any point the defender picks up instead of playing better, the attacker may also press upon him any further cards that he could legally have led – that is, any cards matching one or more ranks of those picked up; but he may not give more than six cards away, including those picked up.

This continues till all twelve cards are played, or one player fails to play the next card. Note that the two follow different requirements: the attacker's lead must always match the rank of any card so far showing, and the defender's reply must always be higher in suit or a trump.

If all cards are played out, the attacker draws six cards from stock, waits for the defender to do likewise, then starts a new bout with any desired lead. But a bout more commonly ends because one player fails to play the next card, in which case . . .

Conceding If the defender fails, he does so by gathering up all cards so far played to the bout and adding them to his hand. He will continue to defend in the next bout.

If the attacker fails, he concedes the bout by turning the played cards face down and pushing them to one side, where they remain out of play for the rest of the game. He then becomes the defender in the next bout.

Drawing and ending If any cards remain in stock before the next bout begins, each player in turn, starting with the attacker, draws cards one at a time from the top of the stock until either he has six cards or the stock runs out with the taking of the trump turn-up. The defender does not draw, of course, if he holds six or more cards.

Play continues without further drawing until one player runs out of cards, thereby winning – or, more precisely, not being left a fool. If the defender's last card beats the attacker's last card, the result is a draw.

Optional rule A player who was dealt †6, or who draws it from stock (but not who acquires it by failing to ward off an attack), may immediately exchange it for the trump turn-up.

Durak for 3–6 players (as individuals)

Deal six cards each. If six play there will be no stock, but the last card is still shown for trumps, though of course it may not be swapped for the †6.

Order In the first bout the player at dealer's left is the principal attacker, the player at attacker's left is the sole defender, and the player at defender's left acts as an auxiliary attacker. Theoretically, other players may also act as auxiliaries, but in practice this makes life unfairly difficult for the defender and it is usual to restrict the attackers to two or three. In any case, the principal attacker has priority and special privileges. No one else may attack without his permission, and he alone is allowed to ask the next auxiliary if he has a good attacking card.

Rules of attack No matter who attacks, the following rules apply:
• each attacking card after the first must match the rank of at least one card already played in the current bout;
• the total number of attacks made in any single bout may not exceed the number of cards held by the defender at the start of the bout, or six, whichever is the lesser.

Each pair of cards is left face up, with the attack card half covered by the defence card, and not combined with any other pair.

> ☛ If more than three play, it is often agreed that first defender (only) cannot be attacked with more than five cards, rather than six, as compensation for his severe positional disadvantage.

Successful defence The defender wins the bout if he:
• beats all the attack cards so far played, and no one makes any further attack; or
• beats six attack cards in succession; or
• having started with fewer than six, beats every attack made and so runs out of cards.

If he wins the bout, all the attack and defence cards are thrown out face down, and the successful defender becomes the principal attacker in the next bout. This begins when everyone has drawn as many cards as needed to restore their hand to six, for which purpose the principal attacker draws first, then the other attackers in rotation, and then the defenders.

Failed defence If unable or unwilling to defend, the defender picks up all the cards so far played in the bout and adds them to his hand. In addition, all those who were entitled to attack may load him with any additional cards which they could legally have played in the same bout. **Ending** As players run out of cards they drop out of play, and the last one left in is the loser, or fool.

McLeod gives this example of procedure from an individual game between four players.

1. West attacks North. North fends off all attacks and runs out of cards.

2. North having no cards, it is for East to attack South, which he does with success.

3. South having picked up, it is for West to attack East. This also succeeds, but West uses all his cards.

4. East having picked up, South must attack East, as the others have no cards.

Partnership Durak

Four may play crosswise as two against two, six as two partnerships of three, each player being flanked by an opponent and sititng opposite one. Play as above, except, of course, that no one attacks their own partner.

Here is an illustration of playing order:

1. West attacks North. North fends off all attacks and runs out of cards.

2. North having succeeded, it is for his side to attack; but as North has no cards South takes his part and attacks East, with success.

3. South now attacks West, but West beats every attack.

4. West must next attack South, in place of North, who has no cards.

5. South picks up the attack card, and now East attacks South.

Note that East and West continue to play alternately as usual, while South gets twice as many turns, since South is standing in for North as well. The order of play is essentially E-S-W-S-E-S-W-S etc. If either East or West runs out of cards next the remaining player will continue playing against South.

As between six players, the same principle applies, though it may seem confusing at first. Given one team consisting of West, North and South-East, the other of North-West, East and South:

1. West attacks North-West and runs out of cards, but North-West picks up.

2. North attacks East and East picks up.

3. South-East attacks South, but South fends this off.

4. South should now attack West, but West has no cards, so South attacks North as the next opponent in rotation.

5. North fends the attack off, and attacks North-West, who has to pick up.

6. Now South-East (the next player of the W-N-SE team) attacks East (the next player of the NW-E-S team), and East picks up.

7. It is now for North to attack South. The order of play, after West runs out of cards, is NW-N-E-SE-S-N-NW-SE-E-N-S-SE-NW-N-E, and so on.

This play of three against two is awkward, but rarely lasts long. In the example above, if a second player of the W-N-SE team runs out of cards next, the remaining player will take the turns of all three team members, the other team continuing to play in rotation. On the other hand, if one of the NW-E-S players runs out of cards, the play reduces to two against two. The actual rotation will depend on just who runs out of cards and when. The principle remains the same: that the remaining players take turns to play for their team. If, for example, at turn 7 (above) South beats off North's attack, running out of cards, it will next be North-West's turn to attack South-East, and the sequence will continue NW-SE-E-N-NW-. . . , which looks similar to a normal four-player game, but played anticlockwise. If, at turn 6, East had beaten off South-East's attack, running out of cards, it would next be South's turn to attack North, leading to the sequence S-N-NW-SE-S-. . . Note that in this case the four surviving players happen to be arranged with partners sitting next to each other, rather than opposite.

When a third player drops out, the situation clarifies. Either one team has lost, or the game has become two against one, with the two players playing alternately for their side.

Challenge (Svoyi Koziri) 2 players, 24–52 cards

Svoyi Koziri, meaning 'One's own trump', first appeared in *Noveyshy russky kartochny igrok* (St Petersburg, 1809) with the implication that it was as popular in Russia as Boston, Whist and Piquet. A variety of it was first described in English under the name 'Challenge' by Hubert Phillips in *The Pan Book of Card Games* (London, 1953), and said then to have been much played at Cambridge under the sponsorship of Professor Besicovitch. Unusually, it is a card game of 'perfect information', being won entirely by foresight and calculation, like Chess. This is described first.

Preliminaries Two play with any number of cards which is a multiple of four, ranking AKQJT98765432 in each suit, as far as it goes. Phillips regarded 32 as standard (Seven low), and this is assumed below.

Object To be the first to run out of cards, leaving them all in the other player's hand.

Trumps and deal To start, each player chooses two suits and nominates one of them as his personal trump. Dealer then deals out half the pack (16 cards) face up in a row, extracts from them those of his own suits, and discards the rest. This gives him approximately half his playing hand. He then distributes to elder, as the first half of his hand, all the cards of elder's two suits which are exactly equivalent to those of his own two.

> Example: Suppose dealer chooses black suits and entrumps spades, leaving elder
> with red suits of which he entrumps hearts. Then the cards might come out:
> Dealer ♠KJ97 ♣AQJ
> Elder ♥KJ97 ♦AQJ

To complete both hands, each player takes all the remaining cards of his opponent's two suits. Each player's hand is therefore a mirror image of the other's, and neither has a strategic advantage other than that of the lead – if such it be. Each hand should include at least two cards in every suit. If not, deal again.

Play At each turn, one player leads a card of his choice. Elder leads first. The other must then either play a better card, in which case he leads next, or else take up all the cards so far played and add them to his hand, in which case his opponent leads next. A 'better' card is a higher card of the suit led, or any card of one's own personal trump (if

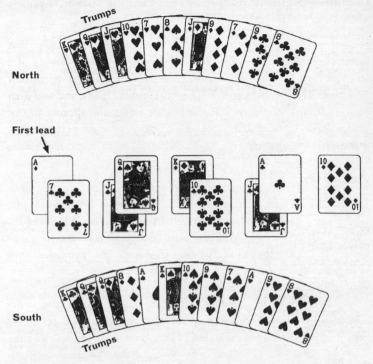

Challenge. North, with hearts as personal trump, leads ♦10 to the fifth 'trick'. South, though able to play ♦Q or a personal trump (clubs), prefers to take all the cards so far played and lead next. This results in a larger but more powerful hand, and it remains to be seen whether it will pay off.

different from the suit led). Note that any card may be led at each turn: it need not relate in any way to the previous card played.

Winning The first to play his last card wins. As this can take hours, it may be agreed that a player who falls asleep during play loses by default, unless the other is also asleep, in which case it is a draw.

Svoyi Koziri

Of the original game, John McLeod says: 'In the version of this game played in Russia (with 36 cards), there are normally three or four players. The players select their trump suits before the game and the cards are dealt out normally, not rigged to make the hands identical. Players normally hold their cards concealed but sometimes when the game is reduced to two players they lay them out on the table, since obviously each knows what the other has. There are versions where when unable to beat the last card played the defender only has to pick up a limited number of cards, rather than the whole pile, and the number of cards to be picked may depend on the top card of the pile.'

Dudak ('Bagpipe') 2–4 players, 32 cards

A Czech game said to be much played by children.

Preliminaries Four players (the best number) each receive eight cards from a 32-card pack ranking AKQJT987 in each suit. The aim is to play out all one's cards. The last player left with cards in hand is the loser.

Play Eldest starts by playing any card face up to the table to start a wastepile. Each in turn thereafter may, if possible, play two cards to the wastepile. The first must be a higher card of the same suit as the top card of the pile, and the second may then be any card at all.

A player unable or unwilling to beat the top card must take it and add it to his own hand, and keep doing so until he uncovers a card which he is able and willing to beat. He does so, adds any second card, and play continues as before. If, however, he thereby takes the whole pile, his turn ends, and the next in turn starts a new pile with a single card.

Trump-making Any player, on his turn to play, may nominate a specific suit as his personal trump. Thereafter, the first of his two discards must be either a higher one of the same suit as the top card, or any card of his personal trump suit. Although each player will normally choose a different suit, it is permitted, and can be tactically interesting, for two or more players to entrump the same one.

A player having once declared a trump is subject to the following rules. First, he may not cancel or change his suit for the rest of the game. Second, whenever he finds himself unable or unwilling to beat the top card, he may not remove cards one by one but must take the whole pile into hand. A new one is then started with a single card by the next in turn to play.

Ending When a player plays his last card to the pile, he drops out of play, and the others continue from the next in turn. If the player who went out did so by playing two cards, play continues exactly as before. If, however, he had only one card at the start of his last turn and so went out by beating the top card, then the current wastepile is turned face down and put to one side. The next in turn then starts a new wastepile by playing one card only, and play continues as before.

Game The overall winner is the one who loses fewest of an agreed number of games. Alternatively, it is the one who has not lost a game when everyone else has lost at least one.

Comment Lacking rules for fewer players, I suggest three receive ten each from a 30-card pack made by removing the black Sevens, and two twelve each from a 24-card pack with Nine low.

Mustamaija ('Black Maria', Spardame)   3–5 players, 52 cards

This is one of several Finnish games sent me by Veikko Lähdesmaki. The Norwegian game of Spardame ('spade Queen') is almost identical, and may be played with a double pack but with one ♠Q removed.

Preliminaries From three to five players receive five cards each (3+2 or 2+3) from a 52-card pack ranking AKQJT98765432 in every suit, except that ♠Q is not a spade but an entirely independent card. Stack the rest face down.

Object To run out of cards, and especially to avoid being the last player left in and holding ♠Q, known as Black Maria.

Opening Eldest starts the first bout by playing face up to the table from one to five cards of the same suit, which may include ♠Q if the others are spades.

Trump Next, dealer turns the top card of the stock for trump. If it is a spade, bury it and turn again until some other suit appears. Then half cover the turn-up with the remainder of the pack face down as a stock.

Play On your turn to play:

1. If the previous player took cards from the table, leaving none face up, start a new bout by playing face up to the table from one to five cards of the same suit.

2. If the previous player left one or more cards on the table, you may beat as many of them as you can and will by placing upon each

one either a higher card of the same suit, or, if it is a plain suit, any trump. Discard face down from the game all the cards you beat, and those you beat them with. In this connection –

- ♠Q can neither beat nor be beaten by any other card, and must therefore always be taken up.
- If you leave any cards unbeaten, add them to your hand.
- If you beat them all, start a new bout (as above).

If at the end of your turn you have fewer than five cards in hand, whether you started a new bout or had to take unbeaten cards, draw from stock until either you have five again or the stock runs out.

Endgame When the stock is empty, the leader to a bout may not play out more cards than are held by the next in turn to play. Players drop out as they run out of cards. The last left in will be holding ♠Q and is designated Black Maria.

Kitumaija ('Wan Maria')   2–5 players, 52 cards

Another Finnish game, a cross between Durak and Mustamaia. *Kitu* means to suffer pain, or pine away.

Preliminaries From two to five players receive five cards each (3+2) from a 52-card pack, of which the next is turned to start the first spread, and the remainder are stacked face down.

Object To run out of cards, and especially to avoid being the last player left in and holding ♠Q, known as Wan Maria.

Trumps Cards rank AKQJT98765432 in each suit, except that ♠Q is entirely independent. Diamonds trump spades and hearts, but not clubs, which are invulnerable.

Play Each in turn, starting with eldest, plays as follows.

- If there are no cards in the spread, play any single card face up to start a new one.
- If the topmost or last-played card of the spread is ♠Q, take into hand the top five cards of the spread, or as many as there are if fewer than five, and end his turn.
- Otherwise, he must first play a bound card and may then play a free card. A bound card is a higher card of the same suit as the top card of the spread, or, if this is a heart or a spade, any diamond, which may be

used as a trump even if the player can follow suit. A free card is any desired card. If unable to beat the top card, he must take into hand the top three cards of the spread (or five if it is headed by ♠Q). The ♠Q may be played only as a free card, not as a bound one.

• Whether or not he beat the top card, end his turn by restoring his hand to five cards if necessary, by drawing from the top of the stock, or as many as remain.

Endgame When the stock is exhausted, no 'free' cards may be played: each in turn must either beat the top card or take the top three into hand, or the top five if headed by ♠Q. Players drop out as they run out of cards. Last in, holding ♠ Queen, is known as Wan Maria, and loses.

Comment As these rules stand, whoever goes into the endgame with ♠Q can never discard it, leaving the outcome a foregone conclusion. It is quite feasible to simply ignore the change of rule and go on playing a bound card followed by a free one. Alternatively, follow the rule but permit ♠Q to be the only card that can be played free.

Hörri ('Fool')

3–7 players, 52 cards

The Finnish equivalent of Durak.

Preliminaries A 52-card pack is distributed randomly and unevenly among two to five players as follows. Set the pack face down, then turn the next eight cards face up and arrange them around the stock. Each in turn draws a card from stock.

If it is a spade, heart or club, and the faced cards include a lower-ranking card of the same suit, he adds both to his hand; but if there is no such lower card, he leaves the turned card face up and takes none.

If it is a diamond, and the faced cards include a lower-ranking diamond, or any spade or heart, he adds both to his hand. If there are several possibilities, he has a free choice, but if there is no such lower card, he leaves the turned diamond face up and takes none.

This continues until the stock is empty. Whoever was the last to take two cards adds any remaining faced cards to his hand. Players now have playing hands of varying lengths, from none upwards. A player with no cards takes no part in the play. This may be boring but at least it means he cannot lose.

Object To avoid having cards left in hand when everyone else has gone out.

Trumps Cards rank AKQJT98765432 in each suit, except that ♠Q is not a spade but entirely independent. Diamonds trump spades and hearts, but not clubs, which are invulnerable.

Play Whoever holds ♣2 plays it face up to the table to start an eventually overlapping spread of discards.

Each in turn may play to the spread either a higher card of the same suit as the top card, or, if it is a spade or heart, any diamond, whether or not able to follow suit. If unable or unwilling to beat the top card, he must take the bottom card of the spread and add it to his hand.

If a player beats the top card and thereby 'completes' the spread, i.e. causes it to contain precisely as many cards as there are active players, he turns it face down, and starts a new one by playing any card face up.

If there is no top card, because the last player has just taken the 'bottom' of a one-card spread, the next in turn may play any card to start a new one.

Skitgubbe (Mas, Mjölnarmatte)   3 players, 52 cards

The legendary Swedish newspaper editor Herbert Tingsten, who was renowned for his stuck-up manners, once found himself seated next to a young woman at a formal dinner and virtually ignored her until coffee was served, when he eyed her speculatively and asked how old she was. 'Twenty-one,' she replied. 'Huh!', said the snob. 'That's not an age, it's a card game.' To which came the prompt rejoinder, 'So is Skitgubbe.'

Source: Dan Glimne

'Sk' in Swedish is pronounced like 'Sh' in English, and the key word means 'dirty old man', in the sense of unwashed rather than obscene.

Preliminaries Three players receive three each from a 52-card pack ranking AKQJT98765432, and the undealt cards are stacked face down.

Object In Part 1, to win good cards for the play of Part 2. In Part 2, to play out all cards won in Part 1. The last player left with cards in hand is a *skitgubbe*.

Play (1) Tricks are played at no trump between two players at a time. Each player draws a card from stock immediately after playing one out. Eldest hand leads to the first trick against his left-hand opponent. Each may play any card regardless of suit, and the trick is taken by the higher card played. If both are equal it is a *stunsa*, or 'bounce': the same leader draws from stock and leads again, and so on until one of them manages to play higher than the other. The trick-winner takes all cards so far played, turns them face down in front of himself and leads to the next trick, to which his left-hand opponent replies. (Even if this is the same player as before.)

Either player may, instead of playing from hand, take a chance by turning the top card of stock and playing that instead. Once turned, it must be played.

When only one card remains in stock, it is taken by the player in turn to draw but remains face down on the table before him. The hands are played out as far as possible, any unplayed cards remaining in hand. If the last trick ends in a 'bounce' the players retrieve the cards they played.

The last card of the stock is then turned up to establish trumps for the play of Part 2, and added to its owner's hand.

The players pick up the cards they won in tricks and use them as their playing hands for Part 2. They probably won't all have the same number, but that doesn't matter. The aim is to play out all one's cards.

Play (2) Whoever took the last card of stock in Part 1 leads to Part 2, and now all three play in turn, not two at a time as before. The leader may play any single card, or a sequence of two or more cards of the same suit. For example, a Three may be led, or 3-4 of a suit, or 3-4-5, and so on. Each in turn thereafter must play a better card or suit-sequence than the previous player. 'Better' means of the same suit but higher in rank – not necessarily consecutive with the previous card – or a trump or trump-sequence to a preceding non-trump play. You may play trumps even if able to follow suit. Throughout Part 2 it is important to keep each player's contributions separate until they are turned down.

A player who can't or won't play better must pick up the card(s) played by the last player – who may have been himself! – and the turn passes to the left. If everyone picks up, leaving no card to beat, the next lead is made by the player to the left of the one who picked up last.

Turning tricks down When a 'trick' contains three contributions in all – whether one each from all three, or more than one by one of them – it is turned down and ignored. Whoever played last to it leads to the next. When one player runs out of cards, the others continue as before until the trick has been played to three times and turned down. Subsequent tricks require only two contributions before being turned down. When a second player plays his last card, the third player has lost, and is a *skitgubbe*.

NLK

John McLeod learnt this from students at Szeged University in Hungary. N is for *nagy* ('big'), L is for any nationality beginning with L, such as Lithuanian, and K is for *kibaszós* ('screwing').

Preliminaries Four players use a 32-card pack ranking AKQJT987 in each suit. For each additional player, add the next lower rank, so nine would use all 52 cards. Play to the right.

Object In Phase 1, to accumulate cards for Phase 2, and in Phase 2 to avoid being left with cards in hand when everyone else has run out.

Deal Choose the first dealer by any agreed means. The loser of each subsequent hand deals the next. Deal one card face up in front of each player, and stack the rest face down as a stock. Each player's faced card forms the base of a stack which, when complete, will constitute his playing hand in Phase 2.

Play (1) On your turn to play:

1. If possible, you may (but need not) play the top card of your stack to the top of another player's stack, provided that it is next higher in rank, regardless of suit. For example, you can play any Seven on top of a Six. On top of an Ace you may play a card of the lowest rank in the pack – a Seven if four play, a Six if five play, and so on. You can keep doing this in the same turn so long as each newly revealed top card of your stack can legally be played to someone else's.

2. You must then complete your turn by drawing the top card of stock and placing it on top of your stack – unless you can legally play it to someone else's, in which case you may do so and then draw again.

Phase 1 ends when someone draws the last card of stock. Its suit becomes trump for Phase 2.

Everyone picks up their cards, and whoever drew the trump card leads to the first trick of Phase 2.

Play (2) The leader to a trick may play any card. Each following player must either beat the previous card played, or take the lowest card in the trick and add it to their hand. The previous card is beaten by playing a higher card of the same suit, or any trump to a plain suit. The 'lowest' card is the lowest of the suit led, or of trumps if only trumps remain. It is permissible to pick up though able to play, and to trump though able to follow suit.

Because each in turn may either play a card or take a card, the number of cards in a trick may rise and fall as play proceeds. A trick ends when it is either full or empty, as follows:

1. It is full when the number of cards it contains equals the number of players who were still in play when it was led. The trick is turned down, and the person who played last (and therefore highest) leads to the next.

2. It is empty when there is only one card in the trick and a player picks it up instead of beating it. In this case the next player in turn leads to the next. Note: If it is your turn to lead, you must do so, unless you have run out of cards, in which case the lead passes to the next in turn.

Players drop out as they run out of cards, thus reducing the number of cards required to complete each subsequent trick (though not the current one).

Ending Play ceases when only one player has any cards, thereby losing. Note that the hand can end in the middle of a trick. For example, if only two players remain, each with just one card, then the player on lead wins, even if the other beats the card led.

Example of trick-play Hearts trump, ♣9 led. Parentheses enclose a card that is picked up, not played.

A	B	C	D	
♣9	♣J	♣A	(♣9)	
♥7	(♣J)	(♣A)	♥8	
(♥7)	(♥8)			Empty trick: C to lead next
		♠7	♠J	
♠Q	♥8			Full trick, turned down: C to lead next

Shithead (Karma, Palace, Shed, many other names)

2–6 players, 52 cards

This folk-game is said to be popular with travelling people and, not surprisingly, is widespread.

Preliminaries Two or more players use a 52-card pack ranking AKQJT98765432 in each suit. Two Jokers are optional, or, if six play, essential.

Additional equipment Brown paper bag. (Warning: do not use a plastic bag.)

Object To avoid being left with cards in hand when everyone else has run out.

Deal Each is dealt three cards face down in a row (down-cards), then one card face up on each of them (up-cards), and finally three cards as a playing hand (hand-cards). The rest are stacked face down. Before play, each player may exchange one or more hand-cards for a corresponding number of his own up-cards.

Play Takes place in two phases. Phase 1 ends when the last card is drawn from stock. In Phase 2, players continue by playing out all their hand-cards, then their three up-cards, and finally their three down-cards.

Eldest hand is the first player to have been dealt a Three as an up-card, or, if no one has, the first to have been dealt a Three as a hand-card. If no one has a Three, it is the person first dealt a Four; and so on as necessary.

Eldest starts by discarding from hand to a common wastepile any single card, or a pair or triplet of the same rank, and restoring his hand to three by drawing from stock. Each in turn thereafter must, if possible, play a single card, or a pair, triplet or quartet of cards, equal or higher in rank than the top card of the wastepile. It isn't necessary to match the *number* of cards played by the previous player, nor to play the whole of a matched set if it seems preferable to hold any back. If this reduces the hand to fewer than three cards, restore it to three by drawing from stock, thus ending the turn.

If unable or unwilling to discard, a player must take all the cards of the wastepile up into hand, leaving the next in turn to start a new series of discards.

Jokers A Joker may be played at any time. It is not wild, but forces a switch in the rotation of play, so that the person who played the card before the Joker now has to match it or beat it himself. The new rotation continues till the next Joker appears.

Special rules Deuces count high and low. You can therefore play one or more Deuces at any time, and the next player in turn can play any other rank.

When a Ten is played, the whole wastepile is turned down and left out of play, and the person who played it ends his turn by drawing up to three cards (if necessary) and starting a new wastepile with one or more matching cards of any rank. (Some schools allow a Ten to be played after a Jack, Queen, King or Ace.)

The same applies when a player leaves four of a kind on the top of the wastepile, whether by playing all four at once, or by duplicating the rank of the previous discard and so bringing the total to four.

Endgame When the stock is exhausted, continue playing from hand. From now on:

A player with no card left in hand must play from his up-cards, if any remain. More than one may be played at a time if they are of the same rank. If forced to take the wastepile, however, he must revert to playing from the hand and may not play from the table until none remain in hand.

When a player has played his three up-cards, and has none left in hand, he must at each turn face one of his down-cards and play it if possible. If it won't go, he must add it and the wastepile to hand, and may not then attempt to play a down-card until no hand-cards remain.

The winner is the first to get rid of his last remaining down-card. The last to do so is a Shithead, and, to illustrate this fact, must wear a brown paper bag until somebody else takes over this role. (Plastic bags are dangerous.)

Variations Many schools have their own special rules. For example, a Seven must be followed by one or more cards of equal or lower rank. If there are no Jokers, Eights switch the rotation, but are 'transparent' – i.e. the next card or cards must beat the rank of the card under the Eight, not necessarily the Eight itself. And so on.

Scapegoat games

Traditional gambling and drinking games in which the aim is to avoid being the last player left with a card in hand, or being left with the lowest card in hand.

Old Maid (Vieux Garçon, Schwarzer Peter)

A famous old Victorian game suitable for three or more. If more than six play, use two packs shuffled together. Remove the ♥Q from the pack before shuffling the cards. Deal the remainder round as far as they will go – it doesn't matter if some receive more than others. The aim is to collect and discard pairs of the same rank and to avoid finishing up with an unmatched Queen in hand.

Everyone starts by discarding from their hand as many pairs of the same rank as they can. If, at this point or any later time in the game, a player manages to get rid of all their cards by pairing, they drop out of play and are safe from loss.

When no more pairing can be done, the player at dealer's left holds his hand of cards out, face down, to the player at his own left, who takes one and adds it to his hand. If this gives him a pair, he discards it face down. He then offers his cards to his left, and so on round the table.

Play continues in this way, with people gradually dropping out as they get rid of their cards in pairs. Eventually they will all be out except for the player left with an unmatched queen, the eponymous Old Maid.

Related games In Vieux Garçon (Old Boy) and Schwarzer Peter (Black Peter), one black Jack is removed and the loser is the player left with the other in hand.

Chase the Ace

(Ranter-go-Round, Cuckoo) A primitive gambling or children's game, called Cuckoo in most European countries, though recorded in Cornwall as Ranter-go-Round. Much played in Scandinavia with special cards, such as Gnav and Killekort. It fits no convenient category, but perhaps most resembles Old Maid.

Players deal in turn. Deal one card each face down from a 52-card pack ranking A23456789TJQK. The aim is to avoid holding the lowest card at end of play. Suits are irrelevant; Ace is always low.

Each in turn, starting with eldest, may either keep his card – and, if it is a King, must turn it face up – or demand to exchange it with that of his left-hand neighbour. The latter may refuse only if he holds a King, which he must then show (saying 'Cuckoo!' in some versions).

The dealer, on his turn, may either stand pat or reject his card and cut a replacement from the pack. The cards are then revealed, and the player with the lowest card loses a life. Players tying for lowest all lose a life. Play up to any agreed number of lives.

Variants If the dealer rejects his card, and then cuts a King, it counts lowest of all, and only he loses a life. Some do not cut, but take the top card of the pack. Some have a rule that a player passing an Ace, Two or Three to his right-hand neighbour must announce that fact.

| **Cheat** (Bullshit, I Doubt It) | 3 or more players, 52 or 104 cards |

This well-known children's game (or students' game, to judge from its cruder American title) theoretically belongs to the first-out-wins type covered in the previous chapter. I place it here because it appears ancestral to a group of 'lying' games which are mostly of the last-in-loses or 'scapegoat' type.

Preliminaries Deal all the cards round as far as they will go. It doesn't matter if some players have one more than others. The aim is to be the first out of cards.

Play The player at dealer's left goes first and everyone plays in turn. The first player discards from one to four cards face down and says 'Aces'. The next does likewise and says 'Twos', the next 'Threes', and so on up to 'Kings', followed by 'Aces' again, and so in rotation.

Challenging In theory, the cards you put out belong to the rank you declare them to be. In practice, you may lie. Indeed, you may have to, since you must play at least one card even if you haven't any of the required rank. Any player may challenge another to show that the cards they just played belong to the stated rank, by calling 'Cheat!' (or whatever else you call the game). The challenged player must turn them face up, and whoever was correct must take up the whole discard pile and add it to their hand. Play then continues from the left of the challenged player. You may not challenge a player once the cards they have played have been covered by the next in turn.

Winning The winner is the first to get rid of all their cards – unless, of course, they are successfully challenged on their last turn and have to take up the discard pile.

Variations Some play that the sequence runs downwards (A-K-Q-J etc.); some that the next in turn may call the next higher or lower rank (e.g. A-K-A-2-3-2 etc.).

Some play that the number of discards must be stated (e.g. 'Three Aces') and that cheating may be attempted by calling a false number of discards. For example, if you are challenged for saying 'Three Aces' when you have actually put out only two Aces, or three Aces and a Jack, then you must take up the discards.

Verish' Ne Verish'

(2–6p, 36-52c) A Russian game: its title may be rendered 'Believe you, believe you not' (source: Leo Broukhis, http://www.pagat.com). It is an ingenious cross between Cheat and Old Maid.

Two or three players use 36 cards, four or more use 52. Remove one card from the pack at random and lay it face down to one side without exposing it. Deal the rest round as far as they will go. It doesn't matter if some players have one more card than others.

The player at the dealer's left starts by playing from one to four cards face down on the table and declaring them to be of any rank – for example 'Jacks'. Each in turn thereafter must either play one or more cards face down and declare the same rank as the previous player, or else challenge the previous player's veracity by saying 'Ne verish' ('Don't believe you') and turning that player's cards face up. Only the person in turn to play may challenge.

The challenger, if mistaken, or the challenged player, if caught lying, must take up all the cards so far played and add them to his hand. He may then, before play proceeds, remove any set of four cards of the same rank from his hand, reveal them to everyone, and discard them face down, thus diminishing the number of cards in play.

The next round is then started by the player to the left of the faulted player (thus the challenger himself, if correct), who may, as before, play and call any desired rank.

Eventually, all complete sets of four will be eliminated, leaving three of the initially discarded rank. Whoever is left with these in hand when everyone else has run out is the loser.

When playing instead of challenging, it is proper, but not compulsory, to say '*Verish*' ('I believe you').

Paskahousu
3 or more players (4–5 best), 52 cards

This more elaborate, and purportedly more strategic, Finnish derivative of Cheat was first communicated to me by Veikko Lähdesmaki. Its name means 'Shitpants'.

Preliminaries Deal five cards each and stack the rest face down.

Object To get rid of your cards and avoid being the last player with cards in hand.

Play The game is started by the first person to initiate a discard pile by playing a card face down to the table and declaring it to be a three, whether or not truthfully. If nobody does so, make it a Four, and so on. Play then proceeds from the left of the starter.

Each in turn plays one or more cards face down to the discard pile, declaring them to be any rank equal to or higher than the last rank announced.

Challenging Whenever somebody makes such a play, and before their cards are covered by the next player, they may be challenged to prove the truthfulness of the call by turning the card or cards in question face up. If they conform to the call, the challenger must add the whole discard pile to his hand, leaving an empty table. If not, the challenged player must do likewise. In either case, the turn then passes to the left of the challenged player.

Special rules Certain rules and restriction govern particular ranks, as follows. (Note: a 'call' means a discard and its accompanying announcement, and reference to 'a' rank means 'one or more' of that rank.)

• You may not call a Jack, Queen or King unless the previous call was an Eight or higher.

- You may not call an Ace unless either the previous call was a Jack, Queen or King, or the discard pile is empty.
- You may call a Two at any time, but a Two may be followed only by another Two.
- Upon calling a Ten (after any lower rank) or an Ace (after a Jack, Queen or King), and not being challenged, you remove the discard pile from play, face down, leaving an empty space. You then start a new pile by playing and calling any card from your hand. If the next player then calls a Ten or an Ace, the player after that must add it to their hand, leaving the next in turn to start a new pile.

Drawing from stock Instead of playing from your hand to the table, you may draw the top card of stock, so long as any remain, and either add it to your hand, thus ending your turn, or play it face down to the table (without first looking at its face) and claim it to be any legal rank. You may even do this at the start of the game and claim it to be a Three.

Outcome The last player left with any cards in hand is designated 'Shitpants', and has to buy the next round.

Don't forget . . .
- Play to the left (clockwise) unless otherwise stated.
- Eldest or Forehand means the player to the left of the dealer in left-handed games, to the right in right-handed games.
- T = Ten, p = players, pp = in fixed partnerships, c = cards, † = trump, ☆ = Joker.

Rummy denotes a wide range of closely related games, few with universally accepted names, let alone a code of rules. The play resembles that of the Chinese game of Mah Jong, and probably derives from it. The oldest western example is the nineteenth-century Mexican game of Conquian, followed a little later by a proprietary game published in England under the name Khan-Hoo. The name Rummy, originally 'Rhum', first appeared in the 1900s, and subsequently became a generic term for the whole family. Rummy games enjoyed an explosion of popularity and development in the first half of the twentieth century, culminating in the highly elaborate partnership game of Canasta in the 1950s. Such rapid evolution in so brief a span of time has left different groups of players, blamelessly ignorant of the historical background, practising a variety of informal games under an equal variety of interchangeable rules and names. To some, all forms of Rummy are 'Gin', to others, they are 'Kalookie'; and so on – just as there are those who call all forms of card-solitaire 'Patience', 'Klondike', 'Canfield', or whatever.

Underlying all true Rummy games are a method of play by *draw and discard*, and the twofold objective of *collecting sets of cards* of the same sort and *eliminating them from the hand* in matching sets called *melds*. Play ceases when one player *goes out* by playing the last card from his hand. Other players are then penalized according to the value of cards remaining in their hands – their so-called *deadwood*.

The family can be broadly divided into positive and negative types. In negative games, which came first, the only scores or pay-offs are penalty points for deadwood: melds score nothing, so the general aim is to go out as soon as possible. In positive games, melds carry plus-scores, so the primary aim is to meld as much as possible, and to delay going out until you can do so most profitably.

This section covers negative or 'out-going' Rummy games, which I classify as follows:

• *Flat-out* games (the oldest type), such as Conquian. No melds are revealed until someone goes out by melding their whole hand in one go. In this respect they resemble shedding games such as Crazy Eights.

• *Knock-out* games, such as Gin. No melds are revealed until someone ends the game by knocking, believing themselves to have the lowest amount of deadwood.

• *Drift-out* games, such as basic Rummy. Melds are revealed as play progresses, and the game ends when someone runs out of cards.

• *Contract* games. The first meld you make in each deal must conform to a statutory pattern (the 'contract'), and the contract requirement gets tougher as further deals ensue.

• *Rearrangement* games, such as Vatican. Melds are revealed as play progresses and are common property, enabling anyone to extend and rearrange their constituent cards to form different melds.

Special terms used in Rummy games

concealed See *go out*.

deadwood Cards left unmelded in your hand at end of play. These always count against you, except, in some games, those that are capable of being melded, or which can be laid off to existing melds. Typically, numerals count at face value and court cards 10 each. Aces usually count 1 in games where they form only low sequences (A-2-3), but 15 or more if they can be used high (Q-K-A). Jokers and other wild cards count higher still.

discard An unwanted card thrown face up to the discard pile, usually at the end of the player's turn. As verb, to throw such a card.

discard pile The pile of discards made during play, also called the *wastepile* or *pack*. In some games they are kept squared up, in some they are spread slightly so all can be identified. The top card is the upcard. An invariable rule of all Rummy games is that, if you draw just the single upcard, you may not immediately discard it (or its twin when more than one pack is used). This would amount to passing one's turn, which is not allowed.

draw To take a card, usually the top card of the stock or the upcard.

escalera A sequence meld. Spanish for 'ladder'. Many Rummy games were developed in Spanish-speaking countries.

face value Numerals Two to Ten have face values of 2 to 10 points respectively. Ace is usually 1, unless otherwise stated.

go out (or *go down*) To play the last card from your hand, thereby ending the play. Whether or not the last card must be a discard depends on the rules of the individual game. Most games impose conditions on when you may go out. To go out by melding all your cards in one turn, without having previously melded any, is called 'going rummy', or 'gin', or 'going out concealed'. In some games this is the only way in which you can go out. In others it is optional, and earns a special reward.

group See *set*.

knock To end the game by knocking on the table. Some games permit this provided that your deadwood does not exceed a certain amount.

lay off Add a card to an existing meld, for example a fourth King to a set of Kings, or a card at either end of a suit sequence. In some games you may lay off cards only to your own or partner's melds, in others to any meld at all. In most games you cannot lay off to another player's meld until you have made at least one of your own.

meld A valid combination of matching cards which you can play from the hand in order to make a score or to go out: either three or more cards of the same rank (called a *set* or a *group*) or three or more cards in suit and sequence (called a *sequence* or a *run*). To meld is to set out such a combination face up on the table for everyone to see. Strictly speaking (since the word comes from German *melden*, meaning to register or declare), a combination in the hand does not become a meld until it is actually revealed; but the habit of referring to undeclared combinations as melds is now too widespread to revoke.

natural card See *wild card*.

pack In Canasta games, the discard pile.

rummy See *go out*.

sequence Three or more cards in suit and sequence. In some games, Ace is low only (A-2-3), in some it is high only (Q-K-A). In some it may be either, and if more than one pack is used it is possible to form a 14-card sequence running A23456789TJQKA. Rarely, it may count simultaneously high and low, permitting a sequence to 'turn the corner' (-K-A-2-); but this should not be assumed permissible unless specifically stated.

set or *group* Three or more cards of the same rank.

stock The stock of undealt cards placed face down at start of play.

turn the corner See *sequence*.

upcard The most recent discard, lying uppermost on the discard pile.

wild card One that may be used to represent any natural card. Jokers (☆) are usually wild, so, for example, a sequence may consist of ♥3-4-☆-6, and a set of ♥3-♠3-☆. In many games, Deuces (Twos) are also wild. Games involving wild cards usually permit you to steal a wild card from any meld on the table provided that you can replace it from your own hand with the natural card it represents, though certain other conditions may also attach to this procedure.

▌ **Rummy** (Basic Rummy) 2–7p, 52 or 104c

The archetypal Rummy dates back to the early 1900s, when it was described under such names as Coon Can, Khun Khan, Colonel. The following rules are typical, but subject to local variations due to the fact that players tend to bring back into it features they have encountered in other games of the same type.

Preliminaries Two or three players use a single pack, seven use a double pack, other numbers may use either. It is usual to add two or more Jokers per pack. Unless otherwise specified, the number of cards dealt should be as follows:

players:	2	3	4	5	6	or: 4–7	
cards:	52	52	52	52	52	104	(+ Jokers)
deal each:	10	7 or 10	7	7	6	10	

Thorough shuffling is essential before each deal. Decide first dealer by any agreed means. The turn to deal and play passes always to the left. Stack the undealt cards face down and turn the next as an upcard. (*Variant*: No upcard until the first discard.)

Object To go out first by getting rid of all your cards in melds, with or without a final discard.

Melds Valid melds are sets and suit-sequences of three or more cards. The lowest sequence is A-2-3 and the highest ends J-Q-K.

☞ This was the original rule. Many now count Ace high or low but not both, thus allowing A-2-3 and Q-K-A (but not K-A-2).

Play On your turn, play as follows:

1. Draw either the top card of the stock, or the upcard, and take it into hand.

2. (If possible and desirable) Meld a set or sequence of cards from the hand, or lay off individual cards to melds already on the table, regardless of who made them. You may make as many melds and lay-offs as you wish.

3. Add a card face up to the discard pile. If you took the upcard, your discard must differ from it.

Wild cards Jokers are wild. For example, a sequence may consist of ♥3-4-☆-6, and a set of ♥3-♠3-☆. You may steal a wild card from any meld on the table provided that you can replace it from your own hand with the natural card it represents.

End of stock If the stock runs out before anyone has gone out, turn the discard pile to form a new one, and turn its top card face up to start a new discard pile.

☞ Most book rules say the stock should not be shuffled before being turned. This favours the player with the best memory. Unless you want to turn it into a memory game, a better rule is that this rule applies only if everyone agrees to it. In case of dispute, shuffle it.

Ending and scoring Play ceases the moment someone goes out by playing the last card from their hand, whether as part of a new meld, a lay-off, or a discard. That player wins, and scores (or is paid) by the other players according to the face value of cards left unmelded in their hands. Numerals at face value, courts 10, and Jokers 15 each. Ace counts 1 unless the Q-K-A sequence is allowed, in which case it counts 11.

Basic Rummy variants

Of the following named variants, many merely denote modifications to the basic rules; they can be put together in almost any combination the players fancy.

Block Rummy

As Basic Rummy, but: If the stock runs out, the discard pile is not turned, and play ceases as soon as all players refuse to take the top discard. Everyone pays or scores negatively according to the amount of their deadwood. This optional extra may be applied to any Rummy game.

Boathouse Rum

As Basic Rummy, but: A player who draws the upcard must also draw the top card of stock. (*Variant*: Or the next upcard. The result, either way, is to take two cards instead of one.) That player may then meld and must discard one card only. Players may thereby increase the number of cards they hold. Turn-the-corner melds are valid, and a deadwood Ace counts 11 against. Nobody melds until one player goes rummy by melding their entire hand, at which point the others meld what they can and the winner scores in the usual way (or, *variant*, one per unmatched card regardless of rank). Cards may not be laid off.

Call Rummy

As Basic Rummy, but: If a player discards a card that could be laid off against a meld, any opponent may immediately call 'Rummy!', lay the discard off, and replace it with a discard from their own hand. If two call simultaneously, priority goes to the next in turn to play.

Discard Rummy

As Basic Rummy, but: You can go out only if you can end your turn by making a discard. Your final card may not be melded or laid off.

Double Rummy

Basic Rummy played with two packs.

One-meld Rummy (Cincinnati Rummy, Queen City Rum)

As Basic Rummy, but: You may may go out only by going rummy, i.e. melding all your cards at once, with or without a discard, and everyone pays you (or you score) the total face value of your melds.

Original Rum

(2–6p, 52c). The most primitive game appears in Donohue, 1905. Deal ten each if two play, seven if three, six if more. Stack the rest face down and turn an upcard. Each in turn draws one card, either from stock or any discard, makes one discard (which must differ from the one taken if a discard was drawn), and may then either make one meld (only) of three or more cards, or lay off one card (only) to any existing meld, but not both. The game ends when somebody melds, lays off, or discards their last card. The others then pay the winner according to their deadwood, counting Ace 1, numerals face value, Jack 11, Queen 12, King 13. If no one has gone out when the stock is depleted, either shuffle the discards and make a new stock, or designate as winner the player with least deadwood.

Variant 1 The discards may be squared up, leaving only the upcard available.

Variant 2 The order of play may be draw-meld-discard instead of draw-discard-meld.

Ramino (Rabino, Remigio)

General term for several Italian varieties of Rummy.

1. One version amounts to seven-card Basic Rummy for two or more players, using 54 cards. Ace counts low or high in a sequence, but not both. Having once melded, you may lay off cards to your own melds, and may take a Joker from any meld in exchange for the appropriate natural card. Deadwood counts at the rate of Aces 1 point, numerals face value, courts 10, Jokers 20 (or 11 by agreement), doubled if the winner went rummy. The first to 101 points loses, or, if more play, drops out.

2. Another version uses two packs with four Jokers and awards side-payments for the following special melds:

Scala reale	Seven in sequence regardless of suit
Sette di seme	Any seven of one suit
Sette figure	Any seven court cards
Pokerissimo	Seven of the same kind

3. A third version is played as above, but with ten cards each. A

single agreed stake is won for going out with a mixed straight, a double for going out with eight of a kind, or quadruple for a straight flush.

Ramino Pokerato
As above, but preceded by a round of Poker-style betting.

Round-the-Corner Rummy (High-Low Rummy)
Any Rummy game in which sequences may turn the corner, i.e. incorporate K-A-2. Ace always counts 11.

Scala Quaranta
(2p, 104c + 4☆). Italian variety of Basic Rummy. Deal thirteen each. One's initial meld must total at least 40 points (whence the title), counting Aces 11 and Jokers 25. Many circles proscribe Jokers in initial melds, and most forbid you to take a Joker for a natural card unless you can meld it immediately.

Skip Rummy
As Basic Rummy, but: Only sets may be melded, not sequences. Having once melded, you may in subsequent turns lay off the fourth of a rank to your own or anyone else's three of the same rank. If left with a pair, you can go out without discarding when you draw a third of the same rank. Play ceases when one player goes out or when the number of cards remaining in stock equals the number taking part. All cards left in hand count against, even if they could have been melded or laid off.

Two-meld Rummy
As Basic Rummy, but: No player may go rummy. Anyone able to do so must hold back one meld to make on the next turn. Consequently, melding with the apparent threat of going out on the next turn may be used as a form of bluff.

Wild-card Rummy
As Basic Rummy, but: Deuces are wild, as are one or more Jokers (optional). Nobody melds until someone can end the game by going rummy. Wild cards left in hand count 25 against.

Loba

This is Argentinian Loba. In Central America the same name (meaning 'she-wolf') denotes Contract Rummy, which in Argentina is called Carioca.

Preliminaries Deal nine cards each from a double pack including four Jokers. Stack the rest face down and turn the next to start a discard pile.

Object To meld cards as you go along and be the first to go out. There are two types of meld.

1. *Pierna* ('leg'). From three to six cards of the same rank and exactly three different suits. Thus a pierna of ♣5 ♦5 ♠5 ♠5 is valid, but not ♦5 ♠5 ♠5 (two suits) or ♣5 ♦5 ♠5 ♥5 (four suits).

2. *Escalera* ('ladder'). Four or more cards in suit and sequence, counting Ace high or low but not both. Thus ♥JQKA and ♠A234 are valid, but not ♣QKA2.

Jokers are wild, but they cannot be used in piernas, and no escalera may contain more than two. A Joker cannot be exchanged for the natural card it represents, but it can be counted as either end of a legal sequence. For example, you can meld ♣345☆, and subsequently add to it either ♣6 or ♣A, leaving ☆ to represent either ♣2 or ♣6. But in ♥A23☆ or ♥23☆5, for example, it can only represent ♥4.

Play At each turn you (1) draw one card, (2) shed cards by making new melds or laying off one or more to your own or other players' melds, and (3) make one discard if you have any left. But:

• you may not draw the upcard unless you can immediately use it to make a new meld in conjunction with other cards from your hand; and

• you may not discard a Joker, unless it is the only card in your hand, in which case you may discard it to go out.

End of deal Play ceases when one player goes out. The others record penalty points equivalent to their deadwood, counting Aces and courts at 10 each and numerals at face value. If you go out by getting rid of all nine (or ten) cards simultaneously, having not previously made any melds or lay-offs, you reduce your penalty score by 10 points.

End of game A player whose penalty score reaches 100 must drop out, but, upon payment of a single stake, may immediately come back in again (*reengancharse*) with the score of the player with the highest current total. No player, however, is allowed more than two *reenganches*. The final winner is the last player left in, or the player with the lowest score if a point is reached at which everybody's score is 100 or more.

Gin

> I will not attempt to describe Gin-Rummy in detail as you can call up any insane asylum and get any patient on the 'phone and learn all about it in no time, as all lunatics are bound to be Gin players, and in fact the chances are it is Gin-Rummy that makes them lunatics.
>
> Damon Runyon, *The Lacework Kid*

Gin Rummy is said to have been perfected in 1909 by a Philadelphian Whist tutor called Elwood T. Baker. A logical development of Conquian/ Coon Can, Gin achieved maximum popularity in the 1930s and 1940s as 'the game of the stars' of both Broadway and Hollywood – as will be well known to all who still enthuse over films of that period. It is subject to many minor variations, and further confused by the fact that many people call almost any form of Rummy 'Gin' even when it isn't. Real Gin is normally played by two and usually for money, though it is undeniably a game of skill. The classic version runs as follows.

Preliminaries Deal two players ten cards each, in ones, from a 52-card pack. Turn the next to start the wastepile, and stack the rest face down.

Object To be the first to knock by laying out all or most of one's cards in melds.

Melds A meld is three or four cards of the same rank, or three or more cards in suit and sequence (Ace low only). A player may knock only if the total face value of unmelded cards left in hand is 10 or less, counting Ace 1, numerals face value, courts 10 each. A 'gin' hand is one in which all ten cards are melded, and scores extra.

Play To start, non-dealer may take the upcard or pass. A pass gives dealer the same option. If both pass, non-dealer must take the top card of stock into hand and make one discard card face up to the wastepile. Each in turn thereafter draws the top card of either the stock or the wastepile and makes one discard to the wastepile. If you take the upcard, you may not discard it in the same turn.

☛ In tournament play the wastepile must be kept squared up and neither player may check through the earlier discards, but in home games this rule may be waived by agreement. However, you are always allowed to spread the stock in order to count how many are left.

Knocking Keep playing till either player knocks, or only two cards remain in stock. In the latter case the game is a no-score draw and the deal passes. You knock by making a final discard face *down* to the wastepile and spreading your other ten cards face up, separated into melds and deadwood. Your opponent then makes whatever melds he can, lays off any cards that match the knocker's melds – unless you went out 'gin', when this is not permitted – and reveals his deadwood.

The knocker normally scores the difference between the values of both players' deadwood, plus a bonus of 25 if he went gin. However, if he didn't go gin, and if his deadwood equals or exceeds that of his opponent, then the latter scores the difference between the two, plus a bonus of 25 for 'undercut'.

Game The deal alternates and scores are kept cumulatively. The winner is the first to reach or exceed a total of 100. Both players then add 25 for each hand they won, and the winner adds a further 100 for the game. The final pay-off is the difference between these end totals, and is doubled if the loser failed to win a single hand.

Variant score Many players score 20 instead of 25 for gin, undercut, and each deal won by the overall winner.

Comment Played well, Gin is a speedy game. Players often knock before half the stock has gone, sometimes after only half a dozen draws. This gradually increases the importance of discarding high unmatched cards rather than low ones in order to reduce deadwood.

Three-hand Gin (Jersey Gin)

Highest cut deals, next highest sits at his left. Play as at two-hand Gin, with the following differences.

1. Eldest must take the first upcard or pass; if he passes, next in turn must take it or pass; if he also passes, eldest draws from stock and play begins.

2. At each turn a player may take either of the two top cards of the discard pile, unless one of them was taken by the previous player, when he may only take the upcard.

3. The winner scores the difference between his own hand and that of each opponent.

4. There is no bonus for undercut; instead, the knocker subtracts 20 (or 25, by agreement) from his score.

5. Opponents may lay off cards only against the knocker's original melds – not against each other's, and not against a card already laid off by the other.

6. The bonus for gin is 50.

7. If no one has melded when only three cards remain in stock, the game is a no-score draw.

8. Game is 200 up.

There are also versions by which only two players are active at a time, but it seems pointless for three players to play a two-hand game. Even more pointless are forms of partnership Gin for any even number of players whereby all play is two-handed but scores are lumped together in teams.

Oklahoma Gin

As two-hand, but the maximum deadwood permitted to the knocker is not necessarily 10 but that of the face value of the initial upcard. For instance, if the upcard is a Seven you may not knock with more than seven. Furthermore, if it is an Ace, you must go gin to knock.

In *The Penguin Book of Card Games* (1979) I mistakenly reported that the maximum deadwood allowed in Oklahoma Gin was that of the *current* upcard. You may like to try this as a variant. It means you can stop your opponent from going out by discarding a card lower than you believe his deadwood to be.

Hollywood Gin

In effect, a method of playing several games simultaneously. Rule up as many double columns as there are deals to be played, and head each pair with the respective initials of the two players. The score for the first deal is entered only in the winner's half of the first double column. That in the second deal is entered at the top of the winner's half of the second column and added to the same player's score in the first. Similarly, each new deal is entered at the top of the next column and accumulated to the score in any previous column that still remains open. When either player reaches a total of 100 in any column, the appropriate bonuses are added and that double column is ruled off, indicating a won game for that player.

Doubling Gin (Open Gin)

This incorporates the doubling principle of Backgammon and other games. Before drawing, a player may offer to double. If the opponent accepts, play proceeds as usual but the winner's score for that hand is doubled, or redoubled if already doubled, and so on. If the double is refused, it doesn't take effect, but the doubler must knock immediately. There are variations on this theme.

Knock Rummy (Poker Rum)

(2–5p, 52c) Multi-player Gin precursor. Deal ten each to two, or seven each to three, four, or five players. No one melds till someone who thinks they have sufficiently low deadwood goes out by drawing a card in turn, knocking on the table, and discarding. Everyone then displays their hands, separated into melds and deadwood. Whoever has the lowest deadwood scores or is paid the difference between their count and that of everyone else. Melding every card scores a bonus of 25. A winning player who undercuts the knocker wins a bonus of 10 from the knocker. The game ends without score if the stock gets reduced to a number of cards equal to the number of players.

Tonk or Tunk

(2–6p, 4–5 best, 52c) Highly variable gambling game with one characteristic feature, namely: If, after the initial deal of five cards (sometimes seven), anyone has a hand worth 49 or more, or 15 or less (counting Ace 1, numerals face value, courts 10 each), they may immediately 'tonk' (knock), thereby winning without play, and receiving a double stake from each opponent. If two players tonk, it is a no-score draw and there is a new deal. No one may tonk once play has begun. Each in turn may draw from stock or discards, may meld or lay off, and must discard unless they have gone out. Play ceases when someone knocks or plays their last card, or the stock runs out. The player with the lowest deadwood wins a single stake from any higher hand. If anyone knocks and is equalled or beaten, they pay double to the winner. Subject to many incidental variations (see Pagat website).

Elimination Rummy (Java Rummy, Freeze-out)

Deuces are wild, as are any Jokers that may be added. Deal seven each. Each in turn draws and discards without melding. This continues until one player, without drawing, goes out by melding all seven cards, or six cards provided that the seventh does not count more than five. Jokers count 25 against, Aces 15, courts 10, others at face value. Going out by melding all seven entitles you to deduct 25 from your current penalty total. Upon reaching 100 penalties, a player drops out and pays a single stake to the pool. The pool eventually goes to the last player left in, or to the player with the lowest score if more than one reach 100 simultaneously.

Kings and Queens

Two-pack basic Rummy with Deuces wild. A player goes out by melding all seven cards in sequences and/or sets of three or more, or by melding six cards provided that the seventh counts not more than seven. Play then ceases, and, if that player has a card unmelded, opponents may lay off their own unmeldable cards of the same rank against it to increase his deadwood. The game is so called because any King forming part of a valid meld reduces a player's penalty score by 5 points, and any Queen similarly by 3 points. Players drop out when they reach 100 penalty points, the last two in sharing the pool between them in proportions of 3:1. Alternatively, the game ends when one reaches 100, and the winner is the player with lowest count (which may be negative).

Mississippi Rummy

(3–8p, 104c, deal ten each) A hard- and soft-score game that limits the amount any player can lose. Assuming a limit of 100p, everyone places that amount on the table to start with. Each player antes 10p before each deal. After the deal, but before play begins, (1) anyone dissatisfied with their hand may lay it face down and decline to play; and (2) anyone dealt 10 of a suit ('Mississippi') or a rummy hand (all cards meldable) shows it, receives 20p from each opponent, adds 20p to the pot, and retires from the play of that hand.

A player may knock on a count of 5 or less. A knocker who goes rummy receives 10p from each other active player and pays 10p to the pot. Otherwise, unless undercut, the knocker receives 5p from each opponent and pays 5p to the pot. If undercut, the knocker pays 20p to anyone who undercut and 5p to each active opponent, and the undercutter adds 10p to the pot.

A player who goes rummy or who goes out without drawing may deduct 10 points from their penalty score, likewise 20 points for a Mississippi.

Upon reaching 100 penalty points a player is eliminated, but may buy in again for 10p and a penalty score equal to that of the second-highest player.

Three Thirteen

(2–4p, 52c) There are 11 deals. The first is of three cards, and Threes are wild; the second of four cards, with Fours wild; and so on, up to a final deal of eleven cards with Kings wild. At each turn draw the top card of stock or the upcard and make one discard. Play ceases when one player goes out by melding all their cards face up, with or without making a final discard. Other players may then meld as many of their cards as possible, but not lay cards off to other players' melds, and score penalty points equivalent to the value of their deadwood. The player with fewest penalty points after 11 deals wins. (From Leah Mathis, via the Pagat website. Related games include Nickel Nickel, the French-Canadian game of Dime, and the Sri Lankan game of Proter.)

Chin-Chón

Spanish Rummy, played by up to three players with 40 cards, or up to five with 48 cards. If 48, cards run A23456789 Sota Caballo Rey, and courts count 10 each; if 40, cards run A234567SCR, and courts count respectively 8, 9, 10. Deal seven each and play as at Gin. A player may knock with deadwood of 5 or less, and whoever has least deadwood deducts 10 from his (penalty) score. Melding one's entire hand is Chin-Chón, and makes everyone else lose double. Players drop out upon reaching 100 penalty points.

Thirty-One Rum (Scat)   2–9 players, 52 cards

> We were playing three-penny-scat, the dullest card game ever invented, but it
> was too hot to think about anything more complicated.
>
> Stephen King, *The Body* (*Different Seasons*)

This popular American game is called Thirty-One (but see separate
entry for this title), or Scat (but it bears no relation to Skat), or Ride
the Bus (related to Stop the Bus – see Bastard Brag). It amounts, in fact,
to Thirty-One played in the manner of Rummy instead of with a spare
hand, for which reason I have added 'Rum' to the title. The differences
are minimal.

Deal three cards each and stack the rest face down, turning the top
one as the first upcard. Each in turn takes the top card of stock, or the
upcard, and makes one discard. The aim is to get cards totalling 31, or
as close as possible, in a single suit. Ace counts 11, courts 10 each,
numerals face value.

Examples: ♠A ♠K ♣J counts 31, ♥5 ♥3 ♥2 counts 10, ♣8 ♣9 ♦J counts 17,
♦A ♣9 ♥9 counts 11.

Play continues until either of the following happens:
• someone gets 31 exactly, in which case they call for an immediate
showdown, and everyone else loses a life; or
• someone with less than 31 knocks instead of drawing a card, in which
case everybody gets one more turn before the showdown, and the player
with the lowest flush score loses a life.

Lose three lives and you're out. The last player left in wins.

Lives are usually represented by pennies or chips, but (to quote from
the Pagat website), 'Ride the Bus has a different way of keeping track
of wins and losses. All players start out "seated" at the back of the bus.
Players who lose a hand move toward the front in a sequence. The
sequence is usually: first, you stand at the back of the bus, then you are
in the middle of the bus, then at the front of the bus, then you are on
the stairs, then you are off the bus. Players who are no longer "riding
the bus" are out of play. Winning a hand simply keeps your position;
you do not move back a step if you win a hand.'

Wushiyi Fen (Fifty-One)   2–8 players, 54 cards

A Chinese game, first described in English by John McLeod in *The Playing-Card* (Vol. VIII, No. 3, February 1980).

Preliminaries Deal from two to eight players five cards each in ones and stack the rest face down. Play to the right.

Object To go out by collecting five cards of the same suit, preferably with a high face value. For this purpose Aces count 11, courts 10 each, and numerals at face value. Jokers belong to any suit and count as any card of that suit not already held.

Play Eldest draws the top card of stock and makes a discard face up. Each in turn thereafter may either:

• draw the top card of stock and add one face up to the discard pile, which should be kept spread out so all are visible; or

• take the whole discard pile after previously discarding the same number of cards from hand to act as a replacement for it.

The pile of discards may never exceed five. When it contains exactly five, each in turn has the further option of drawing any one card from it in exchange for any replacement. As soon as one player draws from stock instead, the five discards are bunched and discarded face down from play. The discard of the player who drew from stock starts a new discard pile, and play proceeds as before.

Going out When you have five of a suit you may, on your turn to play, either draw in the hope of increasing their total face value, or 'knock' by laying all five on the table before you. You may not draw and go out in the same turn.

End of stock If the stock runs out before anyone goes out, the players reveal their cards and everyone scores for their best flush.

Score When someone has knocked, all players reveal their hands. Anyone with five cards of the same suit scores as specified above, making 51 the highest possible total. The knocker scores double, provided that no one else has a higher-scoring five-flush, or one of equal face value but containing fewer Jokers. Anyone who does have such a better hand (or the best of them if more than one player has) scores the value of his own hand plus that of the knocker, who deducts the value of his own hand from his current score.

Game Play up to 1000, or any other agreed target.

Comment I find the above rules unsatisfactory and favour the following modifications. (1) Jokers belong to any suit but have a face value of zero. (2) A player with three or four cards of a suit cannot knock but may, at a showdown, score the face value of the flush, less the face value of any cards of a different suit. This just about makes it possible for a player who knocks with a low five-flush to be beaten, on points, by one with a shorter but higher-scoring flush.

Conquian (Coon Can)

2 players, 40 cards

The earliest true Rummy, a kind of proto-Gin, was first played in Mexico and neighbouring states, especially Texas, from the mid-nineteenth century. The name is a mystery. Some relate it to Spanish *¿con quién?*, literally 'with whom?', but the phrase is totally irrelevant. Like other Rummy names such as Coon Can, Khun Khan, Khan-hoo, Chin-Chón, and so on, it is probably a corruption of an oriental game which I have seen recorded as 'kong-king'.

Preliminaries Deal ten cards each from a 40-card pack ranking A234567JQK and stack the rest face down. The aim is to be the first to go out by melding eleven cards, including the last one drawn. A meld is three or more cards of the same rank or from three to eight cards in suit and sequence. Because Ace is low and Seven and Jack consecutive, both A-2-3 and 6-7-J are valid, but Q-K-A is not.

☞ Technically, you can have a sequence of nine or ten cards, but neither is of any use because you need an eleventh to go out.

Start Non-dealer starts by facing the top card of stock. He may not take it into hand, but must either meld it immediately (with at least two hand-cards) or pass. If he melds, he must balance his hand by making a discard face up. If he passes, dealer must either meld it himself, leaving a discard face up in its place, or else also pass by turning it face down. In the latter event it becomes his turn to draw from stock.

Play Continue in the same way. Whoever turns from stock has first choice of the card turned, and must either meld it, extend one of his existing melds with it, or pass. If both pass, the second turns it down and draws next. If a player declines a faced card which can legally be added to one of his existing melds, he must meld it if his opponent so demands. In this way, it is sometimes possible to force a player into a situation from which he can never go out – a point of considerable strategic interest.

Rearrangement In melding, a player may 'borrow' cards from his other melds to help create new ones, provided that those thereby depleted are not reduced to less than valid three-card melds. After melding, the player's discard becomes available to the opponent, who may either meld it himself or turn it down and make the next draw.

Ending Play ceases when one player melds both the faced card and all cards remaining in his hand, whether by adding to existing melds, making new ones, or both. If neither is out when the last available card has been declined, the game is drawn and the stake carried forward.

Pan (Panguingue)

A multi-player extension of Conquian dating from the early 1900s and still widely played in dedicated gaming establishments in the western United States, especially California. It is exclusively a casino game and has too many complications to justify description here.

▌ Kaluki (Caloochie, etc)   2–6 players, 104 cards

Reportedly most popular in the eastern United States, it is a moot point whether this double-pack Rummy has a greater variety of spellings (Caloochie, Kaloochi, Kaloochie, Kalougie, Kalookie, etc.) or of rules. The following are typical.

Preliminaries From a double 52-card pack plus four Jokers deal fifteen each, or thirteen if five play, or eleven if six. Turn the next to start the wastepile, and stack the rest face down.

Object To be the first out of cards by laying them down in melds, and by laying off individual cards to existing melds (own or others') whenever they match.

Melds A meld is three or four cards of the same rank, or three or more cards in suit and sequence. Sequence order is A23456789TJQKA, Ace counting high or low but not both (K-A-2 is illegal). A Joker may represent any desired card. No meld may contain two identical cards (unless previously agreed otherwise), or simultaneously a Joker and the card it represents.

Play Each in turn draws the top card of either the stock or the wastepile, makes any possible melds, and makes one discard face up to the wastepile. You cannot take the upcard until you have made at least one meld, or can immediately use the upcard to make one.

The first meld made by each player must comprise cards totalling at least 51, counting Ace 15, courts 10, numerals at face value, and Jokers as the cards they represent. You may, however, make a lower-scoring initial meld, provided that you simultaneously lay off a card or cards to other melds which bring the total value of cards played from your hand to 51 or more.

Exchanging Jokers If you hold a natural card which can be substituted for a Joker lying in a meld of your own or anyone else's, you may exchange it for the Joker on your turn to play. If the Joker is ambiguous, any card that leaves a legal meld will do. For example, given ♥4-♥5-♥6-☆, you could exchange the Joker for either ♥3 or ♥7.

Going out Keep playing till someone goes out by melding, laying off, or discarding the last card from their hand.

If playing for hard score, whoever goes out receives from each opponent an agreed stake for each card left in hand. Each Joker counts as two cards, and all stakes are doubled if the winner went 'Kaluki' by going out without having previously made any meld.

If playing for soft score, those who did not go out are penalized by the total face value of cards left in hand, Jokers counting 25. The overall winner is the player with the lowest penalty score when someone loses by reaching an agreed target, such as 150.

Variant Whoever goes out scores the value of all cards left in opponents' hands. Play up to an agreed target score.

Contract Rummy   3–8 players, 2 or 3 × 52 cards

Less a single game than a variety of games based on a single idea – namely, a game consists of several deals, typically seven, each imposing a specific pattern of melds (the contract) to enable a player to go out.

The earliest (Zioncheck) dates from the 1930s. Other names, each denoting a more or less trivial variant, include Hollywood Rummy, Joker Rummy, Liverpool Rummy, May I?, Seven-deal Rummy and Shanghai Rummy. Enthusiasts continue to invent variations on the underlying pattern, often giving them names either knowingly or unwittingly used for obsolete forerunners, making it impossible to keep track of who means what by which.

Preliminaries Three or four players use two packs shuffled together, with one Joker. Five to eight use three such packs and two Jokers. By agreement, Deuces may be declared wild.

Deal Deal ten cards each in the first four deals, twelve each in the last three, stack the rest face down and turn the next to start a discard pile. If the stock is emptied before anyone goes out, shuffle the discards and start a new one.

Object To be the first to go out by melding and laying off all one's cards. But no one may start melding until they can exactly match the pattern of melds required for that deal, which varies as follows (#3 denotes three cards of the same rank; $3 denotes a suit-sequence of three cards. In sequences, cards rank A23456789TJQKA, Ace counting high or low but not both at once):

1. meld 6/10 cards as	#3 #3
2. meld 7/10 cards as	#3 $4
3. meld 8/10 cards as	$4 $4
4. meld 9/10 cards as	#3 #3 #3
5. meld 10/12 cards as	#3 #3 $4
6. meld 11/12 cards as	#3 $4 $4
7. meld all 12 cards as	$4 $4 $4

Two or more requisite sequences may be of the same suit, and may overlap, but they must not be consecutive. For example, ♠2345 ♠4567 or ♠2345 ♥6789 are valid, but not ♠2345 ♠6789. Having melded, a player goes out by subsequently laying off any cards remaining in hand. In this case it is legal to extend suit-sequences, which may contain up to 14 cards (running from Ace low to Ace high).

Play The procedure differs from that of basic Rummy. On your turn you must first either take the upcard or else ask if anyone else wants it. If you offer it, the right to take it passes to each player in rotation until someones takes it or everyone passes. If anyone takes it, they must also draw the top card of stock, but may not discard. This increases their hand as a penalty for gaining a wanted card out of turn.

If you take the upcard, you need not meld it immediately but may add it to your hand. If not, and when everyone has had a chance to take that upcard, you continue by drawing the top card of stock.

Whether or not you meld or lay off, you complete your turn by making a final discard, which must differ from the upcard if that is what you took.

Melding You don't meld anything until you can meld the required pattern of melds for the deal, and you may not meld more than the basic requirement on that turn.

Laying off Having once melded, you may, on subsequent turns, lay off one or more cards to your own or other players' melds, but may not open any new ones.

Wild cards No initial meld may contain more than one wild card. The only wild card you may take in exchange for a natural card is a Joker, and then only when it is being used in a sequence. However, when you hold a natural card that is being represented by a wild card in a sequence, you may add it to the sequence and move the wild card to either end. For example, holding ♥7, you can lay it off to ♥6W89, making the W either ♥5 or ♥T. (W = wild card.)

Ending and Scoring Play ceases when someone either lays off or discards the last card from their hand. Everyone else scores penalties for deadwood at the rate 15 for Aces and wild cards, 10 for courts, and numerals at face value. The player with fewest penalties at the end of seven deals wins.

Zioncheck

(2–6p, 2 × 52c) The earliest form of Contract Rummy, credited to Ruth Armson. Five deals of ten cards each, contract requirements as in deals 1 to 5 above. (From Sifakis.)

King Rummy

(4p, 2 × 52c + 4☆) Four deals of ten cards each. Contract requirements: (1) #3 $4, (2) #3 #3 #3, (3) $4 $4, (4) #3 #3 $4. You may make more than the minimum requirement when you first meld, and may lay off single cards on the same turn. As soon as a Joker is melded, the first player in rotation able to take it in exchange for the natural card it represents may do so, and the person who melded does not discard until this has happened or everyone has passed. Jokers 25, Aces 15, courts 10, numerals face value. (From Sifakis.)

Progressive Rummy

(2–6p, 2 × 52c, Deuces wild) Precursor of Contract Rummy. Seven deals of ten cards each. The contract requirements may be met with sets or sequences or one of each. Meld (1) three cards, (2) four cards, (3) five cards, (4) two threes, (5) three and four, (6) three and five, (7) two fours. Sets of three must be of three different suits; sets of four or more must include all four suits. You can go out only with a discard. Deuces 15, Aces 11, courts 10, numerals face value. Players drop out upon reaching 100 penalty points. (From Phillips.)

Liverpool Rummy

Same as Contract, but the player at dealer's right cuts the pack and deducts 50 from his penalty points if he manages to cut exactly the number of cards required for the complete deal plus one upcard. (From Paul Welty, via Pagat website.)

Carioca

is the Argentine name for a game similar to one played in Central America under the name Loba (which in Argentina is a different Rummy). The differences from Contract Rummy (above) are too slight and probably too variable to justify separate description. (Details on Pagat website.)

Czech Rummy

(2–5p, 104c + 4☆) This interesting variation on a theme of contract was the 'default' Rummy played in Prague in the 1960s (source: Mike Arnautov). Deal twelve each, stack the rest face down, and turn an upcard. At each turn draw from stock or take the upcard, optionally meld or lay cards off to melds (your own only), and discard one. You may also steal a Joker from any meld on the table if you can replace it with the card it represents. A meld is three or more cards of the same rank, or three or more cards in suit and sequence (Ace low). In the first deal, the first meld each player makes must be worth at least 15, counting

Ace 1, numerals face value, Jack 11, Queen 12, King 13. In subsequent deals, the minimum required value of an initial meld depends on one's current score. That of the leading player must count at least 15, of the second player 20, the third 25, and so on up in fives. If two players have the same score, the minimum required of the next player down will be 10 more than that of the tied players. When someone goes out, everyone else counts their unmelded cards as deadwood, even if meldable. Players drop out upon reaching 300 in total. The winner is the last left in, or the player with the lowest score if all pass 300 simultaneously.

Buy Rummy

(2–6p, 52 or 104c) Use one or two packs, depending on the number of players. Deal five each. Play as Basic Rummy but: On your turn to play, either draw the top card of stock or, if you want the upcard, bid for it by stating how many additional cards you will also draw from stock, up to a maximum of six. For example, if you bid 'One', and no one overcalls, you will take the upcard plus one card from stock. But any other player may make a higher bid, and whoever bids highest takes the upcard plus the same number from stock. That player continues by melding, if possible, or, having once melded, by laying a card or cards off to any meld on the table. His turn ends with a discard and passes to his left. First out of cards wins 1 point or stake for each card remaining in other players' hands.

Variant Cards to the number bid are drawn not from stock but from the discard pile, in succession from the upcard downwards, and the maximum bid is the number of cards available. The bidder may continue by melding and laying off, but does not discard.

Push

4 players (2 × 2), 108 cards

A partnership version of Contract Rummy with an unusual method of play. This description is based on one by Paul Welty (via the Pagat website).

Preliminaries Four players sitting crosswise in partnerships use a double 52-card pack plus four Jokers. All Jokers and Deuces are wild.

Deal There are five deals. The first dealer is chosen at random and the turn to deal passes to the left. The number of cards dealt and the initial meld requirement for each deal are as follows:

deal	hand	initial meld
1	6	2 sets of three
2	7	1 set of three, 1 run of four
3	8	2 runs of four
4	9	3 sets of three
5	10	2 runs of five

Deal the appropriate number of cards in ones, turn the next to start a discard pile, and stack the rest face down. If the turn-up is a wild card, bury it in the pack and turn the next instead.

Object In each deal, to meld all your cards, or as many as possible.

Melds A meld is a run of three or more cards in suit and sequence, or a set of three or four cards of the same rank and different in suit. A set may not contain duplicate cards, but any player or side may meld two sets of the same rank.

In a run, Ace counts high or low but not both, and wild cards may count as Twos (permitting A-2-3 ... or ... Q-K-A but not ... K-A-2 ...). You may meld two separate runs in the same suit, for example 4-5-6-7 and 8-9-T-J, or could meld all these together as a run of eight. Once melded, however, runs cannot be split up or joined together, only extended.

Play Each in turn, starting with the player at dealer's left, draws a card, may make a meld, and ends by making a discard.

1. Draw. If you want the upcard, take it and add it to your hand. If not, take the top card of stock, place it face down on top of the upcard, push both cards to your left-hand opponent – who must add them to his hand – and complete your draw by taking the top card of stock.

2. Meld. Having drawn, you may, if able and willing, meld cards by placing them face up on the table. The first meld you make in each deal must meet the initial meld requirements stated in the Table above. This applies to each player individually. If your partner has made an initial meld, this does not qualify you as having made one yourself.

Once you have made a valid initial meld, you may, in the same or subsequent turns, put down any further melds you wish to, or lay off one or more cards to any melds already on the table, regardless of who made them.

3. Discard. End your turn by adding a card to the discard pile.

Wild cards Deuces and Jokers are wild and may be used to represent any desired card, including Twos. A meld must contain at least one natural card. If you make an ambiguous meld, you must clarify what it is. For example, if you meld ♠7-☆-☆, you must state whether it represents ♠5-6-7, or ♠6-7-8, or ♠7-8-9, or three Sevens. If the latter, you need not specify which suits they represent.

If you hold a natural card which is currently being represented by a Joker in any meld on the table, you may, after drawing and before discarding, take the Joker in exchange for that natural card, provided that you can immediately lay the Joker off to another meld or use it in a new one. You may not merely take it into hand.

If a Deuce or Joker is being used as a Two, for example in ♣A-♥2-♣3-♣4, you cannot exchange it (even, in this case, for ♣2).

Going out Play ceases the moment one player goes out by either melding, laying off, or discarding his last card.

Score The side of the player who went out records no penalty points. The other side count penalties for all the cards remaining in both players' hands, as follows:

20 per wild card

15 per Ace

10 per K-Q-J-T

 5 per lower numeral

The winning side is the one with fewest penalty points at the end of the last deal.

Vatican

I was born in Prague to Russian émigré parents. We spoke Russian at home and Czech in the street, but the home culture was largely that of White Russia. Amongst games I learned from my parents and grandmother was Rummy – a version which Czechs didn't seem to play, but were aware of as Vatican. It is a very good game. I suspect that my early mastery of it encouraged mental combinatorial skills which came very handy later in my professional life.

Mike Arnautov, computer systems programmer/architect

Vatican features the novel concept of making melds common property rather than belonging to individual players. It is obviously related to the proprietary tile game Rummikub, which I first encountered in Romania in 1976, and which was first published in Israel. I am grateful to Mike Arnautov for checking this description.

Preliminaries Though playable by two to five, the game works best with three or four. Shuffle together two 52-card packs and two Jokers, making 106 cards in all. Deal thirteen each and stack the rest face down. There is no turn-up and no discard pile.

Object To be the first to go out by playing all your cards from hand to melds on the table.

Melds A meld is three or more cards of the same rank or in suit and sequence. Three or four of the same rank must all be of different suits. Sequence order is A23456789TJQKA. Ace counts both high and low, so -K-A-2- is allowed.

Play At each turn you either draw the top card of stock and add it to hand, or play at least one card from your hand to melds on the table. (If none remain in stock and you cannot play, you must pass.)

The first time you play instead of drawing, you must meld a suit-sequence of at least three cards from hand. Having done so, you may on this and any subsequent turn add one or more cards to the table, and arrange or rearrange melds as you please. The only restriction is that, at the end of your turn, all cards on the table must remain arranged in valid melds of at least three cards.

> ☛ If you find you cannot finish by leaving legal melds, you must retrieve the cards that won't fit. If none of them fit, you must take them all back and draw from stock instead (if any remain).

Jokers A Joker may represent any desired card. Subsequently, it may be replaced by the card it represents, but may not then be taken into hand: it must remain somewhere on the table as part of a valid meld.

Ending If the stock empties before anyone has gone out, each in turn must continue to play if possible, otherwise must pass. The first player out of cards thereby ends and wins the game. There is no scoring.

Carousel

An early member of the Vatican type, Carousel was first recorded by Morehead & Mott-Smith (*Culbertson's Card Games Complete*, 1952), and closely resembles Gin. Two players use 52 cards and one Joker, three 104 and two Jokers. Jokers are wild, and melds in the two-pack game may not include duplicated cards. Deal ten each. Each in turn draws a card from stock and either makes one or more melds or draws again. A player's turn ends after three such draws.

The minimum meld is three or more of a kind or a suit-sequence of three or more (Ace low). In melding, you may steal required cards from opponents' melds provided that all melds remain legal. For example, from 6-7-8-9 you can take only the Six or Nine. There is no discarding.

On your turn to play you may knock to end the game, instead of drawing, provided your deadwood is down to 5 or less. (Originally 10 or less, but 5 is now usual.) There is no laying off. The player with the lowest deadwood (Jokers 25, courts 10 each, Aces and numerals face value) scores the difference between their deadwood and that of each other player. Undercutting the knocker earns a bonus of 10 points. Tied players divide equally. Add 25 for zero deadwood. Game is 150 points, and the winner adds 100 for game. Anyone with a zero score loses double.

Krambambuli

(2–3p, 52c; 4–6p, 104c)

> Des Abends spät, des Morgens früh,
> Trink' ich mein Glas Krambambuli –
> Kram-bim-bam-bambuli, Krambambuli!
>
> German drinking song (trad.)

Deal eleven each and stack the rest face down. At each turn draw from stock or take the upcard, optionally put out melds consisting of at least three cards of the same rank or in suit and sequence (Ace high), and discard one. Having once melded, you may subsequently lay off additional matching cards to your own melds. You may then also, on any future turn, steal a card from another player's meld, provided that (a) the meld from which it is robbed remains valid, (b) you combine it with at least two cards from your own hand to make a new meld, and (c) you do not steal more than one card in any one turn. When one player goes out, the others count their deadwood at the rate of Aces and courts 10 each, numerals face value. Lowest score wins when someone reaches 500. (From Pennycook, *The Book of Card Games*, 1982.)

Shanghai (Manipulation)

In recent versions of this game, played under various names by up to five players, you do not draw if you can meld, and you must meld if you can, rearranging as necessary. (The process of rearrangement is called 'shanghai' in one variant and 'manipulation' in another.) If unable, you keep drawing until either you can meld or the stock runs out. Aces may be used high or low in sequences, and count 15 against, while numerals below Ten each count 5 against.

Don't forget . . .
- Play to the left (clockwise) unless otherwise stated.
- Eldest or Forehand means the player to the left of the dealer in left-handed games, to the right in right-handed games.
- T = Ten, p = players, pp = in fixed partnerships, c = cards, † = trump, ☆ = Joker.

In the original Rummy games described in the previous chapter, the main aim is to 'go out' by melding all your cards, and the only scores are penalties for cards left unmelded in other players' hands. In the 1920s somebody had the bright idea of introducing positive scores for the melds that you make, an early example of this type being 500 Rum. In Canasta and its relatives, this idea is so elaborated that you may wish to keep the game open as long as possible in order to score more and more for melds. Little more than 50 years old at the start of the twenty-first century, Canasta is the most recent card game to have achieved world-wide status as a classic.

Canasta   2–4 players, 108 cards

> It originated in Uruguay ('Canasta' in Spanish means a basket) and is said to have been invented by the ladies of Montevideo as a counter-attraction to Poker which, in their opinion, took up far too much of their menfolk's time.
>
> Albert A. Ostrow, *The Complete Card Player* (1949 edition)

> It puzzles me that people don't seem to play Canasta in South America. They seem to have invented it and then left it to everyone else to take up while they forgot it.
>
> John McLeod (in commenting on this chapter)

Ostrow's account reflects the views of Cecilia and David Salinas, whose card-playing experiences in Montevideo in 1942-7 led them to write *How to Play Canasta del Uruguay* (1949). They add that it was invented there in 1940, codified in 1946, and borrowed and corrupted by the card-clubs of Buenos Aires (which faces Montevideo across the River Plate). According to Ottilie H. Riley, however, whose *Canasta: the Argentine Rummy Game* appeared earlier in 1949, it was invented in Buenos Aires and borrowed and corrupted by the players of Montevideo. Whoever has the right of it, the fact is that the game now played under that name is more distinctly Argentinian than Uruguayan. It certainly reached the USA in 1949, and from 1950 to 1952 was the biggest fad in the history of card games. In Britain, its popularity with the Princess Margaret branch of the royal family ensured equal social success. By the time it pervaded the rest of Europe, practically every other South American state had got in on the act, developing more and more elaborate variations under such names as Chile, Bolivia, Mexicana, and all stations north of Tierra del Fuego.

Canasta has now settled down to the status of a classic. Though no longer a fad, it has notably survived such elaborate descendants as Samba and Bolivia. Even so, the following 'book rules' are subject, in practice, to local variations. Incidentally, while Canasta is invariably regarded as a partnership game – probably because it was developed by Bridge-players – it works remarkably well for two, which one early account claims to have been the original form.

Preliminaries Four players sit crosswise in partnerships. Use two 52-card packs and four Jokers, 108 cards in all. It doesn't greatly matter if the backs are of different colours.

Deal After thorough shuffling and a cut, deal eleven each in ones and stack the rest face down. Turn the top card of the stock to start a discard pile. This pile is known as 'the pack', and its top card as 'the upcard'. If the turned card is a Joker, a Two, or a red Three, cover it with the next card turned from stock. Keep doing so, if necessary, until it is some other card.

Red Threes dealt If you are dealt one or more red Threes, you must, on your first turn to play, lay it or them face up before you and draw replacements from stock. They are bonus cards and take no part in the play.

Object To make and score for melds, especially canastas, and to be the first side to reach 5000 points over as many deals as necessary.

• A meld is three or more cards of the same rank, regardless of suit. Melds can be increased by the addition of natural cards of the same rank or of wild cards represented by Jokers and Deuces. Melds made by both partners are kept together in front of one of them.

• A canasta is a meld of seven or more cards. A side cannot go out until it has made at least one canasta.

Cards Individual cards score as follows:

red Threes	100
Jokers	50
Aces and Deuces	20
each K Q J T 9 8	10
each 7 6 5 4	5
black Threes	5

Threes are special, and are not normally melded. All Jokers and Twos are wild, counting as any desired rank except Threes. A meld must always contain at least two natural cards, and may never contain more than three wild. A canasta must contain at least four naturals but may contain any number of wild cards.

Play Each player's turn consists of three parts: (1) draw, (2) meld (if able and willing), and (3) discard.

1. *Draw.* You may always draw the top card of stock, and either add it to your hand, meld it (subject to rules of melding below), or discard it face up to the pack.

Alternatively, you may take the whole pack (not just part), provided that you immediately use the upcard in a meld. If the pack is not 'frozen' (see below), you may use the upcard to start a new meld by combining it with two cards of the same rank (or one and a wild card) from your hand, or you may lay it off to a meld of that rank belonging to your side.

The pack is frozen to you and your partner until either of you has made an initial meld, and to both partnerships whenever it is headed by a wild card, or when it contains a wild card or a red Three turned at the start of play. In this event, you may use the upcard only to start a new meld with a natural pair of the same rank from your own hand – unless you already have a meld of that rank, in which case you can take the pack and add the top card to that meld.

> ☛ *Black Threes stop for one turn.* Even if the pack is not frozen, you still cannot take it if the upcard is a black Three, as it cannot be melded, except to go out. Discarding a black Three therefore stops the pack to your left-hand opponent for one turn.
> ☛ *Red Threes are simple bonus cards.* If you draw one from stock, lay it face up next to your melds and draw the next card as a replacement. If you are the first player to take the pack, and it includes a red Three, set it out but do not draw a replacement. Subsequent packs will not include red Threes, as they may not be discarded.

2. *Meld.* A new meld is made by laying face up on the table three or more cards of the same rank, of which at least two must be natural and not more than three wild. The first meld made by either side must consist of cards whose combined values reach a minimum requirement, either alone or in connjunction with one or more other melds made at the same time. The minimum requirement depends on the partnership's current score, as follows:

Current score	Minimum
Below 0	15
0 or more	50
1500 or more	90
3000 or more	120

☞ It follows that the minimum requirement is 50 at start of play. If and when a partnership's current score falls below zero there is no minimum requirement. (Fifteen is merely the lowest value possible.)

Once a meld has been made, either partner may extend it by adding one or more cards of the same rank, or wild cards. When it contains seven or more, it becomes a canasta, and is squared up into a pile with a red card on top if it consists entirely of natural cards (*canasta limpia*, 'clean canasta'), otherwise a black one (*canasta sucia*, 'dirty canasta'). Subsequently adding a wild card to a red canasta makes it a black canasta, and its top card is changed accordingly.

On your turn to play you may create and extend as many melds as you like, but you may not do any of the following:

* shift a wild card from one meld to another;
* run more than one meld of a given rank;
* add to a meld belonging to the other side;
* meld or discard the last card from your hand unless you are legally entitled to go out (see below).

3. *Discard.* End your turn by making one discard face up to the top of the pack. This may be any card exept a red Three. Discarding a black Three prevents your left-hand opponent from taking the pack. Discarding a wild card 'freezes' the pack if it is not already frozen. It helps to indicate this fact by placing it sideways and projecting from the pack.

Going out You may go out by melding, laying off or discarding the last card from your hand, provided that your partnership has made at least one canasta. It may be advisable, but is not obligatory, to ask your partner's permission to go out. If you do, the only permissible response is 'Yes' or 'No', and you must abide by it. Any other response entitles the opposing side to grant or withhold the requested permission.

> ☞ You can't go out if, after the draw, you hold two black Threes and nothing else. With just one, you can go out by discarding it. With three or four, you can go out by melding them. Wild cards may not be included in such a meld.
> ☞ If you hold just one card in hand, and the pack also consists of just one card, you cannot go out by taking the pack (unless the stock is empty: see below).

There is a bonus for going out 'concealed' – that is, by going out (with or without a discard) without having previously made any melds or lay-offs. The hand must include a canasta, and no lay-off may be made to any meld made by your partner.

End of stock The stock very occasionally empties before anyone has gone out. If the last card drawn is a red Three it automatically ends the game, except that the player drawing it may first make as many melds and lay-offs as possible. (He may not discard.) If it is not a red Three, play continues without a stock. You each in turn then take the upcard if you can meld or lay it off, and end your turn by discarding or melding out. This continues until someone either goes out or cannot use the previous player's discard, when all play ceases.

Score Each side scores the total value of all cards it has melded, plus any of the following relevant bonuses:

For each natural canasta	500
For each mixed canasta	300
For going out	100 (200 if concealed)
For each red Three declared	100 (200 each if all four held)

From this total subtract the total value of cards left in both partners' hands. If your side has failed to make any meld, or taken but failed to declare any red Three, then every red Three you have taken counts 100 against, or 200 if you took all four. Carry the score forward, and cease play if either side has reached or exceeded 5000. The winning margin is the difference between the two sides' final scores.

Penalties The commonest penalties are the loss of 500 for holding a red Three (it should have been declared and set out), 100 for trying to go out without permission, 100 for being unable to go out after receiving permission to do so, 50 for taking the upcard when unable to use it legally.

Comment Canasta is essentially a point-scoring game. Keep the game open as long as possible by taking the pack frequently, freezing it to

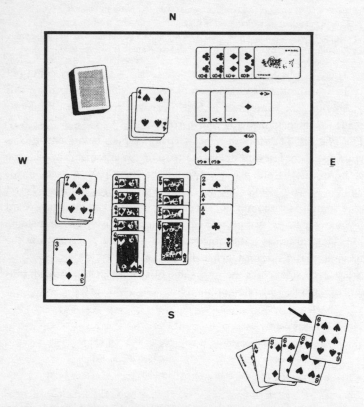

Canasta. South, having just drawn ♠6 from the pack, proposes to go out by melding three Sixes, laying off the Ace and Joker to the meld of Aces, and discarding ♦5. North-South will score 300 for the mixed canasta (Sevens), 50 for Queens, 40 for Kings, 130 for the Ace meld, 15 for the Sixes, 100 for the red Three, and 100 for going out, total 735, less whatever remains in North's hand. East-West have 90 for the meld of Eights, 60 for the Aces and 200 for the red Threes, total 350, less whatever remains in both hands.

your opponents, and not reducing your hand too early in the game. Aim to go out when you are well ahead, or if you can do so before the other side has melded, or as a defensive measure if the other side is doing too well. Use wild cards to freeze the pack when the other side is well ahead, or has made an initial meld before you have. Discard a black Three to stop the pack to your left-hand opponent, especially when your right-hand opponent has just made their side's opening meld.

Canasta for two

Deal fifteen cards each, and at each turn draw two but discard one. Two canastas are required to go out. Penalties need not be so rigidly enforced, as there is no partner to benefit from illegally acquired information.

Canasta for three

As above, but: Deal thirteen each (or cleven), and at each turn draw two but discard one. Each plays for himself. This version should be described as Cut-throat Canasta, but the term is actually reserved for what properly should be called Solo Canasta and plays as follows: The first player to take the pack becomes the lone player, and the others then play as partners against him. The initial meld requirement is fixed by the melder's individual score to date, and red Threes are scored separately instead of in partnership (except that one player is not penalized for red Threes if he has not melded but his partner has); otherwise, each scores the amount made by the partnership. Two canastas are required to go out, and game is 7500. If no one takes the pack, each scores individually. If no one goes out, play ends when the stock runs out. If one goes out before the pack is taken, he scores as the lone player and the others as partners.

Canasta for five

There is an awkward system by which the two who cut high play as partners against the other three, of whom a different one sits out each succeeding hand. But this is not a true five-hander. Experimenters may like to try a version in which all five play and the first to take the pack immediately becomes the partner of the player next but one to his left, the other three combining as opponents of the partnership.

Canasta for six

One version involving six active players splits them into two partnerships of three each, with partners sitting alternately round the table. Deal thirteen each from three 52-card packs plus six Jokers. Two canastas are required to go out. Red Threes count 100 each up to three; four or more count 200 each. Game is 10,000 points, and the initial meld requirement for a side with 7000 or more is increased to 150. Another version involves three partnerships of two each, with partners sitting opposite each other.

Canasta variants

If card games were planets, Canasta would be a belt of asteroids. The following are worth mentioning.

Canasta del Uruguay

Distinctive features of the original game are as follows. Two packs, but only two Jokers. Black Threes are natural and do not serve as stops. Melds and canastas need not contain more than two natural cards. In the partnership game, a side may go out without having melded a canasta. When two to five play as individuals, no one may go out until at least one canasta is on the table, regardless of who made it. A suit-sequence of three or more cards may be melded (black Threes lowest, Ace high). It may contain wild cards, but carries no bonus upon reaching seven, even if all natural. Sequences are called *escaleras* ('ladders'), and mainly serve as an emergency measure for going out.

Samba

Deal fifteen each from three packs and six Jokers, and at each turn draw two from stock and discard one. The pack, whether frozen or un-frozen, may not be taken to start a new escalera. An escalera is a suit-sequence of three or more natural cards (Ace high, Four low, none wild). More may be added until it contains seven, whereupon it becomes a samba, and is turned face down to distinguish it from a canasta. No canasta or samba may contain more than seven cards, but you can have more than one canasta of the same rank or samba of the same sequence.

Sambas and sequences may not contain any wild cards, canastas two at most.

Two seven-card melds are required to go out, regardless of type. Game is 10,000. At 7000 the minimum opening meld requirement is 150. There is a bonus of 200 for going out (open or concealed), and of 1500 for each samba made. Red Threes count 100 each, all six 1000 *in toto*.

Bolivia

As Samba, but sambas are called escaleras, and wild cards may be melded together. Seven wild cards constitute a bolivia, which is stacked with a Joker on top, may not be extended, and carries a bonus of 2500. To go out, a side must have made one escalera and a second major combination, which may be another escalera, a canasta, or a bolivia. Black Threes left unmelded in hand count minus 100 each. Game is 15,000 points.

Brazilian Canasta

An extension of Bolivia. Game is 10,000 up, and initial meld requirements are stepped up as follows:

5000+	150
7000+	150 and a mixed canasta or better
8000+	200 and a mixed canasta or better
9000+	200 and a natural canasta or better

A bolivia counts only 2000. In order to go out, you may lay off one or more properly sequential cards to escaleras. At the end of play any incomplete escalera or bolivia counts 1000 against, face values being ignored. Up to four red Threes count 100 each, five or six 200 each; but these scores are deducted if the side has failed to meld a canasta.

Chilean Canasta

Three-pack Canasta with escaleras, scoring as at Samba, but with wild-card melds (bonus of 2000 for seven) as an alternative to escaleras. That is, a side may meld one or the other type but not both. Only one card is drawn at a time, and one canasta required to go out.

Cuban Canasta (Wild-card Canasta)

A two-pack game without sequences but with wild-card melds. Deal thirteen each. The pack is permanently frozen. Game is 7500, and a side with 5000+ must initially meld at least 150. Three or more wild cards may be melded for their face values, plus 2000 for a wild canasta, or 3000 if it consists of four Jokers and three Deuces, or 4000 for seven Deuces. One red Three counts 100, two or three 200 each, the fourth 500, plus or minus as appropriate. Black Threes behave like red Threes, though not in conjunction with them, and there is a bonus of 100 for getting all four.

Hollywood Canasta

A cross between Samba and Bolivia. Played like Samba but with these differences. A sequence may contain one wild card, a mixed samba counting 1000 instead of 1500 extra. A meld must contain at least three natural cards, but wild-card canastas may be built for a bonus of 2000. Canastas are limited to seven cards. The upcard of an unfrozen pack may be laid off to a meld, but if it is wild it can be taken only with a matching pair (Deuces or Jokers, not one of each).

Italian Canasta

A three-pack game with fifteen dealt to each. Turn the upcard and then deal face down to the table, from the top of the pack, a number of cards equivalent to the rank of the upcard, i.e. three for a Three, up to ten for a Ten, Jack 11, Queen 12, King 13, Ace or wild card 20. Place the upcard face up on the discard pack, so that the first to take the upcard gets the lot. The pack is permanently frozen; it can be taken only with a matching pair. A wild-card canasta carries a bonus of 2000, or 3000 if it consists of Deuces only; in either case the bonus applies only for the side going out, the other scoring only face values. If a wild-card meld is under way, any available deuces must be added to it, instead of to other canastas, until the wild canasta is completed and turned down. Game is 12,000. Up to 7500 the initial meld requirement is 160; up to 10,000 it is 180; beyond that 200. Going out counts 300 (nothing extra for concealed) and two non-wild canastas must have been made. Red Threes count 100 each; four or more count 200 each. Optionally, there is a bonus of 1000 for making five canastas, or 2000 if all are natural.

Mexicana

Three-pack Canasta, thirteen dealt each, in which the first to meld, or the first in each partnership, immediately draws thirteen more cards from stock. Sometimes a canasta of Sevens carries a bonus of 1000 and an upcard Seven cannot be taken. Going out requires two canastas and not less than one red Three per canasta melded.

Quinella

Four-pack Samba with more elaborations.

Tampa

Three-pack Canasta much like Samba but with wild-card melds instead of sequences. A wild canasta carries a bonus of 2000.

Uruguay

as distinct from Canasta del Uruguay (above), denotes a two-pack Canasta with the addition of wild-card melds. Wild canastas count 2000 extra.

Yucatan

Eight-pack Samba. Melds of identical cards are permitted. Seven identical cards constitute a peninsula, carrying a bonus of 1000 per constituent natural card (minimum five). Game is 25,000 up.

Hand and Foot   2–5 players, 104+ cards

First described in the 1990s on the Internet, by Steve Simpson, Hand and Foot is a North American Canasta derivative played by different circles under a variety of rules. The additional features, though not invariable, are generally as follows.

Preliminaries Whether or not played by four in partnerships (the usual form), use one more pack than the number of players, each consisting of 52 cards plus two Jokers. Deal to each player two separate hands of thirteen cards, the first designated the 'hand' and the second the 'foot'. The hand is picked up and played first, and the foot must remain face down and unlooked at until its owner has played the last card from his hand.

Play At each turn you draw two from the stock, and eventually discard one.

There are three types of meld: those consisting entirely of natural cards, those containing one or more wild cards ('mixed'), and those consisting entirely of wild cards ('wild'). A natural meld may become 'mixed' by the addition of wild cards. When a meld contains seven cards – variously designated a 'pile' or a 'canasta' – it is squared up with a red, black or wild card on top, and (in some circles) may not be further extended. A mixed meld must always contain more natural than wild cards, and in some circles may not contain more than two wild.

In some circles there are four deals, for which the initial meld requirements are respectively 50, 90, 120 and 150 points, regardless of your current score.

If you play the last card from your hand to a meld, you may immediately pick up your foot and continue your turn. If, however, you empty your hand by a discard, you don't start playing with your foot until your next turn.

Going out You go out by playing the last card from your foot, but subject to the following restrictions:

• You can't go out by melding black Threes.

• In a partnership game, you must ask and receive your partner's permission, which will almost certainly be withheld if he has not broken into his foot (in case it contains red Threes, which are penalized if not declared).

• You (or your side) must have made at least one wild canasta.

Score Wild canastas score 1500 each. Other scores, bonuses and penalties are as for Canasta. Black Threes left in hand each count 5 points against.

Variants Some versions attach special significance to the number seven. Sevens may not be discarded. You never take the whole pack (unless it contains seven or fewer cards), but only the top seven. In order to go out, you must have made at least one natural meld of Sevens. In some circles you must also have made at least one other natural canasta, one mixed, and one wild.

Pennies from Heaven

(4/6pp, 216c including 8☆) An apparent forerunner of Hand and Foot, typically played in partnerships and preferably by six players, with partners sitting alternately. Jokers and Deuces are wild. Deal to each player thirteen cards as the initial playing hand, then eleven cards face down in a stack. Only when you have completed a canasta do you pick these eleven up and add them to your hand. Though playing in partnership, you keep your own melds in front of you. You may lay cards off to your own or a partner's melds, but the seventh card to your qualifying canasta must come from your own hand before you can take up your eleven 'pennies from heaven'.

At each turn draw two from stock and discard one. If the upcard is wild you cannot take the pack; otherwise, you can take it only by melding the upcard with two natural cards from hand. Wild-card melds are valid, and a wild canasta scores 1000 points.

Sevens are significant. No canasta may contain more than seven cards. Both partnerships must have completed at least one canasta of Sevens before any Seven can be discarded, and you cannot discard a Seven in going out. The canasta of Sevens may be natural or mixed, and in either case scores 1500 points.

---

500 Rum

It was in the 1920s or '30s that players started scoring positively for melds made in Rummy games instead of just negatively for cards left unmelded at end of play. The earliest of its type was Michigan Rum (Michigan now denotes a compendium game comparable to Poch). Five Hundred Rum represents a further development along the road to Canasta. It is a good game for three, and its extension, Persian Rummy, a good partnership game.

Preliminaries From a 52-card pack deal ten each if two play, seven if three or four, six if five or six. Stack the rest face down and turn the top card face up to start a discard pile. Scores are made as play proceeds, thus necessitating a scoresheet ruled into as many columns as players.

Object To meld as many cards as possible, preferably high-scoring ones, and either to go out first or to be left with as little deadwood as possible.

Melds The minimum meld is three of a kind or three cards in suit and sequence. Ace ranks high or low, not both at once. Court cards count 10 each (plus if melded, minus if deadwood), others face value. Ace counts 1 in a low sequence (A-2-3 . . .), otherwise 15 (. . . Q-K-A).

Play On your turn to play you may draw the top card of stock, and either discard it face up to the discard pile or add it to your hand. If you add it, you may then make any melds that you can and will, and finish by adding one to the discard pile. The discards remain slightly spread so that all can be identified.

Alternatively, instead of drawing from stock, you may draw any card from the discard pile, provided that:

• you immediately meld it or lay it off (you can't just add it to your hand), and

• you also take all the other discards lying above it, adding them to your hand or melding or laying them off as the case may be.

Again, you end your turn by discarding one.

Scoring Cards may be laid off against your own or others' melds. Each time you start a meld or lay cards off, note the score for the cards so played, keeping a running total.

Scoring variant No running score is kept. Whenever you lay a card off against another's meld, you merely announce that fact, but play the card face up before you, so that it will count in your favour at the end of play. (It therefore becomes important to keep careful track of extended melds, so as not to miss any opportunity to lay off.)

Going out Play ceases the moment any player melds, lays off, or discards the last card from their hand, or as soon as the last card of stock has been drawn if no one has gone out. (*Variant*: If the stock runs out, players may agree to turn the discards down, without shuffling, to start a new one.)

Score The winner's score is increased by the total value of cards remaining in other players' hands, whether or not they can be melded or laid off. Game is 500 points over as many deals as it takes.

Polish Rummy

lets you take the whole of the discard pile without necessarily melding or laying off the bottom card. But you may not take just part of it except under the conditions prescribed above.

Persian Rummy

An excellent partnership extension of Five Hundred Rum. Deal seven each from a 56-card pack including four Jokers, stack the rest face down and turn an upcard. Play as above until one player goes out, then score as at 500 Rum. Each side's partnership score is that of its two partners combined, plus 25 if one of them went out without having previously melded.

Jokers are not wild but may be melded as a group of three or four, counting 20 each (for or against). Any group of four, if melded in a single turn, scores double its face value. Ace ranks high only and always counts 15.

Game is two deals, and the winning side adds a game bonus of 50.

Arlington (Oklahoma)   2–5 players, 104 cards

Arlington, a name preferable to Oklahoma to avoid confusion with Oklahoma Gin, continues the trend towards greater elaboration in the scoring for melds. A good game for three, it may be thought more complicated than the 500 Rum group, but less interesting than Canasta – or, possibly, less complicated than Canasta but more interesting than 500.

Preliminaries From two to five players receive thirteen cards each from two packs shuffled together, with or without a Joker (104 or 105). Stack the rest face down and turn an upcard from it. Deal the next card face up to found the discard pile, and place the remainder face down to form a stock.

Object To score as much as possible for melds, and either go out, or be left with as little deadwood as possible if somebody else goes out.

Melds Valid melds are three or four cards of the same rank – not necessarily differing in suit, but never exceeding four – and sequences of three or more in the same suit, for which purpose Ace ranks high or low, but not both at once, though two Aces may be used to make a sequence of 14 cards. The Joker and all Deuces are wild. If you draw the natural card being represented by a Joker in one of your own melds, you may put the natural card in its place and take the Joker back into hand, but this privilege does not extend to a Deuce. The owner of a meld containing ambiguous wild cards must indicate what ranks they are intended to represent, either verbally or by arrangement (e.g. 6-7-☆ must be read as 6-7-8), as this determines what cards may be laid off against it.

Spade queens Special value attaches to both Queens of spades. They are melded in groups or sequences in the normal way, but no one is allowed to discard a ♠Q except to go out when no other cards remains in hand.

Play To start, each in turn may take the upcard and then discard or pass. When somebody has taken it, or all have refused, the next in turn begins play proper. At each turn a player may draw from stock, meld and lay off *ad lib.*, and must then discard one card face up to the discard pile, which is kept squared up. Instead of drawing from stock, however, you may take the upcard provided that you:

• immediately meld or lay it off, and

• take the whole of the discard pile into hand, finishing your turn by making any more possible melds and lay-offs, and making one reject to start a new discard pile.

You may lay cards off only against your own melds, not against anyone else's.

Going out Play ceases as soon as anyone goes out by playing their last card, whether by melding, laying off or discarding. There is a bonus for going out 'concealed' – that is, melding your whole hand in one turn, having made no previous melds, and with or without a final discard. But this does not apply if you do so on your first turn.

Scoring Everyone scores the difference between the total value of cards they have melded (plus) and of those left in hand (minus), including various bonuses, as follows:

	plus	*minus*
Joker	100	200
♠Queen	50	100
Ace	20	20
High card (8–K)	10	10
Low card (3–7)	5	5
Deuce	as above	20
Bonus for going out	100	
Going out concealed	250	

☛ The 250-point bonus for going out concealed is held in abeyance until the end of the game. It doesn't count towards the target score.

Game The winner is the first to reach 1000 over as many deals as it takes. The winner adds 200 for game (sharing it equally, if tied), and bonuses for going out concealed are then taken into account before settlements are made on the basis of the final scores.

Fortune Rummy

Basically Arlington (Oklahoma), but with only ten cards dealt to each.

Compartment Full

(4–8p, 104c) Described and probably invented by B. C. Westall (*Games*, *c.*1930), what sounds like a commuter game has several novel features. Deal ten cards each and stack the rest face down without an upcard. The aim is to convert one's hand into one or more melds and go down with all ten cards at once. A meld is three or more cards of the same rank, or three or more numerals in suit and sequence. Sequences run Ace low, Ten high. They may not include courts.

The first player draws from stock and discards one face up. Each in turn thereafter may draw from stock or take any one of the faced discards, which are not piled up but kept separate so all remain visible. If you take a discard you may not discard it in the same turn. If the stock runs out it is not replaced, and play continues with just the discards. Play ceases when one player declares 'Compartment full' by laying down ten cards arranged into one or more valid melds and making one discard. That player scores 50 for going out, plus scores for melds as follows:

eight Aces	50	eight K, Q or J	25	sequence of ten	50
seven . . .	40	seven . . .	20	sequence of nine	25
six . . .	30	six . . .	15	sequence of eight	20
five . . .	20	five . . .	10	sequence of seven	15
four . . .	10	four . . .	5	sequence of six	10
				sequence of five	5

Sets of cards lower than Jack are not permitted. Sequences of three and four are permitted, but score nothing. Everyone else also scores for their melds, and there is no penalty for deadwood.

Note that, although eight of a kind is worth having, it does not enable you to go out. Having got it, therefore, you should so play as to assist another player to go out before everyone gets a high score.

Continental Rummy   2–12 players, 2–4 packs (52 each)

At one time the most popular form of Rummy in women's afternoon games, until in 1950 it lost out to Canasta.

Morehead and Mott-Smith, *Hoyle's Rules of Games*

Be that as it may, Continental has the particular merit of being suitable for a large group of players.

Preliminaries Up to six players use two 52-card packs shuffled together, each containing one or two Jokers to taste. Use three such packs for up to nine players, four for up to twelve.

Deal Deal fifteen each in batches of three. Stack the rest face down and turn the next to start a discard pile. By some accounts, the dealer scores 15 for lifting off exactly the number of cards required to complete the deal.

Object To go out by melding all fifteen cards in sequences of the same suit (sets of the same rank do not count), and in only one of the following patterns: 3-3-3-3-3, 3-4-4-4, or 3-3-4-5.

Rank Ace counts high or low but not both at once. Jokers and Deuces are wild, and Deuces may belong to any suit. For this reason a low sequence may run A-3-4 . . .

Play Each in turn draws from stock or takes the upcard, and discards one.

Ending Keep going till one player melds fifteen cards in one of the specified patterns and makes a final discard. This earns from each opponent the following amount:

    1 for winning

    1 for each Deuce melded

    2 for each Joker melded

    7 for going out on first turn (after one draw)

    10 for going out without having drawn

    10 for using no wild cards in melds

    10 if all natural cards are of the same suit

Two or more such bonuses may be collected simultaneously.

Sequence Rummy

(2–6p, 104c + 2☆). Deal eight each. Your first meld must be a sequence (Ace high or low but not both), and until you have made one you may draw only from stock, not from discards. Having once melded, you may then (a) instead of drawing from stock, take any discard, provided that you meld it immediately and that you also take all those lying above it, and (b) meld sets of three or more of a kind. Score as you go along, counting Jokers 25, Aces 15, courts 10 each and numerals at face value. A Joker may stand for any card provided that there are not already two such natural cards visible in melds. You may steal a Joker from any meld on the table in return for the natural card it represents, provided that you immediately use it in a meld of your own. When one player goes out, everybody deducts from their current score the total face value of cards remaining in hand, even if meldable. Game is any predetermined number of deals.

Pináculo ('Pinnacle') 2–5 players, 2 × 54 cards

This Spanish game, also spelt Pinacle, looks like a forerunner of Canasta and has points of interest meriting separate description. (It is not the same as Pinnacolo, an Italian Rummy of the 1940s.)

Preliminaries Two to five players, four usually in partnerships, play to the right. Double 52-card pack plus four Jokers. Jokers and Deuces are wild. After the shuffle, the player at dealer's left cuts the cards. Deal eleven each in ones from the bottom half, stack the rest face down and turn an upcard. If exactly the right number were cut for the deal – for example, 44 in the four-player game – the cutter scores 50 points.

Object To reach 1500 points over as many deals as necessary, scoring plus for melds and minus for deadwood. A meld is three or more cards of the same rank, or in suit and sequence (*escalera*), and must contain at least two natural cards. In escaleras, Three is low and Ace high.

Play At each turn either draw one from stock or take the whole discard pile (in which case you probably must meld the upcard, but source gives no guidance). You may then start a meld or lay off cards to an existing meld of your own or partner's. End the turn with a discard.

☞ The melds of an individual player or partnership must be kept separate from one another, and no two may be combined even if they match rank or complete a sequence.

Minimum meld A player or side standing at 750 or more points is said to be *barbelé* (French for 'barbed wire'). The first meld they make must contain cards totalling not less than 70 in point-value. A lower meld must be withdrawn and incurs a 50-point penalty.

Premium melds Eleven of a kind is a *pinnacle*. An 11-card escalera is 'complete', and is further described as 'clean' (*limpia*) if it consists entirely of natural cards, 'dirty' (*sucia*) if it contains any Deuce of a different suit, 'unclean' (*semilimpia*) if it contains wild cards that are Deuces of the sequential suit or Jokers.

☞ In partnership play, melding a part-sequence card by card from left to right tells your partner that you hold at least seven to an escalera.

Wild cards If you hold a natural card that is being represented by a wild card in a set of like cards, or at either end of an incomplete escalera (but not within one), you may put the natural card in its place. You do not then take the wild card into hand, but place it sideways at one end of the meld as a reminder to score for it at the end of play.

Ending The game ends if the stock runs out. Otherwise, you may go out at almost any time by melding or laying off all cards remaining in your hand, with or without a discard. When you have only one card in hand you must announce this fact (by calling '*Pumba!*') or lose 50 points. In that situation, you must draw from stock if there is only one discard.

Scoring Each player or side scores plus for melded cards, other than those in premium melds, and minus for deadwood at the following rate: Jokers 30, Deuces 20, Aces 15, high cards (KQJT98) 10, low cards (76543) 5 each.

The following melds carry premium scores in place of their total face value:

pinnacle from one hand (11 of a kind all at once)	3000
pinnacle from one hand (gradual)	1500
clean escalera (suit-sequence of 12 natural cards)	1000
unclean escalera (with one Deuce of matching suit)	800
unclean escalera (with both Deuces of matching suit)	750
dirty escalera (one or more non-suit-matching Deuces)	550
eight natural Aces	1000
eight natural Kings, Queens or Jacks	750
seven natural Aces	400
seven natural Kings, Queens or Jacks	300
six natural Aces	300
six natural Kings, Queens or Jacks	200
six Aces (including a wild card)	180
six Kings, Queens, or Jacks (including a wild card)	120

In addition:
- there is a bonus of 20 for going out;
- going out without the aid of a wild card doubles the face values of all cards played to go out (in addition to the 20-point bonus);
- going out concealed (melding all 11 cards) doubles the face values of all cards played to go out, or, if they are all natural, quadruples them (instead of the 20-point bonus);

- eight natural numerals score 50 plus their total face value;
- each Joker that you replaced with a natural card in course of play scores 30;
- each Deuce that you replaced with a natural card in course of play scores 15 in an escalera, or twice the face value in a set of like ranks.

Don't forget . . .
- Play to the left (clockwise) unless otherwise stated.
- Eldest or Forehand means the player to the left of the dealer in left-handed games, to the right in right-handed games.
- T = Ten, p = players, pp = in fixed partnerships, c = cards, † = trump, ☆ = Joker.

21 Competitive Patiences

The games called Patience in some countries and Solitaire in others, and Cabal in a few, are all slightly misnamed. By definition, a solitaire is any game for one player, though in America it applies specifically to solitaires played with cards, while in Britain it applies specifically to the game known in America as Peg Solitaire.

In a typical card solitaire, you shuffle your pack of cards and then try to put them back into order. The most basic method is to deal cards one by one face up to a wastepile. When an Ace turns up it goes to the centre of the table. Each of the four Aces is then to be built upwards in suit until it supports a 13-card suit-sequence headed by the King. The building is done with the appropriate cards as and when they are turned from stock. When the stock runs out you turn the wastepile to form a new one. Given these rules, the game is bound to 'come out' eventually if the wastepile can be turned often enough. In practice, however, custom decrees a limited number of redeals – hence the factor of real-life 'patience'. Most Patiences are variations on this theme, some involving highly elaborate and imaginative rules and conditions.

First appearing in the late eighteenth century in the Baltic countries, Patience games may have originated as a variety of fortune-telling, along the lines of 'Loves me, loves me not', or 'Tinker, tailor, soldier, sailor . . .'. Interestingly, Tarots were first used for fortune-telling in the same century, and there is an obvious resemblance between tarot and patience layouts.

There are hundreds of different Patiences (I covered some 400 varieties in *The Penguin Book of Patience*), and more continue to be invented, especially since the remarkable revival in their popularity caused by their eminent suitability for computer play. In order to impose practical limitations on the size of this section, I have arbitrarily restricted its contents to competitive Patience games – that is, those that can be practised by two or more players in competition with one another, as distinct from solitarily and in competition with the vagaries of fortune.

▌Spite and Malice (Cat and Mouse)   2 players, 108 cards

This is a reworking of a late nineteenth-century Continental game variously called Crapette, Cripette, Robuse, Rabouge, Russian Bank (etc.). Easley Blackwood in his 1970 treatise on the game says he saw it 'several years ago' being played by various schools in various ways. The following is based on his proposed standard version.

Preliminaries Use two packs of the same size but different back colours or designs. One contains 52 cards, the other 56 by the addition of four Jokers. (But three or even two will suffice.)

Deal Shuffle the 52-card pack very thoroughly and deal twenty-six each. Each player's twenty-six cards form his 'riddance pile' and are placed face down on the table in front of him with the top card turned face up (the 'upcard').

Then shuffle the 56-card pack very thoroughly, deal five each to form a playing hand, and stack the rest face down as a common stockpile.

Sequence order is A23456789TJQK. Whoever has the higher upcard goes first. If equal, bury the upcards and turn the next ones up.

Object To play out all 26 cards from one's riddance pile. The first to do so wins. As each card is played, the one beneath is turned face up. Riddance cards may be played to one of eight piles which are gradually built up in the centre of the table. Each centre pile starts with an Ace, on which is built any Two, then a Three, and so on, until it contains thirteen cards headed by a King. Suit need not be followed. When a centre pile is completed, it is turned face down and put to one side.

Play A turn consists of one or more of the moves described below. On your turn to play, the following rules apply:

• If your upcard is an Ace, you must play it to the centre to start a pile.

• If it is a Two, and an Ace is in place, you must play it to the Ace. If it is any higher playable card, you need not play it if there is any reason why you may prefer not to.

• If you hold (in hand) an Ace or a card playable to a centre pile, you may play it to the centre, but are not obliged to. Playing to a centre pile entitles you to another move.

• If you play off all five cards to centre piles, you draw five more from the common stockpile and continue play.

- When unable or unwilling to play to the centre, end your turn by making one discard face up from your hand to the table. Any card may be discarded except an Ace. You then draw enough cards from the top of the common stockpile to restore your hand to five.

The first discard you make starts your first discard pile. Each subsequent discard may be used to start a new pile, up to a maximum of four. Alternatively, each may be added to the top of a discard pile, provided that it is equal to or one rank lower than the previous card. (For example, you can play a Jack or a Ten to a Jack.) You may never play to or from your opponent's discard piles.

To keep your turn going, you may at any time play off the top card of a discard pile to a centre pile.

End of turn Your turn ends when you make a discard, or if you find you can neither play to a centre pile nor make a legal discard. In the latter case, your hand is said to be 'frozen'.

Frozen hands If one player's hand is frozen, the other keeps playing even after he has made a discard, and continues in this way until the first player announces after a discard that he can now continue.

If both players freeze, there is a re-deal. All the cards in play except the riddance piles are gathered up, and shuffled and reshuffled very thoroughly together. Deal five more each, stack the rest face down, and start again from the beginning.

Jokers You may play a Joker to a centre pile at any time and count it as the required card. For example, it may be called an Ace and used to start a pile, or it may be played as a Two to an Ace, a Three to a Two, and so on. It may not, however, be played on to a King. A Joker once played to a centre pile cannot then be removed.

Alternatively, you may play one to a discard pile, and need not state exactly what it represents until you have to. (Thus if two Jokers are played to a Ten, they may be followed by a Ten, Nine, Eight, or Seven.) Although Aces themselves may not be discarded, any number of Jokers may be discarded on a Two, since they can all be counted as Twos. What a Joker stands for on top of a discard pile does not have to be kept when it is played to a centre pile: it can be played off as anything required.

Forced moves Most moves are optional, and if both players decline to make any move from a given position then it is the same as if both hands were frozen, and a re-deal is made as described above. There are, however, two exceptions:

1. If your upcard is an Ace, you must play it to the centre. If there is a bare Ace in the centre, and you have a natural Two showing as your upcard or on the top of a discard pile, then you must play it to that Ace. (But: a Joker is not so forced even if it logically counts as a Two; and if you also hold a Two you may always play it from hand instead.)

2. If both hands are frozen, or both refuse to play, the next in turn must play an Ace or a Two from hand to the centre if he legally can, and his opponent must then do likewise.

End of stock When the common stockpile is reduced to twelve or fewer cards, there is a pause while a new one is formed. This is done by taking all the centre piles which have been built up to the King, adding them to the existing stock, shuffling the whole lot very thoroughly indeed, and then laying them down as a new stockpile. Incomplete centre piles are not taken for this purpose, unless all are incomplete, in which case all are taken.

End of game The game ends as soon as one person has played off the last card from his riddance pile. The winner scores a basic 5 points, plus 1 for each card left unplayed from that of the loser. Or (my suggestion) the winner scores 1 for the first card left in the loser's hand, 2 for the second, 3 for the third, and so on. Thus four left over would give the winner 10 points, five 15, and so on.

Variations The following local rules are probably commoner than those described above, and must have accounted for some of the 'various ways of playing' referred to by Blackwood.

• The two packs are not separated but shuffled together, so each player may have duplicates within their riddance piles. This makes it unnecessary to deal twenty-six cards to each player's riddance pile, and a more popular number is twenty.

• The number of centre piles varies. Three or four is typical. As soon as a pile is completed it is reshuffled into the stockpile.

• Discard piles need not be packed in sequence: you can throw any card to a discard pile (except an Ace). This means you always end your turn with a discard, and you never get 'frozen'.

• If a game blocks through stalemate, neither player being able or willing to continue play, the game ends, and the winner is the one who

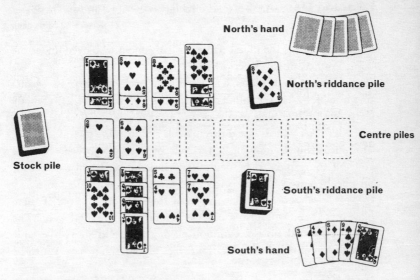

North's hand

North's riddance pile

Centre piles

Stock pile

South's riddance pile

South's hand

Spite and Malice. South could play ♥7 to ♠6, allowing North to play off his ♦8, and then continue the sequence to remove the ♠K from his own riddance pile. But this will be no good if North holds a Nine, as he himself could then block it by playing up to the ♦K. South will therefore play his 3 4 5 to the ♥2, discard ♠9 to ♠10, and draw four new cards, keeping the situation in tension and perhaps improving his hand.

has played off more cards from their riddance pile. If equal, it is a draw.

• If you play without Jokers, you may agree to designate the four Kings 'wild', and use them to represent any desired rank. In this case a centre pile is completed when it contains 12 cards headed by a Queen (or a King in drag).

Russian Bank (Crapette, Robuse, Rabouge)

Several virtually identical games, amounting, in effect, to Spite and Malice played with a single pack each and no Jokers.

Racing Demon (Race Canfield, Pounce, Scramble, Nerts, etc.)
2+ players, 52 cards each

Racing Demon is the oldest name for the game now played under the name Pounce, or (in America) Nerts.

Preliminaries Each player has a complete pack, which must be distinguishable by its back colour or design from everyone else's. Everybody starts by shuffling their own pack and arranging it as follows:

Deal thirteen cards face down in a pile and turn the top one face up. This pile is your Demon, or Pounce pile, or Nerts pile, or whatever else you call the game. To be neutral and descriptive, I will call it your off-pile, because your aim is to be the first to play off all its cards.

Next, deal four cards face up in a row in front of you. If three play, these rows will form a triangle; if four, a square; and so on. The space between them is a common playing area, and should be large enough to contain more than four piles of cards that have yet to be built.

Your four upcards mark the start of four work-piles, each of which will take additional cards spread face up towards you so all are visible. If any of these four is an Ace, play it to the centre space and replace it with the top card of your pack, which you hold face downwards in one hand. If the top card of your off-pile is an Ace, do likewise, and turn up the card beneath it.

Ace-piles Each Ace set out in the common playing area acts as the foundation of a pile which is to be built upwards in suit and sequence until it contains 13 cards, headed by a King. Anyone can play a card to one of these piles whenever they have the next higher card in sequence. If two try playing to the same pile at once, only the card that gets there first stays put and the other goes back to where it came from.

Play At a given signal, everybody starts playing at once. The top card of your off-pile, and the exposed card in each of your work-piles, may be played to one of the Ace-piles when it fits.

Work-piles The cards in your work-piles are to be built downwards in alternating colour (e.g. red Jack on black Queen, etc.). You can also transfer any card from one work-pile to another, together with all the cards lying in alternating sequence on top of it, provided that the join follows the rule. For example, if the exposed card of one pile is ♠9, and another pile contains ♥8, with ♣7 and ♦6 on top, you can play these three to the black Nine.

If you empty a work-pile, you may fill the space it leaves with any available card, whether from the off-pile, another work-pile, your hand, or your wastepile (when it gets going).

Wastepile When stuck, deal the top three cards of your pack face up to a single wastepile and consider the topmost card. If possible, you may play this to one of the Ace-piles (upwards in suit) or to one of your work-piles (downwards in alternating colour), thus revealing the next card for similar play. When stuck, deal the next three cards from your pack face up to the wastepile, and again make whatever plays you can.

When your pack contains only one or two cards, turn them over in the usual way; then, when you get stuck again, turn the wastepile upside down and take it in hand to form a new pack to play from.

Getting stuck If everyone gets stuck, being either unable or unwilling to make any further legal move, everyone turns their wastepile to form a new pack, then transfers the top card of their pack to the bottom before continuing play.

Completed Ace-piles When an Ace-pile is complete, with a King on top, turn it face down to show that nothing else can be played to it.

Going out Play ceases when somebody plays the last card from their off-pile and calls 'Out!' (or 'Nerts', or whatever). Everybody then scores 1 point for each card they managed to work into the Ace-piles (this is why it is necessary for everyone to have a distinctive pack), and deducts 2 points for each card left in their off-pile. It is just possible for the player who went out not to finish with the best score. Play up to 100 points, or any other agreed target.

Variants There are many local variations to these rules, of which the most commendable is to turn cards from the stock one at a time instead of three. (One is natural; three is purposeless.)

In the original version, each starts by dealing thirteen down, then one card face up to act as the first base, then four face up to start the work-piles. Each of the other cards of the same rank as the first base is set out as a base when it becomes available, and these bases are built upwards in suit until they contain 13 cards, turning the corner from King to Ace if necessary. You can play to anyone else's main sequences as and when possible, and it is for each player to note what the terminating rank will be.

Spit (Speed)

I first collected this game from my daughter Lizzi, who was playing it with school-friends in the 1980s. The following is a more elaborate version.

Preliminaries Deal twenty-six cards to each of two players from a well-shuffled 52-card pack. Deal, each of you, from your own twenty-six cards, a layout consisting of five face-down piles of cards, with one card in the first, two in the second, and so on up to five in the fifth. These are the stock piles. Turn the top card of each stock pile face up. Hold your other eleven cards face down in one hand. These eleven are your 'spit' cards.

Object The aim is to be the first to get rid of all your cards over as many deals as necessary. You don't take turns, just play as fast as you can simultaneously.

Play When you are both ready, shout 'Spit!', turn the top card from your hand, and place it face up on the table between both players' stock piles. These two cards form the bases of two piles of cards called the spit piles. What you are aiming to do is to get all the cards played from your stock piles to the spit piles.

At each move, you may play the top card of one of your stock piles to either of the spit piles, provided that it is one rank higher or lower than the card you play it to. On an Ace you can play either a King or a Two. Suits don't matter. Then turn face up the top card of the pile you played from. If one of your stock piles gets emptied, you can fill the space with the top card from another one (but you can never have more than five stock piles).

Sooner or later you will both get stuck. At this point you both shout 'Spit!' again and turn the next card from your hand face up on the spit pile you started before. Then play on as before.

If one player has no spit cards left when play gets stuck, the other one spits alone. They can choose either pile to spit on, but, having chosen it, must stick with it every time the same position is reached.

If neither player has any spit cards when play gets stuck, the player with fewer cards left in their stock piles spits a card from the top of a stock pile.

Next deal When one of you gets rid of all your stock-pile cards, both of you slap your hand over one of the spit piles, ideally the smaller one. Whoever gets there first takes that pile, leaving the larger one for the other player. (If you both choose different piles, of course, there's no dispute.) Whichever of you still has stock-pile cards left unplayed shuffles these in with the pile you took. Both of you shuffle your cards, deal another layout as before, shout 'Spit!' when ready, and play another round.

If one of you has fewer than fifteen cards, you won't be able to deal a complete set of stock piles. In this case you deal them into five piles as far as possible and turn the top card of each. In this case you won't be able to spit, so there is only one spit pile, started by the other player.

End of play When only one spit pile remains, and one player runs out of stock cards, the other plays on until stuck, then gathers up all the cards on the table, deals a new layout, and spits again. The winner is the first player to run out of all spit and stock cards.

Variations Many.

Grabbage (Hasty Patience)   2+ players, 52 cards each

The player who completes a packet with a king must move it from the table; it is generally thrown on the floor, as this game allows no time for small ceremonies.
Mary Whitmore Jones, *Games of Patience* (c.1890)

This hilarious game, a forerunner of Spit, is guaranteed to draw complaints from the neighbours if played late at night, and is best played with worn-out cards, for reasons indicated above.

Cards Each player shuffles a single pack and holds it face down.

Object To be the first to get rid of all your cards.

Play Turn cards rapidly one by one from stock and discard them face up to a personal wastepile unless they can be built.

Building When you turn an Ace, play it face up to the centre to start a sequence. Sequences are common property and are each to be built up to the King regardless of suit. Whoever completes a sequence with the King turns it face down or throws it away. You may add to a sequence, if it fits, a card that you turn from the stock or the current top card of your wastepile. If two try to build simultaneously to the same sequence, the card that gets there first stays put. When you run out of stock, turn your wastepile face down to form a new one.

Variants Whitmore Jones describes Hasty as a two-player game in which each plays to a single wastepile, and Grabbage as a four-player game in which each plays freely to any of four wastepiles.

Pirate

An even sillier game than Spit.

Preliminaries Each takes a complete pack shuffled by the other and cuts it. The lower cut plays to release the Aces as they become available and build them upwards in suit to the Kings, the higher to release the Kings and build them downwards in suit to the Aces.

Object Completed suit-sequences are called ships. The aim is to capture a majority of the eight ships to be built.

Play Both hold their packs face down and play simultaneously. Turn cards from stock one at a time and build them if possible, otherwise discard them face up to a personal wastepile. Building includes putting down an Ace or King as the 'keel' of a new ship. The top card of the wastepile may be built on a ship when it fits. Neither may play to the other's ship. When the two ships of a given suit meet in the middle, the first to play the connecting card captures both. For example, if one has built spades up to the Six and the other spades down to the Eight, the first to play a ♠7 captures that ship. If both play it simultaneously, the two ships are sunk and belong to neither player.

When a ship has been captured or sunk, the two players start a second ship in the same suit, but running in opposite directions. That is, the former Ace-up player now plays King-down, and vice versa. This can result in both players building different suits in opposite directions at the same time.

If you run out of cards first, cease playing, and watch your opponent carefully. Whenever he turns a card you need for one of your own ships, you can claim it and put it in place. When a capturing card is turned, the first to claim it captures both ships – which, as before, are sunk if both claim simultaneously.

Note The first to capture five ships wins, or four if one is sunk. It may be agreed not to sink ships but to keep them in tow, and credit them to whoever unambiguously captures the next ship.

| Conjugal Patience   2 players, 2 x 52 cards

To paraphrase G. B. Shaw, two-player games are popular because they combine the maximum of temptation with the maximum of opportunity. Couples may accordingly be assumed to start with Honeymoon Bridge, progress to Conjugal Patience, and end up with Spite and Malice. (There's also a Patience called Divorce, which we needn't go into here.)

Preliminaries Each shuffles the other's pack, then from your own pack deal six cards face up in front of you as a reserve. Hold the rest face down as a stock.

Object To be first to get rid of all your cards by building them on to the eight 13-card suit-sequences to be built between you.

Play On your turn, play as many cards as you can from your reserve to the centre. You can take an Ace to start a sequence, a Two of the same suit to put on the Ace, and so on, as and when such cards become available, to extend the sequence upwards to the King. Having built any such cards from the reserve, refill the vacancies they leave with cards from the top of your stock, and continue building if possible. Eventually, when the reserve consists of six unplayable cards, end your turn by discarding any one of them face down to a personal wastepile, and filling that vacancy from stock. The space-filler is not available for building until your next turn.

Ending When no cards remain in stock, turn your wastepile upside down to form a new one. Players should agree beforehand whether or not it should be shuffled before use. If not, the last discard will be the first stock-card, and all cards will come out in reverse order of placing – a point to remember whenever discarding during the game. What little skill there is consists in selecting each discard and holding back possible builds that might be more helpful to your opponent than to yourself.

Progressive Patience

Preliminaries Shuffle both packs together and take fifty-two cards each as a stock, which is to be kept face down.

Object To be the first to play off all your cards to the centre.

Play At each turn, face the top card of your stock and play it to the centre if possible, otherwise discard it face up to any one of four wastepiles. Playing it entitles you to turn the next card; discarding it automatically ends your turn.

Central sequences The first to turn an Ace must play it to the centre of the table. Cards are then built on it in sequence, regardless of suit, until it reaches the King. This is followed by another Ace, and the cycle continues until one player runs out of cards. At each turn you may build as many playable cards from your wastepiles as you can before turning a card from stock.

Discarding A turned card not playable to the centre is discarded face up to any one of your wastepiles, regardless of rank or suit. These piles may be spread out in columns so that all cards are visible.

Obligations It is obligatory to start the centre run as soon as the first Ace is turned. After that it is not compulsory to play any playable card. Once a card is turned from stock, it must be immediately built or discarded. This means you are not allowed to look at the next turn-up before deciding whether or not to play from the wastepiles.

Turning the wastepiles When you run out of cards, sweep up your wastepiles and turn them face down as a new stock. (Agree beforehand whether to gather them up at random and shuffle them, or whether to pile them on one another from left to right and turn the newly consolidated stock without disturbing the order of cards.) When you get down to four or fewer cards, you merely turn them all face up, from which it will usually be obvious who gets to win.

Dictation (Sir Tommy)   2+ players, 52 cards each

Almost any form of Patience can be played by the 'dictation' method, one of the most popular being Poker Squares. This lesser-known game is particularly compulsive.

Preliminaries One player, the dictator, shuffles a 52-card pack, and the others arrange theirs face up in such a way as to enable rapid identification of any called card.

Object Each plays a separate game of the patience called Sir Tommy (or any other that may be agreed), but all use cards turned up in the same order. The winner is the player who completes the greater number of thirteen-card sequences, which are built up from Ace to King regardless of suit.

Play At each turn the dictator turns the top card of his pack, announces what it is, and plays it to his own game. Everyone else selects the same card from their own pack and plays it to their own game. When all are ready, the dictator turns the next card, and so on.

Whenever an Ace turns up, set it out as the start of a sequence. You may then, as and when the appropriate cards become available, build it up in sequence towards the King, regardless of suit. Unplayable cards are discarded face up to a personal layout which may contain up to four piles, spread into columns so that all are visible. Any card may be placed on any pile regardless of rank or suit, and you are not obliged to start all four piles at once, but may prefer to hold one or more open until it seems right to start them. No card may be transferred from one column to another, or to a column vacancy, but the exposed card of each column may be built on a main sequence at any time.

When all the cards have been called, everyone can carry on building up their sequences as far as possible by playing off cards from the exposed end of the wastepiles.

Score The usual score is 1 per card played off to your sequences, but I prefer a system whereby everyone scores the combined face values of the uppermost cards on their main sequences, counting for this purpose Jack 15, Queen 20 and King 25. Thus a game completed up to the four Kings scores the maximum of 100, whereas four sequences headed by (say) K-J-9-3 would score 52 – not a bad result, on average.

Dictated Strategy

A Patience much favoured by contemporary players is one called Strategy, invented by Morehead and Mott-Smith. Based on Sir Tommy, it runs as follows, and may be played competitively by the Dictation method.

Set out four Aces to start with. The aim is (eventually) to build each one up in suit and sequence to the King. But not yet.

Instead, as each card is turned and called by the Dictator, place it in any one of eight wastepiles, which may be spread towards you in columns so all are visible. As above, you needn't open all eight immediately, but, unlike the above, you may not yet build any turned card on a main sequence. Not until all 48 cards have been turned from stock, and each discarded to a selected wastepile, do you attempt to complete the game by taking cards from the exposed ends of the wastepiles and using them to build up the sequences.

You can vary this game by reducing or increasing the number of wastepiles. Given a favourable distribution of cards, it can be done in as few as four.

Poker Squares
2+ players, 52 cards each

This is the 'Dictation' version of that perennial favourite, Poker Patience, which runs as follows.

Turn twenty-five cards from a shuffled pack one by one, and place each on the table in such a way as to build up a square of $5 \times 5 = 25$ cards. A card once placed may not be moved so as to alter its position relative to any other placed card. The next card of the stock may not be looked at until the one just turned has been placed. The object is to make the highest-scoring Poker hands in the resultant ten rows and columns.

Treating each row and column as a Poker hand, score for it according to either the British or the American scoring schedule opposite.

British scoring is based on the relative difficulty of forming the various combinations in this particular game, American on their relative ranking in the game of Poker. Playing solitaire, consider yourself to have won with at least 75 British or 200 American points. Playing competitively, obviously, the highest score wins.

	UK	USA
royal flush	30	100
straight flush	30	75
four of a kind	16	50
straight	12	15
full house	10	25
three of a kind	6	10
flush	5	20
two pairs	3	5
one pair	1	2

☞ Reminder: A straight flush is five cards in suit and sequence, counting Ace low or high (A2345 or TJQKA). A royal flush (not distinguished in British practice) is an Ace-high straight flush. A straight is five in sequence but not all in suit, a flush is five in suit but not all in sequence. Four or three of a kind means four or three of the same rank, any other cards being unmatched. Full house is a triplet and pair.

Cribbage Squares   2+ players, 52 cards each

Competitive version of Cribbage Patience, the equivalent of Poker Patience.

Turn one card face up as a starter. If it's a Jack, score 2 for his heels. Then turn sixteen cards from a shuffled pack one by one, and place each on the table in such a way as to build up a square of four rows and four columns. The aim is to make the highest-scoring Cribbage hands in the resultant eight rows and columns, using each line of four in conjunction with the starter to make a five-card hand. Score each hand as at Cribbage. Playing solitaire, consider yourself to have won with at least 61 points. Playing competitively, the highest score wins.

Variant. Deal the square first and then turn the 17th card as a starter. This is more usual, but the above is more authentic.

☞ Reminder: 2 for each combination of cards totalling 15, 2 for a pair, 6 for a prial (three of a kind), 12 for a double pair royal (four of a kind), 1 per card for a run, 4 for a four-card flush or 5 if the starter is of the same suit, 2 for a row or column counting 31 exactly (Ace 1, numerals as marked, courts 10).

Don't forget . . .

- Play to the left (clockwise) unless otherwise stated.
- Eldest or Forehand means the player to the left of the dealer in left-handed games, to the right in right-handed games.
- T = Ten, p = players, pp = in fixed partnerships, c = cards, † = trump, ☆ = Joker.

The first or eldest says, I'le vye the ruff, the next says I'le see it, and the third I'le
see it and revie it . . . then they show their Cards, and he that hath most of a suit
wins six pence or farthings according to the Game of him that holds out the
longest.

John Cotgrave, *The Wit's interpreter* (1662)

The nature of [Brag] is, that you are to endeavour to impose upon the judgment
of the rest that play, and particularly upon the person that chiefly offers to
oppose you, by boasting of cards in your hand, whether Pair Royals, Pairs, or
others, that you are better than his or hers that play against you . . .

Richard Seymour, *The Compleat Gamester* (1725)

Poker heads the family of gambling games in which players vie with one
another as to who holds the best hand. 'Gambling', here, has its literal
meaning of playing for money, not its metaphorical meaning of staking
money on some future event over which you have no control as in casino
or banking games. 'Vying' is the process of claiming that you hold the
best hand, or the makings of the best hand if there are more cards to
come, and backing up the claim by putting your money where your mouth
is. It also includes bluffing, which means backing up a spurious claim
with however much (or little) money as it takes to frighten anyone out of
paying to see your hand – or, literally, 'call your bluff'. Unlike banking
games, few of which offer scope for bluff, Poker and its relatives are
games of psychological and mathematical skill, where you can be dealt
a bad hand yet still win by superior play.

What makes them gambling games is not the element of chance but
the fact that they can reasonably be played only for real money. Strictly
speaking, they are not really card games at all, since they do not involve
any actual play of the cards. It would be truer to describe them as money
games that happen to be played with cards. All the play takes place
with cash, or chips or counters representing cash. The basic principles
underlying Poker can be, and frequently are, applied to other numerically
distinguishable objects, such as bank-notes or dominoes. Nor are they
original to Poker and its relatives, which probably borrowed them from
older games played with dice.

There are two main vying procedures.

- In the first and apparently older type, each in turn either pays money into a pot to assert that he holds the best hand, or drops out of play when convinced he has not. This continues until only two remain in, when one may call for a showdown by matching the previous stake without raising it further. This may be called 'two-down vying', and is typical of Brag.
- In the more sophisticated type, all players can force a showdown by matching the previous stake, thereby preventing the previous raiser from raising it again. This may be called 'all-round vying', and is typical of Poker.

Poker is the only vying game to have transcended its national boundaries and acquired international status. As a national game it remains essentially American. Equivalent national games include Britain's Brag, Italy's Primiera, Spain's Mus, and the now defunct French game of Bouillotte. These and others will be considered in their turn, but there is no doubt as to where we must begin.

▌Poker basics
2 or more players, normally 52 cards

Fields – Poker? Is that the game where one receives five cards? And if there's two alike that's pretty good, but if there's three alike, that's much better?
Hustler – Oh, you'll learn the game in no time.

W. C. Fields, *Never Give a Sucker an Even Break* (1941)

Poker evolved in New Orleans from elements of Brag, Poque, and Bouillotte, and spread along the Mississippi in the steam-boat saloons. It is recorded as having been played under its present name in 1829, and was first described in the 1845 edition of *Hoyle's Games* (Philadelphia) by Henry Anners under the title 'Poker, or Bluff'. A photocopy of the relevant pages, for which I am indebted to Elon Shlosberg, shows that it was played with 52 cards, without a draw, and without straights, making the highest hand four Aces, or four Kings and an Ace kicker. The 1829 game was played, like Bouillotte, with only 20 cards, and this form is said, by Oliver P. Carriere (in *The Great American Pastime,* by Allen Dowling), to have been played as late as 1857 in New York. The draw feature was introduced, from American Brag, in the 1840s, and the straight is first mentioned in *The American Hoyle* of

1864. Stud Poker arose during the Civil War, but, despite these rapid developments, the game as a whole took some time to achieve social respectability. As late as 1897, one commentator noted that, 'The best clubs do not admit the game to their rooms.' It soon reached England, where George Eliot referred in 1855 to the 'game of Brag or Pocher', and Queen Victoria later confessed herself amused by it. American Ambassador Schenk is known to have taught it to the whole Court of St James.

Poker's most characteristic feature is the fact that players bet on a combination of five cards, rather than the three or four of such ancestors as Brag and Pimero. Five also happens to characterize an old Persian game called As Nas, which could have reached America via French settlers who had been in the Persian service, or Persian sailors calling at the port of New Orleans; but to make Poker the direct descendant of As Nas, as some have tried to do, amounts at best to an exaggeration of this particular historical strand.

Poker is practised in three distinct contexts: private play in home and workplace, public play in clubs and casinos, and tournament play wherever it may be held. The following account concentrates on home play, with each player dealing in turn. In public contexts, there is usually a so-called centre dealer, who does all the dealing and takes no part in play.

Dealer's Choice

Poker by its nature invites and receives constant variation in everyday play. Many variations are *ad hoc* and go unrecorded; others become popular over various periods of time and often acquire different names. Here it must suffice to describe the most basic forms, together with the broad lines along which variations occur.

The original game was Straight or 'Cold' Poker, in which five cards were dealt to each player; one period of betting ensued, and the winner of that took the pot. From this developed Draw Poker, in which, after the first betting interval is over, each player can seek to improve his hand by rejecting some of his cards and 'drawing' (= being dealt) replacements, a process followed by a second betting interval before the winner is determined. Draw is still regarded as the basic game for home play and is recommended for beginners, but serious players are now devoted to various forms of the next development, Stud Poker. In these, each player receives five or even more cards, from which he selects any five as his eventual playing hand. Some of these are dealt face down (= hole cards) for his eyes only, others face up (= upcards) for all to see. There is no draw, but betting intervals follow the deal of successive cards, giving more opportunity for betting and for the application of skill.

Both Draw and Stud may be combined with a major variant called Lowball, in which the pot is won by the lowest hand, or, more popularly, High-Low Poker, in which it is shared between the highest and the lowest hand. These and other variants follow the main descriptions of Draw and Stud.

The usual reason quoted for varying the basic game is a desire to speed up the action by increasing the relative frequency of 'good' hands, which otherwise rarely occur. This is only half the story. Each variant also introduces its own schedule of mathematical probabilities. These can hardly be learned by rote, but the skilled player, experienced in several forms of the game, starts out at a considerable advantage over the player whose knowledge stops short at orthodox Draw Poker. It is for this reason that the most popular form of the game is Dealer's Choice, in which each dealer announces exactly what game is to be played for his own deal, or for the round of deals initiated by himself. He is even at liberty to invent new variations and to name them as he pleases. In this way the mathematical variety of the game is given full play almost from deal to deal.

All forms of Poker are based on two principles: a universally recognized hierarchy of five-card combinations called Poker hands, and a universal method of staking and betting ('vying').

Poker hands

In all forms of Poker, players are either betting that they already hold the best hand, or, if more cards have yet to be dealt, that their present cards are so promising that they will finish up with the best hand. A Poker hand, by definition, is five cards. More may be dealt or held, but only five count in a showdown. These five may be totally unmatched, or may form one of the following combinations. (Other combinations are recognized in some games.) The relative rating of each type of hand is determined by the odds against being dealt it on five cards from a thoroughly shuffled pack. Figures above 100 are rounded to the nearest 50.

High card (1–1). No combination. The better of two such hands is the one with the higher top card, or second higher, if tied, etc. Cards rank (high–low) A K Q J T 9 8 7 6 5 4 3 2.

One pair (1½–1). Two of the same rank, the rest unmatched. The better of two such hands is the one with the higher-ranking pair, or the highest non-tying top card if both pairs tie.

Two pairs (20–1). Self-explanatory. The better of two such hands is the one with the higher-ranking pair; if equal, that with the higher-ranking second pair; if still equal, that with the higher odd card.

Threes (triplets, trips) (46–1). Three of a kind, two unmatched.

Straight (250–1). Five cards in numerical sequence, not all in one suit. Ace counts high or low but not both (A2345 or TJQKA, not QKA23). The better of two such hands is the one with the higher-ranking cards.

Flush (500–1). Five cards of the same suit, but not all in sequence. The best of two or more flushes is the one with the highest non-tying top card.

Full house (700–1). A triplet and a pair. The better of two such hands is the one with the higher-ranking triplet.

Fours (4150–1). Four cards of the same rank, the fifth irrelevant.

Straight flush (65,000–1). Five cards in suit and sequence, Ace counting high or low but not both. An Ace-high straight flush, known as a royal flush, is unbeatable, but can be tied, as no suit is better than another in orthodox Poker.

Betting procedure

Play does not take place with cards but with money, or with chips representing money, which are bought from a non-participating *banker* before play. Chips are commonly of three different colours, with whites counting as the basic monetary unit, reds as two, blues as five. Other possible scales begin 1, 5, 10; 1, 5, 20 etc., and there may be more or fewer colours.

To bet, a player moves one or more of the chips from the *stack* in front of him towards the centre of the table, where they become part of the pool or *pot* being played for. Chips once staked cannot be retrieved, except by winning the pot. It helps to keep individual players' stakes separate from one another rather than mingle them all in the pool, but few bother to do so.

In all forms of Poker, someone makes the first or opening bet. Rules vary as to (a) who has the first chance to open, (b) whether the opener must hold at least a specified combination in order to open, and (c) the least and greatest amount that may be made as an opening bet.

In home games, players who are not qualified to open the pot, or do not wish to, may *check* (pass) until somebody does. Public play does not usually allow this, and may require one or more blind bets to get the pot going.

If no one opens the pot, the hands are thrown in and there is a new deal.

Once the pot is open, each in turn to the left of the opener must either call, raise, or fold.

To *call* is to increase your stake so that it matches that of the previous active player.

To *raise* is to match the previous player's stake and increase it.

To *fold* is to place your cards face down on the table, lose what you have staked so far, and relinquish all claim on the pot.

This continues until

• *either*: Nobody calls the last raise and everyone folds. The last raiser thereby wins the pot without having to show his hand.

• *or*: The player who last raised has been called by the other players still left in the pot. All bets now being equal, the last raiser may not raise again, and the betting interval is at an end. Depending on the form of Poker being played, this is followed by the next phase of play or by a final showdown.

In a showdown, those still playing reveal their hands, and the player with the best hand wins the pot. Here, in any form of Poker, there is a rule that 'the cards speak for themselves'. In other words, a hand is what its cards actually are, not what their owner may mistakenly declare them to be.

Draw Poker   2–8 players (5 best), 52 cards

Draw, the oldest form of Poker, is now regarded as antediluvian by all right-thinking Americans, and will be encountered (if at all) only as a home game. Elsewhere, it remains the most basic form for learners and occasional players, standing in relation to 'real' Poker as Whist does to Bridge.

Preliminaries Lower and upper limits should be set on the amount of any opening bet or raise. A logical lower limit is one white. The upper limit may be a fixed amount (e.g. five), or it may be set at the whole or half the amount currently in the pot.

Players deal in turn. Before the deal each player antes one chip. Shuffle thoroughly and deal five cards each, one at a time.

First interval Each in turn, starting from the dealer's left, may open, pass, or fold, until someone opens. If all pass, the hands are thrown in and the pot is carried forward to the next deal. With the pot open, each in turn may call, raise, or fold. Play continues until the last raise has been followed only by calling or folding. If everyone folds following a raise or an opening bet, the last raiser wins the pot. He need not reveal his cards (except, if necessary, to prove he was entitled to open). Otherwise, all the chips staked so far are pushed into the middle of the table and there is a draw. Some schools limit the number of raises – to three, for example, or to the number of players – that may be made in this betting interval.

The draw Each in turn, starting from the dealer's left, may either stand pat or call for cards. In the latter case, he discards from one to three cards face down, announcing clearly how many he is discarding, and is promptly dealt by way of replacement the same number of cards from the top of the pack. Dealer himself is the last to draw, and must himself state clearly how many he is discarding.

Second interval Whoever opened the pot on the first round speaks first in the second. (*Variant*: In home play, first to speak is often the player who raised last in the first round.) Each in turn may check or bet until someone bets. If all check, the original opener must open again. Each in turn thereafter may call, raise, or fold. This continues until the last raise has been followed by calls for a showdown, in which case the player with the best hand wins the pot, or until all but one have folded, in which case the last in wins without showing his hand.

End of game It's advisable to agree a time limit and to finish at the end of the hand being played when that limit is reached.

Out of chips Anyone who runs out of chips in the middle of a pot must fold. In private games, they may be allowed to buy themselves back for the next hand.

Optional extras and variants

Jackpots In the first round, the opener must have at least a pair of Jacks or better (a higher pair or a higher combination). If no one opens, the hands are thrown in. If someone opens and subsequently discards one of his qualifying pair, he must, when the pot is won, prove from his hand and discard that he was entitled to open.

| ☞ When five play, at least one player can be expected to hold Jacks or better.

Hi-Lo Draw The pot is split evenly between the holders of the highest and the lowest hands. A hand lacking any combination is obviously lower than one containing a pair or better. As between two low hands, decide which is the higher on a high-card basis, and the other one is automatically lower. The lowest possible hand is a Seventy-Five (75432 of mixed suits), unless it is agreed to count Ace low, when it is a Sixty-Four (6432A).

Lowball Here the pot is won exclusively by the lowest hand. In Kansas City Lowball, the lowest is a Seventy-Five. In British Lowball, Ace can count low, making the lowest hand 6432A, known as a *royal six*. In California Lowball, straights and flushes are ignored, so the lowest possible is 5432A, known as a *wheel* or *bicycle*.

Seven-Card Draw When fewer than five play the winning hands are mostly rather dull. They can be improved by playing Seven-Card Draw. Each receives seven cards, and, in the draw, discards two more than called for, thereby ending up with a five-card hand.

Strip Poker Whoever has the lowest hand removes an article of clothing specified by the winner. Alternatively, bets are made in terms of clothing, one article being equivalent to one chip; but this is suitable only for players in an urgent hurry. The main problem with Strip Poker is that it is difficult to tell who has won, and why.

Stud Poker

2–8 players, 52 cards

Stud Poker livens the game up by increasing the amount of information available and the number of players to eight – or even more, as several players can usually be expected to fold before more cards need to be dealt.

Five-Card Stud (Short Stud)

The dealer antes as many chips as there are players (unless it's agreed that everyone antes for themselves) and deals each player a hole-card face down and an upcard face up. Everyone examines their hole-card and replaces it face down and half covered by their upcard. First to speak is the player showing the highest card or, if equal, the matching player nearest from the dealer's left. When bets have all been equalized, a second card is dealt face up, then a third, and finally a fourth, with a betting interval after each. At each deal the opening bet is made by

- the player showing the best combination (pair, three of a kind, etc.)
- or, if none, the player showing the highest card or cards
- or, if equal, the player nearest from the dealer's left.

The game ends on the last round when all but one player have folded, or when everyone has called or passed, in which case everyone reveals their hole-card for the showdown.

Canadian Stud

Five-Card Stud admitting four-card straights, flushes and straight flushes as acceptable hands. A fourstraight beats two pairs, a fourflush beats a fourstraight, and a four-card straight flush beats a full house.

Seven-Card Stud (Long Stud)

This variety continues to enjoy world-wide popularity. Deal two hole-cards and one face up. After a betting interval, deal a second, a third, and a fourth face up, then a third face down, with a betting interval after each. In a showdown, everyone selects the best five of their seven cards. Can be played Hi-Lo or Lowball. In Hi-Lo, you can't go for low if any of your upcards is higher than an Eight. ('An awful hybrid, but for some reason fairly well spread in Poker circles in the US and the UK,' says Dan Glimne.)

Razz

Lowball Seven-Card Stud.

English Long Stud

A hybrid of Stud and Draw recorded only in British books. Play as above until everyone has received five cards and the betting interval is closed. Each in turn may then either stand pat or make one discard in return for a replacement. The replacement is dealt face down or up depending on whether the abandoned card was down or up. A betting interval follows. Anyone who discarded on the previous round may then either stand pat or make one more discard, which again matches up or down the card it replaces. A final betting interval follows.

Mexican Stud (Flip Stud, Five-Card Turn-up, Peep-and-Turn)

You get two cards face down and, after looking at them, turn one of them face up. Each of the next three is dealt face down, and you may either 'flip' it (turn it up) or leave it down, in which case you flip the previous hole-card instead. Players must flip simultaneously so as not to influence one another's choice of flip-card.

| ☛ Often played as low card wild. (See Wild-card Poker.)

Baseball

One of the most popular of the 'fancy' games in domestic circles, though despised by the experts. The significance of its various features will be apparent if you know how America's national outdoor sport works, and irrelevant if you don't, so we'll take them as read.

Play as Seven-Card Stud. All Threes and Nines are wild. Anyone dealt a Three face up must immediately double the pot or fold. Anyone dealt a Four face up is immediately dealt an additional hole-card as a bonus, and will therefore enter the showdown (if he doesn't fold) with a choice of five from eight cards instead of seven.

| ☛ Under these rules (there are variations) the average hand is at least four of a kind. Experts say it is one of the best games for 'reading' tight players.

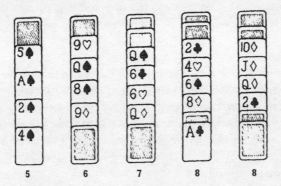

Stud Poker. From five- to eight-card Stud. In each case the first betting interval usually occurs after the deal of the first upcard, and another follows each card subsequently dealt.

Chicago

Seven-Card Stud in which the pot is equally split between the player with the best hand and the player with the highest hole-card of the spade suit. The point is to encourage players with weak hands to stay in the game.

| Flop Poker (Hold 'em, etc.)   2–9 players, 52 cards

There are several varieties of Poker in which one or more cards are dealt face up to the table and counted by each player as if they were part of his own hand. These communal cards form what is called the *flop*.

Hold 'em (Texas Hold 'em, Hold me Darling)

This has been the professionals' high-stakes game for many years now and is annually featured in major tournaments such as The World Series of Poker and the Carnivale of Poker, both at Las Vegas.

Deal two hole-cards to each player. Bet. Deal a three-card flop face up and bet again. Then deal a fourth and fifth card face up to the flop, with a betting interval after each. At a showdown, players may use any five cards out of the seven comprising their own two and the flop. If no one can improve on the complete five-card flop, then no one wins and the pot is shared.

Bedsprings

Deal five hole-cards, bet, then ten flops face down in two rows of five (see illustration). The flop cards are faced one at a time with a betting interval after each. Each player counts any pair of vertically adjacent cards as part of his own hand, and any five of those seven as his final hand.

Cincinnati

Deal five hole-cards, bet, then five flop cards face down. These are faced one at a time with a betting interval after each. Each player chooses any five out of the ten available.

Crossover

Deal five each, bet, then five flop cards face down in a cross (see illustration). These are faced, the arms first and the centre one last, with a betting interval after each. Each player counts any five from the five of his own hand plus either the vertical or the horizontal line of three in the cross.

Omaha

An informal relative of Hold 'em. Deal two hole-cards each, followed by a betting interval, followed by five flop cards face up with a betting interval after each. At a showdown, players must use their two hole-cards and may use any three upcards. Often played hi-lo.

Procter and Gamble

Deal four hole-cards, bet, then three flop cards face down, each of which is flipped (faced) one at a time, with a betting interval after each. The rank of the third flop is wild.

Seven-Card Mutual

As Omaha, but: two hole-cards, a four-card flop, and a third hole-card to each.

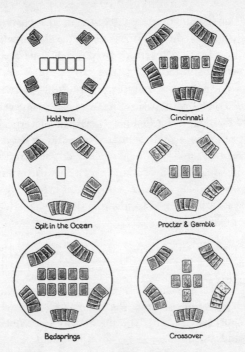

Hold 'em   Cincinnati

Spit in the Ocean   Procter & Gamble

Bedsprings   Crossover

Flop Poker. Layouts for Hold 'em and other varieties of Poker with a flop.

Spit in the Ocean

The ancestral game was basically a variant of Draw designed for more players at a table. Deal four cards each and one face up to the centre. This card, the eponymous 'spit', counts as the fifth card in everybody's hand. For fun, the spit itself, or all four cards of the same rank, may be designated wild.

Wild-card Poker   2 or more players, 52 cards

Any form of Poker may be played with one or more wild cards. A wild card is one which its holder may count as any card lacking from his hand, though sometimes with restrictions. The purpose is to increase the chances of making the higher and more interesting combinations, such as four or five of a kind and a straight flush. Which cards are made wild depends on how many are wanted: the more there are, the higher the winning hands, and the more incalculable the mathematics involved. For one wild card, add a Joker; for two, specify 'one-eyed Jacks'; for four, any given rank; for eight, any two ranks; and so on. Wilder still are *variable* wild cards – for example, Stud is often played with a rule that any card subsequently dealt to a player that matches the rank of his hole-card is wild, but for that player only.

Although wild cards alter the mathematics, they do not normally change the relative ranking of hands. They do, however, introduce a new hand consisting of four of a kind and a wild card counting as the fifth. By agreement, 'five of a kind' either beats everything or is beaten only by a royal flush. Of tied hands, one with fewer wild cards beats one with more.

Short-pack Poker

Poker is often played in countries where short packs are the norm. Like wild cards, short packs change the mathematics but not the relative ranking of hands.

32-card Poker

The French 32-card pack runs AKQJT987, and Ace counts high or low in a straight. In this game by far the commonest hand dealt is one pair. A nothing hand is much rarer, turning up only about three times in ten. This makes 32-card Poker much more interesting for Hi-Lo or Lowball. The most extreme variation occurs with the flush, which is actually harder to get than four of a kind. On the face of it, then, the flush would seem a poor bet and a fourflush not worth drawing to. On the other hand it is not possible to play with more than five at a table (or six at Stud), and four is the best number. The average winning hand is a high two pairs, as in normal Draw Poker, and the reduced number of players virtually halves the frequency of fours and full houses. The fourflush is therefore in fact a very reasonable proposition. Players on the lookout for curiosities will find plenty of scope here. For instance, how about five-player high-low stud with two spits common and wild?

Frequency of Poker hands in a 52-card pack with Deuces wild

The commonly reproduced table for this feature (possibly first published in *Culbertson's Card Games Complete*) is wrong, its most misleading error lying in the rate for straight flushes, quoted as 4,556 instead of the correct 2,552. Only the figures for two pairs, full house, and five of a kind are correct in previous tables. The hands are listed here in order of ascending frequency rather than in correct ranking order. This makes fours commoner than flushes, threes than two pairs, and a nothing hand better than one pair! The figures apply only to a five-card deal as at Five-Card Draw and Stud, not to Seven-Card Stud. A blank indicates that the given combination of cards would in practice be more profitably rated as a hand of higher value. (5S etc. = fives, or five-the-same, meaning five of a kind. NX is nix, meaning no combination.)

com	total	= 1 in	0 wild	1 wild	2 wild	3 wild	4 wild	
5S	672	3868	–	48	288	288	48	(a)
SF	2552	1108	32	544	1320	656	–	(b)
FH	12672	789	3168	9504	–	–	–	(c)
FL	14472	180	3136	7376	3960	–	–	(d)
4S	31552	82	528	8448	19008	3568	–	(e)
ST	62232	42	8160	34272	19800	–	–	(f)
2P	95040	27	95040	–	–	–	–	(g)
3S	355080	7	42240	253440	59400	–	–	(h)
NX	799680	3	799680	–	–	–	–	(i)
1P	1225008	2	760320	464688	–	–	–	(j)
total	2598960	=	1712304	+778320	+103776	+4512	+48	

Notes

(a), (b) If you prefer to rate a royal flush (RF) above five of a kind, the figures become: RF=504, 5S=652, SF=2,068. In this case a hand with four wild cards will be counted as RF if the natural card is Ten or higher, or 5S if Nine or lower.

(c) Two pairs and one wild card make a full house, but with more than one wild card the hand is at least four of a kind.

(d) A flush with three wild cards is at least four of a kind and may be a straight flush. Any other flush is weak because on average it is only half as common as four of a kind.

(e) Four of a kind gets dealt twice as often as a flush.

(f) A straight with three wild cards is at least four of a kind and may be a straight flush.

(g) Two pairs can be made only with natural cards and in most contexts is worthless.

(h) It follows that, if there are seven at a table, at least one player will probably be dealt three of a kind.

(i) A nix hand must consist of natural cards except in Hi-Lo or Lowball.

(j) Worthless alone, 1P stands good chances of conversion into 3S or 4S in a draw.

40-card Poker

Spanish and Italian packs lack Eights, Nines and Tens, so the full sequence runs AKQJ765432. The lowest straight is 5432A and the highest AKQJ7. When a 52-card pack is stripped to 40, it is usual to discard everything lower than Five, making the lowest straight A5678. The probabilities are unaffected by which three ranks are selected for removal. Again, the commonest hand is one pair, which is dealt about five times in ten as opposed to four nothing hands and one of anything higher. Flushes are rarer than full houses, but commoner than fours. A full table would be five or six players at Draw, six or seven at Stud.

48-card Poker

Pinochle enthusiasts have been known to play with a double 24-card pack, running AKQJT9 in each suit. It produces weird results. For instance, there are three distinct flush hands other than a straight flush. A flush containing no duplicated cards is beaten by any flush containing a pair, and a one-pair flush is beaten by any two-pair flush. So, for example, a ♥AKQJ9 falls to ♠KQJJ9, which in turn is beaten by ♦JTT99. This seems logical enough until you calculate the figures and discover that the most commonly dealt flush is the middle-ranking one pair, and the rarest the no-pair. These flushes, though ranking as a whole between a straight and a full house as in the normal game, are in fact rarer than full houses. The top hand is five of a kind, which is only marginally rarer than the straight flush. Ace may count high or low for the purpose of a straight or straight flush, so the three possibilities are: A9TJQ, 9TJQK and TJQKA. The oddest feature of all is the rarity of the nothing hand. It is not merely rarer than a pair, as in other short pack games, but in fact is exactly as rare as the straight – there being 97,920 of each type of hand in the total of 1,712,304 possible hands in the 48-card. To put it another way, the chances of being dealt a nothing hand are approximately 17–1 against. Thus, in the topsy-turvy world of Hi-Lo Pinochle Poker, a nothing is as good as a straight for the high hand, while the best low hand is a pair of Nines accompanied by JQK of mixed suits.

20-card Poker

The earliest form of Poker, current in the Mississippi river-boats of the 1820s, was played with 20 cards ranking AKQJT. The only admissible hands were one pair, two pairs, and three and four of a kind, though the full house soon put in an appearance.

Frequency of Poker hands in short packs

	32 cards		40 cards	
	number	*odds*	*number*	*odds*
SF	20	10068	28	23499
4S	224	898	360	1827
FH	1344	149	2160	304
FL	204	986	980	670
ST	5100	38¹/₂	7140	91
3S	12096	15¹/₂	23040	27¹/₂
2P	24192	7¹/₂	51840	11¹/₂
1P	107520	1	322560	1
NC	50676	3	249900	1¹/₂
Total	201376		658008	

Odds = odds to 1 against being dealt this hand from a properly shuffled pack.

Freak-hand Poker

> The smart gambler will play a game he basically hates if most of the other players have more enthusiasm than skill.
>
> Carl Sifakis, *Encyclopedia of Gambling* (1990)

Freak hands are unorthodox Poker combinations, invented originally to spice up games like basic Draw where most hands are won on two pairs, leaving fours and straight flushes so rare as to risk passing unrecognized when they deign to put in an appearance. Apart from lowball hands described above, freak hands have dropped out of use and are not normally welcomed in Dealer's Choice. This is because it is hard to work out where they should rank in the hierarchy, hard to remember when you have worked them out, and consequently apt to give rise to argument. What they were designed to achieve has been more easily done by introducing wild card, spits, and the deal of more than five cards. The freak hands listed below range from old favourites to complete novelties.

Bent A non-paired, non-flush, non-straight. See *Dutch* and *Irish*.

Bicycle Lowball hand 5432A. Total 1024 including flushes.

Big bobtail Four-card straight flush, plus one idler. Total 2032, of which 948 are not also straights, flushes, or pairs.

Big dog An Ace-high, Nine-low six-card straight with one missing. Relatives include *Big cat* (K–8), *Woolworth,* or *Five and dime* (T–5), *Little cat* (8–3), and *Little dog* (7–2). Cats are also called *Tigers.* There are 4096 of each, of which 16 are flushes.

Blaze Any five court cards. Total 792, of which 24 are fours, 144 full houses, 192 threes, and 432 two pairs.

Bobtail see *Big* and *Little*.

Cherry Five cards of the same colour but not flush. Total 126,412, of which 76,620 are not also pairs, two pairs, or straights.

Dutch straight (Skip straight) An alternating sequence, lowest 9753A, highest AQT86. Total 6144, of which 24 are flushes.

Flash In Joker Poker, the Joker plus any one card of every suit. Total 17,160, of which 264 are wild-card straights.

Fourflush Not uncommon. Usually ranked between two pairs and threes, and above fourstraights, though in defiance of mathematical accuracy. There are 111,540 in all, of which 29,088 are pairs, 600 straights, and 1896 fourstraights.

Fourfright A fourstraight-cum-fourflush, such as ♠A987♥6, other than a bobtail (like ♠A♥9876). Total 3792.

Fourstraight Even more mathematically confused than fourflushes, there are 97,792 of the wretched things.

Irish straight The ultimate *bent*, or non-hand: five different ranks, no two of them consecutive, and not all alternating (otherwise it's a Dutch straight). There are 86,016, of which 336 are flushes.

Kilter or *pelter* Another non-hand: nothing higher than a Nine, and no Ace, pair, straight, or flush. There are 53,040, some overlapping with other freak hands, such as *bents* and *republicans*.

Little bobtail A hand containing an unbroken three-card straight flush. Total 52,260, of which 28,704 are not also pairs or better.

Monkey flush A hand containing three cards of a suit but not in sequence (otherwise it is a *Little bobtail*). Total 812,136, of which 770,160 are not also pairs or better.

Pelter See *Kilter*.

Pet Generic term for any five-card hand equivalent to a one-gap six-card straight (see *Big dog*, etc.).

Republican or *Puritan* Respectively the American and British terms for a hand containing no courts or pairs. There are 258,052, of which 250,924 are neither straight nor flush.

Round-the-corner straight One in which Ace counts high and low simultaneously, allowing such combinations as QKA23. There are 3072, of which 12 are round-the-corner straight flushes. Their introduction does not affect the relative ranking of the straight and straight flush, but has more effect when applied to such freaks as Dutch, cherry, and striped straights.

Skeet A hand consisting of 9-(8 or 7)-5-(4 or 3)-2. Said to rank between threes and a straight, but, with 6120 possibilities (ignoring the 24 flush skeets), it should rank between a straight and a flush.

Skip A Dutch straight.

Squib An Ace (or Jack, or other specified rank) plus exactly one card of each suit.

Striped straight See *Zebra*.

Wheel A low straight, so termed in forms of Lowball where straights are discounted as high hands. The lowest wheel is 5432A, known as a bicycle.

Zebra Five cards that alternate in colour when arranged in numerical order, Ace counting high or low – for example, ♠A ♥J ♣9 ♦4 ♣3 or ♥K ♣Q ♥7 ♣5 ♦A. There being 113,920 of them, they rank between two pairs and threes. An additional 640 that are also in sequence are called striped straights. Another 128 are either straights or zebras but not both, by virtue of the variable Ace. For example, ♠A ♠K ♥Q ♣J ♦T is either an Ace-high straight or an Ace-low zebra.

The relative ranking of these hands depends on which of them are included in the game being played, as they overlap with one another as well as with orthodox hands. Extreme cases of overlapping can produce such freaks as ♠4 ♥2 ♣K ♦J ♠9, which might conceivably be described as a 'round-the-corner Dutch zebra'. Or (afterthought) a Möbius straight, as it forms part of an endless loop that switches seamlessly between odd and even sides.

Dealer's Choice games

The following are not really forms of Poker, but independent and often trivial betting games that are recorded as played in Dealer's Choice.

Beat Your Neighbour (Rollover)

Deal five cards each face down in a pile. The first faces his top card and a betting interval ensues. The second turns his top card. If it is not higher than the previous player's, he turns his second, and so on, until he reaches a higher card. If he reaches a higher card, a second round ensues. If none of his five is higher, he drops out of play. Each in turn does the same, turning cards until he reaches one higher than any before, followed by a betting interval, or dropping out otherwise. Last in wins the pot.

Best Flush

Draw Poker, but only flushes and part flushes count. The best hand is the one with most cards flush. Ties are settled on a high-card basis.

Buddha's Folly

Deal five each and turn the next face up. Eldest hand may either reject the upcard by passing it to the left, or take it and pass a different card to his left. Each in turn, similarly, either passes or exchanges the card offered from the right. Keep going till no one wants the card on offer, then continue as in Guts (below).

Butcher Boy

Keep dealing cards one at a time face up around the table. When a second card of the same rank appears, it goes to the player who received the first. He initiates a round of betting, in which players may drop, check, stay, or raise. More cards are dealt, starting with the player who was next due for a card when the duplicate appeared. The pot is won by the last left in, or the first to receive four of a kind.

Guts

Players receive two cards each and, after examining them, decide whether or not to compete for best. When all are ready, the decisions are announced simultaneously. One way of doing this is to simultaneously unclench fists, showing a chip if you're in or none if you fold. Another is for all to hold their cards face down a small distance above the table, and either drop them to fold or keep hold of them to stay. Either way, those who stay in then reveal their cards. The highest pair wins, or highest card if there are no pairs. The winner takes the pot and the losers must then stake the amount it contained for the next deal. Play continues until only one player will play, thereby winning and emptying the pot.

If no one will play, either keep playing with the same hands until somebody bets (*Hold your Guts*), or reveal hands and make the player who would have won match the pot (*Weenie rule*).

Guts is also played with an additional 'ghost' hand which the otherwise winning hand must also beat if it is to take the pot. Many other variations: see also Buddha's Folly.

Indian Poker

Deal one card face down to each player. You mustn't look at your card – instead, hold it with one finger against your forehead, facing outwards, like the lone feather of an Indian brave. With everyone able to see one another's cards but not their own, there follows a betting interval and showdown in the usual way.

Knock Poker

Played like Knock Rummy, with five each, a stockpile and a wastepile. As soon as one player is satisfied with his Poker hand, he knocks after discarding. Others are permitted one more draw and discard, and the best hand wins. As there is no betting, the players or (preferably) dealer alone should previously ante.

Put and Take

More of a banking than a vying game. All but the dealer receive five cards face up. Dealer turns up the top card of the remaining pack, and anyone who has a card of the same rank pays him 1 chip for it (or for each if he has more than one). Upon turning the second he receives 2 chips for each card of the same rank held, then 3 for the third, 4 for the fourth, 5 for the fifth (or, in some circles, respectively 1, 2, 4, 8, 16). He then turns up the next five, but this time pays out to players with matching cards, following the same schedule as before.

Red and Black (Plus and Minus)

Draw Poker without Poker combinations. Instead, cards count face value from 1 to 10, with courts 10 each. Red cards count plus, black cards minus. The hand with the highest point total wins. Often played High-low.

Rollover Stud

See Beat Your Neighbour.

Three Five Seven

Everyone having anted an agreed amount, deal three cards each and decide who stays and who folds as in Guts. Those who stay in reveal their hands to one another (but not to those who folded) to decide who wins. Threes are wild, straights and flushes don't count. Those who stayed but lost each pay the winner the amount currently in the pot.

Next, deal two more cards to everyone, including those who folded. Play as above, except that Fives are wild, and straights and flushes valid.

Finally, deal two more cards to everyone and play as above. This time Sevens are wild, and each player chooses the best five out of seven cards.

A player who is the only one to stay in for a hand earns a point. The first to get three points takes the pot, ending the game.

Zebra Poker

Draw Poker, in which hands count only if they are zebras (alternating in colour from high to low; see Freak variants). Tied hands are decided on a high-card basis.

Brag

3–7 players, 52 cards

Brag is the traditional vying game of Britain and former colonies, and enjoyed considerable popularity in the United States before being ousted by Poker, to which it contributed several distinctive features. It derives from a family of three-stake games similar to Poch, and formed the subject of a less than adequate treatise by Edmond Hoyle in 1751. Many different versions have been played throughout its long history. Common to all is the fact that they are based on three-card hands, as opposed to the four of Primero and five of Poker.

☞ Most book descriptions of Brag are outdated or inaccurate. For a definitive study, see Jeffrey Burton, 'Bluff English Game – with American Branches', in *The Playing-Card* (Journal of the International Playing-Card Society), XXIV, 3 (Nov.–Dec. 1995) and 4 (Jan.–Feb. 1996).

Basic essentials Brag is normally played with a 52-card pack basically ranking AKQJT98765432, and recognizes the following range of 'Brag hands', from low to high:

Pair. Two cards of the same rank, the third unmatched.

Flush. Three non-consecutive cards of the same suit.

Run. Three consecutive cards, not flush. The highest is 3-2-A, followed by A-K-Q, and so on down to 4-3-2.

Running flush. As above, but in the same suit.

Prial. Three of a kind. The highest is three Threes, followed by Aces, Kings, and so on downwards.

A higher combination beats a lower. If equal, the one with the highest non-tying top card wins.

Wild cards or *floaters*, formerly known as *turners* or *braggers*, are less common in Brag than in Poker. Deuces may be wild, or the Joker added as a wild card. A hand containing one or more wild cards is beaten by one of the same type containing fewer wild cards, regardless of rank. For example, 4-4-4 beats 5-5-W beats 6-W-W.

Several typical versions are described below, all individual rules being variable by agreement. Each can involve as many players as there are cards to go round. All are hard-score games, played for cash or counters.

Three-Card Brag

From three to seven use a 52-card pack basically ranking AKQJT98765432. A game may end by agreement whenever everyone has made the same number of deals. Cards are shuffled before the first deal, but thereafter not between deals until a hand has been won with a prial. Before the deal, players may be required to ante one chip each (desirable if fewer than five play). It may be previously agreed to place a limit on the amount that may be bet at each turn. Deal three cards each, in ones, face down.

Play Each in turn, starting with eldest, may 'stack' (drop out, placing his cards face down under the stock), or make a bet by pushing one or more chips to the kitty. A player may open for any amount. Each in turn thereafter must either stack or match the previous bet, and may raise it. Equalizing the bets does not prevent the last raiser from raising again.

Play continues until only two remain. These continue betting until one player either stacks, leaving the other to win without a showdown, or 'sees' the other by paying twice the amount required to stay in. At a showdown, the kitty goes to the player with the higher hand, or, if equal, to the one who was seen.

The next dealer then gathers in all the hands, including those that have been dropped, and stacks them at the bottom of the pack without mixing them up. Only if the kitty was won on a prial does he shuffle them before dealing.

Betting blind A player may leave his hand face down, untouched, and 'bet blind' for as long as he likes. So long as he does so, he need only add half the amount staked by the previous player, while any raise he makes must be doubled by those who follow. If one of the two final players is betting blind, the other may drop out but may not see him till the blind bettor looks at his cards. 'You can't see a blind man', as the saying goes.

Covering A player who runs out of chips but wishes to stay in may 'cover the kitty' by laying his hand face down. Subsequent players start a new kitty and continue play. When one of them wins, his hand is compared with that of the covering player, and the higher of them wins the original kitty.

Five-Card Brag

As above, but each receives five cards and discards two face down before play begins. A prial of Threes ranks between Deuces and Fours, but, by agreement, the top hand is a prial of Fives.

Seven-Card Brag

All contribute equally to a kitty and receive seven cards face down. Anyone dealt four of a kind wins the kitty and there is a new deal. Otherwise, each discards one card face down and forms the other six into two Brag hands, laying the higher of them face down on his left and the lower face down on his right.

Eldest begins play by turning up his left hand. Each in turn thereafter may pass, or turn his left hand face up if it beats the highest hand showing. Whoever is showing the best hand then turns up his right hand. Again, each in turn thereafter either passes or turns his hand up if it beats all other right hands.

The kitty goes to a player winning on both hands, or winning one and tying for best on the other. In the unlikely event of two players tying for best on left and right, it is divided between them. Otherwise, the kitty is not won but carried forward to the next deal.

A prial of Threes counts between Deuces and Fours, and a prial of Sevens beats all.

Nine-Card Brag

As Seven-Card, except that each receives nine cards and arranges them into three Brag hands, which must be exposed in order from highest to lowest. All three must win (or at least tie for best) for a player to sweep the pool. The best hand is variously set at a prial of Threes or Nines.

Crash

A Lancashire game briefly outlined by Arthur Taylor in *Pub Games* (1976). Four players each receive thirteen cards and arrange them into four Brag hands, ignoring the odd card. Each lays his hands out in a row face down before him. (Source does not say whether they need be in order of superiority.) The hands are revealed strictly in order from left to right, the winner of each marking 1 point. The kitty is won by the first to reach 7 over as many deals as necessary, but a player receiving four of a kind in one deal wins the game outright.

Bastard (Stop the Bus)

A cross between Brag and Commerce or Whisky Poker. Deal three cards each and a spare hand of three face up to the table. Each in turn must exchange one or more cards with the same number on the table – or, in a particularly frustrating variant, one or three cards, but never two. Play continues until someone knocks, whereupon the others may – but need not – make one more exchange. Best hand wins the kitty, or worst hand pays a forfeit, or whatever.

Three-Stake Brag

The original 'Bragg', as described in 1721, was a three-stake game structurally identical with Bone-Ace (= French *Bon As*) and Post & Pair, described in *The Compleat Gamester* of 1674, and with a continental game called Best, Flush and Thirty-One (*Belle, Flux, et Trente-Un*, etc.). Its defining feature was the recognition of one or more wild cards called braggers, of which the first was imported from the game of Loo, where it was called Pamphilus or Mistigris.

Players made three stakes and received two cards face down and one face up from a 52-card pack. The first pot went to the player with the best upcard (Ace highest), or the eldest such player if equal – unless anyone was showing ♦A (*bon Ace*), which won regardless of position. The second went to the winner of a round of vying as to who held the best pair or prial. For this purpose ♣J was a bragger (wild card), and in some circles so also was ♦9. A hand containing one or more braggers was beaten by its equivalent natural hand. Players then revealed their cards and could draw as many more as they wished, the third stake going to the hand counting closest to 31 without exceeding it (Ace 1, numerals face value, courts 10 each).

| **Mus** | 4 players (2 × 2), 40 cards (Spanish) |

Widely played throughout the Spanish-speaking Old and New Worlds, Mus is an extraordinary game of Basque origin and terminology. The uniqueness begins with its basic structure, for, even though it is a gambling game and includes vying, it is normally and best played as a partnership game for four. Not only that, but partners are permitted to indicate the nature of their hands by means of conventional signals – a procedure that would not be countenanced in the wildest of Dealer's Choice Poker. Though simple in structure, it is complicated in detail, making it necessary in the following account to concentrate only on the broad picture. Full details are available from the Pagat website, from which you can link in to playing it on-line.

Scoring and equipment Although a vying game, Mus is played up to a fixed target of 40 points over as many deals as necessary, and a match is the best of three games. Points are represented by *piedras*, 'stones', of which 22 are initially placed in a central container such as a saucer. As stones are won, they are taken by, and stored in front of, one member of the partnership that wins them. For every five stones his side wins, he returns four to the pool and passes one to his partner. This one is called an *amarraco* (apparently from *humarreko*, the Basque for a clutch of ten, presumably reflecting a historically earlier method of scoring). Thus, at any point in the play, each side's score is readily ascertainable as being five times the number of stones being kept by one partner, plus exactly the number of stones kept by the other. When the amarraco-keeper has seven of them, he returns them to the pool and announces this fact, as a warning that his side needs only five more stones to win.

Cards The cards of the 40-card Spanish pack rank from high to low and have face values as follows:

rank	King	Three	Caballo	Sota	Seven	Six	Five	Four	Two	Ace
value	10	3	10	10	7	6	5	4	2	1

However, in the most widespread version of the game all Threes count as Kings and all Deuces as Aces, as to both rank and value. The game is therefore said to be played with eight Kings and eight Aces.

Deal and mus (draw) The player to the dealer's right is eldest hand, and all procedures pass to the right. Deal four cards to each player and stack the rest face down. Each in turn announces '*Mus*' if he wishes to change some or all of his cards, or '*No hay mus*' if satisfied with his hand. If everyone calls '*Mus*', they must then all discard from one to four cards and be dealt replacements from the top of the stock. Further rounds ensue until someone eventually says '*No*'. If the stock runs out before all draws are completed, a new one is formed from the shuffled discards.

Betting intervals The draw (if any) is followed by four rounds of possible betting and vying, each for a particular class of combination. These four classes are followed in a fixed and invariable order, no cards being revealed until all four rounds have been gone through (unless the game is curtailed by the 'sudden death' bid of *Órdago*).

The four classes of combination are bet on in the following order:

1. *Grande.* A bet that you or your partner hold the highest hand, or second highest if equal, and so on. *Example*: K-3-7-6 beats K-C-S-S, as Threes are equivalent to Kings. If tied, priority goes to the elder of tied players.

2. *Chica.* The same, but for the lowest hand. *Example* K-6-2-A beats C-4-4-A because, Aces being equal, its second-lowest card (Two) is lower than the other's Four.

3. *Pares.* The same, but in respect of holding the best paired hand. A pair, worth a basic 1 stone, is beaten by *medias* (three of a kind), worth a basic 2, and *medias* by *dobles* (two pairs), worth a basic 3 stones. No special score attaches to four of a kind, which merely counts as a *dobles.* Thus K-3-2-A would beat C-C-C-C because it is equivalent to K-K-A-A, and Kings beat Caballos. In this and the following rounds the best hand wins the basic value plus the value of the last bet accepted – or, if none, 1 stone.

4. *Juego* or *punto*. Juego is a declaration that you hold cards totalling at least 31 points in face-value, and a bet that you hold the best point. For this purpose the best point is 31, worth 3 stones, followed by 32, worth 2, followed by 40, 37, 36, 35, 34 and 33, all worth 2 stones each. (38 and 39 are impossible.) If no one announces *Juego*, the alternative call is *punto* (or *no juego*). This is a declaration that your cards total 30 or less, and that you have closer to 30 than anyone else. Thus a point of 30 beats 29, which beats 28, and so on downwards. The best *punto* is worth 1 stone.

Procedure On each round players may pass or open for a minimum of 2 stones. An opening bet may be declined ('*No quiero*'), matched ('*Quiero*'), or raised ('*Reenvido*') by either opponent. If declined, the bidder takes the appropriate bonus from the pool, '*porque no*'. If raised, it may be raised by any amount, and re-raised by the other side.

Any player in turn to speak may declare Órdago (from the Basque for 'Here it is'). If the other side accepts it, there is a showdown, and the best hand wins the whole game outright. If not, the other side wins only the bets made on the hand under consideration, plus any appropriate bonus.

When all bets are declined or equalized, the next round begins. On a showdown, no ties are recognized. As between identical combinations the higher-ranking beats the lower, and, if still equal, an elder hand beats a younger.

Partners may signal to each other the holding of certain combinations, provided they stick to accepted convention. At *grande*, for instance, you can show two Kings by biting your lower lip. (To show four Kings, do it twice!)

Mus is equipped with a tremendous array of protocols, technical terms, conventional jokes (if an adversary misbehaves, you can claim a 'Bonus of one stone for playing properly'), and basic Basque vocabulary: *bat, biga, hirur, laur, bortz* are respectively one to five, *bay* 'yes', *ez* 'no'. There is a version in which the Caballo of clubs and Sota of coins are wild cards, known respectively as 'Perico' and 'Perica', and a non-partnership version for four to eight players called Mus Ilustrada.

Primiera (Primero, Prime, Goffo, Bambara)   4–8 players, 40 cards

Italy's national vying game goes back to the sixteenth century. Girolamo Cardano, 'the gambling scholar', knew it as Primiera, Rabelais as Prime, and Shakespeare as Primero. It is still played in central Italy – with Italian-suited cards, of course – under such names as Goffo and Bambara.

Preliminaries The turn to deal and bet passes to the left. Each player antes a previously agreed amount and is dealt four cards, in twos, from a 40-card pack ranking KQJ765432A. Anyone dealt a winning hand calls for an immediate showdown, and the best hand wins the pot.

Winning hands From lowest to highest, the winning hands are:

1. *Primiera* One card of each suit.

2. *Fifty-five* Seven, Six, Ace of a suit, the fourth card any.

3. *Flush* Four cards of the same suit.

Ties are broken in favour of the hand containing the highest point-count. For this purpose, each rank counts as follows:

rank	7	6	A	5	4	3	2	K,Q,J
value	21	18	16	15	14	13	12	10 each

If still equal, the deal is annulled and the pot carried forward to the next. (*Variant*: Flushes and fifty-fives may be decided on a best-suit basis: hearts highest, then diamonds, clubs, spades.)

Example Aldo declares a primiera: ♠K ♥Q ♦4 ♣3. Bruno counters with a fifty-five: ♠7-6-A ♦A. This is beaten by Carlo's flush, ♦7-2-Q-J. Dino, however, sweeps the pool with ♥6-5-4-3, counting 60 to Carlo's 53. (You are, of course, unlikely to see four such hands in a single, honest deal.)

Draw If nobody wins outright, each in turn makes one or more discards and is dealt replacements from the top of the pack. Players may agree to stake again at this stage. If there is still no claim, there is a showdown, and the pot goes to the player with the best *point* – the highest value of cards in one suit. For example: ♥7-4 ♣A ♠K, counting 35 in hearts, beats ♦K-Q-4 ♣7, counting 34 in diamonds.

In some schools, the period between the draw and final showdown sees a round of Poker-style vying, or further draws may ensue until a win is claimed or not enough cards remain.

Variant Though pairs and sequences don't count, three or four of a kind is often rated as a primiera.

Primero

The game played by Elizabeth I and (according to Shakespeare) her father, Henry VIII, is almost certainly identical with the original Primiera described by Cardano. Here, the winning hands from highest to lowest are: *chorus* (fours), *fluxus* (flush), *supremus* (fifty-five), *primiera*, and *numerus* (point).

Poch (Pochen, Glic)   3–8 players, 32 or 52 cards

This popular German family game is one of the oldest known, being first mentioned at Strasbourg in 1441, and appearing shortly afterwards in France under the name Glic (English Gleek). It has always been subject to variation, but its most constant feature is a distinctively tripartite structure. The first stake is won by whoever is dealt the highest cards, or certain specified cards; the second by successfully vying or bragging as to who holds the best combination; and the third for drawing cards to a point value of 31 – or, in a later development, by being the first to play all one's cards out to a sequence, as in Newmarket. The same structure underlies many other historic games, including the earliest version of Brag. The second element, that of vying or bragging, has since become isolated as the sole mechanism of modern Brag and Poker. The word *pochen*, literally meaning to hit or knock, metaphorically means to boast, brag or vie. Poker, therefore, gets its name from its defining method of play, derived ultimately from German *pochen* via French *poque*.

Preliminaries Poch involves a circular board of traditional design containing several staking compartments, one for each winning card or combination. From two to four players use a 32-card pack ranking AKQJT987. More than four use 52 cards.

Part one: best cards Players dress the board by placing chips in the first seven of eight compartments labelled Ace, King, Queen, Jack, Ten, Marriage, Sequence, Poch. Deal five cards each and turn the next for trump. The stakes for Ace, King, Queen, Jack and Ten go respectively to the players dealt those particular trumps. That for marriage goes to the holder of both King and Queen of trumps, in addition to the individual stakes for King and Queen. Sequence is won by anyone dealt the 7-8-9 of trumps. Unclaimed stakes are carried forward to the next deal.

Part two: best combinations Players vie, Poker-style, as to who holds the best combination. A quartet beats a triplet, a triplet a pair, and a pair an unpaired hand, with ties determined by the highest card. The first to bet places a stake in the poch compartment, saying '*Ich poche eins*' ('I bet one', or however many). Each in turn thereafter must either match the best or drop out of this phase of play. The opener may raise it again next time round. If not, there is a showdown, and the best hand wins the contents of the Poch compartment.

Part three: playing out The cards are played out in sequences. Whoever won the previous round starts by playing the lowest card of their longest suit; whoever holds the next higher card of the same suit follows on; and so on. The sequence ends either when the Ace is played, or when no one can follow because the required card has not been dealt. The player of the last card then begins a new sequence, and, in some circles, receives one chip from each opponent. This continues until someone wins by playing out their last card. The others pay that player one chip for each card left in their own hands.

Bouillotte

Reportedly devised by a committee of the French Revolutionary government as a substitute for the officially prohibited game of Brelan, Bouillotte may be named after the heroic Geoffrey de Bouillon, though it also happens to be the French for hot-water bottle. It became popular in nineteenth-century America before Poker won out.

Preliminaries Four players use a 20-card pack, ranking AKQ98 in each suit, and play to the left. Each starts with a *cave* (stack) of 30 chips, five each of reds and whites, a red being worth five whites. The deal and turn to bet pass always to the right. Deal three cards each in ones and turn the next face up.

Play Dealer opens the pot for a previously agreed amount. Each in turn may then fold, straddle, or open. Straddling is equivalent to checking, but involves matching the dealer's ante or previous player's straddle, plus one white. If all pass, the pot is carried forward and the the same dealer deals again. If a straddle is followed by three passes, the straddler wins the pot without further play. If the dealer straddles, eldest must open or fold. If he folds, the next in turn has the same option; and so on.

A player may open for any amount. Each in turn thereafter must either fold, call, or raise. Equalizing the bets does not prevent another round of raising until only two players remain, when a call forces a showdown.

Showdown The best hand is a *brelan* (three of a kind). If tied, the best is one that matches the rank of the turn-up (making a *brelan carré*, or 'brelan squared'). If none matches, that of highest rank wins. Any player with a *brelan* receives a side-payment of one chip – or two for a *carré* – from each opponent.

Failing a *brelan*, the hand with the best point wins. For this purpose, all four players reveal their hands, including those who folded. The face values of all these cards are totalled for each suit, counting Ace 11, courts 10, numerals as marked. The suit with the highest visible total is designated the best suit, and the player holding the highest card of it wins the pot – provided that he did not fold. If he did, the winner is the player holding the greatest face-value of cards in any other suit.

Related vying games

Best, Flush, and Thirty-One

(Belle, Flux, et Trente-un). A French and German game of the seventeenth–eighteenth centuries, resembling Poch, but played without a staking board and with three cards each, one of them dealt face up. The three stakes were won for, respectively, being dealt the highest upcard (*belle*), vying as to who held the best two- or three-card flush, and drawing cards up to 31 in the manner of Pontoon/Blackjack.

Brelan

Classic French vying game widely played from the seventeenth to the nineteenth centuries, but nowhere unambiguously described. From two to five players received three cards each from a pack of 24, 28, 32 or 36, and the next card was turned from stock. The best hand was a *brelan carré*, being four of a kind made with the aid of the *retourne*, followed by a simple *brelan* or prial.

Flush

The flush element of European vying games goes back to a fifteenth–sixteenth century game of probable Italian origin, variously known as Flusso, Frusso, Flux, Fluxus, Flüss, etc. After staking, players received three cards each and vied as to who held the greatest value of cards in a single suit. Courts counted 10 each and Ace originally 1, subsequently 11, giving a maximum of thirty-one.

Flüsslen

Of several descendants of Flusso surviving in Switzerland, Flüsslen is local to Muotatal. Four play in partnerships, using a 20-card Jass pack consisting of Ace, King, Ober, Unter, Banner in each of the suits acorns, bells, shields, flowers. Deal three each. One member of the partnership on lead puts out a two-card flush, but does not turn the third card until the others have tried to beat it with a better two- or three-card flush. The Unter or Banner of acorns counts 11 points, of bells 10$^{1}/_{2}$, of shields 10$^{1}/_{4}$, of flowers 'ten-and-a-bit'. Aces count 11, and Kings and Obers 10 each, but only in combination with one or two other cards of the same suit. Three Aces count as a *Flüss* worth 33, thus beating everything.

Gilet

Old French game variously spelt Gé, J'ai, Je l'ai, Gilet, Gillet, and, in Cardano's Latin text, Geleus. It looks ancestral to Best, Flush, and Thirty-One. Put up two stakes and deal three each, face down, from a 36- or 32-card pack. The first goes to the winner of vying for the best *tricon* (triplet) or *gé* (pair), the second of vying for the best point, meaning the total value of cards in any one suit. The 1777 *Académie des Jeux* says that a pair of Aces counts 20$^{1}/_{2}$ for point, and an Ace and same-suit court card or Ten count 21$^{1}/_{2}$, whether or not the third card is an Ace. Make of this what you will.

Giley

A Spanish Gypsy game, according to Fournier's *Juegos de Naipes Españoles*. Four or five play, to the right, with a 28-card pack counting as follows:

rank	Ace	King	Caballo	Sota	Three	Two	Seven
count	11	10	10	10	10	10	7

The winning hand is the highest flush-point on four cards. A four-card flush ranges in value from 37 to 41, a three-card from 27 to 31, a two-card from 17 to 21. Play to the right. Deal two each in ones, followed by a Poker-style betting interval, then two more, followed by another interval, followed by a Poker-style draw and a final betting interval. Tied hands at a showdown are broken in favour of the eldest player. Some circles acknowledge a best suit, typically oros, which beats an equal point in an ordinary suit. Some rank all suits in descending order oros, copas, espados, bastos (equivalent to ♦-♥-♠-♣).

Golfo

A Spanish vying game comparable to Gilet but more subtle. Four play, to the right, with a 28-card pack consisting only of numerals Three to Nine inclusive. Each in turn deals but sits out, so only three actually vie. The winning hand is the highest-counting flush of up to four cards out of five, which is to say that only two, three, or four of a suit can be counted even if you have five. A higher-counting flush beats a lower, even if it contains fewer cards. The structure is: deal two each, bet, deal three more each, bet, discard and draw, bet, discard and draw again, final bet. Equality in a showdown favours the eldest player. Thus you cannot possibly lose if, as eldest hand, you hold 6-7-8-9 of a suit, counting 30, the highest possible.

Poque (Bog)

The seventeenth–eighteenth century French equivalent of Poch, revived in the nineteenth century under the name Bog. The word Poque, related to *poche* (pocket), also means a staking compartment in the gaming board. The French equivalent of *Ich poche*, recorded as *Je poque*, may suggest that 'poker' was originally pronounced 'pocker'.

Trentnen (Träntnen, Trenta)

This even more elaborate Swiss relative of Flüsslen is played in Appenzell. The procedure is similar, except that each player discards one card, so that only two-card flushes count, and partners may indicate the nature of their hand to each other by means of conventional nods, winks and grimaces.

Don't forget . . .
- Play to the left (clockwise) unless otherwise stated.
- Eldest or Forehand means the player to the left of the dealer in left-handed games, to the right in right-handed games.
- T = Ten, p = players, pp = in fixed partnerships, c = cards, † = trump, ☆ = Joker.

23 **Banking games**

A banking game is a form of gambling in which one or more punters simultaneously play a two-handed game against a banker. The banker deals the cards and generally operates the knobs and levers of play, while the punters, in most cases, have nothing to do but decide how much they want to lose. The banker enjoys a number of advantages, notably that of winning in the event of a tie. Such advantages constitute his 'edge', which can in many cases be calculated as a long-run percentage in the banker's favour. Another characteristic is the fact that many such games require the provision of a betting table marked with a staking layout equivalent to that used in roulette, and, to save time and labour, are played with several packs shuffled together and dealt from a long oblong box called a shoe. This makes banking games ideal activities for casinos, in which the bank is held by the management and the game dealt and controlled by its agents. Casinos, in turn, make ideal sources of revenue for otherwise impecunious political entities. Cardinal Mazarin is said to have turned the seventeenth-century French court at Versailles into one vast casino, virtually operating it as an instrument of state, and to this example the principality of Monte Carlo provides a modern parallel.

Thus banking games are not so much card games as casino games that happen to be played with cards, the casino itself supplying the equipment, funding the bank, and, through its agents (croupiers) generally running the show. A detailed description of banking games therefore belongs not in a book of card games but in a book of casino games. Here, we can safely restrict ourselves to those that can be played anywhere, off the cuff, with a single pack of cards and no special equipment, and for what many regard as the fun of a mild flutter, if indeed they bother to play for cash at all.

Structurally, banking games are little more than dice games adapted to the medium of cards, as shown by the fact that they are fast, defensive rather than offensive, and essentially numerical, suits being often irrelevant. They are divisible into two broad classes:

• turn-up games, in which punters more or less bet on whether or not one card will turn up before another, and stakes are literally won or lost on the turn of a card; and

• point-count games, in which the punters draw cards one by one until their combined face value most nearly reaches, but does not exceed, a given total or 'point'.

| Twenty-One / Pontoon   *n* players, *n* × *52 cards*

Pontoon, the domestic British version of Twenty-One, has been so called since the First World War. The name is almost certainly a corruption of Vingt-et-Un, via a hypothetical form 'Vontoon'. ('Van John' is also attested.) Unlike casino Blackjack, Pontoon has no official rules and varies widely from school to school.

Preliminaries Each player should start with at least twenty chips, counters, matchsticks, or other convenient staking units. Cards have numerical values only, suits being irrelevant. Numerals Two to Ten count as marked, courts 10 each, Aces 1 or 11 as their holders declare.

The bank Select the first dealer/banker at random, such as by dealing cards around face up until someone gets a Jack. Decide how the bank is going to pass. For example:

• each player in turn banks for as many deals as there are players, or
• it automatically goes to the player who gets a pontoon, or
• anyone may offer to buy it from the banker between deals.

Also agree the maximum permissible stake.

Object In each deal, the punter's aim is to end up with cards totalling more in face value than the banker's – but not exceeding 21, otherwise he is 'bust' and loses. A 21 consisting of an Ace and a card worth 10 is a 'pontoon', and pays extra, but a banker's pontoon is unbeatable, as he always wins in cases of equality.

Deal Shuffle the cards thoroughly at start of play. Thereafter, they are not shuffled between deals but only after one in which a player gets a pontoon.

The banker deals one card face down to each player including himself.

Everyone except the banker examines his card and stakes one or more chips on it, up to a previously agreed maximum. The banker then deals a second card to each, but does not yet look at his own. If anyone has a pontoon, he turns the Ace face up and stakes nothing more.

Dealing more cards The banker then addresses himself to each player in turn and asks whether he wants more cards. The punter may do one of the following:

• *Stick.* Decline extra cards, provided that he has a count of 16 or more.

• *Buy.* He increases his stake and is dealt another card face down. The amount staked for each new card must be not less than that staked for the previous one, nor more than the total amount he has staked so far. (*Variant*: Each new buy may be for less but not more than the previous one.)

• *Twist.* He is dealt one card face up free of charge. Having once twisted, he may twist further cards but may not subsequently buy.

Buying or twisting continues until the punter either sticks or busts. On declaring 'bust', he loses his stake and hands his cards to the banker, who places them at the bottom of the pack.

When all have been served, the banker turns his two cards face up, and may, if he wishes, turn more cards face up until he is satisfied with his count, or busts.

Pay-off If the banker gets:

• A pontoon, he wins all the stakes.

• Twenty-one on three or more cards, he pays double to anyone with a pontoon, but wins all the others' stakes.

• Under twenty-one, he pays anyone with a higher count the amount of their stake (doubled for a pontoon), but wins all the other stakes.

• A bust, he keeps the stakes of those who also bust, but pays anyone with a count of 16 to 21 (doubled for a pontoon).

Optional extras

Five-card trick No one may receive more than five cards. A five-card hand worth 21 or less beats everything except a banker's pontoon, and is paid double.

Royal pontoon A hand consisting of three Sevens beats everything except a banker's pontoon, and is paid treble.

Splitting A punter (but not the banker) whose first two cards are of the same rank may split them and play each one as a separate hand, buying a second card for each and generally acting as if he were two people. Some permit only Aces to be split, others permit anything but Aces to be split. (In fact, Aces and Eights are the only rank worth splitting.) Some, if a split Ace becomes a pontoon, do not pay it double or permit that player to take the bank.

Blackjack (Twenty-One)   *n* players, *n* × 52 cards

Using the basic playing strategy, a good card counting system and a sound betting technique, it is possible to obtain a significant advantage over the house.

Dr M. Zadehkoochak, *The Book of British Blackjack*

Anyone playing Blackjack in Northern Nevada should be arrested for stupidity.
Playboy magazine

Blackjack denotes both the American home game and the international casino version. The home game is normally played with one pack and little formality, the casino game with multiple packs shuffled together and a house dealer. In British casinos the rules of play are governed by law, but no such predictability attaches to American procedure, which is governed instead by the laws of a free market. Players will naturally gravitate to the casino offering the most attractive rules, meaning a smaller edge for the house. Inter-house competitiveness, therefore, makes the so-called Strip rules (named after The Strip in Las Vegas, former US Highway 91, along which all the new and modern casinos are situated) the most favourable in the world for the players. They may give the house a tiny edge of approximately 0.5 per cent, but make up for it in increased volume – and plenty of players who are enjoying themselves too much to bother about correct basic strategy, Strip rules or not. If that comment from *Playboy* still applies, it's not entirely the fault of the casinos.

Preliminaries Any number can play, and any number of 52-card packs are shuffled together and dealt from a shoe.

Deal The punters place their bets and the dealer deals two cards face up to each of them. He then deals himself either one card face down (British practice) or one face up and one face down (American).

Object To beat the dealer by ending up with cards whose face values total more than his but do not exceed 21. For this purpose numerals count at face value and face cards 10 each. An Ace normally counts 11, but drops to 1 if 11 would bring the total to more than 21. A 21 consisting of an Ace and a 10-card is a blackjack or a 'natural', and pays extra.

Blackjack If you're dealt a blackjack and the dealer's upcard is a numeral from 2 to 9, you are paid off at 3–2 and your cards are gathered in. If the dealer's upcard is an Ace or 10-card, nothing happens until his second card is turned. You then get 3–2 only if the dealer does not have a blackjack: if he does, it is a stand-off.

Insurance If the dealer's upcard is an Ace, you can make a separate side-bet (usually restricted to half your main stake) that he has a blackjack. If he has, when the time comes to show it, you win this stake double; if not, you lose it single. Insurance is usually a sucker bet, and British rules allow it only if you have a blackjack.

Splitting pairs If dealt two cards of the same rank, you may split them, and play both as two separate hands, after placing the same stake on the second as you did on the first. You then get a second card dealt face up to each of them, and thereafter play them as separate hands. House rules vary as to which ranks you are allowed to split. (British rules prohibit splitting Fours, Fives and Tens, thereby preventing punters from making fools of themselves.)

The following conditions usually apply:

1. You can't re-split a card already split (British rules).
2. If you split Aces, you can't draw more than one more card.
3. In a split, a two-card 21 doesn't count as a blackjack.

Doubling If you have a count of 9, 10 or 11, but not a blackjack, you may double your stake. (British practice. American rules may allow you to double on any first two cards.)

Drawing If you haven't got a blackjack and have neither split pairs nor doubled down, you may then call for more cards to be dealt face up, one at a time, until you either stand (stop drawing) or bust (exceed 21). If you bust, you lose your cards and your stake.

Dealer's count If one or more players remain in play, the dealer deals himself a second card face up (or, in America, turns his hole-card face up).

- If the dealer has a blackjack, he wins the stake of anyone who hasn't.
- If not, he must draw more cards so long as he has a count of 16 or less, and stand when he has 17 or more.
- If he busts, he pays evens to anyone who did not bust.
- If not, he pays evens to anyone showing a higher count and wins the single stake of anyone showing a lower. If equal, it is a stand-off.

Optional extras Some house rules allow you to drop out of play after receiving your first two cards. You then get half your stake back unless the dealer has a blackjack, when you lose it all.

Some allow you to make a side bet that your first two cards will total less than 13, or more than 13. Both pay evens, but both lose if the total is exactly 13.

In home games, some pay double for a twenty-one consisting of 6-7-8 or a five-card hand that is not bust ('five-card Charlie'), treble for three Sevens, and quadruple for a six-card Charlie.

Comment Blackjack is certainly more skill-rewarding than most casino games. Unlike other card games such as Baccara, it offers you millions of probability situations and considerable choice of play; unlike dice and roulette, once a number has turned up it can't turn up again until the pack has been reshuffled. This makes it possible – if you have the requisite single-mindedness – to keep track of which cards have gone, and so make a better estimate of the odds applying to all the cards you can see at any given moment. For example, if so few 10-cards have appeared to date that the rest of the pack must be relatively rich in them, the fact that the dealer must draw to 16 or less means that his chances of busting are relatively greater. 'Card-casing' – which, at its simplest, can come down to just keeping track of the 10-cards – forms the basis of the system famously promoted by Dr Edward O. Thorp in his 1962 best-seller *Beat the Dealer*, though the principle involved is recorded as early as 1900. A more spectacular exponent is Ken Uston, author of *Million Dollar Blackjack*, who was a Senior Vice President of the Pacific Stock Exchange before turning to the game full time and taking the casinos in Las Vegas, Atlantic City and the Caribbean for over four million dollars at the blackjack tables. Card counting, however, besides being hard work, is not the sole guarantee of success. As Zadehkoochak (above) points out, it must be used in conjunction with a good basic playing strategy and a sound betting technique – to which must be added self-discipline and patience – in order to obtain a significant advantage. In the long run, that significant advantage is due to the fact that the dealer has absolutely no choice of play.

Baccara (Baccarat, Chemin de Fer, Chemmy, Punto Banco)

n players, *n* × 52 cards

> To say that the actual play of Baccara is simple is an understatement. Most children's games are infinitely more complicated, and it is doubtful if Baccara played without stakes could hold the attention of any but the most backward child.
>
> Barrie Hughes, *The Educated Gambler* (1976)

Spelt with a 't' in Britain and Las Vegas, Baccara is a more up-market but less intelligent version of Twenty-One. It originated in nineteenth-century France and may be of Oriental inspiration. In basic Baccara, the house is the bank. In Chemin de Fer, or 'Chemmy', the bank passes from player to player. In Punto Banco, it appears to pass from player to player, but is actually held by the house.

Casino play involves three or six 52-card packs shuffled together, but one is enough for anyone daft enough to play it at home. Counting numerals at face value and courts 0, the punter's aim is to receive cards totalling closer to 9 than the banker's, for which purpose 10 or more counts only as its last digit.

The banker deals two cards to the punter and to himself. If either has a point of 8 or 9 (a 'natural') he turns them face up. With 6 or 7 a punter must stand; with less than 5 he must call for a third card, dealt face up; with exactly 5 he may do either (but in most American casinos must draw). The banker must draw to a point under 3, stand with a point above 6, and may do either with a point of 3 to a punter's third-card 9, or 5 to a punter's third-card 4. Otherwise, he must draw or stand as dictated by the most favourable odds.

Macao

Baccara predecessor that remained popular in the USA until the early twentieth century. With cards counting as at Baccara, the aim is to get a count of 9 or less without busting. Punters place their bets and all, including the dealer, receive one card face down. If your first card is a Seven you win the amount you staked, if an Eight you win double, and if a Nine treble – unless, however, the dealer beats your card with an Eight or Nine of his own. All bets are off in case of a tie. When these accounts have been settled, punters counting less than 7 may call for one or more cards, which are dealt face up. Those that are bust drop out, and the dealer tries to beat the totals of those that remain, drawing more cards if necessary.

Farmer (La Ferme)

European game described as *ancien* in the *Académie des Jeux* of 1764, but reportedly played in rural America well into the twentieth century. (Not that the game is essentially rural – *la ferme* metaphorically means the office of professional tax-collector.) Play with 45 cards omitting all Eights and Sixes except ♥6 (originally called *le brillant*). The aim is to get as close to 16 as possible, but not more, counting Ace 1 (only), numerals face value, courts 10. Players ante 1 unit to the farm (pool), and the farmer (or tax-gatherer, or banker) deals one card each face down. Each in turn must call for at least one card and may request more, these being dealt face down. Players may stop when they like, without stating whether or not they are bust. When all are ready, the hands are shown and anyone with a bust pays 1 unit to the farmer. Whoever has 16, or the nearest count below it, collects 1 unit from each non-bust player with a lower total. Two or more players tying for best share this equally between them. The farm and office of 'farmer' transfer to the player who gets exactly 16. In the event of a tie, priority goes to (a) the farmer, (b) the hand containing ♥6, (c) the hand with fewer cards, (d) the tied player next from farmer's left.

Quinze (Quince, Fifteen)

A two-player Pontoon equivalent popular at Crockford's in the early nineteenth century, notable players being Talleyrand and the Duke of Wellington. The key total is 15, counting numerals at face value (Ace 1 only) and courts 10 each. A stake is agreed and one card dealt to each. Non-dealer may stand or keep calling for another card, dealt face up, until he either stands or busts. Dealer does likewise. The player with the better total wins the stake, which, in the event of a tie or two busts, is doubled and carried forward. The deal alternates.

Seven and a Half

Italian Pontoon equivalent played with 40 cards lacking Eights, Nines and Tens. Numerals count face value, courts ½ each, ♦K is wild, and the aim is to get as close as possible to 7½ without exceeding it. Each punter antes and receives a card face down. After looking at it he may either stick or call for more cards, dealt face up, until he either sticks or busts. Banker then does likewise. If he busts, he pays those with less than 8 the amount of their stake, doubled to the player who has a two-card 7½ count. If not, he collects from anyone with a bust hand or a lower count than himself, and pays anyone with a better count. A tie is a stand-off. A two-card 7½ beats one with more than two and entitles its holder to replace the banker, unless the latter also has one.

| Pai Gow Poker   2–7 players, 53 cards

This banking game involving poker combinations is based on Pai Gow, a Chinese Domino game. It has become popular in American casinos. Pai-gow denotes a seven-card hand containing no paired rank, but it has no special part to play.

Preliminaries Agree how the bank is to rotate, assuming you want everyone to have the same number of deals.

Deal The punters each put up a stake and are dealt seven cards face down. All but the dealer examine their cards and split them into two hands, one of five and one of two cards.

Object To make two hands both of which will beat those of the banker when his turn comes to play.

Restrictions The Joker is not completely wild. It may represent an Ace, or whatever card may be necessary to complete a straight, flush, or straight flush, but nothing else. The five-card hand ranks as a poker combination. (Five Aces, including a Joker, beats a royal flush. In some circles, A2345 is the second-best straight after TJQKA.) In the two-card hand, a pair beats a non-pair, but no other combination counts. The five-card hand must outrank the two-card. For example, if the two cards are a pair of Aces, the five cards must contain two pairs or better. Players may not discuss their hands at any time.

Dealer's play When the punters have placed their hands face down, the dealer exposes his seven cards and similarly forms them into a five-card and a two-card hand. The other players may not touch their cards once the dealer's have been shown.

Outcome As between the dealer and each punter, if both the dealer's hands beat both the punter's, the dealer wins the punter's stake; if both the punter's beat the dealer's, the dealer pays the punter the amount of his stake. If either hand is tied, the dealer's beats the punter's. If each of them wins one hand, it is a 'push' (stand-off).

Chinese Poker

(2–4p, 52c) An apparent derivative of Pai Gow, this is neither Poker nor a banking game – nor, as far as I can make out, Chinese. Deal thirteen cards each. Everyone arranges their cards in three tiers, a top row of three and two rows of five beneath. The lowest row must be the highest Poker hand of the three, and the top row the lowest. Each row is then revealed in turn, and each player wins or loses with each other according to their relative ranking. Anyone who fails to arrange their hands in the correct order loses. There is no strategy, no vying, and no sense in it at all.

Yablon (Red Dog, Acey-Deucey, Between the Sheets, etc.)

n players, *n* × 52 cards

Yablon is often called Red Dog, a name that originally applied to High Card Pool. Casino play usually involves anything up to eight packs shuffled together and dealt from a shoe.

Basically, punters bet that the third card dealt from the top of the pack will be intermediate in rank between the first two. Everyone makes an initial stake and the banker deals two cards face up with enough space between them for a third. Unless the first two are of the same rank, or consecutive (running A23456789TJQK) the punters may then raise their stakes, but not by more than the original amount. A third card is then dealt between the first two. If it is intermediate, the punters win; if not, the bank does. The odds paid to a successful punter vary with the 'spread' – that is, the number of ranks intermediate between the first two cards – as follows:

spread	odds
1	5:1
2	4:1
3	2:1
4–11	1:1

If the first two cards are consecutive, it is a tie. No one may raise, and no one wins.

If they are paired, no one may raise, but a third is turned. If it matches the first two, the punters win 11:1, otherwise the bank wins.

Let It Ride

Each player puts up three identical stakes and receives three cards, which he may not show to anyone. The banker deals two face down in front of himself. The hope is that one's own three cards and the banker's two will form a good Poker hand. After examining their cards, each punter may take one bet back or 'let it ride'. The banker exposes one of his two cards and, again, everyone has the option of retrieving another stake or letting it ride. The banker's second card is then faced and everyone shows their hand. Each punter whose three cards make a pair of Tens or better with the banker's two is paid on each of his remaining stakes at the following rate: Tens or better, stake times 1; two pairs × 2; three of a kind × 3; straight × 5; flush × 8; full house × 11; fours × 50; straight flush × 200; royal flush × 1000.

Red Dog (High Card Pool)

'has been the newspaperman's gambling game over the years, rather than Poker' (Sifakis). All contribute equally to a pot, which is replenished when empty. Deal five each, or four if nine or ten play. Each in turn, starting with eldest, either pays a chip and throws his hand in, or bets a specific amount that at least one of his cards will beat the top card turned from the pack, by being a higher card of the same suit (Ace highest). No one may bet more than the pot contains. The banker reveals the top card and each in turn then settles with the pot, withdrawing from it the amount of his stake if he can beat the top card, otherwise paying that amount in.

Variant 1: The actual top card is burnt (replaced at the bottom without being shown), and the next one turned to settle the bet.

Variant 2: A punter may 'copper' his bet – that is, bet that none of his cards will win.

Slippery Sam

(3–15p, 52c). All contribute equally to a pot, which is replenished when empty. Deal three each, which no one may yet look at, and turn the next card face up. If it is a Seven or higher (Ace high), keep turning the next until it is a Six or lower. Everyone then bets whether or not they have been dealt at least one card of the same suit as the turn-up, and higher in rank.

Speculation

n players, 52 cards

Asked to advise on the staging of Speculation for the film production of a Jane Austen novel, I found this late eighteenth-century game surprisingly fun to play, possibly because it rewards competence in calculating probabilities. A banking game to the extent that the dealer has certain advantages, it plays well, and more fairly, if the winner of each hand deals to the next.

Preliminaries Everyone starts with the same number of chips and at the start of each deal antes one to a pot. Deal three cards face down on the table in front of each player in a stack, then turn the next card of the pack to establish a trump suit. (Not that there is any trick-play. 'Trump' here means the only suit that counts.)

Object To be in possession of the highest trump when all cards in play have been exposed. For this purpose cards rank from Two low to Ace high.

Play The trump turn-up belongs by right to the dealer, so if it is an Ace the dealer wins without further play. If it is not an Ace, but is high enough to interest anyone else, they may offer to buy it from the dealer, and the dealer may haggle about it, or auction it, or keep it, as preferred.

Each in turn, starting with the player to the dealer's left – or, if the turn-up was sold, to the purchaser's left – turns up the top card of his own stack. This continues in rotation, but omitting the player who currently possesses the highest trump. If and when a trump is turned that is higher than the one previously showing, the player who turned it may offer it for sale at any mutually agreeable price, or refuse to sell it. Either way, play continues from the left of, and subsequently omitting, the possessor of the highest trump.

Furthermore, anyone at any time may offer to buy not necessarily the best visible trump, but any face-down card or cards belonging to another player. The purchaser may not look at their faces, but must place them face down at the bottom of his stack and turn them up in the normal course of play. (The time to indulge in this piece of speculation is when you currently own the highest trump and want to prevent someone else from turning a higher.)

End The game ends when all cards have been revealed, or when somebody turns the Ace, and whoever has the highest trump wins the pot.

Optional extras

1. Anyone turning up a Five or a Jack adds a chip to the pot. (This looks like an Irish addition – see Twenty-Five.)

2. A spare hand is dealt and revealed at the end of play. If it contains a higher trump than the apparent winner's, the pot remains untaken and is added to that of the next deal.

Other notable banking games

Faro

Reportedly so-called from the likeness of one of the kings to a Pharaoh, this classic banking game originated in eighteenth-century France and spread eastwards to Russia, westwards to America. Casanova, when not more pleasurably engaged, played Faro wherever he went, and by the nineteenth century it had become the world's most widespread casino game. In the twentieth century it has largely been ousted by Blackjack and Baccara.

There is a single layout of thirteen cards, one of each rank, suits being irrelevant. Punters place stakes on individual ranks to turn up in their favour as the banker deals. They can arrange them in various different positions to represent combinations of two or more ranks, and can bet negatively. The banker, after rejecting the top card of the pack (called *soda*, possibly from French *sauter*), turns cards from the pack in twos, the first of each pair being placed at his left and winning for the bank, the second at his right and winning for the punters – unless it matches the rank of the first, in which case, of course, the banker wins. The last card, called *hoc*, is not played. Winning punters can let their bets ride in hopes of a third or fourth card of the same rank turning up later, earning apparently tremendous but in fact unfavourable pay-offs.

Basset

seventeenth-century forerunner of Faro, first mentioned as played by Catherine of Braganza, wife of Charles II. It was a more cumbersome game, in that a separate thirteen-card staking layout was required for each player.

Stuss (Jewish Faro)

The enormous popularity of Faro in the United States led to the development of this simpler and more informal variant. It may still be encountered in low-class American gambling joints.

Trente et Quarante (Rouge et Noir, R & N, Thirty-and-Forty)

This more genteel activity may still be encountered in French casinos, but is declining in popularity because of its low house percentage. Of uncertain age, it was certainly known in 1650 and may have been introduced by Mazarin. A staking layout enables punters to bet on which of two rows respectively marked red and black will come closer to 31, or that the first card dealt will or will not match the colour of the winning row, or both. The banker first deals cards face up in a row marked *rouge*, then again to a row marked *noir*, stopping each row when it reaches or exceeds a point of thirty-one, and paying off accordingly. Punters may also bet that the first card dealt will be of the same colour as the winning row (*couleur*), or of the opposite colour (*inveise*).

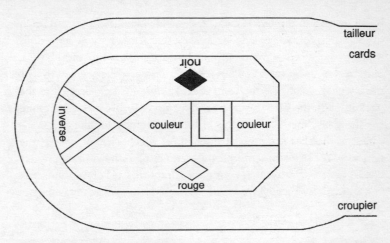

Staking layout for Trent et Quarante. The *tailleur* (dealer) is assisted by one or more croupiers.

A full survey of informal banking games belongs less to a survey of card games than to that of gambling, if not to the annals of crime. For more complete descriptions of banking games, ancient and modern, see especially Carl Sifakis, The Encyclopedia of Gambling *(1990). Entries include Ace-Deuce-Jack, Ambigu, Bango, Banker & Broker, Chase the Ace (or Minoru, after a race-horse of Edward VII), Easy Go, Farmer's Joy, Lansquenet, Monte Bank, Play or Pay, Shoot, Skin, Spanish Monte, Three-Card Monte, Tripoli, Ziginette, and many others that I may have missed.*

Don't forget . . .
- Play to the left (clockwise) unless otherwise stated.
- Eldest or Forehand means the player to the left of the dealer in left-handed games, to the right in right-handed games.
- T = Ten, p = players, pp = in fixed partnerships, c = cards, † = trump, ☆ = Joker.

You can't teach an old dog new tricks.

Anonymous (and untrue)

Why bother to invent a new card game when there are hundreds of good ones already in existence?

The only possible response to this is to adapt George Mallory's answer to the question, 'Why bother to climb Everest?' and reply, 'Because it isn't there.'

Some of the following first appeared in *Original Card Games* (London, 1977) and others in Jaime Poniachik's Spanish translation of it (*Anarquía y Otros Juegos de Cartas*, Madrid & Buenos Aires, 1993), though all have been further modified in the light of extensive play. Two others appear in their appropriate places in the preceding chapters: Ninety-Nine because it has been so widely published elsewhere that it presumably now counts as a real game; and Contract Piquet because it needs the context of its original model to aid comprehension.

Although most are based on traditional features such as trick-taking and Poker combinations, all exploit some novel twist in the mechanism of play, and all, to a greater or lesser degree, are games of skill. Most have short and simple rules, and none requires more than a single pack of cards.

Abstrac
2 players, 25 cards

What happens if you play the matchsticks game with sticks of different value – or, better still, with playing-cards?

Preliminaries Shuffle a 24-card pack consisting of AKQJT9 in each suit, spread them out face up and overlapping, and add a Joker (or a spare card backside up) at the top end.

Object To take cards that form scoring combinations (sets and sequences), without taking more cards than absolutely necessary. The Joker is a penalty card that reduces the inherent advantage of the opening move.

Play Each in turn, starting with the non-dealer, draws either one, two or three consecutive cards from the top end until none remain. Place the cards you take face up on the table before you so that your opponent can always see what they are.

Score The scoring combinations are sequences of three or more cards of the same suit, and sets of three or four cards of the same rank. Any single card may be counted twice, once in a sequence and once in a set. Your full score consists of two parts multiplied together.

First, for combinations, count for each:

> three of a kind 2 points, four of a kind 8 points
>
> suit-sequence of three = 3, four = 4, five = 6, six = 12

Next, multiply this by the number of cards taken by your opponent.

Misère A player who fails to make any combination theoretically scores zero. In this case, however, the two players exchange scores, so it is the one who made combinations that scores zero.

Example: From the sample layout, the number taken at each turn was 2–3, 3–1, 2–3, 1–3, 1–3, 3. This gave the non-dealer, in addition to the worthless Joker, ♠AKQT ♥J ♣AJ9 ♦AKQ, scoring 2 for the Aces and 3 for each sequence of three, times 13 for the number of cards taken by dealer, total 104.

The second took ♠J9 ♥AKQT9 ♣KQT ♦JT9, scoring 2 each for the Nines and Tens, and 3 each for the red sequences, times the other player's 12 cards, total 120.

Game Dealing alternately, play up to 1000, or any other agreed target.

Variant The following variant arose from correspondence with David Levy, an American computer programmer who has tested the game in numerous variations. Spread twenty-five cards out as above. The first player may draw any number of cards up to twelve. Thereafter, the maximum number that may be drawn by each player is one more than the number actually drawn by the previous player. If a player draws only one card, the other may pass; otherwise at least one card must be drawn.

Caterpillar (Court Short)

2 players, 52 cards

An adding-up game that will probably never turn into a butterfly.

Preliminaries Deal each player thirteen cards from a 52-card pack and stack the rest face down.

Object Primarily, to score points by bringing the running total of cards played to a multiple of five. Secondarily, to keep as many court cards as possible in hand.

Play Each in turn plays a card face up to the table and draws a replacement from stock. The cards so played form an overlapping row of cards called the Caterpillar. Non-dealer starts by playing any numeral and announcing its value (Ace =1, Two = 2, etc.). If it is a Five or a Ten, he scores 5 or 10 as appropriate.

At each turn you must play either

- a *numeral* card of the *same suit* as the previous one, or
- a *court* card of *any* suit.

If you play a numeral, you announce the new sum total that it makes, and if that total is a multiple of five you add it to your score.

If you play a court, it adds nothing, and you repeat the same total. If that total is a multiple of five, you score it only if the court you played matches the suit of the previous card – not if it changes the suit to be followed.

Keep going till no cards remain in stock, the caterpillar contains twenty-six, and both of you have thirteen left in hand.

Score Total the amount you scored for multiples, and add 100 for each court left in hand.

Court short If, in course of play, you get stuck because you can neither follow suit nor play a court, you are said to be 'court short', and thereby win. Having shown your cards to prove it, both of you score whatever you made in play, and you who were court short add 100 for each court left in your opponent's hand. That'll teach him to hog all the good cards!

Counterbluff

Poker for two. Yes, it has been done before; but here's another version.

Preliminaries Deal ten cards each from a 52-card pack and stack the rest face down. A game consists of as many hands as it takes to work once through the pack.

Object The aim in each hand is to score points for making the best Poker combination, or for bluffing your opponent into folding (= conceding) before a showdown.

Poker hands Standard Poker hands apply: high card, one pair, two pairs, threes, straight, flush, full house, fours, straight flush. When playing low, standard Lowball hands apply (see page 562).

Play Each in turn, starting with the non-dealer, plays a card face up to the table. Theoretically, this continues until both have played five cards, and the player whose five cards make the better Poker combination wins the hand. If both hands are identical, the second wins. Either player, however, having played at least one card, may on any subsequent turn fold instead of playing a card. The winner marks a score related to the total number of cards played by both players in that hand, at the rate of 1 for the first card, 2 for the second, 3 for the third, and so on. The full schedule is therefore:

cards	2	3	4	5	6	7	8	9	10
score	3	6	10	15	21	28	36	45	55

Drawing from stock Each in turn, starting with the loser of the previous hand, draws from stock until both have ten cards again, or until the stock runs out. The loser then leads to the next hand.

Lowball If you have a low hand, or simply want to get rid of five indifferent cards in hope of drawing better, you can call 'Lowball' on your turn to lead, and play a complete five-card hand either face up or face down. Your opponent then has the choice of playing a five-card hand face up or down, or folding without playing any card. The possible outcomes are:

• *Opponent folds* You score 15 (without having to show your hand if played face down).

• ... *plays face up* Both hands are compared, and the lower-ranking combination scores 30.

- ... *plays face down.* You score 30 if you played face up, 5 if face down.

Last hand When the stock runs out, play continues without drawing until at least one player has fewer than five cards. Both then reveal their unplayed cards as a last hand. In this case combinations do not count. Instead, whoever has the highest non-tying card (Ace high, Two low) wins the hand and scores for it in the usual way.

Full game Play up to 250 points, or any other agreed target.

Dracula   2 players, 54 cards

A two-player game with a bloodthirsty count. It may be played for a small or large stake – preferably through the heart.

Preliminaries Take a 54-card pack including two vampires (or Jokers) and cut a card from the middle. If it's a red card, you deal first, otherwise second. The deal alternates and there are six deals to a game. Numerals count at face value from Ace = 1 to Ten = 10. Face-cards count 0 or 10 (see below).

Deal Deal four each face down, turn the next one face up on the table, and stack the rest face down. The faced card defines the centre of an eventual square of nine cards forming three rows and three columns (as at Noughts & Crosses) which the players gradually build up on the table. This layout is called the coffin, and the initially faced card is the first nail in the coffin.

Object To make the highest-scoring line of three cards in your chosen direction. Decide before play who, when the coffin has been built, will score for the horizontal rows (Queen-player) and who for the vertical columns (King-player.) Whichever you choose will apply throughout the game.

Play Each in turn, starting with the non-dealer, plays a card face up to the table in any of the other eight positions that may be vacant, provided that it goes side by side with a card already in position – corner to corner is not sufficient. Keep going till all are full.

Score Each player scores the value of the highest-scoring line made in their chosen direction, unless tied, when it is the second-highest that counts (or, if still tied, the third-highest). For this purpose:

1. The total face value of any line is doubled if it contains two cards of the same suit, trebled if it contains three of the same colour, or quintupled if it contains three of the same suit.

2. A Queen counts 10 horizontally but 0 vertically. A King counts 10 vertically but 0 horizontally. A Jack counts 0 either way. (But the suit of a card worth zero remains valid for doubling, trebling or quintupling the score of the line in which it appears.)

3. A vampire drains all the score out of the row and column in which it appears, resulting in a whole line counting zero in each direction.

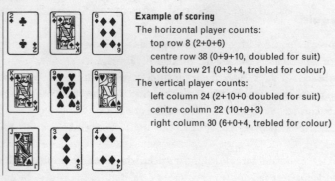

Example of scoring
The horizontal player counts:
    top row 8 (2+0+6)
    centre row 38 (0+9+10, doubled for suit)
    bottom row 21 (0+3+4, trebled for colour)
The vertical player counts:
    left column 24 (2+10+0 doubled for suit)
    centre column 22 (10+9+3)
    right column 30 (6+0+4, trebled for colour)

The scores are therefore 38 to 30. If a vampire had been played in place of ♥Q, the scores would be 21 to 24.

Subsequent Deals The next dealer clears the coffin away and from the stock of unused cards deals four each face down and one face up. Play and score as before.

Game At the end of six deals both players record their totals. Whoever scored more (if not tied) adds a bonus equivalent to the difference between their two totals. Play up to 1000 points.

Duck Soup
2 players, 52 cards

A not too serious trick-taking game designed to drive you quackers.

Deal Shuffle a 52-card pack, deal thirteen each in ones, and stack the rest face down. The game is played in two courses. In the first course (Duck), each player, after playing to a trick, draws the top card of stock to restore the hand to thirteen. The second course (Soup) begins when the stock is empty.

Object The aim is to win tricks in each half of the game. It is better to win a middling number in both halves than many in one half and few in the other.

Play Non-dealer leads to the first trick and the winner of each trick leads to the next. The second may play any card. There is no need to follow suit and there are no trumps.

• In Duck (the first course), the trick is taken by the lowest card of the suit led, and Ace counts low.

• In Soup (second course), the trick is taken by the highest card of the suit led, and Ace counts high.

The winner of a trick containing two cards of the same suit stores it face down. One containing different suits counts double, and is stored face up. The winner of the trick draws first from stock (so long as any cards remain), waits for the other to draw, then leads to the next.

Quacking Peculiar things happen when the second player matches the *rank* of the one led. He must, on this occasion, say 'Quack!' If he fails to do so, the leader simply wins the trick, which counts double and is stored face up.

If the second player quacks, the leader must *either*

• say 'Duck', in which case the other wins the trick and stores it face down; *or*

• play a third card of the same rank and say 'Quack-quack'. In this case the other must play another card. If it is the fourth card of the same rank, he says 'Duck Soup' and wins the trick. If not, the leader wins the trick. In either case the four cards count as two tricks, and both are stored face up.

☛ 1. The leader is not obliged to play a third card of the same rank, but may duck even though able to match it.

☛ 2. Following a quack-quack, each player draws only one card from stock, not two. When the stock is empty, therefore, players may well hold fewer cards than thirteen .

Score At the end of the Duck course, as soon as the last card has been drawn from stock and before the next trick is led, both players note the scores they have made so far, counting one for each face-down trick and two for each face up. These tricks are then piled up to one side so as not to get confused with tricks won in the second half. Tricks won at the end of the Soup course are scored the same way. Each player's final score for the whole deal is found by multiplying together the two scores for the individual halves.

Game Play up to 250 points. A player finishing with less than 125 points is 'in the soup', and pays double. Scoring 125 or more in a single deal wins the game outright.

Galapagos

2 players, 52 or 54 cards

A heady brew, redolent of Gops, Piquet, Whist, and Arsehole, but with a few novelties thrown in. It would take ages to explain the title.

Preliminaries Deal thirteen cards each from a well-shuffled 52-card pack ranking AKQJT98765432. Stack the rest face down and turn the top card face up. The game consists of three phases as follows:

1. *Auction.* Players seek to improve their hands by bidding for new cards from the stock. When the stock is empty, they score for any melds (card combinations) held in their revised hands.

2. *Tricks.* They then play these revised hands to 13 tricks, aiming especially to win the last.

3. *Play-off.* Finally, they each pick up as a new hand the thirteen cards they used in the bidding, and aim to be the first to play them all out.

The hundred bonus If at the end of any scoring phase one player has reached 100 and the other has not, the one who did so gains a bonus. The bonus is 100 if the hundred is reached by the end of Phase 1 (melds), 50 if by the end of Phase 2 (tricks), or 25 if by the end of Phase 3 (play-off).

Phase 1: Auction At each turn the top card of the stock is turned up. Following an auction, one player takes the faced card and the other takes the one below it, sight unseen. The aim of the auction is to win the privilege of choosing whether to take or cede the known top card. Players bid by simultaneously revealing an unwanted bid-card from the hand. The auction is won by the higher card. If tied, it is won by the card of the same suit as the turn-up; or, if neither matches suit, by that of the same colour; or, if neither is of the same colour, by that of the same parity as the turn-up. (Spades and hearts are of *major* parity, clubs and diamonds *minor*.)

Whoever wins the auction may either take the top card and take it into hand, leaving the opponent to take the next, or, if preferred, may cede the top card to the opponent and take the next card down, sight unseen. The bid-cards are then turned down, and the next card of stock is faced and bid for in the same way. Continue thus until the stock is exhausted, when each player will have thirteen cards in hand and thirteen face down on the table.

Scoring for melds Each in turn, starting with the player who took the last card, scores for any sets and sequences they declare. A set is three or more cards of the same kind (Aces, Twos, Kings, etc.). A sequence is three or more cards of the same suit and in ranking order. Ace counts high only (A-K-Q . . . , not A-2-3 . . .). A card may belong to a set and a sequence. Score as follows:

- Sequence of three = 10, four = 20, five = 50, six = 60, and so on up to 13 = 130.
- Set of three = 15, or 30 if the missing card is of one's proposed trump (which should then be announced).
- Set of four = 40, but four Threes = 60, four Twos = 80.

Announce a sequence as 'Three hearts', 'Six clubs', or whatever, and a set as 'Three Aces', 'Four Nines' etc. Any combination scored for must be shown if requested.

If one player has reached 100 and the other has not, the former gets a bonus of 100.

Phase 2: Tricks Play tricks as at Whist or Bridge, except that, before play, each player declares which suit will be their personal trump. Whoever took the last card of stock leads to the first trick. The second player must follow suit if possible, otherwise may play any card. The trick is taken by the higher card of the suit led, or by a personal trump to the lead of a non-trump suit. If one player leads a personal trump and the other cannot follow, the latter can only beat it with a *higher* personal trump – an equal or lower one loses. The winner of each trick leads to the next.

Whoever wins the last trick scores 10 points per trick won, and the other player 5 per trick won. These scores are added to those for melds.

If one player has reached 100, not having done so before, and the other has not, the former gets a bonus of 50.

Phase 3: Play-off Each player now picks up the thirteen cards used in the auction and arranges them as a playing hand. The aim is to be the first to play them all out from the hand in the following way.

The winner of the last trick leads to the first round of play, and the winner of each round leads to the next. The leader may play out a single card, or two or more cards of the same rank, or three or more cards in sequence (not necessarily of the same suit; and Ace counts high or low). The other must either play exactly the same number and combination of cards, but higher in rank, or else pass. If the latter passes, the leader must then match and beat the last combination or pass, and so on. This continues until one player cannot or will not beat the last-played combination. The other player thereby wins the round, turns the played cards down, and leads to the next.

Play stops as soon as one player plays their last card. That player scores 10 for each card left in the other player's hand. Reaching a total of 100 or more by this process, if the other has not, earns a bonus of 25.

Game Keep playing to the end of Phase 3 of the deal in which one player has reached 1000 points or more. After the play-off, the player with the higher point-total scores a single game if the loser reached 1000+, a double if the loser has less than 1000, a treble if less than 750, a quadruple if less than 500.

Optional Jokers In case the game is not elaborate enough, you may add two Jokers, one red and one black. Each player starts with one Joker and twelve cards dealt. Each may play their Joker once only. How it is used depends on when it is played, as follows.

• *In the auction.* Joker played as a bid-card always wins. If both are played simultaneously, that of the same colour as the faced card wins.

• *In melds.* Before scoring for melds, a player who still has a Joker may exchange it for any one of their played-out bid-cards. This may yield a higher meld, or an extra trick.

• *In trick-play,* a player who still has a Joker counts it as a personal trump, ranking lowest (below the Two).

• *In the play-off.* A Joker counts lower than a Two. It is not wild, but may be used in a sequences beginning Joker-2-3 . . . etc.

Garbo ('I Want To Be Alone')   2 players, 32 cards

Many games involve matching cards together. In this one, perversely, you aim to *avoid* putting matched cards together.

Cards Deal four each from a 32-card pack (none lower than Seven) and stack the rest face down. Each suit and rank has a point value as follows:

♠	♥	♣	♦	J	K	7	8	9	10	A	Q
1	2	3	4	5	6	7	8	9	10	11	12

Object To play cards to a layout in such a way as to avoid putting cards of the same suit *next to* each other, and cards of the same rank *in line with* one another. Every match so made gives the opponent a score, which can conveniently be kept on a cribbage board.

Play Each in turn, starting with the non-dealer, plays a card face up to the table. Each subsequent card must go side by side with a card already down. The first sixteen cards played must eventually form a square of four rows and four columns. Leave enough space between the longer edges of adjacent cards to allow a card to be turned sideways without overlapping.

Scoring If the card just played by your opponent matches the suit of any adjacent card, whether diagonally or orthogonally, you score the value of the matching suit. If it matches the rank of any card in the same row, column or diagonal, you score the value of the matching rank. You may claim and score for each and every match so made in one turn, provided that you do so before playing your own next card.

Drawing new cards When both have played four cards, deal each player eight more from stock. Then continue as before till the square contains sixteen cards face up. This completes the first level.

Second level Deal out the rest of the stock so as to restore each hand to eight cards. The leader to the second half of the game is the player with the higher score at the end of the first half, or, if equal, the one who played the last (sixteenth) card. Turns then alternate. At each turn you play a card on top of a card played in level one, which is then turned face down and rotated 90 degrees so that its long edges go the opposite way. This is to show that it has been played on and may not be added to.

Example: In the diagram, playing ♥10 immediately below ♠7 gives nothing away, but playing it below ♣8 gives your opponent 2 for each adjacent heart (Jack, Ace), and 10 for each Ten in line with it, making 24 in all.

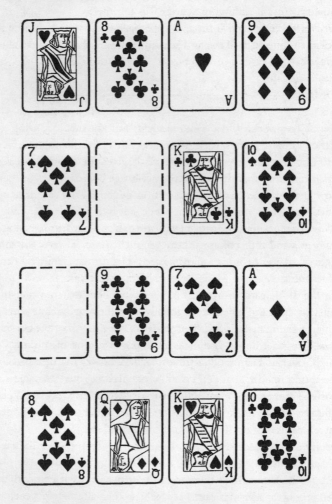

Scores are made as before, but now with an additional penalty. If your opponent plays a card *on top of* a card that matches it by rank or suit, you score *ten times* the value of that rank or suit, in addition to any other scores that may be made in the usual way.

Get Stuck

This one is more of a board game than a card game. If you like mazes, you may find it suitably amazing.

Preliminaries Remove the four Tens from a 52-card pack and add a Joker (or one of the Tens to represent a Joker). Decide in advance who is to play red cards and who black throughout the session. The turn to deal alternates.

Deal Shuffle the remaining 49 cards and deal them all out face up in a square of seven rows and seven columns. Then remove the Joker, whose only purpose was to leave a gap at random.

Object The primary aim is to be the last player legally able to turn a card face down. A secondary aim is to turn down lower rather than higher numerals. For this purpose Ace counts 1 and numerals 2 to 9 at face value. Courts count 10 each to the winner but minus 10 to the loser.

Play To start, non-dealer takes any card of his own colour lying horizontally or vertically in line with the gap, moves it to the gap, and turns it face down, leaving another gap where this card came from. Dealer then does the same thing, moving a card of his own colour in a straight line to the resultant gap and turning it down. The two continue to play alternately in the same way, but with the following special rules:

• In moving to the gap, a numeral (A23456789) may not pass over a card lying face down. Only courts (JQK) may jump over 'dead' cards.

• If you can make a horizontal or vertical move, you must do so.

• When unable to move either horizontally or vertically, you must instead move a card of your own colour that lies in a *diagonal* line with the gap. The same proviso applies, in that only courts can pass diagonally over dead cards.

• If you cannot make any move at all, the game ends, and you have lost.

Score The winner scores the face value of all numerals of his own colour left face up, plus 10 for each of his face-up court cards. The loser scores the face value of all numerals of his own colour left face up, but then subtracts 10 for each of his face-up court cards.

Game Play up to a target score of (say) 250.

Comment The sooner you win, the higher you score. If too many cards get turned down, the nominal winner could finish with a lower score than the loser.

After each trick, players draw from stock alternately until they have 13 cards again, or until the stock runs out. The winner of a trick draws first and leads to the next.

Over the Top

An adding-up game.

Preliminaries Deal thirteen cards each from a 52-card pack and stack the rest face down.

Object To win high-scoring cards in tricks. A trick consists of four cards, whose face values are added and announced as each one is played. The final total determines who wins the trick. Cards count as follows when played to tricks:

2–10	face value
Ace	11 or 1
Queen	10 or 0
Jack	10 if led, otherwise *deducts* the value of the last numeral played
King	10 if led, otherwise *adds* the value of the last numeral played

Play A trick consists of four cards, one of each suit. Each in turn, starting with the non-dealer, plays a card and announces the combined value of all cards so far played. Aces and Queens count 1 and 0 only if 11 and 10 would bring the total to more than 21. A trick counting 22 or more is 'over the top'.

Each card must differ in suit from those already played. If you can't play without duplicating a suit, you must pass, leaving your opponent to play as many more cards as necessary to complete the trick.

A trick counting 21 or less is won by the player of the last card. A trick counting 22 or more is lost by the player who first took it over the top.

Score Scoring is done by removing from the trick the cards whose values are relevant, and discarding the rest to a common waste-pile. A trick counting less than 21 scores the value of its two lowest cards (counting courts 10 each and Ace 11). A trick counting more than 21 scores the value of its two highest cards. A trick counting exactly 21 scores the value of every card it contains.

Umbridge

A two-player Bridge substitute.

Deal The dealer is South and the other player North. Deal four hands of thirteen cards, starting West and finishing South.

Umbrage Both players look at their hands. Either of them, if dissatisfied with their hand, and provided they have not yet started sorting it, may exchange it, sight unseen, for the one on their right. This is called 'Taking umbrage'. If either player takes umbrage, the dealer must then shuffle the two spare hands and deal them out again, face down.

Dummy and bridge The West hand is the eventual dummy. The other is spread out – still face down – in a row of overlapping cards between the two players. This hand is the 'bridge'.

Auction Dealer bids first, and the auction proceeds as at Bridge until either (a) one player passes or (b) a double is followed by a redouble.

When one player passes, whoever last named a contract may make up to six discards face down and draw a like number from the top of the bridge. The other player may then do likewise, but may not exchange more than the first player. After the draw, whoever named the last contract may not pass but must continue the auction by either repeating it or naming a higher one.

The same procedure is followed as long as two or more cards remain in the bridge. Whenever a player passes, the last bidder may draw not more than half the number remaining, and the non-bidder may draw not more than the bidder. If the last bidder at any time declines to draw any cards, then the non-bidder may discard and draw up to as many as remain, and may not then bid higher. The last named bid becomes the contract. It may be doubled and redoubled.

If only one card remains in the bridge when a player passes, the last named bid is the contract, and neither player may bid further, or double or redouble. The Declarer may make one final discard and draw, or else pass that privilege to the Defender.

Play Defender leads to the first trick, then exposes and arranges the dummy on the table. When it is down, Declarer plays a card from hand and Defender contributes a card from dummy.

Throughout play, the dummy is not the exclusive property of either player. It is always played from by the winner of the previous trick, and any trick taken in dummy is added to those of the player who played from it.

Whoever wins the trick in hand leads to the next trick from hand, waits for the other to play, then furnishes the third card from dummy. Whoever wins the trick in dummy leads to the next trick from dummy, waits for the other to play, then furnishes the third card from hand.

Score Score as at Rubber Bridge, except that, if Declarer took umbrage and then went down, the score for undertricks is doubled (in addition to any other doubles that may be applicable).

Tactics It is legal, though sneaky, to keep bidding in an unintended suit in order to induce your opponent to keep discarding from the suit in which you really hope to establish an eventual contract. Defender should always lead an Ace if possible. Both players should be ready to win or discard high in dummy in order to prevent their opponent from eventually cashing dummy's winners.

Throps
3 players, 52 cards

A three-player expansion of Gops. You may think it a bit chancy and uncontrollable at first blush, but there's more to it than meets the eye.

Preliminaries Shuffle a 52-card pack and deal four hands of thirteen. Square one of them up into a stock and turn the top card.

Object To win from the stockpile the greatest possible value of cards in any one suit. The cards you win of one suit score their face value, with courts 10 each and Ace 11, but any cards you win of other suits count the same amount against.

Play At each trick, the top card of the stock is turned up, and everyone takes a bid-card from their hand and lays it face down on the table. When all are ready, the bid cards are revealed. Whoever plays the highest bid-card wins the stock card and places it face up on the table before him.

If there is a tie for highest, it is won by the bid-card of the same suit as the stock card, or, if none, of the same colour, or, if none, of the same parity. (Spades and hearts are major in parity, clubs and diamonds minor.) For example, if the stock card is a spade, the order of precedence is ♠♣♥♦.

The bid-cards are then thrown away and the next stock card turned. This continues until all thirteen have been won.

Score Each player scores as follows:

- the face value of all cards of any one suit,
- *minus* the total face values of all other cards,
- *plus* 10 per void suit.

It follows that a player who wins no card at all scores 40.

Game Play up to 100 points, or any other agreed target.

▌Gooseberry Fool

3 players, 33 cards

The winner of this eccentric trickster is awarded one or more Golden Geese. Agree beforehand what one Golden Goose is worth.

Preliminaries Deal eleven each from a 32-card pack plus Joker. Cards rank AKQJT987 in each suit.

Object To win tricks in such a way as to divide the others as evenly as possible between your opponents.

Play Eldest leads to the first of 11 tricks. You must follow suit if possible, otherwise may play any card. The trick is taken by the 'goose', or odd card out, as follows:

- If all three cards are of the same suit, it is the *middling* card, i.e. second highest. (*Example*: ♠J ♠9 ♠Q is taken by ♠J.)
- If two are of the same suit, it is the card of the *odd suit*. (*Example*: ♥Q ♦A ♥7 is taken by ♦A.)
- If all three are of different suits, it is the card of the *odd colour*. (*Example*: ♣J ♠9 ♥K is taken by ♥K.)

The Joker Holding the Joker, you must play it the first time you can't follow suit to the card led. (You may not lead it unless it is the only card left in your hand.) Although it wins the trick, you needn't keep it yourself but may freely give it to either opponent, who then leads to the next.

Score At end of play, score 1 point for each trick you have won, and 2 for each trick won by the player on your right. (The players' three scores will total 33 and cannot produce a tie.) Whoever scores the middling number of points adds 10 as a bonus.

Game Cease play when one or two players reach 100 points. The winner is the only player to reach 100 points if the other two don't, or the only player *not* to reach it if the others do. Either way, the winner is the gooseberry and the other two are fools.

▌ Bugami (Bleeding Hearts)   3–6 players (4 best), 52 cards

Bugami (accent on the first syllable) is a more cut-throat version of Hearts, in that each player declares which suit they will attempt to take none of. It's especially heart-rending in its so-called 'shotgun wedding' variation, which brings together unintentional partners

Preliminaries Each player nominates a personal 'bug' suit which will count against them if won in tricks. Their aim is then to win 'clean' tricks that don't contain bugs, while trying to avoid tricks that do contain them. Needless to say, everyone will be trying to drop bug cards on everyone else's tricks.

Cards Three players use a 52-card pack from which the Tens, Nines and Eights are removed for use as bid-cards, leaving 40 in play. Four or more use a 52-card pack for play, and an old or incomplete pack for bidding. Each player requires four bid-cards, one of each suit.

Deal Deal all the cards out in ones until everyone has the same number. Any surplus cards remain face down to one side. Cards rank AKQJT98765432.

Bid bugs Everyone looks at their cards, decides on a bug suit, and selects a card of that suit from their bid-cards. When ready, they turn their bid-cards face up so everyone knows everyone else's bug suit. You can bid to take no tricks at all (misère) by leaving all your bid-cards face down.

Play The player at dealer's left leads to the first trick. Tricks are played at no trump. Follow suit if possible, otherwise play any card. A trick is taken by the highest card of the suit led, and the winner of each trick leads to the next. If any cards were left undealt, they are added to the last trick, and go to the player who won it.

Score Each player's score is calculated as follows: count 10 per trick won, and divide this total by the number of bugs taken, ignoring fractions. For example, four tricks containing one bug scores 40, two bugs 20, three 13, and so on. For taking only clean tricks, you don't divide by nought (which is mathematically meaningless) but by one-half, which is the same as doubling the value to 20 each. Winning four clean tricks, therefore, scores 80.

• A player who wins every trick scores 100, regardless of bugs. The others then score nothing unless they bid misère.

• A player who bids misère scores 100 for winning no trick, otherwise zero.

• A player who wins no trick without having bid misère scores 30. Play up to any agreed target, such as 250 points.

Joker variation One or more Jokers may be added to the pack, and these count as bugs when taken in tricks. Any cards left undealt are set face down and go to the winner of the last trick. You can discard a Joker only when unable to follow suit. If you lead one, it wins the trick, and opponents may discard as they please.

Shotgun wedding In this variation, two or more players who bid the same suit automatically become partners. Their tricks are kept together, and each member individually scores the score made by the whole partnership. This does not apply to misère bidders, who continue to play and score as individuals.

Collusion (Take Your Partners)   4 players, 52 cards

This simple, fast, and chatty trick-taking game enables you to wait and see how things develop before deciding who to have as a partner. And if you don't like your final choice, you can always double-cross them and go off with somebody else.

Preliminaries Deal four players thirteen each in ones from a 52-card pack ranking AKQJT98765432 in each suit.

Object Principally, to win the same number of tricks as exactly one other player.

Play Eldest leads to the first trick and the winner of each trick leads to the next. Players must follow suit if possible, otherwise may play any card. A trick is taken by the highest card of the suit led. There are no trumps.

Score Each player scores 1 point per trick won. In addition:

• If exactly two players win the same number of tricks, they each get a bonus of 10.

• If no two players win the same number of tricks, whoever won fewest gets a bonus of 20.

• If three players win the same number of tricks, the fourth gets a bonus of 30.

The target score of 100 may be reached only with the aid of a bonus, not on tricks alone. If you score only for tricks, and that number would bring you to 100 or more, you must deduct it from your total instead of adding it.

If the winner scored a bonus of 10 on the last deal, then the other player who scored 10 automatically comes second, adding as many more points as necessary to bring their score to 100 exactly.

Comment The point of the game is that any two players may collude by arranging to win the same number of tricks as each other. For example, they may say, 'I'm going for four,' or, 'I probably won't take any more,' or may ask another player what suit to lead or avoid leading. All such agreements are informal, and alliances may be broken and re-formed in the light of subsequent events.

Mismatch

A trick-taking game in which you can always play any card you like.

Preliminaries Deal thirteen each in batches of 3-3-3-3-1 from a 52-card pack ranking AKQJT98765432 in each suit.

Object To avoid winning tricks, and especially tricks containing matches. A match is two or more cards of the same rank or suit, or three or more cards in numerical sequence. Penalties are scored for winning tricks and matches, so at end of play the winner is the player with the lowest score.

Play Eldest leads to the first trick and the winner of each trick leads to the next. Each in turn may play any card he likes, but will seek to avoid matching the rank or suit of any card so far played to the trick, or (in the case of the third and fourth players) completing a sequence of three or four.

• If the trick contains NO match, it is taken by the highest card, and its penalty score is that of its lowest card, which will be anything from 2 to 10. The winner places the lowest card face up on the table before him to show his current score, and discards the rest of the trick face down to a common waste-pile.

• If the trick DOES contain a match, it is won by the last player to duplicate a rank or suit, or to make a run of three or four. (Ace counts high or low in a run.) Its penalty value will be a multiple of 10 as follows:

for each pair of the same rank or suit	10
for each triplet (rank or suit) or run of three	30
for each quartet (rank or suit) or run of four	40

Every match counts, even those to which the player of the last matching card did not contribute. For each 10 involved, the winner places any card from the trick face *down* on the table before him and discards the remainder to a common waste-pile. If the penalty is 50 or more, use as counters dead cards taken from the waste-pile.

Game At end of play each player's penalties are recorded at the rate of 10 per face-down card plus the face value of face-up cards. The overall winner is the player with the lowest penalty score at the end of a previously agreed number of deals, or when one player has reached 200 in penalties.

scores 20 (10 each for the pairs of Fives and spades)

40 (30 for the three Eights, 10 for the two diamonds)

50 (10 each for the pairs of hearts and spades, 30 for the run)

100 (10 for the pair, 30 for three diamonds, 60 for two runs of three)

Seconds

4 players, 52 cards

A game for those who never quite make it to the top. And may the second-best man (or woman) win.

Preliminaries There are seven deals. Whoever deals to the first of them is designated South for the whole game, but the turn to deal and play passes always to the left (so North deals to the seventh). Deal thirteen each from a 52-card pack ranking AKQJT98765432 in each suit.

In deal 1, South and North are partners against East and West.

In deal 2, South and West are partners against North and East.

In deal 3, South and East are partners against North and West.

In deal 4, each player's half-partner is their left-hand neighbour.

In deal 5, each player's half-partner is their right-hand neighbour.

In deal 6, there are no partners, and the aim is to win tricks.

In deal 7, there are no partners, and the aim is to lose tricks.

Tricks Eldest leads to the first trick, and the winner of each trick leads to the next. Players must follow suit if possible, otherwise may play any card. There are no trumps.

- A trick is taken by the *second-highest card of the suit led*.
- If no one can follow suit, it is taken by the *second-highest card regardless of suit*.
- If this is tied, it is taken by the *second played of the tying cards*.

Score. In deals 1 to 5, you individually score the number of tricks you won *multiplied by* the number won by your partner or half-partner. (So if either of you wins none, both of you score zero.)

In deal 6 (positive solo), you score the square of the number of tricks you won yourself (0, 1, 4, 9, etc.).

In deal 7 (negative solo), you score the total number of tricks won by the other three players, or (same thing) 13 minus the number you won yourself.

Game Logically, the winner should be the player with the second-highest final score, but you may prefer to ignore this. Note that, although the last two deals are said to be played without partners, they should, in fact, be played by a tacit partnership of three against the player with the highest score at the end of the fifth and sixth deals.

Concerto

4 players, 52 cards

This is for players who like co-operative partnership games and ingenious signalling systems, but don't like trick-taking games such as Bridge. I have modified it since it was first published. Originally, you always scored 15 for a straight flush and 12 for four of a kind. This led excessively cautious players to aim for fours rather than straight flushes. The scores are now variable, and designed to reward good signalling and partnership play.

Preliminaries Four players sitting crosswise in partnerships receive thirteen cards each from a 52-card pack ranking AKQJT98765432 in each suit. The turn to deal and play pass to the left. Each side's aim is to create and score for four five-card Poker hands from the 26 cards between them, and to avoid being left with any such combination in the six cards remaining at end of play.

Poker hands Any five cards together form a Poker hand. Its scoring value, if any, depends on the combination it contains, as follows:

One pair	1
Two pairs	2
Threes	3
Straight	5
Flush	6
Full house	8
Fours	8 if all 4 played from one hand
	12 if 3 cards from one hand
	16 if 2 cards from each hand

Straight flush 10 if 5 played from one hand

15 if 4 cards from either hand

20 if 3 cards from leader, 2 from partner

25 if 2 cards from leader, 3 from partner

Play Assuming West deals, the first hand is played by North–South. Each in turn, starting with North, plays a card face up to the table until five cards have been played. If it forms a Poker combination, they score for it as specified above. North then spreads the completed hand face up on the table before him and the turn passes to East–West, with East leading and playing as described. Note that only one partnership plays at a time: there is no card interaction between the two sides.

Passing The leader to a hand must always play the first card and may not pass. Thereafter, each player, on his turn to play, may either play a card or pass. If he (North, say) passes, the previous player (South) may either play the next card or pass. If, however, South also responds by passing, North must then contribute the next card, as there is a limit of two on the number of consecutive passes that may be made by the two players. This does not, however, prevent an individual player from passing on all his own consecutive turns, leaving his partner to play out a full combination from his own hand.

Forcing Either player, if entitled to pass, may instead say 'Play'. This forces the other player to complete the hand alone, or, lacking enough cards, to play all remaining in hand.

Continuation North having led to the first hand by North–South, and East to the first by East–West, the turn to lead continues in rotation to the left. This continues until eight hands have been played, each player having led to two hands and stored them face up on the table before him. All completed hands remain visible throughout play, as Concerto is not designed to be a memory game.

Round score Each side totals its scores for the four hands. The side with the higher total is eligible for a bonus for 'left-overs' – that is, any combination left in the opponents' unplayed cards. The losers now reveal their last six cards, and the winners score a bonus equivalent to 10 times the value of the highest five-card combination that can be made from them. For example, if the left-overs are ♠J-6 ♥7-5 ♣ 9 ♦8, the winners add 50 for the straight.

If both sides tie for hand-scores, then both reveal their left-overs. In this case the side leaving the higher combination loses, and the other side scores 10 times its value. If both leave the same combination, the losing side is the one whose combination contains the highest card, or second-highest if equal, and so on. In the event of complete equality, neither side scores for left-overs.

Game Each subsequent deal is made by the player to the left of the previous dealer, after very thorough shuffling, and each first lead by the player at the new dealer's left. Play continues until four deals have been made and played, or until either side, after scoring for hands and any left-overs that may accrue, has reached a score of 100 or more.

• If one side finishes with 100+ points and the other does not, the winning side adds a game bonus of 100.

• If fewer than four deals were played, the winning side adds 100 for each deal unplayed – i.e. 100 for winning in three deals, 200 in two, or 300 for winning in one (which is rare, but possible).

All scores are carried forward, and the eventual winners are the first side to reach 1000 points, or any smaller target that may be agreed.

Concerto signals The point of this game is to play or pass in such a way as to convey information about the cards you hold. For example, when your partner has led the first card, you are normally expected to pass. This enables the leader either to pass back, showing a bad hand, or to show by the second card played whether to aim for a straight flush or four of a kind. As leader, you can convey fairly precise information about your hand not only by the relationship between your first two cards, but also by the order in which you play them – whether high-then-low or low-then-high, whether of the same or different suits or colours, and so on.

At start of play it is advisable to go down the following checklist and signal the first one you come to that your hand allows:

    Three or more to a straight flush
    Two sets of three
    Four of a kind
    Full house
    Complete flush or straight
    Two pairs
    Four to a flush or straight

Three to a flush or straight

One pair

First-round or strong signals aim for a straight flush or four of a kind. They are normally played on the first two rounds, and perhaps later, given a good distribution. Second-round or weak signals aim for a straight or flush, possibly a full house, and are normally played on the second two rounds, or on the first two, given a bad distribution.

It is up to the partners to use discretion in following these signals strictly or modifying them in the light of known information, whether visible in the hands already played, or deduced from how the opponents fared in the previous hand.

Straight flush signals Call for a straight flush if holding three or more cards in suit and range. Show your holding by playing upwards or downwards and with one or more gaps (designated x) as follows:

signal	e.g.	meaning (and example)
L x x x H	A-5	5 held, 5 in sequence (A-2-3-4-5)
L x x H	2-5	4 held, 4 in sequence (2-3-4-5)
L x H	3-5	4 held, 3 in sequence, 1 higher or lower (3-4-5 & A or 7)
L H	4-5	3 held, 2 in sequence, one higher (4-5-7 or 4-5-8)
H L	5-4	3 held, 2 in sequence, one lower (5-4-2 or 5-4-A)
H x L	5-3	3 held, 3 in sequence, no other (5-4-3)
H x x L	5-2	4 held, 1 missing between (5-4-2-A)
H x x x L	5-A	3 held, none consecutive (5-3-A)

☞ Some holdings can be shown in more than one way. Thus 5-4-2-A could be signalled 5-2 or 4-A, or even 5-A, since, if your partner holds the missing 3, he will know it cannot mean 5-3-A and will therefore play it. Use your discretion, but, wherever possible, try to avoid playing across a gap.

Same rank signals Call for four of a kind or a full house by playing first and second cards as follows:

from this	play this
four of a kind	same rank, ♥ then ♦
three & three	different rank, same colour
full house	different rank, different colour, from threes first
threes only	red and pass (♥ if possible)

two pairs	same rank, black–red or minor–major, *or* if out of range, different rank, high then low
one pair	black and pass (♦ if both red)

Straights or flushes On the third or fourth rounds, or an initially poor distribution, go for a flush or straight as follows:

to show this:	l-h	h-l	e.g.: l–h	h–l
same suit, out of range	5FL	(2P)	♠4♠J = flush	♠J♠4 = J-J-4-4
same suit, in range	4FL	3FL	♠4♠8 = 4 spades	♠8♠4 = 3 spades
different suit, in range	4/ 5ST*	3ST	♠4♥8 = straight ♠4♥7 = 4 of straight	♠8♥4 = 3 of straight

* With a complete straight, play lowest then highest regardless of suit. With four to a straight, play low-high, but beware giving misleading 5-straight or 4-flush signal.

Summary The three sets of signals listed above (straight flush, same rank, straight or flush) are summarized in the following table. Italics denote weak or second-round signals.

2 cards of:	same suit	same colour	different colour
same rank	-	fours if ♥♦ *or 2 pairs*	two pairs
same range	3 or more to straight flush *or 3 or 4 to flush*	two threes *or 3+ to straight*	FH, threes first *or 3+* to straight
out of range	two threes *or 5 flush*	two threes *or 2 pairs*	full house, threes first

Simplified Concerto Signals

From	Play
5 to SF	lowest, highest
4 to 4S	same ranks, ♥ then ♦
4 to SF	low, high, preferably not over a gap
3+3 to 4S	different ranks, same colour
3+2 to 4S	different ranks, different colour, 3S first
3 to SF	high, low, preferably not over a gap
3S to 4S	same ranks, different colour
pairs	red and pass (♥ if possible)
one pair	black and pass (♦ if both red)

Tantony

4 players (2 × 2), 52 cards

Tantony is a corruption of St Anthony, the patron saint of swineherds, and a Tantony piglet is the smallest one of the litter. What has this got to do with anything? You'll soon see. One amusing feature of this game is the way it automatically stacks the hands to produce the freakish distributions necessary for interesting scores. Another is that it is clearly a game of skill, but I've never been able to work out what skill it requires or whether I have it (whatever it is).

Preliminaries Four players sitting crosswise in partnerships receive thirteen cards each from a 52-card pack ranking AKQJT98765432 in each suit.

Play Eldest leads to the first of 13 tricks played at no trump. Players must follow suit if possible, otherwise may play any card. The trick is taken by the highest card of the suit led, and the winner of each trick leads to the next. There are no trumps.

Each trick carries a score. Its scoring value is that of the lowest card it contains of the suit led (the *runt*). For example, if ♣9 is led, and is followed by ♣5, ♣Q and ♥3, then the trick is taken by the Queen and counts 5 points. For this purpose, courts count 15 and Aces 20 each. (The grand coup in Tantony is to lead an Ace when no one can follow suit.)

Having won a trick, you may either keep it yourself, or give it to any one of the other three players. Theoretically, this enables you to keep fat runts for your own side's score and give the skinny ones away. The catch, however, is that no player may take or be given more than three tricks. This means you can give it only to someone who has not yet filled their quota of three, which in turn means you will sometimes have to give the fat ones away and keep the littl'uns for yourself.

Whoever is given the trick stacks it face down, but with the runt face up, and leads to the next.

End When 12 tricks have been played, everyone turns up their last card. Whoever has the lowest card counts it as a runt, leaving it face up to contribute to their score, while the others turn theirs face down. If there is a tie for lowest, all tied cards score as runts.

Score Each side scores the total face-value of its runts, of which there may be six, seven or eight.

Next deal There is no deal as such. Instead, everybody gathers up their three tricks and, with the addition of the odd card they played to the last trick, re-forms them into a new hand of thirteen cards. The first trick is led by the player to the left of the previous leader.

Game is four deals. For a longer game, play up to 250 or 500 points.

Anarchy

4–6 players, 52 or 60 cards

A fun game with a dubious skill factor.

Deal Four players receive thirteen each from a 52-card pack. Five receive 12 each, or six 10 each, from a 60-card pack. This may be either an Australian '500' pack containing Elevens and Twelves, or a 52-card pack with four extra Twos and Threes from a second pack of identical back design and colour.

Bids Everyone examines their hand and announces how they intend to score for the cards they expect to win in tricks. The possible bids and their scores are:

cards	1 per card
reds (*or* blacks)	2 per card of the colour bid
best	3 per card of whichever suit you take most of
spades (etc.)	4 per card of the suit bid
shorts	5 per card short of the number you were dealt

☞ If you bid shorts, any Ace you hold ranks low (below Two), provided that you call 'Low' upon playing it.

Play When everyone's bid has been written down for future reference, tricks are played as follows. Each player picks out a card and holds it face down on the table. When all are ready, the cards are simultaneously revealed. Then . . .

• If two or more players show the same suit, the highest card of that suit wins any others played of that suit.

• If two or more play singletons (unmatched suits), the highest singleton wins all the other singletons.

• If the highest singletons are equal, or if only one singleton is played, each singleton wins itself.

Examples:
♠8 ♥8 ♠J ♥2 = ♠J wins ♠8, and ♥8 wins ♥2.
♠8 ♥8 ♥J ♥2 = ♥J wins ♥8 and ♥2, and ♠8 wins itself.
♠8 ♥8 ♣7♦2 = each card wins itself.

Undealt cards If five play, the first of the two undealt cards is turned up at the end of the first trick and is won by the first person to play a card of its suit, or the highest if more than one play that suit. The second card is then turned up and won in the same way.

Score Each player scores according to the method they chose. For example, in a four-hand game, a player who finished with ♠KT5 ♥Q3 ♣T982 ♦9 would score 4 for having bid diamonds, 6 for reds, 8 for hearts, 10 for cards, 12 for spades, 12 for best, 14 for blacks, 15 for shorts, or 16 for clubs.

Game Keep playing until one or more players get fed up with it and stop. They are designated anarchists and have 25 points deducted from their final scores.

The bomb A Joker, representing a bomb, may be added to the pack. One odd card is then dealt face up to the table. If it is the Joker, the game explodes (or, at least, ends); if not, the player to whom it is dealt is the anarchist. The anarchist may throw the bomb to any trick. In this trick only, the bomb upsets the values of all the other cards played, so that Deuces rank highest and Aces lowest. The faced card is substituted for the bomb, and whoever wins it also wins the bomb. At end of play, the bomb-holder counts it as any desired card for scoring purposes.

Variations Any of the following additional announcements may be made. They are gambling bids, being hard to predict and likely to yield erratic scores.

uppers	3 per A, K, Q, J, T* taken in tricks
downers	face value of every 5, 4, 3, 2 taken in tricks
fivers	5 times the face value of the lowest card taken
voids	25 per void (none taken of a suit)
doubles	20 for taking the same number of cards in two suits (or 30 for three suits, 40 for four suits)

* T = Twelve if the Australian '500' pack is used.

Minimisère

4–7 players (5 best), 21–36 cards

This snappy little tactical game, Jaime Poniachik tells me, is played in Buenos Aires on a tournament basis. Fame at last!

Cards The size of pack varies with the number of players as follows (☆ = Joker):

players	cards	ranking
four	21	A-K-Q-J-2-☆
five	25	A-K-Q-J-T-2-☆
six	30	A-K-Q-J-T-9-2-☆-☆
seven	36	A-K-Q-J-T-9-8-7-2

Object To win three, four, or none of the five tricks played. Alternatively, to bid and win all five.

Deal If four or seven play, deal the first card face up as the lead to the first trick. If it is an Ace, Deuce or Joker, bury it and deal another. Then deal five each in ones. Anyone who wishes to bid five must do so before playing to the first trick. If two or more players bid five, at least one of them is an idiot.

Play Eldest leads to the first trick, following suit to the faced card if any. Subsequent players must follow suit if possible, otherwise may play any card. The trick is taken by the highest card of the suit led and the winner of each trick leads to the next.

• If a Deuce is led, it wins the trick, and the others must follow suit if possible. If not led, it loses.

• If a Joker is led, it wins the trick, and the others may discard *ad lib*. Otherwise it may be discarded only when its holder cannot follow suit, and loses.

Score Winning no trick scores 5 points, one trick = 1, two = 2, three = 6, four = 8, five = 0 points unless bid verbally. If anyone bid five, they score 10 if successful, and everyone else zero. If unsuccessful, they score zero and everyone else scores 5. Play up to any agreed target, such as 25 or 50.

▍Squint

This was deliberately designed to accommodate five players. It borrows slightly from Skat, but is not a point-trick game and is nowhere near as complicated as it looks at first reading.

Preliminaries Deal five players ten cards each from a 52-card pack ranking AKQJT98765432. Deal the last two face down to the table. These constitute the 'squint'.

Object To win tricks in one of the following ways: by playing alone against the combined efforts of the other four (solo), by playing with a partner against the other three (duo), or with everyone playing for themselves (nolo). Although 10 tricks are played, the last trick counts double, so the number of tricks is reckoned as 11 instead of 10. To remind you of this fact, the squint is placed in front of the last trick winner in such a way as to look like an extra trick.

Bidding Here's how to determine which contract is played. Everyone selects a bid-card of the suit they most favour as trump and holds it face down on the table. When all are ready, the bid-cards are revealed. The contract depends on the particular combination of suits displayed, as follows:

pattern	example	contract
2-2-1 *or* 4-1	♠♠♥♥♣ *or* ♠♠♠♠♥	solo (♣ or ♥ trump)
2-1-1-1 *or* 3-2	♠♠♥♣♦ *or* ♠♠♥♥♥	duo (♠ trump)
3-1-1 *or* 5-0	♠♠♠♥♣ *or* ♠♠♠♠♠	nolo (avoid ♦ or ♠)

The contracts are defined as follows:

• *Solo.* The player showing the odd suit plays solo. As soloist, you can either play with the suit of your bid-card as trump, in which case your aim is to win more tricks than any other single opponent, or you can announce a no-trump misère, in which case your aim is to lose every trick. In either case, you may (but need not) 'squint' – that is, take the squint, add it to your hand, and make any two discards face down. If you squint, you needn't announce your game until you have looked at the two odd cards. If you don't squint, your game value is doubled.

• *Duo.* The two players showing the same suit are partners. Their aim is to win at least six tricks using the suit they bid as trump. Before play, each of them takes one card of the squint (without revealing it) and makes any discard face down.

• *Nolo.* There are no partnerships and no trumps. The aim is to avoid winning tricks containing any card of the penalty suit, which is the one that nobody bid. (Unless all five bid the same suit – most unlikely! – in which case it is the suit they all bid.) Before play, each in turn, starting with eldest, takes the squint and makes any two discards face down to form the squint for the next player. The dealer, who squints last, may not discard from the penalty suit.

Play Eldest leads to the first trick. Players must follow suit if possible, otherwise may play any card. The trick is taken by the highest card of the suit led, or by the highest trump if any are played, and the winner of each trick leads to the next.

Score

• *Solo in trumps.* For winning more tricks than any individual opponent, score 5 points per trick won. If you fail, each opponent scores 5 per trick taken by whichever of them took most. Won or lost, the score is doubled if you played without squinting.

• *Solo misère.* Score 25, or 50 if played without squinting. This goes to the soloist if successful, otherwise to each opponent.

• *Duo.* The winning side is the one that took six or more tricks. Each member of the winning side scores 10 for each trick taken by their side.

• *Nolo.* Score 5 points for each trick you took that did not contain a card of the penalty suit, or 25 for taking no tricks at all. However, if one player takes all 13 penalty cards, the others score zero and the winner scores 50, or 100 for winning every trick.

Game Play up to 250, or any other agreed target.

Variant If three bid the same suit (for example ♠♠♠♥♣ or ♠♠♠♥♥), they become partners in a game called trio. Their bid suit is trump, and they must win all 11 tricks. Whoever showed the lowest trump takes the squint and passes any two cards face down to the one who showed the middling trump, who similarly passes two to the player who showed the highest, who then discards any two face down. A score of 55 goes to each of them if successful, otherwise to each of the two opponents.

Introducing this bid makes it unlikely that a nolo will ever be played. If you want both, play nolo whenever four players bid the same suit.

(You can sometimes force this by deliberately bidding a suit of which you hold only a low singleton.)

Sex

This was designed as a trick-taking game of skill for specifically six players, as described first.

Preliminaries Each player deals in turn and a game is six deals.

Cards Deal nine each from a 54-card pack including two Jokers. Cards rank (A)KQJT98765432(A) in each suit. Ace counts high or low as stated by its holder upon playing to the trick.

Jokers A Joker counts as the Ace of the suit led, and must similarly be declared high or low. If an Ace and a Joker fall to the same trick, whichever is played second must differ in rank from the other. For example, if one person plays a Joker and says 'High', the subsequent player of an Ace to the same trick must say 'Low'.

Object To win an exact multiple of nine cards (0, 9, 18, 27, 36, 45 or 54), or as near as possible below such a multiple, and to get rid of your cards sooner rather than later.

Play Eldest leads to the first trick. He may not pass or lead a Joker. Everybody else in turn may either pass or add a card to the trick, but may play only if they follow suit. A Joker may be played to any trick, as it belongs to any suit; but it may never be led. The trick ends when everyone has either passed or played – there is no second chance.

The trick is taken by the highest card played. The winner places the won cards face down on the table before him in such a way as to show clearly how many he has taken so far. The winner may then either lead to the next trick or pass. If he passes, each in turn has the same opportunity to lead or pass, until either somebody leads or everybody passes. If somebody leads, those next in succession who have not already passed may either pass or play, as before.

If everyone passes, the game ends by deadlock, as no one gets a second chance.

End and score Play continues until at least one player has run out of cards, and the trick to which they last played has been taken and turned down. Calculate your score by multiplying two elements together:

- the number of cards you have played (that is, 10 less the number left in hand)

  multiplied by

- nine if you won a multiple of nine cards, otherwise the remainder when you divide the number you took by nine. In other words:

taken	0	1	2	3	4	5	6	7	8	9	10	11	12	13	14	15	16	17	18
count	9	1	2	3	4	5	6	7	8	9	1	2	3	4	5	6	7	8	9

. . . and so on. The most you can score in one deal is 81, for having played all your cards and won an exact multiple of nine.

Sex for five

Deal ten each from a 52-card pack and two face up to the table. The first player to win a trick in the suit of either of these cards adds it (or them, if both are of the same suit) to the trick. An upturned Ace always counts low. Score as above, except that the aim is to take a multiple of 10 or as near as possible thereunder. The most you can score in one deal is 100, and there are five deals.

Sex for seven

The best way is to use an Australian '500' pack. This contains 63 cards, with Elevens and Twelves in each suit, Thirteens in red suits, and one Joker. You can then deal nine each and play exactly as in the six-hander, except that there are seven deals.

Alternatively, play the nine-card game by adding to the 52-card pack three Jokers plus all Twos and Threes from an identical pack, or the ten-card game by adding two Jokers and extra Twos, Threes, Fours and Fives.

Sex for six Australians ('Neighbours')

Six can play the ten-card game by discarding the Joker and both Thirteens from the Australian '500' pack.

Technical terms

age Order of priority in making the first lead, bid, or bet, as reckoned around the table starting from the player immediately next to the dealer, who is known as eldest and enjoys greatest priority. Also *edge*.

alliance A temporary partnership, lasting only for the current deal (as in 'prop and cop' at Solo Whist).

ante In gambling games, an obligatory stake made before play begins – usually by every player, sometimes only by the dealer.

auction A period of bidding to establish the conditions of the game, such as who is undertaking to win, how many tricks constitute a win, which suit is trump, etc.

bettel An undertaking to win no tricks (also *misère*).

bid An offer to achieve a stated objective (such as a minimum number of tricks) in exchange for choosing the conditions of play (such as a trump suit). If the offer is not overcalled by a higher bid, it becomes a contract.

blank (1) In card-point games, a non-counter, or card worth nothing. (2) A hand without courts, consisting only of numerals.

blaze A non-standard Poker hand, consisting solely of court cards.

card points The point values of cards in point-trick games (as opposed to nominal face values).

carte blanche A hand devoid of face cards (same as *blank*).

carte rouge A hand in which every card counts towards a scoring combination (Piquet).

chicane A hand which, as dealt, contains no trumps.

chip A gaming counter, especially in Poker.

combination A set of cards matching one another by rank or suit and recognized by the rules of the game as a scoring feature.

complex See *point-trick games*.

contract See *bid*.

counter (1) An object representing a pay-off coin or a score. (2) In point-trick games, a card with a point-value.

court (cards) King, Queen, Jack, etc., as opposed to numerals. Also called face-cards, and (originally) *coat cards*.

cut To place the bottom half of the pack on top of the former top half in order to prevent the bottom card from being known.

cut-throat All against all; without partnerships.

dead hand See *widow*.

deadwood (Rummy) Penalty cards remaining in opponents' hands when one player has gone out.

deal (1) To distribute cards to the players at start of play. (2) The play ensuing between one deal and the next.

declare (1) To announce the contract or conditions of play (number of tricks intended, trump suit, etc.). (2) To show and score for a valid combination of cards in one's hand.

declarer The highest bidder, who declares and then seeks to make good the stated contract.

deuce The Two of any given suit.

discard (1) To lay aside an unwanted card or cards from hand. (2) To throw a worthless or unwanted card to a trick.

doubleton Two cards of the same suit in the same hand, no others of that suit being held.

draw To take, or be dealt, one or more cards from a stock or waste-pile.

drinking game One producing not a winner but a loser, whose penalty is to buy the next round.

dummy A full hand of cards dealt face up to the table (or, in Bridge, dealt to one of the players, who eventually spreads them face up on the table) from which the declarer plays as well as from his own hand.

elder, -est. The player to the left of the dealer in left-handed games, or to the right in right-handed, who is obliged or privileged to make the opening bet, bid, or lead. (Also called *age*, *forehand*, *pone*, etc.)

entrump To appoint a suit as the trump.

exchange (1) To discard one or more cards from hand and then draw or receive the same number from stock. (2) To add a specified number of cards to hand and then discard a like number. (3) To exchange one or more cards with a neighbour, sight unseen.

finesse To play a possible winning card instead of a certain winning card, in the hope of making an extra trick.

fish (1) In Fishing games, to capture a card or cards by matching their face values. (2) A gaming counter, originally so shaped.

flip To turn a card face up.

flush A hand of cards all of the same suit.

follow (1) To play second, third, etc. to a trick. (2) Follow suit: to play a card of the same suit as that led.

forehand (German *Vorhand*) Same as eldest.

frog The lowest bid in certain American games of German origin; from German *Frage*, 'request'.

gambling game Technically, one in which cards are not played with but merely bet on. Generally, any game if and when played for money.

game (1) A series of deals or session of play. (2) The contract, or conditions of the game; e.g. 'Solo in hearts'. (3) The target score; e.g. 'Game is 100 points.'

go out To play the last card from one's hand.

grand A bid equivalent to no trump in some games, a slam in others.

hand (1) The cards dealt to an individual player. (2) The period of play of such a hand (same as *deal*).

hard score Pay-off effected with coins, chips or counters.

head To play a higher card than any so far played to the trick.

hit To deal or give a player a card, or force it upon him. (In Blackjack, Hit me is a request for another card.)

honours Cards attracting bonus-scores or side-payments, usually to whoever holds and declares them, occasionally to whoever captures them in play.

kitty (1) The pool or pot being played for. (2) A dead hand or widow.

lead To play the first card; or, the first card played.

line; above/below (Bridge) Scores made for tricks contracted and won are recorded below a line drawn half-way down the sheet, and count towards winning the game; overtricks, honours and other premiums are scored above it and mainly determine the size of the win.

marriage (1) King and Queen of the same suit. (2) In Patience, any two cards in suit and sequence.

matadors Top trumps, sometimes with special privileges.

meld (1) A combination of matching cards attracting scores or privileges, or winning the game. (2) To declare such a combination.

middlehand In three-hand games, the next player round from Forehand.

misère A contract or undertaking to lose every trick.

miss A dead hand (in Loo).

negative game One in which the object is either (1) to avoid taking tricks or penalty cards, or (2) to avoid being the loser, there being no outright winner.

null (1) In point-trick games, a card carrying no point-value; also *blank*. (2) An undertaking to lose every trick (as *misère*).

numerals Number cards, as opposed to courts. Also called pip cards, spot cards, spotters, etc.

ouvert(e) A contract played with one's hand of cards spread face up on the table for all to see.

overcall To bid higher than the previous bidder. *Suit overcall* = bid to entrump a higher-ranking suit; *majority overcall* = to take a higher number of tricks; *value overcall* = to play a game of higher value or to capture a greater total of card-points.

overtrick A trick taken in excess of the number bid or contracted.

pair Two cards of the same rank.

partie A whole game, as opposed to a single deal, especially at Piquet.

partnership Two or more players who play co-operatively and win or lose the same amount. A partnership may be either fixed in advance and last for the whole session, as at Whist and Bridge, or vary from deal to deal, as at Quadrille or Solo, in which case it is better referred to as an *alliance*. Also *side* or *team*.

pass In trick-games, to make no further bid; in vying games, to pass the privilege of betting first but without dropping out of play.

pip A suitmark printed on a card, or the number represented – for example, the Deuce shows two pips. (Originally 'peep'.)

plain suit A suit other than trumps.

plain-trick games Games in which win or loss is determined by the number of tricks taken, regardless of their content (as opposed to *point-trick games*).

point (1) The smallest unit of value, score or reckoning. In various games distinctions may be drawn between *card-points*, which are scoring values attached to certain cards; *score-points*, which are points credited to a player's account; and *game points*, which might loosely be described as 'bundles' of score-points and may be affected by other bonuses. (2) The total face value of all cards held of any one suit (Piquet).

point-trick games Trick-games in which win or loss is determined not by the number of tricks taken but by the total value of counters contained in them (as opposed to *plain-trick games*). Sometimes called 'complex trick' games.

pool See *pot*.

pot A sum of money or equivalent, to which everyone contributes initially or throughout play, and which is eventually awarded (in whole or part) to the winner.

prial (pair royal) Three cards of the same rank; a triplet.

rank (1) the denomination of a card as opposed to its suit. (2) The relative trick-taking power of a card, e.g. 'Ace ranks above King'.

rearhand In three-hand games, the player with least priority, or youngest. (This will be the dealer if there are only three at the table.)

renege To fail to follow suit to the card led, but legally, exercising a privilege granted by the rules of the game.

renounce Strictly, to play a card of any different suit from that led, hence the same as *renege* if done legally, or *revoke* if not. Loosely, to play a non-trump when unable to follow suit, thereby renouncing all hope of winning the trick.

revoke To fail to follow suit to the card led, though able and required to, thereby incurring a penalty.

riffle A method of shuffling. The pack is divided into two halves which are placed corner to corner, lifted, and allowed to fall rapidly together so that they interleave.

round A period or phase of play in which everyone has had the same number of opportunities to deal, bid, play to a trick, etc.

round game One playable by an indefinite number of players, typically from three to seven.

rubber A match consisting (typically) of three games, and therefore won by the first side to win two.

ruff (1) To play a trump to a plain-suit lead. (2) Old term for a flush.

run Same as a *sequence*.

sans prendre A bid to play with the hand as dealt, without benefit of exchanging, thereby increasing the difficulty and scoring value of the game.

sequence A scoring combination consisting of three or more cards in numerical sequence or ranking order.

shuffle To randomize the order of cards in the pack. See also *riffle*.

singleton A card which is the only one of its suit in a given hand.

skat German term for two undealt cards forming a *talon* or *widow*.

slam Grand slam: winning every trick. Small slam: winning every trick bar one.

soft score Score kept in writing or on a scoring device, as opposed to cash or counters (*hard score*).

solo (1) A contract played with the hand as dealt, without exchanging any cards. (2) A contract played alone against the combined efforts of all the other players.

soloist One who plays a solo.

spread A hand of cards spread face up; same as *ouvert*.

squeeze In trick-taking games, a situation in which a player is forced to weaken himself in either of two suits but has no way of deciding which to play from.

stock Cards which are not dealt initially but may be drawn from or dealt out later in the play.

stops Cards which terminate a sequence, in games of the Stops family (Newmarket, Pope Joan, etc.); or those which are not dealt initially and whose absence from play prevents the completion of sequences.

straddle An obligatory stake made, before any cards are dealt, by the second player around, the first having put up an *ante*.

straight In Poker, a five-card sequence.

suit A series of cards distinguished by the presence of a common graphic symbol throughout; or, the symbol (suitmark) itself.

talon The undealt portion of the pack; same as *stock*. (French, meaning (1) heel, (2) the residue of a loaf when one or more slices have been cut from it.)

team Two or more playing as one; a partnership.

tourné(e) A bid or contract to turn the top card of the stock and entrump whatever suit it belongs to.

trey The Three of any suit.

trick A round of cards consisting of one played by each player.

trump (from *triumph*) (1) A superior suit, any card of which will beat any card of a plain suit. (2) To play a trump to a plain-suit lead; to ruff.

turn-up A card turned up at start of play to determine the trump suit.

undertrick A trick less than the number bid or contracted.

upcard A card lying face up on the table, or the faced top card of the waste-pile at Rummy, Patience, etc.

void Having no card of a given suit.

vole The winning of every trick; same as *slam*.

vulnerable (Bridge) Describes a side which, having won one game towards the *rubber*, is subject to increased scores or penalties.

waste-pile A pile of discards, usually face up, as at Rummy, Patience, etc.

widow A hand of cards dealt face down to the table at start of play and not belonging to any particular player. One or more players may subsequently exchange one or more cards with it.

wild card One that may be used to represent any other card, sometimes with certain restrictions. Typically the Joker in Rummy games, Deuces in Poker.

younger, -est The player last in turn to bid or play at the start of a game (usually, in practice, the dealer).

Index of games